상상 그 이상

모두의 새롭고 유익한 즐거움이
비상의 즐거움이기에

아무도 해보지 못한 콘텐츠를 만들어
학교에 새로운 활기를 불어넣고

전에 없던 플랫폼을 창조하여
배움이 더 즐거워지는 자기주도학습 환경을
실현해왔습니다

이제, 비상은
더 많은 이들의 행복한 경험과
성장에 기여하기 위해

글로벌 교육 문화 환경의
상상 그 이상을 실현해 나갑니다

상상을 실현하는 교육 문화 기업 비상

마법같은 블록구문

Memory Book

휴대용 암기장
언제 어디서나 함께하는 내 손안의 블록구문

박세광
실전편

visang

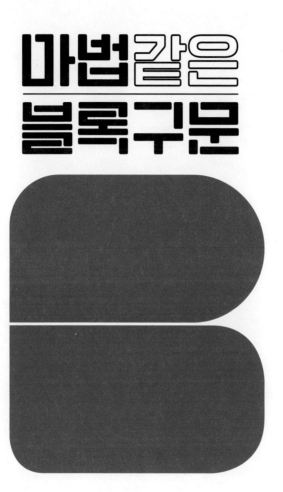

마법같은 블록구문

Memory Book 실전편

STAGE I

문장성분 중심의 구문

Chapter 01 주어의 파악

Chapter 02 동사 구문

Chapter 03 목적어의 파악

Chapter 04 보어의 파악

unit 01 명사구 주어

S TANDARD

01-01 Getting meaningful feedback on your performance is a powerfu
의미 있는 피드백을 얻는 것은 / 당신의 성과에 대해 / 강력한 전략이다

strategy for learning anything.
/ [어떤 것을 배우기 위한]

01-02 To love and to be loved is the greatest happiness of existence.
사랑하고 사랑받는 것은 / 존재의 가장 큰 행복이다

Sydney Smi

A

01-03 Knowing how climate has changed over millions of years is vita
아는 것은 / 기후가 수백만 년 동안 어떻게 변했는지를 / 필수적

to properly assess current global warming trends.
/ 제대로 현재의 지구 온난화 추세를 판단하기 위해

01-04 Giving people the latitude and flexibility to use their judgmer
사람들에게 자유와 융통성을 주는 것은 / [그들의 판단력을 이용하고

and apply their talents **rapidly** accelerates **progress**.
/ 그리고 그들의 재능을 활용하는] / 빠르게 진전을 촉진시킨다

01-05 To think that you know something without actually knowing it is
생각하는 것은 / 당신이 실제로 무언가를 알지 못하면서 그것을 안다고 / 심

serious mistake.
실수이다

B

01-06 Considering issues in an appropriate context will help yo
사안을 고려하는 것이 / 적합한 맥락 속에서 / 도울 것이다 / 당

accurately evaluate the pros and cons of a decision.
정확하게 결정의 찬반양론을 평가하는 것을

01-07 Is passing large sums of wealth on to your children good for them
당신의 자녀들에게 많은 액수의 재산을 물려주는 것이 / 그들에게 좋거나 사회를

or right for society? *Bill Gates*
위해서 옳은가?

01-08 Raising awareness of children about the particular characteristics
아이들의 인식을 높이는 것은 / [SNS의 독특한 특성들에 관한

of SNS and the potential long-term impact of a seemingly trivial
/ 그리고 겉보기에 사소한 행위의 장기적으로 변할 수 있는 영향(에 관한)]

act is crucial.
/ 매우 중요하다

01-09 To conquer oneself is the best and noblest victory; to be
스스로를 정복하는 것은 / 최고의 그리고 가장 숭고한 승리이다 / 자신의

vanquished by one's own nature is the worst and most ignoble
본성에 의해 정복당하는 것은 / 최악의 그리고 가장 수치스러운 패배이다

defeat. *Plato*

C

01-10 Investing regularly in learning opportunities is one of the greatest
정기적으로 투자하는 것은 / 학습 기회에 / 가장 큰 선물 중의 하나이다

gifts you can give yourself.
/ [당신이 스스로에게 줄 수 있는]

01-11 Having a large vocabulary makes **reading** more enjoyable **and**
많은 어휘를 아는 것은 / 독서를 더 즐겁게 만든다 / 그리고

increases **the range of materials that you can explore.**
자료의 영역을 증가시킨다 / [당신이 탐험할 수 있는]

01-12 To say that AI will start doing what it wants for its own purposes
말하는 것은 / AI가 자기가 원하는 것을 하기 시작할 것이라고 / 자신의 목적을 위해서

is like saying a calculator will start making its own calculations.
/ 말하는 것과 같다 / 계산기가 스스로 계산을 하기 시작할 것이라고
Oren Etzioni

5

Unit 02 명사절 주어

02-01 That some organisms must starve in nature is **deeply regrettabl**
일부 유기체가 자연에서 굶주려야 한다는 것은 / 정말 유감스럽고 슬프다

and sad.

02-02 What works for most job seekers is to look through their pas
대부분의 구직자들에게 효과가 있는 것은 / 그들의 과거의 경험을 살펴보는 것이다

experiences to help them build for the future.
/ 그들이 미래를 준비하는 것을 돕기 위해서

A

02-03 Whether an object floats on water depends on **the density of bot**
어떤 물체가 물에 뜨는지는 / 그 물체와 물의 밀도에 달려 있다

the object and the water.

02-04 When Stonehenge was built is known, **but** why it was buil
언제 스톤헨지가 건설되었는지는 알려져 있다 / 그러나 왜 그것이 건설되었는지는

remains a mystery.
미스터리로 남아있다

02-05 Whatever is worth doing at all is worth doing well. *Lord Chesterfield*
어쨌든 할 가치가 있는 것은 무엇이든 / 잘 할 가치가 있다

B

02-06 Whoever acquires knowledge but does not practice it is as on
지식을 습득하지만 그것을 실천하지 않는 사람은 누구나 / 사람과 같다

who ploughs but does not sow. *Saadi*
/ [밭을 갈지만 씨를 뿌리지 않는]

02-07 What we have done for ourselves alone dies **with us**; what we
우리가 우리 자신만을 위해서 해온 것은 　　　　　　　　　　　 / 우리와 함께 사라진다 / 우리가 다른

have done for others and the world remains **and is immortal.**
사람들과 세상을 위해서 해온 것은 　　　　　　 / 남아있다 그리고 영원하다

02-08 How the universe began is a fundamental question **which has**
우주가 어떻게 시작되었는가는 　　　　　 / 근본적인 질문이다 　　　　　 / [사람들의 마음을

occupied the minds of men from prehistoric times.
끌어온 　　　　　　　 / 선사시대부터]

02-09 That witches caused disasters and misfortunes was **widely** believed
마녀들이 재난과 불운을 초래했다는 것은 　　　　　　　 / 널리 믿어졌다

among early American settlers.
/ 초기 미국 정착민들 사이에서

02-10 What makes organisms different from the materials that **compose**
유기체들을 물질과 다르게 만드는 것은 　　　　　　　　　 / [그것들을 구성하는]

them is their level of organization.
/ 그들의 구성의 수준이다

02-11 How successful we are at forming good relationships and how
우리가 좋은 관계를 형성하는 데 얼마나 성공적인지 　　　　　 / 그리고 우리가

valued we feel by other people make **a big difference in how**
다른 사람들에 의해 얼마나 소중하다고 느끼는지는 　　 / 큰 차이를 만든다 　　　　 / 우리가

good we feel about ourselves.
스스로에 대해 얼마나 훌륭하다고 느끼는지에

02-12 Whatever we expect with confidence becomes our own self-
자신감을 가지고 우리가 기대하는 것은 무엇이든 　　　 / 우리 자신의 자기 충족 예언이 된다

fulfilling prophecy.

unit 03 가주어 it

S TANDARD

03-01 It is usual **in this world** for the weak to become the victim of the
(…은) 이 세상에서 흔하다   / 약자가 강자의 희생양이 되는 것은

strong.

03-02 It is a common superstition that a black cat crossing your path is
(…은) 흔한 미신이다   / 검은 고양이가   / [당신의 길을 가로지르는]   /

bad luck.
불운이라는 것은

A

03-03 It's fine to celebrate success **but it is more important to heed the**
(…은) 좋다   / 성공을 축하하는 것은   / 그러나 (…은) 더 중요하다   / 실패의 교훈에

lessons of failure. *Bill Gates*
주의를 기울이는 것은

03-04 It's no use locking the stable door after the horse has bolted.
(…은) 소용없다   / 마구간 문을 잠그는 것은   / 말이 달아난 후에   *Irish Proverb*

03-05 It matters **not what someone is born, but** what they grow to be.
(…이) 중요하다   / 누군가가 어떤 사람으로 태어나는지가 아니라   / 그들이 자라서 어떤 사람이 되는지
the novel <Harry Potter and the Goblet of Fire

B

03-06 It is the essence of scientific thinking to propose alternative ideas
(…은) 과학적 사고의 본질이다   / 대안을 제시하는 것

and then to test them against existing concepts.
/ 그리고 그것을 실험하는 것은   / 기존의 개념과 비교하여

03-07 It was very careless of her to leave the medicine where the
(…은) 아주 조심성이 없었다 / 그녀가 그 약을 둔 것은 / 아이들이 그것을

children could reach it.
집을 수 있는 곳에

03-08 With all the passion for being slim, it is no wonder that many
날씬해지고 싶은 모든 열정으로 / (…은) 놀랄 일이 아니다 / 많은 사람들이

people view any amount of visible fat on the body as something
자신의 몸에 있는 눈에 띄는 지방이 얼마만큼이든 여기는 것은 / 제거해야 할 무언가로

to get rid of.

03-09 It's amazing how much more you learn when you pause, quiet
(…은) 놀랍다 / 얼마나 더 많이 당신이 배우는가는 / 당신이 잠시 멈춰서, 당신의 마음을 진정시키고,

your mind, and listen to what others say.
다른 사람들이 말하는 것을 들을 때

c

03-10 Grown-ups **never** understand **anything by themselves, and it is**
어른들은 **결코** 스스로 아무것도 이해하지 **못한다** / 그리고 (…은)

tiresome for children to be always and forever explaining things to
따분하다 / 아이들이 늘 그리고 끊임없이 상황을 그들에게 설명하고 있는 것은

them. *the novel <The Little Prince>*

03-11 With today's latest virtual reality technologies, it is **now** possible
오늘날의 최신 가상현실 기술로 / (…은) 이제 가능하다

for designers to create real-world situations in a digital environment.
/ 설계자들이 디지털 환경에서 실제 세계의 상황을 만들어내는 것은

03-12 It's **not yet** clear whether the Prime Minister's resignation offer is
(…은) 아직 분명하지 않다 / 그 수상의 사직 의사가 진지한 것인지

a serious one, or whether it's simply a tactical move.
/ 아니면 단순히 전술적인 조치인지는

Unit 04 주어 + 형용사구

04-01 The ability to ask the right question is more than half the battle of
능력은 / [적절한 질문을 하는] / 전투의 절반 이상이다 /

finding the answer. *Thomas J. Watson*
[답을 찾는]

04-02 The candidates applying for the job must know the qualifications
지원자들은 / [그 일자리에 지원하는] / 알아야 한다 / 자격 요건을

required for the job.
/ [그 일자리에 요구되는]

A

04-03 The simple act of typing a few words into a search engine will
간단한 행위는 / [몇 개의 단어를 검색 엔진에 입력하는] / 거의

virtually instantaneously produce links related to the topic at
당장 만들어낼 것이다 / 그 주제와 관련된 링크를 /

hand.
바로 쓸 수 있도록

04-04 The only way to understand a word fully is to see it in use in many
유일한 방법은 / [한 단어를 완전히 이해하는] / 그것이 많은 문맥 속에서 사용되는 것을 보는

contexts.
것이다

04-05 The microwaves emitted from mobile phones can interfere with
극초단파는 / [휴대폰에서 방출되는] / 지장을 줄 수 있다 /

sensitive electronic equipment.
민감한 전자 기기에

B

04-06 An outstanding feature in the evolution of modern man is the
두드러진 특징은 / [현대 인류의 진화에서] /

growth of the size of the brain.
뇌 크기의 증가이다

04-07 Many present efforts to guard and maintain human progress, to
현재의 많은 노력은 / [인류의 발전을 지키고 유지하려는 /

meet human needs, and to realize human ambitions are simply
인간의 요구를 만족시키려는 / 그리고 인간의 야망을 실현하려는] / 도저히 지속할 수

unsustainable—in both rich and poor nations.
없다 —부유한 국가와 가난한 국가 모두에서

04-08 Scientists studying genes in yeast cells recently found a chemical
과학자들은 / [효모 세포 속의 유전자를 연구하는] / 최근에 화학물질을 발견했다

that seems to work with a longevity gene to increase the yeast
/ [장수 유전자와 함께 작동하는 것처럼 보이는 / 효모 세포의 수명을 늘리기 위해서]

cell's lifespan.

04-09 Foreign, or alien, species introduced accidentally or intentionally
외부에서 온, 즉 외래종은 / [우연히 또는 의도적으로 새로운 영역에 유입된]

into new territories often do well in their new homes because
/ 종종 그들의 새로운 서식지에서 잘 생육한다 /

conditions may be highly favorable to their growth and reproduction.
여건이 아마 매우 유리하기 때문에 / 그들의 성장과 번식에

04-10 Speculations about the meaning and purpose of prehistoric art
고찰은 / [선사시대 예술의 의미와 목적에 대한]

rely heavily on analogies drawn with modern-day hunter-gatherer
/ 굉장히 의존한다 / 유사성에 / [현대의 수렵 채집 사회에서 끌어낸]

societies.

04-11 The best way to protect your computer from viruses and spyware
최상의 방법은 / [당신의 컴퓨터를 바이러스와 스파이웨어로부터 보호하기 위한]

is to install a recommended anti-virus program.
/ 권장되는 안티바이러스 프로그램을 설치하는 것이다

04-12 The carbon dioxide given off when coal and oil are burned is
이산화탄소는 / [배출되는 / 석탄과 석유가 연소될 때] /

accumulating in the atmosphere and causing temperatures to
대기 중에 축적되고 있다 / 그리고 기온이 상승하도록 초래하고 (있다)

rise.

unit 05 주어 + 형용사절 1

05-01 Species which have not been able to survive in changing living
종들은 / [생존할 수 없었던 / 변화하는 생활 환경에서]

conditions have become extinct.
/ 멸종되어왔다

05-02 The reason why we have two ears and only one mouth is that we
이유는 / [우리가 두 개의 귀와 오직 하나의 입을 가지고 있는] / ~이다 / 우리

may listen more and talk less.
더 많이 듣고 더 적게 말하려는 것

05-03 The creativity that children possess needs **to be cultivated**
창의성은 / [아이들이 지닌] / 계발될 필요가 있다

throughout their development.
/ 그들의 성장 과정 동안

05-04 A person who works on an assembly line is **well** aware of the
사람은 / [조립 라인에서 일하는] / 잘 알고 있다 / 효율성에

efficiency that can be gained through repetition.
대해 / [반복을 통해 얻어질 수 있는]

05-05 The one area where the Internet could be considered to be an aid to
하나의 영역은 / [인터넷이 사고에 도움이 된다고 여겨질 수 있는]

thinking is the rapid procurement of new information.
/ 새로운 정보의 신속한 입수이다

05-06 People who have a high sense of self-efficacy tend **to pursue**
사람들은 / [높은 자기 효능감을 가진] / 도전적인 목표를 추구하는

challenging goals that may be outside the reach of the average
경향이 있다 / [아마 보통 사람의 도달 범위를 벗어나 있을]

person.

05-07 The idealism that freed men from most of their ancient fetters
이상주의는 / [남성들을 고대의 족쇄 대부분으로부터 자유롭게 만든]

awakened women to a realization of their unequal position in
/ 여성들을 일깨웠다 / 사회에서 그들의 불평등한 위치를 자각하도록

society.

05-08 A classroom where students feel involved and respected will
교실은 / [학생들이 참여하며 존중받는다고 느끼는] / 훈육의

reduce discipline issues, increase student motivation, and
문제를 감소시키고 / 학생의 동기 부여를 증가시키고 / 그리고

ultimately enhance learning.
궁극적으로 학습을 향상시킬 것이다

05-09 The way that we behave in a given situation is often influenced
방식은 / [우리가 주어진 상황 속에서 행동하는] / 종종 영향을 받는다

by how important one value is to us relative to others.
/ 하나의 가치가 우리에게 얼마나 중요한가에 의해 / 다른 가치들에 비해서

C

05-10 Someone who reads only newspapers and books by contemporary
사람은 / [신문과 현대 작가가 쓴 책들만 읽는]

authors looks to me like a near-sighted person.
/ 나에게는 근시안적인 사람처럼 보인다

05-11 The impressions that a child receives from his environment during
인상은 / [아이가 자신의 환경으로부터 받는] / 인생의

the first years of life influence his intellectual development and
처음 몇 해 동안에] / 그의 지적 발달과 성격에 매우 근본적으로 영향을 끼친다

character very basically.

05-12 The period when humans began growing crops, raising animals
기간은 / [인간이 농작물을 재배하고, 식량을 위해 동물을 사육하고, 석기 기술을 사용하기 시작한]

for food, and using stone-tool technology is referred to as Neolithic
/ 신석기라고 일컬어진다

period.

13

unit 06 주어 + 형용사절 2

S TANDARD

06-01 The fact that a book or publication is popular does not
사실이 / [= 어떤 책이나 출판물이 인기가 있다는] / 반드시 만드는

necessarily make it of value.
것은 아니다 / 그것을 가치 있게

06-02 The bodies of flowing ice we call glaciers are the most spectacular
흐르는 얼음 덩어리는 / [우리가 빙하라고 부르는] / 가장 장관을 이루는 것이다

of natural features.
/ [자연의 특징 중]

A

06-03 The rule that nouns form their plural by adding "s" does **not** apply
규칙은 / [= 명사들이 복수형을 만든다는] / 's'를 덧붙임으로써] / 'mouse'라는 단어에는

to the word "mouse."
적용되지 않는다

06-04 The first impressions we form about someone **often** affect ou
첫 인상은 / [우리가 어떤 사람에 대해 만들어 내는] / 종종 우리의 인상에 영향을

impression of subsequent perceptions of that person.
미친다 / [그 사람에 대해 뒤이어 일어나는 인식에 대한]

06-05 One of the most important reasons we need to send humans to
가장 중요한 이유 중의 하나는 / [우리가 화성에 인간을 보낼 필요가 있는]

Mars is to determine whether there ever was or even still is life on
/ 밝혀내는 것이다 / 생명체가 있었는지 또는 아직도 있는지를 /

Mars.
화성에

B

06-06 The announcement that the first stages of human cloning have
발표는 / [= 인간 복제의 첫 단계가 달성되었다는]

been achieved leaves us wondering where it will all end.
/ 우리를 궁금하게 만든다 / 그것이 어디서 완전히 끝날지

06-07 The living organisms we now see **all have their structure based**
살아 있는 유기체들은 / [우리가 지금 보는] / 모두 그들의 구조를 가지고 있다 / [탄소라는

upon the element carbon.
원소에 기반한]

06-08 The words you speak to someone may have **the potential to make**
단어들은 / [당신이 누군가에게 말하는] / 그 사람을 만들거나 깨뜨리는 잠재력을 가지고 있을지도

or break that person, so it is important to choose words carefully.
모른다 / 따라서 (…은) 중요하다 / 단어들을 신중히 선택하는 것은

06-09 The way we wish the world to be is how, in the movies, it more
방식은 / [우리가 세상이 어떻게 되기를 소망하는] / 영화에서 그것(세상)이 대개 결국 존재하게 되는 방식이다

often than not winds up being.

C

06-10 The complaint that immigrants take people's jobs is**, like similar**
불평은 / [= 이민자들이 사람들의 일자리를 앗아간다는] / 기술에 관한 비슷한

complaints about technology, based on an erroneously static
불평처럼 근거하고 있다 / 잘못 고정된 세계관에

view of the world.

06-11 The seemingly impractical knowledge we gain from space probes
겉보기에 비현실적인 지식이 / [우리가 얻는] / 다른 세계로 간 우주 탐사기에서]

to other worlds tells us about our planet and our own role in the
/ 우리에게 말해준다 / 우리의 행성과 우리의 역할에 대해서 / [자연의

scheme of nature.
체계 안에서의]

06-12 The reason people give up so quickly is because they look at how
이유는 / [사람들이 그렇게 빨리 포기하는] / 그들이 바라보기 때문이다 / 그들이

far they still have to go, instead of how far they have come.
여전히 얼마나 멀리 가야 하는지를 / 얼마나 멀리 그들이 왔는지 대신에

15

Review

A

01 Whatever happens, happens **for a reason.**
일어나는 것은 무엇이든지 / 일어난다 / 이유가 있기 때문에

02 What people eat, when they eat, and how they eat are **all** patterned
사람들이 무엇을 먹는지, 그들이 언제 먹는지, 그리고 그들이 어떻게 먹는지는 / 모두 양식이 형성된다

by culture.
/ 문화에 의해서

03 Being able to predict how other people might feel, act, or react is a
예측할 수 있는 것은 / 다른 사람들이 어떻게 느끼고, 행동하고, 반응할지를 / 기술

skill that helps us build better relationships.
이다 / [우리가 더 나은 관계를 형성하도록 돕는]

04 With a bit of unbiased examination of our motives, it is hard to deny
우리의 동기에 대해 좀 공정한 조사를 해 보면 / (…은) 어렵다 / 부인하는 것은

that we have strong bias toward our individual interests.
/ 우리가 개인적인 이익을 향한 강한 성향을 가지고 있다는 것을

B

05 Learning how to persuade people will earn you **the support and respect**
사람들을 설득하는 법을 배우는 것은 / 얻게 할 것이다 / 당신에게 / 지지와 존경을 [당신의 고객, 상사,

of your customers, bosses, co-workers, colleagues and friends.
업무 협력자, 동료, 그리고 친구들의]

06 In nature, there is no such thing as waste. What dies or becomes
자연에는 / 쓰레기와 같은 것은 없다 죽거나 쓸모없게 되는 것은

useless in one part of an ecosystem nourishes **another part.**
/ 생태계의 한 부분에서 / 다른 부분에 영양분을 공급한다

07 Physical and physiological features or behaviors of an organism that
한 유기체의 물리적, 생리적 특징이나 행동은 / [예전에

once may have contributed to its reproductive success but no longer
그 유기체의 번식 성공에 기여했을 수도 있는 / 그러나 더 이상은 그렇지

do so become susceptible to elimination **by natural selection.**
않은] / 자연 선택에 의해 제거되기 쉬워진다

C

08 Learning science through inquiry is a primary principle in education
탐구를 통해 과학을 배우는 것은 / 주된 원칙이다 / 오늘날 교육에서

today.

09 It is difficult to see ourselves through the lenses of others.
(…은) 어렵다 / 다른 사람들의 눈으로 우리 자신을 보는 것은

10 The belly fat disorder caused by lack of physical activity leads to
복부 지방 질환은 / [신체 활동의 부족으로 인한] / 우리 신체의

a decreased rate of metabolism in our body.
신진대사율의 감소로 이어진다

D

11 What traditional entertainment always promised was to transport us
전통적인 오락이 항상 약속한 것은 / 우리를 이동시켜 주는 것이었다

from our daily problems, to enable us to escape from the struggles of
/ 우리의 일상적인 문제들로부터 / 즉 우리가 삶의 고투로부터 벗어날 수 있게 해주는 것

life.

12 The discrepancy between the understanding of the writer and that of
불일치는 / [작가의 이해와 독자의 이해 사이의]

the audience is the single greatest impediment to accurate
/ 정확한 의사소통에 대한 유일한 가장 큰 장애물이다

communication.

13 Any scientist who announces a so-called discovery at a press
과학자는 누구든지 / [기자 회견에서 소위 발견을 발표하는

conference without first permitting expert reviewers to examine his
/ 먼저 전문 검토자들이 그 사람의 주장을 검토하도록 허용하지 않고]

or her claims is automatically castigated as a publicity seeker.
/ 자동적으로 혹평된다 / 명성을 쫓는 사람이라고

unit 07 전치사구와 짝을 이루는 동사 구문

07-01 Many experts in childhood development **think of** play **as the "work**
많은 아동기 발달 전문가들은 / 놀이를 여긴다 / '아이들의 일'로

of children."

07-02 Pride **prevents** individuals **from experiencing their true value or**
자만심은 개인들을 막는다 / 자신들의 참된 가치 또는 다른 사람들의 참된 가치를 경험하는 것을

the true value of others.
로부터

A

07-03 We can **compare** life **to a roller coaster** because it has ups and
우리는 인생을 비유할 수 있다 / 롤러코스터에 / 왜냐하면 그것은 기복이 있기 때문에

downs, but it's your choice **to scream or enjoy the ride.**
/ 그러나 (…은) 당신의 선택이다 / 소리를 지르거나 타는 것을 즐기는 것은

07-04 Future generations may **blame** us **for our wasteful ways, but they**
미래 세대는 우리를 비난할지도 모른다 / 우리의 낭비하는 방식에 대해 / 그러나 그들은

can never **collect on our debt to them.**
결코 징수할 수 없다 / 그들에 대한 우리의 빚을

07-05 Never **deprive** someone **of hope;** it might be all they have.
결코 어떤 사람에게서 희망을 빼앗지 마라 / 그것은 전부일지도 모른다 / [그들이 가진]

B

07-06 The competent, confident, and caring young adults **saw**
유능하고, 자신감 있고, 배려심이 있는 젊은이들은 자기 자신들을 여겼다

themselves as the masters of their own fate and viewed negative
/ 자기 스스로의 운명의 주인으로 / 그리고 부정적인 사건들을 여겼다

events not as threats but as challenges and even opportunities.
/ 위협이 아니라 / 도전과 심지어는 기회로

07-07 Movies provide us with the happy endings and the just solutions
영화는 우리에게 제공한다 / 행복한 결말과 올바른 해결책을

that we cherish in our hearts.
/ [우리가 우리의 마음속에 품고 있는]

07-08 If you feel threatened every time a perceived rival does well, remind
만약 당신이 위협받는다고 느낀다면 / 인지된 경쟁 상대가 잘할 때마다 / 스스로에게

yourself of your own strengths and successes.
상기시켜라 / 당신 자신의 강점과 성공한 것들을

07-09 Throughout history there have been efforts to distinguish the
역사를 통틀어 / 노력이 있어왔다 / [유죄인 사람들을 무죄인 사람들과

guilty from the innocent and to tell the liars from the truthful.
구별하는 / 그리고 거짓말쟁이들을 진실된 사람들과 구별하는]

C

07-10 Nothing can stop the man with the right mental attitude from
어떤 것도 막을 수 없다 / [올바른 정신적 태도를 가진 사람을] / 그의

achieving his goal; nothing on earth can help the man with the
목표를 성취하는 것으로부터 / 지구상의 어떠한 것도 도울 수 없다 / 사람을 / [잘못된 정신적

wrong mental attitude. *Thomas Jefferson*
태도를 가진]

07-11 Most scientists attribute extraordinary memory performance to an
대부분의 과학자들은 비상한 기억력을 덕분으로 여긴다 / 향상된

enhanced ability to associate or organize the information to be
능력의 / [기억될 정보를 연상하거나 조직화하는]

memorized, rather than true photographic memory.
/ 사진처럼 선명한 진정한 기억력이라기보다는

07-12 When individuals have a true sense of self-worth, they do not
개인들이 참된 의미의 자아 존중감을 가질 때 / 그들은 필요가 없다

need to compare themselves with others, to tear others apart or
/ 스스로를 타인과 비교하거나 / 타인들을 헐뜯거나 /

feel superior.
우월하다고 느낄

unit 08 조동사 구문

08-01 You shouldn't have driven that car with the faulty brakes. You
당신은 그 차를 운전하지 말았어야 했다 / [브레이크에 결함이 있는] 당신은

might have had a serious accident.
심각한 사고를 당했을지도 모른다

08-02 I would rather walk with a friend in the dark, than alone in the
나는 차라리 걷겠다 / 어둠 속에서 친구와 함께 / 빛 속에서 혼자 걷느니

light.

A

08-03 I was never top of the class at school, but my classmates must
나는 결코 학창 시절에 학급 수석이 아니었다 / 그러나 나의 급우들은 내게서 잠재력을 봤음

have seen potential in me, because my nickname was "Einstein."
틀림없다 / 왜냐하면 나의 별명은 '아인슈타인'이었으니까 *Stephen Hawking*

08-04 One's true feelings cannot but come through in what one says
사람의 진정한 감정은 전해지지 않을 수 없다 / 사람이 말하고 행하는 것 속에

and does.

08-05 A man may well be condemned, not for doing something, but for
사람은 아마 책망 받을 것이다 / 어떤 일을 해서가 아니라 / 아무것도

doing nothing. *William Barclay*
하지 않기 때문에

B

08-06 It's defeatist to harp on what might have been, and yet, it's hard
(···은) 패배주의적이다 / 무슨 일이 있었을지도 모른다고 되뇌는 것은 / 그렇다 하더라도 (···은) 어렵다

to resist considering what might have been.
/ 무슨 일이 있었을지도 모른다고 생각하는 것을 참는 것은

08-07 The suspect can't have committed the crime as he was in another
그 용의자가 그 범죄를 저질렀을 리가 없다 / 그가 다른 나라에 있었기 때문에

country at the moment of the murder.
/ 살인의 순간에

08-08 You might as well expect rivers to run backwards as any man
당신은 강이 거꾸로 흐르는 것을 기대하는 것이 나을 것이다 / 자유롭게 태어난 어떤

born free to be contented penned up. *Chief Joseph*
사람이 가두어진 채로 만족하는 것을 기대하느니

08-09 *The Brothers Karamazov*, one of the peaks in the literature of the
「카라마조프가의 형제들」은 / 세계 문학의 최고봉 중의 하나인

world, can hardly be valued too highly. *Sigmund Freud*
/ 아무리 높이 평가되어도 지나치지 않다

c

08-10 The universe must have originated from a more compact state
우주는 생겨났음에 틀림없다 / 더 조밀한 어떤 상태로부터

that we call the Big Bang.
/ [우리가 빅뱅이라고 부르는]

08-11 When the epidemic broke out, it claimed many lives. The
그 전염병이 발생했을 때 / 그것은 많은 생명을 앗아갔다 당국이

authorities ought to have taken precautions to prevent the
예방조치를 취했어야 했다 / 그 전염병을 예방하기 위해

epidemic.

08-12 I would rather be a ghost, drifting by your side as a condemned soul,
나는 차라리 유령이 되고 싶다 / 당신 곁을 떠돌면서 / 저주받은 영혼으로서

than enter heaven without you. *the movie <Crouching Tiger, Hidden Dragon 와호장룡>*
/ 당신이 없는 천국에 들어가느니

21

unit 09 수동태 구문

09-01 We are all now connected by the Internet, like neurons in a gian
우리는 모두 지금 연결되어 있다 / 인터넷에 의해 / 마치 거대한 뇌 속의 뉴런들처럼

brain. *Stephen Hawking*

09-02 Solar power and wind power are considered alternatives to fossi
태양 에너지와 풍력은 / 대안으로 여겨진다 / [화석 연료

fuel-based energy generation.
기반의 에너지 생성에 대한]

09-03 The best and most beautiful things in the world cannot be see
세상에서 가장 좋고 가장 아름다운 것은 / 보이거나 심지어는 만져질

or even touched. They must be felt with the heart. *Helen Keller*
수도 없다 그것들은 마음으로 느껴져야 한다

09-04 Unfortunately, the rain forests are being cut down at a shockin
유감스럽게도 / 우림은 잘려져 나가고 있다 / 충격적인 속도로

rate to provide humans with lumber, pasture land, and farm land.
/ 인간들에게 목재, 목초지, 그리고 농지를 제공하기 위해서

09-05 Geysers have often been compared to volcanoes because the
간헐천은 종종 화산으로 비유되어 왔다 / 왜냐하면 그것들은

both emit hot liquids from below the Earth's surface.
둘 다 뜨거운 액체를 분출하기 때문에 / 지구의 표면 아래로부터

09-06 Information is extracted or learned from sources of data, and thi
정보는 추출되거나 학습된다 / 자료의 원천으로부터 / 그리고 이

captured information is then transformed into knowledge that i
입수된 정보는 곧이어 지식으로 바뀐다 / [마침내

eventually used to trigger actions or decisions.
행동 또는 결정을 촉발하기 위해 사용되는]

09-07 Genetic tendencies toward intelligence, sociability, and
유전적 성향은 / [지능, 사교성, 그리고 공격성에 대한]

aggression can be stimulated, controlled, or suppressed by
/ 자극되거나 통제되거나 또는 억압될 수 있다 /

parental response and other environmental influences.
부모의 반응이나 다른 환경적 영향에 의해서

09-08 Hacking is commonly described as the act of re-designing the
해킹은 흔히 묘사된다 / 하드웨어 또는 소프트웨어 시스템의 환경 설정을 재설계

configuration of hardware or software systems to alter their
하는 행위로서 / 그것의 의도된 기능을

intended function.
변경하기 위해

09-09 It is estimated that we have characterized only one percent of all
(…이) 추정된다 / 우리가 모든 박테리아 종들의 겨우 1%만을 규정해왔다는 것이

bacterial species that exist.
/ [존재하는]

C

09-10 Test papers may not be taken out of the examination room.
시험 문제지는 갖고 나가져서는 안 된다 / 시험장 밖으로

09-11 Don't judge people by their covers. Most of their books are still
사람들을 판단하지 마라 / 그들의 겉모습으로 그들의 책 대부분은 여전히 쓰이고 있는 중이다

being written.

09-12 Confirmed scientific theories are often referred to as "laws of nature"
입증된 과학 이론들은 종종 일컬어진다 / '자연의 법칙' 또는 '물리학의

or "laws of physics."
법칙'이라고

Review

A

01 Primitive societies tend to view man and beast, animal and plant,
원시 사회는 경향이 있다 / 사람과 짐승, 동물과 식물, 생물체와 무생물체의 영역을 여기는

organic and inorganic realms, as participants in an integrated,
/ 통합된, 살아있는 총체 속의 참여자로

animated totality.

02 You can fail at what you don't want, so you might as well take a
당신은 실패할 수 있다 / 당신이 원하지 않는 것에   / 따라서 당신은 운에 맡기고 해보는 편이 낫다

chance on doing what you love. *Jim Carrey*
/ 당신이 좋아하는 것을 하는 것을

03 I'd rather be hated for who I am, than loved for who I am not.
나는 차라리 미움을 받겠다 / 내 자신인 것으로 / 사랑받느니 / 내 자신이 아닌 것으로   *Kurt Cobain*

04 Quantum theory states that energy, such as light, is given off and
양자론은 명시한다   / 빛과 같은 에너지는 방출되고 흡수된다는 것을

absorbed in tiny definite units called quanta or photons.
/ 아주 작은 일정한 구성 단위 속에서 / [양자 또는 광자라고 일컬어지는]

B

05 A copyright supplies its holder with a kind of monopoly over the
저작권은 그것의 보유자에게 제공한다   / 일종의 독점을   / [창작된 저작들

created material, and it assures him or her of both control over its
대한]   / 그리고 그것은 그 사람에게 보증한다   / 그것의 이용에 대한 통제권과 그것에서

use and the benefits from it.
나오는 수익 둘 다를

06 The show is all booked up. You should have purchased tickets
그 공연은 모두 예약이 매진되었습니다   당신은 더 일찍 표를 구매했어야 합니다

earlier. Would you like to be put on a waiting list?
당신은 대기자 명단에 오르기를 원하십니까?

07 Scientists assume that Earth must have formed from dry material
과학자들은 추정한다 / 지구는 생겨났음에 틀림없다고 / 물기 없는 물질로부터

and acquired its water through objects from more distant, icy
/ 그리고 물을 얻었음에 틀림없다고 / 물체들을 통해서 / [태양계의 더 먼, 얼음 구간대에서 온]

reaches of the solar system crashing into Earth.
/ [지구로 충돌하는]

08 The personal computer is designed for the general function of
개인용 컴퓨터는 설계된다 / 정보를 다루고 처리하는 일반적인 용도를 위해서

handling and processing information, but exactly how the PC is used is
/ 그러나 정확하게 PC가 어떻게 사용되는지는 미리 결정

not predetermined.
되지 않는다

C

09 I couldn't access the website because it was being updated.
나는 그 웹사이트에 접속할 수 없었다 / 그것이 업데이트 되고 있는 중이었기 때문에

10 It is sometimes alleged, by linguists, that language must have been
(…이) 때때로 주장된다 / 언어학자들에 의해서 / 언어는 발명되었음에 틀림없다는 것이

invented at some recent point in the past.
/ 과거의 어떤 최근 시점에

D

11 The scientist attributed changes in the climate to global warming
그 과학자는 기후 변화를 탓으로 돌렸다 / 지구 온난화와 대기 오염의

and pollution of the atmosphere.

12 A spongy three-pound mass of fatty tissue, the brain has often been
해면 모양으로 생긴 3파운드의 지방 조직 덩어리인 뇌는 종종 비유되어왔다

compared to a super-computer.
/ 슈퍼컴퓨터에

unit 10 명사구 목적어

STANDARD

10-01 Both countries agreed **to abolish their tariff walls within 5 years.**
양국은 동의했다 / 그들의 관세 장벽을 철폐하는 것을 / 5년 내에

10-02 I particularly enjoyed **driving through the countryside with you.**
나는 특히 즐겼다 / 당신과 함께 교외를 드라이브하는 것을

A

10-03 I don't mind **listening to advice that I've asked for,** but I refuse to
나는 조언을 경청하는 것을 싫어하지 않는다 / [내가 요청한] / 그러나 나는 훈계 듣는

be preached at.
것을 거부한다

10-04 I almost forgot **the storyline of the Disney movie** *Frozen*, but I do
나는 디즈니 영화 '겨울왕국'의 줄거리를 거의 잊었다 / 그러나 나는

remember waiting in line to see the movie.
줄을 서서 기다린 것을 정말 기억한다 / 그 영화를 보기 위해

10-05 Politicians are the same all over. They promise **to build a bridge**
정치인들은 어디서나 똑같다 그들은 다리를 놓을 것을 약속한다

even where there is no river. *Nikita Khrushchev*
/ 강이 없는 곳에도

B

10-06 No one's instincts are always correct; so how do you know **when**
어느 누구의 본능도 항상 올바르지는 않다 / 그렇다면 당신은 어떻게 아는가 / 언제

to follow them and when to ignore them?
그것을 따라야 할지 / 그리고 언제 그것을 무시해야 할지를?

10-07 The drunken man admitted **stealing the car, but** denied **driving it**
그 술 취한 남자는 그 차를 훔쳤음을 시인했다 / 하지만 그것을 운전한 것을 부인했다

under the influence of alcohol.
/ 술에 취한 상태로

10-08 Once I forgot **to turn off the oven and** I shall **never forget seeing**
예전에 나는 잊었다 / 오븐을 끄는 것을 / 그리고 나는 결코 잊지 못할 것이다 / 나머지

the expression on the faces of the rest of the family when they
가족의 얼굴 표정을 본 것을 / 그들이 깨달았을

realized they had nothing to eat.
때 / 자신들이 먹을 것이 없다는 것을

10-09 We stopped **checking for monsters under our bed when we**
우리는 괴물들을 살펴보는 것을 그만두었다 / 우리의 침대 아래에서 / 우리가 깨달았을

realized they were inside us. *the movie <The Dark Knight>*
때 / 그것들이 우리 안에 있다는 것을

10-10 After careful **consideration of your proposal, I** regret **to say that**
당신의 제안에 대해서 심사숙고한 후에 / 나는 말하게 되어 유감이다 /

we are unable to accept it.
우리가 그것을 받아들일 수 없다고

10-11 I've **never** regretted **saying a kind word to someone, but I have**
나는 결코 후회하지 않았다 / 누군가에게 다정한 말 한 마디를 한 것을 / 그러나 나는 후회

regretted plenty of mean things I have said and done.
해왔다 / 많은 비열한 것들을 / [내가 말하고 행한]

10-12 Life will knock **us down, but** we can choose **whether or not to**
인생은 우리를 쓰러뜨릴 것이다 / 그러나 우리는 선택할 수 있다 / 우리가 다시 일어설지 말지를

stand back up. *Jackie Chan*

unit **11** 명사절 목적어

S TANDARD

11-01 A judge must decide **whether a person is guilty or innocent of a**
판사는 판결을 내려야 한다 / 어떤 사람이 유죄인지 무죄인지를 / 범행

crime.
대해

11-02 Your present circumstances don't determine **where you can go**
당신의 현재 상황이 결정하지 않는다 / 어디로 당신이 갈 수 있는지를

they merely determine where you start. *Nido Qubein*
/ 그것들은 단지 결정한다 / 어디서 당신이 시작하는지를

A

11-03 The great astronomer Edwin Hubble discovered **that all distant**
위대한 천문학자 에드윈 허블은 발견했다 / 모든 먼 은하들이 멀어지고

galaxies are receding from our Milky Way Galaxy.
있다는 것을 / 우리의 은하로부터

11-04 The woman who was on passport control asked me **if I had any**
그 여자는 / [여권 심사대에 있던] / 내게 물었다 / 내가 또 다른 신분

further identification.
증명 자료를 가졌는지를

11-05 People who are satisfied appreciate **what they have in life and**
사람들은 / [만족하는] / 감사한다 / 그들이 인생에서 가진 것을 / 그리

don't worry about how it compares to what others have.
걱정하지 않는다 / 그것이 어떻게 비교되는지에 대해서 / 다른 사람들이 가진 것과

B

11-06 Perhaps, we've just forgotten **that we are still pioneers, that**
아마도 / 우리는 그저 잊어버렸는지도 모른다 / 우리가 여전히 개척자들이라는 것을 / 우리가

we've barely begun, and that our greatest accomplishments
가까스로 시작했다는 것을 / 그리고 우리의 가장 위대한 성취는 우리의 뒤에 있을 수 없다[이미 일어난 것이

cannot be behind us. *the movie <Interstellar>*
아니라]는 것을

11-07 Actors are **so** fortunate. They can choose **whether they will**
배우들은 아주 운이 좋다 　　　　　　그들은 선택할 수 있다 　　／ 자신들이 비극 또는 희극에 출연할

appear in tragedy or in comedy, whether they will suffer or make
것인지를 　　　　　　　／ 그들이 고통을 겪을 것인지 또는 즐겁게 놀지,

merry, laugh or shed tears. *Oscar Wilde*
웃을지 아니면 눈물을 흘릴 것인지를

11-08 Environmentalists argue **no system of waste disposal can be**
환경 운동가들은 주장한다 　　　　／ 어떠한 쓰레기 처리 시스템도 절대적으로 안전할 수는 없다고

absolutely safe, either now or in the future.
　　　　／ 지금이든 미래든

11-09 Either Saturday or Monday, choose **whichever is more convenient**
토요일이나 월요일 중 　　　／ 선택해라 　／ 어느 것이든 네게 더 편한 쪽을

for you.

11-10 Indeed, a brief look at a dictionary will show you **that the majority**
정말로 　　／ 사전을 잠깐 살펴 보는 것은 당신에게 보여 줄 것이다 　　　／ 대다수의 단어가 사용된다는

of words are used with more than one meaning.
것을 　　　　　　／ 하나 이상의 의미로

11-11 In times of social, cultural or religious sensitivity **one might**
사회적, 문화적 또는 종교적 민감성의 시대에 　　　　　　　　　／ 사람들은 궁금해할

wonder whether it is ethical to avoid, or not to avoid, questions that
수도 있다 　／ (…이) 윤리적인지 　　／ 질문을 피하는 것 또는 피하지 않는 것이 　　　／ [갈등을

might increase conflict.
증가시킬 수도 있는]

11-12 The government will take **whatever action is necessary to achieve**
정부는 취할 것이다 　　　　　／ 필요한 어떤 조치든지 　　　　　　／ 통화와 금융의

monetary and financial stability.
안정성을 확보하기 위해서

unit 12 가목적어 it

12-01 Artificial intelligence makes it possible for machines to learn from
인공지능은 만든다 / (…을) 가능하게 / 기계들이 경험으로부터 배우는 것을

experience and perform human tasks.
/ 그리고 인간의 과제를 수행하는 것을

12-02 We should not take it for granted that classic moral stories wil
우리는 여겨서는 안 된다 / (…을) 당연하게 / 고전적인 교훈적 이야기들이 자동적으로 도덕적

automatically promote moral behaviors.
행동을 촉진할 것임을

A

12-03 The European Union has found it difficult to reach a consensus
유럽연합은 알았다 / (…이) 어렵다는 것을 / 의견 일치에 도달하는 것이

on economic issues.
/ 경제문제에 관해

12-04 Our research makes it evident that many imaginative children
우리의 연구는 만든다 / (…을) 명백하게 / 상상력이 풍부한 많은 아이들이 종종 상상의 놀이 친구를

often invent imaginary playmates.
만들어 낸다는 것을

12-05 Engrave it on your heart that a little help is worth a deal of pity.
새겨라 / (…을) 당신의 마음에 / 작은 도움이 많은 동정의 가치가 있다는 것을

B

12-06 Even if you don't read a newspaper or watch television, and walk
비록 당신이 신문을 읽지 않거나 텔레비전을 시청하지 않는다고 하더라도 / 그리고 눈을

around the streets with your eyes down, you'll find it impossible
내리깐 채로 거리를 걸어 다닌다고 하더라도 / 당신은 알게 될 것이다 / (…이) 불가능하다는

to avoid some form of publicity.
/ 어떤 형태의 광고를 피하는 것이

12-07 I make it a rule not to clutter my mind with simple information
나는 삼는다 / (…을) 규칙으로 / 내 마음을 어지럽히지 않는 것을 / 간단한 정보로

that I can find in a book in five minutes. *Albert Einstein*
/ [내가 책에서 찾을 수 있는 / 5분 이내에]

12-08 We owe it to our children to give them a dignified and hopeful
우리는 의무를 지고 있다 / (…을) 우리의 자녀들에게 / 그들에게 고귀하고 희망찬 미래를 제공할 것을

future. *Giorgio Napolitano*

12-09 Bear it in mind when a life storm breaks that, no matter how
품어라 / (…을) 마음 속에 / 인생의 폭풍이 일 때 / 아무리 맹렬하더라도

violent, it is only temporary and that behind the clouds the sun is
/ 그것은 단지 일시적이라는 것을 / 그리고 구름 뒤에는 태양이 항상 빛나고 있다는 것을

always shining.

C

12-10 The internet has made it easy for us to hear whatever we like the
인터넷은 만들어왔다 / (…을) 쉽게 / 우리가 듣는 것을 / 우리가 가장 좋아하는 무엇이든

most in mere seconds.
/ 단 몇 초 내에

12-11 At certain times in history, cultures have taken it for granted that
역사의 어떤 때에 / 문화는 여겨왔다 / (…을) 당연하게 / 사람이

a person was not fully human unless he or she learned to master
충분하게 인간적이지 않았다는 것을 / 만약 그 사람이 배우지 않았다면 / 생각과 감정을

thoughts and feelings.
억누르는 것을

12-12 Every man who knows how to read has it in his power to magnify
모든 사람은 / [글을 읽는 방법을 아는] / (…을) 그의 수중에 가진다 / 자신을 확장하는 것

himself, to multiply the ways in which he exists, to make his life
/ 방식을 다양화하는 것 / [자신이 존재하는] / 자신의 삶을 충만하고, 중대

full, significant, and interesting. *Aldous Huxley*
하고, 흥미롭게 만드는 것을

Unit 13 목적어 + 형용사구

13-01 Our bodies have the natural ability to fight off bacteria and
우리의 신체는 타고난 능력을 가지고 있다 / [박테리아와 질병을 물리칠

diseases when they enter our bodies.
/ 그것들이 우리의 몸에 들어올 때]

13-02 We often experience unexpected results brought about by words
우리는 종종 예상치 못한 결과를 경험한다 / [말에 의해서 초래되는

carelessly used.
/ [부주의하게 사용된]]

A

13-03 Healthy living in individuals lays the foundation for healthy living
개인들의 건강한 삶은 토대를 놓는다 / [사회와 세계의 모든 곳의

throughout society and the world.
건강한 삶을 위한]

13-04 You have the right to be given a fair trial by a court of law if you
당신은 권리를 가진다 / [공정한 재판을 받을 / 법정에 의해서] / 만약

are accused of a crime.
당신이 범죄로 고발된다면

13-05 I have received an email offering me a job for an unknown
나는 이메일을 받았다 / [내게 무명의 회사의 일자리를 제안하는

company that I don't remember applying to.
/ [내가 지원한 기억이 나지 않는]]

B

13-06 The use of words itself yields, upon analysis, valuable results
단어의 사용 그 자체는 낳는다 / 분석해보면 / 가치 있는 결과를

illustrative of the various temperaments of authors.
/ [작가의 다양한 기질을 분명히 보여 주는]

13-07 At times our own light goes out and is rekindled by a spark from
가끔 우리 자신의 빛이 꺼진다 / 그리고 재점화된다 / 다른 사람으로부터의 불꽃에

another person. Each of us has cause to think with deep gratitude
의해서 우리 각자는 이유를 가지고 있다 / [사람들에 대해 깊이 감사하는 마음으로 생각할

of those who have lighted the flame within us. *Albert Schweitzer*
/ [우리 안의 불꽃에 불을 붙여온]]

13-08 Regular exercise increases the amount of blood flowing through
규칙적인 운동은 피의 양을 증가시킨다 / [당신의 뇌를 통과하여 흐르

your brain.
는]

13-09 We should reduce hazardous and toxic chemicals released into
우리는 위험하고 유독한 화학물질을 줄여야 한다 / [대기와 물속으로 방출

the air and water.
되는]

13-10 Certainly, Leonardo da Vinci had an unusual mind and an uncanny
확실히 레오나르도 다빈치는 남다른 사고방식과 뛰어난 능력을 지녔다

ability to see what others didn't see.
/ [다른 사람들이 보지 못했던 것을 보는]

13-11 Scientists at NASA have spotted six asteroids heading in the
NASA의 과학자들은 여섯 개의 소행성을 발견해왔다 / [지구 쪽으로 향하는]

direction of Earth, with one of them having a size larger than the
/ 그것들 중 하나는 엠파이어 스테이트 빌딩보다 더 큰 크기이다

Empire State Building.

13-12 Google and other carmakers around the world are developing
구글과 전 세계의 다른 자동차 제조사들은 기술을 개발하고 있다

technologies applied to currently "manned" vehicles to permit
/ [현재 '유인' 차량에 적용되는] / 운전자들이

drivers to take their hands off the wheel and focus on other tasks.
운전대로부터 손을 떼고 다른 업무에 집중할 수 있도록

33

Unit 14 목적어 + 형용사절

14-01 We trust leaders who are real, who walk their talk, who act on
우리는 지도자들을 신뢰한다 / [진실된 / 그들이 말한 것을 실행하는 / 그들의 핵심 가치다

their core values, and who tell us the truth.
행동하는 / 그리고 우리에게 진실을 말하는]

14-02 We are approaching the time when machines will be able to
우리는 시대로 다가가고 있다 / [기계가 인간을 능가할 수 있을

outperform humans at almost any task.
/ 거의 모든 업무에서]

A

14-03 Basic scientific research provides the raw materials that
기초 과학 연구는 원료를 제공한다 / [기술

technology and engineering use to solve problems.
공학이 활용하는 / 문제를 해결하기 위해서]

14-04 Personality psychologists had underestimated the extent to
성격 심리학자들은 정도를 과소평가했었다 /

which the social situation shapes people's behavior, independently
[사회적 상황이 사람들의 행동을 형성하는 / 그들의 성격과 관계없이

of their personality.

14-05 The word "fable" frequently denotes a brief tale where animals or
'우화'라는 단어는 빈번하게 짧은 이야기를 뜻한다 / [동물 또는 무생물이 말을 하고

inanimate objects speak and behave like humans, usually to
행동하는 / 사람처럼 / 대개 어떤 교훈적

advance a moral point.
의미를 제시하기 위해서]

B

14-06 I fear not the man who has practiced 10,000 kicks once, but I fear
나는 사람을 두려워하지 않는다 / [한 번에 1만 번의 발차기를 연습한] / 그러나 나는

the man who has practiced one kick 10,000 times. *Bruce Lee*
사람을 두려워한다 / [하나의 발차기를 1만 번 연습한]

14-07 Our atmosphere supplies most of the oxygen which animals must
우리의 대기는 대부분의 산소를 제공한다 / [동물들이 가져야 하는

have to survive, as well as the carbon dioxide needed by plants.
/ 생존하기 위해서] / 이산화탄소뿐만 아니라 / [식물이 필요로 하는]

14-08 Choose words that are more expressive, like 'great' or 'terrific' or
단어들을 선택하라 / [더욱 표현력이 있는 / 'great,' 'terrific,' 또는 'wonderful'

'wonderful' if you want to express pleasure.
처럼] / 만약 당신이 즐거움을 표현하고 싶다면

14-09 We will eventually reach a point at which conflict with the finite
우리는 결국 지점에 이르게 될 것이다 / [자원의 한정성과의 갈등이 불가피한]

nature of resources is inevitable.

C

14-10 'Jack-of-all-trades' means those who claim to be proficient at
'팔방미인'은 사람들을 의미한다 / [셀 수 없이 많은 일들에 능숙하다고 주장하는

countless tasks, but cannot perform a single one of them well.
/ 그러나 그것들 중 단 하나도 잘 해낼 수 없는]

14-11 We are thoroughly enjoying the immediate benefits of attractive
우리는 매력적인 소비재의 목전의 혜택을 잘 누리고 있다

consumer goods that we generate from producing and disseminating
/ [우리가 만들어 내는 / 위험한 화학물질을 생산하고 퍼뜨리는 것으로부터]

hazardous chemicals.

14-12 School physical education programs should offer a balanced
학교 체육 프로그램은 균형 잡힌 다양한 활동을 제공해야 한다

variety of activities that allow young people to develop ability in
/ [젊은이들이 평생 활동 속에서 능력을 개발할 수 있게 하는

lifetime activities that are personally meaningful and enjoyable.
/ [개인적으로 의미 있고 즐거운]]

Review

A

01 Remember to look up at the stars and not down at your feet. Try to
기억해라 / 위로 별을 보고 아래로 네 발을 보지 말 것을 노력해라

make sense of what you see and wonder about what makes the
네가 보는 것을 이해하려고 / 그리고 생각해보라 / 무엇이 우주를 존재하게 만드는가에 대해서

universe exist. *Stephen Hawking*

02 Some people make it difficult for others to tell them the truth
어떤 사람들은 만든다 / (…을) 어렵게 / 다른 사람들이 그들에게 진실을 말하는 것을

because they respond rudely or emotionally to people who tell the
/ 왜냐하면 그들이 무례하게 또는 감정적으로 반응하기 때문이다 / 사람들에게 / [진실을 말하는]

truth.

03 Never tell people how to do things. Tell them what to do and they will
결코 사람들에게 일을 어떻게 해야 할지를 말하지 마라   그들에게 무엇을 해야 할지를 말해라 / 그러면 그들은 당신을

surprise you with their ingenuity. *George S. Patton*
놀라게 할 것이다 / 자신들의 창의력으로

04 People will forget what you said, people will forget what you did, but
사람들은 잊을 것이다 / 당신이 말한 것을 / 사람들은 잊을 것이다 / 당신이 행한 것을 / 그러

people will never forget how you made them feel. *Maya Angelou*
사람들은 절대 잊지 않을 것이다 / 당신이 그들이 어떻게 느끼게 했는지를

B

05 NASA said the satellite stopped working within hours of its launch
NASA는 말했다 / 그 인공위성은 작동을 멈췄다고 / 그것을 발사한 지 몇 시간 내에

and did not respond to attempts to communicate with it.
/ 그리고 그것과 통신하려는 시도에 응답하지 않았다고

06 Do regular maintenance on your vehicles: Do not skimp on or forget
당신의 차량에 정기적인 정비를 하라 지나치게 아끼지 마라 / 또는 잊지 마라

to do regular oil changes.
/ 정기적인 오일 교체를 하는 것을

07 No one knows just what impact the buildup of CO_2 will have, but
아무도 알지 못한다 / 정말 이산화탄소의 축적이 어떤 영향을 미칠지를 / 그러

some scientists fear that the globe will continue to warm up, bringing
일부 과학자들은 염려한다 / 지구가 계속 온난해질 것 / 기후 변화의

on wrenching climatic changes.
왜곡을 야기하면서

08 Focusing on on-line interaction with people who are engaged in the
사람들과 온라인상의 상호작용에 초점을 맞추는 것은 / [동일한 전문화된 분야에 종사하는]

same specialized area can limit potential sources of information and
/ 정보의 잠재적 원천을 제한할 수 있다 / 그리고

thus make it less probable for unexpected findings to happen.
따라서 만들 수 있다 / (…을) 가망이 더 적게 / 예상치 못한 발견이 일어나는 것을

C

09 I realized I had forgotten to lock the door before I'd only gone a few
나는 깨달았다 / 내가 문을 잠그는 것을 잊었다는 것을 / 내가 그 길로 단지 몇 걸음을 채 가기 전에

steps down the road.

10 The law of universal gravitation explains how the force of gravity
만유인력의 법칙은 설명한다 / 어떻게 중력이 우주의 모든 물체에 영향을

affects all objects in the universe.
미치는지를

11 I think it necessary for people to realize what we are doing to the
나는 생각한다 / (…이) 필요하다고 / 사람들이 깨닫는 것이 / 우리가 환경에 무엇을 하고 있는지를

environment each time we throw away plastic.
/ 우리가 플라스틱을 버릴 때마다

D

12 Sometimes in the midst of life's chaos we forget to do the little
때때로 인생의 혼돈의 한가운데에서 / 우리는 작은 것들을 해야 하는 것을 잊는다

things that remind us we're part of something greater than ourselves.
/ [우리에게 상기시켜 주는 / 우리는 우리 자신보다 더 큰 어떤 것의 일부라는 것을]

13 Taking the time to truly understand another's point of view shows
다른 사람의 관점을 진정으로 이해하기 위해서 시간을 들이는 것은 보여 준다

that you value what he says and care about him as a person.
/ 당신이 그가 말하는 것을 소중하게 여긴다는 것을 / 그리고 그를 한 사람으로서 신경 쓴다는 것을

14 Children raised in households that foster communication find it
가정에서 양육된 아이들은 / [소통을 장려하는] / 생각한다 /

easier to talk to others about their emotions later in life.
(…을) 더 쉽게 / 타인들과 얘기하는 것을 / 살면서 나중에 자신들의 감정에 대해서

Unit **15** 주격보어: 구

S TANDARD

15-01 The supreme accomplishment is to blur the line between work
최고의 성취는 ~이다 / 경계를 흐릿하게 만드는 것 / [일과 놀이 사이의]

and play. *Arnold Toynbee*

15-02 The most popular cyber crimes are hacking a person's personal
가장 일반적인 사이버 범죄들은 ~이다 / 개인 계좌를 해킹하는 것

account and spreading a computer virus.
/ 그리고 컴퓨터 바이러스를 유포하는 것

A

15-03 Knowledge of the world is **only** to be acquired in the world, and
세상의 지식은 / **오로지** 세상 속에서 획득될 수 있다 / 벽장

not in a closet. *Lord Chesterfield*
속에서가 아니라

15-04 From the perspective of the individual working person, the key to
근로자 개인의 관점에서 / 훌륭한 직장의

a great workplace is feeling wanted and important.
비결은 ~이다 / 필요로 하고 중요하다고 느끼는 것

15-05 Disease, action that might produce disease, and recovery from
질병, 질병을 유발할 수도 있는 행동, 그리고 질병으로부터의 회복은

disease are of vital concern **to the whole primitive community.**
/ 중대한 관심사이다 / 원시 공동체 전체에게

B

15-06 Average consumers all over the world **still** remain unconvinced of
전 세계의 일반 소비자들은 여전히 확신하지 못하는 상태이다 /

the value and usefulness of cryptocurrencies such as bitcoin.
암호화폐의 가치와 유용성을 / [비트코인과 같은]

15-07 The goal of science is to learn how nature works by observing the
과학의 목적은 / 배우는 것이다 / 자연이 어떻게 작동하는지 / 물리적 세계를 관찰함으로써

physical world, and to understand it through research and
/ 그리고 그것을 이해하는 것(이다) / 연구와 실험을 통해서

experimentation.

15-08 Faith is taking the first step even when you don't see the whole
신뢰는 첫발을 내딛는 것이다 / 당신이 전체의 계단을 보지 못하는 때조차도

staircase. *Martin Luther King Jr.*

15-09 Life isn't about waiting for the storm to pass. It's about learning
삶은 기다리는 것에 관한 것이 아니다 / 폭풍이 지나가길 그것은 배우는 것에 관한 것이다

how to dance in the rain. *Vivian Greene*
/ 빗속에서 어떻게 춤을 추어야 할지

15-10 The only way to understand a word fully is to see it in use in as
단어를 완전히 이해하는 유일한 방법은 / 사용되는 그것을 보는 것이다 / 가능한

many contexts as possible.
한 많은 문맥 속에서

15-11 What the textbooks do not teach you is when to apply the
교과서가 당신에게 가르쳐 주지 못하는 것은 / 그 지식을 언제 적용하느냐이다

knowledge.

15-12 The most important factor in a happy life is having a good social
행복한 삶의 가장 중요한 요소는 / 좋은 사회적 관계를 갖는 것이다

network that you can depend on.
/ [당신이 의지할 수 있는]

unit 16 주격보어: 절

16-01 Life's tragedy is that we get old too soon and wise too late.
인생의 비극은 ~이다 / 우리가 너무 빨리 늙고 너무 늦게 현명해진다는 것
Benjamin Franklin

16-02 Challenges are what make life interesting **and** overcoming them
도전은 ~이다 / 인생을 흥미롭게 만드는 것 / 그리고 도전을 극복하는 것은 ~이다

is what makes life meaningful. *Joshua J. Marine*
/ 인생을 의미 있게 만드는 것

A

16-03 If you don't design your own life plan, chances are you'll fall into
만약 당신이 자신의 인생 계획을 설계하지 않는다면 / 가능성은 ~이다 / 당신이 다른 사람의

someone else's plan. *Jim Rohn*
계획에 빠지게 될 것이라는 것

16-04 Design is **not just** what it looks like and feels like. Design is how it
디자인은 ~아니다 / 단지 그것이 어떻게 보이고 느껴지느냐가 디자인은 ~이다 / 그것이

works. *Steve Jobs*
어떻게 작용하느냐

16-05 The acid test of a good driver is whether he or she remains calm
좋은 운전자를 보여 주는 진정한 척도는 ~이다 / 그 사람이 침착함을 유지하는지 못하는지

in an emergency.
/ 비상시에

B

16-06 A decline of empathy and a rise in narcissism are **exactly** what we
감정이입의 감소와 자아도취의 증가는 정확하게 ~이다 / 우리가 아이들

would expect to see in children who have little opportunity to
에게서 볼 것으로 예상하는 것 / [사회적으로 놀 기회가 거의 없는]

play socially.

16-07 The measure of a true champion is **not how they win. It's how**
진정한 챔피언의 척도는 ~아니다   / 그들이 어떻게 이기느냐가 그것은 ~이다 /

they handle defeat. *Garry Hall*
그들이 어떻게 패배를 다루느냐

16-08 The new processor is **to other processors** what a Ferrari is to
새로운 프로세서는 ~이다   / 다른 프로세서들에 대해서는   / 페라리가 다른 자동차들에 대한 것

other cars: i.e. faster.
   / 즉 더 빠르다

16-09 The meaning of a poem is **whatever the author intends to**
시의 의미는 ~이다   / 작가가 독자에게 전달하려고 의도하는 무엇이나

communicate to the reader by means of the poem.
   / 시에 의하여

16-10 An important lesson to remember is that we should try to see the
기억해야 할 중요한 교훈은 ~이다   / 우리가 인생에서 긍정적인 것들을 보려고 노력해야

positives in life even while we are stuck in the middle of trouble.
한다는 것   / 우리가 곤경의 한 가운데에 빠져 꼼짝 못 할 동안에도

16-11 One key social competence is how well or poorly people express
하나의 중요한 사회적 능력은 ~이다   / 얼마나 잘 또는 형편없이 사람들이 자기 자신의 감정을 표현하

their own feelings.
느냐

16-12 Facts are **to the scientist** what words are to the poet.
사실들은 ~이다 / 과학자에 대해서는   / 단어들이 시인에 대한 것

unit 17 목적격보어 1

17-01 Internet social networking allows **us** to expand our circle of
인터넷 소셜 네트워킹은 가능하게 한다 / 우리가 우리의 친구 범위를 확장하는 것을

friends.

17-02 We must **not** let **the virtual world** take us away from the real world
우리는 허용해서는 안 된다 / 가상세계가 우리를 데리고 떠나게 / 실세계로부터

that doesn't go away with a power outage.
/ [사라지지 않는 / 정전과 함께]

A

17-03 If you used the same password on any other site, we encourage
만약 당신이 어떤 다른 사이트에서 같은 비밀번호를 사용했다면 / 우리는 당신이 당신의

you to change your password there as well.
비밀번호를 바꾸기를 권장한다 / 거기서도 또한

17-04 The realities of growing older and the sense of brevity of our own
늙어간다는 현실 / 그리고 자신의 인생의 덧없음에 대한 의식은

lives **often** make us question the meaning of our existence.
/ 종종 시킨다 / 우리가 우리 존재의 의미를 묻게

17-05 Day after day, I watched **the parent birds** feed their newly hatched
매일 / 나는 지켜봤다 / 어미 새들이 자신들의 갓 부화한 새끼들에게 먹이를 주는 것을

chicks, **and I watched the chicks** grow.
/ 그리고 나는 지켜봤다 / 그 새끼들이 자라는 것을

B

17-06 You can force **the horse** to go to the river **but you cannot force**
당신은 강요할 수 있다 / 말이 강으로 가도록 / 그러나 당신은 강요할 수 없다

the horse to drink from it.
/ 말이 그것에서 마시도록

17-07 **When you read,** focusing on the main idea helps **you understand**
당신이 글을 읽을 때 / 요지에 초점을 맞추는 것은 돕는다 / 당신이 세부사항들을 더 잘

the details better.
이해하도록

17-08 **Most universities have** students fill out an evaluation of every
대부분의 대학들은 시킨다 / 학생들이 모든 강좌의 평가서를 작성하게

course they take.
/ [그들이 수강하는]

17-09 **When the clock said ten minutes to five, punctually as always,**
시계가 5시 10분 전을 가리켰을 때 / 늘 그렇듯 정확하게

she heard **the car** approach and stop outside.
/ 그녀는 들었다 / 그 자동차가 가까이 와서 밖에 멈추는 것을

C

17-10 **To improve their own chances of survival,** some parasites cause
그들 자신의 생존 가능성을 높이기 위해서 / 어떤 기생충들은 시킨다

their hosts to act in ways that are very different from their normal
/ 그들의 숙주들이 방식으로 행동하게 / [그들의 보통 행동과는 아주 다른]

behavior.

17-11 **Before you marry a person,** you should **first** make **them use a**
당신이 어떤 사람과 결혼하기 전에 / 당신은 먼저 시켜야 한다 / 그들이 느린 인터넷

computer with slow Internet service **to see who they really are.**
서비스로 컴퓨터를 사용하게 / 그들이 정말 어떤 사람인지 보기 위해서

17-12 **I've seen couples from different ethnic groups** merge into
나는 보아왔다 / 다른 인종 집단의 커플들이 조화로운 관계로 어울리는 것을

harmonious relationships, **and I've seen people from different**
/ 그리고 나는 보아왔다 / 다른 종교의 사람들이 강하고 지속적인

religions come together for a strong, lasting bond.
유대를 위해 연합하는 것을

43

unit 18 목적격보어 2

S TANDARD

18-01 In the downtown area I often see homeless people begging for
시내에서 / 나는 종종 본다 / 노숙자들이 돈을 구걸하고 있는 것을

money all around the stoplights.
/ 모든 신호등 주변에서

18-02 I saw a car pulled over on the side of the road while I was driving
나는 보았다 / 어떤 자동차가 길 한쪽에 세워진 것을 / 내가 집으로 운전하는 동안에

home.

A

18-03 The front desk clerk was on the phone and kept us waiting to
안내 데스크 직원은 통화중이었다 / 그리고 우리가 체크인하는 것을 계속 기다

check in for a long time.
리게 했다 / 오랫동안

18-04 Many debtors of the bank now find themselves caught in a serious
많은 은행 채무자들은 지금 깨닫는다 / 자신들이 심각한 재정 상태에 빠져 있다는 것을

financial position.

18-05 Unless we take good care of our teeth we may have them all
우리가 우리의 치아에 신경을 쓰지 않는다면 / 우리는 그것들을 모두 뽑히게 할지도 모른다

pulled out and have a set of false teeth made to replace them.
/ 그리고 틀니 세트가 맞춰지게 할지도 모른다 / 그것들을 대신하기 위해서

B

18-06 The air we breathe in and out keeps our hearts beating and our
공기는 / [우리가 들이마시고 내뱉는] / 계속 우리의 심장이 뛰게 한다 / 그리고 우리의

blood moving along our veins and arteries.
피가 우리의 정맥과 동맥을 따라 움직이도록

18-07 I heard the dogs barking fiercely late at night, so I came outside to
나는 들었다 / 개들이 사납게 짖는 것을 / 늦은 밤에 / 그래서 나는 밖으로 나갔다 /

see what was going on.
무슨 일이 일어나고 있는지를 보기 위해서

18-08 Customers want their food delivered fast, and they want it to
고객들은 원한다 / 그들의 음식이 빨리 배달되기를 / 그리고 그들은 원한다 / 그것이

arrive hot.
따끈하게 도착하기를

18-09 Although I have known the judge for a long time, I never heard
비록 내가 그 재판관을 오랫동안 알아 왔지만 / 나는 전혀 듣지 못했다

him spoken ill of by others.
/ 그가 타인에 의해서 나쁘게 말해지는 것을

c

18-10 Winners will have their essays posted on our website. Among the
입상자들은 할 것이다 / 그들의 에세이가 우리의 웹사이트에 게재되게 입상자들 중에서

winners, only the first prize winner will have his or her essay
/ 오직 1등 입상자만이 할 것이다 / 자신의 에세이가 우리의 잡지에

published in our magazine.
실리게

18-11 Up on the green, green shoulder of hill rising to the west I could
언덕의 푸르고 푸른 등성이 위에 / [서쪽으로 솟은] / 나는 볼 수

see a small group of cattle grazing, and, below them on a gentler
있었다 / 작은 소 떼 무리가 풀을 뜯고 있는 것을 / 그리고 / 소 떼보다 아래쪽에 / 보다 완만한 비탈길에

slope, several dozen chickens wandering down to the meadow.
/ 수십 마리의 닭들이 / 아래로 목초지까지 돌아다니고 있는 것을

18-12 Being in the spotlight made Tom feel tense. He tried to deliver his
스포트라이트 속에 있는 것이 만들었다 / Tom이 긴장을 느끼게 그는 자신의 대사를 전달하려고 노력했다

lines as best as he could, but he could feel his voice shaking.
/ 그가 할 수 있는 한 가장 잘 / 그러나 그는 느낄 수 있었다 / 자신의 목소리가 떨리고 있는 것을

45

Unit 19 보어 + 형용사구

S TANDARD

19-01 Painting is **only** a bridge linking the painter's mind with that of the
그림은 다리일 뿐이다 / [화가의 마음을 연결하는 / 보는 사람의 마음과]

viewer. *Eugène Delacroix*

19-02 Rehearsing what you want to say can help **you** find a better way
연습하는 것은 / 당신이 말하고 싶은 것을 / 도울 수 있다 / 당신이 더 나은 방법을 찾는 것을

to say it.
/ [그것을 말하는]

A

19-03 Knowledge workers are the ones responsible for keeping the
지식 근로자들은 사람들이다 / [첨단 기술 경제를 계속 돌아가게 하는 데 책임이 있는]

high-tech economy running.

19-04 In 1953, Jacqueline Cochran became the first woman pilot to
1953년에 / Jacqueline Cochran은 최초의 여성 조종사가 되었다 /

break the sound barrier. **Additionally,** she was the first female to
[음속 장벽을 깬] 게다가 그녀는 최초의 여성이었다 /

pilot a jet across the Atlantic.
[대서양을 횡단하여 제트기를 조종한]

19-05 We should let **our beliefs and values** guide our decisions about
우리는 우리의 신념과 가치관이 우리의 결정을 이끌도록 허용해야 한다 / [우리의

how to live our life.
삶을 어떻게 살아야 할지에 관한]

B

19-06 Improved methods of transportation are forcing **man** to discard
개선된 교통수단은 사람들에게 거리 개념을 버리도록 강요하고 있다

the concept of distance in the past responsible for keeping
/ [과거에 사람들이 따로 떨어지게 한 원인인]

people separated.

19-07 Humans became the only species to acquire guidance on how to
인간은 유일한 종이 되었다 / [살아가는 방법에 관한 지침을 획득한

live from the accumulated knowledge of their ancestors, rather
/ 그들의 조상들의 축적된 지식으로부터 / 단지

than just from their DNA.
자신들의 DNA로부터라기보다는]

19-08 The global village is all the countries of the world thought of as
지구촌은 세계의 모든 나라들이다 / [밀접하게 연결된 것으로

being closely connected by modern communication and trade.
여겨지는 / 현대의 통신과 무역으로]

19-09 A day without a friend is like a pot without a single drop of honey
친구가 없는 하루는 단지 같다 / [안에 남아 있는 꿀이 단 한 방울도 없는]

left inside. *the short story collection <Winnie the Pooh>*

19-10 A mouse is a device making it easier to select different options
마우스는 기구이다 / [(…을) 더 쉽게 만드는 / 컴퓨터 메뉴에서 여러 선택 사항들을 고르는 것을]

from computer menus.

19-11 Hindsight bias is a term used in psychology to explain the
사후인지 편향은 용어이다 / [심리학에서 사용되는 / 사람들의 경향을 설명하기

tendency of people to overestimate their ability to have predicted
위해 / [자신들의 능력을 과대평가하는 / [어떤 결과를 예측했던

an outcome that could not possibly have been predicted.
/ [아마도 예측될 수 없었던]]]]

19-12 Lots of countries wanted **their pharmaceutical companies** to be
많은 나라들은 바랐다 / 자신의 제약회사들이 최초가 되길

the first to succeed in developing vaccines and treatments for
/ [코로나바이러스에 대한 백신과 치료제 개발에 성공하는]

coronavirus.

unit 20 보어 + 형용사절

STANDARD

20-01 Education is the most powerful weapon which you can use to
교육은 가장 강력한 무기이다 / [당신이 세상을 바꾸기 위해서 사용할 수

change the world. *Nelson Mandela*
있는]

20-02 Life is a game where there are multiple winners.
인생은 게임이다 / [다수의 승자가 존재하는]

A

20-03 King Arthur was a legendary king who brought peace to his
아서왕은 전설적인 왕이었다 / [자신의 왕국에 평화를 가져다준

kingdom by vanquishing all forms of evil.
모든 형태의 악을 무찌름으로써]

20-04 In family life, love is the oil that eases friction, the cement that binds
가정생활에서 / 사랑은 윤활유이다 / [마찰을 완화시켜 주는] / 접합제(이다) / [더 가깝게 결속

closer together, and the music that brings harmony. *Eva Burrows*
시키는] / 그리고 음악(이다) / [조화를 가져다주는]

20-05 Nutrition education in schools can help more students eat
학교에서의 영양 교육은 도울 수 있다 / 더 많은 학생들이 균형식을 먹도록

balanced diets that include more vegetables and have a healthy
/ [더 많은 채소를 포함하는] / 그리고 건강한 삶을 살도록

life.

B

20-06 According to one traditional definition, aesthetics is the branch of
하나의 전통적인 정의에 따르면 / 미학은 철학의 한 부문이다

philosophy that deals with beauty, especially beauty in the arts.
/ [미(美)를, 특히 예술에서의 미를 다루는]

20-07 Love is like a beautiful flower which I may not touch, but whose
사랑은 아름다운 꽃과 같다 / [내가 만질 수 없는 / 하지만 그 향기가

fragrance makes the garden a place of delight just the same. *Helen Keller*
정원을 기쁨의 장소로 만드는 / 마찬가지로]

20-08 I consider **nature** a vast chemical laboratory in which all kinds of
나는 **자연**을 광대한 화학 실험실로 여긴다 / [온갖 종류의 합성과 분해가 이뤄지는]

composition and decompositions are formed. *Antoine Lavoisier*

20-09 **At the personal level,** competition allows us to become the best
개인적 수준에서 / 경쟁은 우리가 최고의 개인이 되게 한다

individual we can be.
/ [우리가 될 수 있는]

20-10 **In many situations** the boundary between good and bad is a
많은 상황에서 / 선과 악 사이의 경계는 기준점이다

reference point that changes over time and depends on the
/ [시간에 따라서 바뀌고 당면한 상황에 달려있는]

immediate circumstances.

20-11 **Better** keep yourself clean and bright; you are the window
당신 자신을 깨끗하고 밝게 유지하는 것이 좋다 / 당신은 창문이다

through which you must see the world. *George Bernard Shaw*
/ [당신이 세상을 봐야 하는]

20-12 Every novel is an equal collaboration between the writer and the
모든 소설은 동등한 합작이다 / [작가와 독자 사이의]

reader **and it** is the only place in the world where two strangers
/ 그리고 그것은 세상에서 유일한 곳이다 / [두 명의 낯선 사람이 절대적인 친밀한

can meet on terms of absolute intimacy. *Paul Auster*
사이로 만날 수 있는]

Review

A

01 Words are **to language** what notes are to music.
단어는 ~이다 / 언어에 대해서는 / 음표가 음악에 대한 것

02 Don't let **what you can't do** stop you from doing what you can do.
내버려 두지 마라 / 당신이 할 수 없는 것이 / 당신이 할 수 있는 것을 하지 못하게 하도록
John Wooden

03 A central lesson of science is that we must try to free our minds of
과학의 가장 중요한 교훈은 ~이다 / 우리가 노력해야 한다는 것 / 우리의 정신을 독단으로부터 풀어주

dogma and to guarantee the freedom to publish, to contradict, and to
도록 / 그리고 자유를 보장하도록 / [출판하고, 반박하고, 그리고 실험하는]

experiment.

04 Technological advances will allow **high-performance athletes** to move
기술적 진보는 하게 할 것이다 / 높은 수준의 운동선수들이 더 빨리 움직이도록

faster, jump higher, hit harder, and improve their consistency.
/ 더 높이 뛰도록 / 더 강하게 치도록 / 그리고 그들의 일관성을 향상하도록

B

05 **Walking up the path and back to the car,** they could **still** hear the fish
그 길을 걸어서 그 자동차로 다시 왔다 / (그때) 그들은 여전히 들을 수 있었다 / 물고기

splashing in the water.
들이 물속에서 첨벙거리는 것을

06 I didn't have time to shop **at the market yesterday,** so I phoned the
나는 물건을 살 시간이 없었다 / 시장에서 / 어제 / 그래서 나는 가게에 전화했다

store and had the groceries delivered.
/ 그리고 시켰다 / 식료품들이 배달되게

07 The experience of eating a pile of unwanted cabbage until they feel
원하지 않는 한 무더기의 양배추를 먹는 경험은 / 그들이 물릴 때까지

sick is **hardly** going to make children jump for joy **the next time it is**
/ 좀처럼 아이들이 기쁨으로 펄쩍 뛰게 만들지 않을 것이다 / 다음번에 그것이 제공될 때

served.

C

08 When the man returned to his car, he found car windows broken.
그 남자가 자신의 자동차로 돌아왔을 때 / 그는 알았다 / 차 유리창들이 깨진 것을

09 The growth of scientific knowledge has allowed us to control some
과학 지식의 성장은 해 주었다 / 우리가 삶의 위험들의 일부를 통제

of the risks of life.
하도록

10 One of the most fundamental characteristics of money is that it acts
돈의 가장 근본적인 특징 중 하나는 / 그것이 역할을 한다는 것이다

as an easily transportable store of value.
/ 쉽게 운반 가능한 가치 저장소로서

D

11 Yes and No are the two most important words that determine your
'네'와 '아니오'는 두 개의 가장 중요한 단어들이다 / [인생에서 당신의 운명을 결정하는]

destiny in life.

12 One of the principal aims of the sciences is to extend the range of
과학의 주요한 목표 중 하나는 / 우리의 제한된 감각의 범위를 연장하는 것이다

our limited senses by translating invisible and inaudible phenomena
/ 보이지 않고 들리지 않는 현상을 사건으로 바꿈으로써

into events that can be seen or heard.
/ [보이거나 들릴 수 있는]

13 Nuclear weapons have turned war between superpowers into a mad
핵무기는 전쟁을 바꾸어왔다 / [초강대국 사이의] / 집단 자살이라는

act of collective suicide, and forced the most powerful nations on
광기 어린 행위로 / 그리고 강요해왔다 / 지구상의 가장 강력한 국가들이 평화로운 방법을 찾도록

earth to find peaceful ways to resolve conflicts.
/ [분쟁을 해결할]

51

STAGE II

수식어 중심의 구문

Chapter **05** 명사 수식어: 구

Chapter **06** 명사 수식어: 절

Chapter **07** 부사적 수식어: 구

Chapter **08** 부사적 수식어: 절

Unit 21 명사 + (형용사 +) 전치사구

S TANDARD

21-01 Now the Internet has become a well-integrated technology
현재 인터넷은 잘 통합된 기술이 되었다

essential to global business and culture.
/ [전 세계적 사업과 문화에 필수적인]

21-02 All people have the right to medical care regardless of race,
모든 사람들은 권리를 가지고 있다 / [의료에 대한] / 인종, 종교, 신조 또는 정치적 소속에

religion, creed or political affiliation. *Doctors Without Borders*
관계없이

A

21-03 A small blue car with an unknown driver at the wheel was
작은 파란색 자동차 한 대가 / [모르는 운전자가 핸들을 잡고 있는] / 내 차를

following close behind my car.
바짝 뒤따라오고 있었다

21-04 The greatest scientific discoveries are the product of imagination,
가장 위대한 과학적 발견들은 산물이다 / [상상력, 호기심

curiosity, and years of careful research.
/ 그리고 수년간의 세심한 연구의]

21-05 A global network of non-government organizations works toward
비정부기구들의 전 세계 네트워크는 일한다 / 생산과

eliminating the production and use of toxic chemicals harmful to
사용을 없애기 위해서 / [유독한 화학물질의 / [인간의 건강과

human health and the environment.
환경에 해로운]]

B

21-06 Read the instructions on the front cover of each test carefully.
지시 사항을 읽어라 / [각 시험의 앞장에 있는] / 주의 깊게

21-07 Microsoft Excel is a flexible and user-friendly software suitable for
마이크로소프트의 엑셀은 마음대로 바꿀 수 있고 사용하기 쉬운 소프트웨어이다 / [초보자와 고급

beginners and advanced users alike.
사용자 모두에게 적합한]

21-08 Empathy in the sense of adopting someone's viewpoint is **not** the
다른 사람의 관점을 취한다는 의미에서 공감은 / 동일하지 않다

same as empathy in the sense of feeling compassion toward the
/ 그 사람에 대해 동정심을 느낀다는 의미에서의 공감과

person, but the first can lead to the second by a natural route.
/ 그러나 전자는 후자로 향할 수 있다 / 자연스러운 방법으로

21-09 Love is the only force capable of transforming an enemy into a
사랑은 유일한 힘이다 / [적을 친구로 바꿔 놓을 수 있는]

friend. *Martin Luther King Jr.*

C

21-10 The particular strategies appropriate to an organization depend
특정 전략들은 / [어떤 조직에 적합한] / 크게 달려 있다

to a large extent on the political and financial circumstances of
/ 그 조직의 정치적, 재정적인 상황에

the organization.

21-11 Challenges to new ideas are the legitimate business of science in
도전은 / [새로운 아이디어에 대한] / 과학의 타당한 일이다 /

building valid knowledge.
확실한 지식을 쌓는 데 있어서

21-12 **Often** the difference between feeling fulfilled at work and feeling
종종 차이는 / [일에서 성취감을 느끼는 것과 공허한 것, 어찌할 바를 모르는 것, 짜증이 나는 것,

empty, lost, annoyed, and burned out is **all** about whether or not
그리고 녹초가 되었다고 느끼는 것 사이의] / 모두 당신이 어떤 것을 배우고 있느냐 아니냐에

you're learning anything.
관한 것이다

55

unit 22 명사 + to-v[v-ing ~ / v-ed ~]

S TANDARD

22-01 The human species is unique in its ability to expand its
인간 종은 독특하다 / 그것의 능력에 있어서 / [그것의 기능성을 확대하는

functionality by inventing new cultural tools.
/ 새로운 문화적 도구를 발명함으로써]

22-02 Climate is the total sum of the weather experienced over a long
기후는 날씨의 총합이다 / [충분히 오랜 기간 동안에 걸쳐 경험되는

enough time period for the pattern to be established.
/ 경향이 자리잡을 정도로]

A

22-03 Robots are not equipped with capabilities like humans to solve
로봇은 인간과 같은 능력을 갖추고 있지 않다 / [문제들을

problems as they arise.
해결할] / 그것들이 발생할 때

22-04 The common idea of a creative individual coming up with great
창의적인 개인이라는 통념은 / [대단한 통찰력, 발견, 작품 또는 발명을

insights, discoveries, works, or inventions in isolation is wrong.
생각해내는 / 홀로] / 잘못된 것이다

22-05 The story called *The Strange Case of Dr. Jekyll and Mr. Hyde* is the
이야기는 / [「지킬 박사와 하이드 씨의 이상한 사건,이라고 불리는] / 선량한

famous story of a good man sometimes turning into a horrible
남성에 관한 유명한 이야기이다 / [때때로 끔찍한 괴물로 변하는]

monster.

B

22-06 People judged to be functionally illiterate lack the basic reading
사람들은 / [기능적으로 문맹이라고 판단되는] / 기본적인 읽기와 쓰기 능력이 부족하다

and writing skills required in everyday life.
/ [일상생활에서 요구되는]

22-07 Yeast cells growing on a grape skin obtain energy from nutrient
효모균 세포들은 / [포도 껍질에서 자라는] / 에너지를 얻는다 / 영양소 분자들로부터

molecules originally processed within the grape leaves and
/ [원래 포도 나뭇잎 내부에서 가공되는 / 그리고

stored within the fruit.
열매 안에 저장되는]

22-08 You must pay the past-due balance by the date written on the
당신은 기일을 넘긴 잔금을 지불해야 한다 / 날짜까지 / [당신의 청구서 앞면에

front page of your bill to avoid the late fee.
적혀 있는] / 연체료를 피하기 위해

22-09 On February 9th, 2020, South Korean movie *Parasite* became the
2020년 2월 9일에 / 남한의 영화 '기생충'은 / 최초의 외국어 영화가

first foreign-language film to be crowned Best Picture at the
되었다 / [아카데미 시상식에서 최고 작품상의 영예를 받은]

Academy Awards. *the magazine <The Economist>*

c

22-10 The order to abandon ship automatically assumes two rules:
명령은 / [배를 버리라는] / 자동적으로 두 개의 규칙을 취한다

women and children are first, and the captain is the last to leave
여성과 아이들이 먼저이다 / 그리고 선장은 떠나는 최후의 사람이다

or goes down with his vessel.
/ 또는 자신의 배와 함께 침몰한다

22-11 The company has decided to launch a new campaign targeting
그 회사는 결정했다 / 새로운 캠페인을 시작하기로 / [경력이 없는

inexperienced college graduates preparing to enter the job market
대학 졸업생을 겨냥하는 / [처음으로 취업 시장에 들어가려고 준비하고 있는]]

for the first time.

22-12 The desire to fly is an idea handed down to us by our ancestors
날고자 하는 욕망은 생각이다 / [우리에게 전해진 / 우리 조상에 의해서

who looked enviously on the birds soaring freely through space
/ [새들을 부러운 듯 바라보았던 / [자유롭게 공간을 날아오르는

on the infinite highway of the air. *Orville Wright*
/ 하늘이라는 무한한 고속도로 위에서]]]

57

Review

A

01 We enclose **here a copy of our illustrated catalogue about the main**
저희가 여기에 삽화가 들어간 목록 한 부를 동봉합니다 / [주요 물품들에 관한

items available at present.
/ 현재 구할 수 있는]

02 Two of the hardest tests in life are the patience to wait for the right
인생에서 가장 힘든 두 가지 시험은 ~이다 / 알맞은 순간을 기다리는 인내심

moment and the courage to accept whatever you encounter.
/ 그리고 당신이 맞닥뜨리는 무엇이든 받아들이는 용기

03 We listened **to the sound of the rain beating down on the roof and**
우리는 소리를 들었다 / [지붕을 두드리는 비의 / 그리고

thunder rolling off in the distance.
멀리서 우르릉대는 천둥의]

04 Words acquire **objective meanings because of the "pull" exerted by**
단어들은 객관적인 의미를 얻는다 / '영향력' 때문에 / [사회적 압력에

social pressures to conform to publicly approved usage.
의해서 행사되는 / [대중적으로 인정되는 용법에 순응하게 하는]]

B

05 The Superhero Walkathon is an annual fundraising walking event
Superhero Walkathon은 해마다 열리는 기금 마련 걷기 행사이다

held to support the Active Way, a charity dedicated to granting the
/ [Active Way를 지원하고자 개최되는 / 소원을 들어주기 위한 자선단체인

wishes of terminally ill children.
/ [병이 중증인 어린이들의]]

06 Man's ability to walk upright and use his hands, and his natural
인간의 능력 / [직립 보행하며 손을 사용하는] / 그리고 그 사람의 타고난

capacity to see into the distance instead of looking at the ground,
능력은 / [먼 곳을 보는 / 땅을 보는 대신에]

became weapons of survival.
/ 생존의 무기가 되었다

07 In the information age, reliance on expert intuition will gradually be
정보화 시대에 / 전문가의 직관에 대한 의존은 점차 대체될 것이다

replaced by computer programs processing the relevant data using
/ 컴퓨터 프로그램에 의해 / [관련된 자료를 처리하는 / 규칙들을

rules known as algorithms.
사용하여 / [알고리즘으로 알려진]]

08 The visual preoccupation of early humans with the nonhuman
초기 인류의 시각적 심취는 / [인간이 아닌 생물들에 대한

creatures inhabiting their world becomes profoundly meaningful.
/ [그들의 세상에서 살고 있는]] / 상당히 중요해진다

C

09 Changes to one part of our ecosystem, even a small part, have
우리 생태계의 한 부분에서의 변화는 / 심지어 작은 부분조차도 / 영향을

consequences for everything else.
미친다 / 다른 모든 것에

10 A layer of a gas called ozone in the upper atmosphere protects us
가스층이 / [오존이라고 불리는] / [상층 대기에 있는] / 우리를 보호한다

from harmful rays of the Sun.
/ 태양의 해로운 광선으로부터

11 Facebook and Instagram announced new policy restricting sales and
페이스북과 인스타그램은 발표했다 / 새로운 정책을 / [담배와 주류 상품에 대한 판매와

content for tobacco and alcohol products.
정보를 제한하는]

unit 23 명사 + 관계대명사절

23-01 Social welfare is a set of activities which have, in part, been
사회 복지는 일련의 활동이다   / [부분적으로, 불공평한 분배의 상쇄를 지향해온]

directed to offset unequal distribution.

23-02 A Korean speaker uses different verb forms depending on his or
한국어 사용자는 다른 동사의 형태를 사용한다   / 그 또는 그녀의 관계에 따라서

her relationship to the person whom he or she is speaking to.
/ [그 사람에 대한   / [그 또는 그녀가 이야기하고 있는]]

A

23-03 Birds that in the breeding season fight one another to death over
새들은   / [번식기에 영역을 두고 서로 죽을힘을 다해 싸우는]

territory may end up in the same flock during migration.
/ 결국 있게 될 것이다 / 동일한 무리 속에   / 이주기에는

23-04 Culture shock is the feeling of confusion felt by someone visiting
문화 충격은 혼란의 감정이다   / [어떤 사람이 느끼는   / [어떤 나라

a country or place whose culture they do not know.
또는 장소를 방문하는   / [그곳의 문화를 그들이 알지 못하는]]]

23-05 We define cognitive intrigue as the wonder that stimulates and
우리는 인지적 호기심을 경이로움으로 정의한다   [자극하고

intrinsically motivates an individual to voluntarily engage in an
/ 본질으로 동기를 부여하는   / 개인이 자발적으로 어떤 활동에 참여하도록]

activity.

B

23-06 Time is too slow for those who wait, too swift for those who fear,
시간은 너무 느리다   / 사람들에게는 [기다리는]   / 너무 빠른   / 사람들에게는 [두려워하는]

too long for those who grieve, too short for those who rejoice, but
/ 너무 긴   / 사람들에게는 [슬퍼하는]   / 너무 짧은   / 사람들에게는 [기뻐하는]   / 그러나

for those who love, time is eternity. *Henry Van Dyke*
사람들에게는   [사랑하는]   / 시간은 영원이다

23-07 The man with a toothache thinks that everyone whose teeth are
치통이 있는 사람은 생각한다 / 모든 사람이 / [이가 건강한]

sound is happy. The poverty-stricken man makes the same
/ 행복할 거라고 가난에 시달리는 사람은 같은 실수를 한다

mistake about the rich man. *George Bernard Shaw*
/ 부자에 대해

23-08 The term "placebo" is used to describe a "pill" which contains no
'플라세보'라는 용어는 사용된다 / '알약'을 표현하기 위해 / [약 성분을 포함하지 않는

medical ingredients but which often produces the same effect as
/ 하지만 종종 진짜 약물과 같은 효과를 내는]

genuine medication.

23-09 Flu and colds spread very quickly, especially with the large
독감과 감기는 아주 빠르게 퍼진다 / 특히 많은 접촉으로 인해

amount of contact that people now have with each other.
/ [사람들이 지금 서로 하는]

23-10 Andy Weir wrote *"The Martian"* for science fiction readers who
앤디 위어는 「마션」을 썼다 / 공상 과학 소설 독자들을 위해 / [그들의

want their stories firmly grounded in scientific fact.
이야기가 확고히 근거하고 있기를 바라는 / 과학적 사실에]

23-11 A rain forest is a virtually untapped storehouse of evolutionary
우림은 사실상 미개발의 저장소이다 / [진화적 업적의

achievement that will prove increasingly valuable to mankind as it
/ [점점 더 인류에게 소중한 것으로 판명될 / 그것이

yields its secrets.
자신의 비밀을 밝힘에 따라서]]

23-12 Those people, organizations, and countries that possess the
그 사람들, 조직들, 그리고 국가들은 / [최고급의 정보를 소유하는]

highest-quality information are likely to prosper economically,
/ 경제적으로, 사회적으로, 정치적으로 번영할 것 같다

socially, and politically.

Unit 24 명사 + 전치사 + 관계대명사절

24-01 Many authors **today** are creating fairy stories in which the
많은 작가들이 오늘날 동화를 창작하고 있다   / [여주인공들이 보다

heroines are more active.
적극적인]

A

24-02 It is **often** difficult to get books back from people to whom you
(…은) 종종 어렵다   / 책들을 사람들에게서 돌려받는 것은   / [당신이 그것들을 빌려준

have lent them.
[당신이 그것들을 빌려준

24-03 Sincere apologies are **for those that make them, not for those to**
진정한 사과는 사람들을 위해서이다   / [그것을 하는]   / 사람들을 위해서가 아니라 /

whom they are made. *Greg LeMond*
[그것을 받는]

24-04 Even the exact same question can elicit **very different responses**
완전히 똑같은 질문조차도 매우 다른 반응을 이끌어 낼 수 있다

depending on the context in which the question occurs.
/ 상황에 따라서   / [그 질문이 떠오르는]

24-05 When a seed grows into a tree, it represents **only** a change **in**
씨앗이 나무로 성장할 때   / 그것은 단지 변화를 나타낸다   /

the degree to which its potential, always inherent in its original
정도에 있어서   / [그것의 잠재력이   / (늘 그것의 원래의 본성 속에 내재된)

nature, is realized.
/ 실현되는]

B

24-06 I have **but** one lamp by which my feet are guided, **and** that is the
나는 오직 하나의 램프를 가지고 있다 / [그것으로 나의 발이 인도되는]   / 그리고 그것은 경험의

lamp of experience. *Patrick Henry*
램프이다

24-07 What makes a study scientific is **not** the nature of the things with
어떤 연구를 과학적으로 만드는 것은 / 사물의 본성이 아니다 / [그것이

which it is concerned, **but** the method by which it deals with
관계된] / 방식(이다) / [그것(연구)이 그러한 사물들을 다루는]

those things.

24-08 All human societies have economic systems within which goods
모든 인간 사회는 경제 체제를 가지고 있다 / [그 안에서 재화와 서비스가 만들어

and services are produced, distributed, and consumed.
지고 / 분배되고 / 그리고 소비되는]

24-09 *Spider-Man* was a tremendous hit with readers because it gave
「스파이더맨」은 독자들에게 엄청난 히트였다 / 그것이 수백만의 십 대들에게

millions of teenagers a hero with whom they could identify.
영웅을 선사했기 때문에 / [그들이 동일시할 수 있었던]

24-10 The effectiveness of human society is **largely** dependent **upon the**
인간 사회의 유효성은 크게 의존한다 / 명확성, 정확성,

clarity, accuracy, and efficiency with which language is used or
그리고 효율성에 / [언어가 사용되거나 이해되는]

understood.

24-11 Separation anxiety disorder is defined **as excessive worry and**
분리 불안 장애는 정의된다 / 과도한 걱정과 두려움으로

fear about being apart from individuals to whom a child is most
/ [사람들과 떨어져 있는 것에 대한 / [아이가 가장 애착을 가지고 있는]]

attached.

24-12 Social influence is the process by which individuals adapt their
사회적 영향은 과정이다 / [개인들이 그들의 의견을 조정하거나

opinion, revise their beliefs, or change their behavior as a result of
/ 그들의 신념을 바꾸거나 / 또는 그들의 행위를 변화시키는 / 다른 사람들과 맺는

social interactions with other people.
사회적 상호작용의 결과로]

unit 25 명사 + 관계부사절

25-01 We are living **in the first century when the greatest skills will come**
우리는 첫 번째 세기에 살고 있다 / [가장 위대한 기술들이 인간의 행동에서 생겨날

from human actions rather than from nature.
/ 자연으로부터라기보다는]

25-02 Competition becomes a zero sum game **where one organization**
경쟁은 제로섬 게임이 된다 / [한 조직만 이길 수 있는

can only win at the expense of others.
/ 다른 조직들의 희생으로]

A

25-03 We are embarking **on a time when each individual will have all**
우리는 시기에 들어서고 있다 / [개인 각자가 가지게 될 /

their own medical data and the computing power to process it in
자기 자신의 모든 의료 정보와 / 그리고 그것을 처리하는 컴퓨터 사용 능력을 /

the context of their own world.
자기 자신의 세계라는 맥락 속에서]

25-04 The reason **why worry kills more people than work** is that more
이유는 / [근심이 일보다 더 많은 사람을 죽이는] / 더 많은 사람이 일하기

people worry than work. *Robert Frost*
보다는 근심해서이다

25-05 The way **people act is often influenced by experiences that they**
방식은 / [사람들이 행동하는] / 종종 영향을 받는다 / 경험에 의해서 / [그들이 과거에

had in the past and by the need to fulfill basic human needs.
가진] / 그리고 필요에 의해서 / [기본적인 인간의 욕구를 충족시킬]

B

25-06 We look forward to **the time when the Power of Love will replace**
우리는 때를 기대한다 / [사랑의 힘이 힘에 대한 사랑을 대체할]

the Love of Power. Then will our world know the blessings of
그때는 우리 세계가 평화의 축복을 알게 될 것이다

peace.

25-07 In general, people accept job offers where the monetary
일반적으로 / 사람들은 일자리 제안을 받아들인다 / [금전적인 보수가 그 금액에 가까운

compensation is near the amount that they were hoping for.
/ [그들이 바라고 있었던]]

25-08 Possibly, we all have high points and low points in our creative
아마 / 우리 모두는 높은 지점과 낮은 지점을 지니고 있다 / 우리의 창의적인 주기에

cycles. This may be the reason why we have "good days" and
이것은 이유일 수도 있다 / [우리가 근무 중에 '좋은 날'과 '나쁜 날'이 있는]

"bad days" at work.

25-09 In today's digital environment, appearing in the mainstream news
오늘날의 디지털 환경에서 / 주류 뉴스에 출현하는 것은 여전히 중요한 방법이다

is still an important way that citizens can communicate with a
/ [시민들이 더 넓은 공동체와 소통할 수 있는

broader community about events and issues.
/ 사건과 논쟁점에 대해]

25-10 The best picture books contain words and pictures that
최고의 그림책은 단어와 그림을 담고 있다 / [서로를

complement each other and are dependent upon each other to
보완하는] / 그리고 서로에 의존적이다 /

the point that one would be ineffective without the other.
정도로 / [하나가 다른 하나 없이는 효과가 없게 되는]

25-11 The food industry has made a fortune because we retain Stone Age
식품 산업은 거액을 벌어왔다 / 우리가 석기 시대의 신체를 유지하고 있기 때문에

bodies that crave sugar but live in a Space Age world where sugar is
/ [설탕을 간절히 원하는] / 하지만 우주 시대 세계에 살고 있기 때문에 / [설탕이 저렴하고 풍부한]

cheap and plentiful.

25-12 Friendship is born at that moment when one says to another,
우정은 그 순간에 생겨난다 / [한 사람이 다른 사람에게 말하는

"What! You too? I thought I was the only one." *C. S. Lewis*
/ "뭐라고! 너도야? 나는 생각했어 / 내가 유일한 사람이라고"]

unit 26 명사 + 관계사가 생략된 수식절

S TANDARD

26-01 There are some **among us** fortune smiles on, **and** others she
우리 중에 몇몇이 있다 / [행운의 여신이 미소 짓는] / 그리고 다른 사람들이 (있다)

frowns at.
[그녀가 눈살을 찌푸리는]

26-02 Scientists can answer **when and how the universe began, but**
과학자들은 답할 수 있다 / 언제 그리고 어떻게 우주가 시작되었는지 / 그러나

cannot calculate the reason it began.
이유를 추정할 수는 없다 / [그것이 시작된]

A

26-03 I am writing **to you regarding a price discrepancy I encountered**
나는 당신에게 편지를 쓰고 있다 / 가격 차이에 관하여 / [내가 맞닥뜨린

between an item offered in your retail store and the same item
/ 당신의 매장에서 제공되는 물품과 / 당신의 웹사이트에서 제공되는

offered on your website.
동일한 물품 간의]

26-04 This country imports **about two-thirds of the raw materials it**
이 나라는 수입한다 / 원료의 약 2/3를 /

needs and exports approximately three-fifths of the machinery it
[그 나라가 필요로 하는] / 그리고 수출한다 / 기계류의 약 3/5을 /

produces.
[그 나라가 생산하는]

26-05 The advent of driverless cars and other vehicles promises **to**
운전자 없는 자동차와 다른 차량의 출현은 가망이 있다 /

revolutionize the way the world transports itself goods every day.
방식을 변화시킬 / [세계가 직접 매일 상품을 운송하는]

B

26-06 One of the most effective ways **to calm down from stress is**
스트레스로부터 진정하는 가장 효과적인 방법 중 하나는 /

intimate contact with people you trust and feel comfortable
사람들과의 친밀한 접촉이다 / [주변에 당신이 신뢰하고 그리고 편안하게 느끼는]

around.

26-07 Leaders need to safeguard the faith people have in them by
지도자들은 신념을 보호할 필요가 있다 / [사람들이 지도자들에게서 갖고 있는] /

acting in accordance with the expectations they have raised
행동함으로써 / 기대에 따라 / [그들이 스스로 고양시킨]

themselves.

26-08 One reason most dogs are much happier than most people is that
하나의 이유는 / [대부분의 개들이 대부분의 사람들보다 훨씬 더 행복한] / 개들은

dogs aren't affected by external circumstances the way we are.
영향을 받지 않기 때문이다 / 외부의 환경에 의해서 / 우리가 영향을 받는 것처럼

26-09 An instructor should exemplify the things he seeks to teach. It
강사는 일들에 본보기가 되어야 한다 / [그가 가르치려고 하는] (…은)

will be of great advantage if you yourself can do all you ask of
대단한 이점이 될 것이다 / 만약 당신 스스로 모든 것을 할 수 있다면 / [당신이 당신의

your students and more. *Bruce Lee*
학생들 그리고 그 이상의 사람들에게 요구하는]

C

26-10 Before a job interview, it is a good idea to find out some
구직 면접 전에 / (…은) 좋은 생각이다 / 그 회사에 관한 약간의 배경 정보를

background information about the company you would be working
알아 보는 것은 / [당신이 일하고자 하는]

for.

26-11 Because of the huge volume of clouds it generates, the Amazon
막대한 구름의 양 때문에 / [그것이 생성하는] / 아마존 수계는 중대한

River system plays a major role in the way the sun's heat is
역할을 한다 / 방식에 있어서 / [태양열이 전 지구에 배분되는]

distributed around the globe.

26-12 Do you think that being able to list all the reasons you love a
당신은 생각하는가 / 모든 이유를 열거할 수 있다는 것이 / [당신이 어떤 사람을

person enables you to love that person more or differently?
사랑하는] / 당신이 그 사람을 더 많이 또는 다르게 사랑할 수 있게 해 준다고?

unit 27 명사와 관계사절의 분리

27-01 I can't think of **any good film** at the moment **that I'd like to see.**
나는 어떤 좋은 영화가 생각나지 않는다 / 지금으로서는 / [내가 보고 싶은]

27-02 **That government is best which governs least, because its people**
그러한 정부가 제일이다 / [가장 적게 통제하는] / 왜냐하면 그 국민이 스스로를

discipline themselves. *Thomas Jefferson*
규율하기 때문에

A

27-03 Some people recognize **humans as the only one among the living**
어떤 사람들은 인간을 인지한다 / 유일한 것으로 / 살아 있는 유기체 중에서

organisms that can change its behavior to preserve other
/ [다른 종을 보존하기 위해 자신의 행동을 바꿀 수 있는]

species.

27-04 Courage doesn't always roar. **Sometimes** courage is the little voice
용기가 항상 포효하지는 않는다 때때로 용기는 작은 목소리이다

at the end of the day that says "I'll try again tomorrow." *Mary Anne Radmacher*
/ 하루의 끝에 / ['나는 내일 다시 시도해 볼 거야'라고 말하는]

27-05 Creative solutions are required **which not only answer yesterday's**
창의적인 해결책이 요구된다 / [어제의 질문에 답할 뿐만 아니라

questions but also anticipate tomorrow's needs.
/ 내일의 필요를 예견하기도 하는]

B

27-06 A gene is a part of a cell in a living thing that controls what it
유전자는 세포의 일부이다 / [생명체 안에 있는] / [통제하는 / 그것이

looks like, how it grows, and how it develops.
어떻게 생겼는지 / 그것이 어떻게 자라는지 / 그리고 그것이 어떻게 발달하는지]

27-07 Hospices care for patients suffering from incurable diseases who
호스피스는 환자들을 돌본다 / [불치병으로 고통받고 있는] / [1년

are not expected to live for more than a year.
넘게 살 것으로 예상되지 않는]

27-08 From smart cities to self-driving cars, technology is needed that
스마트 도시부터 자율 주행 자동차까지 / 기술이 요구된다 / [장치와

can allow devices and services to access great volumes of data.
서비스가 대량의 데이터에 접근할 수 있게 해 주는]

27-09 The time will come when people will see that my paintings are
때가 올 것이다 / [사람들이 알게 될 / 나의 그림들이 가치가 있다는 것을

worth more than the price of the paint. *Vincent van Gogh*
/ 물감 가격 이상의]

C

27-10 The ultimate life force lies in tiny cellular factories of energy,
궁극적인 생명력은 아주 작은 에너지 세포 공장에 있다

called mitochondria, that burn nearly all the oxygen we breathe
/ 미토콘드리아라고 불리는 / [거의 모든 산소를 연소시키는 / [우리가 들이마시는]]
in.

27-11 Most professors see themselves in a position of professional
대부분의 교수들은 스스로를 인지한다 / 자신들의 학생들을 넘어서는 전문적인 권위의 입장에서

authority over their students which they earned by many years of
/ [그들이 오랜 세월의 연구로 얻은]
study.

27-12 Art has mostly been considered in terms of seeking beauty, but
예술은 주로 고려되어 왔다 / 아름다움을 추구하는 것의 측면에서 / 그러나

there are other reasons deeply rooted in the human experience that
다른 이유들이 있다 / [인간의 경험 속에 깊이 자리잡은] / [예술에

create needs for art.
대한 필요성을 창조하는]

69

unit 28 명사, 관계사절

S TANDARD

28-01 Costa Rica was discovered and named by Christopher Columbus,
코스타리카는 발견되었다 그리고 명명되었다 / 크리스토퍼 콜럼버스에 의해

who thought it might be a land rich with gold.
/ 그리고 그는 생각했다 / 그것은 금이 풍부한 땅일 것이라고

28-02 Change, which is an essential part of our life, can have both
변화는 / 그것은 우리 삶의 필수적인 부분인데 / 긍정적인 영향과 부정적인

positive and negative effects.
영향을 둘 다 미칠 수 있다

A

28-03 Yesterday is history, tomorrow is a mystery, today is a gift of God,
어제는 역사이다 / 내일은 미스터리이다 / 오늘은 신의 선물이다

which is why we call it the present. *Bill Keane*
/ 그리고 그것이 우리가 오늘을 present(선물)라고 부르는 이유이다

28-04 Urbanization has been taking place since the Neolithic
도시화는 일어나고 있는 중이다 / 신석기 혁명 이래로

Revolution, when agriculture enabled food surpluses to create a
/ 그리고 그때 농업이 잉여 식량으로 정착지에서 분업이 생겨날 수 있게 했다

division of labor in settlements.

28-05 Homer's *Iliad*, which contained descriptions of actual places, was
Homer의 「일리아드」는 / 그것은 실제 장소에 대한 서술을 포함했는데 / 많은

the basis for many early maps.
초기 지도에 대한 기반이었다

B

28-06 Cognitive computing is supported by machine learning and deep
인지 컴퓨팅은 뒷받침된다 / 기계 학습과 딥 러닝 기술에 의해

learning technology, which allows computers to autonomously
그리고 그것은 컴퓨터가 자체적으로 데이터로부터 학습할 수 있게 해 준다

learn from data.

28-07 Maurice Maeterlinck studied law and worked as a lawyer until
Maurice Maeterlinck는 법학을 공부했다 / 그리고 변호사로 일했다 / 1889년

1889, when he decided to devote himself to writing. In 1897, he
까지 / 그리고 그때 그는 결심했다 / 글쓰기에 전념하기로 1897년에 그는 파리로

went to Paris, where he met many of the leading symbolist writers
갔다 / 그리고 거기서 그는 만났다 / 그 당시의 여러 주요한 상징주의 작가들을

of the day.

28-08 Jobs may not be permanent, and you may lose your job for
일자리는 영구적이지 않을 수도 있다 / 그리고 당신은 당신의 일자리를 잃을 수도 있다 /

countless reasons, some of which you may not even be
수많은 이유로 / 그리고 그것들 중의 일부에 대해 당신은 심지어 책임이 없을 수도 있다

responsible for.

28-09 The spontaneous wish to learn, which every normal child has, as
배우고 싶다는 자연스러운 소망은 / 그것은 평범한 아이들 모두가 갖고 있는데 /

shown in their efforts to walk and talk, should be the driving force
아이들의 걷고 말하는 노력에서 보이는 것처럼 / 교육에 있어서 추진력이 되어야 한다

in education.

28-10 The bodies of all living creatures are organized into many
모든 살아 있는 생물의 몸은 조직되어 있다 / 여러 가지 다른

different systems, each of which has a certain function.
체계로 / 그리고 각각의 체계는 특정 기능을 가진다

28-11 One remarkable aspect of aboriginal culture is the concept of
원주민 문화의 한 가지 눈에 띄는 면은 / '토테미즘'이라는 개념이다

"totemism," where the tribal member at birth assumes the soul
/ 그리고 거기(토테미즘)에서 부족 구성원은 출생 시에 자연의 일부의 영혼과 정체성을 취한다

and identity of a part of nature.

28-12 The television crime drama isn't such a hit with police officers,
텔레비전 범죄 드라마는 경찰관들에게는 대단한 히트작이 아니다

who have criticized the series for presenting a highly misleading
/ 그리고 그들은 그 시리즈를 비판해왔다 / 대단히 오해의 소지가 있는 모습을 보여 준다는 이유로

image of how crimes are solved.
/ 범죄가 어떻게 해결되는지에 대한

Review

A

01 **There** is only one thing that makes a dream impossible to achieve:
오직 한 가지가 있다 / [꿈을 이루는 것을 불가능하게 하는]

the fear of failure. *the novel <The Alchemist>*
/ 실패에 대한 두려움

02 Radioactive waste disposal has become one of the key environmental
방사성 폐기물 처리는 주요한 환경 문제의 전쟁터 중 하나가 되어왔다

battlegrounds over which the future of nuclear power has been
/ [원자력의 미래에 맞서 싸워 온]

fought.

03 Fate is like a strange, unpopular restaurant filled with odd little waiters
운명은 이상하고 인기가 없는 식당과 같다 / [이상한 작은 종업원들로 가득찬

who bring you things you never asked for and don't always like.
/ [당신에게 어떤 것들을 갖다주는 / [당신이 결코 요청하지 않은 / 그리고 항상 좋아하는 것은 아닌]]] *Lemony Snicket*

04 Multitasking is another way of saying you are going to complete
멀티태스킹은 말하는 또 다른 방법이다 / 당신이 몇 가지 일을 마무리하려고 하는데

several tasks, none of which are going to be very good.
/ 그러나 그것들 중 어떤 것도 그다지 훌륭하진 않을 것이다라고

B

05 Man is the only animal whose desires increase as they are fed; the
인간은 유일한 동물이다 / [욕망이 증가하는 / 욕망이 충족되었을 때] 즉

only animal that is never satisfied. *Henry George*
유일한 동물 / [결코 만족하지 않는]

06 We're heading **toward a world where an extensive trail of information**
우리는 세상을 향해 나아가고 있다 / [우리에 관한 정보 조각들의 광범위한 자국이

fragments about us will be forever preserved on the Internet,
/ 인터넷상에 영원히 보존될

displayed instantly in a search result.
/ 검색 결과로 즉각 보이는]

07 Angela mentioned **that for a long time she had wanted to get back**
Angela는 언급했다 / 오랫동안 자신은 연극으로 돌아가고 싶어 했다고

into acting, which she used to do in college.
/ 그것을 그녀는 대학 시절에 했었다

08 Penicillin, the first antibiotic to be discovered, kills a broad spectrum
페니실린은 / 발견된 최초의 항생제인 / 광범위의 박테리아를 죽인다

of bacteria, many of which cause disease in humans.
/ 그리고 그것들 중 다수는 인간에게 질병을 유발한다

C

09 Values and their supporting beliefs are lenses through which we see
가치관과 그것들을 뒷받침하는 신념은 렌즈다 / [우리가 세상을 보는]

the world.

10 In this information age when science and technology are developing
이 정보 시대에 / [과학과 기술이 엄청난 속도로 발전하고 있는]

with great rapidity, network has become an important symbol of
/ 네트워크는 현대의 삶에서 중요한 상징이 되어왔다

modern life.

11 The police received a number of bomb warnings, all of which turned
경찰은 다수의 폭발물 예고를 받았다 / 그런데 그것들 모두 허위 신고로

out to be false alarms.
밝혀졌다

D

12 Science operates within the context of the culture it exists in; it does
과학은 작동한다 / 문화의 상황 내에서 / [그것이 존재하는] 그것은

not exist in a vacuum where pure absolute objectivity prevails.
진공에서 존재하지 않는다 / [완전한 절대적 객관성이 지배적인]

13 For every one thing we think we have done on our own, there are a
모든 것에 있어서 / [(우리가 생각하기에) 우리가 스스로 해온] / 수십 개의 일이 있다

dozen things that had to be provided for us by others.
/ [타인들에 의해 우리에게 제공되었어야 하는]

14 The brain modifies its structure in response to the different tasks it is
뇌는 자신의 구조를 수정한다 / 서로 다른 임무에 응하여 / [뇌가

required to do.
수행하도록 요구되는]

unit 29 부사 역할을 하는 전치사구

29-01 By means of photosynthesis, plants convert the radiant energy of
광합성에 의해 / 식물은 태양의 복사 에너지를 전환한다

the sun into chemical energy.
/ 화학 에너지로

29-02 From the moment that we are born, we begin to make sense of
그 순간부터 / [우리가 태어나는] / 우리는 우리 주변의 세상을 이해하기 시작한다

the world around us by associating the unknown with the known.
/ 알려지지 않은 것을 알려진 것과 연관시킴으로써

A

29-03 Fossil fuels form beneath the ground from dead plants and
화석 연료들은 형성된다 / 땅 밑에서 / 죽은 식물과 동물로부터

animals that do not break down completely.
/ [완전히 분해되지 않은]

29-04 Despite its high price, this new cell phone sells like hot cakes
높은 가격에도 불구하고 / 이 신형 휴대폰은 팔린다 / 핫케이크처럼

because of its high quality.
/ 그것의 고품질 때문에

29-05 We borrow environmental capital from future generations with no
우리는 환경 자본을 빌린다 / 미래 세대에서 / 빚을 갚으려

intention or prospect of repaying.
는 의도나 가망도 없이

B

29-06 Each year about 50,000 species of plants and animals disappear
매년 / 약 5만 종의 식물과 동물들이 사라진다

from the planet as a result of human activity.
/ 세상으로부터 / 인간 활동의 결과로

29-07 Sometimes my eyes get jealous of my heart because you always
때때로 / 나의 눈은 내 심장을 질투하게 된다 / 왜냐하면 당신은 항상 나의 심장과

remain close to my heart and far from my eyes.
가까이 있고 나의 눈에서는 멀리 있기 때문이다

29-08 Upon discovering his own passion and talent for architecture,
자기 자신의 열정과 재능을 발견하자마자 / [건축을 향한]

Frank Lloyd Wright dropped out of school and went to work for
/ Frank Lloyd Wright는 학교를 그만두었다 / 그리고 시카고에 있는 건축 회사로

an architectural firm in Chicago.
근무하러 갔다

29-09 Above all, watch with glittering eyes the whole world around you
무엇보다도 / 반짝이는 눈으로 당신 주변의 온 세상을 주시하라

because the greatest secrets are always hidden in the most unlikely
/ 왜냐하면 가장 큰 비밀들은 항상 감춰져 있기 때문이다 / 가장 있을 법하지 않은 곳에

places. *Roald Dahl*

29-10 In a democratic environment, old ideas can be challenged and
민주적인 환경에서 / 오래된 개념은 도전을 받을 수 있다 / 그리고

rigorously criticized, though there are some difficulty due to the
엄격히 비판받을 (수 있다) / 비록 약간의 어려움이 있더라도 / 인간의 욕구 때문에

human desire to hold onto old ideas, especially by the original
/ [오래된 개념을 유지하려는 / 특히 최초 제안자에 의해]

proposers.

29-11 In spite of the rare case of receiving rewarding email, we cannot
가치 있는 이메일을 받을 경우가 드물더라도 / 우리는 이메일을

resist the impulse to check email because our behaviors are
확인하려는 충동을 참지 못한다 / 왜냐하면 우리의 행동이 유지되기 때문이다

maintained with the reward presented in an unpredictable way.
/ 보상으로 / [예측할 수 없는 방식으로 제공되는]

29-12 With the advent of social media, our children become impatient
소셜 미디어의 출현으로 / 우리 아이들은 초조하게 기다리게 되었다

for an immediate answer or "Like" within minutes of sending an
/ 즉각적인 응답 또는 '좋아요'를 / 다급한 정보를 발송하고 수 분 이내에

urgent piece of information out.

unit 30 부사 역할을 하는 to-v의 의미

30-01 Charles Dickens used his desperate experience as a child laborer
찰스 디킨스는 자신의 절망적인 경험을 활용했다 / [빅토리아 시대의 영국에서

in Victorian England to write *David Copperfield*.
아동 노동자로서의] / 「데이비드 코퍼필드」를 쓰기 위해서

30-02 That Friday morning, I awoke to find myself caught in the middle
그 금요일 아침에 / 나는 깨어나서 내가 처해 있다는 것을 알게 되었다 / 소셜 미디어 폭풍의

of a social media storm.
한가운데에

A

30-03 Our brain organizes the available sensory information and
우리의 뇌는 이용 가능한 감각 정보와 환경 자극을 체계화한다

environmental stimuli so as to make sense out of millions of bits
/ 수백만 개의 이런저런 자료들을 이해하기 위해서

and pieces of data.

30-04 When at length the deal was settled, Dr. Paul was delighted to
마침내 그 거래가 합의에 이르렀을 때 / Paul 박사는 기뻤다 /

purchase the carving at a reasonable price.
그 조각품을 적절한 가격에 구입하게 되어

30-05 If an activity is easy to perform, easy to fit into your schedule,
만약 어떤 활동이 하기 쉽고 / 당신의 일정에 맞추기 쉬우며

and easy to love, you're more likely to stick with it.
/ 그리고 좋아하기 쉽다면 / 당신은 그것을 더욱 계속할 것이다

B

30-06 We should carefully think about the reason for someone's
우리는 조심스럽게 생각해야 한다 / 어떤 사람의 행동의 이유에 대해

behavior to avoid coming to a hasty conclusion about it.
/ 성급한 결론에 도달하는 것을 피하기 위해서 / [그것에 대한]

30-07 When temperatures near 0°C, water molecules start bonding with
온도가 섭씨 0도에 가까워질 때 / 물 분자는 서로 결합되기 시작한다

one another to form a crystal structure.
/ 그래서 결정 구조를 형성한다

30-08 We would be honored to have you as a guest at the annual
저희는 영광일 것입니다 / 당신을 손님으로 모신다면 / 해마다 열리는 축제에

festival.

30-09 If you are fortunate to have opportunity, it is your duty to make
만약 당신이 운이 좋다면 / 기회를 가지는 데 / (…은) 당신의 의무이다 / 반드시 하는

sure other people have those opportunities as well. *Kamala Harris*
것은 / 다른 사람들도 또한 그러한 기회를 갖도록

30-10 We can't help but think James must have his head in the clouds
우리는 생각하지 않을 수 없다 / James가 틀림없이 공상에 잠긴 것이라고

to talk like that.
/ 그렇게 말하다니

30-11 Have you ever found yourself speaking to someone at length only
당신은 발견한 적이 있는가 / 자신이 어떤 사람에게 상세히 말하고 있는 것을 / (그러나)

to realize they haven't heard a single thing you've said?
결국 깨닫게 된 / 그들이 하나도 듣지 않았다는 것을 / [당신이 말한]?

30-12 A child who has been repeatedly criticized for poor performance
아이는 / [수학에서의 부진한 (학업) 성취로 인해 반복해서 야단을 맞아온]

on math may learn to dodge difficult math problems in order to
/ 배울지도 모른다 / 어려운 수학 문제들을 피하는 것을 / 더 심한 처벌을

avoid further punishment.
면하기 위해

unit 31 부사적 to-v의 관용 구문

S TANDARD

31-01 Our span of life is brief, but is long enough for us to live well and
우리의 수명은 짧다 / 그러나 길다 / 우리가 멋지게 그리고 정직하게 살기에는 충분히

honestly. *Cicero*

31-02 Some kinds of viruses are too small to be seen by the naked eye.
어떤 종류의 바이러스는 / 너무 작다 / 보이기에는 / 맨눈으로

A

31-03 You are never too old to set another goal or to dream a new
당신은 결코 너무 나이가 많지 않다 / 다른 목표를 정하거나 새로운 꿈을 꾸기에

dream.

31-04 Change is the law of life. And those who look only to the past or
변화는 삶의 법칙이다 그리고 사람은 / [과거 또는 현재만을 바라보는]

present are certain to miss the future. *John F. Kennedy*
/ 반드시 미래를 놓치게 된다

31-05 To make a long story short, Beauty fell in love with the Beast,
간단히 말해서 / 미녀는 야수와 사랑에 빠졌다

who turned out to be a handsome prince.
/ 그리고 그는 잘생긴 왕자인 것으로 밝혀졌다

B

31-06 Copywriters must be versatile enough to adjust to each new
카피라이터는 다재다능해야 한다 / 각각의 새로운 상품과 매체에 적응할 정도로 충분히

product and medium and to vary the language and tone of each
/ 그리고 각 메시지의 용어와 어조를 바꿀 정도로

message.

31-07 People draw **too heavily, too quickly, on already overdrawn**
사람들이 너무 많이, 너무 빠르게 이용한다 / 이미 초과 인출된 환경의 자원 계좌들을

environmental resource accounts to be affordable far into the
/ 먼 미래에 감당하기에는

future without bankrupting those accounts.
/ 그러한 계좌들을 파산시키지 않고서는

31-08 It is **not** fair to ask of others what you are **not** willing to do
(…은) 공정하지 않다 / 타인들에게 요구하는 것은 / 당신이 직접 기꺼이 하려고 하지 않는 것을

yourself.

31-09 The team has **lost** the last two games and, **to make matters**
그 팀은 마지막 두 경기를 졌다 / 그리고 설상가상으로

worse, two of its best players are injured.
/ 최고 선수들 중 두 명이 부상 중이다

C

31-10 I **always** like to look on the optimistic side of life, but I am realistic
나는 항상 좋아한다 / 인생의 낙관적인 면을 보는 것을 / 그러나 나는 현실적이다

enough to know that life is a complex matter. *Walt Disney*
/ 알 정도로 충분히 / 인생은 복잡한 문제라는 것을

31-11 The bargain must **truly stand out** in the consumer's mind as a
염가판매는 정말로 눈에 띄어야 한다 / 소비자의 마음속에 / 좋은

good deal that is just too exceptional to pass up.
거래로서 / [정말 너무나 파격적이어서 놓칠 수 없는]

31-12 Pollution has **a negative effect** on the health of everyone living in
오염은 부정적인 영향을 미친다 / 모든 사람의 건강에 / [도시에 살고

the city, not to mention the damage to the environment.
있는] / 환경에 대한 손상은 말할 것도 없이

unit 32 부사 역할을 하는 분사구문의 의미

S TANDARD

32-01 Tapping his fingers loudly on the desk top, he made his
자신의 손가락으로 시끄럽게 톡톡 두드렸다 / 책상 위를 / (그러면서) 그는 자신의

impatience and dissatisfaction known.
성급함과 불만이 알려지게 했다

32-02 Pressed for time and stuck in a deadlock, she had no idea how to
시간에 쫓기고 교착 상태에 갇혔다 / (그래서) 그녀는 알지 못했다 / 그 논문을

finish the paper.
어떻게 끝내야 할지

A

32-03 Being a hybrid art as well as a late one, film has always been in a
혼합 예술이다 / 후발 예술일 뿐만 아니라 / (그래서) 영화는 항상 대화를 해왔다

dialogue with other narrative genres.
/ 다른 서사 장르와

32-04 Taken daily, according to a new study, vitamin D can help treat
매일 섭취된다 / 새로운 연구에 따르면 / (그러면) 비타민 D는 심한 천식을 치료하는

severe asthma.
것을 도울 수 있다

32-05 Originally raised mainly for their meat, sheep and goats became
원래 주로 고기를 위해 사육되었다 / (그러나) 양과 염소는 귀중하게 되었다

valuable also for their milk and wool.
/ 그것들의 우유와 털 때문에도

B

32-06 Children at play often take on other roles, pretending to be
놀이 중인 아이들은 종종 다른 역할을 맡는다 / Walsh 교장 선생님이나

Principal Walsh or Josh's mom, happily forcing themselves to
Josh의 엄마인 체하면서 / (그러면서) 행복하게 스스로가 상상하도록 한다

imagine how someone else thinks and feels.
/ 다른 사람이 어떻게 생각하고 느끼는지

32-07 A mother is a person who seeing there are only four pieces of pie
어머니는 사람이다 / [다섯 명이 있는데 파이가 네 조각만 있는 것을 본다

for five people, promptly announces she never did care for pie.
/ (그때) 바로 알리는 / 자신은 한 번도 파이를 좋아한 적이 없었다고]

32-08 Assumed to have a substantial amount of water, Mars is probably
상당한 양의 물을 가진 것으로 추정된다 / (그래서) 화성은 아마도 가장

most habitable out of all the planets in our solar system.
살기에 적합할 것이다 / 우리 태양계의 모든 행성들 중에서

32-09 When I find myself in times of trouble, mother Mary comes to me,
내 자신이 곤경에 처한 것을 알게 될 때 / 어머니 Mary가 내게 오신다

speaking words of wisdom, "Let it be." And in my hour of
/ (그리고 나서) 지혜의 말씀을 주신다 / "내버려 두라" 그리고 내가 어둠의 시간에 있을 때

darkness she is standing right in front of me, speaking words of
/ 그녀는 내 바로 앞에 서 계신다 / (그리고 나서) 지혜의 말씀을 주신다

wisdom, "Let it be." *the song <Let It Be>*
/ "내버려 두라"

32-10 Fueled by drought and development, wildfires in the West are
가뭄과 개발로 부채질된다 / (그래서) (미국) 서부의 들불은 점점 더 커지고

getting bigger and more aggressive.
더 강력해 지고 있다

32-11 Seconds after its spectacular launch, the spacecraft with seven
극적인 발사 수초 후에 / 일곱 명의 우주비행사들이 탑승한 그 우주선은

astronauts on board blew up and came apart, striking the viewers
폭발하였다 / 그리고 부서졌다 / (그래서) 시청자들이 갑자기 충격으로

dumb with shock.
말문이 막히게 했다

32-12 The very real genetic differences between races or genders are
매우 실질적인 유전적 차이들은 / [인종 또는 성별 사이의] / 사소

insignificant compared with the similarities in our minds.
하다 / 우리의 정신적 유사성과 비교될 때

unit 33 분사구문의 다양한 형태 1

33-01 Not having been to the city before, I needed some tourist
전에 그 도시에 가본 적이 없었다 / (그래서) 나는 몇 개의 여행자용 팸플릿이

pamphlets.
필요했다

33-02 Can we sustain our standard of living in the same ecological
우리는 우리의 생활 수준을 유지할 수 있을까 / 동일한 생태적 공간에서

space while consuming the resources of that space?
/ 그 공간의 자원을 소비하면서?

A

33-03 The fundamental problem most patients face is an inability to love
근본적인 문제는 / [대부분의 환자들이 직면하는] / 자신을 사랑하지 못하는 것이다

themselves, having been unloved by others during some crucial
/ (왜냐하면) 사랑받지 못했다 / 다른 사람들에 의해서 / 그들의 삶의 어떤 결정적인 기간

part of their lives.
동안에

33-04 I sat quietly in a chair, my only actions consisting of taking notes
나는 의자에 조용히 앉아 있었다 / (그러면서) 나의 유일한 행동은 필기를 하는 것이었고

and stuffing my ears with wadded toilet paper.
/ 그리고 내 귀를 똘똘 뭉친 화장지로 채우는 것이었다

33-05 Though seriously injured, the pilot crawled out of the wreckage
비록 심하게 다쳤지만 / 그 조종사는 잔해에서 기어나왔다

and was flown by helicopter to a nearby medical center.
/ 그리고 헬리콥터에 태워져 이송되었다 / 근처의 의료 센터로

B

33-06 Turned down for countless jobs, Jenny didn't give up hope and is
무수한 일자리를 거절당했다 / (그러나) Jenny는 희망을 포기하지 않았다 / 그리고

now a successful architect.
지금은 성공한 건축가이다

33-07 In recent history, countries with the highest net inward migration
최근의 역사에서　　　　　/ 순유입이 가장 높았던 나라들이

have also had the highest growth rates, the two factors clearly
/ 또한 가장 높은 성장률을 보였다　　　　　/ (그래서) 그 두 요소는 분명 조화롭게 연결

being linked in harmony.
되어 있다

33-08 When faced with a bunch of watermelons, all promising delicious
한 무더기의 수박을 마주 대하게 될 때　　　　　/ 모두 속에 맛있는 과즙이 있을 것 같은데

juiciness inside, how do you know which one to pick?
/ 당신은 어떻게 아는가　　/ 어느 것을 골라야 할지?

33-09 The time spent in lamenting their lot, if applied to honest
시간은　　/ [자신의 운명을 한탄하면서 보낸]　　　　/ 만약 정직한 노력에 쓰인다면

endeavor, would yield splendid results and give them proper
/ 정말 멋진 결과를 낳을 텐데　　　　/ 그리고 그들에게 세상에서 적절한 자리를

places in the world.
줄 텐데

33-10 The making of a contract requires the mutual agreement of two or
계약을 하는 것은 필요로 한다　　　　/ 둘 이상의 사람이나 단체의 상호 합의를

more persons or parties, one of them ordinarily making an offer
/ 그들 중 한쪽이 보통 제안을 한다

and another accepting.
/ 그리고 다른 한쪽은 받아들인다

33-11 There being a dispute over a topic of environment, the country is
환경이라는 주제에 대해서 논쟁이 있다　　　　　/ (그래서) 그 나라는 효과

to make an effective law for its sustainable development.
적인 법률을 만들 예정이다　　　/ 지속 가능한 개발을 위해서

33-12 When expelled from the nucleus of an atom, a neutron is unstable
원자핵에서 방출되었을 때　　　　/ 중성자는 불안정하다

and decayed to form a proton and an electron.
/ 그리고 자연 붕괴된다　/ 그 결과 양성자와 전자를 형성한다

unit 34 분사구문의 다양한 형태 2

34-01 Adolescents have been quick to immerse themselves in
청소년들은 재빨랐다 / 기술에 몰두하는 것에

technology with most using the Internet to communicate.
/ 대부분 인터넷을 사용하면서 / 소통하기 위해서

34-02 Judging from his latest novel that I have read, he seems to be a
그의 최신 소설로 판단하건대 / [내가 읽은] / 그는 꽤 유망한 작가인 것 같다

fairly promising writer.

A

34-03 While afloat, the reindeer is uniquely vulnerable, moving slowly
물에 떠 있는 동안 / 순록은 특히 공격받기 쉽다 / (왜냐하면) 천천히 움직인다

with its antlers held high as it struggles to keep its nose above
/ 뿔을 높이 받쳐 든 채로 / 순록이 코를 유지하려고 애쓰면서 / 물 위로

water.

34-04 Desperate to keep himself and his family from starving, Erich
필사적이었다 / 자기 자신과 가족이 굶주리지 않게 하려고 / (그래서)

took any available job.
Erich는 구할 수 있는 어떠한 일자리라도 취했다

34-05 Granted that you've made some progress, you should not be
네가 어느 정도 진전을 이루었다는 것이 인정된다 / (그러나) 너는 자만해서는 안 된다

conceited.

B

34-06 With the industrial society evolving into an information-based
산업 사회가 진화하면서 / 정보 기반 사회로

society, the concept of information as a product, a commodity
/ 정보의 개념이 / [생산물로서 / 즉 그 자체의 가치를

with its own value, has emerged.
가진 상품(으로서)] / 나타났다

34-07 Unable to write, or even to speak clearly, Stephen Hawking was
쓸 수도 혹은 명확하게 말을 할 수도 없었다   / (그러나) 스티븐 호킹은 도약하고 있었다

leaping beyond relativity, beyond quantum mechanics, beyond
/ 상대성 이론을 넘어   / 양자 역학을 넘어   / 빅뱅을 넘어

the Big Bang, to the 'dance of geometry' that created the
/ '기하학의 춤'으로   / [우주를 창조한]

universe.

34-08 Some pioneers in computer usage see the ultimate relation
일부 개척자들은   / 컴퓨터 사용에 있어서   / 인간과 컴퓨터 사이의 궁극적인 관계를 여긴다

between man and computer as a symbiotic union of two living
/ 두 개의 살아 있는 종의 공생 결합으로

species, each completely dependent on the other for survival.
/ (왜냐하면) 각각은 완전히 상대방에 의존하고 있다   / 생존을 위해

34-09 Strictly speaking, Great Britain consists of Scotland, Wales and
엄격히 말하자면   / Great Britain은 스코틀랜드, 웨일스, 그리고 잉글랜드로 구성된다

England, and the United Kingdom consists of Great Britain and
/ 그리고 the United Kingdom은 Great Britain과 북아일랜드로 구성된다

Northern Ireland.

34-10 The role of science can sometimes be overstated, with its advocates
과학의 역할은 때때로 과장될 수 있다   / 그 지지자들이 과학(만능)주의에

slipping into scientism.
빠져들면서

34-11 Taking into account growing population numbers, climate change
늘어나는 인구의 수, 기후 변화, 자연재해를 고려할 때

and natural disasters, global food security is under threat.
/ 전 세계의 식량 안보가 위협받고 있다

34-12 With so much data collected about us and with anybody being
우리에 관해 너무나 많은 자료가 수집된 상태에서   / 그리고 누구라도 그것을 유포할 수 있는 상태

able to disseminate it around the globe, is there anything we really
에서   / 전 세계에   / 어떤 것이 있는가   / [우리가 정말로

can do to protect privacy?
할 수 있는]   / 사생활을 보호하기 위해서?

Review

A

01 Holding on to anger is like grasping a hot coal **with the intent of**
분노를 계속 유지하는 것은 뜨거운 석탄을 쥐고 있는 것과 같다 　　　　　 / 그것을 누군가에게 던지려는

throwing it at someone else; you are the one who gets burned. *Buddha*
의도로 　　　　　　　　　　　　 당신이 사람이다 　　 / [화상을 입게 되는]

02 I can't change the direction of the wind, but I can adjust **my sails to**
나는 바람의 방향을 바꿀 수 없다 　　　　　　　 / 그러나 나는 돛을 조정할 수 있다 　　　 /

always reach my destination. *Jimmy Dean*
항상 나의 목적지에 도착하기 위해

03 The virus is **too small** to carry all the molecular machinery **required**
바이러스는 너무 작다 　　　 / 모든 분자적 조직을 갖기에는 　　　　　 / [스스로를

to replicate itself, which is why it needs a host cell to multiply.
복제하는 데 필요한] 　 / 그리고 그것이 바이러스가 숙주 세포를 필요로 하는 이유이다 / 증식하기 위해서

04 Plants communicate, **signaling to remote organs within an individual,**
식물들은 소통한다 　　　　 / 개체 내에서 멀리 떨어진 기관에 신호를 보내면서

eavesdropping on neighboring individuals, and exchanging information
/ 이웃하는 개체의 이야기를 엿들으면서 　　　　　　　　 / 그리고 다른 유기체와 정보를 교환하면서

with other organisms.

B

05 A foreign exchange market gets influenced **by a real world event,**
외환 시장은 영향을 받는다 　　　　　　 / 실제 세상의 사건에

and has an impact on the economy of a nation, causing the value of
/ 그리고 영향을 끼친다 　 / 한 나라의 경제에 　　　　 / 그 나라의 화폐 가치가 오르내리게

its money to rise and fall.
하면서

06 With so many people getting their information online, there **may not**
너무나 많은 사람들이 온라인에서 정보를 얻고 있어서 　　　　　 / 수요가 없을지도 모른다

be a need for traditional newspapers.
/ [전통적인 신문에 대한]

07 When seen near the horizon, the moon appears **strikingly larger than**
지평선 근처에서 보일 때 　　　　　 / 달은 현저하게 더 커 보인다 　　　　 / 머리

when viewed overhead.
위로 보일 때보다

C

08 Teachers need to know their students well in order to teach them
교사들은 자신의 학생들을 잘 알 필요가 있다 / 학생들을 효과적으로 가르치기 위해서

effectively.

09 The Internet is a modern luxury abounding with information, allowing
인터넷은 현대의 사치품이다 / [정보가 풍부한] / (그래서)

you access to any information, all with the ease of a simple finger
여러분이 모든 정보에 접근할 수 있게 해준다 / 단지 간단한 손가락 클릭만으로 쉽게

click.

10 It took me a little while to get used to this job, but now I could do it
(…은) 내게 잠깐의 시간이 걸렸다 / 이 일에 익숙해지는 것은 / 하지만 이제 나는 그 일을 할 수 있다

with my eyes closed.
/ 눈을 감은 채로

D

11 All species are seen as having rights as people do, environmental
모든 종은 여겨진다 / 권리를 가진 것으로 / 사람들처럼 / (따라서) 환경적 복지는

welfare thus coming before human welfare.
인간의 복지에 우선한다

12 Have you ever experienced the frustration of offering to help
너는 좌절을 경험해 본 적이 있니 / [누군가를 도와주겠다고 제안하였는데

someone only to be told to mind your own business?
/ 그러나 결국 네 자신의 일에나 신경 쓰라는 말을 듣게 된]?

13 Faced with information that relates to what the old already know, their
정보에 직면한다 / [노인들이 이미 알고 있는 것과 관계가 있는] / (그때)

brains tend to work quicker and smarter, discerning patterns and
그들의 뇌는 더 빠르고 더 현명하게 작동하는 경향이 있다 / 양상을 구분하고 논리적인 결론 부분으로 도약

jumping to the logical end point.
하면서

unit 35 시간의 부사절

S TANDARD

35-01 Once you replace negative thoughts with positive ones, you'll start
일단 당신이 부정적인 생각을 긍정적인 생각으로 대체하면 / 당신은 긍정적인

having positive results. *Willie Nelson*
결과를 가지기 시작할 것이다

35-02 You never really understand a person until you consider things
당신은 결코 정말로 어떤 사람을 이해하지 못한다 / 당신이 그의 관점으로 상황을 고려할 때까지

from his point of view. *the novel <To Kill a Mockingbird>*

A

35-03 We must be ready to abandon or modify our hypothesis as soon
우리는 준비가 되어 있어야 한다 / 우리의 가설을 폐기하거나 수정할 / 가설이 사실과

as it is shown to be inconsistent with the facts.
일치하지 않는다는 것으로 증명되자마자

35-04 Lunar eclipses occur each time the Earth blocks the sun's light
월식은 일어난다 / 지구가 태양의 빛을 막을 때마다

from the moon during the moon's full phase.
/ 달로부터 / 달의 만월 단계 동안에

35-05 No sooner had I spoken the words than I felt an icy chill creep to my
내가 그 말을 내뱉자마자 / 나는 얼음 같은 냉기가 서서히 다가오는 것을 느꼈다

heart. *the short story <The IMP of the Perverse>*
나의 심장으로

B

35-06 The moment you doubt whether you can fly, you cease forever to
당신이 의심하자마자 / 당신이 날 수 있는지를 / 당신은 영원히 멈춘다 /

be able to do it. *the novel <Peter Pan>*
그것을 할 수 있는 것을

35-07 Since the Industrial Revolution began in the eighteenth century,
산업 혁명이 18세기에 시작된 이래로

CO$_2$ released during industrial processes has greatly increased
/ 산업 공정 중에 배출된 이산화탄소는 크게 증가시켰다

the proportion of carbon in the atmosphere.
/ 대기 중의 탄소의 비율을

35-08 Each player must accept the cards life deals him or her; but once
각각의 경기자는 카드들을 받아들여야 한다   / [인생이 그 사람에게 나눠주는]   / 그러나 일단

they are in hand, he or she alone must decide how to play the
그것들이 수중에 있으면   / 그 사람은 홀로 결정해야 한다   / 그 카드들을 어떻게 사용할

cards in order to win the game. *Voltaire*
것인지   / 그 게임을 이기기 위해서

35-09 You can't just ask customers what they want and then try to give
당신은 단지 고객에게 물어볼 수 없다   / 그들이 원하는 것을   / 그러고 나서 그들에게 그것을 주려고

that to them. By the time you get it built, they'll want something
시도할 (수는 없다)   당신이 그것이 만들어지게 할 무렵에는   / 그들은 새로운 어떤 것을 원할 것이다

new. *Steve Jobs*

35-10 Art does not come to life until a spectator, a listener, or an audience
예술은 살아 움직이지 않는다   / 관객, 청취자, 혹은 청중이 그것에 생명을 불어넣을 때까지

breathes life into it by experiencing it.
/ 그것을 경험함으로써

35-11 Hardly had everybody taken their seats when the professor began
모든 사람이 자기 자리에 앉자마자   / 그 교수는 자신의 강의를 시작했다

his lecture.

35-12 Whenever a geneticist unlocks new secrets of the DNA molecule,
유전학자가 DNA 분자의 새로운 비밀들을 밝힐 때마다

it adds to our knowledge base and enables us to better the
/ 그것은 우리의 지식 기반에 더해진다   / 그리고 우리가 인간의 여건을 개선하는 것을 가능하게

human condition.
한다

Unit 36 이유의 부사절

36-01 As people are walking all the time, in the same spot, a path
사람들이 늘 걷고 있기 때문에 / 같은 장소에서 / 길이 생긴다

appears. *John Locke*

36-02 Don't take the wrong side of an argument just because your
논쟁의 잘못된 면을 선택하지 마라 / 단지 당신의 상대방이 올바른 면을

opponent has taken the right side. *Baltasar Gracian*
취했다고 해서

A

36-03 Knowing another language is a window into another culture,
다른 언어를 아는 것은 다른 문화를 보는 창문이다

since how a society thinks and views the world is expressed
/ 한 사회가 세상을 어떻게 생각하고 바라보는지가 표현되기 때문에

through its language.
/ 그것의 언어를 통해서

36-04 The time scales of geological activity are important for
지질학적 활동의 시간 척도들은 중요하다 / 환경

environmental geologists because they provide a way to measure
지질학자들에게 / 그것들이 방법을 제공하기 때문에 / [인간의 영향을

human impacts on the natural world.
측정하는 / [자연계에 미친]]

36-05 Now that tablet PCs, 3D VR glasses, and interactive whiteboards
태블릿 PC, 3차원 가상현실 안경, 그리고 쌍방향의 화이트보드는 현대 교실에서 너무나도 많은 부분이기 때문에

are so much a part of the modern classroom, many people fear
/ 많은 사람들은 염려한다

reading books will no longer be as important.
/ 책을 읽는 것이 더 이상 중요하지 않을까 봐

B

36-06 Words can carry meanings beyond those consciously intended
단어들은 의미를 전달할 수 있다 / 의식적으로 의도된 의미를 넘어서

by speakers or writers because listeners or readers bring their
/ 화자 또는 필자에 의해 / 청자 또는 독자가 그들 자신의 시각을 언어에 가져오기 때문에

own perspectives to the language they encounter.
/ [그들이 맞닥뜨리는]

36-07 Just because you can hear your robins, goldfinches, and sparrows
단지 당신이 울새, 오색방울새, 그리고 참새가 행복하게 지저귀는 것을 들을 수 있다는 이유로

chirping away happily in the garden every morning, don't be
/ 매일 아침 정원에서 / 생각하도록

fooled into thinking that all is well in 'birdworld.'
속아 넘어가지 마라 / '조류 세상'에서는 모든 것이 다 괜찮다고

36-08 As the nature of sarcasm implies a contradiction between intent
빈정거림의 본질은 모순을 암시하기 때문에 / [의도와 메시지 사이의]

and message, nonverbal cues may "leak" and reveal the
/ 비언어적 신호는 '새어나가게' 그리고 드러나게 할지도 모른다 / 화자의

speaker's true mood.
진정한 기분을

36-09 Now that genetically modified foods are on our supermarket
유전자 조작 식품이 우리의 슈퍼마켓 선반에 있기 때문에

shelves, the genie is out of the bottle and cannot be put back in.
/ genie는 병 밖으로 나와 있다 / 그리고 안으로 다시 넣어질 수 없다

36-10 As price is decided by bringing demand and supply into equilibrium,
가격은 결정되기 때문에 / 수요와 공급을 균형에 맞춰놓음으로써

an increase in supply leads to a fall in price and increase in
/ 공급의 증가는 이어진다 / 가격의 하락과 균형 생산량의 증가로

equilibrium quantity.

36-11 If we are not to become 'slaves to the machine', we should keep
만약 우리가 '기계의 노예'가 되지 않으려면 / 우리는 명심해야 한다

in mind that since computer programs are designed by people,
/ 컴퓨터 프로그램은 사람에 의해서 설계되므로

they, too, are fallible.
/ 그것들도 또한 틀릴 수 있다는 것을

36-12 Now that labor's clout has significantly diminished, knowledge
노동의 영향력이 상당히 줄어들었기 때문에 / 지식 근로자들이

workers have become the more important group in the economic
더 중요한 집단이 되었다 / 경제 방정식에서

equation.

unit 37 조건의 부사절

37-01 Differences of habit and language are nothing **at all if our aims are**
습관과 언어의 차이는 전혀 아무것도 아니다 / 만약 우리의 목표가 같다면

identical and our hearts are open. *the novel <Harry Potter and the Goblet of Fire>*
/ 그리고 우리의 마음이 열려 있다면

37-02 A life devoted to the acquisition of wealth is useless, **unless we**
부의 획득에 바쳐진 인생은 쓸모없다 / 만약 우리가 알지

know how to turn it into joy.
못한다면 / 어떻게 그것을 즐거움으로 바꾸는지

A

37-03 In so far as changes in interest rates affect expectations, **lower**
이자율의 변화가 기대에 영향을 미치는 한에서 / 더 낮은

interest rates may still contribute to higher investment.
이자율은 여전히 기여할 것이다 / 더 높은 투자에

37-04 I don't care who you are, where you're from or what you did **as**
나는 상관없다 / 당신이 누구인지 / 당신이 어디 출신인지 / 또는 당신이 무엇을 했는지 /

long as you love me. *the song <As Long As You Love Me>*
당신이 나를 사랑하는 한

37-05 A motion may be withdrawn **by its proposer at any time before**
발의는 철회될 수도 있다 / 그 제안자에 의해서 / 언제라도 / 그것에

voting on it has commenced, provided that the motion has not
대한 투표가 시작되기 전에 / 만약 그 발의가 수정되지 않았다면

been amended.

B

37-06 If you wait for the mango fruits to fall, you'd be wasting **your time**
당신이 망고 열매가 떨어지기를 기다린다면 / 당신은 당신의 시간을 낭비하고 있는 것이다

while others are learning how to climb the tree. *Michael Bassey Johnson*
/ 다른 사람들이 배우고 있는 동안에 / 어떻게 그 나무에 올라갈지를

37-07 You can't think creatively about information unless you have
당신은 정보에 대해서 창의적으로 생각할 수 없다 / 만약 당신이 머릿속에 생각할

information in your head to think about.
정보가 없다면

37-08 As far as we can discern, the sole purpose of human existence is
우리가 식별할 수 있는 한 / 인간 존재의 유일한 목적은 빛을 밝게 하는 것이다

to kindle a light in the darkness of mere being. *Carl Jung*
/ 단순한 존재의 어둠 속에서

37-09 Mediation parallels advocacy in so far as it tends to involve a
중재는 옹호와 유사하다 / 그것이 협상의 과정을 수반하는 경향이 있다는 점에서

process of negotiation, but differs in so far as mediation involves
/ 그러나 다르다 / 중재가 중립적인 역할을 취하는 것을 수반한다는 점에서

adopting a neutral role between two opposing parties rather than
/ 대립하는 두 당사자들 사이에서 / 한쪽 편의 입장을

taking up the case of one party against another.
취하기보다는 / 다른 편에 반대하여

37-10 An object that is moving at constant speed will eventually slow
물체는 [일정한 속도로 움직이고 있는] / 마침내 느려지고 멈추게 될 것이다

down and come to a stop unless there is something to keep it moving
/ 만약 어떤 것이 없다면 / [그것을 일정한 속도로 계속

at constant speed.
움직이게 하는]

37-11 Change may hurt us a little when it occurs, but if we accept it as
변화는 우리를 약간 아프게 할 수도 있다 / 그것이 일어날 때 / 그러나 만약 우리가 그것을 성장 과정

a growth process, it will bring benefits in the long run.
으로 받아들인다면 / 그것은 결국에는 이익을 가져다줄 것이다

37-12 There is no fee for the card and no interest is charged provided
카드에 대한 수수료가 없다 / 그리고 이자가 청구되지 않는다 / 만약 그 계좌가

that the account is settled in full every month.
결제된다면 / 매월 전액

93

unit 38 목적 · 결과의 부사절

38-01 We do what we have to do so that we can do what we want to
우리는 한다 / 우리가 해야 하는 것을 / 우리가 할 수 있도록 / 우리가 하고 싶은 것을

do.

38-02 It was so quiet in the room that I could hear the leaves being
방안이 아주 조용했다 / 그래서 나는 들을 수 있었다 / 바깥에서 나뭇잎들이 나무들

blown off the trees outside.
로부터 날리고 있는 것을

A

38-03 A scientific understanding of emotional intelligence may allow us
정서 지능의 과학적 이해는 우리가 우리의 감성적 기술들을 훈련하게 할 수도 있을 것이다

to train our emotional skills so that we can live more fulfilling and
/ 우리가 살아갈 수 있도록 / 더 성취감을 주고 더 생산적인

productive lives.
삶을

38-04 The personal computer becomes far smaller and much more
개인용 컴퓨터는 훨씬 더 작고 훨씬 더 휴대하기 쉽게 된다

portable, so that some people such as writers or stock dealers
/ 그래서 일부 사람들은 / [작가 또는 증권 중개인과 같은]

are able to work wherever they are.
/ 일할 수 있다 / 그들이 있는 어디서나

38-05 Some people are making such thorough preparation for rainy days
어떤 사람들은 하고 있다 / 아주 철저한 준비를 / [비 오는 날을 대비하는]

that they aren't enjoying today's sunshine. *William Feather*
/ 그래서 그들은 오늘의 햇빛을 즐기지 못하고 있다

B

38-06 In 1936, King Edward VIII became the very first British monarch
1936년에 / 국왕 에드워드 8세는 바로 최초의 영국 군주가 되었다

to voluntarily give up his throne when he abdicated so that he
/ [자발적으로 자신의 왕위를 포기한] / 그가 퇴위했을 때 / 그가 이혼한 미국인

could marry Mrs. Simpson, a divorced American woman.
여성, Simpson 부인과 결혼하기 위해서

38-07 Her eyes are nothing but a pure emerald shining in the rays of the
그녀의 눈은 바로 순수한 에메랄드이다 / [햇살과 달빛 속에서 빛나는]

sun and the moon so that you can't take your eyes off her.
/ 그래서 당신은 그녀에게서 눈을 뗄 수 없다

38-08 When one door of happiness closes, another opens; but often we
행복의 한쪽 문이 닫히면 / 또 다른 문이 열린다 / 그러나 종종 우리는

look so long at the closed door that we do not see the one which
아주 오래 닫힌 문을 바라본다 / 그래서 우리는 그것(문)을 보지 못한다 / [우리를

has been opened for us. *Helen Keller*
위해 열린]

38-09 The witness described the suspect in such detail that the police
목격자는 용의자를 묘사했다 / 아주 상세하게 / 그래서 경찰은 그의 위치를

were able to locate him in no time.
알아낼 수 있었다 / 즉시

38-10 Rights and obligations should be so inseparable that a demand
권리와 의무는 아주 불가분적이어야 한다 / 그래서 하나에 대한 요구는

for one is always accompanied by a statement of the other.
항상 수반되게 / 다른 하나의 표명에 의해

38-11 If you live to be a hundred, I want to live to be a hundred minus
만약 당신이 100세까지 산다면 / 나는 100세에서 하루를 뺀 날까지 살고 싶다

one day so I never have to live without you. *the short story <Winnie the Pooh>*
/ 내가 결코 살아야 하지 않도록 / 당신 없이

38-12 When you are reading for study purposes, it is critical to read
당신이 학습 목적으로 글을 읽고 있을 때 / (…은) 중요하다 / 체계적으로

systematically, so you are able to integrate the new knowledge
읽는 것은 / 당신이 새로운 지식을 통합할 수 있도록

you acquire with what you already know.
/ [당신이 획득하는] / 당신이 이미 알고 있는 것과

unit 39 반전 · 대조의 부사절

39-01 **Even though a speech can be effective,** all the words in the world
비록 연설이 효과적일 수 있을지라도 / 세상의 모든 말은 필적할 수 없다

cannot measure up to the example of a leader.
/ 지도자의 본보기에

39-02 **However hard you shop for an item, after you've bought it,** it will
아무리 열심히 당신이 어떤 물품을 사러 가더라도 / 당신이 그것을 사고 난 후에 / 그것은

be on sale somewhere cheaper.
할인 중일 것이다 / 어딘가에서 더 싸게

A

39-03 **Even if it turns out that time travel is impossible,** it is important
비록 (…이) 판명될지라도 / 시간 여행이 불가능하다는 것이 / (…은) 중요하다

that we understand why it is impossible. *Stephen Hawking*
/ 우리가 이해하는 것은 / 왜 그것이 불가능한가를

39-04 **Before sound recording,** classical music was passed down
음원 녹음 이전에 / 고전 음악은 전해졌다

through written scores, whereas early jazz mainly relied on live
/ 기록된 악보를 통해서 / 반면에 초기의 재즈는 주로 라이브 공연에 의존했다

performance.

39-05 **Strange as it may sound,** the diamond, so clear and transparent,
비록 이상하게 들릴 수도 있지만 / 다이아몬드는 / 아주 깨끗하고 투명한데

is composed of the same material as coal and soot, namely
/ 동일한 물질로 구성되어 있다 / 석탄과 검댕과 / 즉 탄소로

carbon.

B

39-06 **No matter what emotion you're feeling right now,** you can count
당신이 어떤 감정을 느끼고 있다 하더라도 / 바로 지금 / 당신은 한 가지를 믿을 수

on one thing—it will change.
있다 / 즉, 그것은 바뀔 것이다

39-07 If we don't have the power to choose where we come from, we
비록 우리가 선택할 힘은 없을지라도 / 우리가 어디서 오는지를 / 우리는

can still choose where we go from there.
여전히 선택할 수 있다 / 우리가 거기에서 어디로 갈지를

39-08 Newton imagined that masses affect each other by exerting a
뉴턴은 상상했다 / 질량은 서로 영향을 미친다고 / 힘을 씀으로써

force, while in Einstein's theory the effects occur through a
/ 반면에 아인슈타인의 이론에서는 / 그 영향이 일어난다 / 공간과 시간의

bending of space and time and there is no concept of gravity as
휘어짐을 통해 / 그리고 중력의 개념은 없다 /

a force.
힘으로서

39-09 I'll do whatever it takes to win games, whether it's sitting on a bench
나는 할 것이다 / 게임을 이기는 데 필요로 하는 것은 무엇이든 / 그것이 벤치에 앉아 있는 것이든

waving a towel, handing a cup of water to a teammate, or hitting
/ 수건을 흔들면서 / 팀 동료에게 물 한 잔을 건네는 것이든 / 결승 슛을 하는

the game-winning shot. *Kobe Bryant*
것이든

39-10 Though most people agree that clothes do not make the person,
비록 대부분의 사람들이 동의할지라도 / 옷이 사람을 만들지 않는다는 것에

they spend considerable time and money dressing themselves in
/ 그들은 상당한 시간과 돈을 쓴다 / 스스로 옷을 차려 입는 데 /

the newest fashion.
최신 패션으로

39-11 Whereas science is concerned with finding and stating the facts,
과학은 관련이 있는 반면에 / 사실들을 찾고 진술하는 것과

poetry's task is to give you the look, the smell, the taste, and the
/ 시의 과제는 당신에게 주는 것이다 / 모양, 냄새, 맛, 그리고 '느낌'을

"feel" of those facts.
/ [그러한 사실들의]

39-12 Whatever you want to do, if you want to be great at it, you have
당신이 무엇을 하고 싶든지 간에 / 만약 당신이 그것에 뛰어나길 원한다면 / 당신은 그것을

to love it and be able to make sacrifices for it. *Maya Angelou*
사랑해야 한다 / 그리고 희생할 수 있(어야 한다) / 그것을 위해서

Unit 40 양태의 부사절

S TANDARD

40-01 A mind needs books **as a sword needs a whetstone, if it is to**
정신은 책을 필요로 한다 / 칼이 숫돌을 필요로 하는 것처럼 / 그것이 날을

keep its edge. *the novel <A Game of Thrones>*
유지하려고 한다면

40-02 Most textbooks are written **as if science is a set of truths to be**
대부분의 교과서는 쓰여 있다 / 마치 과학이 일련의 사실들인 것처럼 / [암기되

memorized.
어야 할]

A

40-03 The horse-drawn carriage was **itself** a technological innovation,
말이 끄는 마차는 그 자체로 기술적 혁신이었다

as were the horseless carriage and later automobiles.
/ 말이 없는 차와 나중의 자동차가 그랬듯이

40-04 Just as a flesh-and-blood beast influences and is influenced by
꼭 현재 살아 있는 짐승이 영향을 주고 받는 것처럼 /

its environment, so too do science and society **mutually influence**
환경과 / 과학과 사회도 또한 / 상호간에 서로 영향을 미친다

one another.

40-05 Live **as though you intend to live forever, and** work **as though your**
살아라 / 마치 당신이 영원히 살고자 하는 것처럼 / 그리고 일하라 / 마치 당신의 힘이 무한한

strength were limitless.
것처럼

B

40-06 We need to see people **as they are, not as we would like them to**
우리는 사람들을 볼 필요가 있다 / 있는 그대로 / 우리가 그들이 어떠하길 바라는 대로가 아니라

be.

40-07 Just as darkness comes at the end of each day, so also comes
꼭 어둠이 오듯이 / 하루의 끝에 / 또한 새벽이 온다

the dawn to spread light across the land. Just as plants must die
/ 온 땅에 빛을 퍼뜨리기 위해 꼭 식물들이 틀림없이 죽는 것처럼

at the end of their life cycle, the seeds they have produced will
/ 생명 주기의 끝에 / 씨들이 / [그들이 만들어 낸] / 나타날

emerge as new plants in the spring.
것이다 / 봄에 새로운 식물들로

40-08 Act as if what you do makes a difference. It does. *William James*
행동하라 / 마치 당신이 하는 것이 변화를 가져오는 것처럼 그것은 그러하다(변화를 가져온다)

40-09 Even when you feel as though there isn't a lot you can do to change
당신이 느낄 때조차도 / 마치 많은 것이 있지 않은 것처럼 / [당신이 할 수 있는 / 불행 또는

unhappiness or problems, you can always do a little—and a little
문제를 바꾸기 위해서] / 당신은 항상 작은 것을 할 수 있다 / 그리고 한 번에

at a time eventually makes a big difference.
조금씩은 / 결국 큰 변화를 만들어 낸다

C

40-10 As there are differing tastes and preferences among different
다른 취향과 선호가 있는 것처럼 / 세상의 여러 민족과 지역 사이에

peoples and regions of the world, so do tastes and preferences
/ 취향과 선호는 진화한다

evolve over the course of centuries.
/ 수 세기에 걸쳐서

40-11 We usually take for granted our ability to produce and understand
우리는 대개 우리의 능력을 당연한 것으로 여긴다 / [말을 만들어 내고 이해하는]

speech, just as we are not particularly aware of the action of our
/ 마치 우리가 작동을 특히 알아차리지 못하는 것처럼 / [우리의

hearts, brains, or other essential organs.
심장, 뇌, 또는 다른 필수적인 기관들의]

40-12 Once you have listened to the gossip for some time, you will soon
일단 당신이 소문에 귀를 기울여왔다면 / 얼마간 / 당신은 곧 느낄 것이다

feel as if you know everyone, even if you have never met them.
/ 마치 당신이 모두를 아는 것처럼 / 비록 당신은 결코 그들을 만난 적이 없을지라도

Review

A

01 Celebrate what you've accomplished, but raise the bar a little higher
축하하라 / 당신이 성취한 것을 / 하지만 장애물을 약간 더 높여라

each time you succeed.
/ 당신이 성공할 때마다

02 A broken heart is just the growing pains necessary so that you can
상심은 단지 필요한 성장통이다 / 당신이 더 완전하게 사랑할

love more completely when the real thing comes along. *J. S. B. Morse*
수 있기 위해서 / 진정한 것이 다가올 때

03 The rights guaranteed in the Bill of Rights—freedom of speech,
권리장전에 보장된 권리들은 / —언론, 집회, 종교, 기타 등등의 자유—

assembly, religion, and so on—fall within negative rights, as do the
/ 소극적인 권리에 해당한다 / 상해로부터의

rights to freedom from injury and to privacy.
그리고 사생활의 자유에 대한 권리들이 그런 것처럼

04 Food unites as well as distinguishes eaters because what and how
음식은 먹는 사람들을 구별짓을 뿐만 아니라 결속시킨다 / 왜냐하면 사람이 무엇을 어떻게 먹느냐가

one eats forms much of one's emotional tie to a group identity, be it
형성하기 때문이다 / 그 사람의 감정적 유대의 많은 것을 / [집단 정체성에 대한] / 그것이

a nation or an ethnicity.
국가이든 민족 집단이든

B

05 The noise of barking and yelling from the park at night is so loud and
밤중에 공원에서 개가 짖어대는 소리와 (사람들이) 소리치는 소음이 / 너무 시끄럽고 불편하게

disturbing that I cannot relax in my apartment.
한다 / 그래서 나는 나의 아파트에서 쉴 수 없다

06 The teacher had no sooner gone out of the classroom than all of the
그 선생님이 교실 밖으로 나가자마자 / 모든 학생들이 갑자기

students burst out laughing.
웃기 시작했다

07 If you are stuck in a pattern of doing the same things every day and
만약 당신이 패턴 속에 갇혀 있다면 / [매일 똑같은 것들을 하는] / 그리고

you feel as though you are becoming dull, perhaps it is time to stop
당신이 느낀다면 / 마치 당신이 무뎌지고 있는 것처럼 / 아마도 시간일 것이다 / [멈춰서

and sharpen your axe.
당신의 도끼를 갈아야 할]

C

08 Now that we are all part of the global village, everyone becomes a
우리는 모두 지구촌의 일원이기 때문에 / 모든 사람이 이웃이 된다

neighbor.

09 Much as I sympathize with your difficulties, there is little I can do to
나는 너의 어려움에 매우 공감하지만 / 내가 너를 돕기 위해 할 수 있는 것이 거의

help you.
없다

10 Leave things as they are until the police arrive.
물건들을 둬라 / 있는 그대로 / 경찰이 도착할 때까지

D

11 Adolescents are so primed to learn that they are also extremely
청소년들은 배울 준비가 아주 잘 되어 있다 / 그래서 그들은 또한 극히 취약하다

vulnerable to learning the wrong things.
/ 잘못된 것들을 배우는 것에도

12 Unless an actor speaks and moves in the manner in which the
만약 배우가 말하고 움직이지 않는다면 / 방식으로 / [가상의 등장인물이

imaginary character whose part he is playing would do, the story will
/ [그 역할을 그가 연기하고 있는] / 할 것 같은] / 그 이야기는 분명하게

not be clearly communicated to the audience.
전달되지 않을 것이다 / 관객에게

13 While physics and mathematics may tell us how the universe began,
물리학과 수학이 우리에게 말해 줄 수도 있는 반면에 / 우주가 어떻게 시작되었는지

they are not much use in predicting human behavior because there
/ 그것들은 그다지 소용이 없다 / 인간의 행동을 예측함에 있어서는 / 풀어야 할 너무나 많은

are far too many equations to solve. *Stephen Hawking*
방정식이 있기 때문에

STAGE III

주요 구문의 독파

Chapter **09** 가정법 구문

Chapter **10** 비교 구문

Chapter **11** 특수 구문

Chapter **12** 기타 주요 구문

Unit 41 if 가정법 과거 구문

S TANDARD

41-01 **If people knew how hard I had to work to gain my mastery, it**
만약 사람들이 안다면 / 내가 얼마나 열심히 일해야 했는지 / 나의 숙련된 솜씨를 얻기 위해 /

would not seem so wonderful at all. *Michelangelo*
그것은 전혀 매우 놀랍게 보이지 않을 텐데

41-02 **If thunder should occur, it would be better to find a shelter as**
혹시라도 천둥이 친다면 / (…이) 더 나을 것이다 / 대피소를 찾는 것이 /

soon as possible and avoid dangerous places.
가능한 한 빨리 / 그리고 위험한 장소를 피하는 것이

A

41-03 **I heard a young boy on television say, "If I were President, I'd give**
나는 텔레비전에서 어린 남자아이가 말하는 것을 들었다 / 제가 만약 대통령이라면 / 저는 모든

everybody enough money to buy whatever they want."
사람에게 줄 거예요 / 사기에 충분한 돈을 / 그들이 원하는 무엇이든

41-04 **If an asteroid with a diameter of 30 km were to collide with the**
만약 직경 30km의 소행성이 지구와 충돌한다면

Earth, it would probably bring an end to human civilization.
/ 그것은 아마 종말을 초래할 텐데 / 인간 문명에

41-05 **Should you meet a jaguar in the jungle, just turn slowly, walk**
만약 당신이 정글에서 재규어를 만난다면 / 그저 천천히 돌아서 / 걸어가고

away, and never look back.
/ 그리고 결코 뒤돌아보지 마라

B

41-06 **If young people understood how doing well in school makes the**
만약 젊은이들이 이해한다면 / 어떻게 학교에서 잘하는 것이 / 그들의 여생을

rest of their life so much interesting, they would be more
정말 흥미롭게 만드는지를 / 그들은 더욱 동기부여가 될 텐데

motivated. *Bill Gates*

41-07 Many species of animals could not survive were it not for the strong
많은 종의 동물들은 생존할 수 없을 것이다 / 강한 모성 본능이 없다면

maternal instinct to protect the young.
/ [새끼를 보호하려는]

41-08 If the universe were to rewind back to the beginning and the laws
만약 우주가 처음으로 되돌아간다면 / 그리고 자연의 법칙이

of nature were the same, would everything happen in the exact
동일하다면 / 모든 것이 일어날까 / 정확히 같은 방식으로?

same way?

41-09 Should you find our service useful, further information can be
만약 당신이 저희의 서비스가 유용하다고 생각하시면 / 추가 정보가 얻어질 수 있습니다

obtained by contacting our office.
/ 저희 사무실에 연락함으로써

41-10 When Stephen Douglas, Abraham Lincoln's opponent in the
에이브러햄 링컨의 경쟁자였던 스티븐 더글러스가 / 대통령

presidential election, accused Lincoln of being two-faced during
선거에서 / 링컨을 위선적이라고 비난했을 때 / 토론 중에

a debate, Lincoln self-deprecatingly responded like this. "Honestly,
/ 링컨은 자조적으로 이렇게 응답했다 / 솔직히 말해서

if I were two-faced, would I be wearing this one?"
/ 만약 내가 얼굴이 두 개라면 / 내가 이 얼굴을 하고 있겠는가?

41-11 Delicious autumn! My very soul is wedded to it, and if I were a
달콤한 가을! 나의 영혼은 가을과 결혼했다 / 그리고 만약 내가 새라면

bird I would fly about the earth seeking the successive autumns.
/ 나는 지구 여기저기를 날아다닐 텐데 / 이어지는 가을을 찾아서

George Eliot

41-12 If a man were to come back from the past and watch the modern
만약 어떤 남자가 과거로부터 돌아와서 현대 세계를 지켜본다면

world, he would note any number of things that would intoxicate
/ 그는 주목하게 될 것이다 / 꽤 많은 것들을 / [그를 경이로움과 환희에 열광하게 할]

him with wonder and delight.

unit 42 if 가정법 과거완료 구문

S TANDARD

42-01 He wouldn't have stopped smoking if his doctor hadn't told him
그는 흡연을 중단하지 않았을 텐데 / 만약 그의 의사가 그에게 말해주지 않았더라면

about the condition of his lungs.
/ 그의 폐 상태에 대해

42-02 In my own travels, had I taken packaged tours I never would have
내 자신의 여행에서 / 내가 패키지여행을 했다면 / 나는 결코 놀랄 만한 경험을 할

had any eye-opening experiences.
수 없었을 텐데

A

42-03 If the truck driver had only taken a few minutes to get the nail
만약 그 트럭 운전사가 단 몇 분을 들였더라면 / 그 못을 제거하기 위해서

removed, he most likely would not have had a flat tire yesterday.
/ 그는 아마도 어제 타이어 펑크를 겪지 않았을 텐데

42-04 As a firefighter, I have seen many people die in fires. Most could
소방관으로서 / 나는 많은 사람들이 화재 속에서 죽는 것을 봐왔다 / 대부분은 자신을 구할

have saved themselves had they been prepared.
수 있었을 텐데 / 그들이 준비되어 있었더라면

42-05 Can you imagine what the world today would be like if Leonardo
너는 상상할 수 있니 / 오늘날 세상이 어떠할지를 / 만약 레오나르도

da Vinci had become a farmer or Wolfgang Amadeus Mozart a
다빈치가 농부가 되었다면 / 또는 볼프강 아마데우스 모차르트가 은행원이 되었다면?

banker?

B

42-06 If I am a great man, it is all thanks to my mother. Hadn't she
만약 내가 위대한 인물이라면 / 그것은 모두 나의 어머니 덕분이다 / 그녀가 나를 부양하는

devoted herself to supporting me, I could never have become
데 헌신하지 않았더라면 / 나는 결코 현재의 내가 될 수 없었을 것이다

what I am.

42-07 **We must assume that we had one chance each for** *The Divine*
우리는 생각해야 한다 / 우리가 「신곡」과 「리어 왕」에 대해 각각 한 번의 기회가 있었다고

Comedy and King Lear. **If Dante and Shakespeare had died before**
만약 단테와 셰익스피어가 사망했다면 / 그들이 그

they wrote those works, nobody ever would have written them.
작품들을 쓰기 전에 / 아무도 지금까지 그것들을 쓰지 않았을 것이다

42-08 **Some economists discovered that gym goers would have been**
어떤 경제학자들은 발견했다 / 헬스클럽에 가는 사람들은 더 나았을 것이라는 것을

better off, financially, had they chosen to pay per workout rather
/ 금전적으로 / 만약 그들이 운동할 때마다 지불하는 것을 선택했더라면 / 월 또는

than signing up for monthly or annual memberships.
연 단위의 회원권을 신청하는 대신에

42-09 **If Louise had not learned the effective parenting skills taught in**
만약 Louise가 효과적인 양육 기술을 배우지 않았더라면 / [세미나에서

the seminars, she would probably be using similarly ineffective
교수 받은] / 그녀는 아마도 비슷하게 비효율적인 위협하는 기술을 사용하고 있을 것이다

threatening techniques with her own children today.
/ 오늘날 자신의 자녀들에게

C

42-10 **If our ancestors hadn't agonized over losses and instead had**
만약 우리의 조상이 손실에 대해 고심하지 않았다면 / 그리고 대신에 너무나 많은

taken too many chances in going after the big gains, they'd have
위험을 무릅썼다면 / 큰 이익을 추구하면서 / 그들은 실패하여 결코

been more likely to lose out and never become anyone's ancestor.
어떤 사람의 조상이 되지 못했을 가능성이 더욱 컸을 것이다

42-11 **Had it not been for Newton, Einstein might never have had his**
만약 뉴턴이 없었더라면 / 아인슈타인은 결코 자신의 기적의 해를 갖지 못했을 것이다

own miracle year that completely revolutionized our view of gravity,
/ [완전히 근본적으로 바꾼 / 중력, 공간, 물질 그리고 시간에

space, matter, and time.
대한 우리의 시각을]

42-12 **Copernicus doubted that the earth was the center of the universe.**
코페르니쿠스는 의심했다 / 지구가 우주의 중심이라는 것을

If it had not been for doubt, we should be now even more ignorant
만약 의심이 없었더라면 / 우리는 지금 훨씬 더 무지할 것이다

than we really are.
/ 실제의 우리보다

Unit 43 wish·as if 가정법 구문

43-01 I wish I were endowed with an artistic talent for painting
나는 좋을 텐데 / 내가 예술적 재능을 타고났다면   / [걸작을 그리기 위한

masterpieces like Pablo Picasso's.
/ [파블로 피카소의 것과 같은]]

43-02 The woman smiled and he felt as if she lit up the world around
그 여자는 미소를 지었다   / 그러자 그는 느꼈다 / 마치 그녀가 밝히는 것처럼 / 그녀 주변의 세상을

her.

A

43-03 I wish I had accepted your invitation, rather than running away
나는 좋을 텐데 / 내가 너의 초대를 받아들였다면   / 도망치는 것 대신에

with my tail between my legs.
/ 겁을 먹고

43-04 Even though I don't personally believe in the Lord, I try to behave
비록 내가 개인적으로 하느님을 믿지 않을지라도   / 나는 행동하려고 노력한다

as though He was watching. *Christopher Reeve*
/ 마치 그가 지켜보고 있는 것처럼

43-05 He burst into a high-pitched laugh, as though he'd said
그는 갑자기 고음의 웃음을 터뜨렸다   / 마치 자신이 웃긴 어떤 것을 말했던 것처럼

something funny.

B

43-06 I wish I could turn the clock back and give Mom a fraction of
나는 좋을 텐데 / 내가 예전으로 돌아갈 수 있다면   / 그래서 엄마에게 일부라도 드릴 수 있다면   /

what she gave to me.
[그녀가 내게 준 것의]

43-07 No one on his deathbed ever said, "I wish I had spent more time
임종에 어느 누구도 지금껏 말한 적이 없었다 / 나는 좋을 텐데 / 내가 나의 사업에 더 많은 시간을
on my business."
썼다면

43-08 To achieve great things we must live as though we were never going
위대한 것들을 성취하기 위해서 / 우리는 살아야 한다 / 마치 우리가 절대 죽지 않을 것처럼
to die. *Marquis de Vauvenargues*

43-09 Men occasionally stumble over the truth, but most of them pick
사람들은 가끔 진실에 발이 걸린다 / 그러나 그들 대부분은 스스로 일어선다
themselves up and hurry off as if nothing had happened. *Winston Churchill*
/ 그리고 서둘러 떠난다 / 마치 아무 일도 일어나지 않았던 것처럼

43-10 I've lived my life taking risks and I wish I could tell you they were
나는 내 인생을 위험을 감수하며 살아왔다 / 그리고 나는 좋을 텐데 / 내가 당신에게 말할 수 있다면 / 그것들은
all successful, but they weren't.
모두 성공적이었다고 / 그러나 그것들은 그렇지 않았다

43-11 Toward the end of their administrations, every president I think I've
집권 정부가 끝날 무렵에 / 모든 대통령은 / [내가 생각하기에 /
ever known was disappointed and wished they had done some
내가 알아온] / 실망했었다 / 그리고 바랐다 / 그들이 어떤 것들을 달리했었기를
things differently. *Billy Graham*

43-12 All told, every second, our senses transmit an estimated 11
모두 통틀어 / 매 초 / 우리의 감각은 어림잡아 천백만 비트의 정보를 전송한다
million bits of information to our poor brains, as if a giant fiber-optic
/ 우리의 불쌍한 뇌에 / 마치 거대한 광섬유 케이블이 뇌에 직접
cable were plugged directly into them, firing information at full
연결된 것처럼 / 정보를 전속력으로 쏘면서
speed.

unit 44 if가 없는 가정법 구문

S TANDARD

44-01 Dreams come true. **Without that possibility,** nature would not
꿈은 실현된다   그런 가능성이 없다면   / 본성은 우리가 꿈을 가지도록

incite us to have them. *John Updike*
자극하지 **않을** 것이다

44-02 In different circumstances, I would have enjoyed that journey. My
다른 상황이었다면   / 나는 그 여행을 즐겼을 텐데   / 내

legs were **very** tired and sore.
다리가 너무 피곤하고 아팠다

A

44-03 Coronavirus is a completely different type of virus. **Otherwise it**
코로나는 완전히 다른 형태의 바이러스이다   그렇지 않다면   /

would be called flu.
그것은 독감이라고 불릴 것이다

44-04 Only a fool would ignore his past experience **when confronted**
오직 바보만이 자신의 과거 경험을 무시할 것이다   / 새로운 상황에 직면했을 때

with a new situation.

44-05 To see her walking around in her old clothes, you'd never guess she
그녀가 자신의 낡은 옷을 입고 걸어 다니는 것을 본다면   / 당신은 결코 추측하지 못할 것이다 /

owned a multi-million dollar business.
그녀가 수백만 달러의 사업체를 가지고 있다는 것을

B

44-06 We would **not** have had men on the Moon but for Wells and Verne
우리는 인간을 달에 있게 할 수 없었을 것이다   / 만약 웰스와 베른 그리고 사람들이 없었더

and the people who write about this and made people think about
/ [이것에 대해서 쓰고   / 그리고 사람들이 그것에 대해서 생각하게 만든]

it. *Arthur C. Clarke*

44-07 All great achievers in past ages possessed singleness of purpose
위대한 성취자들은 / [옛날의] / 단 하나의 목적을 갖고 있었다

without exception. Without it, Columbus wouldn't have started
/ 예외 없이 그것이 없었다면 / 콜럼버스는 항해를 출발하지 않았을 것이다

upon the voyage that made his name immortal.
/ [그의 이름을 영원히 기억되게 한]

44-08 A hundred years ago not a doctor in the world could have
백 년 전이라면 / 세상의 어떤 의사도 환자에게 장담할 수 없었을 것이다

assured a patient that an operation would be painless.
/ 어떤 수술이 고통스럽지 않을 거라고

44-09 Born in better times, he would have done credit to society.
더 좋은 시대에 태어났더라면 / 그는 사회에 명예로운 인물이 되었을 텐데

C

44-10 In the past it never occurred to me that every casual remark of
과거에 / (…이) 내게 결코 떠오르지 않았다 / 나의 모든 무심코 한 말이

mine would be snatched up and recorded. Otherwise I would
/ 집아채여지고 / 그리고 기록될 것임이 그렇지 않았다면 / 나는 기어갔을

have crept further into my shell. *Albert Einstein*
텐데 / 더 한층 나의 껍질 속으로

44-11 With the right software, I could help students form a concrete
알맞은 소프트웨어가 있다면 / 나는 도울 수 있을 텐데 / 학생들이 사회에 대한 구체적인 인상을 형성

idea of society by displaying on-screen a version of the city in
하도록 / 화면으로 도시의 형태를 보여 줌으로써 /

which they live.
[그들이 살고 있는]

44-12 Ironically, while many of us perceive insects as harmful pests—
역설적이게도 / 우리 중 많은 사람들이 곤충을 해충으로 인지하는 반면에 / —

dangerous, ugly, and disease-ridden—in reality, without the
위험한, 흉한, 그리고 질병이 들끓는 / —실제로는 / 수분의 공로가 없다면

service of pollination which they provide, humankind might cease
/ [그들이 제공하는] / 인류는 존재하기를 멈출지도 모른다

to exist.

Review

A

01 If everything given to us by research were to be taken away,
만약 연구에 의해서 우리에게 주어진 모든 것이 빼앗긴다면

civilization would collapse and we would stand naked, searching for
/ 문명은 무너질 것이다   / 그리고 우리는 벌거벗은 상태가 될 것이다   / 다시 동굴을 찾으면서

caves again.

02 It was wonderful to find America, but it would have been more
(…은) 멋졌다   / 아메리카를 발견한 것은   / 그러나 (…은) 더 멋졌을 텐데

wonderful to miss it. *Mark Twain*
/ 그것을 지나쳤다면

03 He drowsed off, but then woke up abruptly, as though someone had
그는 졸았다   / 그러나 그때 갑자기 깨어났다   / 마치 누군가가 그의 이름을 불렀던 것처럼

called his name.

04 The sun, the moon and the stars would have disappeared long ago,
태양, 달, 그리고 별들은 사라졌을 것이다   / 오래전에

had they happened to be within reach of predatory human hands.
/ 만약 그것들이 마침 있었다면   / 인간의 약탈하는 손이 미치는 범위 내에   *Havelock Ellis*

B

05 When two cultures come into contact, they do not exchange every
두 문화가 접촉할 때   / 그것들이 모든 문화적 항목을 교환하지는 않는다

cultural item. If that were the case, there would be no cultural
만약 그것이 사실이라면   / 어떠한 문화적 차이도 없을 것이다

differences in the world today.
/ 오늘날 세계에는

06 Indeed, if our early African ancestors hadn't been good at fixing all
정말로   / 만약 우리의 초기 아프리카의 조상들이 능숙하지 않았다면   / 그들의 모든 주의를

their attention on the just-ripened fruit or the approaching predators,
고정하는 것에   / 막 익은 열매 또는 다가오는 포식자들에게

we wouldn't be here.
/ 우리는 여기에 없을 것이다

07 I wish I could have called my family more often while I was away
나는 좋을 텐데   / 내가 나의 가족들에게 더 자주 전화했다면   / 내가 집에서 떠나 있던 동안에

from home.

08 If we had stopped at the service station, we wouldn't have run out of
만약 우리가 주유소에 들렀다면 　　　　　　　　　　　/ 우리는 가솔린이 바닥나지 않았을 텐데

gas.

09 I wish I had known there was a sale. I would have gone with you.
나는 좋을 텐데 / 내가 할인 판매가 있다는 것을 알았다면　　　나는 너와 함께 갔을 텐데

10 Had it not been for antibiotics, medicine would not have made such
만약 항생제가 없었다면　　　　　　　　　/ 의학은 이루지 못했을 것이다　　　　　　　　/ 그런

remarkable progress.
놀라운 발전을

11 Without your donations, many more children would go hungry.
만약 너의 기부가 없다면　　　　　　　　/ 더욱 많은 아이들이 굶주리게 될 것이다

= If it were not for your donations, many more children would go
hungry.

= Were it not for your donations, many more children would go
hungry.

12 You told me how the film ends; it would have been better if you had
당신은 내게 그 영화가 어떻게 끝나는지 말했다　　/ (…이) 더 나았을 텐데　　　　　/ 만약 당신이 내게

not told me.
얘기하지 않았다면

= I wish you hadn't told me how the film ends.
나는 좋을 텐데 / 당신이 내게 얘기하지 않았다면 / 그 영화가 어떻게 끝나는지

13 I got caught in a traffic jam; otherwise I would have been here
나는 교통 체증에 걸렸다　　　　　　/ 그렇지 않았다면 / 나는 도착했을 텐데　　　　　/ 여기에

sooner.
더 일찍

= I got caught in a traffic jam; if I had not got caught in a traffic jam, I
나는 교통 체증에 걸렸다　　　　　　/ 내가 교통 체증에 걸리지 않았다면　　　　　　/

would have been here sooner.
나는 도착했을 텐데　　　/ 여기에 더 일찍

unit 45 원급 구문

45-01 What you get by achieving your goals is **not as** important **as what**
당신이 얻는 것은 / 당신의 목표를 성취함으로써 / 중요하지 않다 / 당신이 되는

you become by achieving your goals. *Zig Zigler*
것만큼 / 당신의 목표를 성취함으로써

45-02 The human brain cell can hold **five times as** much information **as**
인간의 뇌세포는 보유할 수 있다 / 5배 많은 정보를 /

the Encyclopaedia Britannica.
브리태니커 백과사전보다

A

45-03 To ask what is the use of poetry should be **as absurd as** asking
묻는 것은 / 시의 효용이 무엇인지를 / 아마 어리석을 것이다 / 묻는 것만큼

what is the use of a rainbow, or the sea, or a nice dress. *Cecil Day-Lewis*
/ 무지개나 바다 또는 근사한 옷의 효용이 무엇인지를

45-04 The International Space Station is **almost four times as** large **as the**
국제 우주 정거장은 거의 네 배만큼 크다 / 러시아의

Russian space station Mir and about five times as large as the U.S.
우주 정거장 Mir보다 / 그리고 약 5배만큼 크다 / 미국의 스카이랩보

Skylab.

45-05 It is important **not so much** to give a man bread, **as** to put him in
(…은) 중요하다 / 어떤 사람에게 빵을 주는 것보다는 / 오히려 그 사람이 스스로 그

the way of earning it for himself.
빵을 얻을 수 있도록 해주는 것이

B

45-06 A person's choice and use of words tells **as much about him or**
어떤 사람의 단어 선택과 사용은 말한다 / 그 사람에 대해 많이

her as do manners, dress, and general behavior.
/ 예의, 복장, 그리고 일반적인 행동이 말하는 만큼

45-07 Happiness is produced **not so much by** great pieces of good
행복은 만들어진다 / 행운이라는 큰 조각들에 의해서가 아니라

fortune that seldom happen, **as by** little advantages that occur
/ [드물게 생기는] / 작은 좋은 점들에 의해서 / [매일 일어나는]

every day. *Benjamin Franklin*

45-08 While people today have twice as much spending power as they
오늘날 사람들이 두 배 더 많은 구매력을 가지고 있는 반면에 / 그들이

did in the 1950s, they are ten times more likely to be depressed.
1950년대에 그랬던 것보다 / 그들은 10배 더 우울한 것 같다

45-09 A hero can be anyone, even a man doing something as simple and
영웅은 누구든지 될 수 있다 / 심지어 어떤 사람도 / [간단하고 안심시켜주는 무언가를 하는

reassuring as putting a coat on a young boy's shoulders to let him
/ 어린 소년의 어깨에 외투를 걸쳐주는 것만큼 / 그에게 알려주기

know that the world hadn't ended. *the movie <The Dark Knight Rises>*
위해서 / 세상이 끝나지 않았다는 것을]

---

c

45-10 The consequences of interaction can be difficult to foresee
상호작용의 결과는 예측하기 어려울 수 있다

because they depend as much on the behavior of others as on
/ 왜냐하면 그것들은 타인의 행동에 많이 달려 있기 때문이다 / 자기

oneself.
자신에 만큼

45-11 Singapore has nearly 8,000 people per km², and is more than 200
싱가포르는 평방킬로미터 당 거의 8,000명을 보유하고 있다 / 그리고 200배 이상 밀집되어 있다

times as dense as the U.S.
/ 미국보다

45-12 Most insomnia is not an illness or a physical condition so much
대부분 불면증은 질환이나 건강 문제가 아니다 / 오히려 다른

as a symptom of another problem that may simply be a reaction
문제에 대한 증상(이다) / [단순히 특정한 약물에 대한 반응

to certain medications, anxiety about travel, or stress before a
/ 여행에 대한 불안 / 또는 취업 면접 전의 스트레스일

job interview.
수 있는]

Unit 46 비교급 구문 1

46-01 According to recent research, the universe is expanding faster
최근의 연구에 의하면 / 우주는 오늘날 더 빠르게 팽창하고 있다

today than it did in its infancy.
/ 우주가 초기에 그랬던 것보다

46-02 The energy in sunlight arriving on earth contains about twelve
햇빛 속의 에너지는 / [지구에 도달하는] / 약 12,000배 더 많은 에너지를 포함하고

thousand times more energy than humanity uses in a year.
있다 / 인류가 1년에 사용하는 에너지보다

A

46-03 It is more important to be honorable and trustworthy than to look
(…은) 더 중요하다 / 명예롭고 신뢰할 수 있는 것은 / 대단해 보이는 것보다

important for one small minute.
/ 짧은 순간 동안에

46-04 Learning to study effectively is even more important than merely
효과적으로 공부하는 것을 배우는 것이 / 훨씬 더 중요하다 / 단지 특정한 양의

acquiring a particular body of information.
정보를 습득하는 것보다

46-05 Champion golfers are much less likely than average golfers to
챔피언 골프 선수들은 일반 골프 선수들보다 자신들의 문제들을 훨씬 덜 탓할 것 같다

blame their problems on the weather, the course, or chance
/ 날씨, 코스, 또는 뜻밖의 요소에 대해

factors. Instead they focus relentlessly on their own performance.
대신에 그들은 가차없이 초점을 맞춘다 / 자신들의 실력에

B

46-06 Medical procedures may sound scarier when presented in terms
의료 시술은 더 무섭게 들릴 수도 있다 / 제시될 때 / 사망 위험의

of the risk of dying, rather than the likelihood of coming through
관점에서 / 무사히 성공할 가능성보다

unharmed.

46-07 We are **always** **more** anxious **to be distinguished for a talent which**
우리는 늘 유명해지기를 더욱 열망한다 / 한 가지 재능으로 / [우리가

we do not possess, than to be praised for the fifteen which we do
갖고 있지 않은] / 15개의 재능으로 칭찬받기보다는 / [우리가 정말 가지고

possess. *Mark Twain*
있는]

46-08 What **some call health**, **if purchased by perpetual anxiety about**
일부가 건강이라고 부르는 것이 / 만약 식단에 대한 끊임없는 불안으로 얻어지는 것이라면

diet, isn't much better than tedious disease. *George Prentice*
/ 훨씬 더 좋지는 않다 / 시시한 병보다

46-09 It takes **two to six times more grain** to produce food value
(…은) 두 배에서 여섯 배 더 많은 곡물을 필요로 한다 / 영양가를 만들어 내는 것은

through animals than to get the equivalent value directly from
/ 동물을 통해서 / 직접 동등한 영양가를 얻는 것보다 / 식물에서

plants.

46-10 Astronomers observe **that the sun's diameter is more than one**
천문학자들은 말한다 / 태양의 직경은 100배 이상 더 크다고

hundred times larger than the earth's.
/ 지구의 직경보다

46-11 Insights are **far** more **likely** **to come when you are in the mind-**
통찰력은 생길 가능성이 훨씬 더 높다 / 당신이 멍한 상태일 때

wandering mode than in the task-focused mode.
/ 과제에 집중하는 상태일 때보다

46-12 Big cars that use a lot of petrol are **less** popular **now than twenty**
대형차들은 / [많은 휘발유를 사용하는] / 현재 덜 인기가 있다 / 20년 전보다

years ago.

unit 47 비교급 구문 2

47-01 The more we use certain parts of our brain, the more developed
더 많이 　／ 우리가 뇌의 특정 부분들을 사용할수록 　　　／ 더욱더 발달하고 더 효율적이게

and efficient those parts of the brain become.
／ 뇌의 그 부분들이 된다

47-02 A collection of facts is no more science than a dictionary is
사실들의 모음은 과학이 아니다 　　　　　　／ 사전이 시가 아닌 것만큼

poetry.

A

47-03 According to Einstein's Special Theory of Relativity, the faster a
아인슈타인의 특수 상대성 이론에 따르면 　　　　　　／ 우주선이 더 빠르게

spaceship goes, the slower its clock ticks and the shorter its
갈수록 　　　　／ 그것의 시계는 더 느리게 움직인다 　　／ 그리고 그것의 이동 방향의 길이가

length in the direction of travel gets.
더 짧아진다

47-04 Man is no more than a reed, the weakest in nature, but he is a
인간은 갈대에 불과하다 　　　　　／ 자연에서 가장 연약한 존재 　　／ 그러나 그는 생각

thinking reed. *Blaise Pascal*
하는 갈대이다

47-05 Air pollution does no less harm to birds and animals than it does
대기 오염은 조류와 동물에게 마찬가지로 해를 끼친다 　　　　　／ 그것이 인간에게

to human beings.
해를 끼치는 것과

B

47-06 Anyone who has tried to complete a jigsaw puzzle as the clock
누구든 　／ [조각 그림 퍼즐을 완성하려고 애썼던 　　　　　／ 시계가 마감 시간을

ticked on toward a deadline knows that the more they struggle to
향해 째깍째깍 움직일 때] 　　／ 안다 　／ 그들이 더욱더 안달복달할수록 　／

find the missing pieces, the harder it is to find them.
빠진 조각들을 찾느라 　　／ 더욱더 힘들다는 것을 　／ 그것들을 찾는 것이

47-07 We have called upon the people to set their air conditioners at no
우리는 사람들에게 그들의 에어컨을 설정하도록 요청해왔다 / 여름에는

lower than 28 degrees Celsius in the summer and no higher than
섭씨 28도보다 조금도 낮지 않게 / 그리고 겨울에는 20도보다 조금도

20 in the winter.
높지 않게

47-08 We can no more explain a passion to a person who has never
우리는 어떤 이에게 열정을 설명할 수 없다 / [그것을 한 번도 경험하지

experienced it than we can explain light to the blind. *T. S. Eliot*
않은] / 마치 우리가 눈이 먼 사람에게 빛을 설명할 수 없는 것만큼

47-09 Organic farmers grow crops that are no less plagued by pests
유기 농법을 사용하는 농부들은 작물을 재배한다 / [마찬가지로 해충에 시달리는

than those of conventional farmers; insects generally do not
/ 재래 농법을 사용하는 농부들의 작물과] / 곤충들은 대개 구별하지 않는다

discriminate between organic and conventional as well as we do.
/ 유기 농법인지 재래 농법인지를 / 우리가 그런 것만큼 잘

47-10 The closer the people in the world become, the more frequently
세상 사람들이 더 가까워질수록 / 그들은 더욱더 자주 노출된다

they are exposed to people from other cultures.
/ 다른 문화권의 사람들에게

47-11 If all our knowledge stopped at the level of the senses, we would
만약 우리의 모든 지식이 멈춘다면 / 감각의 수준에서 / 우리는 조금도

be no better off than the subhuman members of the animal
더 낫지 않을 것이다 / 동물 세계의 유인원보다

kingdom.

47-12 Mind is not to be found in molecules any more than the works of
정신은 분자 속에서 발견될 수 없다 / 셰익스피어의 작품들이 그의

Shakespeare were to be found in his genes.
유전자 속에서 발견될 수 없었던 것만큼

Unit 48 최상급 구문

S TANDARD

48-01 Global warming is considered to be the most serious threat facing
지구온난화는 여겨진다 / 가장 심각한 위협으로 / [인류를

humanity **by many environmentalists.**
향한] / 많은 환경 운동가들에 의해

48-02 Nothing in all the world is more dangerous **than sincere ignorance**
세상의 어떤 것도 더 위험하지는 않다 / 성실하면서 무지한 것과

and conscientious stupidity. *Martin Luther King Jr.*
양심적이면서 어리석은 것보다

A

48-03 Personal computers have become the most empowering tool
개인용 컴퓨터는 되었다 / 가장 힘을 더해 주는 도구가

we've ever created. *Bill Gates*
/ [우리가 지금껏 만들어 낸 것 중]

48-04 Next to religion, baseball has had a greater impact on our American
종교 다음으로 / 야구는 우리 미국인의 생활 방식에 더 큰 영향을 미쳐왔다

way of life than any other American institution. *Herbert Hoover*
/ 다른 어떤 미국의 제도보다

48-05 No other writer's plays have been produced so many times or
다른 어떤 작가의 희곡도 여러 번 상연되거나 널리 읽히지 않았다

read so widely in so many countries as Shakespeare's.
/ 아주 많은 국가에서 / 셰익스피어의 희곡만큼

B

48-06 Nobody is so miserable as he who longs to be somebody and
어느 누구도 비참하지는 않다 / 사람만큼 / [누군가 그리고 무언가가 되기를 바라는

something other than the person he is in body and mind. *Angelo Patri*
/ 자기 자신이 아닌 / 몸과 마음에서]

48-07 One of the hardest things in this world is to admit you are wrong.
이 세상에서 가장 어려운 것들 중의 하나는 　　　　　　/ 받아들이는 것이다 / 당신이 틀렸다는 것을

And nothing is more helpful in resolving a situation than its frank
/ 그리고 어떤 것도 더 도움이 되지는 않는다 　/ 어떤 상황을 해결하는 데 　　　/ 그것의 솔직한 인정보다

admission. *Benjamin Disraeli*

48-08 The most exciting phrase to hear in science, the one that heralds
가장 흥미진진한 말은 　　　　　　/ [과학에서 듣는] 　　　/ 즉 새로운 발견을 알리는 말은

new discoveries, is not "Eureka!"(I found it!) but "That's funny."
　　　　　　/ '유레카!'(내가 그걸 찾았어!)가 아니라 '그거 신기하네'이다 　　　*Isaac Asimov*

48-09 The Amazon's aquatic life, such as freshwater dolphins,
아마존의 수생 생물은 　　　　　/ 민물 돌고래, 400 파운드의 메기, 거대한 뱀장어와 같은

400-pound catfish, giant eels, is larger and more diverse than
　　　　　　　　/ 더 크고 더 다양하다 　　　　　/

that of all the other river systems in the world.
세계의 다른 모든 하천 수생 생물보다

48-10 Of all the wonderful and unique characteristics of man, his ability to
인간의 모든 놀랍고 독특한 특성들 중에서 　　　　　　/ 인간의 의사소통

communicate through the use of language is perhaps the most
능력은 　　　/ [언어의 사용을 통한] 　　　/ 아마 가장 중요할 것이다

important.

48-11 Although humans are not the only animals who use tools, our
비록 인간이 유일한 동물은 아닐지라도 　　　　　　/ [도구를 사용하는] 　/

species has developed this skill to a far greater extent than any
인류는 이 기술을 발전시켜왔다 　　　　/ 훨씬 더 훌륭한 정도로 　/ 다른 어떤

other animal.
동물보다

48-12 In today's industry, where technology and speed of information
오늘날의 산업에서 　　　/ 거기서는 기술과 정보의 속도가 중대한 요소인데

are critical factors, nothing is more valuable to our clients than
　　　　　　/ 어떤 것도 우리의 고객에게 더 유용하지는 않다 　/

providing timely and accurate information.
시기 적절하고 정확한 정보를 제공하는 것보다

Review

A

01 An individual neuron sending a signal in the brain uses **as much**
개별적인 뉴런은 　　　　　　／ [뇌에서 신호를 보내는]　　　　.　　　　　　／ 많은 에너지를 사용한다
energy as a leg muscle cell running a marathon.
／ 다리 근육 세포만큼　　　／ [마라톤을 뛰는]

02 Knowledge can **no more** be planted in the human mind without labor
지식은 심겨질 수 없다　　　　　　／ 인간의 정신 속에　　　　／ 노력 없이
than a field of wheat can be produced without the previous use of
／ 밀밭이 만들어질 수 없는 것만큼　　　　　　／ 쟁기를 먼저 쓰지 않고서
the plow.

03 126 different studies of more than 36,000 people found **that the more**
36,000명 이상의 사람들에 대한 126개의 여러 연구들이 밝혀냈다　　　　　　／ 어떤 사람이 불안해하는
prone to anxieties a person is, the poorer his or her academic
성향일수록　　　　　　／ 그 사람의 학업 성취는 더 떨어진다는 것을
performance is.

04 **There is no other quality so** essential to success of any kind **as the quality**
다른 어떤 자질은 없다　　　／ [어떤 종류의 성공에 필수적인]　　　　　　／ 끈기라는 자질만큼
of perseverance. It overcomes almost everything, even nature. *John D. Rockefeller*
그것은 거의 모든 것을 극복한다　　　　　　／ 심지어 본성조차도

B

05 **Solids, like wood for example, transfer sound waves much better**
고체는　　／ 예를 들어 목재와 같은　　　　　　／ 음파를 훨씬 더 잘 전달한다
than air typically does because the molecules in a solid substance are
／ 공기가 일반적으로 하는 것보다　　　／ 왜냐하면 고체 물질 속의 분자들은 훨씬 더 가깝기 때문이다
much closer and more tightly packed together than they are in air.
／ 그리고 더욱 밀집되게 채워져 있기 (때문이다)　　　　　　／ 그것들이 공기 속에서 그런 것보다

06 **The more effectively parents communicate their loving authority, the**
더 효과적으로　　　　／ 부모가 자신의 애정 어린 권위를 전할수록　　　　　　／ 더
more secure the child feels.
안전하게　　　／ 그 자녀는 느낀다

07 The brain's running costs are about eight to ten times as high, per
뇌의 유지 비용은 약 8~10배 높다   / 단위

unit mass, as those of the body's muscles.
질량당   / 신체 근육의 유지 비용보다

08 Having children makes you no more a parent than having a piano
자녀가 있는 것은 당신을 부모로 만들지 않는다   / 피아노가 있는 것이

makes you a pianist.
당신을 피아니스트로 만들지 않는 것만큼

C

09 Recycling plastic saves twice as much energy as it takes to burn it.
플라스틱을 재활용하는 것은 절약시켜 준다 / 두 배 많은 에너지를   / 그것을 소각하는 데 필요로 하는 것보다

10 The more experience you have, the more job opportunities you'll
더 많은 경험을   / 네가 가질수록   / 더 많은 일자리 기회를   / 너는 찾을

find.
것이다

11 No bread in the world is so sweet as that earned by his own labor.
세상의 어떤 빵도 달콤하지 않다   / 자신의 노동으로 얻은 빵만큼

D

12 Fear defeats more people than any other one thing in the world.
두려움은 패배시킨다   / 더 많은 사람들을   / 세상에서 다른 어떤 것보다

= Nothing in the world defeats so many people as fear.
세상의 어떤 것도 패배시키지 않는다   / 많은 사람들을   / 두려움만큼

13 Just as a horse is not a fish, a whale is not a fish either.
말이 물고기가 아닌 것처럼   / 고래도 또한 물고기가 아니다

= A whale is no more a fish than a horse is.
고래가 물고기가 아닌 것은 말이 물고기가 아닌 것과 같다

= A whale is not a fish any more than a horse is.
고래가 물고기가 아닌 것은 말이 물고기가 아닌 것과 같다

14 She is a realist rather than a pessimist.
그녀는 오히려 현실주의자이다 / 비관론자라기보다는

= She is not so much a pessimist as a realist.
그녀는 비관론자라기보다는   / 현실주의자이다

= She is not a pessimist so much as a realist.
그녀는 비관론자라기보다는   / 현실주의자이다

Unit 49 도치 구문 1

S TANDARD

49-01 On no account must you give your banking details to anyone over
결코 당신은 당신의 은행 정보를 줘서는 안 된다 / 누군가에게 /
the phone or by email.
전화로 또는 이메일로

49-02 Trustworthy are those who give not only compliments but also
신뢰할 수 있는 것은 사람들이다 / [칭찬뿐만 아니라 쓴 조언도 주는]
bitter advice.

A

49-03 Not until the rise of ecology at the beginning of the twentieth
생태학이 등장하고 나서야 비로소 / 20세기 초에
century did people begin to think seriously of land as a natural
/ 사람들은 땅을 진지하게 여기기 시작했다 / 서로 연결된 부분들을
system with interconnecting parts.
가진 자연계로서

49-04 Every cell is a triumph of natural selection, and we're made of
모든 세포는 자연 선택의 업적이다 / 그리고 우리는 수조 개의 세포로
trillions of cells. Within us, is a little universe. *Carl Sagan*
이뤄져 있다 우리 안에 / 작은 우주가 있다

49-05 Natural ability is necessary to become an expert in anything, but
타고난 재능은 필수적이다 / 어떤 것에서 전문가가 되기 위해 / 그러
no less important is the willingness to study.
기꺼이 연구하려는 의사가 마찬가지로 중요하다

B

49-06 For a computer to solve a problem, not only must the solution be
컴퓨터가 어떤 문제를 해결하기 위해서 / 해결 방법이 아주 자세해야 할 뿐만 아니라
very detailed, but it must also be written in a form the computer
/ 그것은 또한 쓰여야 한다 / 형태로 / [그 컴퓨터가 이해할 수
can understand.
있는]

49-07 Under no circumstances will anyone's personal information be
어떤 상황에서도 누군가의 개인 정보는 배포되지 않을 것이다

given out to any third party without the express permission of the
/ 제3자에게 / 명시적 허락 없이는 / [관계자의]

person concerned.

49-08 Out of the fundamentals of elementary algebra evolved the abstract
기초 대수학의 원리로부터 / 오늘날 사용되는 추상 대수학과 대수

algebra used today and the concept of an algebraic structure.
구조의 개념이 발전했다

49-09 Included in this chapter is a list of frequently misspelled words,
이 장(章)에 포함되어 있다 / 자주 철자를 틀리는 단어들의 목록이

which you may find it helpful to memorize.
/ 그리고 당신은 그것을 암기하는 것이 유용하리라는 것을 알게 될 것이다

49-10 Only in the last few decades, in the primarily industrially developed
겨우 지난 몇 십 년 동안에서야 / 주로 산업적으로 발전된 국가에서

economies, has food become so plentiful and easy to obtain as to
/ 음식은 아주 풍부하고 얻기 용이하게 되었다 / 지방과

cause fat-related health problems.
관련된 건강 문제를 일으킬 만큼

49-11 Fundamental to most moral approaches is the idea that human
대부분의 도덕적 접근의 근간이 되는 것은 / 생각이다 / [= 인간의 삶은 특별한

life has a special dignity and value that is worth preserving even
존엄성과 가치를 가진다는 / [보존할 가치가 있는 / 심지어

at the expense of self-interest.
자기 이익을 희생하고서라도]]

49-12 Laid before me was, I realized, a scene of almost classical rural
내 앞에 놓여졌다 / 나는 깨달았다 / 거의 전형적인 시골의 아름다운 장면이—

beauty—the meadows dotted with contented animals, the woods
/ (배불러) 만족한 동물들이 점점이 있는 목초지 / 그 뒤편의 숲

in the background, a twisting stream threading through it all.
/ 그 모두의 사이를 구불구불 흘러 지나가는 시냇물

125

Unit **50** 도치 구문 2

S TANDARD

50-01 The present moment does **not** exist **in the equations of physics,**
현재의 순간은 존재하지 않는다 / 물리학 방정식에

and therefore neither does the flow of time.
/ 따라서 시간의 흐름도 그렇지 않다

50-02 What the caterpillar calls the end of the world the world calls a
애벌레가 세상의 종말이라고 부르는 것을 / 세상은 나비라고 부른다

butterfly. *Richard Bach*

A

50-03 Such was the power of his voice that even those at the back of
그의 목소리의 힘은 대단했다 / 그래서 그 방의 뒤쪽에 있는 사람들조차도 그 연사를

the room gazed at the speaker in awe.
경탄하며 응시했다

50-04 Philosophy, which is understood to be the desire to acquire
철학은 / 그것은 욕망으로 이해되는데 / [지혜를 얻으려는]

wisdom, is a fundamental part of the human being, and so is
/ 인간의 근원적인 부분이다 / 그리고 과학도

science.
역시 그러하다

50-05 The release of atomic energy has **not** created a new problem. It
원자 에너지의 방출이 새로운 문제를 만들어 내지 않았다 그

has **merely** made more urgent the necessity of solving an existing
단지 더 긴급하게 만들었을 뿐이다 / 기존의 문제를 해결해야 하는 필요성을

one.

B

50-06 So closely is sniffing tied to odor perception that people routinely
매우 밀접하게 / 코를 킁킁거리는 것은 냄새 지각과 연관되어 있다 / 그래서 사람들은 일상적으로 코를 킁

sniff when they are asked to imagine a smell.
거린다 / 그들이 어떤 냄새를 상상해 보라는 요청을 받을 때

50-07 People often say that motivation doesn't last. Well, neither does
사람들은 종종 말한다 / 동기 부여는 오래가지 않는다고 음, 목욕하는 것도 역시 그렇지 않다—

bathing—that's why we recommend it daily. *Zig Ziglar*
/ 그것이 우리가 그것을 매일 권장하는 이유이다

50-08 We carry home what we have bought in some vessel, but learning
우리는 집으로 가져간다 / 우리가 구매한 것을 / 용기에 담아서 / 그러나 배운 것을

we cannot put in any other vessel but our minds.
우리는 둘 수 없다 / 다른 어떤 용기 속에 / [우리의 정신 이외의]

50-09 How on earth are you ever going to explain in terms of chemistry
도대체 당신은 어떻게 설명할 것인가 / 화학과 물리학의 관점에서

and physics so important a biological phenomenon as first love?
/ 첫사랑과 같은 중요한 생물학적인 현상을? *Albert Einstein*

C

50-10 So quickly did he rush out of the office that he forgot to lock up
아주 서둘러서 / 그는 사무실에서 나왔다 / 그래서 그는 잊어버렸다 / 문을 잠그고 경보

and set the alarm.
장치를 설정하는 것을

50-11 Unlike animals, plants cannot pick up their roots and race for
동물과 달리 / 식물은 자신의 뿌리를 집어 들 수 없다 / 그리고 안전을 위해서 질주할

safety. Nor have many plants taken the offensive and become
(수 없다) 많은 식물은 공격 태세를 취한 적이 없다 / 그리고 포식자가 된

predators.
(적도 없다)

50-12 The large part of our thoughts and feelings that we do not know and
우리의 생각과 감정의 커다란 부분을 / [우리가 알지 못하고 통제할 수 없는]

cannot control Sigmund Freud called the unconscious.
/ 지그문트 프로이트는 무의식이라고 불렀다

unit **51** 강조 구문

S TANDARD

51-01 **It is** the interaction between our genes and the environment tha|
(…은) 바로 상호작용이다 / [우리의 유전자와 환경 사이의] / 결정|

determines whether we develop an illness.
하는 것은 / 우리가 병이 생길지 어떨지

51-02 **It was not until** the twelfth century **that** the magnetic compas|
(…은) 바로 12세기가 될 때까지는 아니었다 / 자기 나침반이 사용된 것은

was used for navigation.
/ 항해를 위해

A

51-03 Success **is not** final, failure **is not** fatal: **it is** the courage t|
성공은 최종적이지 않다 / 실패는 결정적이지 않다 / (…은) 바로 계속하려는 용기이다

continue **that** counts. *Winston Churchill*
/ 중요한 것은

51-04 **It is not** the number of books which a young man reads tha|
(…은) 바로 책의 권수가 아니다 / [젊은이가 읽는] / 그를|

makes him intelligent and well-informed, **but** the number of well|
지적이고 박식하게 만드는 것은 / 정선된 책의 권수(이다)

chosen ones that he has mastered.
/ [그가 완전히 익힌]

51-05 **It is** through his untiring effort **that** the singer has succeeded i|
(…은) 바로 그의 지칠 줄 모르는 노력을 통해서이다 / 그 가수가 성공한 것은 /

becoming what he is now, getting out of what he was.
현재의 그가 되는 것에 / 예전의 자신의 상태에서 벗어나

B

51-06 **It is not** work, **but** overwork, **that** is hurtful; and **it is not** hard wor|
(…은) 바로 일이 아니라 과로이다 / 상하게 하는 것은 / 그리고 (…은) 바로 힘든 일이 아니다

that is injurious so much as unwilling work.
/ 해롭게 하는 것은 / 오히려 마음이 내키지 않는 일(이다)

51-07 Heritage is **more** concerned with meanings **than material**
유산은 의미와 더욱 관련이 있다 / 물질적인 인공물보다는

artefacts. **It is** the **former that** give value, **either cultural or**
(…은) 바로 전자이다 / 가치를 주는 것은 / 문화적이든 금전적이든

financial, **to the latter and** explain **why they have been selected**
/ 후자에게 / 그리고 설명하는 (것은) / 왜 그것들이 선택되었는지를

from the near infinity of the past.
/ 거의 무한에 가까운 과거의 산물에서

51-08 It's not until we're being massaged by warm water, unable to
(…은) 바로 우리가 따뜻한 물로 마사지를 받고 있을 때까지는 아니다 / 우리의 이메일을

check our e-mail, that we're **finally** able to hear the quiet voices
확인할 수 없는 상황에서 / 우리가 마침내 조용한 목소리를 들을 수 있는 것은

in the backs of our heads telling us about the insight.
/ 우리의 머리 뒤편에서의 / [통찰에 대해 우리에게 말을 건네는]

51-09 I've made the most important discovery of my life. It's only in the
나는 내 인생의 가장 중요한 발견을 해냈다 (…은) 바로 사랑이라는

mysterious equation of love that any logical reasons can be
신비한 방정식 속에서뿐이다 / 어떤 논리적 이유도 발견될 수 있는 것은

found. *John Nash*

51-10 It is the biography of Steve Jobs that[which] I have been looking
(…은) 바로 스티브 잡스의 전기이다 / 내가 찾고 있었던 것은

for.

51-11 Some people say science deprives man of his dreams and of his
어떤 사람들은 말한다 / 과학이 인간에게서 꿈과 시를 빼앗는다고

poetry, but we can also say it is poetry and dreams that[which]
/ 그러나 우리는 또한 말할 수 있다 / (…은) 바로 시와 꿈이라고 / 과학을 발전시켜 온

have developed science.
것은

51-12 It is only in our darkest hours that we may discover the true
(…은) 바로 오직 우리의 가장 어두운 시간 속에서이다 / 우리가 눈부신 빛의 진정한 힘을 발견할 수 있는 것은

strength of the brilliant light within ourselves.
/ 우리 자신의 내부에서

unit 52 동격 구문

52-01 Alpha rhythm, a brain wave frequency of moderate voltage, is
알파 리듬은 / = 적당한 전압의 뇌파 진동수인

characteristic of a person who is awake but relaxed.
사람의 특징이다 / [깨어 있지만 안정된]

52-02 Coevolution is the concept that two or more species of organisms
공진화는 개념이다 / [= 둘 이상의 유기체 종들이 서로 상대방의 진화 방향에 영향을 줄

can reciprocally influence the evolutionary direction of the other.
있다고 하는]

A

52-03 Throughout history, people have been intrigued by the question
역사를 통틀어 / 사람들은 질문에 강한 흥미를 느껴왔다

of whether there is intelligent life elsewhere in the universe.
/ [= 지적생명체가 있는지의 / 우주 어딘가 다른 곳에]

52-04 Scientists tried to extract knowledge by devising theories, that is
과학자들은 지식을 끌어내려고 노력했다 / 이론을 고안해 냄으로써 / = 즉,

building models to explain the data they observed.
자료를 설명하는 모델을 만듦으로써 / [그들이 관찰한]

52-05 As humans, we respond to everything in our environment in one
인간으로서 / 우리는 모든 것에 반응한다 / 환경 속에서 / 두 가지

of two basic ways: we either approach stimuli or we avoid stimuli
기본 방식 중의 하나로 / = 우리는 자극에 다가간다 / 또는 우리는 자극을 피한다

B

52-06 Don't try to be a jack-of-all-trades, I-can-do-anything job applicant
만물박사가 되려고 하지 마라 / = 나는 무엇이든 할 수 있다는 구직자

also known as a "slash" person.
/ [또한 '여기 저기 발을 걸친' 사람으로 알려진!]

52-07 The so-called Mozart effect—listening to Mozart will make your
이른바 모차르트 효과는   / —모차르트 음악을 듣는 것이 당신의 자녀를 더 영리하게 만들

child smarter—is a good example of a scientific finding being
것이라는   / —과학적 결과의 좋은 예이다   / [대중

distorted by the media through hype not warranted by the
매체에 의해서 왜곡되고 있는   / 과장 광고를 통해서   / [연구 조사에 의해 보장되지 않은]]

research.

52-08 We are survival machines, robot vehicles blindly programmed to
우리는 생존 기계들이다   / = 로봇 매개체들   / [맹목적으로 프로그램된   /

preserve the selfish molecules known as genes. *Richard Dawkins*
이기적 분자들을 보존하기 위해서   / [유전자로 알려진]]

52-09 The first time rock 'n' roll came into being, it received much
로큰롤이 처음 출현했을 때   / 그것은 많은 비판을 받았다

criticism on the grounds that it could be a threat to the traditional
/ 이유로   / [= 그것이 전통적인 문화에 위협이 될 수 있다는]

culture, just as jazz did thirty-five years ago.
/ 35년 전에 재즈가 그랬듯이

52-10 Only the smallest fraction of the human race has **ever** acquired
인류의 오직 가장 적은 일부만이 획득한 적이 있었다

the habit of taking an objective view of the past.
/ 과거에 대해서 객관적인 견해를 취하는 습관을

52-11 There is a growing interest in computer programs that can
늘어나는 관심이 있다   / 컴퓨터 프로그램에   / [자료를 분석하고

analyze data and extract information automatically from them—in
그것들부터 자동적으로 정보를 뽑아낼 수 있는   / 다시

other words, learn.
말해서   / = 배울 수 있는]

52-12 In writing or speaking English, there is only the general principle
영어를 쓰거나 말하는 데 있어   / 일반적인 원칙이 있을 뿐이다

that concrete words are better than abstract ones, and that the
/ [= 구체적인 단어들이 추상적인 단어들보다 더 낫다는   / 그리고 어떤 것을

shortest way of saying anything is always the best.
말하는 가장 짧은 방식이 항상 최선이라는]

131

unit 53 삽입 구문

53-01 The little reed, **bending to the force of the wind, soon** stood upright
작은 갈대는 / (바람의 힘에 구부러지는) / 곧 다시 똑바로 섰다

again when the storm had passed over. *Aesop*
/ 폭풍이 지나갔을 때

53-02 A fallacy is an idea that **a lot of people think** is true but which is
오류는 생각이다 / [(많은 사람들이 생각하기에) / 진실인 / 그러나 잘못된]

false.

A

53-03 What's dangerous about the Internet is, **because it has the aura**
인터넷에 대해 위험한 것은 ~이다 / (그것이 기술이라는 기운을 두르고 있기

of technology around it, it has a totally undeserved instant
때문에) / 그것이 전혀 자격이 없는. 즉각적인 신뢰성을 지닌다는 것

credibility.

53-04 An idealist is one who, **on noticing that a rose smells better than**
이상주의자는 사람이다 / [(알아차리자마자 / 장미가 양배추보다 더 좋은 냄새가 난다는 것을)

a cabbage, concludes that it will also make better soup. *Henry L. Mencken*
/ 결론을 내리는 / 그것(장미)이 또한 더 좋은 수프가 될 것이라고]

53-05 Your work is going to fill **a large part of your life, and** the only way
당신의 일은 당신의 인생의 큰 부분을 채울 것이다 / 그리고 진정으로 만족하는

to be truly satisfied is to do what **you believe** is great work. *Steve Jobs*
유일한 방법은 하는 것이다 / (당신이 믿기에) 멋진 일인 것을

B

53-06 Words are, **in my not so humble opinion,** our most inexhaustible
말은 ~이다 / (나의 주제넘은 의견으로는) / 우리의 가장 무궁무진한 마법의 원천

source of magic, capable of both influencing injury, and
/ [마음의 상처에 영향을 줄 수도 있고, 그것을 치료할 수도 있는]

remedying it. *the novel <Harry Potter and the Deathly Hallows>*

53-07 We can share what we know, however little it might be, with
우리는 공유할 수 있다 / 우리가 알고 있는 것을 / (그것이 아무리 작을지라도) / 사람과

someone who has need of that knowledge.
/ [그 지식을 필요로 하는]

53-08 There are computer programs which, when they are fed patients'
컴퓨터 프로그램들이 있다 / [(그 컴퓨터들이 환자의 병력을 제공받았을 때)

medical histories, can predict health issues such as heart attacks
/ 심장 마비와 같은 건강 문제들을 예측할 수 있는

more reliably than doctors.
/ 의사들보다 더 확실하게]

53-09 It looks like water was on Mars, because the surface features
(…이) 보인다 / 물이 화성에 있었던 것처럼 / 왜냐하면 표면 지형들이 지구상의 지형들과 닮았기 때문에

resemble those on Earth that we know are made by water.
/ [(우리가 알기로는) / 물에 의해서 만들어진]

53-10 Our judgments are so liable to be influenced by many considerations,
우리의 판단들은 많은 고려 사항들에 의해서 영향을 받기 무척 쉽다

which almost, without our knowing it, are unfair, that it is necessary
/ (그것들은 거의 / (우리가 그것을 알지 못한 채로) / 불공정하다) / 그래서 (…이) 필요하다

to keep a guard upon them.
/ 그것들에 대해 경계하는 것이

53-11 People may change the kinds of games they are playing, but an
사람들은 게임의 종류를 바꿀지도 모른다 / [그들이 하고 있는] / 그러나

interest in interactive entertainment media, once acquired,
쌍방향의 오락 매체에 대한 흥미는 / (일단 습득되면)

seems never to fade.
/ 결코 사라지지 않는 것 같다

53-12 I recently saw a news interview with an acquaintance who I was
나는 최근에 지인과의 뉴스 인터뷰를 보았다 / [(내가 확신하기로는)

certain was going to lie about a few particularly sensitive issues,
/ 몇 가지 특히 민감한 문제들에 대해서는 거짓말을 할]

and lie she did.
/ 그리고 그녀는 정말 거짓말을 했다

Unit 54 생략·공통 구문

54-01 It is found that puppies only a few weeks old could interpret
(…이) 발견된다 / 강아지들이 / [겨우 몇 주밖에 안 된] / 인간의 신호를 해석할 수

human signals, while full-grown wolves raised by humans coul
있다는 것이 / 반면에 다 자란 늑대들은 / [인간에 의해서 양육된] / (인간의

not.
신호를 해석)할 수 없다는 것이

54-02 The object of education is, or ought to be, to provide exercise fo
교육의 목적은 / ∼이다 / 또는 ∼여야 한다 / 훈련을 제공하는 것 /

student's potential capacities.
[학생의 잠재력을 위한]

A

54-03 Marshall McLuhan noted that clothes are people's extended skin
마셜 매클루언은 언급했다 / 옷은 사람들의 연장된 피부이고

wheels extended feet, camera and telescopes extended eyes.
/ 바퀴는 연장된 발(이며) / 카메라와 망원경은 연장된 눈(이라고)

54-04 A snack with the label "99% natural" seems more appealing tha
'99% 천연인'이라는 라벨이 붙은 과자는 더욱 매력적으로 보인다 / 그것

it would if labeled "1% unnatural."
그럴 것보다 / 만약 '1% 천연이 아닌'이라고 라벨이 붙여진다면

54-05 Mathematics is an area of study that I'm attracted to, interested
수학은 학문의 한 분야이다 / [내가 끌리는, 관심이 있는, 그리고 잘하는]

in, and good at, though I have not explored it in depth.
/ 비록 내가 그것을 탐구하지 않았지만 / 깊게

B

54-06 Sleep is to the brain what food is to the body. That is to say, i
수면은 ∼이다 / 뇌에 대해 / 음식과 신체의 관계 다시 말해서 /

deprived of adequate sleep, the brain cannot function properly.
만약 (뇌가) 적절한 수면을 빼앗긴다면 / 뇌는 제대로 기능할 수 없다

54-07 Scientific beliefs are supported **by evidence, and** they get results.
과학적 신념은 증거에 의해 뒷받침된다 / 그리고 그것들은 결과를 얻는다

Myths and faiths are not and do not. *Richard Dawkins*
신화와 신앙은 (증거에 의해서 뒷받침되지) 않으며, (결과를 얻지) 못한다

54-08 In the realm of human psychology, research has **long** noted the
인간 심리학의 영역에서 / 연구는 오랫동안 주목해왔다 /

essential trait of adapting to life's events, whether happy or
본질적인 특성을 / [인생의 사건들에 적응하는] / (그 사건들이) 행복한 것이든

tragic.
매우 슬픈 것이든

54-09 It takes **a great deal of bravery** to stand up to our enemies, **but**
(…은) 많은 용기를 필요로 한다 / 우리의 적에게 맞서는 것은 / 그러나

just as much to stand up to our friends. *the novel <Harry Potter and the Sorcerer's Stone>*
꼭 같은 양의 (용기를 필요로 한다) / 우리의 친구에게 맞서는 것은

54-10 The computer is **only** a fast idiot; it has **no imagination;** it **cannot**
컴퓨터는 단지 빠른 멍청이일 뿐이다 / 그것은 상상력이 없다 / 그것은 행동을

originate action. It is, **and will remain, only** a tool of man.
일으킬 수 없다 / 그것은 ~이다 / 그리고 남아 있을 것이다 / 단지 인간의 도구로

54-11 Pride causes **individuals** to be out of touch with the reality of who
자만심은 개인들이 현실성과 접촉하지 못하게 만든다 / [= 자신들이]

they truly are and of what really brings happiness.
진정으로 누구인지의 / 그리고 무엇이 정말로 행복을 가져다주는지의]

54-12 Only after the immediate concerns of the unconscious have been
무의식의 즉각적인 관심사들이 충족된 후에서야

satisfied can the conscious mind begin to be convinced of, or
/ 의식적인 마음은 어떤 것이든 확신하거나 흥미를 갖기 시작할 수 있다

interested in, anything.

135

Review

A

01 At the heart of individualism lies the belief that each indivic
개인주의의 핵심에 / 신념이 놓여 있다 / [= 각 개인은 자신의 우주의 중

person constitutes the center of one's universe.
구성한다는]

02 It is not what he has, nor even what he does, which dired
(…은) 바로 그가 가진 것이 아니다 / 심지어는 그가 하는 것도 아니다 / 어떤 사람의 가치를

expresses the worth of a man, but what he is. *Henri-Frédéric Amiel*
나타내는 것은 / 그가 어떤 사람인지이다

03 It's a common misconception that money is every entreprenec
(…은) 흔한 오해이다 / 돈이 성공에 대한 모든 기업인의 측정 기준이라는 것은

metric for success. It's not, and nor should it be.
그것은 아니다 / 그리고 그것이 그래서도 안 된다

04 Don't get caught up in thinking that any success you experience a
생각하는 것에 말려들지 마라 / 어떠한 성공이 / [당신이 학생으로서 경험하는

student has no bearing on, or relationship to, future success in the "re
/ 관련이나 관계가 없다고 / '현실' 세계에서 미래의 성공과

world.

B

05 Break the 'big, fat, terrible book' down into sections that you
'크고, 두툼하고, 지겨운 책'을 부분들로 쪼개라 / [(당신이 느끼기

are more manageable and read through them one at a time.
/ 보다 감당할 수 있는] / 그리고 하나씩 그것들을 통독하라

06 Even more significant than the ability to communicate knowledge
훨씬 더 중요한 것은 / 지식을 전달하는 능력보다

means of signs and sounds was the development of a means
기호와 음성으로 / 수단의 발전이었다

preserving the knowledge through written records.
[문서 기록을 통해 지식을 보존하는]

07 It is in our ancient myths that many writers find the core of
(…은) 바로 우리 고대의 신화 속이다 / 많은 작가들이 인간의 분투의 핵심을 발견하는 것은

human struggle to make sense of the world and to find one's rol
/ [세상을 이해하고 자신의 역할을 찾으려는]

in short, a road map to the human psyche.
(간단히 말해) / 인간 정신세계로 가는 도로 지도를

08 The police arrested a man who they suspected had been at the
경찰은 한 남자를 체포했다 / [(그들이 의심했던) / 범행 현장에 있었던 것으로]

crime scene.

09 It's the possibility of having a dream come true that makes life
(···은) 바로 꿈을 실현하는 가능성이다 / 인생을 흥미롭게 만드는 것은

interesting.

10 Scarcely had we started out before the sky became overcast and
우리가 출발하자마자 / 하늘이 흐려졌다 / 그리고

down came the rain again.
비가 다시 내렸다

11 Any discussion of coevolution quickly runs into what philosophers
공진화에 대한 어떠한 토론도 곧 충돌한다 / 철학자들이 '인과 관계 딜레마'라고

call a "causality dilemma," a problem we recognize from the
부르는 것과 / = 문제인 / [우리가 질문에서 인식하는

question, "Which came first, the chicken or the egg?"
/ = 어떤 것이 먼저냐 / 닭이냐 달걀이냐?]

12 The wise are instructed by reason; ordinary minds, by experience;
현명한 사람들은 이성에 의해 교육된다 / 평범한 사람들은 경험에 의해서 (교육된다)

the stupid, by necessity; and brutes, by instinct.
/ 어리석은 사람들은 필요에 의해서 (교육된다) / 그리고 짐승 같은 사람들은 본능에 의해서 (교육된다)

13 In my experience, it's not what happens to you in life, but how you
나의 경험으로는 / (···은) 바로 인생 동안 당신에게 일어나는 것이 아니라 / 당신이 그것을 어떻게

deal with it, that makes you a survivor and a winner.
처리하느냐이다 / 당신을 생존자이자 승자로 만드는 것은

137

unit **55** 등위접속사 구문

55-01 Be thankful **for what you have and** you'll end up **having more.**
감사하라 / 당신이 가진 것에 대해서 / 그러면 당신은 결국 더 많이 갖게 될 것이다
Oprah Wi

55-02 I am the wisest man alive, **for I know** one thing, **and that is th**
나는 현존하는 가장 현명한 사람이다 / 왜냐하면 나는 한 가지를 알기 때문이다 / 그리고 그것은 ~이다

know nothing. *Socrates*
내가 아무것도 모른다는 것

A

55-03 Cut your coat **according to your cloth, or** you'll repent **some da**
네 코트를 잘라라 / 네 옷감에 맞춰서 / 그렇지 않으면 너는 언젠가 후회할 것이다
Pro

55-04 Everyone admits **that love is wonderful and necessary, yet no o**
모두가 인정한다 / 사랑은 아름답고 필연적인 것임을 / 하지만 아무

agrees on just what it is. *Diane Ackerman*
의견이 일치하지 않는다 / 정확하게 그것이 무엇인지에 대해

55-05 Criminalizing a behavior does **not make it immoral, nor is**
어떤 행동을 범죄로 간주하는 것이 만들지 않는다 / 그 행동을 비도덕적으로 / 그리고

immoral behavior necessarily criminalized.
비도덕적 행동이 반드시 범죄로 간주되지도 않는다

B

55-06 Change the way **you look at things and** the things **you look**
방식을 바꿔라 / [당신이 상황을 바라보는] / 그러면 상황은 / [당신이 바라보

change. *Wayne Dyer*
바뀐다

55-07 When a finger is pointing a way to the moon, don't concentrate
손가락이 달 쪽을 향해 가리키고 있을 때 / 그 손가락에 집중하지 마라

on the finger or you will miss all that heavenly glory!
/ 그렇지 않으면 당신은 저 모든 하늘의 장관을 놓치게 될 것이다!

55-08 I will love the light for it shows me the way, yet I will endure the
나는 빛을 사랑할 것이다 / 왜냐하면 그것은 내게 길을 보여 주기 때문에 / 하지만 나는 어둠을 견딜 것이다

darkness for it shows me the stars. *Og Mandino*
/ 왜냐하면 그것은 내게 별들을 보여 주기 때문에

55-09 Appreciation is the highest form of prayer, for it acknowledges
감사는 가장 고귀한 형식의 기도이다 / 왜냐하면 그것은 선의 존재를 인정

the presence of good wherever you shine the light of your thankful
하기 때문에 / 당신이 감사하는 마음의 빛을 비추는 어디서나

thoughts. *Alan Cohen*

55-10 The rough times must be endured and taken as they come, but
힘든 시간들은 견뎌져야 하고 감수되어야 한다 / 그것들이 올 때 / 그러나

they are not constant, nor do they last forever.
그것들이 계속되지는 않는다 / 그리고 그것들은 영원히 지속되지도 않는다

55-11 We sometimes think of aging as a process applying uniformly to
우리는 때때로 노화를 여긴다 / 과정으로 [유기체 전체에 균일하게 적용되는]

the whole organism, yet physiological studies show that different
/ 하지만 생리학 연구들은 보여 준다 / 신체의 여러 부분들이

parts of the body age at different rates.
노화한다는 것을 / 별개의 속도로

55-12 The old maxim "I'll sleep when I'm dead" is unfortunate. Adopt
'나는 죽을 때 잠에 들 것이다'라는 옛 격언은 유감스럽다 이러한 마음

this mindset, and you will be dead sooner and the quality of that
가짐을 취해 보라 / 그러면 당신은 더욱 빨리 죽게 될 것이다 / 그리고 그 삶의 질은 더욱 나빠질 것이다

life will be worse.

139

unit 56 상관접속사 구문

56-01 The athletes competed to gain honor both for themselves and fo
그 운동선수들은 경쟁했다 / 명예를 얻기 위해서 / 자기 자신들을 위해서도 / 그리고

their countries rather than achieve great wealth.
자신들의 나라를 위해서도 / 큰 부를 성취하기 위해서라기보다는

56-02 The Internet is the greatest tool we have **not only** for making
인터넷은 가장 위대한 도구이다 / [우리가 가진 / 사람들을 더 빨리 더 똑똑하게 만들

people smarter quicker, **but also** for making people dumbe
위해서일 뿐만 아니라 / 사람들을 더 빨리 더 멍청하게 만들기 위해서도]

faster.

A

56-03 The stupid **neither** forgive **nor** forget; the naive forgive **and** forget
어리석은 자는 용서하지도 잊지도 않는다 / 순진한 자는 용서하고 잊어버린다

the wise forgive **but** do not forget. *Thomas Szasz*
/ 현명한 자는 용서하지만 잊지 않는다

56-04 A word isn't ambiguous **by itself but** is used **ambiguously**: it i
어떤 단어는 그 자체로 애매한 것이 아니라 / 애매하게 사용되는 것이다 / 그

ambiguous **when** one cannot tell from the context what sense i
단어는 애매하다 / 사람이 문맥에서 알 수 없을 때 / 어떤 의미가 쓰이고 있

being used.
지를

56-05 Life on a desert island is wretched. You **either** starve to death o
무인도에서의 삶은 비참하다 당신은 굶주려서 죽게 된다 /

live **like** Robinson Crusoe, waiting for a boat which never comes.
또는 로빈슨 크루소처럼 산다 / 보트를 기다리면서 / [결코 오지 않는]

B

56-06 As fruit needs **not only** sunshine **but** cold nights and chilling
열매가 햇살뿐만 아니라 서늘한 밤과 차가운 소나기도 필요로 하듯이

showers to ripen it, so character needs **not only** joy **but** trial and
/ 그것을 익히기 위해서 / 인격은 기쁨뿐만 아니라 시련과 곤경도 필요하다

difficulty to mellow it.
/ 그것을 원숙하게 하기 위해서

56-07 Mishaps are like knives that **either** serve us **or** cut us as we grasp
불행은 칼과 같다 / [우리에게 쓸모가 있거나 또는 우리를 베는 / 우리가 그것을 붙잡

them by the handle or blade.
을 때 / 손잡이 또는 날로]

56-08 The true mark of heroes lies **not necessarily in the result of their**
영웅들의 진정한 특징은 있다 / 반드시 그들의 행동의 결과에가 아니라

actions, **but in what they are willing to do for others and for their**
/ 그들이 기꺼이 하고자 하는 것에 / 남을 위해서 그리고 자신들이 선택한

chosen causes.
대의를 위해서

56-09 Movies offer **both the happy ending that we love and the more**
영화는 제공한다 / 행복한 결말과 / [우리가 사랑하는] / 그리고 주류 문화에 대한

conservative support of the dominant culture that guides
더욱 보수적인 지지를 / ['현실 세계'에서의

behavior in "the real world."
행동을 좌우하는]

56-10 **Neither** a wise man **nor** a brave man lies down **on the tracks of**
현명한 사람도 용감한 사람도 누워 있지 않는다 / 역사라는 철로 위에

history to wait for the train of the future to run over him.
/ 미래라는 기차가 자신을 치고 가기를 기다리기 위해   *Dwight D. Eisenhower*

56-11 The whole aim of good teaching is to turn the young learner into
훌륭한 교육의 완전한 목표는 젊은 학습자를 독립적인 사람으로 바꾸는 것이다

an independent man, **who doesn't merely learn but works by**
/ 그리고 그 사람은 배울 뿐만 아니라 스스로 공부한다

himself.

56-12 The language which every human being speaks is **not an individual**
언어는 / [모든 인간이 말하는] / 개인적 유산이 아니라

inheritance, **but a social acquisition from the group in which he**
/ 집단으로부터 사회적으로 습득된 것이다 / [인간이 성장한]

grows up. **Both language and** environment help **to determine the**
언어와 환경 둘 다 도움을 준다 / 인간의 사고의 성격을 결정

character of his thought.
짓는 데

141

unit 57 병렬 구문

S TANDARD

57-01 Creative solutions come from viewing something differently an(
창의적인 해결책은 나온다 / 어떤 것을 다르게 보는 것으로부터 / 그(

discovering what others have missed.
발견하는 것으로부터 / 다른 사람들이 놓친 것을

57-02 Testing allows us not merely to confirm our theories but to weed ou(
실험은 우리가 우리의 이론을 입증하도록 해 줄 뿐만 아니라 / 이론들을 제거하게도 해(

those that do not fit the evidence.
/ [그 증거에 부합하지 않는]

A

57-03 Some drug companies have frequently been caught making fals(
몇몇 제약 회사들은 자주 목격되어왔다 / 자신들의 제품에 대(

claims about their products or hiding information to cover u(
허위 주장을 하는 것이 / 또는 그것들의 위험을 감추기 위해서 정보를 은폐하는 것이

their dangers.

57-04 Many people who have type II diabetes are advised to contro(
많은 사람들은 / [제2형 당뇨병을 가진!] / 그들의 혈당 수준을 통제하라고 조언을

their blood sugar levels by following a healthy diet, takin(
받는다 / 건강한 식단을 실천함으로써, 운동을 함으로써,

exercise and losing weight.
/ 그리고 살을 뺌으로써

57-05 The world is a dangerous place to live; not because of the peopl(
세상은 살기에 위험한 곳이다 / 사람들 때문이 아니라

who are evil, but because of the people who don't do anythin(
/ [악한] / 사람들 때문에 / [악에 대해서 아무것도 하지 않는]

about it. *Albert Einstein*

B

57-06 In music, cacophony is discordant sounds, false harmony, (
음악에서 / 불협화음은 ~이다 / 조화되지 않는 소리 / 잘못된 화음 /

noisy and inharmonious combinations of sounds.
또는 시끄럽고 가락이 맞지 않는 음들의 조합

57-07 Teachers cannot seat children all behind desks in a classroom,
교사들은 ~할 수 없다 / 아이들 모두를 앉게 하고 / 교실에서 책상 뒤에

dictate information to them and expect them to absorb all of it
/ 그들에게 지식을 받아쓰게 하고 / 그리고 그들이 스펀지처럼 그것 모두를 흡수하기를 기대할

like a sponge.

57-08 The value of life is not in the length of days, but in the use we make
인생의 가치는 날들의 길이에 있는 것이 아니라 / 우리가 그 날을 사용하는 데 있다

of them; a man may live long yet very little. *Michel de Montaigne*
사람은 오래 살 수도 있지만 아주 적게 살 수도 있다

57-09 The law about a contract considers such questions as whether it
계약에 관한 법은 문제들을 고려한다 / [계약이 존재하는지

exists, what the meaning of it is, whether it has been broken, and what
/ 그것의 의미가 무엇인지 / 그것이 깨졌는지 / 그리고 어떤

compensation is due to the injured party.
보상이 피해를 입은 당사자에게 지불되어야 하는지와 같은]

57-10 By sensing whether people are in the house or which rooms they
감지함으로써 / 사람들이 집에 있는지 / 또는 그들이 어떤 방에 있는지를

are in, a smart thermostat can either switch off heating or cooling
/ 똑똑한 자동 온도 조절기는 난방 또는 냉방장치를 완전히 끌 수 있거나

completely or concentrate on the rooms where the people are.
/ 또는 방에 집중할 (수 있다) / [그 사람들이 있는]

57-11 Electric cars have several limitations that reduce their popularity.
전기차는 몇 가지 한계를 지니고 있다 / [그들의 인기를 떨어뜨리는]

Some of these disadvantages are that the autos are expensive,
이러한 불리한 점들의 일부는 ~이다 / 그 자동차들이 비싸고

are relatively slow, and require constant recharging.
/ 상대적으로 느리고 / 그리고 끊임없는 재충전이 필요하다는 것

57-12 Recently, researchers have suggested that the purpose of
최근에 / 연구자들은 시사했다 / 웃음의 목적은 전달하는 것일 뿐만

laughter is not just to communicate that one is in a playful state,
아니라 / 어떤 이가 쾌활한 상태에 있다는 것을

but to induce this state in others as well.
/ 이 상태를 남들에게서 또한 유도해내려는 것이기도 하다는 것을

143

unit 58 부정 구문

S TANDARD

58-01 "Judging from the scene, there is little chance of there being an
"현장으로 판단하건대 / 가능성은 거의 없다 / [생존자가 있을]

survivors," an airport official said.
/ 한 공항 관리자가 말했다

58-02 I think dreams can come true, but not necessarily like fairy-tale
나는 생각한다 / 꿈은 이루어질 수 있다고 / 그러나 반드시 동화처럼은 아니라고

It's not always so perfect like that. *Patrick Dempsey*
그것은 항상 그렇게 완벽하지는 않다 / 그처럼

A

58-03 There have been few, if any, human societies that have not ha
거의 없었다 / 있다 하더라도 / 인간 사회는 / [그들 자신의 윤리 규범이 없었

their own codes of ethics. There are few, if any, human beings no
/ 거의 없다 / 있다 하더라도 / 인간은 / [

interested in distinctions between right and wrong.
것과 그른 것 사이의 구별에 관심이 없는]

58-04 When the ancestors of the cheetah first began pursuing th
치타의 조상이 처음 가젤의 조상을 뒤쫓기 시작했을 때

ancestors of the gazelle, neither of them could run as fast as the
/ 그들 중 어느 쪽도 달릴 수 없었다 / 그들이 오늘날 할 수 있

can today. *Richard Dawkins*
만큼 빠르게

58-05 No sensible decision can be made any longer without taking int
합리적인 결정은 더 이상 내려질 수 없다 / 고려하지 않고서는

account not only the world as it is, but the world as it will be.
/ 세상을 현재 그대로 뿐만 아니라 / 세상이 앞으로 어떻게 될 것인지도 *Isaac Asim*

B

58-06 All that is gold does not glitter. Not all those who wander are los
금으로 된 모든 것이 반짝이는 것은 아니다 방황하는 사람들 모두가 길을 잃은 것은 아니다
the movie <The Lord of the Rings: The Fellowship of the Rin

58-07 With free capital flows, monetary policy could be directed **either at**
자유로운 자본 흐름으로 / 통화 정책은 방향지게 될 수 있다 / 환율을 안정화

stabilizing an exchange rate or controlling inflation, but not both.
하는 것으로 / 또는 인플레이션을 통제하는 것으로 / 그러나 둘 다는 아니다

58-08 A new idea comes **suddenly and in a rather intuitive way. But**
새로운 아이디어는 찾아온다 / 갑자기 그리고 다소 직관적인 방식으로 / 그러나

intuition is nothing but the outcome of earlier intellectual
직관은 결과일 뿐이다 / [이전의 지적 경험의]

experience. *Albert Einstein*

58-09 No one has given **so much care to the study of composition as I.**
어느 누구도 많은 관심을 주지는 않았다 / 작곡 연구에 / 나만큼

There is scarcely a famous master in music whose works I have
음악계에서 유명한 거장은 거의 없다 / [그들의 작품을 내가 자주 그리고

not frequently and diligently studied. *Wolfgang Amadeus Mozart*
부지런하게 연구하지 않은]

58-10 People **rarely succeed unless they have fun in what they are doing.**
사람들은 좀처럼 성공하지 못한다 / 그들이 즐거움을 느끼지 않으면 / 자신이 하고 있는 것에

58-11 Hardly any discovery is possible **without making use of**
거의 어떠한 발견도 가능하지 않다 / 지식을 활용하지 않고서

knowledge gained by others.
/ [다른 사람들에 의해 얻어진]

58-12 Geniuses **don't necessarily have a higher success rate than other**
천재들이 반드시 더 높은 성공률을 가진 것은 아니다 / 다른 창작자들보다

creators; they simply do more—and they do a range of different
그들은 단지 더 많은 것을 한다 / —그리고 그들은 여러 다양한 것들을 한다

things.

unit **59** 동명사 관용 구문

S TANDARD

59-01 We are used **to thinking of light as always going in straight lines**
우리는 빛을 생각하는 것에 익숙하다 / 항상 직선으로 가는 것이라고

But it doesn't.
그러나 그것은 그렇지 않다

59-02 It's no use carrying an umbrella **if your shoes are leaking.** *Irish Proverb*
(…은) 소용없다 / 우산을 갖고 다니는 것은 / 만약 당신의 신발이 새고 있다면

A

59-03 Those who don't set goals, will have a difficult time figuring ou
목표를 설정하지 않는 사람들은 어려움을 겪을 것이다 / 그것에 어떻게 도

how to reach them. *JJ Goldwag*
할지 알아내는 데

59-04 Don't waste your time looking back at what you lost. Move or
당신의 시간을 낭비하지 마라 / 되돌아보는 데 / 당신이 잃은 것을 나아가라

Life is not meant to be traveled backwards.
인생은 뒤로 돌아가도록 되어 있지 않다

59-05 It goes **without saying that stating a problem is not the sam**
(…은) 말할 것도 없다 / 어떤 문제를 명시하는 것이 같은 것이 아니라는 것은

thing as solving it in practice.
/ 그것을 실제로 해결하는 것과

B

59-06 During sleep, while the body rests, the brain is busy processin
자는 동안 / 몸은 쉬고 있는 반면에 / 뇌는 바쁘다 / 낮에 만들어진

information from the day and forming memories.
정보를 처리하느라 / 그리고 기억을 구성하느라

59-07 She made a point of sending thank-you notes to everyone who
그녀는 감사 편지 보내는 일을 반드시 했다 / 모두에게 / [자신의

attended her party.
파티에 참석한]

59-08 It is no use saying, "We are doing our best." You have got to
(…은) 소용없다 / 말하는 것은 / "우리는 최선을 다하고 있다"고 당신은 성공해야 한다

succeed in doing what is necessary. *Winston Churchill*
/ 필요한 일을 하는 것에

59-09 It's a dangerous business, Frodo, going out your door. You step
(…은) 위험한 일이야 / 프로도 / 문 밖으로 나가는 것은 네가 길을 나서면

onto the road, and if you don't keep your feet, there's no knowing
/ 그리고 만약 네가 똑바로 서 있지 않으면 / 아는 것은 불가능해

where you might be swept off to.
/ 네가 어디로 휩쓸려 가게 될지 *the movie <The Lord of the Rings: The Fellowship of the Ring>*

59-10 A good book enlightening your mind is worth reading over again
좋은 책은 / [당신의 정신을 깨우치게 하는] / 반복해서 읽을 가치가 있다

and again.

59-11 There is no telling how far science and technology will have
말하는 것은 불가능하다 / 과학과 기술이 어디까지 진보했을지

progressed by the end of this century.
/ 금세기 말에

59-12 People have a hard time letting go of their suffering. Out of a fear
사람들은 어려움을 겪는다 / 자신들의 고통을 놓아주는 데 미지에 대한 두려움으로

of the unknown, they prefer suffering that is familiar. *Thich Nhat Hanh*
/ 그들은 고통을 더 좋아한다 / [익숙한]

unit 60 전치사 + 명사절

60-01 There have been many debates as to whether cryptocurrenc
많은 토론이 있어왔다 / [암호화폐가 분류되어야 하는지에 관한

should be classified as property, commodity, money, or security.
/ 자산, 상품, 돈, 또는 유가증권으로서]

60-02 Ecosystems are dynamic in that their various parts are alway
생태계는 역동적이다 / 그것의 다양한 부분들이 항상 변하고 있다는 점에서

changing.

A

60-03 One day President Roosevelt told me that he was asking publicl
어느 날 루즈벨트 대통령이 내게 말했다 / 자신이 공개적으로 의견을 구하고 있다고

for suggestions about what the war should be called. I said a
/ [그 전쟁이 무엇으로 불려야 하는지에 대한] 나는 바로

once "The Unnecessary War." *Winston Churchill*
'불필요한 전쟁'이라고 말했다

60-04 Technology is the basis of many of our metaphors and i
기술은 우리의 은유 대부분의 토대이다 / 그리고

important in terms of how we think and how our ideas progress.
중요하다 / 어떻게 우리가 생각하는가 그리고 어떻게 우리의 생각이 나아가는가의 관점에서

60-05 What you do for a living is critical to where you settle and how
생계를 위해 당신이 하는 것은 대단히 중요하다 / 당신이 어디에 정착하는지와 어떻게 사는지에—

you live—and the converse is also true.
/ 그리고 그 반대 또한 진실이다

B

60-06 The success of the talks is up to whether both sides are willing t
대화의 성공은 / 양측이 기꺼이 약간의 양보를 하려고 하는지에 달려 있다

make some concessions.

60-07 In biology, the "niche" of a species is broadly defined by what it
생물학에서 / 어떤 종의 '적합한 환경'은 폭넓게 정의된다 / 그것이 무엇을

eats and how it reproduces.
먹는지와 그것이 번식하는 방식에 의해

60-08 Competition is basically concerned with how the availability of
경쟁은 기본적으로 관련된다 / 어떻게 자원의 입수 가능성이

resources, such as food and space, is reduced by other
/ [먹이와 공간 같은] / 다른 생물체로 인해 줄어드는지와

organisms.

60-09 Winning is important to me, but what brings me real joy is the
승리하는 것은 내게 중요하다 / 그러나 내게 진정한 기쁨을 주는 것은 완전히 몰입하고 있는

experience of being fully engaged in whatever I'm doing. *Phil Jackson*
경험이다 / 무엇이든지 내가 하고 있는 것에

60-10 In choosing which path to take with some of life's decisions,
선택할 때 / 어느 길을 취할 것인가 / 인생의 몇몇 결정들에

ethics are often at the center; heavily influencing our choices
윤리가 종종 중심에 있다 / 우리의 선택에 크게 영향을 미치면서

between what is right and what is wrong.
/ [옳은 것과 그릇 것 사이의]

60-11 We hunger to understand, so we invent myths about how we
우리는 이해하는 데 굶주려 있다 / 그래서 우리는 신화들을 지어낸다 / [우리가 상상하기에 세상이

imagine the world is constructed. *Carl Sagan*
어떻게 구성되었는지에 관한]

60-12 The knowledge you have acquired will enable you to be successful
지식은 / [당신이 습득한] / 당신이 성공할 수 있게 해 줄 것이다

in whatever field you may enter.
/ 당신이 진입하게 될 어떠한 분야에서든지

149

Review

01 People are **often** blinded **by love, making bad judgments and wron**
사람들은 종종 사랑에 눈이 먼다 / 부적절한 판단과 잘못된 선택을 하면서

choices, or doing stupid and foolish things, under the influence c
/ 또는 어리석고 바보 같은 일을 하면서 / 사랑의 영향으로

love.

02 Blockchain technology is **not** a company, **nor** is it an app, **but rathe**
블록체인 기술은 회사가 아니다 / 그것은 응용 프로그램도 아니다 / 오히려

an entirely new way of documenting data on the Internet.
인터넷상에서 자료를 기록하는 완전히 새로운 방식(이다)

03 Material wealth **in and of itself** does **not necessarily** generat
물질적인 부유함은 그 자체로 그리고 저절로 / 반드시 의미를 만들어 내거나 감정적인 부유함으로 이끌지

meaning or lead to emotional wealth.
않는다

04 You **probably** wouldn't worry **about what people think of you if yo**
당신은 아마 걱정하지 않을 텐데 / 사람들이 당신을 어떻게 생각하는지에 대해 / 만약

could know how seldom they do.
당신이 알 수 있다면 / 그들이 얼마나 드물게 그렇게 하는지

05 Energy can **neither** be created **nor** destroyed, **but can merely b**
에너지는 창조될 수도 파괴될 수도 없다 / 단지 변형될 수 있을 뿐이다

transformed from one state to another.
/ 하나의 상태로 다른 상태로

06 Just walking through a garden or, for that matter, seeing one out you
단지 정원을 걷는 것 / 또는 실제로 / 창밖으로 정원을 보는 것은

window, can lower blood pressure, reduce stress, and ease pain.
/ 혈압을 낮출 수 있다 / 스트레스를 줄인다 / 그리고 고통을 완화시킨다

07 Having grown up in a culture that appreciates modesty and reserve, h
문화에서 성장했기 때문에 / [겸손함과 신중함을 높이 평가하는]

was not accustomed to expressing emotions in public.
익숙하지 않았다 / 공개적으로 감정을 표현하는 것에

08 Introducing drones to our emergency services could save lives by
드론을 우리의 긴급 구조대에 도입하는 것은 생명을 구할 수 있다 /

transporting materials like blood and AEDs more quickly, locating
혈액과 AED와 같은 물자를 더 빨리 운송함으로써 / 화재가 난 건물

people inside burning buildings, and helping the police track suspects.
안에 있는 사람들의 위치를 알아냄으로써 / 그리고 경찰이 용의자를 추적하는 것을 도움으로써

C

09 You can move the cursor either by using the mouse or by using the
당신은 커서를 움직일 수 있다 / 마우스를 사용함으로써 / 또는 키보드 위의 화살표

arrow keys on the keyboard.
키를 사용함으로써

10 Advertisements do not always tell you everything you need to know
광고가 항상 당신에게 말해 주지는 않는다 / 모든 것을 [당신이 알 필요가 있는]

in order to make a wise choice.
/ 당신이 현명한 선택을 하기 위해서

11 True love cannot be found where it does not exist, nor can it be
진정한 사랑은 발견될 수 없다 / 그것이 존재하지 않는 곳에서 / 그리고 그것은 부인될

denied where it does. *Torquato Tasso*
수도 없다 / 그것이 존재하는 곳에서

D

12 A hypothesis not only should fit the facts which brought about its
가설은 사실에 들어맞아야 할 뿐만 아니라 / [그 가설을 생겨나게 한]

creation but should also be compatible with the rest of the body of
/ 또한 양립할 수 있어야 한다 / 과학의 대다수의 나머지 것들과

science.

13 When people are overwhelmed with the volume of information
사람들이 압도당할 때 / 그들과 마주하고 있는 정보의 양에

confronting them, they have difficulty knowing what to focus on.
/ 그들은 어려움을 겪는다 / 무엇에 집중해야 할지 판단하는 데

14 Where the degree of competition is particularly intense, a zero-sum
경쟁의 정도가 특히 치열한 곳에서 / 제로섬 게임은

game can quickly become a negative sum game, in that everyone in
곧 네거티브섬 게임이 될 수 있다 / 시장에 있는 모든 이가 추가 비용에

the market is faced with additional costs.
직면한다는 점에서

Memo

마법같은
블록구문

마법같은 블록구문

Marvel Book 실전편

Preview

Marvel Book 구문 집중 학습을 위한 본책

영어 문장 완전 독파를 위해 정교하게 설계된 Stage별 단계적 학습 시스템

1. 전체 구문 조망 ➔ 2. 기본 문장성분 ➔ 3. 수식어의 이해 ➔ 4. 주요 구문의 이해 ➔ 5. 전체 구문 복습

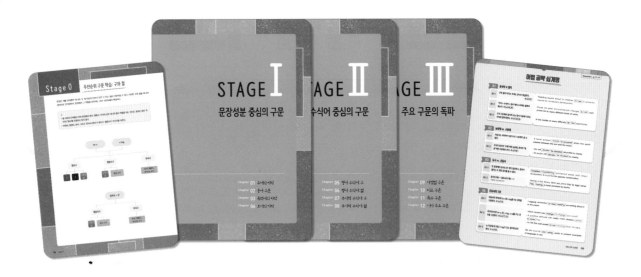

'블록+컬러'의 이미지를 통한 구문의 시각화

1. Chapter 목표 구문의 핵심을 블록으로 정리 ➔ 2. Unit별 구문 학습 ➔ 3. Chapter 종합문제

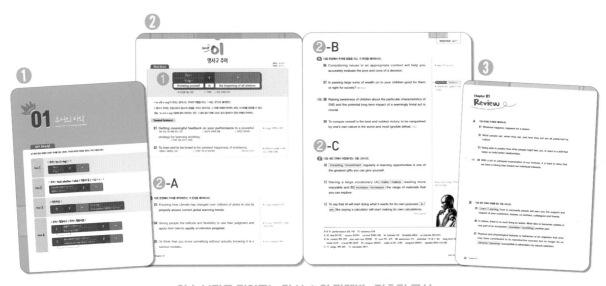

학습 부담을 덜어주는 각 Unit의 단계별 · 점층적 구성

- 1. Block Board: 블록과 컬러로 기본 문장 구조를 직관적으로 이해
- 2. A, B, C의 3단계로 이루어진 점층적 학습 활동

Rainbow Book 완벽한 자학자습용 해설서

쉽고 편하게 학습할 수 있도록 본책과 동일하게 설계된 페이지 구성

- Unit별 핵심 어휘 정리
- 모든 문장에 문장성분별 컬러를 적용하여 직관적 학습 강화
- 문장 구조의 이해를 돕는 끊어읽기와 직독직해

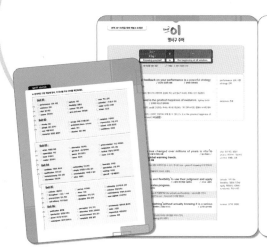

Memory Book 휴대용 문장 모음집

암기 또는 반복 학습을 위한 포켓북

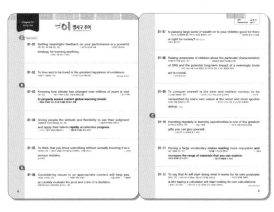

Colors & Abbreviations [Symbols]

문장성분별 컬러

컬러	문장성분
파랑	주어
빨강	동사
초록	주격보어
진갈색	(직접)목적어
연갈색	간접목적어 / 목적격보어
검정	부사어
회색	두 가지 이상의 문장성분

- 검정색 처리:
  - 부사절 내의 주어와 동사 등
  - 삽입어구, 보충 설명하는 관계사절 (계속적 용법)
- Block Board의 블록에서 해당 구문의 주요 요소는 노란색 망으로 강조
- Unit의 학습 목표 구문은 볼드체로 강조

약호

- **S** 주어
- **V** 동사
- **O** 목적어
- **C** 보어
- **O'** 전치사의 목적어
- **to-v** to부정사
- **v-ing** 동명사 / 현재분사
- **v-ed** 과거분사
- **ⓥ** 동사원형

기호

- **/** : 끊어 읽기
- **[ ]** : 대체 가능어
- **=** : 같음, 동격
- **( )** : 생략 가능
- **⌐⌐|** : 수식 어구
- **✔** : 생략된 어구

Contents

Appendixes

Colors in Block	9
Structures in Block	10
Rules in Block	15
Answer Key	215

Stage 0 우선순위 구문 학습

구와 절

Stage 1 문장성분 중심의 구문

Chapter 01. 주어의 파악

		중요도 / 난이도
Unit 01 명사구 주어	28	★★☆ / ★☆☆
Unit 02 명사절 주어	30	★★☆ / ★★☆
Unit 03 가주어 it	32	★★★ / ★★★
Unit 04 주어 + 형용사구	34	★★☆ / ★★☆
Unit 05 주어 + 형용사절 1	36	★★★ / ★★★
Unit 06 주어 + 형용사절 2	38	★★★ / ★★★
Chapter 01 Review	40	

Chapter 02. 동사 구문

Unit 07 전치사구와 짝을 이루는 동사 구문	44	★★☆ / ★☆☆
Unit 08 조동사 구문	46	★★☆ / ★★☆
Unit 09 수동태 구문	48	★★☆ / ★★☆
Chapter 02 Review	50	

Chapter 03. 목적어의 파악

Unit 10 명사구 목적어	54	★☆☆ / ★☆☆
Unit 11 명사절 목적어	56	★★★ / ★★☆
Unit 12 가목적어 it	58	★★★ / ★★★
Unit 13 목적어 + 형용사구	60	★☆☆ / ★☆☆
Unit 14 목적어 + 형용사절	62	★☆☆ / ★★☆
Chapter 03 Review	64	

Chapter 04. 보어의 파악

Unit 15 주격보어: 구	68	★★☆ / ★☆☆
Unit 16 주격보어: 절	70	★★☆ / ★★☆
Unit 17 목적격보어 1	72	★★☆ / ★☆☆
Unit 18 목적격보어 2	74	★★☆ / ★★☆
Unit 19 보어 + 형용사구	76	★★☆ / ★☆☆
Unit 20 보어 + 형용사절	78	★★☆ / ★★☆
Chapter 04 Review	80	

Stage 2 수식어 중심의 구문

Chapter 05. 명사 수식어: 구

Unit 21 명사 + (형용사 +) 전치사구	86	★★☆ / ★☆☆
Unit 22 명사 + to-v[v-ing / v-ed]	88	★★☆ / ★★☆
Chapter 05 Review	90	

Chapter 06. 명사 수식어: 절

Unit 23 명사 + 관계대명사절	94	★★☆ / ★★☆
Unit 24 명사 + 전치사 + 관계대명사절	96	★★☆ / ★★★
Unit 25 명사 + 관계부사절	98	★★☆ / ★★☆
Unit 26 명사 + 관계사가 생략된 수식절	100	★★★ / ★★☆
Unit 27 명사와 관계사절의 분리	102	★★☆ / ★★★
Unit 28 명사, 관계사절	104	★★☆ / ★★☆
Chapter 06 Review	106	

Chapter 07. 부사적 수식어: 구

Unit 29 부사 역할을 하는 전치사구	110	★★☆ / ★★☆

Unit 30 부사 역할을 하는 to-v의 의미   112   ★★☆ / ★★★

Unit 31 부사적 to-v의 관용 구문   114   ★★☆ / ★★☆

Unit 32 부사 역할을 하는 분사구문의 의미   116   ★★☆ / ★★★

Unit 33 분사구문의 다양한 형태 1   118   ★★☆ / ★★★

Unit 34 분사구문의 다양한 형태 2   120   ★☆☆ / ★★☆

Chapter 07 Review   122

Chapter 08. 부사적 수식어: 절

Unit 35 시간의 부사절   126   ★★☆ / ★★☆

Unit 36 이유의 부사절   128   ★★☆ / ★★☆

Unit 37 조건의 부사절   130   ★★☆ / ★★☆

Unit 38 목적 · 결과의 부사절   132   ★★☆ / ★★☆

Unit 39 반전 · 대조의 부사절   134   ★★☆ / ★★☆

Unit 40 양태의 부사절   136   ★★☆ / ★★☆

Chapter 08 Review   138

Stage 3   주요 구문의 독파

Chapter 09. 가정법 구문

Unit 41 if 가정법 과거 구문   144   ★☆☆ / ★☆☆

Unit 42 If 가정법 과거완료 구문   146   ★★☆ / ★★☆

Unit 43 wish · as if 가정법 구문   148   ★★☆ / ★★☆

Unit 44 if가 없는 가정법 구문   150   ★★☆ / ★★★

Chapter 09 Review   152

Chapter 10. 비교 구문

Unit 45 원급 구문   156   ★★☆ / ★★☆

Unit 46 비교급 구문 1   158   ★★☆ / ★★☆

Unit 47 비교급 구문 2   160   ★★☆ / ★★☆

Unit 48 최상급 구문   162   ★★☆ / ★★☆

Chapter 10 Review   164

Chapter 11. 특수 구문

Unit 49 도치 구문 1   168   ★★★ / ★★☆

Unit 50 도치 구문 2   170   ★★☆ / ★★☆

Unit 51 강조 구문   172   ★★☆ / ★★☆

Unit 52 동격 구문   174   ★★☆ / ★★☆

Unit 53 삽입 구문   176   ★★☆ / ★★☆

Unit 54 생략 · 공통 구문   178   ★★☆ / ★★☆

Chapter 11 Review   180

Chapter 12. 기타 주요 구문

Unit 55 등위접속사 구문   184   ★☆☆ / ★★☆

Unit 56 상관접속사 구문   186   ★★☆ / ★★☆

Unit 57 병렬 구문   188   ★★★ / ★★☆

Unit 58 부정 구문   190   ★★☆ / ★★☆

Unit 59 동명사 관용 구문   192   ★★☆ / ★★☆

Unit 60 전치사 + 명사절   194   ★★☆ / ★★☆

Chapter 12 Review   196

Special Stage   구문 복습을 위한 어법 72제

어법 공략 십계명   199

Special Unit 01   202

Special Unit 02   208

3-Step Course

Warming-up Course

- Colors in Block
- Structures in Block
- Rules in Block
- Stage 0 우선순위 구문 학습

Main Course

Stage 1
문장성분 중심의 구문
주어 / 동사 / 목적어 / 보어

Stage 2
수식어 중심의 구문
형용사적 수식어 / 부사적 수식어

Stage 3
주요 구문의 독파
비교 구문 / 특수 구문 등

Review Course

- 어법 공략 십계명
- 어법 72제

Preface

영어교과서 또는 수능 수준의 영어 문장의 해석에 어려움을 겪는다면,
여러분은 다음 세 가지 중의 하나 또는 둘 이상이 문제라는 진단을 받게 될 것이다.

① 어휘력이 부족하다.
② 문장의 구조를 파악하지 못한다.
③ 추상적인 내용에 대한 이해력 또는 배경지식이 부족하다.

여러분의 진단결과가 주로 ②라면, 영어 닥터는 여러분에게 이 책을 처방할 것이다.^^
그리고 여러분이 이 책으로 꾸준히 학습하면, **확실하게 & 흥미롭게 & 효율적으로** 영어
문장의 구조를 습득하게 될 것이라고 격려할 것이다. (ㅋㅋ)

한국인이 영문의 구조를 파악하는 데 어려움을 겪는 이유는 영어의 어순이 우
리말의 어순과 다르기 때문이다. 예컨대, 국어는 동사가 문장의 끝에 오지만,
영어는 동사가 주어 다음에 온다. 국어는 어떤 명사를 수식하는 말이 아무리
길어도 그 명사 앞에 오지만, 영어는 대개 긴 명사 수식어가 그 명사 뒤에 온다.
이와 같은 어순의 차이를 극복하려면 영어 문장의 기본 구조를 익히고, 영어와
국어가 어떻게 다른지를 파악하고, 충분한 영어 문장의 독해를 통해 숙달하는
과정이 필요하다.

영문의 구조 이해를 돕기 위한 구문 학습용 교재들이 시중에 다수 나와 있음에도
상당수의 학습자들이 여전히 영문의 구조 파악에 어려움을 겪고 있는 것은 학
습자의 문제라기보다는 학습 교재 및 학습 과정의 문제일 수 있다. 본 교재는
학습자 중심의 교재, 즉, 학습자의 눈높이에 맞고 학습자가 흥미를 가지고 완
독할 수 있는 교재를 지향한다. 이를 위해서 다음과 같은 세 가지의 학습 장치
를 고안하고, 교재의 구성에 반영했다.

1. 구문의 시각화

본 교재는 블록과 색으로 영문의 구조를 시각화했다. image가 text보다 훨씬
더 효과적인 설명·이해 방식이며, 요즘 세대의 학습자들은 text보다 image가
더 익숙하다.

2. 점층적 학습 과정

본문의 마주보는 두 페이지는 해당 Unit의 목표 구문의 제시·이해·적용이 단계적으로 이루어지도록 구성되었으며, 해당 구문에 최적화된 학습 활동이 각 단계별로 주어졌다.

3. 자학자습용 해설서 Rainbow Book

본책인 Marvel Book은 수강용, 해설서인 Rainbow Book은 자학자습용이다. Rainbow Book은 실제적인 자기 주도적 학습이 가능하도록 Marvel Book의 내용과 구성을 그대로 옮겨온 상태에서 입체적인 해설을 덧붙였다.

"왜 영어 구문을 컬러블록으로 학습하는가?"

백문(百聞)이 불여일견(不如一見)!
아무리 여러 번 들어도 실제로 한 번 보는 것보다는 못하다.

문장을 이루는 요소를 문장성분이라고 하는데, 여기에는 주어, 동사, 목적어, 보어, 수식어 등이 있다. 이러한 문장성분이 결합해서 하나의 문장이 된다. 이러한 문장성분의 결합 순서, 즉 규칙을 말 또는 글로 설명한다면, 여러분은 벌써 머리가 아파올 것이다.

복잡한 결합의 규칙 설명 대신에, 레고를 가지고 놀 듯 영문을 이해하면 어떨까?

본 교재는 영어 구문의 기본 규칙을 컬러블록으로 제시하여 image 세대인 학습자들이 친근하게 접근할 수 있도록 하였다. 각 문장성분을 컬러블록으로, 문장성분의 결합을 컬러블록간의 결합으로 시각화하여 학습자들이 영문의 구조를 직관적으로 인식할 수 있도록 설계했다. 문장의 패턴을 컬러블록의 형태로 입체적으로 인지하면서, 본 교재에서 제시된 흐름대로 학습 활동을 하다보면, 어느새 여러분의 머릿속에 영어 구문이 image, 즉 블록 패턴으로 펼쳐질 것이다.

How to Use the Book 〈실전편〉

Book	Contents	Page	Features
Marvel Book	**Colors in Block / Structures in Block**	9~14	컬러블록으로 이미지화된 영어 구문의 숲! 5형식을 바탕으로 구와 절, 수식어의 위치 등을 직관적으로 이해하자!
	⬇		
	Rules in Block	15~17	구문독해에서 가장 핵심인 10가지 규칙을 컬러블록으로 우선 숙지하자!
	⬇		
	Stage 0 우선순위 구문 학습 (구와 절)	18~23	영어 구문의 가장 기본 덩어리인 구와 절의 종류와 쓰임을 미리 짚어보고 가자!
	⬇		
	Stage 1 주요 문장성분 20개 Unit / 240개 예문	24~81	주어 / 동사 / 목적어 / 보어를 살펴보고, 문장의 골격을 파악하자!
	⬇		
	Stage 2 수식어 20개 Unit / 240개 예문	82~139	형용사적 수식어 / 부사적 수식어를 확인하며, 수식어를 가려내자!
	⬇		
	Stage 3 주요 구문 20개 Unit / 240개 예문	140~197	가정법 구문, 비교 구문, 특수 구문 등 주요 영어 구문의 패턴을 익히자!
	⬇		
	Special Stage 어법 공략 십계명 / 어법 72제	198~214	앞에서 학습한 구문을 적용하여 어법 문제를 풀면서 고난도 구문을 독파하자!

Book	Contents	Features
Rainbow Book	자학자습용 해설서	• Unit별 핵심 어휘만 모아 한 번에 정리 • 모든 문장에 문장성분별 컬러 적용 • 꼼꼼한 직독직해 & 친절한 구문·내용 해설

Book	Contents	Features
Memory Book	휴대용 예문 모음집	암기 또는 반복 학습을 도와 주는 주머니 속의 마법 기억책

Colors in Block

문장성분	블록	품사
● **주어** 동사의 주체가 되는 말	S	← 명사(구, 절)
● **동사** 주어의 동작이나 상태를 나타내는 말	V	← 동사(구)
● **목적어** 동사가 나타내는 동작의 대상이 되는 말	O	← 명사(구, 절)
● **주격보어** 주어를 보충 설명하는 말	C	← 명사(구, 절) / 형용사(구)
● **목적격보어** 목적어를 보충 설명하는 말	C	← 명사(구, 절) / 형용사(구)
● **부사어** 동사, 형용사, 부사 등을 꾸며주는 말	부사어	← 부사(구, 절)

문장의 형식+색

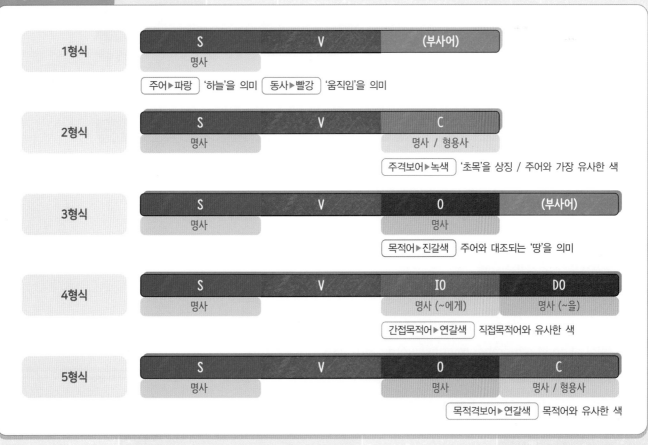

1형식
S 명사 / V / (부사어)
주어▶파랑 '하늘'을 의미　동사▶빨강 '움직임'을 의미

2형식
S 명사 / V / C 명사 / 형용사
주격보어▶녹색 '초목'을 상징 / 주어와 가장 유사한 색

3형식
S 명사 / V / O 명사 / (부사어)
목적어▶진갈색 주어와 대조되는 '땅'을 의미

4형식
S 명사 / V / IO 명사 (~에게) / DO 명사 (~을)
간접목적어▶연갈색 직접목적어와 유사한 색

5형식
S 명사 / V / O 명사 / C 명사 / 형용사
목적격보어▶연갈색 목적어와 유사한 색

Structures in Block

1. 문장의 기본 구조: 5형식

S: 주어(subject) V: 동사(verb) O: 목적어(object)
C: 보어(complement) IO: 간접목적어(indirect object)
DO: 직접목적어(direct object) OC: 목적격보어(object complement)

문장성분이 결합하여 유의미한 문장을 구성하는 방식은 크게 다섯 가지로 나눌 수 있다.

1형식

| S | V | (부사어) |
| 명사 | | |

• S는 V하다

2형식

| S | V | C |
| 명사 | | 명사 / 형용사 |

• S는 C이다[C하다]

3형식

| S | V | O | (부사어) |
| 명사 | | 명사 | |

• S는 O를 V하다

4형식

| S | V | IO | DO |
| 명사 | | 명사 | 명사 |

• S는 IO에게 DO를 V하여 주다

5형식

| S | V | O | OC |
| 명사 | | 명사 | 명사 / 형용사 |

• S는 O를 C라고[C하도록] V하다

Structures in Sentence

• **1형식** Blood flows **through our bodies.** 피는 흐른다 / 우리의 신체를 통과하여

• **2형식** Kind words are the music of the world. 친절한 말은 세상의 음악이다

• **3형식** I can't remember my password. 나는 내 암호를 기억할 수 없다

• **4형식** Santa Claus will **not** give crying children **presents.** 산타클로스는 우는 아이들에게 선물을 주지 않을 것이다

• **5형식** We should keep Earth clean. 우리는 지구를 깨끗하게 유지해야 한다

10 Structures in Block

2. 5형식 X 구와 절

to-v: to부정사(to infinitive) ⓥ: 원형부정사(bare infinitive)
v-ing: 동명사/현재분사(gerund / present participle) **v-ed**: 과거분사(past participle)

영어 문장의 독해가 어려운 이유 중 하나는 문장이 개별 단어뿐만 아니라 그것들의 덩어리인 구 또는 절로 이루어진 경우가 많기 때문이다. (• 구: to-v ~ / v-ing ~ / 전치사 + 명사 • 절: 접속사 + s + v ~)

Structures in Sentence

- **1형식** Keeping a positive attitude matters. 긍정적인 태도를 유지하는 것은 중요하다

- **2형식** The problem is that no one knows the truth. 문제는 ~이다 / 아무도 진실을 모른다는 것

- **3형식** I can't understand what you are saying. 나는 이해할 수 없다 / 네가 말하고 있는 것을

- **4형식** Understanding other cultures gives us a big edge over others.
  다른 문화를 이해하는 것은 준다 / 우리에게 타인들에 대한 큰 우위를

- **5형식** Big data allows us to learn more about our daily lives.
  빅데이터는 가능하게 한다 / 우리가 우리의 일상생활에 관해 더 많이 아는 것을

3. 5형식 X 후치수식어

● 후치수식어

to-v ~ / v-ing[v-ed] ~ 전치사 + 명사
that[wh-] + (s) + v ~

영어 문장의 독해가 어려운 또 다른 이유는 명사를 수식하는 긴 수식어가 우리말과는 달리 명사의 뒤에 오기 때문이다. 이런 긴 수식어인 to-v ~, v-ing[v-ed] ~, 전치사 + 명사, 접속사 + s + v ~를 하나의 덩어리로 익히는 훈련이 필요하다.

Structures in Sentence

● **1형식** The efforts **to understand the world around us** began several thousand years ago.
노력들은 / [우리 주변의 세상을 이해하려는] / 수천 년 전에 시작되었다

● **2형식** Today **which I spent vainly** is tomorrow **which the dead longed.**
오늘은 / [내가 헛되이 보낸] / 내일이다 / [죽은 사람들이 갈망했던]

● **3형식** We all have a tendency **to look at our own flaws with a magnifying glass.**
우리 모두는 경향을 가지고 있다 / [자신의 결점을 돋보기를 가지고 들여다보는]

● **4형식** I have told you everything **that happened.**
나는 너에게 모든 것을 말했다 / [일어났던]

● **5형식** The challenges **in your life** require you to call on the inner resources **residing deep inside you.** 어려움들은 / [여러분의 삶에 있어서의] / 요구한다 / 여러분이 내적인 자원을 요청하도록 / [여러분의 내면의 깊은 곳에 자리하고 있는]

4. 5형식 X 부사수식어

부사어는 동사, 형용사, 다른 부사, 또는 문장 전체를 수식하는 말이다. 부사(구/절)는 문장의 앞, 중간, 끝을 가리지 않고 불쑥불쑥 등장하여 문장의 구조를 파악하기 어렵게 만들므로 이를 식별해내면 구조를 파악하기 수월해진다.

문장 앞에 오는 경우
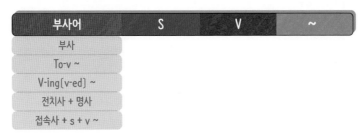

문장 뒤에 오는 경우

문장 앞·뒤에 오는 경우
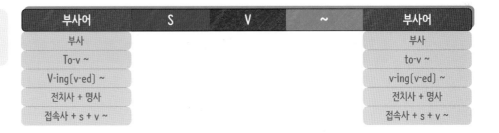

Structures in Sentence

- **문장 앞** **Feeling frustrated,** she began to think about giving up on the race.
  좌절감을 느껴서 / 그녀는 경주를 포기하는 것을 생각하기 시작했다

- **문장 뒤** I fell asleep **as soon as my head hit the pillow.**
  나는 잠들었다 / 내 머리에 베개를 베자마자

- **문장 앞·뒤** **To secure your seat,** please arrive **at least 15 minutes prior to departure.**
  당신의 좌석을 확보하기 위해서는 / 도착하십시오 / 적어도 출발 15분 전에

5. 어순의 변화

의문문이나 도치 구문 등에서는 앞에서 다룬 일반적인 평서문 문장과 어순이 달라지므로 그 규칙을 잘 익혀두어야 한다.

의문문

● 의문사가 없는 경우

be동사	S	~

조동사	S	본동사	~

● 의문사가 있는 경우

의문사	be동사	S	~

의문사	조동사	S	본동사	~

도치 구문

● 부정어가 문두에 오는 경우

부정어	be동사	S	~

부정어	조동사	S	본동사	~

● 부사어(장소·방향 등)가 문두에 오는 경우

부사어	V	S	~

● 주격보어가 문두에 오는 경우

C	V	S	~

Structures in Sentence

● **의문문**　Are you hungry? / Did you eat lunch?
　　　　너는 배가 고프니?　　　　너는 점심을 먹었니?

　　　　Where is the nearest subway station? / What do you want to have for dinner?
　　　　가장 가까운 지하철역이 어디에 있니?　　　　너는 저녁으로 무엇을 먹기를 원하니?

● **도치 구문**　Not a word has she written since the exam started.
　　　　한 단어도 그녀는 쓰지 않았다 / 시험이 시작된 이후로

　　　　At the center of non-violence stands the principle of love.
　　　　비폭력의 중심에는 / 사랑의 원리가 놓여 있다

　　　　Happy is the man who is contented with his lot.
　　　　행복하다 / 사람은 / [자신의 운명에 만족하는]

Rules in Block

영어 문장을 빠르고 정확하게 파악할 수 있도록 해주는
구문의 10가지 기본 규칙을 먼저 빠르게 익혀보세요!
해당 Unit으로 가면 각 규칙을 상세하게 학습할 수 있습니다.

Rule 01 주어를 덩어리로 파악하라. → unit 01~06

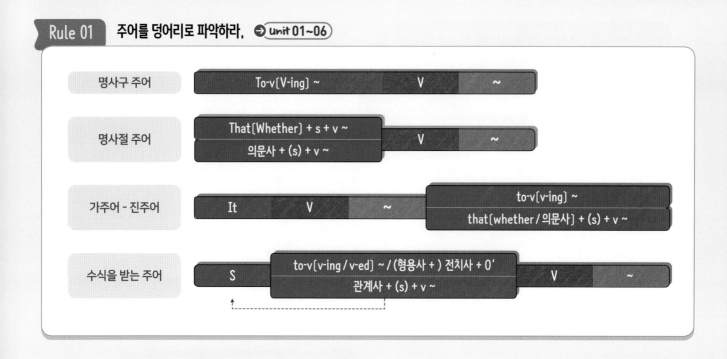

Rule 02 동사 이후를 예측하면서 읽어라. (※ 평서문 기준)

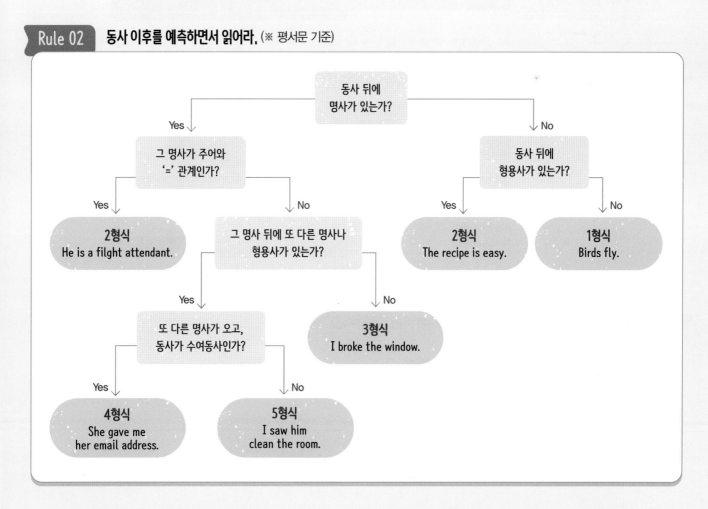

Rule 03 동사의 형태에 주목하라. → unit 07~09

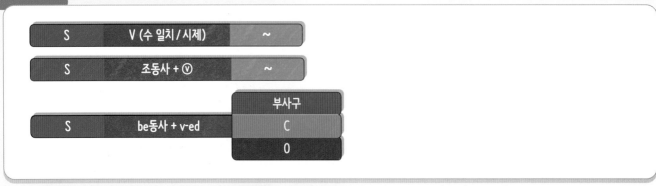

Rule 04 목적어를 덩어리로 파악하라. → unit 10~14

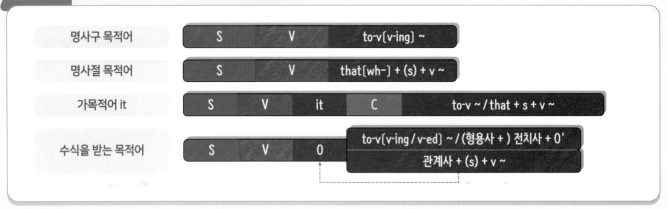

Rule 05 보어를 덩어리로 파악하라. → unit 15~20

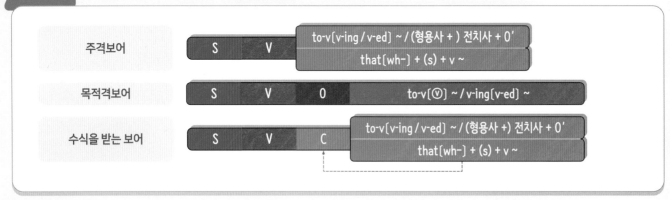

Rule 06 부사구와 부사절의 앞 또는 뒤에서 끊어라. → unit 29~34, 35~40

Rule 07 보충 설명은 가볍게 처리하라. ➡ unit 28, 53

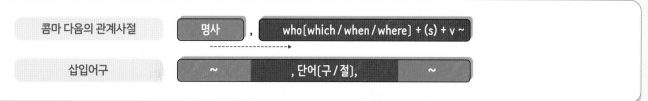

| 콤마 다음의 관계사절 | 명사 | , | who[which / when / where] + (s) + v ~ |
| 삽입어구 | ~ | , 단어(구 / 절), | ~ |

Rule 08 주요 구문의 패턴을 익혀라. ➡ unit 41~42, 45~48

● 가정법: if절과 주절의 동사의 형태에 유의하라.

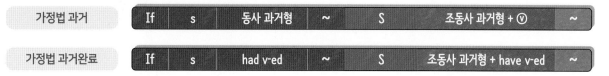

| 가정법 과거 | If | s | 동사 과거형 | ~ | S | 조동사 과거형 + ⓥ | ~ |
| 가정법 과거완료 | If | s | had v-ed | ~ | S | 조동사 과거형 + have v-ed | ~ |

● 비교구문: 비교 표현을 익혀라.

원급 구문	S	V	as	형용사 / 부사	as + s + v ~
비교급 구문	S	V	비교급		than ~
최상급 구문	S	V	the + 최상급	in [of] + 명사 / (that +) s + have (ever) v-ed

Rule 09 특수 구문의 규칙을 파악하라. ➡ unit 49~54

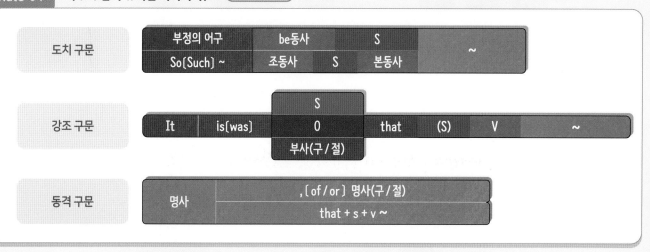

| 도치 구문 | 부정의 어구 | be동사 | S | ~ |
| | So[Such] ~ | 조동사 | S | 본동사 | |

| 강조 구문 | It | is[was] | S / O / 부사(구 / 절) | that | (S) | V | ~ |

| 동격 구문 | 명사 | , [of / or] 명사(구 / 절) / that + s + v ~ |

Rule 10 관용적인 표현은 따로 암기하라.

- 전치사구와 짝을 이루는 동사 구문 ➡ unit 07
- 부사적 to-v의 관용 구문 ➡ unit 31
- 동명사의 관용 구문 ➡ unit 59
- 분사구문의 관용 구문 ➡ unit 34
- 상관접속사 구문 ➡ unit 56

우선순위 구문 학습: 구와 절

문장은 개별 단어뿐만 아니라, 두 개 이상의 단어가 모인 구 또는 절로 이루어질 수 있다. 이러한 구와 절을 하나의 덩어리로 인식하면서, 문장에서 그 역할을 파악하는 것이 구문독해의 핵심이다.

구
- 둘 이상의 단어들이 모여 문장에서 명사, 형용사, 부사와 같은 하나의 품사 역할을 하는 것으로, 절과는 달리 '주어'와 '동사'를 포함하고 있지 않다.
- 부정사, 동명사, 분사, 그리고 '전치사+명사'가 명사구, 형용사구, 부사구를 이끈다.

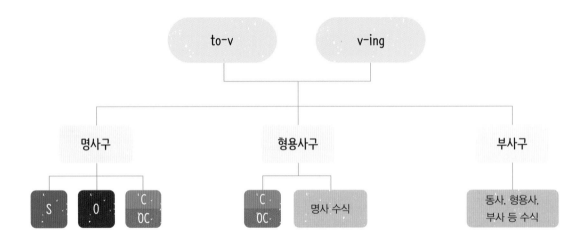

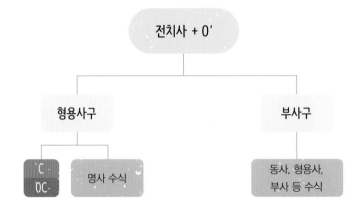

1 명사구

주어, 목적어, 보어 역할을 한다. 부정사와 동명사가 이끄는 구가 여기에 해당된다.

[주어]

01 **To marry a knight in shining armor** was the dream of some girls.
빛나는 갑옷을 입은 기사와 결혼하는 것은   / 일부 소녀들의 꿈이었다

02 **Sending text messages** is a fast and cheap communication channel.
텍스트 메시지를 보내는 것은   / 빠르고 저렴한 통신 수단이다

[목적어]

03 Most parents want **to give their children the best start in life.**
대부분의 부모들은 원한다   / 자신의 자녀들에게 인생에서 최상의 출발을 주는 것을

04 The suspect finally admitted **committing that crime.**
그 용의자는 마침내 인정했다   / 그 범죄를 저질렀다는 것을

[보어]

05 The essential role of hand gestures is **to mark the points of emphasis**
손짓의 본질적인 역할은 ~이다   / 우리의 발언에 강조점들을 나타내는 것
in our speech.

06 Our goal is **expanding the business to the international level.**
우리의 목표는 ~이다 / 그 사업을 국제적 수준으로 확장하는 것

2 형용사구

보어의 역할을 하거나 명사를 수식한다. 부정사나 분사가 이끄는 구, 전치사구가 여기에 해당된다.

[보어]

07 The man's alibi turned out **to be false.**
그 남자의 알리바이는 거짓인 것으로 드러났다

08 The movie was **beyond my imagination.**
그 영화는 나의 상상력을 넘어섰다

09 You will see flowers **dancing in the wind.**
너는 보게 될 것이다   / 꽃들이 바람에 춤추고 있는 것을

[명사 수식]

10 Fiber has the ability **to keep your digestive system working smoothly**.

식이섬유는 능력을 가지고 있다   / [당신의 소화계가 부드럽게 작동하게 하는]

11 The number of people **visiting museums** increased slightly last year.

사람들의 수가   / [박물관을 방문하는]   / 작년에 약간 증가했다

12 Behaviors **stopped by mild punishment** almost always reappear later.

행동들은   / [가벼운 처벌에 의해서 중단된]   / 거의 언제나 나중에 다시 나타난다

13 The topic **under discussion** was relevant to the current issues **about**

토론 중인 주제는 관련되었다   / 시사 문제들과   / [지구

global warming.

온난화에 관한]

3 부사구

동사, 형용사 등을 수식한다. 부정사, 분사구문, 또는 전치사구가 부사구로 쓰인다.

14 Advertisers want to use colorful language **to get the customer's interest**.

광고업자들은 다채로운 언어를 사용하기를 원한다   / 소비자의 관심을 끌기 위해서

15 This chapter is difficult **to understand**.

이 장은 어렵다   / 이해하기에

16 They sailed open ocean in large canoes, **navigating by the sun and**

그들은 망망대해를 항해했다   / 큰 카누를 타고서   / 해와 별들에 의지하여 항해하면서

stars.

―――――――― 문장 전체 수식 ――――――――

17 **By good fortune**, everything worked out **all right in the end**.

다행스럽게도   / 모든 것이 마침내 잘 해결되었다

> 절
> • 절은 주어와 동사를 포함하는 둘 이상의 단어들이 모인 것이다.
> • 하나의 문장은 두 개 이상의 절로 구성될 수 있다. 이 때, 두 절의 관계가 대등하면 등위절이라고 하고, 대등하지 않으면 주절과 종속절로 나뉜다.

1 등위절

등위접속사(and, but, or, for, so 등)에 의해서 대등하게 연결되는 두 개의 절을 말한다.

01 The weather was perfect **and** the sun never stopped shining.
　　　　〈등위절 1〉　　　　　------ 대등 ------　　　〈등위절 2〉
　　　　날씨는 완벽했다　　　　　　　　　　/ 그리고 태양은 **결코** 빛나는 것을 멈추지 **않았다**

02 She's very upset now, **so** we had better leave her alone.
　　　　〈등위절 1〉　　------ 대등 ------　　　〈등위절 2〉
　　　　그녀는 지금 아주 심란하다　　　　/ 따라서 우리는 그녀를 혼자 있도록 두는 게 더 낫겠다

2 종속절

하나의 절이 다른 절 안에 포함되어 명사, 형용사, 부사의 역할을 할 때 이 절을 종속절이라고 하고, 종속절을 거느리는 절을 주절이라고 한다. 종속절에는 명사절, 형용사절, 부사절이 있다.

[명사절]
주어, 목적어, 보어 등의 역할을 하는 절이다. 접속사 that, whether, 의문사(who, what, when, how 등), wh-ever 등이 명사절을 이끈다.

명사절의 형태	that+ s + v ~ whether[if] + s + v ~ 의문사[wh-ever] + (s) + v ~

03 What comes from soil returns to soil.

땅에서 오는 것은 　　　　　　　 / 땅으로 돌아간다

| 목적어 |

04 I can't remember **how the film ends.**

나는 기억할 수 없다 　　　 / 그 영화가 어떻게 끝나는지를

| 보어 |

05 The question is **whether technology is going to be our servant or our**

그 문제는 ~이다 　　　 / 기술이 우리의 종이 되느냐 우리의 주인이 되느냐

master.

| 동격 |

06 People once mocked the idea **that the earth is round.**

사람들은 예전에 생각을 조롱했다 　　　　　　 / [= 지구가 둥글다는]

| 전치사의 목적어 |

07 Focus on **what we have in common,** not on our differences.

　　　　전치사　　　　　　 전치사의 목적어

초점을 맞춰라 / 우리가 공통으로 가진 것에 　　　　 / 우리의 차이점이 아니라

[형용사절]

명사를 수식하는 절이다. 관계대명사 who, which, that과 관계부사 when, where, why 등이 형용사절을
이끈다.

형용사절의 형태	명사 + who[which / that] + (s) + v ~
	명사 + when[where / why / that] + s + v ~

| 관계대명사가 이끄는 형용사절 |

08 Hope is a wing **that gives you victory over obstacles.**

희망은 날개이다 　 / [당신에게 장애물에 대한 승리를 선사하는]

| 관계부사가 이끄는 형용사절 |

09 Nature is the only place **where you can feel unconditionally loved.**

자연은 유일한 곳이다 　　　　 / [당신이 무조건적으로 사랑받는 것을 느낄 수 있는]

| 관계사가 생략된 형용사절 |

10 Someone's potential is an ability ✔**they have not yet discovered.**

어떤 사람의 잠재력은 능력이다 　　　　 / [그들이 아직 발견하지 못한]

[부사절]

문장에서 부사 역할을 하면서 시간, 이유, 조건, 목적, 결과, 반전, 양태 등의 뜻을 나타낸다.

부사절의 형태	접속사 + S + V ~
부사절을 이끄는 접속사	• 시간: when, while(~ 하는 동안에), since, until[till], as(~할 때, ~하면서), as soon as(~하자마자) • 이유: because, since(~때문에), as, now that(~이니까) • 조건: if, unless(~하지 않는다면) • 목적·결과: so that(~하기 위해서), so ~ that ...(아주 ~해서 …하다) • 반전·대조: though, although, while(~인 반면에), whether A or B(A이든 B이든) • 양태: as(~처럼), as if(마치 ~인 것처럼)

11 My subconscious works on things **while I'm asleep.** 시간

나의 잠재의식은 일들에 작용한다　　　　　　　　　／ 내가 잠들어 있는 동안에

12 **Now that you've grown up,** you must stop this childish behavior. 이유

네가 다 컸으니까　　　　　　　　　／ 너는 이런 유치한 행동을 그만둬야 한다

13 A moving object continues to move **unless some force is used to stop**

움직이는 물체는 움직이기를 계속한다　　　　　／ 어떤 힘이 그것을 멈추기 위해서 사용되지 않는다면

it. 조건

14 They grow vegetables in the backyard **so that they can have fresh**

그들은 뒤뜰에서 채소를 재배한다　　　　　　　　　／ 그들이 신선한 채소를 먹을 수 있도록 하기 위해서

vegetables all year round. 목적

　　　　　／ 일년 내내

15 **Whether we like it or not,** the world we live in has changed a great deal. 반전

우리가 좋아하든 그렇지 않든　　　／ 세상은　　　／ [우리가 사는] / 변해왔다　　　／ 많이

16 **Just as there are rules for driving on ordinary highways,** there are rules

규칙들이 있는 것처럼　　　　　　　／ [보통의 고속도로에서 운전하기 위한]　　　／ 규칙들이 있다

for "driving" on the Internet. 양태

／ [인터넷상에서 '운전하기' 위한]

STAGE I

문장성분 중심의 구문

Chapter 01 주어의 파악

Chapter 02 동사 구문

Chapter 03 목적어의 파악

Chapter 04 보어의 파악

주어의 파악

☑ 영어 문장 독해의 시작은 주어를 찾는 것이다. 주어의 파악이 어려운 경우는 주로 다음과 같다.

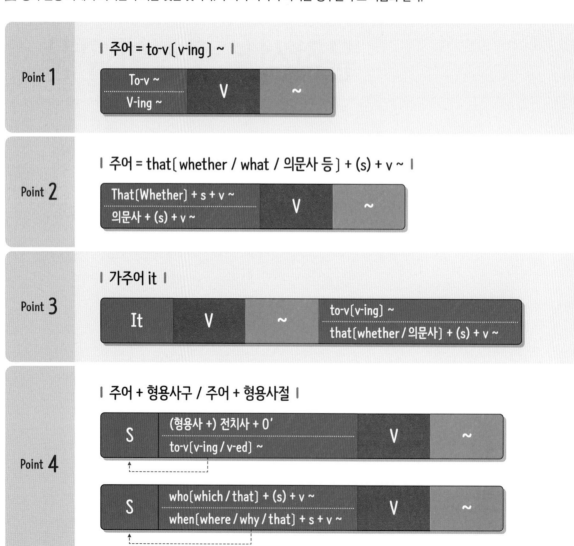

Point 1

| 주어 = to-v [v-ing] ~ |

| To-v ~ / V-ing ~ | V | ~ |

Point 2

| 주어 = that[whether / what / 의문사 등] + (s) + v ~ |

| That[Whether] + s + v ~ / 의문사 + (s) + v ~ | V | ~ |

Point 3

| 가주어 it |

| It | V | ~ | to-v[v-ing] ~ / that[whether / 의문사] + (s) + v ~ |

Point 4

| 주어 + 형용사구 / 주어 + 형용사절 |

| S | (형용사 +) 전치사 + O' / to-v[v-ing / v-ed] ~ | V | ~ |

| S | who[which / that] + (s) + v ~ / when[where / why / that] + s + v ~ | V | ~ |

- unit 01   명사구 주어
- unit 02   명사절 주어
- unit 03   가주어 it
- unit 04   주어+형용사구
- unit 05   주어+형용사절 1
- unit 06   주어+형용사절 2

명사구 주어
→ unit 01

▷ 명사 역할을 하는 to-v와 v-ing는 주어 자리에 올 수 있다. 단, to-v는 주로 '가주어−진주어' 구문을 취한다.

명사절 주어
→ unit 02

▷ 접속사 that, whether, what, 의문사 등은 명사절을 이끌어 주어 자리에 올 수 있다.

가주어 it
→ unit 03

▷ 명사구 또는 명사절이 주어일 때 주어 자리에 it을 쓰고, 해당되는 구와 절을 문장의 뒤로 보내 '가주어−진주어' 구문을 취하는 경우가 많다.

주어를 꾸미는 형용사적 수식어
→ unit 04, 05, 06

▷ 주어가 명사나 대명사인 경우, 그 뒤에 주어를 꾸며주는 형용사적 수식어가 올 수 있다.
▷ 형용사적 수식어로는 전치사구, 준동사구, 그리고 관계사절이 있다.

명사구 주어

중요도 ★★★
난이도 ★★★

Block Board

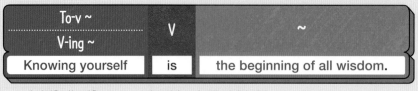

To-v ~ / V-ing ~	V	~
Knowing yourself	is	the beginning of all wisdom.
네 자신을 아는 것은	/ ~이다	/ 모든 지혜의 시작

- to-v와 v-ing가 이끄는 명사구는 주어의 역할을 하고, '~하는 것'으로 해석한다.
- 명사구 주어는 준동사로서 동사의 성질을 가지고 있으므로, 그 뒤에 자체의 목적어, 보어, 수식어를 동반할 수 있다.

  Tip to-v나 v-ing 다음에 절이 이어지는 경우, 그 절이 끝난 뒤에 나오는 동사 앞까지가 문장 전체의 주어이다.

Standard Sentences

01 **Getting meaningful feedback on your performance** is a powerful
의미 있는 피드백을 얻는 것은　　　　　　　 / 당신의 성과에 대해　　　　　 / 강력한 전략이다

strategy for learning anything.
　　　　 / [어떤 것을 배우기 위한]

▶「v-ing + 목적어」가 주어

02 **To love and to be loved** is the greatest happiness of existence.
사랑하고 사랑받는 것은　　　　 / 존재의 가장 큰 행복이다　　　　　 *Sydney Smith*

▶ 등위접속사 and로 두 개의 to-v가 병렬 연결됨

A 다음 문장에서 주어를 파악하면서, 각 문장을 해석하시오.

03 Knowing how climate has changed over millions of years is vital to properly assess current global warming trends.

▶「v-ing + how절」이 주어

04 Giving people the latitude and flexibility to use their judgment and apply their talents **rapidly** accelerates **progress**.

▶「v-ing + 간접목적어 + 직접목적어」가 주어

05 To think that you know something without actually knowing it is a serious mistake.

▶「to-v + that절」이 주어

B 다음 문장에서 주어에 밑줄을 치고, 각 문장을 해석하시오.

06 Considering issues in an appropriate context will help you accurately evaluate the pros and cons of a decision.

▶ help + O + to-v(ⓥ)

07 Is passing large sums of wealth on to your children good for them or right for society? *Bill Gates*

◀ **Know More** **Rainbow p.7** ▶
▶ 의문문의 어순: 「be동사 + 주어 + 보어」

(수능) **08** Raising awareness of children about the particular characteristics of SNS and the potential long-term impact of a seemingly trivial act is crucial.

09 To conquer oneself is the best and noblest victory; to be vanquished by one's own nature is the worst and most ignoble defeat. *Plato*

C 다음 네모 안에서 어법에 맞는 것을 고르시오.

10 [Investing / Investment] regularly in learning opportunities is one of the greatest gifts you can give yourself.

11 Having a large vocabulary (A) [make / makes] reading more enjoyable and (B) [increase / increases] the range of materials that you can explore.

▶ to-v 또는 v-ing가 이끄는 주어는 단수 취급

12 To say that AI will start doing what it wants for its own purposes [is / are] like saying a calculator will start making its own calculations.
Oren Etzioni

S·S 01 performance 성과, 수행   02 existence 존재
A 03 vital 필수적인   assess 판단하다   current 현재의; 흐름   04 latitude 자유   flexibility 융통성   accelerate 촉진시키다
B 06 context 맥락, 문맥   pros and cons 찬반양론   07 sum 액수, 금액   08 awareness 인식   potential ~이 될 수 있는   long-term 장기적인   trivial 사소한   crucial 매우 중요한   09 conquer 정복하다   noble 숭고한, 고귀한   vanquish 정복하다   ignoble (일이) 수치스러운
C 11 range 영역, 범위   12 calculator 계산기

명사절 주어

Block Board

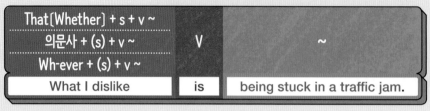

That[Whether] + s + v ~		
의문사 + (s) + v ~	V	~
Wh-ever + (s) + v ~		
What I dislike	is	being stuck in a traffic jam.

내가 싫어하는 것은 / ~이다 / 교통 혼잡에 꼼짝 못하게 되는 것

- 「접속사 + 주어 + 동사」가 명사 역할을 할 때, 문장의 주어로 쓰일 수 있다.
  Form ▷ That + s + v ~: ~라고 하는 것　　　　▷ Whether + s + v ~: ~인지 아닌지
  　　　 ▷ What + (s) + v ~: ~하는 것, 무엇을 ~하는지　▷ Who[Where / When / Why] + (s) + v ~: 누가[어디에 / 언제 / 왜] ~하는지
  　　　 ▷ Whoever[Whichever / Whatever] + (s) + v ~: ~하는 사람은 누구나[것은 어느 것이나 / 것은 무엇이나]
  Tip 명사절이 끝난 후 나오는 동사 앞까지가 주어이며, 명사절 주어는 보통 단수로 취급한다.

Standard Sentences

[모의] 01 **That some organisms must starve in nature is deeply** regrettable
일부 유기체가 자연에서 굶주려야 한다는 것은 / 정말 유감스럽고 슬프다

and sad.

▶ 주어가 that절인 경우, 대개 '가주어-진주어' 구문으로 쓰인다. **● unit 03**

[모의] 02 **What works for most job seekers is to look through their past**
대부분의 구직자들에게 효과가 있는 것은 / 그들의 과거의 경험을 살펴보는 것이다

experiences **to help them build for the future.**
/ 그들이 미래를 준비하는 것을 돕기 위해서

▶ What + (s) + v ~
① ~하는 것
② 무엇이[무엇을] ~하는 것

A 다음 문장에서 주어를 파악하면서, 각 문장을 해석하시오.

03 Whether an object floats on water depends on the density of both
the object and the water.

04 When Stonehenge was built is known, **but** why it was built remains
a mystery.

･･･ **Know More**　Rainbow p.8
▶ 간접의문문의 어순: 「의문사 + s + v」

05 Whatever is worth doing at all is worth doing well. *Lord Chesterfield*

B 다음 문장에서 주어에 밑줄을 치고, 각 문장을 해석하시오.

06 Whoever acquires knowledge but does not practice it is as one who ploughs but does not sow. *Saadi*

07 What we have done for ourselves alone dies with us; what we have done for others and the world remains and is immortal.

08 How the universe began is a fundamental question which has occupied the minds of men from prehistoric times.

09 That witches caused disasters and misfortunes was widely believed among early American settlers.

··▶ **Know More**   Rainbow p.9

C 다음 네모 안에서 어법에 맞는 것을 고르시오.

10 What makes organisms different from the materials that compose them is / are their level of organization.

11 How successful we are / are we at forming good relationships and how valued we feel by other people make a big difference in how good we feel about ourselves.

▶ 두 개의 명사절이 주어

12 Whatever / However we expect with confidence becomes our own self-fulfilling prophecy.

*self-fulfilling prophecy 자기 충족적 예언

▶ however가 이끄는 절은 부사절이며, 명사절로 쓸 수 없음

A 03 float 뜨다   density 밀도   **05** be worth v-ing ~할 가치가 있다   at all (긍정문) 어쨌든
B 06 plough 갈다, 일구다   sow 씨를 뿌리다   **07** immortal 영원한, 불멸의   **08** occupy (마음·주의를) 끌다, 차지하다   prehistoric times 선사시대
09 witch 마녀   disaster 재난, 재해   misfortune 불운   settler 정착민
C 10 compose 구성하다   organization 구성, 조직   **11** valued 소중한; 중요한   **12** confidence 자신감

가주어 it

Block Board

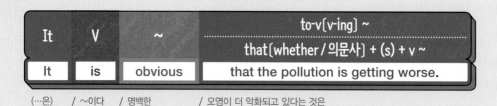

It	V	~	to-v[v-ing] ~
			that[whether / 의문사] + (s) + v ~
It	is	obvious	that the pollution is getting worse.

(…은) / ~이다 / 명백한 / 오염이 더 악화되고 있다는 것은

- 명사구나 명사절이 주어로 쓰여 길어지는 경우, 주어 자리에 It을 쓰고 명사구나 명사절은 문장 뒤로 보낸다.

Form To-v[V-ing] ~ + V + … ➡ It + V + … + to-v[v-ing] ~

That[Whether / 의문사] + (s) + v ~ + V … ➡ It + V + … + that[whether / 의문사] + (s) + v ~

Tip 문장의 앞에 있는 It이 대명사가 아니라면, 뒤에 오는 명사구나 명사절을 대신하는 가주어일 수 있다.

Standard Sentences

01 It is usual in this world for the weak to become the victim of the
(…은) 이 세상에서 흔하다 / 약자가 강자의 희생양이 되는 것은

strong.

▶ to-v의 의미상의 주어: to-v
앞에 「for[of] + O」로 씀

02 It is a common superstition that a black cat crossing your path is
(…은) 흔한 미신이다 / 검은 고양이가 [당신의 길을 가로지르는] /

bad luck.
불운이라는 것은

A 다음 문장에서 가주어 It이 가리키는 것을 파악하면서, 각 문장을 해석하시오.

03 It's fine to celebrate success but it is more important to heed the lessons of failure. *Bill Gates*

04 It's no use locking the stable door after the horse has bolted. *Irish Proverb*

05 It matters not what someone is born, but what they grow to be.

the novel <Harry Potter and the Goblet of Fire>

▶ It = what + s + v ~

B 다음 문장에서 가주어 It[it]이 가리키는 것에 밑줄을 치고, 각 문장을 해석하시오.

(모의) **06** It is the essence of scientific thinking to propose alternative ideas and then to test them against existing concepts.

07 It was very careless of her to leave the medicine where the children could reach it.

▶ It + be동사 + 성질·태도를 나타내는 형용사 + of + O' + to-v

(모의) **08** With all the passion for being slim, it is no wonder that many people view any amount of visible fat on the body as something to get rid of.

(모의) **09** It's amazing how much more you learn when you pause, quiet your mind, and listen to what others say.

▶ pause, quiet ~, and listen to ~: A, B, and C 병렬구조

C 다음 네모 안에서 어법에 맞는 것을 고르시오.

10 Grown-ups never understand anything by themselves, and it is tiresome for / of children to be always and forever explaining things to them. *the novel <The Little Prince>*

11 With today's latest virtual reality technologies, it is now possible for designers create / to create real-world situations in a digital environment.

12 It's not yet clear that / whether the Prime Minister's resignation offer is a serious one, or whether it's simply a tactical move.

▶ 확실한 내용은 that절, 불확실한 내용은 whether절을 씀

S·S 01 victim 희생양; 희생   **02** superstition 미신

A 03 heed ~에 주의를 기울이다   **04** stable 마구간   bolt 달아나다   **05** matter 중요하다

B 06 essence 본질   alternative 대신하는   **07** careless 조심성이 없는   **08** get rid of ~을 제거하다   **09** pause 잠시 멈추다   quiet 진정시키다

C 10 tiresome 따분한   **11** latest 최신의   virtual reality 가상현실   **12** prime minister 수상, 국무총리   resignation 사직, 사임   offer 의사(표시), 제안   tactical 전술의, 전략적인   move 조치; 이동

주어 + 형용사구

중요도 ★★☆
난이도 ★★☆

Block Board

S	(형용사 +) 전치사 + O' to-v[v-ing / v-ed] ~	V	~
The difference	between ordinary and extraordinary	is	that little extra.
차이는	/ [평범과 비범 사이의]	/ ~이다	/ 저 작은 extra

- 주어는 전치사구, 준동사구(to-v, v-ing, v-ed), 관계사절의 수식을 받아 길어질 수 있다.

  Tip 뒤에서 주어를 수식하는 어구를 괄호로 묶고 동사를 찾는다. 특히 수식어구로 과거분사(v-ed)가 쓰인 경우, 동사 과거형과 헷갈리지 않도록 유의해야 한다. (→ 주어를 수식하는 과거분사는 주어와 수동의 의미 관계이며, 뒤에 진짜 동사가 등장한다.)

Standard Sentences

01 The ability **to ask the right question** is more than half the battle of
능력은 　　/ [적절한 질문을 하는]　　　　 / 전투의 절반 이상이다　　　　　　　　 /

finding the answer. *Thomas J. Watson*
[답을 찾는]
▶ S + to-v ~ + V

02 The candidates **applying for the job** must know the qualifications
지원자들은 　　/ [그 일자리에 지원하는]　　 / 알아야 한다　 / 자격 요건을

required for the job.
/ [그 일자리에 요구되는]
▶ S + v-ing ~ + V

A 다음 문장에서 주어를 수식하는 형용사구를 파악하면서, 각 문장을 해석하시오.

모의 **03** The simple act of typing a few words into a search engine will
virtually instantaneously produce links related to the topic at hand.
▶ S + 전치사구 + V

04 The only way to understand a word fully is to see it in use in many
contexts.

05 The microwaves emitted from mobile phones can interfere with
sensitive electronic equipment.
▶ S + v-ed ~ + V

B 다음 문장에서 주어를 수식하는 형용사구를 괄호로 묶고, 각 문장을 해석하시오.

06 An outstanding feature in the evolution of modern man is the growth of the size of the brain.

(수능) **07** Many present efforts to guard and maintain human progress, to meet human needs, and to realize human ambitions are simply unsustainable—in both rich and poor nations.

▶ 세 개의 to-v ~가 주어를 수식함

08 Scientists studying genes in yeast cells recently found a chemical that seems to work with a longevity gene to increase the yeast cell's lifespan.

09 Foreign, or alien, species introduced accidentally or intentionally into new territories often do well in their new homes because conditions may be highly favorable to their growth and reproduction.

C 다음 네모 안에서 어법에 맞는 것을 고르시오.

(수능) **10** Speculations about the meaning and purpose of prehistoric art rely / relies heavily on analogies drawn with modern-day hunter-gatherer societies.

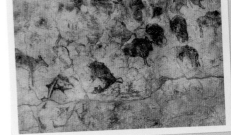

▲ Prehistoric Altamira Cave Painting

11 The best way to protect your computer from viruses and spyware is / are to install a recommended anti-virus program.

*spyware 스파이웨어(인터넷 사용자를 염탐하는 악성 소프트웨어 프로그램)

12 The carbon dioxide given off when coal and oil are burned is / are accumulating in the atmosphere and causing temperatures to rise.

S·S 01 battle 전투, 싸움　**02** candidate 지원자, 후보자　qualification 자격 요건
A 03 virtually 거의　instantaneously 바로, 당장　at hand 바로 쓸 수 있도록　**05** microwave 극초단파　interfere with ~에 지장을 주다
B 06 outstanding 두드러진, 눈에 띄는　**07** simply (부정문) 도저히, 결코　unsustainable 지속할 수 없는　**08** yeast 효모　longevity 장수
　　lifespan 수명　**09** alien 외래의　territory 영역, 지역　favorable 유리한
C 10 speculation 고찰, 추측　analogy 유사성　hunter-gatherer 수렵 채집　**11** install 설치하다　**12** give off ~을 배출하다

주어 + 형용사절 1

Block Board

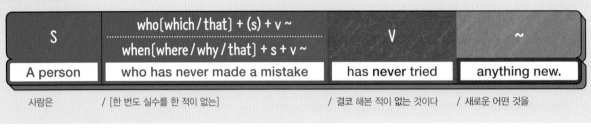

S	who[which/that] + (s) + v ~	V	~
	when[where/why/that] + s + v ~		
A person	who has never made a mistake	has never tried	anything new.
사람은	/ [한 번도 실수를 한 적이 없는]	/ 결코 해본 적이 없는 것이다	/ 새로운 어떤 것을

- 주어는 형용사절의 수식을 받아 길어질 수 있으며, 관계대명사 또는 관계부사가 형용사절을 이끈다.
  ▷ 관계대명사: who, which, that   ▷ 관계부사: when, where, why, that

  Tip 주어를 뒤에서 수식하는 형용사절을 괄호로 묶어 주어를 파악하고, 동사를 찾는다.

Standard Sentences

01 Species **which have not been able to survive in changing living**
종들은   / [생존할 수 없었던   / 변화하는 생활 환경에서]

conditions have become extinct.
                / 멸종되어왔다

▶ S + 관계대명사절 + V

02 The reason **why we have two ears and only one mouth** is that we
이유는   / [우리가 두 개의 귀와 오직 하나의 입을 가지고 있는]   / ~이다 / 우리가

may listen more and talk less.
더 많이 듣고 더 적게 말하려는 것

▶ S + 관계부사절 + V

Ⓐ 다음 문장에서 주어를 수식하는 절을 파악하면서, 각 문장을 해석하시오.

(수능!) **03** The creativity that children possess needs to be cultivated throughout
their development.

(모의) **04** A person who works on an assembly line is **well** aware of the
efficiency that can be gained through repetition.

05 The one area where the Internet could be considered to be an aid
to thinking is the rapid procurement of new information.

B 다음 문장에서 주어를 수식하는 절을 괄호로 묶고, 각 문장을 해석하시오.

[모의] **06** People who have a high sense of self-efficacy tend to pursue challenging goals that may be outside the reach of the average person.

07 The idealism that freed men from most of their ancient fetters awakened women to a realization of their unequal position in society.

···➤ **Know More** Rainbow p.15 ◁

08 A classroom where students feel involved and respected will reduce discipline issues, increase student motivation, and ultimately enhance learning.

[모의] **09** The way that we behave in a given situation is often influenced by how important one value is to us relative to others.

▶ S + 관계부사절 + V: the way 뒤에는 관계부사 how 대신 that 을 씀 ● **Unit 25**

C 다음 네모 안에서 어법에 맞는 것을 고르시오.

[수능] **10** Someone who reads only newspapers and books by contemporary authors | looks / looking | to me like a near-sighted person.

11 The impressions that a child receives from his environment during the first years of life | influence / influences | his intellectual development and character very basically.

12 The period when humans began growing crops, raising animals for food, and using stone-tool technology | is / are | referred to as the Neolithic period.

*Neolithic period 신석기

A 03 cultivate 계발하다   throughout ~ 동안, ~ 내내   **04** assembly line (공장의 대량 생산) 조립 라인   **05** procurement 입수, 확보
B 06 self-efficacy 자기 효능감   pursue 추구하다   **07** idealism 이상주의   fetter 족쇄   awaken A to B A에게 B를 일깨우다   realization 자각, 인식   **08** discipline 훈육; 징계   ultimately 궁극적으로, 결국   enhance 향상시키다   **09** relative to ~에 비하여; ~에 관하여
C 10 contemporary 현대의; 동시대의   near-sighted 근시안적인   **12** refer to A as B A를 B라고 부르다

주어 + 형용사절 2

중요도 ★★☆
난이도 ★★★

Block Board

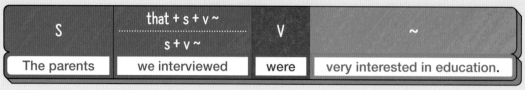

S	that + s + v ~ ········· s + v ~	V	~
The parents	we interviewed	were	very interested in education.

부모님들은 / [우리가 인터뷰한] / ~였다 / 교육에 아주 관심이 많은

- 주어 뒤에 오는 that절은 동격의 의미를 나타낼 수 있다. ● unit 52
  (동격의 that절은 문법상 명사절이나, 절을 동반하는 주어의 구문으로 보아 편의상 Unit 06에서 다루었다.)
  Form S + | that + s + v ~ | + V ~
  ┊ = ┊
  Tip 관계대명사 that 뒤에는 불완전한 절이 오고, 동격의 접속사 that 뒤에는 완전한 절이 온다.

- 주어 뒤에 관계사절이 올 때, 목적격 관계대명사와 관계부사는 종종 생략된다. ● unit 26
  Form S ✔ s + v ~ + V ~
  Tip 주어 다음에 「s + v」가 오면 그 사이에 관계사가 생략되었을 가능성이 높다.

Standard Sentences

01 The fact **that a book or publication is popular** does not necessarily
사실이 / [= 어떤 책이나 출판물이 인기가 있다는] / 반드시 만드는 것은 아니다

make it of value.
/ 그것을 가치 있게

▶ the fact + that + s + v ~
: ~라는 사실

모예 02 The bodies of flowing ice **we call glaciers** are the most spectacular
흐르는 얼음 덩어리는 / [우리가 빙하라고 부르는] / 가장 장관을 이루는 것이다

of natural features.
/ [자연의 특징 중]

A 다음 문장에서 주어를 수식하는 절을 파악하면서, 각 문장을 해석하시오.

03 The rule that nouns form their plural by adding "s" does not apply to
the word "mouse."

⋯ **Know More** Rainbow p.16

모예 04 The first impressions we form about someone often affect our
impression of subsequent perceptions of that person.

▶ impressions ✔ we form ~

05 One of the most important reasons we need to send humans to Mars
is to determine whether there ever was or even still is life on Mars.

▶ reasons ✔ we need ~

B 다음 문장에서 주어를 수식하는 절을 괄호로 묶고, 각 문장을 해석하시오.

06 The announcement that the first stages of human cloning have been achieved leaves us wondering where it will all end.

07 The living organisms we now see all have their structure based upon the element carbon.

(모의) **08** The words you speak to someone may have the potential to make or break that person, so it is important to choose words carefully.

(수능) **09** The way we wish the world to be is how, in the movies, it more often than not winds up being.

C 다음 네모 안에서 어법에 맞는 것을 고르시오.

(모의) **10** The complaint that immigrants take people's jobs is / are , like similar complaints about technology, based on an erroneously static view of the world.

(수능) **11** The seemingly impractical knowledge we gain from space probes to other worlds tell / tells us about our planet and our own role in the scheme of nature.

12 The reason people give up so quickly is / are because they look at how far they still have to go, instead of how far they have come.

S·S 01 publication 출판물   of value 가치 있는, 귀중한   02 glacier 빙하   spectacular 장관을 이루는
A 03 noun 명사   plural 복수형; 복수형의   04 subsequent 뒤이어 일어나는, 다음의   perception 인식, 지각   05 determine 밝히다, 알아내다
B 06 announcement 발표, 공고   clone 복제하다   08 potential 잠재력   09 more often than not 대개, 자주   wind up v-ing 결국 ~으로 되다
C 10 complaint 불평, 불만   immigrant 이민자   erroneously 잘못되게, 틀리게   static 고정된   11 impractical 비현실적인   scheme 체계

Review

A 다음 문장을 우리말로 해석하시오.

01 Whatever happens, happens for a reason.

02 What people eat, when they eat, and how they eat are all patterned by culture.

03 Being able to predict how other people might feel, act, or react is a skill that helps us build better relationships.

(모의) **04** With a bit of unbiased examination of our motives, it is hard to deny that we have a strong bias toward our individual interests.

B 다음 네모 안에서 어법에 맞는 것을 고르시오.

05 Learn / Learning how to persuade people will earn you the support and respect of your customers, bosses, co-workers, colleagues and friends.

06 In nature, there is no such thing as waste. What dies or becomes useless in one part of an ecosystem nourishes / nourishing another part.

07 Physical and physiological features or behaviors of an organism that once may have contributed to its reproductive success but no longer do so become / becomes susceptible to elimination by natural selection.

C 다음 괄호 안의 말을 우리말과 같은 뜻이 되도록 배열하여 문장을 완성하시오.

08 탐구를 통해 과학을 배우는 것은 오늘날 교육에서 주된 원리이다.
(through inquiry, is, learning science, a primary principle)

→ _____ in education today.

09 다른 사람들의 눈으로 우리 자신을 보는 것은 어렵다.
(the lenses of others, difficult, through, to see ourselves)

→ It is _____.

(Up!) **10** 신체 활동의 부족으로 인한 복부 지방 질환은 우리 신체의 신진대사율 감소로 이어진다.
(of physical activity, by lack, caused, the belly fat disorder)

→ _____ leads to
a decreased rate of metabolism in our body.

D 다음 문장의 빈칸에 들어가기에 가장 적절한 것을 고르시오.

11 What traditional entertainment always promised was to transport us from
our daily problems, to enable us to _____ the struggles of life.
① overcome ② prepare for ③ escape from

12 The discrepancy between the understanding of the writer and that of the
audience is the single greatest impediment to _____.
① critical reading ② accurate communication ③ commercial success

(모의) **13** Any scientist who announces a so-called discovery at a press conference
without first permitting expert reviewers to examine his or her claims is
automatically castigated as a _____.
① publicity seeker ② theoretical physicist ③ lonely pioneer

A 02 pattern 양식을 형성시키다 **04** unbiased 공정한, 편견이 없는 **B 05** colleague (함께 일하는) 동료 **07** physiological 생리
적인 susceptible to ~되기 쉬운 natural selection 자연 선택 **C 08** inquiry 탐구 primary 주된, 주요한 **10** disorder (가벼
운) 질환 metabolism 신진대사 **D 11** entertainment 오락 **12** discrepancy 불일치, 차이 impediment 장애물
13 so-called 소위, 이른바 press conference 기자 회견 castigate 혹평하다 publicity 명성, 평판 theoretical 이론적인

Get Ready!

☑ 동사는 문장에서 주어를 나머지 문장성분과 연결하는 '다리' 역할을 한다.
☑ 동사는 시제와 태가 바뀌거나 조동사와 결합하기도 하므로 동사와 관련된 어구를 하나의 덩어리로 파악해야 한다.

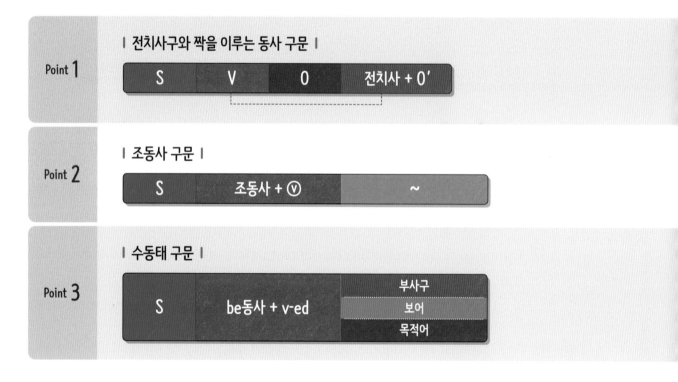

Point 1

ㅣ 전치사구와 짝을 이루는 동사 구문 ㅣ

| S | V | O | 전치사 + O' |

Point 2

ㅣ 조동사 구문 ㅣ

| S | 조동사 + ⓥ | ~ |

Point 3

ㅣ 수동태 구문 ㅣ

S	be동사 + v-ed	부사구
		보어
		목적어

- Unit 07 전치사구와 짝을 이루는 동사 구문
- Unit 08 조동사 구문
- Unit 09 수동태 구문

전치사구와 짝을 이루는 동사 구문 Unit 07	▷ 어떤 타동사는 목적어 다음에 전치사구와 함께 쓰이므로, 이런 동사 구문은 숙어처럼 익혀 두어야 한다.
조동사 구문 Unit 08	▷ 조동사는 본동사 앞에 와서 동사의 기능 또는 의미를 확장시켜준다. ▷ 빠르고 정확한 문장 독해를 위해 조동사 관용 구문을 숙지해야 한다.
수동태 구문 Unit 09	▷ 수동태는 「be동사＋v-ed」의 형태로 쓰며 '~되다, ~ 당하다'로 해석한다. ▷ 수동태 동사 뒤에는 부사(구), 보어, 또는 목적어가 올 수 있고, 「by＋O」는 종종 생략된다.

전치사구와 짝을 이루는 동사 구문

Block Board

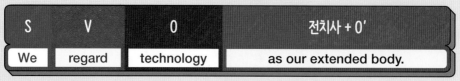

S	V	O	전치사 + O'
We	regard	technology	as our extended body.
우리는	/ 여긴다	/ 기술을	/ 우리의 확장된 신체로서

- **전치사구와 짝을 이뤄 의미를 나타내는 동사**
  - ▷ regard(look upon / think of / see / view) A as B: A를 B로 여기다[간주하다]
  - ▷ blame(scold) A for B: A를 B라는 이유로 비난하다[꾸짖다]
  - ▷ prevent(stop / keep / discourage) A from v-ing: A가 ~하는 것을 막다[하지 못하게 하다]
  - ▷ distinguish(tell / know) A from B: A를 B와 구별하다
  - ▷ rob(deprive / relieve) A of B: A에게서 B를 빼앗다[덜다]
  - ▷ remind / inform / convince A of B: A에게 B를 상기시키다 / 알리다 / 확신시키다
  - ▷ owe(attribute / ascribe) A to B: A는 B의 덕분이다, A를 B의 탓으로 돌리다
  - ▷ provide(supply) A with B: A에게 B를 제공하다 (= provide B for[to] A)
  - ▷ compare A with B: A를 B와 비교하다 ⒸⒻ compare A to B: A를 B에 비유[비교]하다

Standard Sentences

(모의) **01** Many experts in childhood development **think of play** **as the "work**
많은 아동기 발달 전문가들은 / 놀이를 여긴다 / '아이들의 일로

of children."

(모의) **02** Pride **prevents individuals** **from experiencing their true value or the**
자만심은 개인들을 막는다 / 자신들의 참된 가치 또는 다른 사람들의 참된 가치를 경험하는 것으로부터

true value of others.

Ⓐ 다음 문장에서 동사와 짝을 이루는 전치사구를 파악하면서, 각 문장을 해석하시오.

03 We can compare life to a roller coaster because it has ups and downs, but it's your choice to scream or enjoy the ride.

(수능!) **04** Future generations may blame us for our wasteful ways, but they can **never** collect on our debt to them.

▶ blame A for B
= blame B on A

05 **Never** deprive someone of hope; it might be all they have.

ℬ 다음 문장에서 밑줄 친 단어와 짝을 이루는 전치사구를 동그라미하고, 각 문장을 해석하시오.

(모예) **06** The competent, confident, and caring young adults <u>saw</u> themselves as the masters of their own fate and <u>viewed</u> negative events not as threats but as challenges and even opportunities.

▶ not A but B: A가 아니라 B

07 Movies <u>provide</u> us with the happy endings and the just solutions that we cherish in our hearts.

08 If you feel threatened every time a perceived rival does well, <u>remind</u> yourself of your own strengths and successes.

▶ every time: s + v: ~할 때마다

09 Throughout history there have been efforts to <u>distinguish</u> the guilty from the innocent and to <u>tell</u> the liars from the truthful.

▶ the + 형용사: ~한 사람들
cf. the guilty = guilty people

ℭ 다음 문장의 빈칸에 알맞은 것을 보기 에서 고르시오.

┌─ 보기 ●
│   with   to   from
└─

10 Nothing can stop the man with the right mental attitude _____ achieving his goal; nothing on earth can help the man with the wrong mental attitude. *Thomas Jefferson*

(모예) **11** Most scientists attribute extraordinary memory performance _____ an enhanced ability to associate or organize the information to be memorized, rather than true photographic memory.

(모예) **12** When individuals have a true sense of self-worth, they do not need to compare themselves _____ others, to tear others apart or feel superior.

A 03 ups and downs 기복, (길의) 오르내림   **04** generation 세대   collect on 징수하다   debt 빚
B 06 competent 유능한   caring 배려하는   fate 운명   **07** cherish (마음속에) 품다, 간직하다   **08** perceive 인지하다   **09** guilty 유죄인
C 10 mental 정신적인   **11** extraordinary 비상한, 놀라운   enhance 향상시키다   associate 연상하다   photographic (사진처럼) 선명한, 생생한
   12 self-worth 자아 존중감, 자부심   tear apart 헐뜯다   superior 우월한

조동사 구문

Block Board

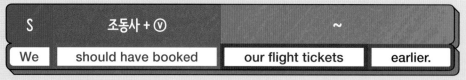

S	조동사 + ⓥ	~	
We	should have booked	our flight tickets	earlier.

우리는 / 예약했어야 했다 / 우리의 비행기 표를 / 더 일찍

- **조동사 + have v-ed**: 과거에 대한 추측 또는 후회
  - ▷ may[might] have v-ed: ~했을지도 모른다
  - ▷ can't[couldn't] have v-ed: ~했을 리가 없다
  - ▷ must have v-ed: ~했음에 틀림없다
  - ▷ should[ought to] have v-ed: ~했어야 했는데 (하지 않았다)

- **조동사 관용 구문**
  - ▷ cannot (help) but + ⓥ: ~하지 않을 수 없다 (= cannot help v-ing)
  - ▷ may well + ⓥ: 아마 ~일 것이다, ~하는 것은 당연하다
  - ▷ would rather A (than B): (B하느니) 차라리 A하겠다[하고 싶다]
  - ▷ cannot + ⓥ + too: 아무리 ~해도 지나치지 않다
  - ▷ may[might] as well A (as B): (B하느니) A하는 편이 좋다

Standard Sentences

01 You **shouldn't have driven** that car with the faulty brakes. You
당신은 그 차를 운전하지 말았어야 했다 / [브레이크에 결함이 있는] 당신은

▶ should not have v-ed:
~하지 말았어야 했는데 (했다)

might have had a serious accident.
심각한 사고를 당했을지도 모른다

02 I **would rather walk** with a friend in the dark, **than** alone in the light.
나는 차라리 걷고 싶다 / 어둠 속에서 친구와 함께 / 빛 속에서 혼자 걷느니

▶ than (walk) alone ~

Ⓐ 다음 문장에서 조동사 구문을 파악하면서, 각 문장을 해석하시오.

03 I was **never** top of the class at school, but my classmates **must have seen** potential in me, because my nickname was "Einstein."

Stephen Hawking

04 One's true feelings **cannot but come through** in what one says and does.

▶ cannot but come ~
= cannot help coming ~

05 A man **may well** be condemned, **not** for doing something, **but** for doing nothing. *William Barclay*

▶ not A but B: A가 아니라 B

B 다음 문장에서 조동사 구문에 밑줄을 치고, 각 문장을 해석하시오.

06 It's defeatist to harp on what might have been, and yet, it's hard to resist considering what might have been.

▸ to-v 이하를 대신하는 가주어 it이 쓰임 ➔ **Unit 03**

07 The suspect can't have committed the crime as he was in another country at the moment of the murder.

08 You might as well expect rivers to run backwards as any man born free to be contented penned up. *Chief Joseph*

▸ ~ as (expect) any man born free ...

09 *The Brothers Karamazov*, one of the peaks in the literature of the world, can hardly be valued too highly. *Sigmund Freud*

▸ cannot ~ too ...
= can hardly(barely) ~ too ...

C 다음 네모 안에서 어법에 맞는 것을 고르시오.

10 The universe must │ originate / have originated │ from a more compact state that we call the Big Bang.

11 When the epidemic broke out, it claimed many lives. The authorities ought to │ take / have taken │ precautions to prevent the epidemic.

12 I would rather be a ghost, drifting by your side as a condemned soul, than │ enter / entering │ heaven without you.

the movie <Crouching Tiger, Hidden Dragon 와호장룡>

S·S 01 faulty 결함이 있는; 그릇된
A 03 potential 잠재력 **04** come through 전해지다, 통하다 **05** condemn 책망하다, 비난하다
B 06 defeatist 패배주의적인 harp on ~을 되뇌다 resist 참다, 삼가다 **07** suspect 용의자 commit a crime 범죄를 저지르다 murder 살인
08 content 만족시키다 pen 가두다, 감금하다 **09** peak 최고점, 절정 literature 문학 value 평가하다
C 10 originate 생기다, 유래하다 compact 조밀한 state 상태 **11** epidemic 전염병 break out 발생하다 claim (목숨을) 앗아가다 authority
(pl.) 당국 precaution 예방조치 **12** drift 떠돌다 condemned 저주받은; 비난받은

수동태 구문

중요도 ★★★
난이도 ★★★

Block Board

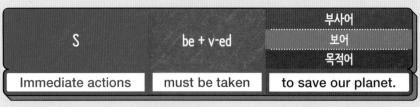

S	be + v-ed	부사어
		보어
		목적어
Immediate actions	must be taken	to save our planet.
즉각적인 조치가	/ 취해져야 한다	/ 우리의 행성을 구하기 위해서

- **수동태의 기본 형태**: 「be동사 + v-ed」 (~되다, ~당하다)
  Form ▷ be being v-ed: ~되고 있는 중이다 ▷ have been v-ed: ~되어져 왔다
  ▷ will[can / may / must] be v-ed: ~될 것이다[될 수 있다 / 될지도 모른다 / 되어야 한다]

- **수동태의 패턴**
  ▷ S + be v-ed + (by + O'): S가 ~되다
  ▷ S + be v-ed + C + (by + O'): S가 C로 ~되다
  ▷ S + be v-ed + O + (by + O'): S가 O를 ~받게 되다

Standard Sentences

01 We **are** all now **connected** by the Internet, like neurons in a giant
우리는 모두 지금 연결되어 있다 / 인터넷에 의해 / 마치 거대한 뇌 속의 뉴런들처럼

brain. *Stephen Hawking*

▶ S + be v-ed + by + O'

02 Solar power and wind power **are considered** alternatives to fossil-
태양 에너지와 풍력은 / 대안으로 여겨진다 / [화석 연료

fuel-based energy generation.
기반의 에너지 생성에 대한]

▶ S + V + O + C
→ S + be v-ed + C (+ by + O')

A 다음 문장에서 수동태 구문을 파악하면서, 각 문장을 해석하시오.

03 The best and most beautiful things in the world cannot be seen or
even touched. They must be felt with the heart. *Helen Keller*

▶ 「조동사 + ⓥ」의 수동태:
조동사 + be + v-ed

04 Unfortunately, the rain forests are being cut down at a shocking rate
to provide humans with lumber, pasture land, and farm land.

▶ 진행형의 수동태:
be being v-ed

05 Geysers have often been compared to volcanoes because they
both emit hot liquids from below the Earth's surface.

▶ **Know More** Rainbow p.26
▶ 완료형의 수동태:
have been v-ed

B 다음 문장에서 수동태 구문에 밑줄을 치고, 각 문장을 해석하시오.

06 Information is extracted or learned from sources of data, and this captured information is then transformed into knowledge that is eventually used to trigger actions or decisions.

모의 **07** Genetic tendencies toward intelligence, sociability, and aggression can be stimulated, controlled, or suppressed by parental response and other environmental influences.

08 Hacking is commonly described as the act of re-designing the configuration of hardware or software systems to alter their intended function.

09 It is estimated that we have characterized only one percent of all bacterial species that exist.

▶ 긴 주어를 대신하는 가주어 It
Unit 03

C 다음 괄호 안의 말을 이용하여 우리말과 같은 뜻이 되도록 고쳐 쓰시오.

10 시험 문제지는 시험장 밖으로 갖고 나가져서는 안 된다.

Test papers _____ out of the examination room. (may, take, not)

11 사람들을 그들의 겉모습으로 판단하지 마라. 그들의 책 대부분은 여전히 쓰이고 있는 중이다.

Don't judge people by their covers. Most of their books _____ _____. (still, write)

12 입증된 과학 이론들은 종종 '자연의 법칙' 또는 '물리학의 법칙'이라고 일컬어진다.

Confirmed scientific theories _____ "laws of nature" or "laws of physics." (often, refer to A as B)

S·S 01 connect 연결하다   neuron 뉴런, 신경세포   02 solar 태양의   alternative 대안   fossil fuel 화석 연료   generation 생성, 발전
A 04 rate 속도; 비율   lumber 목재   pasture land 목초지   05 geyser 간헐천   emit 내뿜다   surface 표면
B 06 extract 추출하다   capture 획득하다   trigger 촉발하다   07 sociability 사교성   aggression 공격성   stimulate 자극하다   suppress 억압
하다   08 configuration (시스템의) 환경 설정, 구성   alter 변경하다   09 characterize 규정하다, 특징짓다
C 11 judge 판단하다   12 confirm 입증하다   refer to A as B A를 B라고 일컫다(-referred-referred)

Chapter 02

Review

A 다음 문장을 우리말로 해석하시오.

01 Primitive societies tend to view man and beast, animal and plant, organic and inorganic realms, as participants in an integrated, animated totality.

02 You can fail at what you don't want, so you might as well take a chance on doing what you love. *Jim Carrey*

03 I'd rather be hated for who I am, than loved for who I am not. *Kurt Cobain*

04 Quantum theory states that energy, such as light, is given off and absorbed in tiny definite units called quanta or photons.

B 다음 네모 안에서 어법에 맞는 것을 고르시오.

모의 **05** A copyright supplies its holder (A) to / with a kind of monopoly over the created material, and it assures him or her (B) of / with both control over its use and the benefits from it.

06 The show is all booked up. You must / should have purchased tickets earlier. Would you like to be put on a waiting list?

07 Scientists assume that Earth must / should have formed from dry material and acquired its water through objects from more distant, icy reaches of the solar system crashing into Earth.

모의 **08** The personal computer (A) designs / is designed for the general function of handling and processing information, but exactly how the PC is used is not (B) predetermining / predetermined .

C 다음 괄호 안의 단어를 우리말과 같은 뜻이 되도록 고쳐 쓰시오.

09 나는 그 웹사이트가 업데이트 되고 있는 중이었기 때문에 그것에 접속할 수 없었다. (update)

→ I couldn't access the website because it _____.

10 언어는 과거의 어떤 최근 시점에 발명되었음에 틀림없다는 것이 때때로 언어학자들에 의해서 주장된다. (invent)

→ It is sometimes alleged, by linguists, that language _____
_____ at some recent point in the past.

D 다음 괄호 안의 말을 이용하여 우리말과 같은 뜻이 되도록 문장을 완성하시오. (필요하면 어형을 바꿀 것)

11 그 과학자는 기후 변화를 지구 온난화와 대기 오염의 탓으로 돌렸다.
(changes in the climate, global warming, to, attribute)

→ The scientist _____ and pollution
of the atmosphere.

12 해면 모양으로 생긴 3파운드의 지방 조직 덩어리인 뇌는 종종 슈퍼컴퓨터에 비유되어왔다.
(a super-computer, compare, often, to)

→ A spongy three-pound mass of fatty tissue, the brain _____
_____.

A 01 tend to-v ~하는 경향이 있다 primitive 원시의 realm 영역 integrate 통합하다 animate 생명을 주다 **02** take a chance on ~을 운에 맡기고 해보다 **04** quantum 양자(*pl.* quanta) state 명시하다 give off 방출하다 definite 일정한 photon 광자 **B 05** copyright 저작권 monopoly 독점 benefit 수익, 혜택 **06** be booked up 예약이 매진되다 put ~ on a waiting list ~을 대기 명단에 올리다 **07** assume 추정하다 **08** predetermine 미리 결정하다 **C 09** access 접속하다 **10** allege 주장하다, 단언하다 linguist 언어학자 **D 11** atmosphere 대기 **12** spongy 해면 모양의 mass 덩어리 fatty tissue 지방 조직

03 목적어의 파악

☑ 목적어는 문장의 동사가 나타내는 동작의 대상으로 명사, 대명사, 명사구, 명사절이 목적어 역할을 할 수 있다.

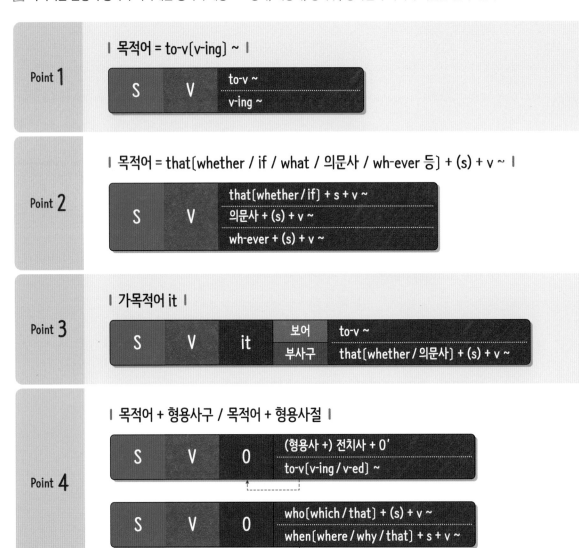

Point 1

❙ 목적어 = to-v[v-ing] ~ ❙

| S | V | to-v ~ |
| | | v-ing ~ |

Point 2

❙ 목적어 = that[whether / if / what / 의문사 / wh-ever 등] + (s) + v ~ ❙

S	V	that[whether / if] + s + v ~
		의문사 + (s) + v ~
		wh-ever + (s) + v ~

Point 3

❙ 가목적어 it ❙

| S | V | it | 보어 | to-v ~ |
| | | | 부사구 | that[whether / 의문사] + (s) + v ~ |

Point 4

❙ 목적어 + 형용사구 / 목적어 + 형용사절 ❙

| S | V | O | (형용사 +) 전치사 + O' |
| | | | to-v[v-ing / v-ed] ~ |

| S | V | O | who[which / that] + (s) + v ~ |
| | | | when[where / why / that] + s + v ~ |

- **unit 10** 명사구 목적어
- **unit 11** 명사절 목적어
- **unit 12** 가목적어 it
- **unit 13** 목적어 + 형용사구
- **unit 14** 목적어 + 형용사절

명사구 목적어 → Unit 10	▷ to-v와 v-ing는 명사 역할을 할 수 있으므로 목적어 자리에 올 수 있다. ▷ 동사에 따라 목적어로 to-v 또는 v-ing를 취하므로 그 용법을 잘 익혀 두어야 한다.
명사절 목적어 → Unit 11	▷ 접속사 that, whether, if, 의문사, wh-ever 등은 명사절을 이끌어 목적어 자리에 올 수 있다.
가목적어 it → Unit 12	▷ 5형식에서 목적어가 to-v 또는 명사절인 경우에는 그 자리에 it을 쓰고, to-v 또는 명사절은 문장의 뒤로 보내는 '가목적어-진목적어' 구문을 취한다.
목적어를 꾸미는 형용사적 수식어 → Unit 13, 14	▷ 목적어가 명사 또는 대명사인 경우, 뒤에 그 목적어를 수식하는 전치사구, to-v, v-ing, v-ed가 올 수 있다. ▷ 목적어가 명사 또는 대명사인 경우, 뒤에 그 목적어를 수식하는 관계사절이 올 수 있다.

명사구 목적어

Block Board

S	V	to-v ~
		v-ing ~
He	wants	to spend more time with his family.

그는 / 원한다 / 자신의 가족과 더 많은 시간을 보내기를

- to-v나 v-ing가 이끄는 명사구는 타동사의 목적어 역할을 할 수 있고, '~하는 것을, ~하기를'로 해석한다.
  Plus⊕ 「의문사 + to-v」는 명사구로서 주어, 목적어, 보어로 쓰인다.
  ▷ what to do 무엇을 ~할지　　▷ how to do 어떻게 ~할지　　▷ when to do 언제 ~할지

- to-v 또는 v-ing만 목적어로 취하는 동사

decide, choose, plan, agree, refuse, promise 등	+ to-v	미래를 나타냄 (~할 것을)
enjoy, mind, finish, admit, deny, avoid, suggest, imply, give up, put off 등	+ v-ing	현재·과거를 나타냄 (~하는 것을, ~한 것을)

- to-v와 v-ing 둘 다 목적어로 취하는 동사

remember ⌈ to-v: ~할 것을 기억하다　　forget ⌈ to-v: ~할 것을 잊다　　regret ⌈ to-v: ~하게 되어 유감이다
　　　　　└ v-ing: ~한 것을 기억하다　　　　　└ v-ing: ~한 것을 잊다　　　　　└ v-ing: ~한 것을 후회하다

Standard Sentences

01 Both countries agreed **to abolish their tariff walls within 5 years.**
양국은 동의했다 / 그들의 관세 장벽을 철폐하는 것을 / 5년 내에

02 I particularly enjoyed **driving through the countryside with you.**
나는 특히 즐겼다 / 당신과 함께 교외를 드라이브하는 것을

Know More Rainbow p.32
▶ agree + to-v
▶ enjoy + v-ing

Ⓐ 다음 문장에서 명사구 목적어를 파악하면서, 각 문장을 해석하시오.

03 I don't mind listening to advice that I've asked for, but I refuse to be preached at.

▶ mind + v-ing
▶ refuse + to-v

04 I almost forgot the storyline of the Disney movie *Frozen*, but I do remember waiting in line to see the movie.

▶ remember + v-ing: ~한 것을 기억하다

05 Politicians are the same all over. They promise to build a bridge even where there is no river. *Nikita Khrushchev*

B 다음 문장에서 명사구 목적어에 밑줄을 치고, 각 문장을 해석하시오.

수능 **06** No one's instincts are always correct; so how do you know when to follow them and when to ignore them?

▶ 의문사＋to-v

07 The drunken man admitted stealing the car, but denied driving it under the influence of alcohol.

08 Once I forgot to turn off the oven and I shall never forget seeing the expression on the faces of the rest of the family when they realized they had nothing to eat.

09 We stopped checking for monsters under our bed when we realized they were inside us.

the movie <The Dark Knight>

C 다음 네모 안에서 어법에 맞는 것을 고르시오.

10 After careful consideration of your proposal, I regret to say / saying that we are unable to accept it.

11 I've never regretted to say / saying a kind word to someone, but I have regretted plenty of mean things I have said and done.

12 Life will knock us down, but we can choose whether or not to stand / standing back up. *Jackie Chan*

▶ whether or not to-v: ~을 할지 말지

S·S 01 abolish (법률·제도·관습을) 폐지하다 tariff wall 관세 장벽 02 countryside 시골 지역, 전원
A 03 mind 싫어하다; 주의하다 preach at ~에 훈계하다 04 storyline (소설·연극·영화 등의) 줄거리 05 politician 정치인
B 06 instinct 본능 07 admit 시인하다, 인정하다 deny 부인하다 under the influence of alcohol 술에 취한 상태로 08 turn off ~을 끄다 expression 표정; 표현 the rest 나머지
C 10 consideration 숙고, 고려 proposal 제안 11 plenty of 많은 mean 비열한, 심술궂은 knock down 쓰러뜨리다, 무너뜨리다

unit 11
명사절 목적어

중요도 ★★★
난이도 ★★☆

Block Board

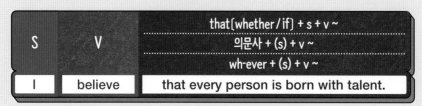

S	V	that[whether / if] + s + v ~
		의문사 + (s) + v ~
		wh-ever + (s) + v ~
I	believe	that every person is born with talent.

나는 / 믿는다 / 모든 사람은 재능을 갖고 태어난다는 것을

- 접속사(that, whether, if), what, 의문사, wh-ever 등은 명사절을 이끌어 타동사의 목적어 역할을 할 수 있다.

  Form ▷ that + s + v ~: ~라고 하는 것 　　▷ whether[if] + s + v ~: ~인지 아닌지

  　　　 ▷ what + (s) + v ~: ~하는 것 　　▷ 의문사(who, what, when …) + (s) + v ~: 누가[무엇이 / 언제 …] ~하는 것

  　　　 ▷ whoever[whichever / whatever] + (s) + v ~: ~하는 누구나[어느 것이나 / 무엇이나]

Standard Sentences

01 A judge must decide **whether a person is guilty or innocent of a**
판사는 판결을 내려야 한다 　　　　／ 어떤 사람이 유죄인지 무죄인지를 　　　　　／ 범행에

crime.
대해

02 Your present circumstances don't determine **where you can go**: they
당신의 현재 상황이 결정하지 않는다 　　　　　　　　／ 어디로 당신이 갈 수 있는지를 / 그것들은

merely determine where you start. *Nido Qubein*
단지 결정한다 　　　／ 어디서 당신이 시작하는지를

A 다음 문장에서 명사절 목적어를 파악하면서, 각 문장을 해석하시오.

03 The great astronomer Edwin Hubble discovered that all distant
galaxies are receding from our Milky Way Galaxy.

04 The woman who was on passport control asked me if I had any
further identification.

▶ if + s + v ~: ~인지 아닌지(= whether + s + v ~)
cf. 부사절로 쓰이면 '만약 ~라면'

05 People who are satisfied appreciate what they have in life and don't
worry about how it compares to what others have.

B 다음 문장에서 명사절 목적어에 밑줄을 치고, 각 문장을 해석하시오.

06 Perhaps, we've just forgotten that we are still pioneers, that we've barely begun, and that our greatest accomplishments cannot be behind us. *the movie <Interstellar>*

07 Actors are so fortunate. They can choose whether they will appear in tragedy or in comedy, whether they will suffer or make merry, laugh or shed tears. *Oscar Wilde*

08 Environmentalists argue no system of waste disposal can be absolutely safe, either now or in the future.

▶ 목적어절을 이끄는 접속사 that이 생략됨

09 Either Saturday or Monday, choose whichever is more convenient for you.

C 다음 문장의 빈칸에 들어가기에 알맞은 것을 보기에서 고르시오.

┌─ 보기 ─────────────────────────────┐
│   that   whether   whatever   │
└─────────────────────────────────────┘

[모의] **10** Indeed, a brief look at a dictionary will show you _____ the majority of words are used with more than one meaning.

11 In times of social, cultural or religious sensitivity one might wonder _____ it is ethical to avoid, or not to avoid, questions that might increase conflict.

▶ 긴 주어를 대신하는 가주어 it

12 The government will take _____ action is necessary to achieve monetary and financial stability.

S·S 01 guilty 유죄의   innocent 무죄의   crime 범행, 범죄   **02** circumstance 상황, 환경   merely 단지, 그저
A 03 astronomer 천문학자   galaxy 은하   recede 멀어지다   **04** passport control 여권 심사대   further 여분의, 추가의   identification 신분증명서   **05** appreciate 제대로 알다, 진가를 인식하다
B 06 pioneer 개척자   barely 가까스로, 겨우   **07** make merry 즐겁게 놀다   shed tears 눈물을 흘리다   **08** disposal 처리, 폐기   absolutely 절대적으로   **09** convenient 편리한
C 10 indeed 정말로   **11** religious 종교적인   sensitivity 민감성   ethical 윤리적인   **12** monetary 통화의, 재정의   stability 안정성

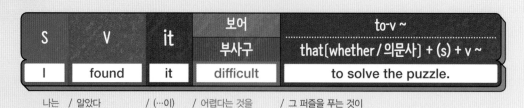

unit 12

가목적어 it

중요도 ★★☆
난이도 ★★★

Block Board

S	V	it	보어	to-v ~
			부사구	that[whether / 의문사] + (s) + v ~
I	found	it	difficult	to solve the puzzle.

나는 / 알았다 / (…이) / 어렵다는 것을 / 그 퍼즐을 푸는 것이

- 5형식에서 목적어로 to-v나 that절이 오면 목적어 자리에는 가목적어 it을 쓰고, 진목적어인 to-v나 that절은 보어 뒤에 위치시킨다.
  Form S + V + it + C + to-v[that + s + v]
- 3형식에서 목적어로 to-v나 that절이 온 경우, '가목적어(it)-진목적어' 구문을 쓰기도 한다.
  Form S + V + it + 부사구 + to-v[that + s + v]
  Tip it이 앞에 나온 것을 가리키는 것이 아니라면, 뒤에 온 to-v나 that절을 받는 가목적어일 가능성이 높다.

Standard Sentences

01 Artificial intelligence makes **it** possible **for machines to learn from**
인공지능은 만든다 / (…을) 가능하게 / 기계들이 경험으로부터 배우는 것을

▶ for + O': to-v의 의미상 주어

experience and perform human tasks.
/ 그리고 인간의 과제를 수행하는 것을

02 We should **not** take **it** for granted **that classic moral stories will**
우리는 여겨서는 안 된다 / (…을) 당연하게 / 고전적인 교훈적 이야기들이 자동적으로 도덕적인

▶ take it for granted that ~: ~을 당연한 것으로 여기다

automatically promote moral behaviors.
행동을 촉진할 것임을

A 다음 문장에서 가목적어와 진목적어를 파악하면서, 각 문장을 해석하시오.

03 The European Union has found it difficult to reach a consensus on economic issues.

··· Know More Rainbow p.36

04 Our research makes it evident that many imaginative children often invent imaginary playmates.

05 Engrave it on your heart that a little help is worth a deal of pity.

B 다음 문장에서 밑줄 친 it이 가리키는 것을 찾아 동그라미하고, 각 문장을 해석하시오.

06 Even if you don't read a newspaper or watch television, and walk around the streets with your eyes down, you'll find it impossible to avoid some form of publicity.

07 I make it a rule not to clutter my mind with simple information that I can find in a book in five minutes. *Albert Einstein*

▶ make it a rule to-v: ~하는 것을 규칙으로 삼다

08 We owe it to our children to give them a dignified and hopeful future. *Giorgio Napolitano*

09 Bear it in mind when a life storm breaks that, no matter how violent, it is only temporary and that behind the clouds the sun is always shining.

C 다음 네모 안에서 어법에 맞는 것을 고르시오.

10 The internet has made it │ easy / easily │ for us to hear whatever we like the most in mere seconds.

모의 **11** At certain times in history, cultures have taken it for granted │ which / that │ a person was not fully human unless he or she learned to master thoughts and feelings.

12 Every man who knows how to read has │ it / this │ in his power to magnify himself, to multiply the ways in which he exists, to make his life full, significant, and interesting. *Aldous Huxley*

S·S 01 artificial intelligence 인공지능   perform 수행하다   task 과제   **02** moral 교훈적인; 도덕적인
A 03 consensus (의견의) 일치   **04** evident 명백한   imaginative 상상력이 풍부한   **05** engrave 새기다, 명심하다   a deal of 많은   pity 동정
B 06 publicity 광고, 홍보   **07** clutter 어지럽히다   **08** owe A to B A를 B에게 빚지고 있다   dignified 고귀한, 위엄 있는   **09** bear ~ in mind ~을 명심하다   violent 맹렬한, 폭력적인   temporary 일시적인
C 10 mere 단지, 겨우 ~의   **11** master (감정을) 억누르다   **12** magnify 확장하다   multiply 다양화하다   significant 중대한

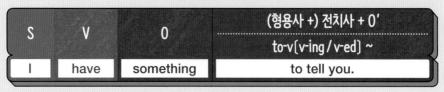

목적어 + 형용사구

unit 13

중요도 ★★★
난이도 ★★★

Block Board

S	V	O	(형용사 +) 전치사 + O' to-v[v-ing / v-ed] ~
I	have	something	to tell you.

나는 / 가지고 있다 / 어떤 것을 / [너에게 말할]

- 목적어가 명사 또는 대명사인 경우에 이를 수식하는 형용사구가 이어질 수 있다.

Form

목적어
(명사 / 대명사) + ── (형용사 +) 전치사 + O': ~한
── to-v: ~해야 하는, ~할
── v-ing: ~하는, ~하고 있는 (능동·진행)
── v-ed: ~되는, ~된 (수동·완료)

Tip 분사가 단독으로 명사를 수식할 때는 명사의 앞에 오며, 분사 뒤에 딸린 어구가 있어서 분사구가 되면 명사의 뒤에 온다.

a **dancing** girl (명사 앞)　　　a girl **dancing** on the ice (명사 뒤)

Standard Sentences

[수능] **01** Our bodies have the natural ability **to fight off bacteria and diseases**
우리의 신체는 타고난 능력을 가지고 있다 　　　　/ [박테리아와 질병을 물리칠

when they enter our bodies.
/ 그것들이 우리의 몸에 들어올 때]

02 We **often** experience unexpected results **brought about by words**
우리는 종종 예상치 못한 결과를 경험한다 　　　　/ [말에 의해서 초래되는

carelessly used.
/ [부주의하게 사용된]]

▶ 명사 + v-ed ~: 명사와 분사가
수동의 관계

Ⓐ 다음 문장에서 목적어를 수식하는 형용사구를 파악하면서, 각 문장을 해석하시오.

[모의] **03** Healthy living in individuals lays the foundation for healthy living
throughout society and the world.

04 You have the right to be given a fair trial by a court of law if you are
accused of a crime.

···· **Know More** Rainbow p.38

05 I have received an email offering me a job for an unknown company
that I don't remember applying to.

B 다음 문장에서 목적어를 수식하는 어구에 밑줄을 치고, 각 문장을 해석하시오.

06 The use of words itself yields, upon analysis, valuable results illustrative of the various temperaments of authors.

07 At times our own light goes out and is rekindled by a spark from another person. Each of us has cause to think with deep gratitude of those who have lighted the flame within us. *Albert Schweitzer*

▶ those who ~: ~하는 사람들

08 Regular exercise increases the amount of blood flowing through your brain.

09 We should reduce hazardous and toxic chemicals released into the air and water.

C 다음 네모 안에서 어법에 맞는 것을 고르시오.

[모의] **10** Certainly, Leonardo da Vinci had an unusual mind and an uncanny ability | to see / seeing | what others didn't see.

···< Know More | Rainbow p.39 ⟨

11 Scientists at NASA have spotted six asteroids | heading / head | in the direction of Earth, with one of them having a size larger than the Empire State Building.

▶ with + 명사 + v-ing(v-ed): ~ 가 …채로 ➡ Unit 34

12 Google and other carmakers around the world are developing technologies | applying / applied | to currently "manned" vehicles to permit drivers to take their hands off the wheel and focus on other tasks.

S·S 02 bring about ~을 초래하다   carelessly 부주의하게
A 03 foundation 토대   **04** a fair trial 공정한 재판   a court of law 법정   accuse A of B A를 B의 이유로 고발하다   **05** apply 지원하다, 신청하다
B 06 yield (결과를) 낳다, 산출하다   illustrative 분명히 보여 주는   temperament 기질   **07** at times 가끔   go out (불·전깃불이) 꺼지다
    rekindle 다시 불붙이다   spark 불꽃   cause 이유, 원인   gratitude 감사하는 마음   flame 불꽃   **09** hazardous 위험한   toxic 유독한
C 10 uncanny 뛰어난, 신비로운   **11** spot 발견하다   asteroid 소행성   head 향하다   **12** manned 유인의, 사람이 탑승한   permit 허용하다

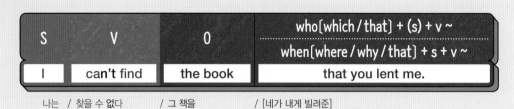

목적어 + 형용사절

중요도 ★★☆
난이도 ★★☆

Block Board

S	V	O	who[which / that] + (s) + v ~ when[where / why / that] + s + v ~
I	can't find	the book	that you lent me.

나는 / 찾을 수 없다 / 그 책을 / [네가 내게 빌려준]

- 목적어가 명사 또는 대명사인 경우에 이를 수식하는 형용사절이 이어질 수 있다.
- 형용사절은 관계대명사 또는 관계부사가 이끈다.
- 관계대명사가 전치사의 목적어일 때, 전치사는 관계대명사의 앞 또는 관계사절의 끝에 온다. ▶ unit 24

Standard Sentences

모의 **01** We trust leaders **who are real, who walk their talk, who act on their**
우리는 지도자들을 신뢰한다 / [진실된 / 그들이 말한 것을 실행하는 / 그들의 핵심 가치대로 행동하는

core values, and who tell us the truth.
/ 그리고 우리에게 진실을 말하는]

02 We are approaching the time **when machines will be able to**
우리는 시대로 다가가고 있다 / [기계가 인간을 능가할 수 있을

outperform humans at almost any task.
/ 거의 모든 업무에서]

A 다음 문장에서 목적어를 수식하는 절을 파악하면서, 각 문장을 해석하시오.

수능! **03** Basic scientific research provides the raw materials that technology and engineering use to solve problems.

모의 **04** Personality psychologists had underestimated the extent to which the social situation shapes people's behavior, independently of their personality.

▶ 명사 + 전치사 + 관계대명사 ~

05 The word "fable" frequently denotes a brief tale where animals or inanimate objects speak and behave like humans, usually to advance a moral point.

B 다음 문장에서 목적어를 수식하는 절에 밑줄을 치고, 각 문장을 해석하시오.

06 I fear not the man who has practiced 10,000 kicks once, but I fear the man who has practiced one kick 10,000 times. *Bruce Lee*

07 Our atmosphere supplies most of the oxygen which animals must have to survive, as well as the carbon dioxide needed by plants.

▶ A as well as B: B뿐만 아니라 A도

(모의) **08** Choose words that are more expressive, like 'great' or 'terrific' or 'wonderful' if you want to express pleasure.

(모의) **09** We will eventually reach a point at which conflict with the finite nature of resources is inevitable.

▶ at which = where

C 다음 문장의 빈칸에 들어갈 내용으로 알맞은 것을 보기에서 고르시오.

```
보기
ⓐ that we generate
ⓑ who claim to be proficient at countless tasks
ⓒ that allow young people to develop ability
```

10 'Jack-of-all-trades' means those _____ but cannot perform a single one of them well.

(모의) **11** We are thoroughly enjoying the immediate benefits of attractive consumer goods _____ from producing and disseminating hazardous chemicals.

(모의) **12** School physical education programs should offer a balanced variety of activities _____ in lifetime activities that are personally meaningful and enjoyable.

S·S 01 walk the talk 말한 것을 실천하다　**02** approach 다가가다　outperform 능가하다
A 03 raw material 원료, 원자재　**04** underestimate 과소평가하다　independently of ~와 관계없이　**05** fable 우화　denote 뜻하다　advance 제시하다
B 07 carbon dioxide 이산화탄소　**08** expressive 표현력이 있는　**09** conflict 갈등　finite 한정된　inevitable 불가피한
C 보기 claim 주장하다; 요구하다　proficient 능숙한　**10** jack-of-all-trades 팔방미인, 무엇이나 잘하는 사람　**11** thoroughly 잘, 아주; 완전히
immediate 목전의, 즉시의　consumer goods 소비재　disseminate 퍼뜨리다　**12** physical education 체육　balanced 균형 잡힌

Chapter 03

Review

A 다음 문장을 우리말로 해석하시오.

01 Remember to look up at the stars and not down at your feet. Try to make sense of what you see and wonder about what makes the universe exist.

Stephen Hawking

(수능!) **02** Some people make it difficult for others to tell them the truth because they respond rudely or emotionally to people who tell the truth.

03 Never tell people how to do things. Tell them what to do and they will surprise you with their ingenuity. *George S. Patton*

04 People will forget what you said, people will forget what you did, but people will never forget how you made them feel. *Maya Angelou*

B 다음 네모 안에서 어법에 맞는 것을 고르시오.

05 NASA said the satellite stopped to work / working within hours of its launch and did not responded to attempts to communicate with it.

06 Do regular maintenance on your vehicles: Do not skimp on or forget to do / doing regular oil changes.

07 No one knows just what impact the buildup of CO_2 will have, but some scientists fear that / what the globe will continue to warm up, bringing on wrenching climatic changes.

(수능!) **08** Focusing on on-line interaction with people who are engaged in the same specialized area can limit potential sources of information and thus make it less probable for unexpected findings happen / to happen .

C 다음 괄호 안의 말을 이용하여 우리말과 같은 뜻이 되도록 문장을 완성하시오. (필요하면 어형을 바꿀 것)

09 내가 그 길로 단지 몇 걸음을 채 가기 전에 나는 문을 잠그는 것을 잊었다는 것을 깨달았다.
(I, the door, lock, had forgotten)

→ I realized _____ before I'd only gone a few
steps down the road.

10 만유인력의 법칙은 중력이 어떻게 우주의 모든 물체에 영향을 미치는지를 설명한다.
(the force of gravity, affect, how, all objects)

→ The law of universal gravitation explains _____
in the universe.

11 나는 우리가 플라스틱을 버릴 때마다 환경에 무엇을 하고 있는지를 사람들이 깨닫는 것이 필요하다고 생각한다.
(people, to realize, necessary, it, think, for)

→ I _____ what we are doing to the environment
each time we throw away plastic.

D 다음 문장의 빈칸에 들어갈 내용으로 알맞은 것을 보기 에서 고르시오.

> • 보기 •
> ⓐ that you value what he says and care about him as a person
> ⓑ that remind us we're part of something greater than ourselves
> ⓒ to talk to others about their emotions later in life

12 Sometimes in the midst of life's chaos we forget to do the little things
_____.

(모의) **13** Taking the time to truly understand another's point of view shows _____
_____.

(모의) **14** Children raised in households that foster communication find it easier
_____.

A 01 make sense of ~을 이해하다   **02** rudely 무례하게   emotionally 감정적으로   **03** ingenuity 창의력, 재간
B 05 satellite 인공위성   launch 발사   **06** maintenance 정비, 보수   skimp 지나치게 아끼다, 인색하게 굴다   **07** buildup 축적
bring on ~을 야기하다   wrench 왜곡하다; 비틀다   **08** be engaged in ~에 종사하다   potential 잠재적인   probable 가망이
있는   **C 10** the law of universal gravitation 만유인력의 법칙   gravity 중력   **11** each time ~할 때마다   **D** 보기 value
소중하게 여기다   **12** chaos 혼돈, 혼란   **13** point of view 관점   **14** foster 장려하다, 촉진하다

04 보어의 파악

Get Ready!

☑ 보어는 주어 또는 목적어를 보충 설명하여 문장의 의미를 완전하게 하는 것으로, 주어를 보충하면 주격보어, 목적어를 보충
  하면 목적격보어이다.
☑ 보어로는 명사와 형용사 및 그 상당어구가 쓰인다.

Point 1

| 주격보어 = to-v[v-ing / v-ed / 전치사 + 0'] ~ /
              that[whether / what / 의문사] + (s) + v ~ |

| S | V | to-v[v-ing / v-ed] ~ |
| | | (형용사 +) 전치사 + 0' |

| S | V | that[whether] + s + v ~ |
| | | 의문사 + (s) + v ~ |

Point 2

| 목적격보어 = to-v[ⓥ] ~ / v-ing[v-ed] ~ |

| S | V | 0 | to-v[ⓥ] ~ |

| S | V | 0 | v-ing[v-ed] ~ |

Point 3

| 보어 + 형용사구 / 보어 + 형용사절 |

| S | V | C | (형용사 +) 전치사 + 0', to-v[v-ing / v-ed] ~ |
| | | | who[which / that / when / where / why] + (s) + v ~ |

| S | V | 0 | C | (형용사 +) 전치사 + 0', to-v[v-ing / v-ed] ~ |
| | | | | who[which / that / when / where / why] + (s) + v ~ |

• unit 15   주격보어: 구

• unit 16   주격보어: 절

• unit 17   목적격보어 1

• unit 18   목적격보어 2

• unit 19   보어 + 형용사구

• unit 20   보어 + 형용사절

주격보어
→ Unit 15, 16

▷ 명사 또는 형용사의 역할을 하는 준동사와 전치사구는 주격보어 자리에 올 수 있다.

▷ 접속사 that, whether, 의문사 등이 이끄는 명사절은 주격보어 자리에 올 수 있다.

목적격보어
→ Unit 17, 18

▷ 준동사는 목적격보어 자리에 올 수 있다.

▷ 동사의 성격에 따라 목적격 보어로 to-v, ⓥ 또는 v-ing를 취한다.

▷ 목적어와의 관계가 수동인 경우에는 v-ed가 온다.

보어를 꾸미는 형용사적 수식어
→ Unit 19, 20

▷ 보어가 명사 또는 대명사인 경우에 그 뒤에 보어를 수식하는 전치사구, 준동사구, 형용사절이 올 수 있다.

주격보어: 구

Block Board

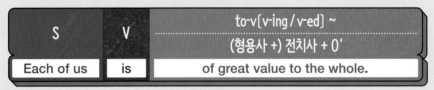

S	V	to-v[v-ing / v-ed] ~
		(형용사 +) 전치사 + O'
Each of us	is	of great value to the whole.

우리들 각각은 / ~이다 / 전체에 대단히 중요한

- 주어를 보충하는 주격보어로는 명사(구, 절)와 형용사(구) 등이 올 수 있다.
- 주격보어로 쓰이는 명사구는 주어와 '=' 관계에 있으며, 주격보어로 쓰이는 형용사구는 주어의 성질·상태를 나타낸다.

Tip S + V + C: S는 C이다[하다]

Standard Sentences

01 The supreme accomplishment is **to blur the line between work and**
최고의 성취는 ~이다 / 경계를 흐릿하게 만드는 것 / [일과 놀이 사이의]

play. *Arnold Toynbee*

02 The most popular cyber crimes are **hacking a person's personal**
가장 일반적인 사이버 범죄들은 ~이다 / 개인 계좌를 해킹하는 것

account and spreading a computer virus.
/ 그리고 컴퓨터 바이러스를 유포하는 것

A 다음 문장에서 주격보어를 파악하면서, 각 문장을 해석하시오.

03 Knowledge of the world is **only** to be acquired in the world, and not in a closet. *Lord Chesterfield*

> ••• **Grammar Plus** Rainbow *p.46*
> ▶ be to-v 용법 중 '가능'의 뜻으로 쓰임

04 From the perspective of the individual working person, the key to a great workplace is feeling wanted and important.

수능 **05** Disease, action that might produce disease, and recovery from disease are of vital concern to the whole primitive community.

> ▶ of + 추상명사: 형용사구

B 다음 문장에서 주격보어에 밑줄을 치고, 각 문장을 해석하시오.

06 Average consumers all over the world still remain unconvinced of the value and usefulness of cryptocurrencies such as bitcoin.

Know More Rainbow p.47

*crytocurrency 암호화폐

07 The goal of science is to learn how nature works by observing the physical world, and to understand it through research and experimentation.

08 Faith is taking the first step even when you don't see the whole staircase. *Martin Luther King Jr.*

09 Life isn't about waiting for the storm to pass. It's about learning how to dance in the rain. *Vivian Greene*

C 다음 괄호 안의 단어를 우리말과 같은 뜻이 되도록 배열하여 문장을 완성하시오.

10 단어를 완전히 이해하는 유일한 방법은 가능한 한 많은 문맥 속에서 사용되는 그것을 보는 것이다.
(it, is, in use, to see)

→ The only way to understand a word fully _____

in as many contexts as possible.

11 교과서가 당신에게 가르쳐 주지 못하는 것은 그 지식을 언제 적용하느냐이다.
(the knowledge, to, is, apply, when)

→ What the textbooks do not teach you _____.

▶ 의문사 + to-v

12 행복한 삶의 가장 중요한 요소는 당신이 의지할 수 있는 좋은 사회적 관계를 갖는 것이다.
(a, having, good, is, social network)

→ The most important factor in a happy life _____

that you can depend on.

S·S 01 supreme 최고의, 최상의 blur 흐릿하게 만들다 **02** hack 해킹하다 account 계좌 spread 유포하다, 퍼뜨리다
A 03 closet 벽장 **04** perspective 관점 **05** vital 중대한 concern 관심사; 염려 primitive 원시의
B 06 average 일반적인, 보통의 unconvinced of ~을 확신하지 못하는 bitcoin 비트코인(디지털 화폐) **07** observe 관찰하다
C 10 fully 완전히 context 문맥, 상황 **11** apply 적용하다 **12** factor 요소

주격보어: 절

중요도 ★★★
난이도 ★★☆

Block Board

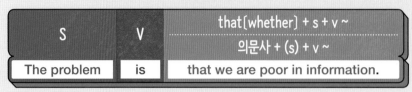

	S	V	that[whether] + s + v ~
			의문사 + (s) + v ~
	The problem	is	that we are poor in information.

우리의 문제는 / ∼이다 / 우리가 정보가 부족하다는 것

• 주격보어로는 접속사 that, whether, 의문사, wh-ever 등이 이끄는 명사절이 올 수 있다.

Tip 보어절을 이끄는 접속사 that은 생략되기도 한다.

Standard Sentences

01 Life's tragedy is **that we get old too soon and wise too late.**
인생의 비극은 ∼이다 / 우리가 너무 빨리 늙고 너무 늦게 현명해진다는 것

▶ that + s + v: ∼라는 것

Benjamin Franklin

02 Challenges are **what make life interesting** and overcoming them is
도전은 ∼이다 / 인생을 흥미롭게 만드는 것 / 그리고 도전을 극복하는 것은 ∼이다

▶ what + (s) + v:
① ∼하는 것
② 무엇이[무엇을] ∼하는 것

what makes life meaningful. *Joshua J. Marine*
/ 인생을 의미 있게 만드는 것

Ⓐ 다음 문장에서 주격보어를 파악하면서, 각 문장을 해석하시오.

03 If you don't design your own life plan, chances are you'll fall into
someone else's plan. *Jim Rohn*

▶ 보어절을 이끄는 접속사 that이 생략됨

04 Design is **not just** what it looks like and feels like. Design is how it
works. *Steve Jobs*

••● **Know More** Rainbow p.48

05 The acid test of a good driver is whether he or she remains calm in
an emergency.

▶ 접속사 whether의 의미:
① 명사절: ∼인지 (아닌지)
② 부사절: ∼이든 아니든

B 다음 문장에서 주격보어에 밑줄을 치고, 각 문장을 해석하시오.

[모예] **06** A decline of empathy and a rise in narcissism are exactly what we would expect to see in children who have little opportunity to play socially.

07 The measure of a true champion is not how they win. It's how they handle defeat. *Garry Hall*

08 The new processor is to other processors what a Ferrari is to other cars: i.e. faster.

▶ A is to B what[as] C is to D: A와 B의 관계는 C와 D의 관계와 같다

09 The meaning of a poem is whatever the author intends to communicate to the reader by means of the poem.

C 다음 괄호 안의 단어를 우리말과 같은 뜻이 되도록 배열하여 문장을 완성하시오.

[모예] **10** 기억해야 할 중요한 교훈은 우리가 곤경의 한 가운데에 빠져 있을 동안에도 우리가 인생의 긍정적인 것들을 보려고 노력해야 한다는 것이다. (we, is, to see, should try, that)

An important lesson to remember _____ the positives in life even while we are stuck in the middle of trouble.

[수능!] **11** 하나의 중요한 사회적 능력은 얼마나 잘 또는 형편없이 사람들이 자기 자신의 감정을 표현하느냐이다. (how, people, is, express, well or poorly)

One key social competence _____ their own feelings.

12 사실들과 과학자의 관계는 단어들과 시인과의 관계와 같다. (words, the poet, are, what, to)

Facts are to the scientist _____.

S·S 01 tragedy 비극　**02** challenge 도전　overcome 극복하다
A 03 design 설계하다, 계획하다　fall into ~에 빠지다　**05** acid test 진정한 척도, 시금석　calm 침착한　in an emergency 비상시에
B 06 empathy 감정이입, 공감　narcissism 자아도취　**07** measure 척도　defeat 패배　**08** processor (컴퓨터의) 프로세서　i.e. 즉
　　09 author 작가　by means of ~에 의하여, ~의 도움으로
C 10 be stuck 꼼짝 못 하다, 갇혀 있다　**11** competence 능력, 능숙함

Unit 17
목적격보어 1

Block Board

S	V	O	to-v[ⓥ] ~
The gunman	forced	the pilot	to land in Miami.

그 총기소지자는 / 강요했다 / 그 비행사가 / 마이애미에 착륙하도록

- 목적어를 보충 설명하는 목적격보어로는 명사, 형용사, to-v, ⓥ, v-ing, v-ed, 전치사구 등이 올 수 있다.
- 주요 동사에 따른 목적격보어의 형태

want, ask, allow, encourage, cause, enable, order, tell, advise, help 등 (* help는 ⓥ도 가능)	to-v
사역 V make, have, let	ⓥ
지각 V see, watch, hear, feel, notice, observe 등	

Tip S + V + O + to-v[ⓥ]: S는 O가 ~하도록 V하다

Standard Sentences

모의 **01** Internet social networking allows us to expand our circle of friends.
인터넷 소셜 네트워킹은 가능하게 한다 / 우리가 우리의 친구 범위를 확장하는 것을

수능! **02** We must not let the virtual world take us away from the real world
우리는 허용해서는 안 된다 / 가상세계가 우리를 데리고 떠나게 / 실세계로부터

that doesn't go away with a power outage.
/ [사라지지 않는 / 정전과 함께]

Ⓐ 다음 문장에서 목적격보어를 파악하면서, 각 문장을 해석하시오.

모의 **03** If you used the same password on any other site, we encourage
you to change your password there as well.

04 The realities of growing older and the sense of brevity of our own
lives often make us question the meaning of our existence.

모의 **05** Day after day, I watched the parent birds feed their newly hatched
chicks, and I watched the chicks grow.

B 다음 문장에서 목적격보어에 밑줄을 치고, 각 문장을 해석하시오.

06 You can force the horse to go to the river but you cannot force the horse to drink from it.

07 When you read, focusing on the main idea helps you understand the details better.

▶ help + O + (to) ⓥ

(모의) **08** Most universities have students fill out an evaluation of every course they take.

09 When the clock said ten minutes to five, punctually as always, she heard the car approach and stop outside.

C 다음 네모 안에서 어법에 맞는 것을 고르시오.

(모의) **10** To improve their own chances of survival, some parasites cause their hosts | act / to act | in ways that are very different from their normal behavior.

11 Before you marry a person, you should first make them | use / to use | a computer with slow Internet service to see who they really are.

(수능) **12** I've seen couples from different ethnic groups (A) | merge / to merge | into harmonious relationships, and I've seen people from different religions (B) | come / to come | together for a strong, lasting bond.

S·S 01 expand 확장하다　circle (교제의) 범위　**02** virtual 가상의　power outage 정전
A 04 brevity 덧없음, 짧음　existence 존재　**05** feed 먹이를 주다　hatch 부화하다　chick 새끼 새; 병아리
B 07 main idea 요지　detail 세부사항　**08** fill out ~을 작성하다　evaluation 평가(서)　**09** punctually 정확하게　approach 가까이 다가오다
C 10 parasite 기생충　host 숙주　normal 보통의　**12** ethnic group 인종 집단　merge 어우러지다　lasting 지속적인　bond 유대; 접착

목적격보어 2

Block Board

S	V	O	v-ing[v-ed] ~
She	watched	her little girl	swimming in the lake.

그녀는 / 지켜보았다 / 자신의 어린 딸이 / 호수에서 수영하고 있는 것을

- 목적어와 목적격보어의 관계가 능동인지 수동인지에 따라 목적격보어로 쓰이는 분사의 형태가 달라진다.

Form S + 지각 V / find, keep, leave 등 + O + v-ing ~: O가 ~하고 있는, ~하는 〔능동·진행〕

S + 지각 V / 사역 V (make, have) / find, keep, leave 등 + O + v-ed ~: O가 ~된[당한] 〔수동·완료〕

Standard Sentences

모의 01 In the downtown area I often see homeless people begging for
시내에서 / 나는 종종 본다 / 노숙자들이 돈을 구걸하고 있는 것을

money all around the stoplights.
/ 모든 신호등 주변에서

▶ see + O + v-ing

02 I saw a car pulled over on the side of the road while I was driving
나는 보았다 / 어떤 자동차가 길 한쪽에 세워진 것을 / 내가 집으로 운전하는 동안에

home.

▶ see + O + v-ed

A 다음 문장에서 목적격보어를 파악하면서, 각 문장을 해석하시오.

03 The front desk clerk was on the phone and kept us waiting to check
in for a long time.

04 Many debtors of the bank now find themselves caught in a serious
financial position.

05 Unless we take good care of our teeth we may have them all pulled
out and have a set of false teeth made to replace them.

▶ have + O + v-ed

B 다음 문장에서 목적격보어에 밑줄을 치고, 각 문장을 해석하시오.

06 The air we breathe in and out keeps our hearts beating and our blood moving along our veins and arteries.

07 I heard the dogs barking fiercely late at night, so I came outside to see what was going on.

(모의) **08** Customers want their food delivered fast, and they want it to arrive hot.

09 Although I have known the judge for a long time, I never heard him spoken ill of by others.

C 다음 네모 안에서 어법에 맞는 것을 고르시오.

(모의) **10** Winners will have their essays (A) | post / posted | on our website. Among the winners, only the first prize winner will have his or her essay (B) | publish / published | in our magazine.

(모의) **11** Up on the green, green shoulder of hill rising to the west I could see a small group of cattle (A) | to graze / grazing |, and, below them on a gentler slope, several dozen chickens (B) | to wander / wandering | down to the meadow.

(모의) **12** Being in the spotlight made Tom (A) | feel / feeling | tense. He tried to deliver his lines as best as he could, but he could feel his voice (B) | to shake / shaking |.

S·S 01 beg 구걸하다   stoplight 신호등, 정지 신호   02 pull over (차를) 길가에 세우다
A 04 debtor 채무자, 빚진 사람   financial 재정의, 재무의   05 unless ~하지 않는다면   pull out ~을 뽑다   false teeth 틀니, 의치
B 06 beat (심장이) 뛰다   vein 정맥   artery 동맥   07 bark 짖다   fiercely 사납게   09 speak ill of ~을 욕하다, ~에 대해 나쁘게 말하다
C 10 post 게재하다, 게시하다   publish 싣다; 출판하다   11 graze 풀을 뜯다   slope 비탈, 경사지   meadow 목초지   12 tense 긴장된

보어 + 형용사구

Block Board

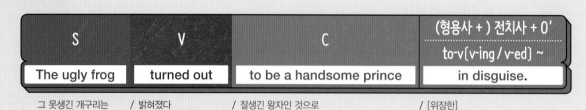

S	V	C	(형용사 +) 전치사 + O' to-v[v-ing / v-ed] ~
The ugly frog	turned out	to be a handsome prince	in disguise.
그 못생긴 개구리는 /	밝혀졌다 /	잘생긴 왕자인 것으로 /	[위장한]

- 보어로 명사가 쓰이거나 보어에 명사가 포함된 경우, 그 명사를 수식하는 형용사구가 이어질 수 있다.

- 수식하는 형용사구로는 「(형용사 +) 전치사 + O'」, to-v, v-ing, v-ed가 올 수 있다.

Standard Sentences

01 Painting is **only** a bridge **linking the painter's mind with that of the**
그림은 다리일 뿐이다 / [화가의 마음을 연결하는 / 보는 사람의 마음과]

viewer. *Eugène Delacroix*

··· ▶Know More Rainbow p.54

02 Rehearsing what you want to say can help you find a better way **to**
연습하는 것은 / 당신이 말하고 싶은 것을 / 도울 수 있다 / 당신이 더 나은 방법을 찾는 것을 /

say it.
[그것을 말하는]

▶ help + O + (to) ⓥ

A 다음 문장에서 보어를 수식하는 형용사구를 파악하면서, 각 문장을 해석하시오.

03 Knowledge workers are the ones responsible for keeping the high-tech economy running.

(모의) **04** In 1953, Jacqueline Cochran became the first woman pilot to break the sound barrier. Additionally, she was the first female to pilot a jet across the Atlantic. *sound barrier 음속 장벽(비행기의 속도가 음속에 가까워질 때 충격파가 발생하는 현상)

05 We should let our beliefs and values guide our decisions about how to live our life.

B 다음 문장에서 보어를 수식하는 형용사구를 괄호로 묶고, 각 문장을 해석하시오.

06 Improved methods of transportation are forcing man to discard the concept of distance in the past responsible for keeping people separated.

07 Humans became the only species to acquire guidance on how to live from the accumulated knowledge of their ancestors, rather than just from their DNA.

08 The global village is all the countries of the world thought of as being closely connected by modern communication and trade.

09 A day without a friend is like a pot without a single drop of honey left inside. *the short story collection <Winnie the Pooh>*

C 다음 네모 안에서 어법에 맞는 것을 고르시오.

10 A mouse is a device makes / making it easier to select different options from computer menus.

▶ 긴 목적어(to select ~)를 대신하는 가목적어 it이 쓰임

Up! **11** Hindsight bias is a term using / used in psychology to explain the tendency of people to overestimate their ability to have predicted an outcome that could not possibly have been predicted.

＊hindsight bias 사후인지 편향

··· **Know More** Rainbow p.55

12 Lots of countries wanted their pharmaceutical companies to be the first succeed / to succeed in developing vaccines and treatments for coronavirus.

S·S 02 rehearse 연습하다
A 03 responsible for ~에 책임이 있는; ~의 원인이 되는　high-tech 첨단 기술의　04 pilot 조종사; 조종하다　05 value (pl.) 가치관; 가치, 진가
B 06 discard 버리다　separate (따로) 떨어지다, 분리시키다　07 accumulate 축적하다　ancestor 조상　08 trade 무역, 거래　09 pot 단지, 항아리
C 10 device 기구, 장치　11 term 용어　outcome 결과　12 pharmaceutical company 제약회사　vaccine 백신　treatment 치료제

보어 + 형용사절

중요도 ★★★
난이도 ★★★

Block Board

S	V	O	C	who[which / that] + (s) + v ~ when[where / why / that] + s + v ~
He	asked	us	to help students	who can't read.
그는	/ 요청했다	/ 우리가	/ 학생들을 도울 것을	/ [읽지 못하는]

- 보어는 형용사절의 수식을 받아 길어질 수 있다.
- 형용사절은 관계대명사(who, which, that) 또는 관계부사(when, where, why, that)가 이끈다. ➔ Unit 23~26

Standard Sentences

01 Education is the most powerful weapon **which you can use to change**
교육은 가장 강력한 무기이다 / [당신이 세상을 바꾸기 위해서 사용할 수 있는]

the world. *Nelson Mandela*

수능! **02** Life is a game **where there are multiple winners.**
인생은 게임이다 / [다수의 승자가 존재하는]

Ⓐ 다음 문장에서 보어를 수식하는 형용사절을 파악하면서, 각 문장을 해석하시오.

03 King Arthur was a legendary king who brought peace to his kingdom by vanquishing all forms of evil.

⋯ Know More Rainbow p.56

04 In family life, love is the oil that eases friction, the cement that binds closer together, and the music that brings harmony. *Eva Burrows*

모의 **05** Nutrition education in schools can help **more students** eat balanced diets that include more vegetables and have a healthy life.

▶ help + O + (to) ⓥ

B 다음 문장에서 보어를 수식하는 형용사절을 괄호로 묶고, 각 문장을 해석하시오.

모의 **06** According to one traditional definition, aesthetics is the branch of philosophy that deals with beauty, especially beauty in the arts.

07 Love is like a beautiful flower which I may not touch, but whose fragrance makes the garden a place of delight just the same. *Helen Keller*

08 I consider nature a vast chemical laboratory in which all kinds of composition and decompositions are formed. *Antoine Lavoisier*

09 At the personal level, competition allows us to become the best individual we can be.

C 다음 문장의 빈칸에 들어갈 내용으로 알맞은 것을 보기에서 고르시오.

> • 보기 •
> ⓐ through which you must see the world
> ⓑ where two strangers can meet on terms of absolute intimacy
> ⓒ that changes over time and depends on the immediate circumstances

수능! **10** In many situations the boundary between good and bad is a reference point _____.

11 Better keep yourself clean and bright; you are the window _____
_____. *George Bernard Shaw*

··· **Know More** Rainbow p.57
▶ You had better + ⓥ
= You better + ⓥ
= Better + ⓥ (구어체)

12 Every novel is an equal collaboration between the writer and the reader and it is the only place in the world _____
_____. *Paul Auster*

A 03 vanquish 무찌르다 evil 악 **04** ease 완화하다, 덜다 friction 마찰 cement 접합(접착)제 bind 결속시키다, 묶다
B 06 aesthetics 미학 **07** fragrance 향기 **08** composition 합성; 구성 decomposition 분해; 부패
C 보기 on terms of intimacy 친한 사이로 immediate 당면한 **10** boundary 경계선 a reference point 기준점 **12** collaboration 합작, 협력

Chapter 04

Review

A 다음 문장을 해석하시오.

01 Words are to language what notes are to music.

02 Don't let what you can't do stop you from doing what you can do. *John Wooden*

03 A central lesson of science is that we must try to free our minds of dogma and to guarantee the freedom to publish, to contradict, and to experiment.

04 Technological advances will allow high-performance athletes to move faster, jump higher, hit harder, and improve their consistency.

B 다음 네모 안에서 어법에 맞는 것을 고르시오.

(수능!) **05** Walking up the path and back to the car, they could still hear the fish to splash / splashing in the water.

06 I didn't have time to shop at the market yesterday, so I phoned the store and had the groceries deliver / delivered .

(모의!) **07** The experience of eating a pile of unwanted cabbage until they feel sick is hardly going to make children jump / to jump for joy the next time it is served.

C 다음 괄호 안의 말을 이용하여 우리말과 같은 뜻이 되도록 문장을 완성하시오. (필요하면 어형을 바꿀 것)

08 그 남자가 자신의 자동차에 돌아왔을 때, 그는 차 유리창들이 깨진 것을 알았다.
(car windows, break, find)

→ When the man returned to his car, he _____.

09 과학 지식의 성장은 우리가 삶의 위험들의 일부를 통제하도록 해 주었다.
(some of the risks of life, control, allow, us)

→ The growth of scientific knowledge has _____.

10 돈의 가장 근본적인 특징 중 하나는 그것이 쉽게 운반 가능한 가치 저장소로서의 역할을 한다는 것이다.
(act, it, be, that)

→ One of the most fundamental characteristics of money _____
as an easily transportable store of value.

D 다음 문장의 빈칸에 들어갈 내용으로 알맞은 것을 보기 에서 고르시오.

> • 보기 •
> ⓐ that determine your destiny in life
> ⓑ to find peaceful ways to resolve conflicts
> ⓒ to extend the range of our limited senses

11 Yes and No are the two most important words _____
_____.

12 One of the principal aims of the sciences is _____
_____ by translating invisible and inaudible phenomena into events
that can be seen or heard.

13 Nuclear weapons have turned war between superpowers into a mad act of
collective suicide, and forced the most powerful nations on earth _____
_____.

A 01 note 음표　**03** dogma 독단, 신조　guarantee 보장하다　contradict 반박하다　**04** advance 진보　consistency 일관성
B 05 splash (물속에서) 첨벙거리다　**06** grocery 식료품　**07** a pile of 한 무더기의　cabbage 양배추　**C 10** store 저장소
D 보기 destiny 운명　resolve 해결하다　**12** principal 주요한　translate (다른 상태·성질로) 바꾸다, 변형하다　invisible 보이지 않는
inaudible 들리지 않는　phenomenon 현상 (*pl.* phenomena)　**13** nuclear weapon 핵무기　collective suicide 집단 자살

STAGE Ⅱ
수식어 중심의 구문

Chapter 05 명사 수식어: 구
Chapter 06 명사 수식어: 절
Chapter 07 부사적 수식어: 구
Chapter 08 부사적 수식어: 절

Chapter

05 명사 수식어: 구

Get Ready!

☑ 명사 수식어는 문장의 주요 성분인 주어, 목적어, 보어 등으로 쓰이는 명사를 꾸며준다.

☑ 명사를 수식하는 전치사구, to-v, v-ing ~, v-ed ~는 수식하는 명사 뒤에 온다.

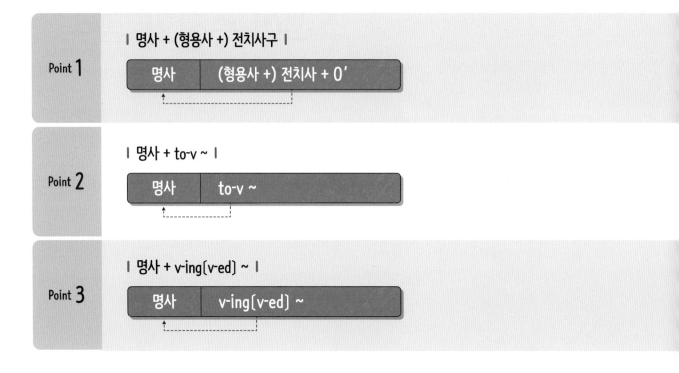

Point 1

❘ **명사 + (형용사 +) 전치사구** ❘

| 명사 | (형용사 +) 전치사 + O′ |

Point 2

❘ **명사 + to-v ~** ❘

| 명사 | to-v ~ |

Point 3

❘ **명사 + v-ing[v-ed] ~** ❘

| 명사 | v-ing[v-ed] ~ |

- **unit 21** 명사 + (형용사 +) 전치사구
- **unit 22** 명사 + to-v[v-ing ~ / v-ed ~]

명사 + (형용사 +) 전치사구 ➔ Unit 21	▷ 형용사에 이어지는 어구가 있으면 명사를 뒤에서 수식한다. ▷ 형용사 역할을 하는 전치사구는 명사를 뒤에서 수식한다.
명사 + to-v ~ ➔ Unit 22	▷ 형용사 역할을 하는 to-v는 명사를 뒤에서 수식한다.
명사 + v-ing[v-ed] ~ ➔ Unit 22	▷ 분사는 형용사의 역할을 할 수 있으며, 단독으로 쓰이면 명사의 앞에서 수식하고, 뒤에 딸린 어구가 있으면 뒤에서 명사를 수식한다. ▷ 수식을 받는 명사와의 관계가 능동일 때는 현재분사(v-ing)를 쓰고, 수동일 때는 과거분사(v-ed)를 쓴다.

unit 21
명사 + (형용사 +) 전치사구

중요도 ★★★
난이도 ★★★

Block Board

~		명사	(형용사 +) 전치사 + O'
He	has developed	software	useful to designers.
그는	/ 개발해왔다	/ 소프트웨어를	/ [디자이너들에게 유용한]

- 형용사는 보통 명사 앞에 오지만, 형용사구는 뒤에서 명사를 수식한다. 형용사 역할을 하는 전치사구 또한 명사 뒤에 온다.

Form 명사 + (형용사 +) 전치사 + O'

Tip 명사를 수식하는 「(형용사 +) 전치사구」를 괄호로 묶는다.

Standard Sentences

01 Now the Internet has become a well-integrated technology **essential**
현재 인터넷은 잘 통합된 기술이 되었다 / [전 세계적

to global business and culture.
사업과 문화에 필수적인]

02 All people have the right **to medical care** regardless of race, religion,
모든 사람들은 권리를 가지고 있다 / [의료에 대한] / 인종, 종교, 신조 또는 정치적 소속에 관계없이

creed or political affiliation. *Doctors Without Borders*

A 다음 문장에서 명사 뒤의 수식어를 파악하면서, 각 문장을 해석하시오.

03 A small blue car with an unknown driver at the wheel was following close behind my car.

04 The greatest scientific discoveries are the product of imagination, curiosity, and years of careful research.

05 A global network of non-government organizations works toward eliminating the production and use of toxic chemicals harmful to human health and the environment.

B 다음 문장에서 명사 뒤의 수식어를 괄호로 묶고, 각 문장을 해석하시오.

06 Read the instructions on the front cover of each test carefully.

07 Microsoft Excel is a flexible and user-friendly software suitable for beginners and advanced users alike.

(모의) **08** Empathy in the sense of adopting someone's viewpoint is not the same as empathy in the sense of feeling compassion toward the person, but the first can lead to the second by a natural route.

09 Love is the only force capable of transforming an enemy into a friend. *Martin Luther King Jr.*

··· **Know More** Rainbow p.65

"Love is the only force capable of transforming an enemy into a friend."

C 다음 네모 안에서 어법에 맞는 것을 고르시오.

10 The particular strategies appropriate to an organization depend / depends to a large extent on the political and financial circumstances of the organization.

(모의) **11** Challenges to new ideas is / are the legitimate business of science in building valid knowledge.

(모의) **12** Often the difference between feeling fulfilled at work and feeling empty, lost, annoyed, and burned out is / are all about whether or not you're learning anything.

S·S 01 integrate 통합하다   02 regardless of ~에 관계없이   race 인종   creed 신조, 신념   affiliation 소속
A 03 at the wheel (자동차의) 핸들을 잡고, 운전하여   follow close behind 바짝 뒤따르다   05 toxic 유독한
B 06 instruction (*pl.*) 지시 사항, 설명   07 flexible 마음대로 바꿀 수 있는   user-friendly 사용하기 쉬운   suitable 적합한   08 empathy 공감
adopt 취하다, 채택하다   compassion 동정심   09 transform A into B A를 B로 바꾸다   enemy 적; 장애물
C 10 to a large extent 크게   11 legitimate 타당한; 합법적인   valid (근거가) 확실한   12 fulfilled 성취감을 느끼는   burn out 녹초가 되게 하다

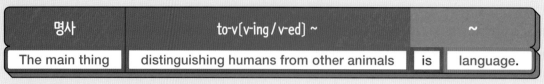

unit 22

명사 + to-v[v-ing ~ / v-ed ~]

중요도 ★★☆
난이도 ★★★

명사	to-v[v-ing / v-ed] ~		~
The main thing	distinguishing humans from other animals	is	language.

주요한 것은 / [인간을 다른 동물들과 구별하는] / ~이다 / 언어

- to-v, v-ing, v-ed는 명사를 수식하는 형용사 역할을 할 수 있다. to-v는 항상 명사 뒤에서 수식하며, v-ing와 v-ed는 딸린 어구(목적어, 보어, 부사 등)가 있을 때 명사 뒤에서 수식한다.

  Form 명사 + to-v : ~할, ~해야 하는

  명사 + v-ing ~ / v-ed ~ : ~하는, ~하고 있는 (능동) / ~되는, ~된 (수동)

  Tip 명사를 뒤에서 수식하는 부정사구 또는 분사구를 괄호로 묶는다.

Standard Sentences

수능! 01 The human species is unique in its ability **to expand its functionality**
인간 종은 독특하다 / 그것의 능력에 있어서 / [그것의 기능성을 확대하는
▶ 명사 + to-v ~

by inventing new cultural tools.
/ 새로운 문화적 도구를 발명함으로써]

02 Climate is the total sum of the weather **experienced over a long**
기후는 날씨의 총합이다 / [충분히 오랜 기간 동안에 걸쳐 경험되는
▶ 명사 + v-ed ~

enough time period for the pattern to be established.
/ 경향이 자리잡을 정도로]

A 다음 문장에서 명사 뒤의 수식어를 파악하면서, 각 문장을 해석하시오.

수능! 03 Robots are not equipped with capabilities like humans to solve problems as they arise.

모의 04 The common idea of a creative individual coming up with great insights, discoveries, works, or inventions in isolation is wrong.

05 The story called *The Strange Case of Dr. Jekyll and Mr. Hyde* is the famous story of a good man sometimes turning into a horrible monster.

··· **Know More** Rainbow p.66

B 다음 문장에서 명사 뒤의 수식어를 괄호로 묶고, 각 문장을 해석하시오.

06 People judged to be functionally illiterate lack the basic reading and writing skills required in everyday life.

(모의) **07** Yeast cells growing on a grape skin obtain energy from nutrient molecules originally processed within the grape leaves and stored within the fruit.

08 You must pay the past-due balance by the date written on the front page of your bill to avoid the late fee.

09 On February 9th, 2020, South Korean movie *Parasite* became the first foreign-language film to be crowned Best Picture at the Academy Awards. *the magazine <The Economist>*

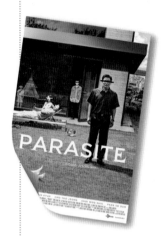

C 다음 네모 안에서 어법에 맞는 것을 고르시오.

10 The order to abandon ship automatically assumes two rules: women and children are first, and the captain is the last │ to leave / left │ or goes down with his vessel.

11 The company has decided to launch a new campaign (A)│ targeting / targeted │ inexperienced college graduates (B)│ preparing / prepared │ to enter the job market for the first time.

(Up!) **12** The desire to fly is an idea (A)│ handing / handed │ down to us by our ancestors who looked enviously on the birds (B)│ soaring / soared │ freely through space on the infinite highway of the air. *Orville Wright*

S·S 01 functionality 기능성   02 sum 총합, 합계   establish (기록, 습관 등이) 자리를 잡다; 확립하다
A 03 be equipped with ~을 갖추고 있다   arise 발생하다, 생기다   04 come up with 생각해내다   in isolation 홀로, 고립되어   05 case 사건, 사례
B 06 illiterate 문맹의, 읽고 쓸 줄 모르는   08 past-due 기일을 넘긴   balance 잔금, 지불 잔액   late fee 연체료   09 crown (영예를) 지니게 하다
C 10 abandon 버리다   assume (태도를) 취하다   vessel 배, 선박   11 launch 시작하다   12 hand down 전하다, 물려주다   soar 날아오르다

Chapter 05

Review

A 다음 문장을 우리말로 해석하시오.

01 We enclose here a copy of our illustrated catalogue about the main items available at present.

02 Two of the hardest tests in life are the patience to wait for the right moment and the courage to accept whatever you encounter.

03 We listened to the sound of the rain beating down on the roof and thunder rolling off in the distance.

(모의) **04** Words acquire objective meanings because of the "pull" exerted by social pressures to conform to publicly approved usage.

B 다음 네모 안에서 어법에 맞는 것을 고르시오.

(모의) **05** The Superhero Walkathon is an annual fundraising walking event (A)│ holding / held │ to support the Active Way, a charity (B)│ to dedicate / dedicated │ to granting the wishes of terminally ill children.

06 Man's ability to walk upright and use his hands, and his natural capacity │ sees / to see │ into the distance instead of looking at the ground, became weapons of survival.

07 In the information age, reliance on expert intuition will gradually be replaced by computer programs (A)│ processing / processed │ the relevant data using rules (B)│ knowing / known │ as algorithms.

(수능) **08** The visual preoccupation of early humans with the nonhuman creatures │ inhabiting / inhabited │ their world becomes profoundly meaningful.

C 다음 괄호 안의 말을 이용하여 우리말과 같은 뜻이 되도록 문장을 완성하시오.

09 우리 생태계의 한 부분, 심지어 작은 부분에서의 변화는 다른 모든 것에 영향을 미친다.
(of our ecosystem, one part, changes, to)

→ _____, even a small part, have consequences for everything else.

10 상층 대기에 있는 오존이라고 불리는 가스층이 태양의 해로운 광선으로부터 우리를 보호한다.
(protects, called ozone, in the upper atmosphere)

→ A layer of a gas _____ us from harmful rays of the Sun.

11 페이스북과 인스타그램은 담배와 주류 상품에 대한 판매와 정보를 제한하는 새로운 정책을 발표했다.
(restricting, sales and content, new policy)

→ Facebook and Instagram announced _____

_____ for tobacco and alcohol products.

A 01 enclose 동봉하다   illustrate 삽화를 넣다   at present 현재   **02** encounter 맞닥뜨리다   **03** beat 두드리다   roll off (천둥이) 우르릉대다; 굴러떨어지다   in the distance 멀리서   **04** objective 객관적인   pull 영향력   exert (영향력을) 행사하다   conform 순응하다   approve 인정하다   **B 05** fundraising 기금 마련, 모금   dedicate 바치다   grant (소원, 간청을) 들어주다   terminally ill (병이) 중증인, 말기인   **07** reliance 의존   intuition 직관   relevant 관계가 있는   algorithm 알고리즘(문제 해결 절차 및 방법)   **08** preoccupation 심취   inhabit 살다, 거주하다   profoundly 상당히   **C 09** have consequences for ~에 영향을 미치다   **10** layer 층   ray 광선, 빛살   **11** announce 발표하다   restrict 제한하다   content (인터넷이나 컴퓨터 통신에서 제공되는) 정보, 내용물

06 명사 수식어 절

☑ 명사를 수식하는 형용사절은 관계대명사 또는 관계부사가 이끈다.
☑ 관계사가 생략된 관계사절, 수식받는 명사와 떨어져 있는 관계사절 등의 문장 구조 파악에 특히 유의해야 한다.

Point 1

| 명사 + 관계대명사절 |

| 명사 | who[which/that] + (s) + v ~ |

Point 2

| 명사 + 관계부사절 |

| 명사 | when[where/why/that] + s + v ~ |

Point 3

| 명사 + (관계사 +) s + v ~ |

| 명사 | s + v ~ |

Point 4

| 명사, 관계사절 |

| 명사 |, who[which/when/where] + (s) + v ~ |

- **unit 23** 명사 + 관계대명사절
- **unit 24** 명사 + 전치사 + 관계대명사절
- **unit 25** 명사 + 관계부사절
- **unit 26** 명사 + 관계사가 생략된 수식절
- **unit 27** 명사와 관계사절의 분리
- **unit 28** 명사, 관계사절

명사 + 관계대명사절 Unit 23	▷ 관계대명사 who와 which는 명사를 뒤에서 수식하는 형용사절을 이끈다. ▷ who 또는 which를 대신해서 관계대명사 that을 쓸 수 있다.
명사 + 관계부사절 Unit 25	▷ 관계부사 when(시간), where(장소), why(이유)는 명사를 뒤에서 수식하는 관계부 사절을 이끈다. ▷ 관계부사 when, where, why, how를 대신해서 that을 쓸 수도 있다.
명사 + (관계사 +) s + v ~ Unit 26	▷ 목적격 관계대명사 또는 관계부사는 종종 생략된다.
명사, 관계사절 Unit 28	▷ 앞에 나온 명사에 대해서 보충 설명을 할 때는 콤마 다음에 관계대명사 who, which와 관계부사 when, where가 이끄는 관계사절이 온다.

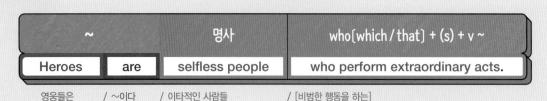

unit 23
명사 + 관계대명사절

중요도 ★★☆
난이도 ★★☆

~	명사	who[which / that] + (s) + v ~
Heroes	are	selfless people	who perform extraordinary acts.

영웅들은 / ~이다 / 이타적인 사람들 / [비범한 행동을 하는]

- 관계대명사 who, which, that이 이끄는 형용사절은 그 앞에 오는 명사(선행사)를 뒤에서 수식한다.

  Form 명사 + 관계대명사[who / which / that] + (s) + v ~ : (…가) ~하는 명사

  Tip 관계대명사는 명사를 수식하는 형용사절을 이끄는 역할이며, 그 자체는 해석하지 않는다.

Standard Sentences

01 Social welfare is a set of activities **which have, in part, been directed**
사회 복지는 일련의 활동이다 / [부분적으로, 불평등한 분배의 상쇄를 지향해온]

to offset unequal distribution.

02 A Korean speaker uses different verb forms **depending on his or her**
한국어 사용자는 다른 동사의 형태를 사용한다 / 그 또는 그녀의 관계에 따라서

relationship to the person whom he or she is speaking to.
/ [그 사람에 대한 / [그 또는 그녀가 이야기하고 있는]]

A 다음 문장에서 관계대명사절을 파악하면서, 각 문장을 해석하시오.

모의 **03** Birds that in the breeding season fight one another to death over territory may end up in the same flock during migration.

04 Culture shock is the feeling of confusion felt by someone visiting a country or place whose culture they do not know.

▶ whose는 소유격 관계대명사로 '~의 …'로 해석함

수능 **05** We define cognitive intrigue as the wonder that stimulates and intrinsically motivates an individual to voluntarily engage in an activity.

B 다음 문장에서 관계대명사절을 괄호로 묶고, 각 문장을 해석하시오.

06 Time is too slow for those who wait, too swift for those who fear, too long for those who grieve, too short for those who rejoice, but for those who love, time is eternity. *Henry Van Dyke*

07 The man with a toothache thinks that everyone whose teeth are sound is happy. The poverty-stricken man makes the same mistake about the rich man. *George Bernard Shaw*

08 The term "placebo" is used to describe a "pill" which contains no medical ingredients but which often produces the same effect as genuine medication.   *placebo 가짜 약, 위약

모의 **09** Flu and colds spread very quickly, especially with the large amount of contact that people now have with each other.

C 다음 네모 안에서 어법에 맞는 것을 고르시오.

모의 **10** Andy Weir wrote "*The Martian*" for science fiction readers who / whom want their stories firmly grounded in scientific fact.

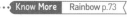 ··· **Know More** Rainbow p.73

11 A rain forest is a virtually untapped storehouse of evolutionary achievement it / that will prove increasingly valuable to mankind as it yields its secrets.

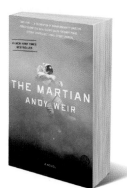

수능! **12** Those people, organizations, and countries that possess the highest-quality information is / are likely to prosper economically, socially, and politically.

S·S 01 social welfare 사회 복지   offset 상쇄하다   distribution 분배   **02** verb 동사
A 03 breeding season 번식기   territory 영역   end up 결국 (어떤 처지에) 처하게 되다
   04 culture shock 문화 충격   **05** cognitive 인지의   intrigue 호기심, 흥미   intrinsically 본질적으로   voluntarily 자발적으로
B 06 swift 빠른, 신속한   grieve 슬퍼하다   rejoice 기뻐하다   eternity 영원   **07** sound 건강한, 이상 없는   poverty-stricken 가난에 시달리는
C 10 firmly 확고하게   ground 근거를 두다; 땅   **11** virtually 사실상, 거의   untapped 미개발의   yield (비밀을) 밝히다   **12** prosper 번영하다

명사 + 전치사 + 관계대명사절

중요도 ★★★
난이도 ★★★

Block Board

명사	전치사 + whom[which] + s + v ~	~	
The music	to which I'm listening	is	nice.
음악은	/ [내가 듣고 있는]	/ ~이다	/ 멋진

- 관계대명사가 전치사의 목적어로 쓰일 때, 전치사는 관계대명사의 바로 앞이나 관계사절의 끝에 온다. 전치사가 관계대명사와 떨어져 있을 때는 관계대명사를 생략할 수 있다. ▶ unit 26

  Form 명사 + 전치사 + 관계대명사 + s + v ~ = 명사 + (관계대명사) + s + v + 전치사 ~

  Plus⊕ 관계대명사가 생략된 경우에는 전치사는 문장의 뒷부분에 위치하며, 관계대명사 that은 전치사 다음에 쓸 수 없다.

  Tip 명사를 수식하는 「전치사 + 관계대명사절」을 괄호로 묶는다.

Standard Sentences

01 Many authors **today** are creating fairy stories **in which the heroines**
많은 작가들이 오늘날 동화를 창작하고 있다   / [여주인공들이 보다 적극적인]

are more active.

▶ in which = where

02 It is **often** difficult to get books back from people **to whom you**
(…은) 종종 어렵다   / 책들을 사람들에게서 돌려받는 것은   / [당신이 그것들을

have lent them.
빌려준]

Ⓐ 다음 문장에서 「전치사 + 관계대명사」절을 파악하면서, 각 문장을 해석하시오.

03 Sincere apologies are for those that make them, not for those to
whom they are made. *Greg LeMond*

04 Even the exact same question can elicit very different responses
depending on the context in which the question occurs.

모의 **05** When a seed grows into a tree, it represents only a change in the
degree to which its potential, always inherent in its original nature,
is realized.

B 다음 문장에서 「전치사＋관계대명사」절에 밑줄을 치고, 각 문장을 해석하시오.

06 I have but one lamp by which my feet are guided, and that is the lamp of experience. *Patrick Henry*

07 What makes a study scientific is not the nature of the things with which it is concerned, but the method by which it deals with those things.

모의 **08** All human societies have economic systems within which goods and services are produced, distributed, and consumed.

09 *Spider-Man* was a tremendous hit with readers because it gave millions of teenagers a hero with whom they could identify.

C 다음 문장의 빈칸에 들어갈 내용으로 알맞은 것을 보기에서 고르시오.

> ─ 보기 •
> ⓐ to whom a child is most attached
> ⓑ with which language is used or understood
> ⓒ by which individuals adapt their opinion

10 The effectiveness of human society is largely dependent upon the clarity, accuracy, and efficiency _____.

모의 **11** Separation anxiety disorder is defined as excessive worry and fear about being apart from individuals _____.

 ···▶ **Know More** Rainbow p.75

12 Social influence is the process _____, revise their beliefs, or change their behavior as a result of social interactions with other people.

S·S 01 author 작가, 저자　fairy story 동화　heroine 여주인공
A 03 sincere 진정한, 진심의　apology 사과　**04** elicit 이끌어 내다　context 상황　**05** potential 잠재력　inherent 내재된, 내재하는
B 06 but 오직, 단지　**07** concern 관계하다　deal with ~을 다루다　**08** consume 소비하다　**09** tremendous 엄청난　identify with ~와 동일시하다
C 보기 be attached to ~에 애착을 가지다　**10** clarity 명확성　accuracy 정확성　**11** separation anxiety 분리 불안　**12** revise 바꾸다, 변경하다

unit 25
명사 + 관계부사절

중요도 ★★★
난이도 ★★☆

Block Board

명사	when[where / why / (how)] + s + v ~	~
The reason	why I'm calling	is	to make an appointment.

이유는 / [내가 전화하고 있는] / ~이다 / 약속을 정하는 것

- 관계부사 when(시간), where(장소), why(이유)는 명사를 뒤에서 수식하는 형용사절을 이끌며, 관계부사 how(방법)는 명사(선행사)와 함께 쓰지 않고 둘 중 하나만 쓴다.

  Form 명사 + 관계부사[when / where / why / that] + s + v ~

  Plus⊕ 관계부사 that은 when, where, why, how를 대신할 수 있다.

  Tip 명사를 수식하는 관계부사절을 괄호로 묶고, 관계부사 자체는 해석하지 않는다.

Standard Sentences

01 We are living in the first century **when the greatest skills will come**
우리는 첫 번째 세기에 살고 있다 / [가장 위대한 기술들이 인간의 행동에서 생겨날

from human actions rather than from nature.
/ 자연으로부터라기보다는]

02 Competition becomes a zero sum game **where one organization**
경쟁은 제로섬 게임이 된다 / [한 조직만 이길 수 있는

can only win at the expense of others.
/ 다른 조직들의 희생으로]

▶ 관계부사 where의 선행사: 물리적 장소 외에 point, case, situation 등과 같은 추상적인 장소 개념도 가능함

A 다음 문장에서 관계부사절을 파악하면서, 각 문장을 해석하시오.

(모의) **03** We are embarking on a time when each individual will have all their own medical data and the computing power to process it in the context of their own world.

04 The reason why worry kills more people than work is that more people worry than work. *Robert Frost*

05 The way people act is often influenced by experiences that they had in the past and by the need to fulfill basic human needs.

▶ The way + (that) + people act

B 다음 문장에서 관계부사절을 괄호로 묶고, 각 문장을 해석하시오.

06 We look forward to the time when the Power of Love will replace the Love of Power. Then will our world know the blessings of peace.

(모의) **07** In general, people accept job offers where the monetary compensation is near the amount that they were hoping for.

08 Possibly, we all have high points and low points in our creative cycles. This may be the reason why we have "good days" and "bad days" at work.

(모의) **09** In today's digital environment, appearing in the mainstream news is still an important way that citizens can communicate with a broader community about events and issues.

C 다음 문장의 빈칸에 들어갈 내용으로 알맞은 것을 보기에서 고르시오.

> ● 보기 ●
> ⓐ when one says to another   ⓑ where sugar is cheap and plentiful
> ⓒ that one would be ineffective without the other

(모의) **10** The best picture books contain words and pictures that complement each other and are dependent upon each other to the point _____ _____.

11 The food industry has made a fortune because we retain Stone Age bodies that crave sugar but live in a Space Age world _____ _____.

12 Friendship is born at that moment _____, "What! You too? I thought I was the only one." *C. S. Lewis*

S·S **02** at the expense of ~의 희생으로
A **03** embark ~에 들어서다, 착수하다   **05** fulfill 충족시키다
B **06** look forward to ~을 기대하다   replace 대체하다, 대신하다   **07** in general 일반적으로   compensation 보수, 급여; 보상   **08** cycle 주기; 순환
C **10** contain 담고 있다, 포함하다   complement 보완하다   **11** make a fortune 거액을 벌다, 재산을 모으다   crave 간절히 원하다, 갈망하다

unit 26

명사 + 관계사가 생략된 수식절

중요도 ★★★
난이도 ★★★

Block Board

명사	s + v ~	~
The information	we get from the Internet	is | not always | reliable.
정보는	/ [우리가 인터넷에서 얻는]	/ 항상 신뢰할 수 있는 것은 아니다

- 목적격 관계대명사 whom, which, that과 관계부사 when, why는 생략될 수 있다. the way를 선행사로 하는 관계부사 how도 생략된다.

  Form 명사 + (관계사) s + v ~ : ～가 …하는 명사

  Tip 명사 다음에 「주어 + 동사 ～」의 절이 이어지면, 관계사가 생략되었을 가능성이 높다.

Standard Sentences

01 There are some among us ✔fortune smiles on, and others ✔she
우리 중에는 몇몇 사람들이 있다 / [행운의 여신이 미소 짓는] / 그리고 다른 사람들이 (있다) /

frowns at.
[그녀가 눈살을 찌푸리는]

▶✔ 자리에 whom 또는 that이 생략됨

02 Scientists can answer when and how the universe began, but
과학자들은 답할 수 있다 / 언제 그리고 어떻게 우주가 시작되었는지 / 그러나

cannot calculate the reason ✔it began.
이유를 추정할 수는 없다 / [그것이 시작된]

▶✔ 자리에 why가 생략됨

A 다음 문장에서 생략된 관계사를 파악하면서, 각 문장을 해석하시오.

모의 **03** I am writing to you regarding a price discrepancy I encountered between an item offered in your retail store and the same item offered on your website.

04 This country imports about two-thirds of the raw materials it needs and exports approximately three-fifths of the machinery it produces.

05 The advent of driverless cars and other vehicles promises to revolutionize the way the world transports itself goods every day.

▶ the way와 관계부사 how는 같이 쓸 수 없음

B 다음 문장에서 관계사가 생략된 자리에 ∨ 표시를 하고 형용사절을 괄호로 묶은 후, 해석하시오.

06 One of the most effective ways to calm down from stress is intimate contact with people you trust and feel comfortable around.

07 Leaders need to safeguard the faith people have in them by acting in accordance with the expectations they have raised themselves.

(수능) **08** One reason most dogs are much happier than most people is that dogs aren't affected by external circumstances the way we are.

▶ the way는 접속사로 '~처럼' 의 뜻으로 쓰임

09 An instructor should exemplify the things he seeks to teach. It will be of great advantage if you yourself can do all you ask of your students and more. *Bruce Lee*

C 다음 문장의 빈칸에 들어갈 내용으로 알맞은 것을 보기 에서 고르시오.

> • 보기 •
> ⓐ you love a person   ⓑ you would be working for
> ⓒ the sun's heat is distributed

10 Before a job interview, it is a good idea to find out some background information about the company _____.

11 Because of the huge volume of clouds it generates, the Amazon River system plays a major role in the way _____ around the globe.   *river system 수계(한 지역을 흐르는 지표면의 하천이나 고여 있는 표층수 및 지류)

(모의) **12** Do you think that being able to list all the reasons _____ _____ enables you to love that person more or differently?

S·S 01 fortune 행운의 여신; 행운; 재산   frown 눈살을 찌푸리다   **02** calculate 추정하다; 계산하다
A 03 regarding ~에 관하여   discrepancy 차이; 불일치   retail store 매장, 소매 상점   **04** raw material 원료, 원자재   approximately 대략
machinery 기계류   **05** advent 출현   promise ~할 가망이 있다   revolutionize 혁명을 일으키다
B 06 intimate 친밀한   **07** safeguard 보호하다   in accordance with ~에 따라   **08** external 외부의   **09** exemplify ~의 좋은 예가 되다
C 보기 distribute 배분하다   **11** huge 거대한   volume 분량   generate 발생시키다   **12** list 열거하다

명사와 관계사절의 분리

중요도 ★★★
난이도 ★★★

~	명사	수식어	관계사 + (s) + v ~
I saw	a dress	in a shop	that my daughter would love.

나는 / 보았다 / 드레스를 / 가게에서 / [내 딸이 아주 좋아할]

• 명사와 그 명사를 수식하는 관계사절은 경우에 따라 떨어져 있을 수 있다.

Form 명사 뒤에 수식어가 있는 경우

명사 + 수식어 + 관계사 + (s) + v ~

주어를 수식하는 관계사절이 길고, 서술어가 짧아서 관계사절을 뒤로 보낸 경우

명사 + 서술어 + 관계사 + (s) + v ~

Standard Sentences

01 I can't think of any good film at the moment **that I'd like to see.**
나는 어떤 좋은 영화가 생각나지 않는다 / 지금으로서는 / [내가 보고 싶은]

▶ any good film + 수식어 + 관계사절

02 That government is best **which governs least**, because its people
그러한 정부가 제일이다 / [가장 적게 통제하는] / 왜냐하면 그 국민들은 스스로를

discipline themselves. *Thomas Jefferson*
규율하기 때문에

▶ That government + 서술어 + 관계사절

Ⓐ 다음 문장에서 명사를 수식하는 관계사절을 파악하면서, 각 문장을 해석하시오.

(모의) **03** Some people recognize humans as the only one among the living organisms that can change its behavior to preserve other species.

04 Courage doesn't always roar. Sometimes courage is the little voice at the end of the day that says "I'll try again tomorrow." *Mary Anne Radmacher*

05 Creative solutions are required which not only answer yesterday's questions but also anticipate tomorrow's needs.

B 다음 문장에서 명사와 그 명사를 수식하는 관계사절에 밑줄을 치고, 각 문장을 해석하시오.

06 A gene is a part of a cell in a living thing that controls what it looks like, how it grows, and how it develops.

07 Hospices care for patients suffering from incurable diseases who are not expected to live for more than a year.

08 From smart cities to self-driving cars, technology is needed that can allow devices and services to access great volumes of data.

09 The time will come when people will see that my paintings are worth more than the price of the paint. *Vincent van Gogh*

C 다음 네모 안에서 어법에 맞는 것을 고르시오.

(수능) **10** The ultimate life force lies in tiny cellular factories of energy, called mitochondria, that burn / burns nearly all the oxygen we breathe in.

11 Most professors see themselves in a position of professional authority over their students whom / which they earned by many years of study.

(모의) **12** Art has mostly been considered in terms of seeking beauty, but there are other reasons deeply rooted in the human experience that create / creates needs for art.

S·S **01** at the moment 지금으로서는, 바로 지금   **02** govern 통제하다; 통치하다   discipline 규율하다; 훈련하다
A **03** recognize A as B A를 B로 인지하다   **04** roar 포효하다, 으르렁거리다   **05** anticipate 예견하다, 예상하다
B **07** hospice 호스피스(말기 환자들을 전문으로 돌보는 특수 병원)   care for ~을 돌보다   suffer from ~으로 고통받다   incurable 불치의
C **10** ultimate 궁극적인   **11** authority 권위; 권한   **12** in terms of ~의 면에서, ~의 관점에서   rooted 자리잡은, 고착한

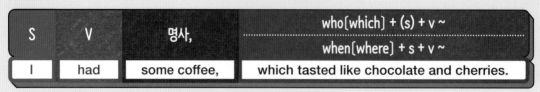

unit 28
명사, 관계사절

Block Board

S	V	명사,	who[which] + (s) + v ~
			when[where] + s + v ~
I	had	some coffee,	which tasted like chocolate and cherries.

나는 / 마셨다 / 약간의 커피를 / 그리고 그것은 초콜릿과 체리 같은 맛이 났다

- 관계사 앞에 콤마가 있는 경우, 관계사절은 앞에 나온 명사(선행사)를 보충 설명한다.

  Form 명사, who[which] + (s) + v ~ : 그리고[그런데] 그 사람은[그것은] ~

  명사, when[where] + s + v ~ : 그리고[그런데] 그때[거기서] ~

- 관계사 앞에 「부정대명사 + of」가 있을 경우, 부정대명사의 의미를 살려 해석한다.

  Form 명사, 부정대명사 + of + whom[which] + (s) + v ~ *cf* 부정대명사: some, any, most, few, all, both, none 등

- 명사 뒤에 온 관계사절의 앞과 뒤에 콤마가 있을 경우, 관계사절은 삽입절로 쓰인 것이다.

  Form 명사, 관계사 + (s) + v ~ , ~

Standard Sentences

모의 01 Costa Rica was discovered and named by Christopher Columbus,
코스타리카는 발견되었다 그리고 명명되었다 / 크리스토퍼 콜럼버스에 의해서

who thought it might be a land rich with gold.
/ 그리고 그는 생각했다 / 그것은 금이 풍부한 땅일 것이라고

모의 02 Change, **which is an essential part of our life,** can have both positive
변화는 / 그것은 우리 삶의 필수적인 부분인데 / 긍정적인 영향과 부정적인 영향을

and negative effects.
둘 다 미칠 수 있다

A 다음 문장에서 콤마 뒤의 관계사절을 파악하면서, 각 문장을 해석하시오.

03 Yesterday is history, tomorrow is a mystery, today is a gift of God,
which is why we call it the present. *Bill Keane*

▶ which의 선행사는 앞의 절 today ~ God임

모의 04 Urbanization has been taking place since the Neolithic Revolution,
when agriculture enabled food surpluses to create a division of
labor in settlements.

05 Homer's *Iliad*, which contained descriptions of actual places, was
the basis for many early maps.

··· **Know More** Rainbow p.82

B 다음 문장에서 콤마 뒤의 관계사절에 밑줄을 치고, 각 문장을 해석하시오.

06 Cognitive computing is supported by machine learning and deep learning technology, which allows computers to autonomously learn from data. *machine learning 기계 학습(자신의 동작을 스스로 개선할 수 있는 슈퍼컴퓨터의 능력)

(모의) **07** Maurice Maeterlinck studied law and worked as a lawyer until 1889, when he decided to devote himself to writing. In 1897, he went to Paris, where he met many of the leading symbolist writers of the day.

(수능) **08** Jobs may not be permanent, and you may lose your job for countless reasons, some of which you may not even be responsible for.

09 The spontaneous wish to learn, which every normal child has, as shown in their efforts to walk and talk, should be the driving force in education.

C 다음 문장의 빈칸에 들어갈 내용으로 알맞은 것을 보기 에서 고르시오.

> • 보기 •
> ⓐ who have criticized the series   ⓑ each of which has a certain function
> ⓒ where the tribal member at birth assumes

10 The bodies of all living creatures are organized into many different systems, _____.

(모의) **11** One remarkable aspect of aboriginal culture is the concept of "totemism," _____ the soul and identity of a part of nature. *totemism 토테미즘(원시 사회에서 동식물이나 자연을 신성시함으로써 형성되는 종교 및 사회 체제)

(모의) **12** The television crime drama isn't such a hit with police officers, _____ for presenting a highly misleading image of how crimes are solved.

A **04** urbanization 도시화   surplus 잉여, 나머지   division of labor 분업   settlement 정착지; 해결
B **06** cognitive 인지의   autonomously 자체적으로   **07** devote oneself to ~에 전념하다   symbolist 상징주의자   **08** permanent 영구적인
C 보기 tribal 부족의, 종족의   assume 취하다   **11** remarkable 눈에 띄는   aboriginal 원주민의   **12** misleading 오해의 소지가 있는

Chapter 06

Review

A 다음 문장을 우리말로 해석하시오.

01 There is only one thing that makes a dream impossible to achieve: the fear of failure. *the novel <The Alchemist>*

02 Radioactive waste disposal has become one of the key environmental battlegrounds over which the future of nuclear power has been fought.

03 Fate is like a strange, unpopular restaurant filled with odd little waiters who bring you things you never asked for and don't always like. *Lemony Snicket*

(모의) **04** Multitasking is another way of saying you are going to complete several tasks, none of which are going to be very good.

B 다음 네모 안에서 어법에 맞는 것을 고르시오.

05 Man is the only animal ⎡ who / whose ⎤ desires increase as they are fed; the only animal that is never satisfied. *Henry Georges*

(모의) **06** We're heading toward a world ⎡ which / where ⎤ an extensive trail of information fragments about us will be forever preserved on the Internet, displayed instantly in a search result.

(모의) **07** Angela mentioned that for a long time she had wanted to get back into acting, ⎡ which / that ⎤ she used to do in college.

08 Penicillin, the first antibiotic to be discovered, kills a broad spectrum of bacteria, many of ⎡ them / which ⎤ cause disease in humans.

C 다음 괄호 안의 말을 우리말과 같은 뜻이 되도록 배열하여 문장을 완성하시오.

09 가치관과 그것들을 뒷받침하는 신념은 우리가 세상을 보는 렌즈다.
(we, through, see the world, which)

→ Values and their supporting beliefs are lenses _____

_____ .

10 과학과 기술이 엄청난 속도로 발전하고 있는 이 정보 시대에, 네트워크는 현대의 삶에서 중요한 상징이 되어왔다.
(science and technology, with great rapidity, are developing, when)

→ In this information age _____

_____ , network has become an important symbol of modern life.

11 경찰은 다수의 폭발물 예고를 받았는데, 그것들 모두 허위 신고로 밝혀졌다.
(all, to be false alarms, of, turned out, which)

→ The police received a number of bomb warnings, _____

_____ .

D 다음 문장의 빈칸에 들어갈 내용으로 알맞은 것을 보기 에서 고르시오.

> **보기**
> ⓐ it is required to do
> ⓑ that had to be provided for us by others
> ⓒ where pure absolute objectivity prevails

12 Science operates within the context of the culture it exists in; it does not exist in a vacuum _____ .

13 For every one thing we think we have done on our own, there are a dozen things _____ .

14 The brain modifies its structure in response to the different tasks _____ .

A 02 radioactive 방사성의   disposal 처리, 처분   battleground 전쟁터   nuclear power 원자력   03 fate 운명   odd 이상한
B 05 feed 충족시키다   06 extensive 광범위한   trail 자국   fragment 조각   instantly 즉각   07 mention 언급하다
08 antibiotic 항생제   spectrum 범위   C 10 with great rapidity 엄청난 속도로   11 turn out ~으로 밝혀지다
D 보기 absolute 절대적인   prevail 지배적이다, 만연하다   12 vacuum 진공   14 modify 수정하다   in response to ~에 응하여

07 부사적 수식어: 구

Get Ready!

☑ 전치사구, to-v, 분사구문은 동사, 형용사, 부사 또는 문장 전체를 수식하는 부사의 역할도 한다. 부사적으로 쓰이는 to-v와
  분사구문의 의미를 잘 파악해야 한다.

Point 1

| 부사 역할을 하는 전치사구 |

| S | V | ~ | 전치사 + O' ~ |

Point 2

| 부사 역할을 하는 to-v |

| S | V | ~ | to-v ~ |

Point 3

| to-v의 관용 구문 |

| S | V | 형용사[부사] | enough to-v ~ |

| S | V | too + 형용사[부사] | to-v ~ |

Point 4

| 분사구문의 의미 |

| V-ing[V-ed] ~, | S | V | ~ |

| S | V | ~ | v-ing[v-ed] ~ |

Point 5

| 분사구문의 다양한 형태 |

Having v-ed ~
명사 + v-ing[v-ed] ~ | S | V | ~ |
접속사 + v-ing[v-ed] ~

- unit 29 부사 역할을 하는 전치사구
- unit 30 부사 역할을 하는 to-v의 의미
- unit 31 부사적 to-v의 관용 구문
- unit 32 부사 역할을 하는 분사구문의 의미
- unit 33 분사구문의 다양한 형태 1
- unit 34 분사구문의 다양한 형태 2

부사 역할을 하는 전치사구
> Unit 29

▷ 문장 내에서 전치사구의 위치는 다양하다. 수식하는 내용에 따라 문장의 맨 앞이나 뒤, 수식받는 동사 또는 형용사의 뒤에 위치한다.

부사 역할을 하는 to-v
> Unit 30

▷ 부사 역할을 하는 to-v는 '목적', '원인', '결과' 등의 의미로 쓰인다.

to-v의 관용 구문
> Unit 31

▷ ~ enough to-v, too ~ to-v 등의 관용 구문을 잘 익혀 두어야 한다.

분사구문의 의미
> Unit 32

▷ 분사구문은 주절의 앞 또는 뒤에 쓰이며, 주어와 동사 사이에 삽입되기도 한다.
▷ 분사구문은 주절과의 문맥상 의미 관계에 따라 '시간', '원인', '조건' 등의 의미를 나타낸다.

분사구문의 다양한 형태
> Unit 33, 34

▷ 분사구문의 분사는 시제, 태에 따른 변화형이 있다.
▷ 분사구문의 앞에 의미상 주어를 명시하거나 접속사를 덧붙이기도 한다.

unit 29
부사 역할을 하는 전치사구

Block Board

전치사 + O' ~	S	V	전치사 + O' ~
After an hour	I	arrived	at the airport.
한 시간 후에	/ 나는	/ 도착했다	/ 공항에

- 전치사는 목적어로 명사, 대명사, 동명사, 명사절 등을 취하며, 전치사구는 형용사 또는 부사의 역할을 한다. 부사 역할을 하는 전치사구 (= 전치사 + 목적어)는 동사, 형용사, 또는 문장 전체를 수식한다. **○ unit 21, 60**

- 전치사구는 문장의 앞 또는 끝에 올 수 있고, 동사나 형용사의 뒤에 위치하기도 한다.

Standard Sentences

01 **By means of photosynthesis,** plants convert the radiant energy of
광합성에 의해   / 식물은 태양의 복사 에너지를 전환한다

the sun **into chemical energy.**
     / 화학 에너지로

02 **From the moment that we are born,** we begin to make sense of the
그 순간부터   / [우리가 태어나는]   / 우리는 우리 주변의 세상을 이해하기 시작한다

world around us **by associating the unknown with the known.**
     / 알려지지 않은 것을 알려진 것과 연관시킴으로써

▶ by + v-ing: ~함으로써

Ⓐ 다음 문장에서 부사 역할을 하는 전치사구를 파악하면서, 각 문장을 해석하시오.

03 Fossil fuels form beneath the ground from dead plants and animals that do not break down completely.

04 Despite its high price, this new cell phone sells like hot cakes because of its high quality.

▶ because of + O
cf. because + s + v

수능 **05** We borrow environmental capital from future generations with no intention or prospect of repaying.

B 다음 문장에서 부사 역할을 하는 전치사구에 밑줄을 치고, 각 문장을 해석하시오.

06 Each year about 50,000 species of plants and animals disappear from the planet as a result of human activity.

07 Sometimes my eyes get jealous of my heart because you always remain close to my heart and far from my eyes.

(모의) **08** Upon discovering his own passion and talent for architecture, Frank Lloyd Wright dropped out of school and went to work for an architectural firm in Chicago.

▶ upon v-ing: ~하자마자

09 Above all, watch with glittering eyes the whole world around you because the greatest secrets are always hidden in the most unlikely places. *Roald Dahl*

C 다음 문장의 빈칸에 들어가기에 가장 적절한 것을 고르시오.

10 In a democratic environment, old ideas can be challenged and rigorously criticized, though there are some difficulty _____ the human desire to hold onto old ideas, especially by the original proposers.

① due to   ② regardless of   ③ for the sake of

(모의) **11** In spite of the rare case of receiving rewarding email, we cannot resist the impulse to check email because our behaviors are maintained _____ presented in an unpredictable way.

① by nature   ② to our taste   ③ with the reward

(모의) **12** With the advent of social media, our children _____ for an immediate answer or "Like" within minutes of sending an urgent piece of information out.

① go outside   ② become impatient   ③ make preparation

S·S 01 by means of ~에 의해서   photosynthesis 광합성   convert 전환하다   radiant energy 복사 에너지   **02** make sense of ~을 이해하다
A 03 fossil fuel 화석 연료   break down 분해되다   **04** sell like hot cakes 날개 돋친 듯이 팔리다   **05** prospect 가망, 가능성   repay 빚을 갚다
B 06 planet 세상; 행성   **08** drop out of school 학교를 그만두다, 중퇴하다   **09** glitter 반짝이다   unlikely 있을 법하지 않은
C 10 rigorously 엄격히   hold onto ~을 계속 유지하다   **11** resist 참다   impulse 충동   **12** advent 출현   impatient 초조하게 기다리는

unit 30
부사 역할을 하는 to-v의 의미

중요도 ★★★
난이도 ★★★

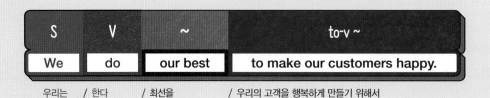

S	V	~	to-v ~
We	do	our best	to make our customers happy.

우리는 / 한다 / 최선을 / 우리의 고객을 행복하게 만들기 위해서

- 부사 역할을 하는 to-v는 문맥에 따라 다양한 의미를 나타낸다.

  ▷ 목적: ~하기 위해 (※ 이 의미로 가장 많이 쓰임)

    = in order to-v, so as to-v (목적의 의미를 더 명확히 함)

  ▷ 감정의 원인: ~해서, ~하게 되어

    감정의 어구 (glad, happy, sad, sorry ...) + to-v

  ▷ 조건·가정: ~한다면(~할 것이다)

    조동사 (will / would ~) + to-v

  ▷ 결과: ~해서[결국] ···하다, ~하게 되다

    awake, grow up, live ... + to-v / only, never + to-v

  ▷ 판단의 근거: ~하다니, ~하는 것을 보니

    판단·추측의 어구 + to-v

  ▷ 형용사 수식: ~하기에, ~하는 데

    형용사 (easy, hard ...) + to-v

Standard Sentences

수능! 01 Charles Dickens used his desperate experience as a child laborer in
찰스 디킨스는 자신의 절망적인 경험을 활용했다 / [빅토리아 시대의 영국에서 아동

Victorian England **to write** *David Copperfield*.
노동자로서의] / 「데이비드 코퍼필드」를 쓰기 위해서

> **Know More** Rainbow p.90

02 That Friday morning, I awoke **to find myself caught in the middle**
그 금요일 아침에 / 나는 깨어나서 내가 처해 있는 것을 알게 되었다 / 소셜 미디어 폭풍의

of a social media storm.
한가운데에

▶ to-v: '결과'의 의미

A 다음 문장에서 부사 역할을 하는 to-v를 파악하면서, 각 문장을 해석하시오.

03 Our brain organizes the available sensory information and environmental stimuli so as to make sense out of millions of bits and pieces of data.

▶ 목적의 의미를 명확히 할 때 to-v 앞에 so as 또는 in order를 붙임

수능! 04 When at length the deal was settled, Dr. Paul was delighted to purchase the carving at a reasonable price.

05 If an activity is easy to perform, easy to fit into your schedule, and easy to love, you're more likely to stick with it.

B 다음 문장에서 부사 역할을 하는 to-v가 이끄는 어구에 밑줄을 치고, 각 문장을 해석하시오.

06 We should carefully think about the reason for someone's behavior to avoid coming to a hasty conclusion about it.

07 When temperatures near 0℃, water molecules start bonding with one another to form a crystal structure.

08 We would be honored to have you as a guest at the annual festival.

09 If you are fortunate to have opportunity, it is your duty to make sure other people have those opportunities as well. *Kamala Harris*

C 다음 문장의 빈칸에 들어갈 내용으로 알맞은 것을 보기에서 고르시오.

> • 보기 •
> ⓐ only to realize　　　　　ⓑ to avoid further punishment
> ⓒ to talk like that

10 We can't help but think James must have his head in the clouds _____.

▶ cannot (help) but + ⓥ: ~ 하지 않을 수 없다

(모의) **11** Have you ever found yourself speaking to someone at length _____ they haven't heard a single thing you've said?

(수능) **12** A child who has been repeatedly criticized for poor performance on math may learn to dodge difficult math problems in order _____ _____.

S·S 01 desperate 절망적인　laborer 노동자
A 03 stimulus 자극(*pl.* stimuli)　bits and pieces 이런저런 것들, 일부분　**04** at length 마침내; 상세히　settle 합의를 보다　carving 조각품
reasonable (가격이) 적절한; 합리적인　**05** fit into ~에 맞추다　stick with ~을 계속하다
B 06 hasty 성급한　come to a conclusion 결론에 도달하다　**07** near 가까워지다　crystal 결정, 결정체　**09** make sure 반드시 ~하도록 하다
C 보기 further 더 심한　punishment 처벌　**10** have one's head in the clouds 공상에 잠기다　**12** criticize 지적하다　dodge 피하다, 기피하다

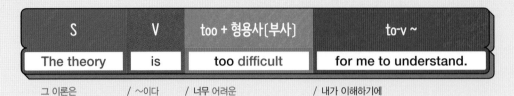

unit 31
부사적 to-v의 관용 구문

중요도 ★★☆
난이도 ★★☆

Block Board

S	V	too + 형용사[부사]	to-v ~
The theory	is	too difficult	for me to understand.

그 이론은 / ~이다 / 너무 어려운 / 내가 이해하기에

- **~ enough to-v / too ~ to-v**
  - ▷ 형용사[부사] + enough to-v: ~할 정도로[하기에] 충분히 …한[하게]
  - ▷ too + 형용사[부사] + to-v: 너무 ~해서 …할 수 없는 (= so ~ that + s + can't …)

- **be + 형용사 + to-v**
  - ▷ be eager[anxious] to-v: ~하기를 갈망하다
  - ▷ be sure[certain] to-v: 반드시 ~하다
  - ▷ be likely[unlikely] to-v: ~할 것 같다[같지 않다]
  - ▷ be willing to-v: 기꺼이 ~하다

- **문장 전체를 수식하는 to-v**
  - ▷ to be frank, to be honest: 솔직히 말해서
  - ▷ to make matters worse: 설상가상으로
  - ▷ to begin with: 우선적으로
  - ▷ not to mention: ~은 말할 것도 없이
  - ▷ to be brief, to put it simply, to make a long story short: 간단히 말해서

Standard Sentences

01 Our span of life is brief, but is **long enough for us to live well and**
우리의 수명은 짧다 / 그러나 길다 / 우리가 멋지게 그리고 정직하게 살기에는 충분히

honestly. *Cicero*

▶ to-v 앞의 'for + O'는 to-v의 의미상 주어

02 Some kinds of viruses are **too small to be seen by the naked eye.**
어떤 종류의 바이러스는 / 너무 작다 / 보이기에는 / 맨눈으로

Know More Rainbow p.92

A 다음 문장에서 to-v의 관용 구문을 파악하면서, 각 문장을 해석하시오.

03 You are **never too old** to set another goal or to dream a new dream.

04 Change is the law of life. And those who look only to the past or present are **certain to miss the future.** *John F. Kennedy*

05 **To make a long story short,** Beauty fell in love with the Beast, who turned out to be a handsome prince.

B 다음 문장에서 to-v의 관용 구문에 밑줄을 치고, 각 문장을 해석하시오.

(모의) **06** Copywriters must be versatile enough to adjust to each new product and medium and to vary the language and tone of each message.

*copywriter 카피라이터, 광고의 글귀를 만드는 사람

(수능) **07** People draw too heavily, too quickly, on already overdrawn environmental resource accounts to be affordable far into the future without bankrupting those accounts.

08 It is not fair to ask of others what you are not willing to do yourself.

09 The team has lost the last two games and, to make matters worse, two of its best players are injured.

C 다음 괄호 안의 말을 의미가 통하도록 배열하여 문장을 완성하시오.

10 I always like to look on the optimistic side of life, but I _____ _____ that life is a complex matter. *Walt Disney*

(enough, know, to, realistic, am)

••• Know More   Rainbow p.93

(모의) **11** The bargain must truly stand out in the consumer's mind as a good deal that _____.

(to, exceptional, is just, pass up, too)

12 Pollution has a negative effect on the health of everyone living in the city, _____.

(the environment, the damage, to, not, mention, to)

S·S 01 span of life 수명   **02** naked eye 맨눈
B 06 versatile 다재다능한   medium 매체   tone 어조   **07** draw on ~을 이용하다   overdrawn 초과 인출된   bankrupt 파산시키다
C 10 optimistic 낙관적인   **11** stand out 눈에 띄다, 두드러지다   deal 거래   exceptional 파격적인, 예외적인   **12** mention 언급하다

unit 32
부사 역할을 하는 분사구문의 의미

중요도 ★★☆
난이도 ★★★

Block Board

V-ing(V-ed) ~,	S	V	~
Walking on the street,	I	met	a friend of mine.
길을 걸었다		/ (그때) 나는 / 만났다	/ 내 친구 한 명을

- v-ing 또는 v-ed가 이끄는 분사구문은 보통 문장의 앞이나 뒤에 오며, 중간에 삽입될 수도 있다.

- 문장의 주어와 능동의 관계이면 분사구문에 v-ing를 쓰고, 수동의 관계이면 v-ed를 쓴다.

- 분사구문의 의미는 문맥, 즉 주절과의 논리적 관계를 통해 파악해야 한다.

┌─ 논리적 관계 ─┐   ┌─ 논리적 관계 ─┐
Form V-ing(V-ed) ~, S + V ...   S + V ... v-ing(v-ed) ~

〈시간〉 그때 / 그러면서 / 그러고 나서   〈시간〉 그때 / 그러면서 / 그러고 나서 / ~할 때
〈인과〉 그래서   〈인과〉 그래서 / 왜냐하면
〈조건〉 그러면
〈역접〉 그러나

Standard Sentences

01 **Tapping his fingers loudly on the desk top,** he made his impatience
자신의 손가락으로 시끄럽게 톡톡 두드렸다 / 책상 위를   / (그러면서) 그는 자신의 성급함과 불만이

and dissatisfaction known.
알려지게 했다

(모의) **02** **Pressed for time and stuck in a deadlock,** she had no idea how to
시간에 쫓기고 교착 상태에 갇혔다   / (그래서) 그녀는 알지 못했다 / 그 논문을

finish the paper.
어떻게 끝내야 할지

Ⓐ 다음 문장에서 분사구문을 파악하면서, 각 문장을 해석하시오.

(수능) **03** Being a hybrid art as well as a late one, film has always been in a
dialogue with other narrative genres.

04 Taken daily, according to a new study, vitamin D can help treat severe
asthma.
▶ help + ⓥ: ~하는 것을 돕다

05 Originally raised mainly for their meat, sheep and goats became
valuable also for their milk and wool.

B 다음 문장에서 분사구문에 밑줄을 치고, 각 문장을 해석하시오.

(모의) **06** Children at play often take on other roles, pretending to be Principal Walsh or Josh's mom, happily forcing themselves to imagine how someone else thinks and feels.

▶ 이중의 분사구문

07 A mother is a person who seeing there are only four pieces of pie for five people, promptly announces she never did care for pie.

▶ 관계사절 속의 분사구문

08 Assumed to have a substantial amount of water, Mars is probably most habitable out of all the planets in our solar system.

09 When I find myself in times of trouble, mother Mary comes to me, speaking words of wisdom, "Let it be." And in my hour of darkness she is standing right in front of me, speaking words of wisdom, "Let it be." *the song <Let It Be>*

··· **Know More** Rainbow p.95

Let it be~

C 다음 네모 안에서 어법에 맞는 것을 고르시오.

10 Fueling / Fueled by drought and development, wildfires in the West are getting bigger and more aggressive.

11 Seconds after its spectacular launch, the spacecraft with seven astronauts on board blew up and came apart, striking / struck the viewers dumb with shock.

12 The very real genetic differences between races or genders are insignificant comparing / compared with the similarities in our minds.

S·S 01 tap 톡톡 두드리다　impatience 성급함　dissatisfaction 불만　**02** be pressed for time 시간에 쫓기다　deadlock 교착 상태
A 03 hybrid 혼합의　narrative 서사의　**04** asthma 천식　**05** originally 원래　raise (가축을) 사육하다
B 06 take on ~을 맡다　**07** promptly 바로　care for ~을 좋아하다　**09** assume 추정하다　substantial 상당한　habitable 살기 적합한
C 10 fuel 부채질하다　**11** spectacular 극적인　come apart 부서지다　strike 갑자기 ~가 되게 하다　**12** gender 성별　insignificant 사소한

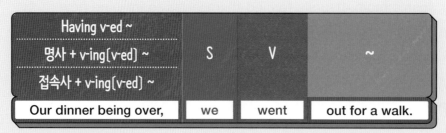

unit 33

분사구문의 다양한 형태 1

중요도 ★★☆
난이도 ★★★

Block Board

Having v-ed ~			
명사 + v-ing(v-ed) ~	S	V	~
접속사 + v-ing(v-ed) ~			
Our dinner being over,	we	went	out for a walk.

우리의 저녁 식사가 끝났다 / (그리고 나서) 우리는 / 나갔다 / 밖으로 산책을 하러

- **완료분사구문**: 분사구문이 문장의 동사보다 앞서 일어난 일을 나타낼 때, having v-ed를 쓴다. 이때, 주어와 능동의 관계이면 having v-ed, 수동의 관계이면 having been v-ed가 되어야 한다.

  Form [Having v-ed(Having been v-ed) ~,] S + V ...

- **독립분사구문**: 문장의 주어와 분사구문의 의미상 주어가 서로 다를 때, 분사 앞에 의미상 주어를 밝혀 준다.

  Form [명사 + v-ing(v-ed) ~,] S + V ...

  (명사 ≠ S)

- **접속사 + 분사구문**: 분사구문의 의미를 분명히 하기 위해, 문맥에 맞는 접속사를 덧붙이기도 한다.

  Form [접속사 + v-ing(v-ed) ~,] S + V ...

Standard Sentences

01 **Not having been to the city before**, I needed some tourist pamphlets.
전에 그 도시에 가본 적이 없었다 / (그래서) 나는 몇 개의 여행자용 팸플렛이 필요했다

▶ 분사구문의 부정형:
not(never) + v-ing/v-ed

(모의) **02** Can we sustain our standard of living in the same ecological space
우리는 우리의 생활수준을 유지할 수 있을까 / 동일한 생태적 공간에서

while consuming the resources of that space?
/ 그 공간의 자원을 소비하면서?

Ⓐ 다음 문장에서 분사구문을 파악하면서, 각 문장을 해석하시오.

03 The fundamental problem most patients face is an inability to love themselves, having been unloved by others during some crucial part of their lives.

(모의) **04** I sat quietly in a chair, my only actions consisting of taking notes and stuffing my ears with wadded toilet paper.

05 Though seriously injured, the pilot crawled out of the wreckage and was flown by helicopter to a nearby medical center.

118 Chapter 07

B 다음 문장에서 분사구문에 밑줄을 치고, 각 문장을 해석하시오.

06 Turned down for countless jobs, Jenny didn't give up hope and is now a successful architect.

(모의) **07** In recent history, countries with the highest net inward migration have also had the highest growth rates, the two factors clearly being linked in harmony. *net inward migration 순유입(인원이 빠져나간 것보다 많이 들어옴)

(모의) **08** When faced with a bunch of watermelons, all promising delicious juiciness inside, how do you know which one to pick?

▶ 이중의 분사구문

09 The time spent in lamenting their lot, if applied to honest endeavor, would yield splendid results and give them proper places in the world.

C 다음 네모 안에서 어법에 맞는 것을 고르시오.

(수능!) **10** The making of a contract requires the mutual agreement of two or more persons or parties, one of them ordinarily ⏐ makes / making ⏐ an offer and another accepting.

11 There ⏐ is / being ⏐ a dispute over a topic of environment, the country is to make an effective law for its sustainable development.

12 When ⏐ expelling / expelled ⏐ from the nucleus of an atom, a neutron is unstable and decayed to form a proton and an electron.

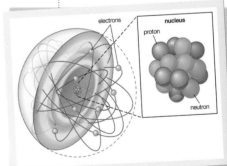

S·S 01 pamphlet 팸플릿, 소책자   02 sustain 유지하다   standard 수준, 표준   ecological 생태적인   consume 소비하다
A 04 consist of ~으로 구성되다   stuff A with B A를 B로 채우다   wad ~을 뭉치다   05 crawl 기어가다   wreckage (사고 자동차·비행기 등의) 잔해
B 06 turn down 거절하다   08 bunch 무더기, 다발   09 lament 한탄하다   lot 운명, 운   yield (결과를) 낳다   splendid 정말 멋진
C 10 contract 계약   mutual 상호의   agreement 합의   party 단체, 일행   11 dispute 논쟁   sustainable 지속 가능한   12 nucleus 핵
neutron 중성자   unstable 불안정한   decay (방사능 물질이) 자연 붕괴하다   proton 양성자

분사구문의 다양한 형태 2

중요도 ★★★
난이도 ★★★

(Being[Having been]) 명사[형용사] ~	S	V	~
Anxious to avoid visitors,	she	didn't answer	the door bell.
방문객들을 피하고 싶었다	/ (그래서) 그녀는	/ 응답하지 않았다	/ 초인종 소리에

- **명사 또는 형용사로 시작하는 분사구문:** 명사 또는 형용사 앞에 being 또는 having been이 생략된 형태이다.

  Form (Being / Having been) 명사[형용사] ~, S + V ...

- **with + 명사 + v-ing[v-ed]:** ~가 …한 채로, ~가 …하여

  with 뒤에는 분사의 의미상 주어가 오며, 명사와 분사의 관계가 능동이면 v-ing, 수동이면 v-ed가 온다.

- **분사구문의 관용표현**
  ▷ judging from: ~으로 판단하건대　　　　　▷ granting[granted] (that): ~을 인정한다고 하더라도
  ▷ generally[frankly/strictly/roughly] speaking: 일반적으로[솔직하게/엄격하게/대략] 말해서
  ▷ taking ~ into account[consideration]: ~을 고려하면(= considering)

Standard Sentences

모의 **01** Adolescents have been quick to immerse themselves in technology
청소년들은 재빨랐다 　　　　　　　　　　/ 기술에 몰두하는 것에

with most using the Internet to communicate.
/ 대부분 인터넷을 사용하면서 　　　　　　/ 소통하기 위해서

02 Judging from his latest novel that I have read, he seems to be a
그의 최신 소설로 판단하건대 　　　　　　　/ [내가 읽은] 　　　　/ 그는 꽤 유망한 작가인 것 같다

fairly promising writer.

Ⓐ 다음 문장에서 분사구문을 파악하면서, 각 문장을 해석하시오.

수능 **03** While afloat, the reindeer is uniquely vulnerable, moving slowly with
its antlers held high as it struggles to keep its nose above water.

모의 **04** Desperate to keep himself and his family from starving, Erich took
any available job.

05 Granted that you've made some progress, you should not be
conceited.

B 다음 문장에서 분사구문에 밑줄을 치고, 각 문장을 해석하시오.

(수능!) **06** With the industrial society evolving into an information-based society, the concept of information as a product, a commodity with its own value, has emerged.

07 Unable to write, or even to speak clearly, Stephen Hawking was leaping beyond relativity, beyond quantum mechanics, beyond the Big Bang, to the 'dance of geometry' that created the universe.

(Up!) **08** Some pioneers in computer usage see the ultimate relation between man and computer as a symbiotic union of two living species, each completely dependent on the other for survival.

09 Strictly speaking, Great Britain consists of Scotland, Wales and England, and the United Kingdom consists of Great Britain and Northern Ireland.

C 다음 괄호 안의 주어진 단어를 문맥에 맞게 고쳐 쓰시오.

(수능!) **10** The role of science can sometimes be overstated, with its advocates _____ into scientism. (slip)

11 _____ into account growing population numbers, climate change and natural disasters, global food security is under threat. (take)   *food security 식량 안보(국가가 필요로 하는 식량을 항상 확보하여 유지하는 것)

12 With so much data (A)_____ about us and with anybody (B)_____ able to disseminate it around the globe, is there anything we really can do to protect privacy? (collect, be)

S·S 01 adolescent 청소년   immerse oneself in ~에 몰두하다, 열중하다   **02** fairly 꽤   promising 유망한
A 03 afloat (물에) 뜬   reindeer 순록   vulnerable 공격받기 쉬운   antler (가지진) 뿔   **04** desperate 필사적인   **05** conceited 자만하는
B 07 relativity 상대성 이론; 상대성   quantum mechanics 양자 역학   geometry 기하학   **08** ultimate 궁극적인   symbiotic 공생의
C 10 overstate 과장하다   scientism 과학(만능)주의   **11** under threat 위협받고 있는   **12** disseminate 유포하다, 퍼뜨리다

Chapter 07
Review

A 다음 문장을 우리말로 해석하시오.

01 Holding on to anger is like grasping a hot coal with the intent of throwing it at someone else; you are the one who gets burned. *Buddha*

02 I can't change the direction of the wind, but I can adjust my sails to always reach my destination. *Jimmy Dean*

03 The virus is too small to carry all the molecular machinery required to replicate itself, which is why it needs a host cell to multiply.

04 Plants communicate, signaling to remote organs within an individual, eavesdropping on neighboring individuals, and exchanging information with other organisms.

*eavesdrop 이야기를 엿듣다

B 다음 네모 안에서 어법에 맞는 것을 고르시오.

05 A foreign exchange market gets influenced by a real world event, and has an impact on the economy of a nation, causing / caused the value of its money to rise and fall.

*foreign exchange market 외환 시장

06 With so many people getting / got their information online, there may not be a need for traditional newspapers.

07 When seeing / seen near the horizon, the moon appears strikingly larger than when viewed overhead.

C 다음 괄호 안의 말을 이용하여 우리말과 같은 뜻이 되도록 문장을 완성하시오. (필요하면 어형을 바꿀 것)

08 교사들은 학생들을 효과적으로 가르치기 위해 자신의 학생들을 잘 알 필요가 있다.
(to, them, teach, effectively, in order)

→ Teachers need to know their students well _____.

09 인터넷은 정보가 풍부한 현대의 사치품으로, 단지 간단한 손가락 클릭만으로 쉽게 여러분이 모든 정보에 접근할 수 있게 한다.
(any information, access to, you, allow)

→ The Internet is a modern luxury abounding with information, _____ _____, all with the ease of a simple finger click.

10 내가 이 일에 익숙해지는 데 잠깐 시간이 걸렸지만, 이제 나는 그 일을 눈을 감은 채로 할 수 있다.
(close, my eyes, with)

→ It took me a little while to get used to this job, but now I could do it _____.

D 다음 문장의 빈칸에 들어갈 내용으로 알맞은 것을 보기에서 고르시오.

> • 보기 •
> ⓐ only to be told to mind your own business
> ⓑ discerning patterns and jumping to the logical end point
> ⓒ environmental welfare thus coming before human welfare

11 All species are seen as having rights as people do, _____ _____.

12 Have you ever experienced the frustration of offering to help someone _____ _____?

13 Faced with information that relates to what the old already know, their brains tend to work quicker and smarter, _____ _____.

A **01** hold on to ~을 유지하다   grasp 꽉 쥐다   coal 석탄   **02** adjust 조정하다   sail 돛; 항해(하다)   **03** replicate 복제하다   host 숙주; 주인   multiply 증식[번식]하다   **04** signal 신호를 보내다   remote 멀리 떨어진   organ 기관   B **07** horizon 지평선, 수평선   strikingly 현저하게, 두드러지게   C **09** luxury 사치품   abound with ~이 풍부하다   access 접근   D 보기 mind 신경 쓰다   discern 구분하다, 식별하다   welfare 복지   **12** frustration 좌절   **13** relate to ~와 관계가 있다

08 부사적 수식어: 절

Get Ready!

☑ 부사절은 주절의 의미를 보충 설명하기 위해 쓰는 것으로, 이끄는 접속사에 따라, 시간, 이유, 조건, 목적, 결과, 반전 등의 의미를 갖는다.

☑ 부사절로 시작하는 문장은 부사절의 끝에서, 문장의 뒤에 이어지는 부사절은 부사절의 앞에서 끊는다.

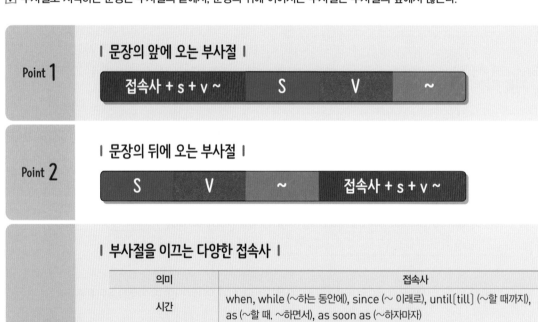

Point 1 | **문장의 앞에 오는 부사절**

접속사 + s + v ~ | S | V | ~

Point 2 | **문장의 뒤에 오는 부사절**

S | V | ~ | 접속사 + s + v ~

Point 3 | **부사절을 이끄는 다양한 접속사**

의미	접속사
시간	when, while (~하는 동안에), since (~ 이래로), until[till] (~할 때까지), as (~할 때, ~하면서), as soon as (~하자마자)
이유	because, since, as, now that (~이므로)
조건	if, unless (~하지 않는다면)
목적·결과	so that (~하기 위해서), so ~ that ... (아주 ~해서 …하다)
반전·대조	though, although (~일지라도), while (~인 반면에)
양태	as (~처럼), as if (마치 ~인 것처럼)

- unit 35 시간의 부사절
- unit 36 이유의 부사절
- unit 37 조건의 부사절
- unit 38 목적 · 결과의 부사절
- unit 39 반전 · 대조의 부사절
- unit 40 양태의 부사절

| **문장의 앞에 오는 부사절** | ▷ 접속사로 시작하는 절은 명사절이거나 부사절일 수 있다. |
| | ▷ 시간, 이유, 조건, 반전 등을 나타내는 접속사로 문장이 시작하면 부사절이다. |

| **문장의 뒤에 오는 부사절** | ▷ 주어와 동사를 포함하는 절 다음에 시간, 이유, 조건, 목적, 결과, 반전 등을 나타내는 접속사가 오면 부사절이 이어진다는 신호이다. |

| **부사절을 이끄는 다양한 접속사** | ▷ 각 접속사의 의미를 살려 부사절을 해석한다. |

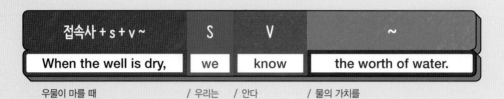

unit 35
시간의 부사절

중요도 ★★★
난이도 ★★★

Block Board

접속사 + s + v ~	S	V	~
When the well is dry,	we	know	the worth of water.
우물이 마를 때	/ 우리는	/ 안다	/ 물의 가치를

- **시간을 나타내는 접속사**
  - ▷ when: ~할 때
  - ▷ while: ~하는 동안에
  - ▷ as: ~할 때, ~하면서
  - ▷ since: ~ 이래로
  - ▷ once: 일단 ~하면, ~하자마자
  - ▷ by the time: ~할 무렵에는
  - ▷ every time / each time / whenever: ~할 때마다
  - ▷ until[till]: ~할 때까지
  - ▷ as soon as / the moment / the minute: ~하자마자
  - ▷ no sooner ~ than ... / hardly[scarcely] ~ when[before] ...: ~하자마자 …하다

Standard Sentences

01 **Once you replace negative thoughts with positive ones,** you'll
일단 당신이 부정적인 생각을 긍정적인 생각으로 대체하면 / 당신은

start having positive results. *Willie Nelson*
긍정적인 결과를 가지기 시작할 것이다

▶ Once + s + v ~, S + V ...

02 You never really understand a person **until you consider things**
당신은 결코 정말로 어떤 사람을 이해하지 못한다 / 당신이 그의 관점으로 상황을 고려할 때까지

from his point of view. *the novel <To Kill a Mockingbird>*

···• Know More Rainbow p.104

▶ S + V ~ until + s + v ...

A 다음 문장에서 시간의 부사절을 파악하면서, 각 문장을 해석하시오.

모의 03 We must be ready to abandon or modify our hypothesis as soon as
it is shown to be inconsistent with the facts.

04 Lunar eclipses occur each time the Earth blocks the sun's light from
the moon during the moon's full phase.

05 No sooner had I spoken the words than I felt an icy chill creep to
my heart. *the short story <The IMP of the Perverse>*

B 다음 문장에서 시간의 부사절에 밑줄을 치고, 각 문장을 해석하시오.

06 The moment you doubt whether you can fly, you cease forever to be able to do it. *the novel <Peter Pan>*

(모의) **07** Since the Industrial Revolution began in the eighteenth century, CO_2 released during industrial processes has greatly increased the proportion of carbon in the atmosphere.

08 Each player must accept the cards life deals him or her; but once they are in hand, he or she alone must decide how to play the cards in order to win the game. *Voltaire*

09 You can't just ask customers what they want and then try to give that to them. By the time you get it built, they'll want something new. *Steve Jobs*

C 다음 네모 안에서 어법에 맞는 것을 고르시오.

10 Art does not come to life until / since a spectator, a listener, or an audience breathes life into it by experiencing it.

11 Hardly had everybody taken their seats when / while the professor began his lecture.

(수능) **12** Whenever / By the time a geneticist unlocks new secrets of the DNA molecule, it adds to our knowledge base and enables us to better the human condition.

A **03** abandon 폐기하다   hypothesis 가설   **04** lunar eclipse 월식   phase 단계   **05** chill 냉기, 서늘함   creep 서서히 다가오다
B **06** cease 멈추다, 중단하다   **07** release 배출하다   proportion 비율   carbon 탄소   **09** deal (카드를) 나눠주다, 돌리다
C **10** come to life 살아 움직이다   spectator 관객   **11** lecture 강의   **12** unlock (비밀 등을) 밝히다   molecule 분자   better 개선하다

unit 36
이유의 부사절

Block Board

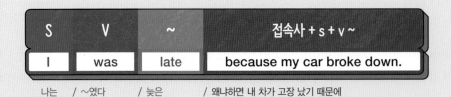

S	V	~	접속사 + s + v ~
I	was	late	because my car broke down.

나는 / ~였다 / 늦은 / 왜냐하면 내 차가 고장 났기 때문에

- 이유를 나타내는 접속사
  ▷ because, since, as: ~이기 때문에
  ▷ now (that): ~이기 때문에, ~이므로
  ▷ not A because B: B이기 때문에 A는 아니다; B라고 해서 A는 아니다

Standard Sentences

01 **As people are walking all the time, in the same spot,** a path appears.
사람들이 늘 걷고 있기 때문에 / 같은 장소에서 / 길이 생긴다
John Locke

02 Don't take the wrong side of an argument **just because your**
논쟁의 잘못된 면을 선택하지 마라 / 단지 당신의 상대방이 올바른 면을

opponent has taken the right side. *Baltasar Gracian*
취했다고 해서

Ⓐ 다음 문장에서 이유의 부사절을 파악하면서, 각 문장을 해석하시오.

03 Knowing another language is a window into another culture, since how a society thinks and views the world is expressed through its language.

(모의) **04** The time scales of geological activity are important for environmental geologists because they provide a way to measure human impacts on the natural world.

05 Now that tablet PCs, 3D VR glasses, and interactive whiteboards are so much a part of the modern classroom, many people fear reading books will no longer be as important.

B 다음 문장에서 이유의 부사절에 밑줄을 치고, 각 문장을 해석하시오.

수능 **06** Words can carry meanings beyond those consciously intended by speakers or writers because listeners or readers bring their own perspectives to the language they encounter.

모의 **07** Just because you can hear your robins, goldfinches, and sparrows chirping away happily in the garden every morning, don't be fooled into thinking that all is well in 'birdworld.' *robin 울새 goldfinch 오색방울새

모의 **08** As the nature of sarcasm implies a contradiction between intent and message, nonverbal cues may "leak" and reveal the speaker's true mood.

09 Now that genetically modified foods are on our supermarket shelves, the genie is out of the bottle and cannot be put back in.

C 다음 네모 안에서 문맥에 맞는 것을 고르시오.

10 As price is decided by bringing demand and supply into equilibrium, an | increase / decrease | in supply leads to a fall in price and increase in equilibrium quantity.

11 If we are not to become 'slaves to the machine', we should keep in mind that since computer programs are designed by people, they, too, are | fallible / perfect |.

12 Now that labor's clout has significantly diminished, knowledge workers have become the more | important / trivial | group in the economic equation.

S·S 02 argument 논쟁; 주장   opponent 상대, 적수
A 04 scale 척도   geological 지질학의   **05** interactive 쌍방향의, 대화형의   fear 염려하다   no longer 더 이상 ~ 않는
B 06 consciously 의식적으로   encounter 맞닥뜨리다, 마주치다   **07** chirp (새가) 지저귀다   **08** sarcasm 빈정거림, 비꼼   contradiction 모순
nonverbal 비언어적인   **09** genetically modified food 유전자 조작 식품   the genie is out of the bottle 돌이킬 수 없는 문제가 발생하다
C 10 demand and supply 수요와 공급   equilibrium 균형   **11** fallible 틀릴 수 있는   **12** clout 영향력   diminish 줄어들다   equation 방정식

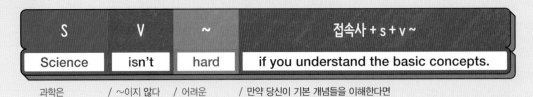

unit 37
조건의 부사절

중요도 ★★☆
난이도 ★★☆

Block Board

S	V	~	접속사 + s + v ~
Science	isn't	hard	if you understand the basic concepts.

과학은 / ~이지 않다 / 어려운 / 만약 당신이 기본 개념들을 이해한다면

- 조건을 나타내는 접속사
  ▷ if: 만약 ~라면　　　　　▷ unless: 만약 ~가 아니라면, 만약 ~하지 않으면 (= if ... not)
  ▷ suppose[supposing / providing / provided] (that): 만약 ~라면
  ▷ as[so] long as: ~하는 한, ~하기만 하면 (= if only)
  ▷ as[so] far as: ~하는 한; ~까지
  ▷ in so far as: ~하는 한에 있어서, ~한다는 점에서

Standard Sentences

01 Differences of habit and language are nothing **at all if our aims are**
습관과 언어의 차이는 전혀 아무것도 아니다 / 만약 우리의 목표가 같다면

identical and our hearts are open. *the novel <Harry Potter and the Goblet of Fire>*
/ 그리고 우리의 마음이 열려 있다면

02 A life devoted to the acquisition of wealth is useless, **unless we**
부의 획득에 바쳐진 인생은 쓸모없다 / 만약 우리가 알지 못한다면

know how to turn it into joy.
/ 어떻게 그것을 즐거움으로 바꾸는지

A 다음 문장에서 조건의 부사절을 파악하면서, 각 문장을 해석하시오.

03 In so far as changes in interest rates affect expectations, lower interest rates may still contribute to higher investment.

04 I don't care who you are, where you're from or what you did as long as you love me. *the song <As Long As You Love Me>*

05 A motion may be withdrawn by its proposer at any time before voting on it has commenced, provided that the motion has not been amended.

B 다음 문장에서 조건의 부사절에 밑줄을 치고, 각 문장을 해석하시오.

06 If you wait for the mango fruits to fall, you'd be wasting your time while others are learning how to climb the tree. *Michael Bassey Johnson*

(모의) **07** You can't think creatively about information unless you have information in your head to think about.

08 As far as we can discern, the sole purpose of human existence is to kindle a light in the darkness of mere being. *Carl Jung*

(수능) **09** Mediation parallels advocacy in so far as it tends to involve a process of negotiation, but differs in so far as mediation involves adopting a neutral role between two opposing parties rather than taking up the case of one party against another.

C 다음 문장의 빈칸에 들어갈 내용으로 알맞은 것을 보기에서 고르시오.

> • 보기 •
> ⓐ if we accept it as a growth process
> ⓑ provided that the account is settled in full every month
> ⓒ unless there is something to keep it moving at constant speed

10 An object that is moving at constant speed will eventually slow down and come to a stop _____.

11 Change may hurt us a little when it occurs, but _____
_____, it will bring benefits in the long run.

12 There is no fee for the card and no interest is charged _____
_____.

A **03** interest rate 이자율   contribute 기여하다   **05** motion 발의, 제안; 움직임   withdraw 철회하다   commence 시작되다   amend 수정하다
B **08** discern 식별하다   kindle 밝게 하다; (불을) 붙이다   **09** mediation 중재   parallel ～와 유사하다   advocacy 옹호   take up (입장을) 취하다
C 보기 settle 결제하다   constant 일정한   **10** eventually 마침내   **11** in the long run 결국에는   **12** charge 청구하다

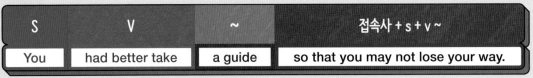

unit 38
목적·결과의 부사절

Block Board

S	V	~	접속사 + s + v ~
You	had better take	a guide	so that you may not lose your way.

너는 / 가져가는 게 나을 것이다 / 여행 안내서를 / 네가 길을 잃지 않기 위해서

- **목적을 나타내는 접속사**
  ▷ so (that) + s + can[will / may] + ⓥ ~: ~하도록, ~하기 위해서 (= in order that ~)

- **결과를 나타내는 접속사**
  ▷ ...(,) so (that) + s + v ~: ···해서 ~하다
  ▷ so + 형용사[부사] + (that) + s + v ~: 아주 ···해서 ~하다
  ▷ such + (a) + (형용사) + 명사 + (that) + s + v ~: 아주 ···해서 ~하다

Standard Sentences

01 We do what we have to do **so that we can do what we want to do.**
우리는 한다 / 우리가 해야 하는 것을 / 우리가 할 수 있도록 / 우리가 하고 싶은 것을

02 It was **so** quiet in the room **that I could hear the leaves being**
방안이 아주 조용했다 / 그래서 나는 들을 수 있었다 / 바깥에서 나뭇잎들이 나무들로

blown off the trees outside.
부터 날리고 있는 것을

Ⓐ 다음 문장에서 목적 또는 결과의 부사절을 파악하면서, 각 문장을 해석하시오.

모의 **03** A scientific understanding of emotional intelligence may allow us to train our emotional skills so that we can live more fulfilling and productive lives.

04 The personal computer becomes far smaller and much more portable, so that some people such as writers or stock dealers are able to work wherever they are.

05 Some people are making such thorough preparation for rainy days that they aren't enjoying today's sunshine. *William Feather*

B 다음 문장에서 목적 또는 결과의 부사절을 나타내는 부분에 밑줄을 치고, 각 문장을 해석하시오.

06 In 1936, King Edward VIII became the very first British monarch to voluntarily give up his throne when he abdicated so that he could marry Mrs. Simpson, a divorced American woman.

07 Her eyes are nothing but a pure emerald shining in the rays of the sun and the moon so that you can't take your eyes off her.

08 When one door of happiness closes, another opens; but often we look so long at the closed door that we do not see the one which has been opened for us. *Helen Keller*

09 The witness described the suspect in such detail that the police were able to locate him in no time.

▲ King Edward VIII and Wallis Simpson were married on June 3rd, 1937.

C 다음 문장의 빈칸에 들어갈 내용으로 알맞은 것을 보기에서 고르시오.

┌─ 보기 ─────────────────────────────────┐
ⓐ so you are able to integrate   ⓑ so I never have to live without you
ⓒ that a demand for one is always accompanied
└──┘

10 Rights and obligations should be so inseparable _____ _____ by a statement of the other.

11 If you live to be a hundred, I want to live to be a hundred minus one day _____. *the short story <Winnie the Pooh>*

12 When you are reading for study purposes, it is critical to read systematically, _____ the new knowledge you acquire with what you already know.

A 03 emotional intelligence 정서 지능   fulfilling 성취감을 주는   **04** portable 휴대용의   stock dealer 증권 중개인   **05** thorough 철저한
B 06 monarch 군주   throne 왕위   abdicate (왕위·권리를) 포기하다   divorce 이혼하다   **07** nothing but 바로 ~인   **09** in no time 즉시, 당장
C 보기 integrate 통합하다   accompany 수반하다   **10** obligation 의무   inseparable 분리할 수 없는   statement 표명; 진술   **12** critical 중요한

unit 39

반전 · 대조의 부사절

중요도 ★★☆
난이도 ★★☆

Block Board

S	V	~	접속사 + s + v ~
I	love	music	although I can't play a musical instrument.

나는 / 사랑한다 / 음악을 / 비록 내가 악기를 연주할 수 없을지라도

- 반전·대조를 나타내는 접속사
  - ▷ though, although: ～이지만, ～일지라도
  - ▷ even though + 사실의 내용: 비록 ～일지라도　　▷ (even) if + 가정의 내용: 비록 ～일지라도
  - ▷ whether A or B: A이든 B이든　　　　　　　　▷ while(whereas): ～인 반면에
  - ▷ 형용사(부사 / (무관사) 명사) + as + s + v ~: 비록 ～이지만
  - ▷ whoever / whatever / whichever: 누가 / 무엇을 / 어느 것을 ～하더라도 (= no matter who / what / which)
  - ▷ whenever / wherever / however: 언제 / 어디서 / 아무리 ～하더라도 (= no matter when / where / how)

Standard Sentences

수능! 01 **Even though a speech can be effective,** all the words in the world
비록 연설이 효과적일 수 있을지라도　　　　　　　　　　　/ 세상의 모든 말은

cannot measure up to the example of a leader.
필적할 수 없다　　　　　/ 지도자의 본보기에

02 **However hard you shop for an item,** after you've bought it, it will
아무리 열심히 당신이 어떤 물품을 쇼핑하더라도　　　/ 당신이 그것을 사고 난 후에　　　/ 그것은

　　　　　　　　　　　　　　　　　　　　　　　　　　　　▶ However + 부사 + s + v ~:
　　　　　　　　　　　　　　　　　　　　　　　　　　　　아무리 ～하더라도

be on sale somewhere cheaper.
할인 중일 것이다 / 어딘가에서 더 싸게

A 다음 문장에서 반전 또는 대조의 부사절을 파악하면서, 각 문장을 해석하시오.

03 Even if it turns out that time travel is impossible, it is important that
we understand why it is impossible. *Stephen Hawking*

수능! 04 Before sound recording, classical music was passed down through
written scores, whereas early jazz mainly relied on live performance.

05 Strange as it may sound, the diamond, so clear and transparent, is
composed of the same material as coal and soot, namely carbon.

B 다음 문장에서 반전 또는 대조의 부사절에 밑줄을 치고, 각 문장을 해석하시오.

06 No matter what emotion you're feeling right now, you can count on one thing—it will change.

▶ No matter what + 명사 + s + v ~, S + V ...

07 If we don't have the power to choose where we come from, we can still choose where we go from there.

(수능!) **08** Newton imagined that masses affect each other by exerting a force, while in Einstein's theory the effects occur through a bending of space and time and there is no concept of gravity as a force.

09 I'll do whatever it takes to win games, whether it's sitting on a bench waving a towel, handing a cup of water to a teammate, or hitting the game-winning shot. *Kobe Bryant*

C 다음 문장의 빈칸에 들어가기에 알맞은 것을 보기 에서 고르시오.

┌── 보기 ──
│ Whatever   Though   However   Whereas   Whether
└──

10 _____ most people agree that clothes do not make the person, they spend considerable time and money dressing themselves in the newest fashion.

11 _____ science is concerned with finding and stating the facts, poetry's task is to give you the look, the smell, the taste, and the "feel" of those facts.

12 _____ you want to do, if you want to be great at it, you have to love it and be able to make sacrifices for it. *Maya Angelou*

S·S 01 measure up to ~에 필적하다, ~에 달하다 **02** on sale 할인 중인; 판매 중인
A 04 pass down 전하다   score 악보   **05** transparent 투명한   be composed of ~으로 구성되다   soot 검댕, 매연   namely 즉
B 06 count on ~을 믿다   **08** mass 질량   exert (힘 따위를) 쓰다   theory 이론   **09** hand 건네다
C 10 considerable 상당한   **11** be concerned with ~와 관련되다   state 진술하다   poetry (집합적) 시   **12** make sacrifices 희생하다

양태의 부사절

중요도 ★★★
난이도 ★★★

Block Board

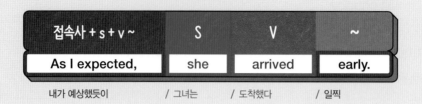

접속사 + s + v ~	S	V	~
As I expected,	she	arrived	early.
내가 예상했듯이	/ 그녀는	/ 도착했다	/ 일찍

- 양태를 나타내는 접속사

  ▷ as: ～처럼, ～이듯이, ～ 대로

  ▷ (just) as ~, so ...: (꼭) ～인 것처럼 …하다

  ▷ as if[as though]: 마치 ～인 것처럼　㏄ as if[as though] + 가정법 ➜ Unit 43

Standard Sentences

01 A mind needs books **as a sword needs a whetstone**, if it is to keep
정신은 책을 필요로 한다　　　/ 칼이 숫돌을 필요로 하듯이　　　　　/ 그것이 날을 유지하려고

⋯ **Know More**　Rainbow p.114

its edge. *the novel <A Game of Thrones>*
한다면

02 Most textbooks are written **as if science is a set of truths to be**
대부분의 교과서는 쓰여 있다　　　　/ 마치 과학이 일련의 사실들인 것처럼　　　　　/

memorized.
[암기되어야 할]

Ⓐ 다음 문장에서 양태의 부사절을 파악하면서, 각 문장을 해석하시오.

(모의) **03** The horse-drawn carriage was itself a technological innovation, as
were the horseless carriage and later automobiles.

▶「as + v + s」의 형태로 도치됨

(모의) **04** Just as a flesh-and-blood beast influences and is influenced by its
environment, so too do science and society mutually influence one
another.

▶「Just as + s + v ~, so + V + S」의 형태로 도치됨

05 Live as though you intend to live forever, and work as though your
strength were limitless.

B 다음 문장에서 양태의 부사절에 밑줄을 치고, 각 문장을 해석하시오.

06 We need to see people as they are, not as we would like them to be.

[모의] **07** Just as darkness comes at the end of each day, so also comes the dawn to spread light across the land. Just as plants must die at the end of their life cycle, the seeds they have produced will emerge as new plants in the spring.

08 Act as if what you do makes a difference. It does. *William James*

09 Even when you feel as though there isn't a lot you can do to change unhappiness or problems, you can always do a little—and a little at a time eventually makes a big difference.

C 다음 문장의 빈칸에 들어갈 내용으로 알맞은 것을 보기에서 고르시오.

> ─● 보기 ●─
> ⓐ as if you know everyone   ⓑ so do tastes and preferences evolve
> ⓒ just as we are not particularly aware of the action

[모의] **10** As there are differing tastes and preferences among different peoples and regions of the world, _____ over the course of centuries.

11 We usually take for granted our ability to produce and understand speech, _____ of our hearts, brains, or other essential organs.

12 Once you have listened to the gossip for some time, you will soon feel _____, even if you have never met them.

S·S 01 sword 칼   whetstone 숫돌   edge (칼의) 날; 예리함
A 03 carriage 마차, 차   **04** flesh-and-blood 현재 살아 있는   mutually 상호간에, 서로   **05** intend ~하려고 하다, 의도하다
B 07 dawn 새벽   spread 퍼뜨리다   seed 씨   emerge 나타나다   **08** make a difference 변화를 가져오다   **09** at a time 한 번에
C 보기 preference 선호   be aware of ~을 알다   particularly 특히   **11** take ~ for granted ~을 당연한 것으로 여기다   **12** gossip 소문, 험담

Chapter 08

Review

A 다음 문장을 우리말로 해석하시오.

01 Celebrate what you've accomplished, but raise the bar a little higher each time you succeed.

02 A broken heart is just the growing pains necessary so that you can love more completely when the real thing comes along. *J. S. B. Morse*

03 The rights guaranteed in the Bill of Rights—freedom of speech, assembly, religion, and so on—fall within negative rights, as do the rights to freedom from injury and to privacy. *the Bill of Rights (영국) 권리장전

(모의) **04** Food unites as well as distinguishes eaters because what and how one eats forms much of one's emotional tie to a group identity, be it a nation or an ethnicity.

B 다음 네모 안에서 적절한 것을 고르시오.

(수능) **05** The noise of barking and yelling from the park at night is so / such loud and disturbing that I cannot relax in my apartment.

06 The teacher had no sooner gone out of the classroom when / than all of the students burst out laughing.

(모의) **07** If you are stuck in a pattern of doing the same things every day and you feel as though / even though you are becoming dull, perhaps it is time to stop and sharpen your axe.

C 다음 괄호 안의 말을 우리말과 같은 뜻이 되도록 배열하여 문장을 완성하시오.

08 우리는 모두 지구촌의 일원이기 때문에 모든 사람이 이웃이 된다.

(of the global village, now, all part, are, that, we)

→ _____, everyone becomes a neighbor.

09 나는 너의 어려움에 매우 공감하지만, 내가 너를 돕기 위해 할 수 있는 것이 거의 없다.

(I, sympathize with, much, your difficulties, as)

→ _____, there is little I can do to help you.

10 경찰이 도착할 때까지 물건들을 있는 그대로 둬라.

(things, they, as, are, leave)

→ _____ until the police arrive.

D 다음 문장의 빈칸에 들어갈 내용으로 알맞은 것을 보기 에서 고르시오.

┌─ 보기 ●────────────────────────────────
ⓐ they are also extremely vulnerable
ⓑ they are not much use in predicting human behavior
ⓒ the story will not be clearly communicated to the audience
└──────────────────────────────────────

11 Adolescents are so primed to learn that _____ to learning the wrong things.

12 Unless an actor speaks and moves in the manner in which the imaginary character whose part he is playing would do, _____ _____.

13 While physics and mathematics may tell us how the universe began, _____ because there are far too many equations to solve. *Stephen Hawking*

A 01 celebrate 축하하다　bar 장애물; 막대기　**02** growing pains 성장통　**03** guarantee 보장하다　assembly 집회　negative rights 소극적 권리(침해받지 않을 권리)　**04** identity 정체성　ethnicity 민족 집단; 민족성　**B 05** yell 소리 지르다　disturb 불편하게 하다　**06** burst out v-ing 갑자기 ~하기 시작하다　**07** be stuck in ~에 갇혀 있다　dull 무딘　ax(e) 도끼　**C 09** sympathize 공감하다　**D** 보기 vulnerable 취약한　audience 관객, 청중　**11** primed 준비가 되어 있는, ~할 의향이 있는

STAGE III

주요 구문의 독파

Chapter **09** 가정법 구문

Chapter **10** 비교 구문

Chapter **11** 특수 구문

Chapter **12** 기타 주요 구문

Chapter **09** 가정법 구문

☑ 가정법 문장은 사실과 반대되거나, 일어날 가능성이 희박한 일에 대해 가정·상상·소망을 나타낼 때 쓰는 것으로, 사실을 나타내는 직설법 문장과 구분하기 위해 특정한 동사 패턴을 가진다.

☑ 가정법 문장의 의미를 정확히 파악하기 위해서는 가정법 구문의 기본 패턴을 익히고 나아가서 if가 없는 가정법 구문을 숙지하는 것이 필요하다.

Point 1 | if 가정법 과거 |

| If | s | 동사 과거형 | ~ | S | 조동사 과거형 + ⓥ | ~ |

Point 2 | if 가정법 과거완료 |

| If | s | had v-ed | ~ | S | 조동사 과거형 + have v-ed | ~ |

Point 3 | wish 가정법 |

| S | wish | (that +) s | 동사 과거형 / had v-ed | ~ |

Point 4 | as if[as though] 가정법 |

| S | V | ~ | as if[as though] | s | 동사 과거형 / had v-ed | ~ |

Point 5 | if가 없는 가정법 |

| 부사(구) To-v[V-ing / V-ed] ~ | S | 조동사 과거형 + ⓥ / have v-ed | ~ |

- unit 41   if 가정법 과거 구문
- unit 42   if 가정법 과거완료 구문
- unit 43   wish·as if 가정법 구문
- unit 44   if가 없는 가정법 구문

if 가정법 과거 ➔ Unit 41	▷ 현재 사실과 반대로 가정·상상하거나, 현실에서 일어날 것 같지 않은 일을 가정·상상할 때 쓴다.
if 가정법 과거완료 ➔ Unit 42	▷ 과거 사실과 반대로 가정·상상할 때 쓴다.
wish 가정법 ➔ Unit 43	▷ 「S + wish」 다음에 오는 that절은 소망의 내용이므로 가정법의 동사 형태가 온다.
as if[as though] 가정법 ➔ Unit 43	▷ as if 또는 as though 뒤에 사실과 반대의 내용이 오면 가정법의 동사 형태가 온다.
if가 없는 가정법 ➔ Unit 44	▷ 가정법에서 if가 이끄는 부사절 대신에, 부사(구), 부정사, 주어 등에 가정의 의미가 함축되어 있을 수 있다.

unit 41
if 가정법 과거 구문

중요도 ★★★
난이도 ★★☆

Block Board

If	s	동사 과거형	~	S	조동사 과거형 + ⓥ	~
If	I	had	a time machine,	I	would go back	yesterday.

만약 ~라면 / 내가 / 가지고 있다 / 타임머신을 / 나는 / 돌아갈 텐데 / 어제로

- **가정법 과거**: 현재 사실과 반대의 일이나, 실제로 일어날 것 같지 않은 일을 가정·상상할 때 쓴다.

  Form If + s + 동사 과거형 ~, S + 조동사 과거형 + ⓥ ...: 만약 ~라면, …할 텐데

- **were to 가정법**: 있을 법하지 않은 가상의 미래 상황을 가정할 때 쓴다.

  Form If + s + were to + ⓥ ~, S + 조동사 과거형 + ⓥ ...: (불가능한 일이지만) 만약 ~라면, …할 텐데

- **should 가정법**: 가능성이 낮은 미래의 일을 가정할 때 쓴다.

  Form If + s + should + ⓥ ~, ┌ S + 조동사(현재형 / 과거형) + ⓥ ...: (혹시라도) 만약 ~라면, …할 텐데
  └ 명령문: (혹시라도) 만약 ~라면, …해라

Standard Sentences

01 **If people knew how hard I had to work to gain my mastery,** it
만약 사람들이 안다면 / 내가 얼마나 열심히 일해야 했는지 / 나의 숙련된 솜씨를 얻기 위해서 /

would not seem so wonderful at all. *Michelangelo*
그것은 전혀 매우 놀랍게 보이지 않을 텐데

02 **If thunder should occur, it would be** better to find a shelter as soon
혹시라도 만약 천둥이 친다면 / (…이) 더 나을 것이다 / 대피처를 찾는 것이 / 가능한 한 빨리

as possible and avoid dangerous places.
/ 그리고 위험한 장소를 피하는 것이

A 다음 문장에서 가정법 과거 구문을 파악하면서, 각 문장을 해석하시오.

03 I heard a young boy on television say, "If I were President, I'd give everybody enough money to buy whatever they want."

▶ 가정법 과거의 조건절에서는 주어가 3인칭 단수일 때도 was 대신 were를 쓰는 것이 원칙임

04 If an asteroid with a diameter of 30 km were to collide with the Earth, it would probably bring an end to human civilization.

05 Should you meet a jaguar in the jungle, just turn slowly, walk away, and never look back.

▶ If + s + should + ⓥ ~
= Should + s + ⓥ ~

B 다음 문장에서 가정법 과거를 나타내는 동사에 밑줄을 치고, 각 문장을 해석하시오.

06 If young people understood how doing well in school makes the rest of their life so much interesting, they would be more motivated.

Bill Gates

07 Many species of animals could not survive were it not for the strong maternal instinct to protect the young.

▶ if it were not for ~
= were it not for ~

08 If the universe were to rewind back to the beginning and the laws of nature were the same, would everything happen in the exact same way?

09 Should you find our service useful, further information can be obtained by contacting our office.

C 다음 네모 안에서 어법에 맞는 것을 고르시오.

10 When Stephen Douglas, Abraham Lincoln's opponent in the presidential election, accused Lincoln of being two-faced during a debate, Lincoln self-deprecatingly responded like this. "Honestly, if I am / were two-faced, would I be wearing this one?"

▲ The Lincoln-Douglas debates of 1858 in Illinois, USA

11 Delicious autumn! My very soul is wedded to it, and if I were a bird I will / would fly about the earth seeking the successive autumns. *George Eliot*

12 If a man were to / should come back from the past and watch the modern world, he would note any number of things that would intoxicate him with wonder and delight.

A 04 asteroid 소행성 diameter 직경 collide 충돌하다 **05** jaguar 재규어, 아메리카 표범
B 06 the rest of one's life ~의 여생 **07** maternal instinct 모성 본능 **08** rewind 되돌리다, 되감다 laws of nature 자연의 법칙
C 10 opponent 경쟁자, 상대 accuse A of B A를 B라는 이유로 비난하다 two-faced 위선적인, 두 얼굴을 가진 self-deprecatingly 자조적으로
　11 wed 결혼하다 successive 이어지는 **12** note 주목하다 any number of 꽤 많은 intoxicate 열광하게 하다 delight 환희, 기쁨

unit 42
if 가정법 과거완료 구문

Block Board

If	s	had v-ed	~	S	조동사 과거형 + have v-ed	~
If	I	had taken	the subway,	I	would have arrived	sooner.
만약	/ 내가	/ 탔더라면	/ 지하철을	/ 나는	/ 도착했을 텐데	/ 더 빨리

- **가정법 과거완료**: 과거 사실과 반대로 가정·상상할 때 쓴다.

  Form If + s + [had v-ed] ~, S + [조동사 과거형 + have v-ed] ...: 만약 ~했다면, ...했을 텐데

- **혼합 가정법**: 조건절과 주절이 가정하는 시점이 다를 때 쓰며, 과거 사실을 반대로 가정하여 현재를 상상하는 가정법이 주로 쓰인다.

  Form If + s + [had v-ed] ~, S + [조동사 과거형 + ⓥ] ...: 만약 (과거에) ~했다면, (지금) ...할 텐데

  Tip 조건절에서 if가 생략되면 「had + s + v-ed」의 형태로 도치된다.

Standard Sentences

01 He **wouldn't have stopped** smoking **if his doctor hadn't told him**
그는 흡연을 중단하지 않았을 텐데   / 만약 그의 의사가 그에게 말해주지 않았다면

about the condition of his lungs.
/ 그의 폐 상태에 대해

(모의) **02** In my own travels, **had I taken packaged tours** I never **would have**
내 자신의 여행에서   / 내가 패키지 여행을 했다면   / 나는 결코 놀랄 만한 경험을 할

had any eye-opening experiences.
수 없었을 텐데

▶ had I taken packaged tours
= if I had taken packaged tours

Ⓐ 다음 문장에서 가정법 과거 완료 구문을 파악하면서, 각 문장을 해석하시오.

03 If the truck driver had only taken a few minutes to get the nail removed, he most likely would not have had a flat tire yesterday.

04 As a firefighter, I have seen many people die in fires. Most could have saved themselves had they been prepared.

▶ had they been prepared
= if they had been prepared

(모의) **05** Can you imagine what the world today would be like if Leonardo da Vinci had become a farmer or Wolfgang Amadeus Mozart a banker?

▶ 혼합 가정법

ⓑ 다음 문장에서 가정법 과거 완료를 나타내는 동사에 밑줄을 치고, 각 문장을 해석하시오.

06 If I am a great man, it is all thanks to my mother. Hadn't she devoted herself to supporting me, I could never have become what I am.

(모의) **07** We must assume that we had one chance each for *The Divine Comedy* and *King Lear*. If Dante and Shakespeare had died before they wrote those works, nobody ever would have written them.

08 Some economists discovered that gym goers would have been better off, financially, had they chosen to pay per workout rather than signing up for monthly or annual memberships.

(모의) **09** If Louise had not learned the effective parenting skills taught in the seminars, she would probably be using similarly ineffective threatening techniques with her own children today.

▲ Dante Alighieri

▶ 혼합 가정법

ⓒ 다음 네모 안에서 어법에 맞는 것을 고르시오.

10 If our ancestors hadn't agonized over losses and instead had taken too many chances in going after the big gains, they'd ┃ be / have been ┃ more likely to lose out and never become anyone's ancestor.

11 Had it not been for Newton, Einstein might never ┃ have / have had ┃ his own miracle year that completely revolutionized our view of gravity, space, matter, and time.

▶ Had it not been for Newton
= If it had not been for Newton

12 Copernicus doubted that the earth was the center of the universe. If it had not been for doubt, we should ┃ be / have been ┃ now even more ignorant than we really are.

S·S 01 lung 폐   02 eye-opening 놀랄 만한, 눈이 휘둥그레지는
A 03 nail 못; 손톱   remove 제거하다   flat tire 펑크난 타이어   04 save 구하다; 절약하다
B 06 devote oneself to ~에 헌신하다   07 assume 생각하다, 가정하다   08 better off 더 나은   workout 운동   sign up for ~을 신청하다
C 10 agonize 고심하다   take chance 위험을 무릅쓰다   go after ~을 추구하다   11 gravity 중력   matter 물질   12 ignorant 무지한

unit 43

wish·as if 가정법 구문

중요도 ★★☆
난이도 ★★☆

Block Board

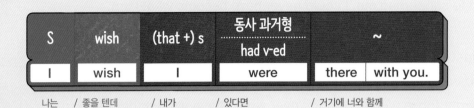

S	wish	(that +) s	동사 과거형 had v-ed	~
I	wish	I	were	there | with you.

나는 / 좋을 텐데 / 내가 / 있다면 / 거기에 너와 함께

- **wish 가정법**: 현재 또는 과거의 이룰 수 없는 소망을 나타낸다.

  Form S + wish (that) + s + (조)동사 과거형 + ~: ~하면 좋을 텐데 (주절과 같은 시점)

  S + wish (that) + s + had v-ed[조동사 과거형 + have v-ed] + ~: ~했다면 좋았을 텐데 (주절보다 앞선 시점)

- **as if[as though] 가정법**: 사실에 반하는 현재 또는 과거의 상상·가정을 표현한다.

  Form as if[as though] + s + (조)동사 과거형 + ~: 마치 ~인[하는] 것처럼 (주절과 같은 시점)

  as if[as though] + s + had v-ed + ~: 마치 ~였던[했던] 것처럼 (주절보다 앞선 시점)

  Tip as if[as though] + 직설법: 일어날 가능성이 있는 상황을 서술할 때 '~처럼'의 의미의 직설법이 올 수 있다. ▶ Unit 39

Standard Sentences

01 I wish I **were endowed** with an artistic talent for painting masterpieces
나는 좋을 텐데 / 내가 예술적 재능을 타고났다면 / [걸작을 그리기 위한

like Pablo Picasso's.
/ [파블로 피카소의 것과 같은]]

모의 **02** The woman smiled and he felt **as if she lit up the world around her.**
그 여자가 미소를 지었다 / 그러자 그는 느꼈다 / 마치 그녀가 밝히는 것처럼 / 그녀 주변의 세상을

A 다음 문장에서 가정법 구문을 파악하면서, 각 문장을 해석하시오.

03 I wish I had accepted your invitation, rather than running away with my tail between my legs.

04 Even though I don't personally believe in the Lord, I try to behave as though He was watching. *Christopher Reeve*

▶ as if[as though] 가정법에서도 가정법 과거일 때 구어체인 경우 was를 쓰기도 함

05 He burst into a high-pitched laugh, as though he'd said something funny.

B 다음 문장에서 wish 가정법 또는 as if 가정법을 나타내는 동사에 밑줄을 치고, 각 문장을 해석하시오.

06 I wish I could turn the clock back and give Mom a fraction of what she gave to me.

07 No one on his deathbed ever said, "I wish I had spent more time on my business."

08 To achieve great things we must live as though we were never going to die. *Marquis de Vauvenargues*

09 Men occasionally stumble over the truth, but most of them pick themselves up and hurry off as if nothing had happened.

Winston Churchill

C 다음 네모 안에서 어법에 맞는 것을 고르시오.

(모의) **10** I've lived my life taking risks and I wish I | can / could | tell you they were all successful, but they weren't.

11 Toward the end of their administrations, every president I think I've ever known was disappointed and wished they | did / had done | some things differently. *Billy Graham*

(모의) **12** All told, every second, our senses transmit an estimated 11 million bits of information to our poor brains, | as if / even if | a giant fiber-optic cable were plugged directly into them, firing information at full speed.

S·S 01 endow A with B A에게 B(재능, 자질, 권리 등)를 주다(부여하다) masterpiece 걸작 **02** light 밝게 하다
A 03 with one's tail between one's legs 겁을 먹고, 기가 죽어서 **05** burst into 갑자기 ~을 터뜨리다 high-pitched (음이) 아주 높은; 격렬한
B 06 turn the clock back 예전으로 돌아가다 fraction 일부, 작은 부분 **07** on one's deathbed ~의 임종에 **09** stumble 발이 걸리다
pick oneself up 일어나다 hurry off 서둘러 떠나다
C 10 take risk 위험을 감수하다 **11** administration (미국) 집권 정부; 관리 **12** all told 모두 통틀어 fiber-optic cable 광섬유 케이블
plug ~와 연결하다; 플러그를 꽂다 fire 쏘다, 발사하다

unit 44
if가 없는 가정법 구문

중요도 ★★☆
난이도 ★★★

Block Board

부사(구) To-v(V-ing / V-ed) ~	S	조동사 과거형 + $\overset{\text{ⓥ}}{\text{have v-ed}}$	~
Without music	our life	would be	dry as a desert.
음악이 없다면	/ 우리 삶은	/ ~일 것이다	/ 사막처럼 건조한

- if 또는 if절이 없더라도 부사(구) 또는 주어에 가정의 의미가 함축되어 있을 수 있다. 그럴 경우, 조동사 과거형이 가정법 구문을 파악하는 단서가 될 수 있다.
  - ▷ without(but for) ~ ┌ 만약 ~이 없다면 (= if it were not for ~, were it not for ~)
                        └ 만약 ~이 없었다면 (= if it had not been for ~, had it not been for ~)
  - ▷ otherwise: 그렇지 않으면 / 그렇지 않았다면
  - ▷ to부정사 또는 분사구문에 가정의 뜻이 포함된 경우
    - to-v(v-ing / v-ed) ~, S + 조동사 과거형 + ⓥ(have v-ed) ...

Standard Sentences

01 Dreams come true. **Without that possibility,** nature **would not incite**
꿈은 실현된다 ·   그런 가능성이 없다면   / 본성은 우리가 꿈을 가지도록 자극하지

us to have them. *John Updike*
않을 것이다

▶ Without that possibility
= If it were not for that
possibility

02 **In different circumstances,** I **would have enjoyed** that journey. My
다른 상황이었다면   나는 그 여행을 즐겼을 텐데   내

legs were **very** tired and sore.
다리가 너무 피곤하고 아팠다

▶ In different circumstances
= If I had been in different
circumstances

Ⓐ 다음 문장에서 가정법을 함축하는 어구를 파악하면서, 각 문장을 해석하시오.

03 Coronavirus is a completely different type of virus. Otherwise it
would be called flu.

04 Only a fool would ignore his past experience when confronted with
a new situation.

▶ 주어가 가정의 의미를 나타냄

05 To see her walking around in her old clothes, you'd never guess she
owned a multi-million dollar business.

▶ to부정사가 가정의 의미를 나타냄

B 다음 각 문장에서 가정법을 함축하고 있는 어구에 밑줄을 치고, 문장을 해석하시오.

06 We would not have had men on the Moon but for Wells and Verne and the people who write about this and made people think about it. *Arthur C. Clarke*

● ● ● Know More Rainbow p.129

07 All great achievers in past ages possessed singleness of purpose without exception. Without it, Columbus wouldn't have started upon the voyage that made his name immortal.

08 A hundred years ago not a doctor in the world could have assured a patient that an operation would be painless.

09 Born in better times, he would have done credit to society.

C 다음 문장의 빈칸에 알맞은 것을 보기 에서 고르시오.

┌─ 보기 ●
│   with   without   otherwise
└─

10 In the past it never occurred to me that every casual remark of mine would be snatched up and recorded. _____ I would have crept further into my shell. *Albert Einstein*

11 _____ the right software, I could help students form a concrete idea of society by displaying on-screen a version of the city in which they live.

모의 **12** Ironically, while many of us perceive insects as harmful pests— dangerous, ugly, and disease-ridden—in reality, _____ the service of pollination which they provide, humankind might cease to exist.

S·S 01 come true 실현되다   incite 자극하다   02 circumstance 상황   sore 아픈
A 04 confront 직면하다   05 own 가지다, 소유하다   multi-million 수백만의
B 07 voyage 항해   immortal 영원히 기억되는, 불후의   08 assure 장담하다   operation 수술   09 do credit to ~에 명예로운 인물이 되다
C 10 casual remark 무심코 한 말   snatch 잡아채다   creep 기어가다   11 concrete 구체적인   12 disease-ridden 질병이 들끓는   pollination 수분

Chapter 09

Review

A 다음 문장을 우리말로 해석하시오.

01 If everything given to us by research were to be taken away, civilization would collapse and we would stand naked, searching for caves again.

02 It was wonderful to find America, but it would have been more wonderful to miss it. *Mark Twain*

03 He drowsed off, but then woke up abruptly, as though someone had called his name.

04 The sun, the moon and the stars would have disappeared long ago, had they happened to be within reach of predatory human hands. *Havelock Ellis*

B 다음 네모 안에서 어법에 맞는 것을 고르시오.

(수능!) **05** When two cultures come into contact, they do not exchange every cultural item. If that is / were the case, there would be no cultural differences in the world today.

(모의) **06** Indeed, if our early African ancestors hadn't been good at fixing all their attention on the just-ripened fruit or the approaching predators, we wouldn't be / have been here.

07 I wish I could call / have called my family more often while I was away from home.

C 다음 괄호 안의 말을 이용하여 우리말과 같은 뜻이 되도록 문장을 완성하시오. (필요하면 형태를 바꿀 것)

08 만약 우리가 주유소에 들렀다면, 우리는 가솔린이 바닥나지 않았을 텐데.
(gas, run out of, wouldn't)

→ If we had stopped at the service station, we _____.

09 내가 할인 판매가 있다는 것을 알았다면 좋을 텐데. 나는 너와 함께 갔을 텐데.
(I, know, a sale, be, there)

→ I wish _____. I would have gone with you.

10 만약 항생제가 없었다면, 의학은 그런 놀라운 발전을 이루지 못했을 것이다.
(antibiotics, it, had, not, for, be)

→ _____, medicine would not have made such remarkable progress.

D 다음 주어진 문장들이 같은 의미가 되도록 빈칸에 알맞은 말을 쓰시오.

11 Without your donations, many more children would go hungry.

= If _____, many more children would go hungry.

= Were _____, many more children would go hungry.

12 You told me how the film ends; it would have been better if you had not told me.

= I wish _____ how the film ends.

13 I got caught in a traffic jam; otherwise I would have been here sooner.

= I got caught in a traffic jam; if _____, I would have been here sooner.

A 01 take away ~을 빼앗다　collapse 무너지다　naked 발가벗은　**03** drowse 졸다　abruptly 갑자기　**04** reach (팔이) 미치는 범위[거리]　predatory 약탈하는　**B 05** come into contact 접촉하다, 만나다　the case 사실, 실정　**06** indeed 정말로　ancestor 조상　ripen 익다　predator 포식자　**C 08** service station 주유소　run out of ~을 바닥내다, ~을 다 써 버리다　**10** antibiotic 항생제　remarkable 놀라운, 주목할 만한　**D 11** donation 기부　**13** traffic jam 교통 체증

Chapter

10 비교 구문

Get Ready!

☑ 비교 구문은 둘 이상의 대상을 비교하여 그 정도의 같음이나 차이를 나타내며, 원급, 비교급, 최상급의 세 가지 기본 형태가 있다.

☑ 비교 구문을 독해할 때는 먼저 비교 구문의 형태가 어떤 것인지, 무엇과 무엇이 비교되는지를 파악해야 한다.

☑ 관용적으로 쓰이는 비교 구문의 형태와 의미를 익혀두어야 한다.

Point 1 | **원급 구문** |

| S | V | as | 형용사[부사] | as + s + v ~ |

Point 2 | **비교급 구문** |

| S | V | 비교급 | than ~ |

| The + 비교급 | s + v ~ | the + 비교급 | S | V | ~ |

Point 3 | **최상급 구문** |

| S | V | the + 최상급 | in(of) + 명사 / (that +) s + have (ever) v-ed |

- unit **45** 원급 구문
- unit **46** 비교급 구문 1
- unit **47** 비교급 구문 2
- unit **48** 최상급 구문

원급 구문	둘을 비교하여 그 정도가 서로 같거나 비슷함을 나타낸다.
→ Unit 45	▷ as + 형용사[부사] + as ~: ~만큼 …한[하게]
	▷ 부정 표현 not + as[so] + 형용사[부사] + as ~: ~만큼 …하지 않은[않게]

비교급 구문	둘을 비교하여 그 정도의 차이를 나타낸다.
→ Unit 46, 47	▷ 비교급 + than ~: ~보다 더 …한[하게]
	▷ the + 비교급 ~, the + 비교급 …: ~하면 할수록, 더욱더 …하다

최상급 구문	셋 이상을 비교하여 그 정도가 가장 높은 것을 나타낸다.
→ Unit 48	▷ the + 최상급 + ┌ in[of] + 명사: ~ 중에서 가장 …한
	└ that절: ~해 본 중에서 가장 …한

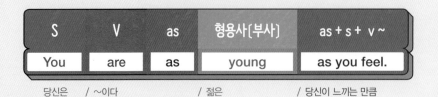

unit 45
원급 구문

중요도 ★★☆
난이도 ★★☆

Block Board

S	V	as	형용사[부사]	as + s + v ~
You	are	as	young	as you feel.

당신은 / ~이다 / 젊은 / 당신이 느끼는 만큼

- 서로 비슷하거나 같은 두 대상을 설명할 때 원급 구문을 쓴다.

  Form as + 형용사[부사] + as ~: ~만큼 …한[하게]   **부정 표현** not + as[so] + 형용사[부사] + as ~: ~만큼 …하지 않은[않게]

- **배수 표현**: 배수사(twice, half, … times 등) + as + 형용사[부사] + as ~ (~보다 몇 배 더 …한[하게])

- **원급을 이용한 관용표현:**

  not so much A as B: A라기보다는 오히려 B (= not A so much as B = B rather than A)

  Tip 「as + 형용사[부사]」가 나오면 뒤의 as를 찾아 무엇과 무엇을 비교하고 있는지 파악한다.

Standard Sentences

01 What you get by achieving your goals is **not as** important **as** what
당신이 얻는 것은 / 당신의 목표를 성취함으로써 / 중요하지 않다 / 당신이 되는

you become by achieving your goals. *Zig Zigler*
것만큼 / 당신의 목표를 성취으로써

02 The human brain cell can hold **five times as** much information **as**
인간의 뇌세포는 보유할 수 있다 / 5배 많은 정보를 /

the Encyclopaedia Britannica.
브리태니커 백과사전보다

A 다음 문장에서 원급 구문을 파악하면서, 각 문장을 해석하시오.

03 To ask what is the use of poetry should be as absurd as asking
what is the use of a rainbow, or the sea, or a nice dress. *Cecil Day-Lewis*

04 The International Space Station is almost four times as large as the
Russian space station Mir and about five times as large as the U.S.
Skylab.

05 It is important not so much to give a man bread, as to put him in
the way of earning it for himself.

B 다음 문장에서 원급 구문에 밑줄을 치고, 각 문장을 해석하시오.

06 A person's choice and use of words tells as much about him or her as do manners, dress, and general behavior.

▶ as ~ as + v + s: 두 번째 as 뒤에 도치가 일어날 수 있음

07 Happiness is produced not so much by great pieces of good fortune that seldom happen, as by little advantages that occur every day. *Benjamin Franklin*

08 While people today have twice as much spending power as they did in the 1950s, they are ten times more likely to be depressed.

09 A hero can be anyone, even a man doing something as simple and reassuring as putting a coat on a young boy's shoulders to let him know that the world hadn't ended.

the movie <The Dark Knight Rises>

A hero can be anyone!

C 다음 네모 안에서 어법에 맞는 것을 고르시오.

모의 **10** The consequences of interaction can be difficult to foresee because they depend as / so much on the behavior of others as on oneself.

11 Singapore has nearly 8,000 people per km², and is more than 200 times as dense / densely as the U.S.

12 Most insomnia is not an illness or a physical condition so many / much as a symptom of another problem that may simply be a reaction to certain medications, anxiety about travel, or stress before a job interview.

▶ not A so much as B = not so much A as B

A 03 poetry (집합적) 시 absurd 어리석은; 불합리한 04 space station 우주 정거장 05 put A in the way of A가 ~할 수 있도록 해주다

B 06 manners 예의 07 fortune 행운 advantage 좋은 점, 이점 08 depressed 우울한 09 reassuring 안심시키는

C 10 consequence 결과, 결론 interaction 상호작용 foresee 예측하다, 예견하다 11 nearly 거의 dense 밀집한, 고밀도의

12 insomnia 불면증 symptom 증상; 징후 medication 약물; 투약 anxiety 불안; 갈망

비교급 구문 1

중요도 ★★☆
난이도 ★★☆

Block Board

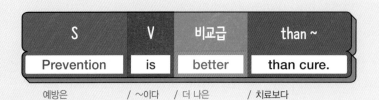

S	V	비교급	than ~
Prevention	is	better	than cure.

예방은 / ~이다 / 더 나은 / 치료보다

- 서로 차이가 나는 두 대상을 비교하여 설명할 때 비교급 구문을 쓴다.

  Form 형용사[부사] 비교급 + than ~: ~보다 더 …한[하게]

  Plus⊕ 비교급 앞에 even, far, much, still, a lot을 쓰면 비교급을 강조하여 '훨씬 더 ~한[하게]'의 의미를 나타낸다.

- **배수 표현**: 배수사 + 비교급 + than ~ (~보다 몇 배 더 …한[하게]) **Unit 45**

- **열등 비교**: less + 원급 + than ~ (~보다 덜 …한[하게])

  Tip 형용사 또는 부사의 비교급이 나오면 뒤의 than을 찾아 무엇과 무엇이 비교되는지 파악한다.

Standard Sentences

01 According to recent research, the universe is expanding **faster**
최근의 연구에 의하면 / 우주는 오늘날 더 빠르게 팽창하고 있다

today **than** it did in its infancy.
/ 우주가 초기에 그랬던 것보다

02 The energy in sunlight arriving on earth contains **about twelve**
햇빛 속의 에너지는 / [지구에 도달하는] / 약 12,000배 더 많은 에너지를 포함하고 있다

thousand times more energy **than** humanity uses in a year.
/ 인류가 1년에 사용하는 에너지보다

A 다음 문장에서 비교급 구문을 파악하면서, 각 문장을 해석하시오.

03 It is more important to be honorable and trustworthy than to look important for one small minute.

04 Learning to study effectively is even more important than merely acquiring a particular body of information.

05 Champion golfers are much less likely than average golfers to blame their problems on the weather, the course, or chance factors. Instead they focus relentlessly on their own performance.
모의

B 다음 문장에서 비교급 구문에 밑줄을 치고, 각 문장을 해석하시오.

모의 **06** Medical procedures may sound scarier when presented in terms of the risk of dying, rather than the likelihood of coming through unharmed.

07 We are always more anxious to be distinguished for a talent which we do not possess, than to be praised for the fifteen which we do possess. *Mark Twain*

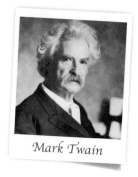
Mark Twain

08 What some call health, if purchased by perpetual anxiety about diet, isn't much better than tedious disease. *George Prentice*

모의 **09** It takes two to six times more grain to produce food value through animals than to get the equivalent value directly from plants.

··· **Know More** Rainbow p.137 ⟨

C 다음 괄호 안의 말을 우리말과 같은 뜻이 되도록 배열하여 문장을 완성하시오.

10 천문학자들은 태양의 직경은 지구의 직경보다 100배 이상 더 크다고 말한다.
(than, the earth's, larger, one hundred times, more than)
Astronomers observe that the sun's diameter is ＿＿＿＿＿＿＿＿＿
＿＿＿＿＿＿＿＿＿＿＿.

11 통찰력은 당신이 과제에 집중하는 상태일 때보다 멍한 상태일 때 생길 가능성이 훨씬 더 높다.
(to come, likely, more, far)
Insights are ＿＿＿＿＿＿＿＿＿ when you are in the mind-wandering mode than in the task-focused mode.

12 많은 휘발유를 사용하는 대형차들은 현재 20년 전보다 덜 인기가 있다.
(twenty years, now than, popular, ago, less)
Big cars that use a lot of petrol are ＿＿＿＿＿＿＿＿＿＿＿＿.

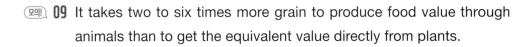

S·S 01 infancy (발달의) 초기; 유아기   **02** contain 포함하다   humanity 인류; 인간성
A 03 honorable 명예로운   trustworthy 신뢰할 수 있는   **04** body of ～의 (많은) 양   **05** factor 요소   relentlessly 가차없이
B 06 procedure (의학) 시술, 수술   in terms of ～의 관점에서   likelihood 가능성   come through 성공하다, 극복하다   **07** distinguished 유명한
   08 perpetual 끊임없는   tedious 시시한, 따분한   **09** grain 곡물; 낟알   food value (식품의) 영양가   equivalent 동등한
C 10 observe (소견을) 말하다, 진술하다   diameter 직경   **11** insight 통찰력   mind-wandering 멍한, 딴 생각하는   **12** petrol 휘발유, 가솔린

비교급 구문 2

Block Board

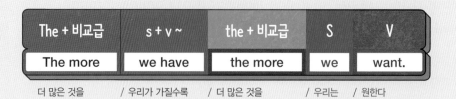

The + 비교급	s + v ~	the + 비교급	S	V
The more	we have	the more	we	want.
더 많은 것을	/ 우리가 가질수록	/ 더 많은 것을	/ 우리는	/ 원한다

- the + 비교급 ~, the + 비교급 …: ~하면 할수록, 더욱더 …하다
- no + 비교급 + than ~: ~보다 조금도 …하지 않은[않게] • not + 비교급 + than ~: ~보다 더 …하지 않은[않게]

  Plus⊕ no[not] + more[less] + than 관용표현

no more than	① 겨우 (= as few as) ② ~일 뿐 (= only)
no less than	① ~만큼이나 (= as much[many] as) ② ~와 마찬가지로
not more than	기껏해야, 많아도 (= at most)
not less than	적어도 (= at least)

- **A no more ~ than B …:** 양자 부정 A가 ~이 아닌 것은 B가 …이 아닌 것과 같다 (= A not ~ any more than B …)

  A no less ~ than B …: 양자 긍정 A가 ~인 것은 B가 …인 것과 같다, A는 B와 마찬가지로 ~이다

Standard Sentences

01 **The more** we use certain parts of our brain, **the more** developed
더 많이   / 우리가 뇌의 특정 부분들을 사용할수록   / 더욱더 발달하고 더 효율적이게

and efficient those parts of the brain become.
         / 뇌의 그 부분들이 된다

02 A collection of facts is **no more** science **than** a dictionary is poetry.
사실들의 모음은 과학이 아니다   / 사전이 시가 아닌 것만큼

▶ A no more ~ than B …
: 양자 부정

A 다음 문장에서 비교급 구문을 파악하면서, 각 문장을 해석하시오.

03 According to Einstein's Special Theory of Relativity, the faster a
spaceship goes, the slower its clock ticks and the shorter its length
in the direction of travel gets.

04 Man is no more than a reed, the weakest in nature, but he is a
thinking reed. *Blaise Pascal*

05 Air pollution does no less harm to birds and animals than it does to
human beings.

▶ A no less ~ than B …
: 양자 긍정

B 다음 문장에서 비교급 구문에 밑줄을 치고, 각 문장을 해석하시오.

(모의) **06** Anyone who has tried to complete a jigsaw puzzle as the clock ticked on toward a deadline knows that the more they struggle to find the missing pieces, the harder it is to find them.

07 We have called upon the people to set their air conditioners at no lower than 28 degrees Celsius in the summer and no higher than 20 in the winter.

08 We can no more explain a passion to a person who has never experienced it than we can explain light to the blind. *T. S. Eliot*

··· **Know More** Rainbow p.139 ⟨

(모의) **09** Organic farmers grow crops that are no less plagued by pests than those of conventional farmers: insects generally do not discriminate between organic and conventional as well as we do.

C 다음 괄호 안의 말을 우리말과 같은 뜻이 되도록 배열하여 문장을 완성하시오.

10 세상 사람들이 더 가까워질수록, 그들은 더욱더 자주 다른 문화권의 사람들에게 노출된다.
(they, more frequently, the, are exposed)
The closer the people in the world become, _____
_____ to people from other cultures.

11 만약 우리의 모든 지식이 감각의 수준에서 멈춘다면, 우리는 동물 세계의 유인원보다 조금도 더 낫지 않을 것이다. (better off, would be, than, no)
If all our knowledge stopped at the level of the senses, we _____
_____ the subhuman members of the animal kingdom.

(Up!) **12** 정신이 분자 속에서 발견될 수 없는 것은 셰익스피어의 작품들이 그의 유전자 속에서 발견될 수 없었던 것과 같다. (to be found, not, in molecules, any more than)
Mind is _____ the works of Shakespeare were to be found in his genes.

A 03 tick (시계가 째깍째깍) 움직이다   length 길이   travel 이동   **04** reed 갈대   **05** harm 해, 손상
B 06 jigsaw puzzle 조각 그림 퍼즐   struggle 안달복달하다, 몸부림치다   **07** call upon 요청하다   **08** passion 열정   blind 눈이 먼, 맹인의
09 organic 유기 농법의   plague 괴롭히다   pest 해충   conventional 재래 농법의   discriminate 구별하다; 차별하다
C 10 expose 노출시키다   **11** be better off 더 낫다, 더 좋은 상태이다   subhuman 유인의, 사람에 가까운   **12** molecule 분자   work (집합적) 작품

최상급 구문

중요도 ★★☆
난이도 ★★☆

Block Board

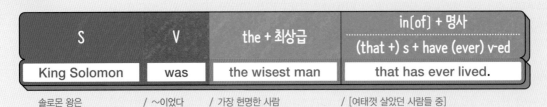

S	V	the + 최상급	in[of] + 명사 (that +) s + have (ever) v-ed
King Solomon	was	the wisest man	that has ever lived.
솔로몬 왕은	/ ~이었다	/ 가장 현명한 사람	/ [여태껏 살았던 사람들 중]

- 셋 이상 중에 '정도'가 가장 높은 하나를 나타낼 때 최상급 구문을 쓴다.

  Form the + 최상급 + ┌ in[of] + 명사: ~ 중에서 가장 …한
  └ (that +) s + have (ever) v-ed: (지금껏) ~해 본 중에서 가장 …한

- **최상급의 의미를 나타내는 원급·비교급 표현**
  ▷ 비교급 + than + any other + 단수 명사: 다른 어떤 ~보다 더 …한
  ▷ 비교급 + than + (all) the other + 복수 명사: 다른 (모든) ~보다 더 …한
  ▷ 부정 주어 + ~ 비교급 + than …: 어떤 것도 …보다 더 ~하지 않은
  ▷ 부정 주어 + ~ as[so] + 원급 + as …: 어떤 것도 …만큼 ~하지 않은

Standard Sentences

01 Global warming is considered to be **the most serious** threat facing
지구온난화는 여겨진다 / 가장 심각한 위협으로 / [인류를 향한]

humanity by many environmentalists.
/ 많은 환경 운동가들에 의해

02 **Nothing** in all the world is **more dangerous than** sincere ignorance
세상의 어떤 것도 더 위험하지는 않다 / 성실하면서 무지한 것과

and conscientious stupidity. *Martin Luther King Jr.*
양심적이면서 어리석은 것보다

▶ 부정 주어 ~ + 비교급 +
than …

Ⓐ 다음 문장에서 최상급 구문을 파악하면서, 각 문장을 해석하시오.

03 Personal computers have become the most empowering tool we've
ever created. *Bill Gates*

04 Next to religion, baseball has had a greater impact on our American
way of life than any other American institution. *Herbert Hoover*

05 No other writer's plays have been produced so many times or read
so widely in so many countries as Shakespeare's.

B 다음 문장에서 최상급의 의미를 나타내는 부분에 밑줄을 치고, 각 문장을 해석하시오.

06 Nobody is so miserable as he who longs to be somebody and something other than the person he is in body and mind. *Angelo Patri*

07 One of the hardest things in this world is to admit you are wrong. And nothing is more helpful in resolving a situation than its frank admission. *Benjamin Disraeli*

▶ one of the 최상급 + 복수형: 가장 ~한 … 중의 하나

08 The most exciting phrase to hear in science, the one that heralds new discoveries, is not "Eureka!" (I found it!) but "That's funny."

Isaac Asimov

Isaac Asimov

09 The Amazon's aquatic life, such as freshwater dolphins, 400-pound catfish, giant eels, is larger and more diverse than that of all the other river systems in the world.

C 다음 네모 안에서 어법에 맞는 것을 고르시오.

10 Of all the wonderful and unique characteristics of man, his ability to communicate through the use of language is perhaps the more / the most important.

11 Although humans are not the only animals who use tools, our species has developed this skill to a far greater extent than any other animal / animals .

12 In today's industry, where technology and speed of information are critical factors, nothing is more valuable to our clients as / than providing timely and accurate information.

S·S 01 humanity 인류; 인간성 **02** sincere 진실한, 진정한   ignorance 무지   conscientious 양심적인; 진지한   stupidity 어리석음
A 03 empower 힘을 더해주다   **04** religion 종교   institution 제도, 관습; 기관   **05** produce 상연하다
B 06 miserable 비참한, 불쌍한   long 바라다, 갈망하다   other than ~이 아닌   **07** admit 인정하다 *cf.* admission 인정   frank 솔직한
  08 phrase 말; 어구   herald 알리다   funny 신기한, 이상한   **09** aquatic 수생의, 물의   catfish 메기   eel 뱀장어
C 11 to ~ extent ~한 정도로   **12** critical 중대한   valuable 귀중한   client 고객   timely 시기적절한, 때맞춘   accurate 정확한

Chapter 10

Review

A 다음 문장을 우리말로 해석하시오.

(모의) **01** An individual neuron sending a signal in the brain uses as much energy as a leg muscle cell running a marathon.

02 Knowledge can no more be planted in the human mind without labor than a field of wheat can be produced without the previous use of the plow.

(수능) **03** 126 different studies of more than 36,000 people found that the more prone to anxieties a person is, the poorer his or her academic performance is.

04 There is no other quality so essential to success of any kind as the quality of perseverance. It overcomes almost everything, even nature.

John D. Rockefeller

B 다음 네모 안에서 어법에 맞는 것을 고르시오.

05 Solids, like wood for example, transfer sound waves much better than air typically (A) | is / does | because the molecules in a solid substance are much closer and more tightly packed together (B) | as / than | they are in air.

(수능) **06** The more (A) | effective / effectively | parents communicate their loving authority, the more (B) | secure / securely | the child feels.

(모의) **07** The brain's running costs are about eight to ten times as high, per unit mass, as | that / those | of the body's muscles.

08 Having children makes you no more a parent than having a piano | makes / doesn't make | you a pianist.

C 다음 괄호 안의 말을 우리말과 같은 뜻이 되도록 배열하여 문장을 완성하시오.

09 플라스틱을 재활용하는 것은 그것을 소각하는 데 필요로 하는 것보다 두 배 많은 에너지를 절약시켜 준다.
(energy, much, twice, as, as)

→ Recycling plastic saves _____ it takes to burn it.

10 네가 더 많은 경험을 가질수록, 너는 더 많은 일자리 기회를 찾을 것이다.
(job opportunities, you, find, more, will, the)

→ The more experience you have, _____.

11 세상의 어떤 빵도 자신의 노동으로 얻은 빵만큼 달콤하지 않다.
(bread, in the world, no, sweet, so, as, is)

→ _____ that earned by his own labor.

D 다음 주어진 문장들이 같은 의미가 되도록 빈칸에 알맞은 말을 쓰시오.

12 Fear defeats more people than any other one thing in the world.

= _____ in the world defeats so many people _____.

13 Just as a horse is not a fish, a whale is not a fish either.

= A whale is no more a fish _____ a horse is.

= A whale is not a fish _____ a horse is.

14 She is a realist rather than a pessimist.

= She is not so much a pessimist _____ a realist.

= She is not a pessimist _____ a realist.

A **01** individual 개별적인; 개인의   signal 신호   **02** plant 심다   wheat 밀   previous 먼저의, 이전의   plow 쟁기; (밭을) 갈다
03 prone to ~하는 경향이 있는, ~하기 쉬운   academic performance 학업 성취   **04** quality 자질, 특성   perseverance 끈기, 인내
B **05** solid 고체   transfer 전달하다   typically 일반적으로   molecule 분자   substance 물질   **06** authority 권위, 권한
secure 안전한, 확실한   **07** running cost 유지비   per ~당, ~마다   unit 단위   mass 질량; 다수   C **11** labor 노동, 수고
D **12** defeat 패배시키다   **14** realist 현실주의자   pessimist 비관주의자

Chapter 11 특수 구문

☑ 문장에서 어순이 뒤바뀌거나, 특정 어구를 강조하거나, 어떤 어구가 덧붙여지거나 빠지거나 하는 경우를 특수 구문이라고 한다.

☑ 각 특수 구문의 고유한 패턴을 익혀 두면 실전에서 문장의 구조와 의미를 더 쉽고 정확하게 파악할 수 있다.

Point 1

| 도치 구문 |

| 부정의 어구 | be동사 | S | ~ |
| So[Such] ~ | 조동사 | S | 본동사 |

Point 2

| 강조 구문 |

| It | is[was] | S / O / 부사(구/절) | that | (S) | V | ~ |

Point 3

| 동격 구문 |

| 명사 | ,[of / or] + 명사(구/절) / that + s + v ~ |

Point 4

| 삽입 구문 |

| ~ | , 단어[구/절], | ~ |

Point 5

| 생략·공통 구문 |

| S₁ | V₁ | ~ | 연결사 | S₂ | (V₂) | ~ |

└─ 동사의 생략

| S₁ | V₁ | 연결사 | V₂ | ~ |

└─ 공통의 주어

- unit **49** 도치 구문 1
- unit **50** 도치 구문 2
- unit **51** 강조 구문
- unit **52** 동격 구문
- unit **53** 삽입 구문
- unit **54** 생략·공통 구문

도치 구문
`unit 49, 50`

▷ 강조하고자 하는 어구가 문장의 맨 앞으로 올 때 주어와 동사의 어순이 바뀌는 도치가 일어날 수 있다.

강조 구문
`unit 51`

▷ It is와 that 사이에 강조하고자 하는 어구를 넣어 표현할 수 있다.

동격 구문
`unit 52`

▷ 앞에 온 명사 또는 대명사에 대한 의미를 보충하기 위해 콤마(,), 하이픈(—), 콜론(:), of, or, that 등의 뒤에 어구가 올 수 있다.

삽입 구문
`unit 53`

▷ 문장의 중간에 설명을 덧붙이거나 의미를 보충하기 위해서 콤마 사이에 단어, 구, 절이 삽입되기도 한다.

생략·공통 구문
`unit 54`

▷ 반복되는 어구, 또는 빠지더라도 의미 전달에 문제가 없는 어구는 종종 생략된다.
생략 구문: A ...... (A)

▷ 생략의 결과로 두 개 이상의 어구가 하나의 어구에 공통으로 연결되는 공통 구문이 생겨난다.
공통 구문: AX + BX → X(A + B) 또는 (A + B)X

unit 49
도치 구문 1

중요도 ★★★
난이도 ★★★

Block Board

부정의 어구	be동사		S	~
	조동사	S	본동사	
Never	will	I	forget	your kindness.
결코 ~ 않는	/ ~할 것이다	/ 나는	/ 잊지	/ 너의 친절을

- **도치 구문**: 강조하고자 하는 어구가 문장의 앞으로 올 때 주어와 동사의 어순이 바뀌는 도치가 일어날 수 있다.

  Form 부정의 어구 + be동사 + S / 부정의 어구 + 조동사 + S + 본동사
    ↳ no, not, never, none, little, few, seldom, hardly, scarcely, rarely 등

  Plus⊕ only를 포함하는 부사어가 문장의 맨 앞에 올 때도 주어와 동사가 도치된다.

  ▷ 장소·방향의 부사 + (장소·이동의) V + S　　**cf** 장소·이동의 동사: be동사, come, go 등

  ▷ 보어 + V + S

  ▷ 분사 + be동사 + S

Standard Sentences

01 **On no account** must you give your banking details to anyone over
결코 당신은 당신의 은행 정보를 줘서는 안 된다　　　　　　　　　　　　/ 누군가에게 /

the phone or by email.
전화로 또는 이메일로

▶ 부정의 어구 + 조동사 + S + 본동사

02 **Trustworthy** are those who give not only compliments but also
신뢰할 수 있는 것은 사람들이다　　　　/ [칭찬뿐만 아니라 쓴 조언도 주는]

bitter advice.

▶ 보어 + be동사 + S

A 다음 문장에서 도치 구문을 파악하면서, 각 문장을 해석하시오.

[모의] **03** Not until the rise of ecology at the beginning of the twentieth
century did people begin to think seriously of land as a natural
system with interconnecting parts.

▶ not A until B → not until
B A (A 부분에서 도치 발생)

04 Every cell is a triumph of natural selection, and we're made of
trillions of cells. Within us, is a little universe. *Carl Sagan*

⋯▶ **Know More** Rainbow p.146
▶ 장소의 부사 + V + S

05 Natural ability is necessary to become an expert in anything, but no
less important is the willingness to study.

▶ 보어 + be동사 + S

B 다음 문장에서 도치된 주어와 동사에 밑줄을 치고, 각 문장을 해석하시오.

06 For a computer to solve a problem, not only must the solution be very detailed, but it must also be written in a form the computer can understand.

07 Under no circumstances will anyone's personal information be given out to any third party without the express permission of the person concerned.

08 Out of the fundamentals of elementary algebra evolved the abstract algebra used today and the concept of an algebraic structure.

09 Included in this chapter is a list of frequently misspelled words, which you may find it helpful to memorize.

▶ 분사 ~ + be동사 + S

C 다음 네모 안에서 어법에 맞는 것을 고르시오.

(모의) **10** Only in the last few decades, in the primarily industrially developed economies, food has / has food become so plentiful and easy to obtain as to cause fat-related health problems.

▶ so + 형용사 + as + to-v: ~할 정도로 …한

(모의) **11** Fundamental to most moral approaches is / are the idea that human life has a special dignity and value that is worth preserving even at the expense of self-interest.

(모의) **12** Laid before me was / were , I realized, a scene of almost classical rural beauty—the meadows dotted with contented animals, the woods in the background, a twisting stream threading through it all.

S·S 01 on no account 결코[무슨 일이 있어도] ~ 않는 **02** trustworthy 신뢰할 수 있는
A 03 ecology 생태학 interconnect 서로 연결하다 **04** triumph 업적 natural selection 자연 선택 trillion 조(兆)
B 07 under no circumstances 어떠한 상황에서도 ~ 않는 third party 제3자 express 명시된 the person concerned 관계자
  08 fundamental 원리; 근본적인 elementary 기초의 abstract 추상적인 algebra 대수학 **09** misspell 철자를 틀리다, 철자를 잘못 쓰다
C 10 economy (경제 주체로서의) 국가; 경제 **11** at the expense of ~을 희생하여 **12** meadow 목초지 dotted 점점이 있는 contented 만족한

도치 구문 2

중요도 ★★★
난이도 ★★★

Block Board

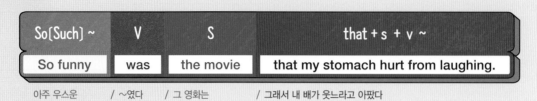

So[Such] ~	V	S	that + s + v ~
So funny	was	the movie	that my stomach hurt from laughing.

아주 우스운 / ~였다 / 그 영화는 / 그래서 내 배가 웃느라고 아팠다

- **So / Such ~ that 구문**

  > So + 형용사[부사]
  > Such (+a+형용사+명사)
  > + be동사+S+that+s+v ~
  > 조동사+S+본동사+that+s+v ~

- **So / Neither / Nor 구문**
  - ▷ So + 조동사[be동사] + S: S도 역시 그렇다　　ⓒⓕ So + S + V: S는 정말 그렇다
  - ▷ Neither[Nor] + 조동사[be동사] + S: S도 역시 그렇지 않다

- **목적어의 도치**: 목적어가 긴 경우, 목적어가 목적격보어나 부사의 뒤로 갈 수 있다.
  - ▷ S+V+O+O·C ➡ S+V+O·C+O
  - ▷ S+V+O+부사 ➡ S+V+부사+O

Standard Sentences

모의 01 The present moment does not exist in the equations of physics, and
현재의 순간은 존재하지 않는다　　　　　　　/ 물리학 방정식에　　　　　/ 따라서

therefore **neither** does the flow of time.
시간의 흐름도 그렇지 않다

02 What the caterpillar calls the end of the world the world calls a
애벌레가 세상의 종말이라고 부르는 것을　　　　　　　　　　　　/ 세상은 나비라고 부른다

butterfly. *Richard Bach*

▶ O+S+V ~: 목적어가 맨 앞으로 나오더라도 주어와 동사는 도치되지 않음

A 다음 문장에서 도치 구문을 파악하면서, 각 문장을 해석하시오.

03 Such was the power of his voice that even those at the back of the room gazed at the speaker in awe.

▶ = The power of his voice was such that ~

04 Philosophy, which is understood to be the desire to acquire wisdom, is a fundamental part of the human being, and so is science.

05 The release of atomic energy has **not** created a new problem. It has **merely** made more urgent the necessity of solving an existing one.

▶ 긴 목적어와 목적격보어의 도치

B 다음 문장에서 도치된 부분에 밑줄을 치고, 각 문장을 해석하시오.

(모의) **06** So closely is sniffing tied to odor perception that people routinely sniff when they are asked to imagine a smell.

07 People often say that motivation doesn't last. Well, neither does bathing—that's why we recommend it daily. *Zig Ziglar*

08 We carry home what we have bought in some vessel, but learning we cannot put in any other vessel but our minds.

09 How on earth are you ever going to explain in terms of chemistry and physics so important a biological phenomenon as first love?

Albert Einstein

▶ so + 형용사 + a(n) + 명사 = such + a(n) + 형용사 + 명사

C 다음 괄호 안의 말을 우리말과 같은 뜻이 되도록 배열하여 문장을 완성하시오.

10 그는 아주 서둘러서 사무실에 나오느라 문을 잠그고 경보 장치를 설정하는 것을 잊어버렸다.
(did, quickly, he, rush)

So ＿＿＿＿＿＿＿＿＿＿＿＿ out of the office that he forgot to lock up and set the alarm.

(모의) **11** 동물과 달리, 식물은 자신의 뿌리를 집어 들고 안전을 위해 질주할 수 없다. 많은 식물은 공격 태세를 취해서 포식자가 된 적도 없었다. (taken, many plants, the offensive, have)
Unlike animals, plants cannot pick up their roots and race for safety.
Nor ＿＿＿＿＿＿＿＿＿＿＿＿ and become predators.

12 우리가 알지 못하고 통제할 수 없는 우리의 생각과 감정의 커다란 부분을 지그문트 프로이트는 무의식이라고 불렀다. (the unconscious, Sigmund Freud, called)
The large part of our thoughts and feelings that we do not know and cannot control ＿＿＿＿＿＿＿＿＿＿＿＿.

S·S 01 equation 방정식, 등식 02 caterpillar 애벌레
A 03 such (that과 함께 쓰여) 대단한, 굉장한 gaze 응시하다 in awe 경탄하며 04 fundamental 근원적인 05 atomic 원자의 existing 기존의
B 06 sniff 코를 킁킁거리다 odor 냄새 perception 지각, 인식 routinely 일상적으로 08 vessel 용기, 그릇 but ～ 이외에 09 on earth 도대체 in terms of ～의 관점에서
C 11 offensive 공격 태세; 공격적인 predator 포식자; 약탈자 12 unconscious 무의식

강조 구문

It	is[was]	S / O / 부사(구/절)	that	(S)	V	~
It	was	a UFO	that	we	saw	last night.
(…은)	/ ~이었다	/ 미확인 비행물체		/ 우리가	/ 본 것은	/ 어젯밤에

- 「It is ~ that ....」 강조 구문: It is와 that 사이에 주어, 목적어, 부사(구/절)가 들어가 강조되어 '…하는 것은 바로 ~이다'의 의미를 나타낸다.

    Plus⊕ 강조되는 어구가 사람이면 that 대신 who, 사물이면 that 대신 which를 쓸 수 있다.

- 「It is ~ that ....」 강조 구문은 It is와 that을 빼면, 나머지 요소들만으로도 완전한 의미를 갖는 문장으로 쓸 수 있다.

Standard Sentences

01 **It is** the interaction between our genes and the environment **that**
(…은) 바로 상호작용이다 / [우리의 유전자와 환경 사이의] / 결정

determines whether we develop an illness.
하는 것은 / 우리가 병이 생길지 어떨지

▶ 주어 강조

02 **It was** not until the twelfth century **that** the magnetic compass was
(…은) 바로 12세기가 될 때까지는 아니었다 / 자기 나침반이 사용된 것은

used for navigation.
/ 항해를 위해

▶ 부사구 강조

Ⓐ 다음 문장에서 강조 구문을 파악하면서, 각 문장을 해석하시오.

03 Success is not final, failure is not fatal: it is the courage to continue
that counts. *Winston Churchill*

04 It is not the number of books which a young man reads that makes
him intelligent and well-informed, but the number of well-chosen
ones that he has mastered.

05 It is through his untiring effort that the singer has succeeded in
becoming what he is now, getting out of what he was.

B 다음 문장에서 강조되는 부분에 밑줄을 치고, 각 문장을 해석하시오.

Up! **06** It is not work, but overwork, that is hurtful; and it is not hard work that is injurious so much as unwilling work.

▸ not A so much as B: A라기보다는 오히려 B

수능! **07** Heritage is more concerned with meanings than material artefacts. It is the former that give value, either cultural or financial, to the latter and explain why they have been selected from the near infinity of the past.

모의! **08** It's not until we're being massaged by warm water, unable to check our e-mail, that we're finally able to hear the quiet voices in the backs of our heads telling us about the insight.

09 I've made the most important discovery of my life. It's only in the mysterious equation of love that any logical reasons can be found.
John Nash

▲ *A Beautiful Mind*: The Life of Mathematical Genius and Nobel Laureate John Nash

C 다음 문장의 밑줄 친 부분을 강조하도록 「It is ~ that ...」 구문을 사용하여 다시 쓰시오.

10 I have been looking for the biography of Steve Jobs.

→ _____

11 Some people say science deprives man of his dreams and of his poetry, but we can also say poetry and dreams have developed science.

→ but we can also say _____.

12 We may discover the true strength of the brilliant light only in our darkest hours within ourselves.

→ _____

S·S **01** develop an illness 병이 생기다, 발병하다   **02** magnetic compass 자기 나침반
A **03** fatal 결정적인   count 중요하다   **04** well-informed 박식한   well-chosen 정선된, 잘 골라낸   **05** untiring 지칠 줄 모르는, 지치지 않는
B **06** unwilling 마음이 내키지 않는, 마지못해 하는   **07** heritage 유산   artefact 인공물   the former 전자   the latter 후자   infinity 무한
  08 insight 통찰(력)   **09** logical 논리적인
C **10** biography 전기   **11** deprive A of B A에게서 B를 빼앗다   **12** brilliant 눈부신, 반짝반짝 빛나는

unit 52

동격 구문

Block Board

명사	**,[of / or] + 명사 (구/절)** ┄┄┄┄┄┄┄┄┄┄ **that + s + v ~**	~
Psychology	, or the science of the mind,	**helps** · **to understand human behavior.**

심리학은 / = 마음에 관한 과학인 / 도와준다 / 인간의 행동을 이해하는 것을

- **동격 구문**: 앞선 명사 또는 대명사의 의미를 보충하기 위해 콤마(,), 대시(—), 콜론(:), of, or, that 등의 뒤에 다른 명사 상당 어구를 덧붙이는 것을 '동격(=)'이라고 한다.
  ▷ 동격의 구두점: 명사, 명사 , 명사—명사 , 명사: 명사
  ▷ 동격어구와 동격절: 명사 + of + 명사 , 명사, or 명사 , 명사 + that + s + v ~
  ▷ 동격의 관용표현: in other words, that is (to say), namely 등

Standard Sentences

01 Alpha rhythm, **a brain wave frequency of moderate voltage,** is
알파 리듬은 / = 적당한 전압의 뇌파 진동수인 /

characteristic of a person who is awake but relaxed.
사람의 특징이다 / [깨어 있지만 안정된]

▶ 명사, 명사

(모의) **02** Coevolution is the concept **that two or more species of organisms**
공진화는 개념이다 / [= 둘 이상의 유기체 종들이 서로 상대방의 진화 방향에 영향을 줄 수

can reciprocally influence the evolutionary direction of the other.
있다고 하는]

▶ 명사 + that + s + v ~

Ⓐ 다음 문장에서 동격 구문을 파악하면서, 각 문장을 해석하시오.

03 Throughout history, people have been intrigued by the question of whether there is intelligent life elsewhere in the universe.

▶ 명사 + of + 명사절

(모의) **04** Scientists tried to extract knowledge by devising theories, that is, building models to explain the data they observed.

▶ 명사구, 동격의 관용표현, 명사구

05 As humans, we respond to everything in our environment in one of two basic ways: we either approach stimuli or we avoid stimuli.

▶ 명사: 명사절

ⓑ 다음 문장에서 굵게 표시한 어구와 동격인 부분에 밑줄을 치고, 각 문장을 해석하시오.

06 Don't try to be **a jack-of-all-trades**, I-can-do-anything job applicant, also known as a "slash" person.

··· **Know More** Rainbow p.153

07 **The so-called Mozart effect**—listening to Mozart will make your child smarter—is a good example of a scientific finding being distorted by the media through hype not warranted by the research.

▶ 명사—명사절

08 We are **survival machines**, robot vehicles blindly programmed to preserve the selfish molecules known as genes. *Richard Dawkins*

Rock'n'roll~

09 The first time rock 'n' roll came into being, it received much criticism on **the grounds** that it could be a threat to the traditional culture, just as jazz did thirty-five years ago.

▲ Elvis Presley is widely known as the "King of Rock 'n' Roll".

ⓒ 다음 문장에서 동격 관계에 있는 두 부분에 각각 밑줄을 치시오.

10 Only the smallest fraction of the human race has ever acquired the habit of taking an objective view of the past.

(모의) **11** There is a growing interest in computer programs that can analyze data and extract information automatically from them—in other words, learn.

12 In writing or speaking English, there is only the general principle that concrete words are better than abstract ones, and that the shortest way of saying anything is always the best.

S·S 01 brain wave 뇌파   frequency 진동수   moderate 적당한   voltage 전압   02 coevolution 공진화   reciprocally 서로
A 03 intrigue 강한 흥미를 불러일으키다   elsewhere (어딘가) 다른 곳에   04 devise 고안하다   observe 관찰하다   05 stimulus 자극 (*pl.* stimuli)
B 06 jack-of-all-trades 만물박사   slash 사선(/)   07 so-called 이른바, 소위   distort 왜곡하다   hype 과장 광고, 과대 선전   warrant 보장하다
    08 vehicle 매개체, 수단   blindly 맹목적으로, 무분별하게   09 come into being 출현하다   ground 이유; 땅
C 10 fraction 일부, 부분   objective 객관적인   11 extract 뽑아내다; 추출   12 concrete 구체적인   abstract 추상적인

unit 53
삽입 구문

중요도 ★★☆
난이도 ★★★

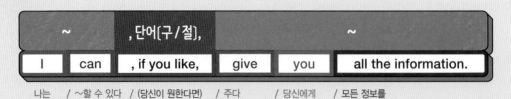

~	,단어[구 / 절],			~
I	can	, if you like,	give	you	all the information.

나는 / ~할 수 있다 / (당신이 원한다면) / 주다 / 당신에게 / 모든 정보를

- **삽입 구문**: 문장의 중간에 설명을 덧붙이거나 의미를 보충하기 위해서 단어, 구, 절이 삽입될 수 있다. 삽입어구의 앞뒤에 대개 콤마(,), 대시(—), 관용표현이 오지만, 아무 표시 없이 삽입될 수도 있다. 특히 관계대명사 다음에 「s + v」 형태의 절이 삽입되기도 한다.

(Tip) 삽입어구를 괄호로 묶으면 문장의 구조를 잘 파악할 수 있다.

Standard Sentences

01 The little reed, **bending to the force of the wind**, soon stood upright
작은 갈대는 / (바람의 힘에 구부러지는) / 곧 다시 똑바로 섰다

again when the storm had passed over. *Aesop*
/ 폭풍이 지나갔을 때

02 A fallacy is an idea that **a lot of people think** is true but which is
오류는 생각이다 / [(많은 사람들이 생각하기에) / 진실인 / 그러나 잘못된]

false.

▶ ~ 관계대명사 + (s + v) ...

Ⓐ 다음 문장에서 삽입된 부분을 파악하면서, 각 문장을 해석하시오.

(수능!) **03** What's dangerous about the Internet is, because it has the aura of technology around it, it has a totally undeserved instant credibility.

04 An idealist is one who, on noticing that a rose smells better than a cabbage, concludes that it will also make better soup. *Henry L. Mencken*

05 Your work is going to fill a large part of your life, and the only way to be truly satisfied is to do what you believe is great work. *Steve Jobs*

B 다음 문장에서 삽입된 부분을 괄호로 묶고, 각 문장을 해석하시오.

06 Words are, in my not so humble opinion, our most inexhaustible source of magic, capable of both influencing injury, and remedying it. *the novel <Harry Potter and the Deathly Hallows>*

···◖Grammar Plus Rainbow p.155 ◗
▶ 전치사구의 삽입

07 We can share what we know, however little it might be, with someone who has need of that knowledge.

08 There are computer programs which, when they are fed patients' medical histories, can predict health issues such as heart attacks more reliably than doctors.

09 It looks like water was on Mars, because the surface features resemble those on Earth that we know are made by water.

C 다음 네모 안에서 어법에 맞는 것을 고르시오.

▶ 관계대명사절의 삽입

Up! **10** Our judgments are so liable to be influenced by many considerations, which almost, without our knowing it, are unfair, that / what it is necessary to keep a guard upon them.

모의 **11** People may change the kinds of games they are playing, but an interest in interactive entertainment media, once acquired, seems / seeming never to fade.

모의 **12** I recently saw a news interview with an acquaintance who / whom I was certain was going to lie about a few particularly sensitive issues, and lie she did.

S·S **01** reed 갈대   upright 똑바로   **02** fallacy 오류
A **03** aura 기운, 분위기   undeserved 자격이 없는   instant 즉각적인   credibility 신뢰성   **04** idealist 이상주의자, 공상가   conclude 결론짓다
B **06** humble 겸손한; 보잘 것 없는   inexhaustible 무궁무진한, 다 쓸 수 없는   remedy 치료하다   **08** feed (정보를) 제공하다   medical history 병력
heart attack 심장 마비   reliably 확실하게, 믿을 수 있게   **09** feature 지형; 특징   resemble 닮다
C **10** liable ~하기 쉬운   consideration 고려 사항   **11** acquire (몸에) 익히다, 지니게 되다   fade 사라지다, 약해지다   **12** acquaintance 지인, 아는 사람

unit 54

생략·공통 구문

중요도 ★★☆
난이도 ★★☆

Block Board

S₁	V₁	~	연결사	S₂	(V₂)	~
The sun	shines	in the daytime	and	the stars	(shine)	at night.
태양은	/ 빛난다	/ 낮에	/ 그리고	/ 별들은		/ 밤에

- **생략 구문**: 문장 내의 어떤 어구가 빠져도 의미 파악에 지장을 주지 않는 경우에 '생략'이 일어난다.
  ▷ 문장에서 반복되는 어구 생략
  ▷ 부사절의 주어가 주절의 주어와 동일한 경우 「S + be동사」 생략

- **공통 구문**: 문장에서 생략이 일어난 후, 두 개 이상의 어구가 한 어구에 공통으로 연결될 수 있다.
  AX + BX → X A + B 또는 A + B X
  ▷ 주어 동사 + 동사 / 동사 보어 + 보어 / 동사 목적어 + 목적어
  ▷ 동사 + 동사 목적어 / 전치사 + 전치사 목적어

Standard Sentences

모의 **01** It is found that puppies only a few weeks old could **interpret human**
(…이) 발견된다 / 강아지들이 / [겨우 몇 주밖에 안 된] / 인간의 신호를 해석할 수 있다는 것이

signals, while full-grown wolves raised by humans could not ✔.
/ 반면에 다 자란 늑대들은 / [인간에 의해서 양육된] / (인간의 신호를 해석)할 수 없다는 것이

▶ ✔ 자리에 interpret ~ signals가 생략됨

02 The object of education is, **or ought to be, to provide exercise for**
교육의 목적은 / ~이다 / 또는 ~여야 한다 / 훈련을 제공하는 것 /

student's potential capacities.
[학생의 잠재력을 위한]

▶ 공통의 보어

A 다음 문장에서 생략되거나 공통으로 쓰인 부분을 파악하면서 각 문장을 해석하시오.

모의 **03** Marshall McLuhan noted that clothes are people's extended skin,
wheels extended feet, camera and telescopes extended eyes.

 **Know More** Rainbow p.156

모의 **04** A snack with the label "99% natural" seems more appealing **than it**
would if labeled "1% unnatural."

05 Mathematics is an area of study that I'm attracted to, interested in,
and good at, **though I have not explored it in depth.**

B 다음 문장에서 생략된 부분에 √ 표시를 한 후 생략된 어구를 쓰고, 각 문장을 해석하시오.

06 Sleep is to the brain what food is to the body. That is to say, if deprived of adequate sleep, the brain cannot function properly.

▶ A is to B what C is to D: A의 B에 대한 관계는 C의 D에 대한 관계와 같다

07 Scientific beliefs are supported by evidence, and they get results. Myths and faiths are not and do not. *Richard Dawkins*

(모의) **08** In the realm of human psychology, research has long noted the essential trait of adapting to life's events, whether happy or tragic.

(Up!) **09** It takes a great deal of bravery to stand up to our enemies, but just as much to stand up to our friends. *the novel <Harry Potter and the Sorcerer's Stone>*

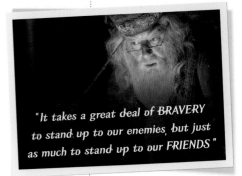

"It takes a great deal of BRAVERY to stand up to our enemies, but just as much to stand up to our FRIENDS"

C 다음 문장에서 공통으로 쓰인 부분에 동그라미로 표시하시오.

10 The computer is only a fast idiot; it has no imagination; it cannot originate action. It is, and will remain, only a tool of man.

(모의) **11** Pride causes individuals to be out of touch with the reality of who they truly are and of what really brings happiness.

(모의) **12** Only after the immediate concerns of the unconscious have been satisfied can the conscious mind begin to be convinced of, or interested in, anything.

S·S 01 interpret 해석하다   02 object 목적, 목표   potential capacity 잠재력
A 03 extend 연장하다   telescope 망원경   04 snack 과자, 간식   appealing 매력적인   05 attract 끌다; 매혹하다
B 06 deprive 빼앗다, 박탈하다   adequate 적절한, 충분한   07 myth 신화; 통념   faith 신앙, 신념   08 realm 영역   psycology 심리학
trait 특성, 특징   adapt to ~에 적응하다   tragic 매우 슬픈, 비극적인   09 a great(good) deal of (양이) 많은   stand up to ~에게 맞서다
C 10 idiot 멍청이, 바보   originate 일으키다   12 immediate 즉각적인   concern 관심사   be convinced of ~을 확신하다

Review

A 다음 문장을 우리말로 해석하시오.

(모의) **01** At the heart of individualism lies the belief that each individual person constitutes the center of one's universe.

02 It is not what he has, nor even what he does, which directly expresses the worth of a man, but what he is. *Henri-Frédéric Amiel*

03 It's a common misconception that money is every entrepreneur's metric for success. It's not, and nor should it be.

04 Don't get caught up in thinking that any success you experience as a student has no bearing on, or relationship to, future success in the "real" world.

B 다음 네모 안에서 어법에 맞는 것을 고르시오.

05 Break the 'big, fat, terrible book' down into sections that you feel is / are more manageable and read through them one at a time.

06 Even more significant than the ability to communicate knowledge by means of signs and sounds was / were the development of a means of preserving the knowledge through written records.

(Up!) **07** It is in our ancient myths which / that many writers find the core of the human struggle to make sense of the world and to find one's role—in short, a road map to the human psyche.

C 다음 괄호 안의 말을 우리말과 같은 뜻이 되도록 배열하여 문장을 완성하시오.

08 경찰은 범행 현장에 있었던 것으로 그들이 의심했던 한 남자를 체포했다.
(they, who, had been, suspected)

→ The police arrested a man _____ at the crime scene.

09 인생을 흥미롭게 만드는 것은 바로 꿈을 실현하도록 하는 가능성이다.
(life, interesting, makes, that)

→ It's the possibility of having a dream come true _____.

10 우리가 출발하자마자 하늘이 흐려졌고 비가 다시 내렸다.
(we, started out, before, had)

→ Scarcely _____ the sky became overcast and down came the rain again.

D 다음 문장의 빈칸에 들어갈 내용으로 알맞은 것을 보기 에서 고르시오.

┌─ 보기 ●─────────────────────────────────┐
ⓐ the stupid, by necessity
ⓑ that makes you a survivor and a winner
ⓒ a problem we recognize from the question
└──────────────────────────────────────┘

(모의)
11 Any discussion of coevolution quickly runs into what philosophers call a "causality dilemma," _____, "Which came first, the chicken or the egg?"

12 The wise are instructed by reason; ordinary minds, by experience; _____; and brutes, by instinct.

13 In my experience, it's not what happens to you in life, but how you deal with it, _____.

A **01** constitute 구성하다 **03** misconception 오해, 오인 entrepreneur 기업인 metric 측정 기준 **04** get caught up in ~에 말려들다 bearing 관련, 영향 B **05** manageable 감당할 수 있는, 처리하기 쉬운 one at a time 하나씩, 차례로 **06** significant 중요한, 의미심장한 by means of ~으로, ~을 수단으로 하여 **07** core 핵심 in short 간단히 말해 psyche 정신(세계) C **08** suspect 의심하다, 혐의를 두다 crime scene 범행 현장 **10** overcast 흐린 D **11** coevolution 공진화 run into ~와 충돌 하다 causality 인과 관계 dilemma 딜레마, 진퇴양난 **12** instruct 교육하다, 가르치다 mind 사람; 마음 brute 짐승 같은 사람; 짐승

12 기타 주요 구문

Get Ready!

Point 1

| 등위접속사 구문 |

| 단어[구/절] | and[but/or/for] | 단어[구/절] |

Point 2

| 상관접속사 구문 |

| both/either/neither ~ | 단어[구/절] | and/or/nor ... | 단어[구/절] |

Point 3

| 병렬 구문 |

| 단어[구/절] | and[but/or] | 단어[구/절] |

동등한 형태

Point 4

| 부정 구문 |

▷ 의미에 유의해야 할 부정어: few, little, seldom, anything but ~

▷ 부분 부정: not + both[all / every / always / necessarily] ~

▷ 이중 부정: not[never] ~ without[unless] ...

Point 5

| 동명사 관용 구문 |

▷ be used to v-ing   ▷ spend[waste] + 시간[돈] + v-ing   ▷ have difficulty v-ing

▷ There is no v-ing   ▷ It is no use v-ing

Point 6

| 전치사 + 명사절 |

| 전치사 + that[whether/의문사 등] + (s) + v ~ |

- **Unit 55** 등위접속사 구문
- **Unit 56** 상관접속사 구문
- **Unit 57** 병렬 구문
- **Unit 58** 부정 구문
- **Unit 59** 동명사 관용 구문
- **Unit 60** 전치사 + 명사절

등위접속사 구문	▷ 등위접속사(and, but, or, for 등)는 대등한 두 개 이상의 단어, 구, 절을 연결한다.
Unit 55	

상관접속사 구문	▷ 상관접속사는 떨어져 있는 두 개의 어구가 짝을 이루어 접속사 역할을 한다.
Unit 56	

병렬 구문	▷ 등위접속사나 상관접속사로 연결되는 어구들은 대등한 개념을 나타내기 위해서 문법적으로 동등한 형태를 취한다.
Unit 57	

부정 구문	▷ 부정어가 포함된 구문은 전체 부정, 부분 부정, 이중 부정 등의 의미를 나타내므로, 의미 파악에 유의해야 한다.
Unit 58	

동명사 관용 구문	▷ 동명사 관용 구문은 오랫동안 하나의 형태로 쓰인 표현들이므로 숙어처럼 따로 암기해야 한다.
Unit 59	

전치사 + 명사절	▷ 전치사의 목적어로 명사절이 올 수 있다.
Unit 60	▷「전치사 + 명사절」은 형용사 또는 부사의 역할을 한다.
	cf. 전치사 + 명사(구) **Unit 21, 29**

등위접속사 구문

Block Board

단어 [구 / 절]			and[but / or / for]	단어 [구 / 절]	
He	plays	the guitar	and	his sister	sings.
그는	/ 연주한다	/ 기타를	/ 그리고	/ 그의 여동생은	/ 노래한다

- **등위접속사**: 두 개 이상의 단어, 구, 절을 대등한 관계로 연결한다.

- **명령문, and[or] + S + V ~**: …해라, 그러면[그렇지 않으면] ~할 것이다

- **for + S + V ~**: 왜냐하면 ~이기 때문에   ⒸⒻ for가 이끄는 절은 앞서 말한 것에 대한 부가적 이유·근거에 해당한다.

- **(not[never] ~), nor + V + S**: …도 또한 아니다

Standard Sentences

01 Be thankful **for what you have and** you'll end up having more. *Oprah Winfrey*
감사하라   / 당신이 가진 것에 대해서   / 그러면 당신은 결국 더 많이 갖게 될 것이다

▶ 명령문, and + S + V ~

02 I am the wisest man alive, **for** I know one thing, **and** that is that I
나는 현존하는 가장 현명한 사람이다   / 왜냐하면 나는 한 가지를 알기 때문이다 / 그리고 그것은 ~이다   /

know nothing. *Socrates*
내가 아무것도 모른다는 것

🅐 다음 문장에서 등위접속사의 의미를 파악하면서, 각 문장을 해석하시오.

03 Cut your coat according to your cloth, or you'll repent some day. *Proverb*

04 Everyone admits that love is wonderful and necessary, yet no one
agrees on just what it is. *Diane Ackerman*

▶ S + V ~, yet + s + v …

05 Criminalizing a behavior does not make it immoral, nor is all immoral
behavior necessarily criminalized.

▶ nor + V + S

B 다음 문장에서 등위접속사에 밑줄을 긋고, 각 문장을 해석하시오.

06 Change the way you look at things and the things you look at change. *Wayne Dyer*

07 When a finger is pointing a way to the moon, don't concentrate on the finger or you will miss all that heavenly glory!

08 I will love the light for it shows me the way, yet I will endure the darkness for it shows me the stars. *Og Mandino*

09 Appreciation is the highest form of prayer, for it acknowledges the presence of good wherever you shine the light of your thankful thoughts. *Alan Cohen*

▲ Jean-Francois Millet, *The Angelus* (1859)

C 다음 네모 안에서 어법에 맞는 것을 고르시오.

(모의) **10** The rough times must be endured and taken as they come, but they are not constant, nor ⌐they / do they⌐ last forever.

11 We sometimes think of aging as a process applying uniformly to the whole organism, ⌐for / yet⌐ physiological studies show that different parts of the body age at different rates.

(모의) **12** The old maxim "I'll sleep when I'm dead" is unfortunate. ⌐Adopt / Adopting⌐ this mindset, and you will be dead sooner and the quality of that life will be worse.

S·S 01 end up 결국 ~하게 되다
A 03 according to ~에 맞춰서   repent 후회하다   05 criminalize 범죄로 간주하다   immoral 비도덕적인   necessarily 반드시
B 07 heavenly 하늘의   glory 장관   08 endure 견디다, 참다   09 appreciation 감사; 감상   acknowledge 인정하다   presence 존재; 참석
C 10 rough 힘든, 고된   constant 계속되는; 일정한   11 aging 노화 (*cf.* age 노화하다)   uniformly 균일하게, 한결같이   physiological 생리학의
    12 maxim 격언, 금언   unfortunate 유감스러운; 불행한   adopt (자세·입장을) 취하다

unit 56
상관접속사 구문

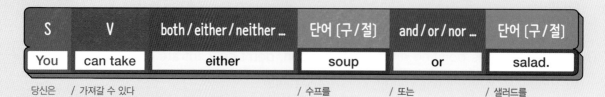

중요도 ★★☆
난이도 ★★★

Block Board

S	V	both / either / neither ...	단어 [구 / 절]	and / or / nor ...	단어 [구 / 절]
You	can take	either	soup	or	salad.
당신은	/ 가져갈 수 있다		/ 수프를	/ 또는	/ 샐러드를

- **상관접속사**: 등위접속사 and, but, or, nor를 사용해 서로 떨어져 있는 두 개의 어구가 짝을 이루어 접속사 역할을 한다.
  - ▷ both A and B: A와 B 둘 다
  - ▷ either A or B: A이거나 B
  - ▷ neither A nor B: A도 B도 아닌
  - ▷ not A but B: A가 아니라 B
  - ▷ not only[just / merely] A but (also) B: A뿐만 아니라 B도 역시 (= B as well as A)

Standard Sentences

01 The athletes competed to gain honor **both** for themselves **and** for
그 운동선수들은 경쟁했다 / 명예를 얻기 위해서 / 자기 자신들을 위해서도 / 그리고

their countries rather than achieve great wealth.
자신들의 나라를 위해서도/ 큰 부를 성취하기 위해서라기보다는

(수능) **02** The Internet is the greatest tool we have **not only** for making people
인터넷은 가장 위대한 도구이다 / [우리가 가진 / 사람들을 더 빨리 더 똑똑하게 만들기

smarter quicker, **but also** for making people dumber faster.
위해서일 **뿐만 아니라** / 사람들을 더 빨리 더 멍청하게 만들기 위해서도]

A 다음 문장에서 상관접속사가 이끄는 어구를 파악하면서, 각 문장을 해석하시오.

03 The stupid **neither** forgive **nor** forget; the naive forgive **and** forget;
the wise forgive **but** do not forget. *Thomas Szasz*

(모의) **04** A word isn't ambiguous by itself **but** is used ambiguously: it is
ambiguous when one cannot tell from the context what sense is
being used.

05 Life on a desert island is wretched. You **either** starve to death **or** live
like Robinson Crusoe, waiting for a boat which never comes.

···▶ **Know More** Rainbow p.164

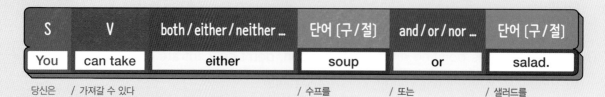

B 다음 문장에서 상관접속사가 연결하는 부분에 밑줄을 치고, 각 문장을 해석하시오.

06 As fruit needs not only sunshine but cold nights and chilling showers to ripen it, so character needs not only joy but trial and difficulty to mellow it.

07 Mishaps are like knives that either serve us or cut us as we grasp them by the handle or blade.

(수능!) 08 The true mark of heroes lies not necessarily in the result of their actions, but in what they are willing to do for others and for their chosen causes.

09 Movies offer both the happy ending that we love and the more conservative support of the dominant culture that guides behavior in "the real world."

C 다음 네모 안에서 어법에 맞는 것을 고르시오.

10 Neither a wise man | or / nor | a brave man lies down on the tracks of history to wait for the train of the future to run over him. *Dwight D. Eisenhower*

11 The whole aim of good teaching is to turn the young learner into an independent man, who doesn't merely learn | and / but | works by himself.

(모의) 12 The language which every human being speaks is not an individual inheritance, (A) | or / but | a social acquisition from the group in which he grows up. (B) | Either / Both | language and environment help to determine the character of his thought.

A **03** naive 순진한 **04** ambiguous 애매한 tell (정확히) 알다 **05** desert island 무인도 wretched 비참한, 끔찍한 starve to death 굶어 죽다
B **06** chilling 서늘한, 냉랭한 ripen 익히다 trial 시련 mellow 원숙하게 하다 **07** mishap 불행, 재난 grasp 붙잡다 blade (칼 등의) 날
08 cause 대의, 목적 **09** conservative 보수적인 dominant 주류의 guide (사상·감정을) 좌우하다; 안내하다
C **10** track 선로 run over (차 등이) ~을 치다 **11** aim 목적, 목표 **12** inheritance 유전; 상속

unit 57
병렬 구문

Block Board

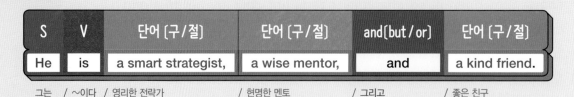

S	V	단어 [구/절]	단어 [구/절]	and[but/or]	단어 [구/절]
He	is	a smart strategist,	a wise mentor,	and	a kind friend.

그는 / ~이다 / 영리한 전략가   / 현명한 멘토   / 그리고   / 좋은 친구

- **병렬 구문**: 두 개 이상의 단어, 구, 절이 등위접속사 and, but, or로 연결될 때, 그 어구들은 문법적으로 농능한 형태를 취한다.

Form   A   [등위접속사 and / but / or]   B   └── 동등한 형태 ──┘

Form   [both / not (only) / either]   A   [등위접속사 and / but / or]   B   └── 동등한 형태 ──┘

Tip   and, but, or로 연결되는 어구들을 각각 하나의 덩어리로 인식하면서 무엇과 무엇이 대등하게 연결되고 있는지 파악한다.

Standard Sentences

01 Creative solutions come from **viewing something differently and**
창의적인 해결책은 나온다   / 어떤 것을 다르게 보는 것으로부터   / 그리고

discovering what others have missed.
발견하는 것으로부터 / 다른 사람들이 놓친 것을

(수능) **02** Testing allows us **not merely** to confirm our theories **but to weed**
실험은 우리가 우리의 이론을 입증하도록 해 줄 뿐만 아니라   / 이론들을 제거하게도

out those that do not fit the evidence.
해 준다   / [그 증거에 부합하지 않는]

▶ not only(just / merely) A but (also) B: A뿐만 아니라 B도

Ⓐ 다음 문장에서 병렬 구문을 파악하면서, 각 문장을 해석하시오.

(모의) **03** Some drug companies have **frequently** been caught making false claims about their products **or** hiding information to cover up their dangers.

04 Many people who have type II diabetes are advised to control their blood sugar levels by following a healthy diet, taking exercise **and** losing weight.

*type II diabetes 제2형 당뇨병

05 The world is a dangerous place to live; **not** because of the people who are evil, **but** because of the people who don't do anything about it. *Albert Einstein*

B 다음 문장에서 병렬 구문으로 연결되는 부분에 밑줄을 치고, 각 문장을 해석하시오.

06 In music, cacophony is discordant sounds, false harmony, or noisy and inharmonious combinations of sounds.   *cacophony 불협화음

07 Teachers cannot seat children all behind desks in a classroom, dictate information to them and expect them to absorb all of it like a sponge.

08 The value of life is not in the length of days, but in the use we make of them; a man may live long yet very little. *Michel de Montaigne*

수능! **09** The law about a contract considers such questions as whether it exists, what the meaning of it is, whether it has been broken, and what compensation is due to the injured party.

▶ such A as B: B와 같은 A

C 다음 네모 안에서 어법에 맞는 것을 고르시오.

10 By sensing whether people are in the house or which rooms they are in, a smart thermostat can either switch off heating or cooling completely or ⟨ concentrate / concentrating ⟩ on the rooms where the people are.

모의 **11** Electric cars have several limitations that reduce their popularity. Some of these disadvantages are that the autos are expensive, are relatively slow, and ⟨ require / requiring ⟩ constant recharging.

모의 **12** Recently, researchers have suggested that the purpose of laughter is not just to communicate that one is in a playful state, but ⟨ to induce / inducing ⟩ this state in others as well.

S·S 02 confirm 입증하다, 확인하다   weed out ~을 제거하다   fit 부합하다
A 03 false 허위의, 틀린   claim 주장   cover up ~을 은폐하다[감추다]   **04** blood sugar 혈당   **05** evil 악한; 악
B 06 discordant 조화되지 않는   inharmonious 가락이 맞지 않는   **07** dictate 받아쓰게 하다   **09** contract 계약   compensation 보상
  due 지불되어야 할   party 당사자, 상대방
C 10 sense 감지하다   thermostat 자동 온도 조절기   **11** recharging 재충전   **12** suggest 시사하다; 제안하다   induce 유도하다; 유발하다

부정 구문

중요도 ★★☆
난이도 ★★★

Block Board

S	V	not + both[all / always]		~
The rich	are	not always	happier	than the poor.
부자들이	/ ~이다	/ 항상 ~이지는 않은	/ 더 행복한	/ 가난한 사람들보다

- **의미에 유의해야 할 부정어**
  ▷ few(수), little(양): 거의 없는 ⓒⓕ a few(수), a little(양): 약간의　▷ seldom, rarely, hardly, scarcely, barely: 거의 ~ 않는
  ▷ anything but, far from, by no means: 결코 ~ 않는 (= never)

- 【부분 부정】 not + both[all / every / always / necessarily]: 둘 다[모두 / 모든 / 항상 / 반드시] ~인 것은 아니다

- 【이중 부정】 not[never / hardly] ~ without[unless / but] …: …하지 않고는 ~하지 않다 (~하면 반드시 …한다)
  Tip 이중 부정은 「부정어 + 부정어」로 강한 긍정을 나타낼 수 있다.

Standard Sentences

01 "Judging from the scene, there is **little** chance of there being any
"현장으로 판단하건대　　　　　　　/ 가능성은 거의 없다　　　　/ [생존자가 있을]

survivors," an airport official said.
　　　　　　　/ 한 공항 관리자가 말했다

02 I think dreams can come true, but **not necessarily** like fairy-tales.
나는 생각한다 / 꿈은 이루어질 수 있다고　　　/ 그러나 반드시 동화처럼은 아니라고

It's **not always** so perfect like that. *Patrick Dempsey*
그것은 항상 그렇게 완벽하지는 않다　/ 그처럼

Ⓐ 다음 문장에서 부정 구문을 파악하면서, 각 문장을 해석하시오.

03 There have been few, if any, human societies that have not had their
own codes of ethics. There are few, if any, human beings not interested
in distinctions between right and wrong.

04 When the ancestors of the cheetah first began pursuing the
ancestors of the gazelle, neither of them could run as fast as they
can today. *Richard Dawkins*

05 No sensible decision can be made any longer without taking into
account not only the world as it is, but the world as it will be. *Isaac Asimov*

B 다음 문장에서 부정 구문에 밑줄을 치고, 각 문장을 해석하시오.

06 All that is gold does not glitter. Not all those who wander are lost.

the movie <The Lord of the Rings: The Fellowship of the Ring>

07 With free capital flows, monetary policy could be directed either at stabilizing an exchange rate or controlling inflation, but not both.

08 A new idea comes suddenly and in a rather intuitive way. But intuition is nothing but the outcome of earlier intellectual experience. *Albert Einstein*

▶ nothing but: ~일 뿐

Up! 09 No one has given so much care to the study of composition as I. There is scarcely a famous master in music whose works I have not frequently and diligently studied. *Wolfgang Amadeus Mozart*

▲ Wolfgang Amadeus Mozart

C 다음 괄호 안의 말을 우리말과 같은 뜻이 되도록 배열하여 문장을 완성하시오.

10 사람들은 자신이 하고 있는 것에 즐거움을 느끼지 않으면 좀처럼 성공하지 못한다.
(they, succeed, have fun, rarely, unless)

People _____ in what they are doing.

Up! 11 거의 어떠한 발견도 다른 사람들에 의해 얻어진 지식을 활용하지 않고서는 가능하지 않다.
(possible, without, hardly, any discovery, is)

_____ making use of knowledge gained by others.

모의 12 천재들이 반드시 다른 창작자들보다 더 높은 성공률을 가진 것은 아니다. 그들은 단지 더 많은 것을 한다―그리고 그들은 여러 다양한 것들을 한다. (necessarily, have, don't, a higher success rate)

Geniuses _____ than other creators; they simply do more―and they do a range of different things.

S·S 01 judging from ~으로 판단하건대   official 관리자   **02** fairy-tale 동화
A 03 code of ethics 윤리 규범   distinction 구별   **04** gazelle 가젤, 영양   **05** sensible 합리적인   take ~ into account ~을 고려하다
B 06 glitter 반짝이다   wander 방황하다   **07** capital 자본   monetary 통화[화폐]의   stabilize 안정시키다   exchange rate 환율
  08 intuitive 직관적인(cf. intuition 직관)   outcome 결과, 성과   **09** composition 작곡, 작문; 구성   diligently 부지런하게

59
동명사 관용 구문

Block Board

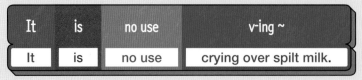

It	is	no use	v-ing ~
It	is	no use	crying over spilt milk.

(…은) / ~이다 / 소용없는 / 엎질러진 우유를 두고 우는 것은

- **동명사 관용 구문**
  ▷ be used to v-ing: ~하는 데 익숙하다 (= be accustomed to v-ing)
  ▷ be busy v-ing: ~하느라 바쁘다　　　　　▷ be worth v-ing: ~할 가치가 있다
  ▷ have difficulty[trouble / a hard time] (in) v-ing: ~하는 데 어려움을 겪다
  ▷ make a point of v-ing: 반드시[으레] ~하다, ~을 규칙적으로 하다 (= make it a rule to-v)
  ▷ spend[waste] + 시간[돈] + v-ing: ~하는 데 …을 쓰다[낭비하다]
  ▷ It is no use v-ing: ~해도 소용없다 (= There is no use (in) v-ing, It is of no use to-v)
  ▷ There is no v-ing: ~하는 것은 불가능하다, ~할 수 없다 (= It is impossible to-v)
  ▷ It goes without saying that ~: ~은 말할 것도 없다 (= It is needless to say that ~)

  Tip 동명사 관용 구문에서 쓰인 전치사 to를 to-v의 to와 혼동하지 않도록 유의해야 한다.

Standard Sentences

[모의] 01 We are used **to thinking** of light as always going in straight lines.
우리는 빛을 생각하는 것에 익숙하다　　　　　　　 / 항상 직선으로 가는 것이라고

But it doesn't.
그러나 그것은 그렇지 않다

02 It's no use carrying an umbrella if your shoes are leaking. *Irish Proverb*
(…은) 소용없다　 / 우산을 갖고 다니는 것은　　　 / 만약 당신의 신발이 새고 있다면

A 다음 문장에서 동명사 관용 구문을 파악하면서, 각 문장을 해석하시오.

03 Those who don't set goals, will have a difficult time figuring out how to reach them. *JJ Goldwag*

04 Don't waste your time looking back at what you lost. Move on. Life is **not** meant to be traveled backwards.

05 It goes **without saying** that stating a problem is not the same thing as solving it in practice.

B 다음 문장에서 동명사 관용 구문에 밑줄을 치고, 각 문장을 해석하시오.

06 During sleep, while the body rests, the brain is busy processing information from the day and forming memories.

07 She made a point of sending thank-you notes to everyone who attended her party.

08 It is no use saying, "We are doing our best." You have got to succeed in doing what is necessary. *Winston Churchill*

09 It's a dangerous business, Frodo, going out your door. You step onto the road, and if you don't keep your feet, there's no knowing where you might be swept off to.

the movie *<The Lord of the Rings: The Fellowship of the Ring>*

C 다음 괄호 안의 말을 이용하여 우리말과 같은 뜻이 되도록 문장을 완성하시오. (필요하면 형태를 바꿀 것)

10 당신의 정신을 깨우치게 하는 좋은 책은 반복해서 읽을 가치가 있다.
(your mind, enlightening, read, is, worth)

A good book _____ over again and again.

11 금세기 말에 과학과 기술이 어디까지 진보했을지 말하는 것은 불가능하다. (tell, no, is, there)

_____ how far science and technology will have progressed by the end of this century.

12 사람들은 자신의 고통을 놓아주는 데 어려움을 겪는다. 미지에 대한 두려움으로, 그들은 익숙한 고통을 더 좋아한다. (have, their suffering, let go of, a hard time)

People _____. Out of a fear of the unknown, they prefer suffering that is familiar. *Thich Nhat Hanh*

S·S 02 leak 새다
A 03 figure out 알아내다, 이해하다 **04** mean 의도하다; 의미하다 **05** state 명시하다, 말하다 in practice 실제로
B 07 attend 참석하다 **08** succeed in ~에 성공하다 **09** keep one's feet 똑바로 서 있다[걷다], 넘어지지 않다 sweep 휩쓸어 가다; 쓸다
C 10 enlighten 깨우치게 하다; 계몽하다 **12** let go of ~을 놓아주다 familiar 익숙한

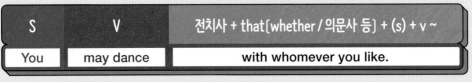

unit 60
전치사 + 명사절

Block Board

S	V	전치사 + that[whether / 의문사 등] + (s) + v ~
You	may dance	with whomever you like.

너는 / 춤춰도 된다 / 네가 좋아하는 누구나와

- 전치사는 목적어로 명사, 대명사, 동명사 외에 명사절을 취할 수 있다. **unit 29**

- 「전치사 + 명사절」은 형용사 또는 부사의 역할을 한다.
  └→ 명사절은 접속사 that, whether, 의문사, 그리고 복합관계대명사 등이 이끈다.

  Form S + V + 전치사 + 명사절   명사 + 전치사 + 명사절

          부사 역할 – 동사 수식   형용사 역할 – 명사 수식

Standard Sentences

01 There have been many debates **as to whether cryptocurrency**
많은 토론이 있어왔다 / [암호화폐가 분류되어야 하는지에 관한

should be classified as property, commodity, money, or security.
/ 자산, 상품, 돈, 또는 유가증권으로서]   ＊cryptocurrency 암호화폐

02 Ecosystems are dynamic **in that their various parts are always**
생태계는 역동적이다 / 그것의 다양한 부분들이 항상 변하고 있다는 점에서

changing.

▶ 전치사 in과 except만
that절 앞에 올 수 있음

 다음 문장에서 「전치사 + 명사절」 구문을 파악하면서, 각 문장을 해석하시오.

03 One day President Roosevelt told me that he was asking publicly
for suggestions about what the war should be called. I said at once
"The Unnecessary War." *Winston Churchill*

(모의) **04** Technology is the basis of many of our metaphors and is important
in terms of how we think and how our ideas progress.

05 What you do for a living is critical to where you settle and how you
live—and the converse is also true.

Ⓑ 다음 문장에서 「전치사 + 명사절」 구문에 밑줄을 치고, 각 문장을 해석하시오.

06 The success of the talks is up to whether both sides are willing to make some concessions.

07 In biology, the "niche" of a species is broadly defined by what it eats and how it reproduces.

(모의) **08** Competition is basically concerned with how the availability of resources, such as food and space, is reduced by other organisms.

09 Winning is important to me, but what brings me real joy is the experience of being fully engaged in whatever I'm doing. *Phil Jackson*

Ⓒ 다음 문장의 빈칸에 들어갈 내용으로 알맞은 것을 보기에서 고르시오.

```
• 보기 •
ⓐ in whatever field you may enter
ⓑ between what is right and what is wrong
ⓒ about how we imagine the world is constructed
```

10 In choosing which path to take with some of life's decisions, ethics are often at the center: heavily influencing our choices _____ _____.

11 We hunger to understand, so we invent myths _____ _____. *Carl Sagan*

12 The knowledge you have acquired will enable you to be successful _____.

S·S 01 classify 분류하다   commodity 상품, 산물   security 유가증권; 안전   **02** dynamic 역동적인
A 03 publicly 공개적으로   at once 바로, 즉시   **04** metaphor 은유   **05** critical 대단히 중요한   settle 정착하다   converse 반대의; 대화하다
B 06 be up to ~에 달려 있다   concession 양보   **07** niche 적합한 환경, 적소   **08** be concerned with ~와 관련되다   **09** be engaged in ~에 몰입하다
C 보기 field 분야; 들판   construct 구성하다   **10** path 길, 경로   ethics 윤리, 도덕   **11** myth 신화; 통념

Chapter 12
Review

A 다음 문장을 우리말로 해석하시오.

01 People are often blinded by love, making bad judgments and wrong choices, or doing stupid and foolish things, under the influence of love.

02 Blockchain technology is not a company, nor is it an app, but rather an entirely new way of documenting data on the Internet.

(수능!) **03** Material wealth in and of itself does not necessarily generate meaning or lead to emotional wealth.

04 You probably wouldn't worry about what people think of you if you could know how seldom they do.

B 다음 네모 안에서 어법에 맞는 것을 고르시오.

(모의) **05** Energy can neither be created | or / nor | destroyed, but can merely be transformed from one state to another.

(수능!) **06** Just walking through a garden or, for that matter, | see / seeing | one out your window, can lower blood pressure, reduce stress, and ease pain.

07 Having grown up in a culture that appreciates modesty and reserve, he was not accustomed to | express / expressing | emotions in public.

08 Introducing drones to our emergency services could save lives by transporting materials like blood and AEDs more quickly, locating people inside burning buildings, and | help / helping | the police track suspects.

*AED(Automated External Defibrillator) 심장 충격기

C 다음 괄호 안의 말을 이용하여 우리말과 같은 뜻이 되도록 문장을 완성하시오.

09 당신은 마우스를 사용하거나 키보드 위의 화살표 키를 사용함으로써 커서를 움직일 수 있다.
(the arrow keys, using, or, by)

You can move the cursor either by using the mouse _____
on the keyboard.

10 광고가 항상 당신에게 당신이 현명한 선택을 하기 위해서 알 필요가 있는 모든 것을 말해 주지는 않는다.
(you, tell, do, everything, not always)

Advertisements _____ you need to know in order to
make a wise choice.

11 진정한 사랑은 존재하지 않는 곳에서 발견될 수 없으며, 존재하는 곳에서 부인될 수도 없다.
(be denied, it, nor, can)

True love cannot be found where it does not exist, _____
_____ where it does. *Torquato Tasso*

D 다음 문장의 빈칸에 들어갈 내용으로 알맞은 것을 보기에서 고르시오.

┌─ 보기 ───┐
ⓐ they have difficulty knowing what to focus on
ⓑ in that everyone in the market is faced with additional costs
ⓒ but should also be compatible with the rest of the body of science
└──┘

12 A hypothesis not only should fit the facts which brought about its creation
_____.

13 When people are overwhelmed with the volume of information confronting
them, _____.

14 Where the degree of competition is particularly intense, a zero-sum game
can quickly become a negative sum game, _____
_____.

*negative sum game 참여한 모든 사람이 손해를 보는 게임

A 02 app 응용 프로그램   entirely 완전히   document 기록하다   **03** in itself 그 자체로   of itself 저절로   **B 06** for that matter
실제로   blood pressure 혈압   **07** appreciate 높이 평가하다   modesty 겸손함; 소박함   reserve 신중함, 자제   **08** emergency
services 긴급 구조대   locate 위치를 알아내다   track 추적하다   **C 09** cursor (컴퓨터 화면의) 커서   **11** deny 부인하다
D 보기 compatible 양립할 수 있는   body 대다수, 대부분   **12** hypothesis 가설   **13** volume 양; 부피   **14** intense 치열한

Special
Stage

구문 복습을 위한 어법 72제

구문 중심의 어법 72문항을 풀어보면서,
Chapter 1~12에서 학습한 구문을 종합적으로 복습하고,
고난도 문장의 구문독해에 도전해 보세요!

- **어법 공략 십계명**
- **Special Unit 01** ·········· 01 - 36제
- **Special Unit 02** ·········· 37 - 72제

어법 공략 십계명

01 동사의 수 일치

01-1 구와 절이 이끄는 주어는 단수로 취급한다.
➡ Unit 01

Reading books aloud to children is / are a powerful source for vocabulary development.

01-2 '주어 + 수식어 + 동사'에서 수식어는 괄호로 묶는다. ➡ Unit 04, 05

Clues (to past environmental change) is / are well preserved in many different kinds of rocks.

01-3 도치 구문에서 동사의 수는 동사 다음에 나오는 주어에 일치시킨다. ➡ Unit 49, 50

In the middle of every difficulty lie / lies opportunity.

02 능동태 vs. 수동태

02-1 자동사는 목적어가 없으므로 수동태로 쓸 수 없다.

A lunar eclipse occurs / is occurred when the earth passes between the sun and the moon.

02-2 주어가 동사의 '주체'이면 능동태, 동사의 '대상'이면 수동태로 쓴다. ➡ Unit 09

• We will donate / be donated all profits to charity.
• All profits will donate / be donated to charity.

03 동사 vs. 준동사

03-1 한 문장에서 동사는 한 개가 필요하고, 접속사 없이는 두 개의 동사를 쓸 수 없다.

Establish / Establishing protected areas with intact ecosystems is essential for species conservation.

03-2 동사의 개수 = 접속사의 개수 + 1
* 생략된 접속사에 유의

Having a fine library does not prove that its legal owner has / having a mind enriched by books.

04 준동사의 구분

04-1 타동사의 목적어로 to-v와 v-ing를 쓰는 경우를 구분한다. ➡ Unit 10

I vaguely remember to read / reading something about it in the paper.

04-2 목적격보어로 to-v, ⓥ, v-ing, v-ed를 쓰는 경우를 구분한다. ➡ Unit 17, 18

• What caused you change / to change your mind?
• A positive attitude can really make dreams come / to come true.
• He felt the cold sweat to run / running down his back.

04-3 to 다음에 ⓥ 대신 v-ing가 오는 경우에 유의한다. ➡ Unit 59

We are used to use / using audio to present examples of language in use.

05 준동사의 시제와 태

준동사	완료형	수동형	완료수동형
부정사(to-v)	to have v-ed	to be v-ed	to have been v-ed
동명사(v-ing)	having v-ed	being v-ed	having been v-ed
분사(v-ing)	having v-ed	v-ed	having been v-ed

05-1 준동사의 시제와 태의 변화에 유의한다.
➡ unit 22, 32, 33

– 완료형: 문장의 동사보다 앞선 일
– 수동형: 의미상 주어·수식하는 명사와 수동 관계
– 완료수동형: 문장의 동사보다 앞선 일 + 의미상 주어·수식하는 명사와 수동 관계

- My son dislikes | treating / being treated | like a son.
- The earth is only a baby | comparing / compared | with many other stars.
- Judging from his appearance, he seems | to be / to have been | ill for quite a long time.

06 병렬구조

06-1 and, but, or로 연결된 어구들은 동등한 형태를 취한다. ➡ unit 57

Computer buyers expect versatility, simplicity, and energy | efficient / efficiency | as essential components of new equipment.

06-2 비교 구문에서 비교되는 대상은 동등한 형태를 취한다. ➡ unit 45~47

Recycling is much more energy efficient than | to make / making | from raw materials.

07 접속사와 관계사의 구분

07-1 확실한 사실 앞에는 that을, 불확실하거나 의문시되는 내용 앞에는 whether나 if를 쓴다.

- We think | that / whether | the company has a bright future.
- Please decide | that / whether | the following statements are true or false.

07-2 '선행사 + 관계사'에서 뒤에 이어지는 절이 불완전하면 관계대명사, 완전하면 관계부사가 온다. ➡ Unit 23, 25

- We'll go to a restaurant | which / where | has a children's menu.
- I'd like to go to a restaurant | which / where | I will be offered great services.

07-3 앞에 선행사가 없고 이어지는 절이 불완전하면 what이 온다. ➡ unit 02, 11, 16

* that은 접속사, 관계대명사, 관계부사 등으로 쓸 수 있다.

- Don't discount | that / what | you might consider "small" successes.
- *cf.* Toys are cultural objects | that / what | children learn to play with.

08 가정법

| if 가정법 | 과거 | If + s + 동사 과거형 ~, S + 조동사 과거형 + ⓥ ...: 만약 ~라면 …할 텐데 |
| | 과거완료 | If + s + had v-ed ~, S + 조동사 과거형 + have v-ed ...: 만약 ~했다면, …했을 텐데 |

08-1 가정법 과거 vs. 가정법 과거완료 ➡ unit 41, 42

- If I were in your shoes, I | would accept / would have accepted | the invitation.
- Emma would have gotten the job if she | were / had been | better prepared.

주장, 요구, 명령, 제안 등의 표현	that절 ('의향·소망'의 내용)
insist, ask, order, suggest, recommend, require 등	that + s + (should) + ⓥ * that절의 내용이 '일반적 사실'인 경우, 시제 일치에 적합한 동사를 쓴다.

08-2 that절의 '(should) + ⓥ'

- The piano teacher required that her student | practice / practiced | every day.
- *cf.* Sam insisted that he | do / had done | nothing wrong.

09 형용사·부사 및 비교 표현

09-1 형용사는 보어로 쓰이거나 명사를 수식하고, 부사는 동사, 형용사, 부사 등을 수식한다.

Deleting unnecessary words will make your writing more | clear / clearly |.

09-2 비교 구문에서 원급, 비교급 및 최상급의 패턴을 확인한다. ➡ unit 45~48

The modern adult owes more to the experience of his culture | as / than | does primitive man.

10 어순

10-1 간접의문문: 의문사 + s + v ➡ unit 02, 11, 16
* 의문사가 이끄는 절이 명사절로 쓰인 경우

Computer technology can improve | how a work is / how is a work | performed, broadcast, and experienced.

10-2 부정어[장소의 부사, 보어] + V[조동사] + S ➡ unit 49, 50

Little | he knew / did he know | that he was giving his son unseen stress.

Special Unit 01

01~12 다음 문장의 네모 안에서 어법상 바른 것을 고르시오.

Unit Link

모의 01 According to Pierre Pica, understanding quantities approximately in terms of estimating ratios is / are a universal human intuition.

❯ Unit 01, 십계명 01-1

02 The truth is not simply what you think it is; it is also the circumstances which / in which it is said, and to whom, why and how it is said.

Vaclav Havel

❯ Unit 24

03 Sometimes we are so used to (A) do / doing the things that we think we should do, (B) which / that we can forget about the things that we really want to do.

(A) ❯ Unit 59, 십계명 04-3
(B) ❯ Unit 38

04 The airline requests that all baggage is / be kept in the overhead compartments.

❯ 십계명 08-2

05 Most of the animal-training practices considered / are considered good and normal in our world do not take the animals' viewpoint into account.

❯ Unit 22, 십계명 03-1

06 It is a paradoxical but profoundly true and important principle of life that / which the most likely way to reach a goal is to be aiming not at that goal itself but at some more ambitious goal beyond it. *Arnold Tonybee*

❯ Unit 03

---

01 quantity 수량, 양   in terms of ~의 관점에서   estimate 어림잡다, 가늠하다   ratio 비율   intuition 직관   02 circumstance 상황   04 airline 항공사   baggage 수하물   compartment (보관용) 칸   05 viewpoint 관점   take ~ into account ~을 고려하다   06 paradoxical 역설적인   profoundly 깊게   aim at ~을 겨누다   ambitious 야심적인

(모의) **07** The tendency to give more attention and weight to data that support our beliefs than we do to contrary data is / are especially dangerous when our beliefs are little more than prejudices.

→ Unit 01, 십계명 01-2

(모의) **08** If one looks at the Oxford definition, one gets the sense that post-truth is not so much a claim that truth does not exist as / so that facts are subordinate to our political point of view.

→ Unit 45

09 People, Homo sapiens and our past ancestors and relatives, must always (A) be / have been managing water in some manner as far back as six million years, the date (B) which / at which we shared a common ancestor with the chimpanzee.

(A) → Unit 08
(B) → Unit 24

(모의) **10** Children learn the meanings of words by trial and error, by hypothesizing a fit between word and object and use / using the feedback they get from others to refine the abstract category for which the word stands.

→ Unit 57

(모의) **11** It (A) has said / has been said that eye movements are windows into the mind, because where people look (B) reveal / reveals what environmental information they are attending to.

(A) → Unit 09
(B) → Unit 02, 십계명 01-1

12 Supplies of salts that plants use to build up their substance can only be maintained through the activities of bacteria (A) breaking / broken down the organic matter (B) leaving / left in the soil by other living things.

(A) → Unit 22, 십계명 05-1
(B) → Unit 22, 십계명 05-1

---

07 weight 중요성 contrary 반대의 little more than ~에 지나지 않는(= only) prejudice 편견 **08** post-truth 탈진실(왜곡된 정보, 개념, 인식 등) claim 주장, 요구 subordinate 하위의, 종속적인 **09** ancestor 조상 relative 친척 **10** trial and error 시행착오 hypothesize 가설을 세우다 fit 적합(성) refine ~를 다듬다, 세련되게 하다; 정제하다 abstract 추상적인 stand for ~을 나타내다 **11** reveal 드러내다 attend to ~에 주의를 기울이다 **12** substance 물질 maintain 유지하다 break down 분해하다; 고장나다

Unit Link

13~24 다음 문장의 네모 안에서 어법상 바른 것을 고르시오.

(수능!) **13** If you are known as someone who is easily offended, you will never know that / what others are really thinking or feeling because they will distort the truth to escape from your negative reaction.

⊙ Unit 11, 십계명 07-3

14 Many people, in their rise to success, are so busy (A) to run / running to the top, stepping on their competitors, stepping on their enemies, and saddest of all, stepping on their friends and loved ones, (B) that / what when they get to the top, they look around and discover that they are extremely lonely and unhappy. *Berry Gordy*

(A) **⊙ Unit 59, 십계명 04-3**
(B) **⊙ Unit 38**

(모의) **15** It is not at all rare for investigators to adhere to their broken hypotheses, turn / turning a blind eye to contrary evidence, and not altogether unknown for them to deliberately suppress contrary results.

⊙ Unit 32

16 Whoever it was who searched the heavens with a telescope and found no God would not have found the human mind if he searched / had searched the brain with a microscope. *George Santayana*

⊙ Unit 42, 십계명 08-1

(모의) **17** Whether we develop effective communication skills that (A) promote / promotes healthy interactions (B) depend / depends largely on how we learn to communicate.

(A) **⊙ Unit 23**
(B) **⊙ Unit 02, 십계명 01-1**

18 The use of artificial intelligence technology makes it possible for repetitive but hazardous activities to take / to be taken over by computers or robots.

⊙ 십계명 05-1

---

13 offend 기분을 상하게 하다   distort 왜곡하다   **14** be busy v-ing ~하느라 바쁘다   step on ~을 밟다   competitor 경쟁자   extremely 극도로   **15** investigator 조사원, 수사관   adhere to ~을 고수하다   hypothesis 가설(*pl.* hypotheses)   turn a blind eye to ~을 못 본 체하다   altogether 완전히, 전적으로   deliberately 고의로   suppress (정보 등을) 은폐하다   **16** telescope 망원경   microscope 현미경   **17** promote 증진시키다   interaction 상호작용   **18** artificial intelligence 인공지능   repetitive 반복적인   hazardous 위험한   take over ~을 인계받다

19 One of the greatest discoveries a man makes, one of his great surprises, is / are to find he can do what he was afraid he couldn't do. *Henry Ford*

십계명 01-2

20 Concerning charity, it means not only providing immediate assistance to the impoverished, but also helps / helping the poor in ways that will enable them to support themselves and no longer need help.

Unit 56, 57

모의 **21** The brain wants rewards and anything that is learned, good or bad, that stimulates the production of dopamine interprets / is interpreted by the brain as a reward.

*dopamine 도파민(신경 전달 기능을 하는 체내 유기 화합물)

Unit 09, 십계명 02-2

모의 **22** A sovereign state is usually defined as one which / whose citizens are free to determine their own affairs without interference from any agency beyond its territorial borders.

Unit 23

23 Students often perceive a textbook as a huge, insurmountable obstacle that sits on their desk softly (A) whisper / whispering their name just to make them (B) feel / to feel guilty every time they walk past it.

(A) Unit 32
(B) Unit 17

24 Although commonsense knowledge may have merit, it also has drawbacks, not the least of them / which is that it often contradicts itself.

Unit 28

---

20 concerning ~에 관한　charity 자선 (단체)　assistance 도움, 원조　impoverished 빈곤한　enable ~할 수 있게 하다　no longer 더 이상 ~ 않는
21 reward 보상　stimulate 자극하다　interpret 해석하다　22 sovereign state 주권국, 독립국　affair 일, 문제　interference 방해, 간섭
agency 정부 기관; 대행사　territorial 영토의　23 perceive A as B A를 B로 인식하다　insurmountable 넘을 수 없는, 극복할 수 없는　obstacle 장애물
whisper 속삭이다　guilty 가책을 느끼는; 유죄의　24 commonsense 상식적인　merit 장점　drawback 결점　contradict 모순되다

Unit Link

25~36 다음 문장의 네모 안에서 어법상 바른 것을 고르시오.

25 In childhood, a considerable number of languages may be learned one after another, without the preceding language | leaves / leaving | any trace of its grammar or sound system on the one that succeeds.

⊙ Unit 29

모의 26 Individuals who believe they control their own destinies and generally expect the best from life | is / are |, in fact, more likely to gain control of their stressors and experience positive stress rather than distress.

⊙ Unit 05, 십계명 01-2

27 Hidden within every astronomical investigation, sometimes so deeply buried that the researcher himself is unaware of its presence, | lies / lying | a kernel of awe. *Carl Sagan*

⊙ Unit 49, 십계명 10-2

모의 28 Creativity is strange in that it finds its way in any kind of situation, no matter how | restricting / restricted |, just as the same amount of water flows faster and stronger through a narrow strait than across the open sea.

*strait 해협

⊙ Unit 39, 십계명 05-1

29 Making new paper from recycled materials uses less energy than (A)| to produce / producing | paper from virgin tree products and (B)| leave / leaves | more trees to absorb excess carbon dioxide.

(A) ⊙ 십계명 06-2
(B) ⊙ Unit 57, 십계명 06-1

모의 30 With the evolution of more settled rural societies based on agriculture, other characteristics, other traditions of form appropriate to the new patterns of life, rapidly | emerged / emerging |.

⊙ 십계명 03-1

---

25 considerable 상당한   one after another 차례로   precede 선행하다, 앞서다   trace 자취, 흔적   succeed 이어지다, 뒤에 오다   **26** destiny 운명   stressor 스트레스 요인   distress 고통, 골칫거리   **27** astronomical 천문학의   investigation 연구, 조사   be unaware of ~을 알지 못하다   presence 존재; 출석   kernel 핵심, 알맹이   awe 경외감, 두려움   **28** creativity 독창성, 창의력   in that ~라는 점에서   restrict 제한하다   **29** material 물질, 재료   virgin 쓰인 적이 없는; 처녀의   absorb 흡수하다   excess 초과한   carbon dioxide 이산화탄소   **30** evolution 발전, 진전   settled 안정된, 자리를 잡은   agriculture 농업   characteristic 특징   appropriate 적합한   emerge 나타나다

(모의) **31** Lie detector tests base judgments of honesty on blood pressure, pulse, respiration, and vocal pitch, which the test assumes differ / differs when people lie and when they tell the truth.

Unit 23, 53

(모의) **32** With pests often (A) consuming / consumed up to 40 percent of the crops grown in the United States, most organic farmers cannot but (B) rely / to rely on chemicals as necessary supplements to their operations.

(A) Unit 34
(B) Unit 08

33 Only a man who knows what it is like to be defeated can reach down to the bottom of his soul and come / comes up with the extra ounce of power it takes to win when the match is even. *Muhammad Ali*

Unit 57, 심계명 06-1

34 Our expectations are often deceived. Things which we feared might do us hurt (A) turn / turning out to be our advantage, and what we thought would save us (B) proves / proving our ruin.

(A) Unit 53, 심계명 03-1, 2
(B) Unit 53, 심계명 03-1, 2

(모의) **35** Modern psychological theory states that the process of understanding is a matter of construction, not reproduction, (A) which / it means that the process of understanding takes the form of the interpretation of data coming from the outside and (B) generating / generated by our mind.

Unit 28
Unit 22

(수능) **36** At the root of many of our blind spots is / are a number of emotions or attitudes—fear being the most obvious, but also pride, self-satisfaction, and anxiety.

Unit 49, 심계명 10-2

---

31 lie detector 거짓말 탐지기 base A on B A의 기초를 B에 두다 pulse 맥박 respiration 호흡 vocal pitch 목소리의 높이 assume 추정하다
32 pest 해충 consume 먹어버리다; 소비하다 crop 농작물 organic 유기농의 chemical 화학물질 supplement 보충물, 보충제 operation 조업, 운용, 경영 33 defeat 패배시키다 come up with ~을 만들어내다 ounce 아주 적은 양 34 deceive 기만하다, 속이다 hurt 손해, 피해 advantage 이득, 이익 ruin 파멸(의 원인) 35 psychological 심리적인 state 분명히 말하다 construction 구성 reproduction 재생 interpretation 해석 generate 발생시키다, 일으키다 36 blind spot 맹점 obvious 명백한 anxiety 불안; 갈망

Special Unit 02

37~47 다음 문장의 밑줄 친 부분 중, 어법상 어색한 것을 고르시오.

Grammar Point

수능 **37** When we learn to say no to ① what we don't feel like ② to do in order to say yes to our true self, we feel ③ empowered, and our relationships with others ④ improve.

① what이 이끄는 명사절
② 동명사 관용 구문
③ 보어 역할을 하는 v-ed
④ 동사의 파악

모의 **38** Every parent ① knows that lying to their kids about everything from the arrival of Santa Claus to the horrible things that will happen ② if they don't eat their peas ③ are a key component of ④ raising a child.

① 동사의 수 일치
② 부사절을 이끄는 접속사
③ 동사의 수 일치
④ 전치사의 목적어

모의 **39** ① Making a choice that is 1 percent better or 1 percent worse seems ② insignificantly in the moment, but over the span of moments that ③ make up a lifetime these choices ④ determine the difference between who you are and who you could be.

① 주어 역할을 하는 v-ing
② 보어의 형태
③ 동사의 수 일치
④ 동사의 파악

40 Understanding the trait of human nature ① is essential to ② realizing why people click on a link, hit the "like" button, share a post, or ③ comment on something someone else ④ has been said on social media.

① 동사의 수 일치
② 전치사의 목적어
③ 병렬구조
④ 동사의 태

모의 **41** When ① delighted by the way one's beautiful idea ② offers promise of further advances, it is tempting to overlook an observation ③ that does not fit into the pattern woven, or ④ trying to explain it away.

① '주어 + be동사' 생략
② 동사의 파악
③ 관계사의 쓰임
④ 병렬구조

42 ① What astounds and dismays us is ② that, knowing so well that war is wrong, and fearing and ③ hating it more than anything else, we seem ④ compelling, in spite of ourselves, to go on waging it.

① what의 쓰임
② 접속사 that의 쓰임
③ 병렬구조
④ 분사의 형태

---

37 empowered 권한이 주어진　38 horrible 끔찍한　pea 완두콩　component 구성 요소　39 span (어떤 일이 지속되는) 기간　make up ~을 구성하다
40 trait 특징　comment on ~에 의견을 달다　41 advance 진전, 발전　tempting 솔깃한, 유혹하는　overlook 간과하다　observation 관찰　fit
into ~에 부합하다　weave 짜다, 엮다(-wove-woven)　explain away ~을 둘러대다, 해명하다　42 astound 경악하다, 크게 놀라게 하다　dismay 당황
하게 하다　compel 강요하다, 억지로 시키다　in spite of oneself 자기도 모르게　wage (전쟁 등을) 벌이다

43 An interesting aspect of human psychology is ① what we tend to like things more and find them more ② appealing if everything about those things ③ is not obvious the first time we experience ④ them.

① 보어절을 이끄는 접속사
② 목적격보어의 형태
③ 동사의 수 일치
④ 대명사의 수 일치

(모의) **44** ① Deciding ② whether to spend Saturday afternoon relaxing with your family or ③ to exercise will be determined by the relative importance ④ that you place on family versus health.

① 주어 역할을 하는 v-ing
② whether + to-v
③ 병렬구조
④ 관계사의 쓰임

(모의) **45** ① It is no coincidence that countries ② which sleep time has declined most dramatically over the past century ③ are also those ④ suffering the greatest increase in rates of physical diseases and mental disorders.

① 가주어-진주어
② 관계사의 쓰임
③ 동사의 수 일치
④ 명사를 수식하는 분사의 형태

46 The fact ① that life evolved out of nearly nothing, some 10 billion years after the universe evolved out of literally nothing, ② are a fact so staggering ③ that I ④ would be mad to attempt words to do it justice. *Richard Dawkins*

① 접속사 that의 쓰임
② 동사의 수 일치
③ 부사절을 이끄는 접속사
④ 가정법 과거

(수능) **47** The Chinese saw the world as ① consisting of continuously ② interacting substances, so their attempts to understand it ③ causing them ④ to be oriented toward the complexities of the entire "field," that is, the context or environment as a whole.

① 전치사의 목적어
② 명사를 수식하는 분사의 형태
③ 동사의 파악
④ 목적격보어의 형태

---

43 aspect 측면   psychology 심리   tend to-v ~하는 경향이 있다   appealing 매력적인   obvious 명백한   **44** relative 상대적인   versus ~ 대(對), ~에 대한   place (중요성·가치 등을) 두다   **45** coincidence 우연의 일치   dramatically 극적으로   suffer 고통 받다, 겪다   rate 비율   disorder 질환 **46** evolve 진화하다, 발달하다   nearly 거의   literally 문자 그대로   staggering 충격적인, 믿기 어려운   do ~ justice ~을 정당하게 대하다 **47** continuously 계속해서, 끊임없이   interact 상호작용하다   substance 물질   orient (수동태로) ~을 지향하게 하다, ~을 향해 있다   complexity 복잡성 that is 다시 말해서   context 문맥, 맥락

48~57 다음 문장의 밑줄 친 부분 중, 어법상 어색한 것을 고르시오.

Grammar Point

48 Only through accurately understanding our feelings ① we can learn to free ② ourselves from negative emotions, ③ which provides more creative energy, as well as the opportunity for limitless personal growth, and, ultimately, ④ connects us to our higher selves.

① 도치 구문
② 재귀대명사
③ 관계사의 쓰임
④ 병렬구조

49 ① Knowing that the depth of our thought ② is tied directly to the intensity of our attentiveness, it's hard not ③ to conclude that as we adapt to the intellectual environment of the Net our thinking ④ becoming shallower.

① 분사구문
② 동사의 태
③ 가주어-진주어
④ 동사의 파악

모에 **50** As with a crossword, so with the physical universe, we find that the solutions to independent clues ① link together in a consistent and supportive way ② to form a coherent unity, ③ so that the more clues we solve, ④ the more easily we find it to fill in the missing features.

① 동사의 수 일치
② to-v의 부사적 용법
③ 부사절을 이끄는 접속사
④ 목적격보어의 형태

51 Helping a child ① to acknowledge what they can change, and ② explore how to change the way ③ how they respond to permanent situations, ④ will create a shift in outlook and life experience.

① 목적격보어의 형태
② 병렬구조
③ 관계사의 쓰임
④ 동사의 파악

52 How the universe as we know it now ① evolved ② being a complex question ③ involving study by vastly different branches of physics ④ including particle physics, nuclear physics and cosmology.

① 동사의 파악
② 동사의 파악
③ 명사를 수식하는 분사의 형태
④ 전치사의 쓰임

---

48 accurately 정확하게   limitless 무한한   ultimately 궁극적으로   self 자기, 자아(*pl.* selves)   **49** intensity 강도, 세기   attentiveness 주의력, 조심성   adapt to ~에 적응하다   intellectual 지능의, 지적인   the Net 인터넷   shallow 피상적인, 얕은   **50** consistent 한결같은, 일관된   supportive 지지하는, 힘을 주는   coherent 일관성 있는, 논리 정연한   unity 통일(성)   feature 생김새; 특징   **51** acknowledge 인정하다   explore 탐험하다, 조사하다   permanent 영구적인, 불변의   shift 변화, 전환   outlook 관점, 견해; 전망   **52** involve 포함하다; 관련시키다   vastly 대단히, 엄청나게   branch 부문   including ~을 포함하여   particle physics 입자물리학   cosmology 우주론

53 It is common knowledge ① that walnuts, also ② called "super food" and "food for the gods," ③ contains more antioxidants of higher quality than ④ any other nut.

① 가주어–진주어
② 명사를 수식하는 분사의 형태
③ 동사의 수 일치
④ 비교 구문

[모의] 54 Evolution is largely the result of natural selection that ① takes place because humans, during their history of development as a species, ② have been part of biotic communities ③ which their interactions with other species of animals and plants have decided ④ whether or not they survived and reproduced.

① 동사의 수 일치
② 동사의 파악
③ 관계사의 쓰임
④ 목적어절을 이끄는 접속사

55 Patents for novel ideas, processes and methodologies ① are simply the tangible results of someone ② seen something differently ③ than the world had ever seen ④ it before.

① 동사의 수 일치
② 전치사의 목적어
③ 접속사 than
④ 대명사의 수 일치

56 An instrument is efficient to the extent ① to which the using of it ② enables the purpose, ③ for which the instrument was designed, ④ to achieve.

① 전치사＋관계대명사
② 동사의 수 일치
③ 전치사＋관계대명사
④ to-v의 태

[모의] 57 When she reached her car, it occurred to her that she ① might have forgotten ② turning off the gas range. With a sigh, she climbed breathlessly up the stairs, only ③ to find that the range ④ had been turned off.

① 과거에 대한 추측
② forget to-v(v-ing)
③ to-v의 부사적 용법
④ 동사의 시제와 태

---

53 common 흔한   antioxidant 항산화제   quality 질   54 evolution 진화   natural selection 자연 선택   take place 일어나다, 발생하다
biotic community 생물 군집   interaction 상호작용   survive 생존하다   reproduce 번식하다   55 patent 특허(권)   novel 참신한, 새로운
methodology 방법론, 절차   tangible 실재하는, 분명히 보이는   56 instrument 기구, 도구   efficient 효율적인   extent 정도   achieve 성취하다
57 occur (생각이) 떠오르다   turn off ~을 끄다   sigh 한숨   breathlessly 숨을 헐떡이며

58~67 다음 문장의 밑줄 친 부분 중, 어법상 어색한 것을 고르시오.

[모의] 58 The reason ① that we keep making the same error repeatedly ② is that associations form between the ideas in the chain of thoughts and become ③ more firmly each time they are used, until finally the connections are so well established ④ that the chain is very difficult to break.

① 관계사의 쓰임
② 동사의 파악
③ 보어의 형태
④ 부사절을 이끄는 접속사

[모의] 59 Psychological studies indicate ① that it is knowledge possessed by the individual ② what determines which stimuli become the focus of that individual's attention, ③ what significance he or she assigns to these stimuli, and ④ how they are combined into a larger whole.

① 접속사 that의 쓰임
② 강조 구문
③ 의문형용사
④ 명사절을 이끄는 의문사

[모의] 60 In response to variations in chemical composition, temperature and most of all pressure, volatile substances ① containing in the magma like water or carbon dioxide ② can be released to form gas bubbles, ③ producing great changes in the properties of the magma and in many cases ④ leading to an eruption.

① 명사를 수식하는 분사의 형태
② 동사의 태
③ 분사구문
④ 병렬구조

61 The ability to see the situation as the other side sees ① it, as ② difficult as it may be, ③ being one of the most important ④ skills a negotiator has to possess.

① 대명사의 수 일치
② 보어의 형태
③ 동사의 파악
④ 명사의 수 일치

[수능] 62 In addition to ① protecting the rights of authors ② so as to encourage the publication of new creative works, copyright ③ also supposed to place reasonable time limits on those rights so that outdated works ④ may be incorporated into new creative efforts.

① 전치사의 목적어
② to-v의 부사적 용법
③ 동사의 태
④ 동사의 태

---

58 association 연계, 연관   firm 굳은, 견고한   connection 연결   establish 확립하다   **59** psychological 심리적인   indicate 나타내다   possess 소유하다   stimulus 자극(*pl.* stimuli)   significance 중요성   assign 부여하다   combine 결합하다   **60** variation 변화   composition 구성 volatile 휘발성의   substance 물질   release 방출하다   property 속성, 특성   eruption 분출   **61** negotiator 교섭자, 협상가   **62** in addition to ~에 더하여, ~뿐만 아니라   publication 출판   copyright 저작권   outdated 기한이 지난; 구식의   incorporate 통합하다

63 It is not men's faults ① that ruin them so much ② as the manner ③ which they conduct themselves after the faults ④ have been committed.

① 강조 구문
② not A so much as B
③ 관계사의 쓰임
④ 동사의 태

64 There is no good reason why we should fear the future, but there is every reason why we should face ① it seriously, neither ② hiding from ourselves the gravity of the problems before us ③ or fearing to approach these problems with the unbending, unflinching purpose to solve ④ them aright. *Theodore Roosevelt*

① 대명사의 수 일치
② 분사구문
③ 상관접속사의 쓰임
④ 대명사의 수 일치

〔모의〕 **65** There is a widely ① accepted theory in social psychology known as the pratfall effect, ② that actually states that making certain kinds of mistakes ③ makes you more ④ likable because you are relatable in your vulnerability. *pratfall 엉덩방아 찧기

① 명사를 수식하는 분사의 형태
② 관계사의 쓰임
③ 동사의 파악
④ 목적격보어의 형태

66 ① Despite our precision mathematics and experiments, new surprises in modern physics and cosmology ② have emerged that ③ compel some of the most able physicists ④ resort to myth making to try and explain the mind-bending information they have uncovered about the nature of the universe.

① 전치사의 쓰임
② 동사의 파악
③ 동사의 수 일치
④ 목적격보어의 형태

〔모의〕 **67** The objection to ① include ethics among the sciences ② is that, ③ whereas science deals with what is, ethics, it is said, ④ is concerned with what ought to be.

① 전치사의 목적어
② 동사의 수 일치
③ 부사절을 이끄는 접속사
④ 동사의 태

---

63 fault 잘못, 책임 ruin 망가뜨리다 conduct 행동하다, 처신하다 commit 저지르다 64 gravity 중대함, 심각성; 중력 approach 접근하다, 다가서다 unbending 굽히지 않는, 불굴의 unflinching (위험한 상황에도) 움츠리지 않는 purpose 의지력, 결단력 aright 올바르게, 틀림없이 65 relatable 공감대를 형성하는 vulnerability 취약함 66 despite ~에도 불구하고 precision 정확, 정밀 cosmology 우주론 emerge 나타나다 compel 강요하다 resort to ~에 의지하다 myth 근거 없는 믿음, 통념; 신화 mind-bending (마음·상황을) 혼란스럽게 하는, 환각성의 uncover (비밀 등을) 알아내다, 밝혀내다 67 objection 반대 ethics 윤리(학) whereas ~임에 반하여 deal with ~을 다루다

Special Unit 02

68~72 다음 문장의 밑줄 친 부분 중, 어법상 어색한 것을 고르시오.

Grammar Point

수능! **68** ① <u>Based</u> on a complex sensory analysis that is not only restricted to the sense of taste but also ② <u>included</u> smell, touch, and hearing, the final decision ③ <u>whether</u> to swallow or reject food ④ <u>is made</u>.

① 분사구문
② 병렬구조
③ whether + to-v
④ 동사의 태

69 Blockchain owes its name to ① <u>how does it work</u> and the manner ② <u>in which</u> it stores data, namely ③ <u>that</u> the information is packaged into blocks, ④ <u>which</u> link to form a chain with other blocks of similar information.

① 간접의문문이 어순
② 전치사 + 관계대명사
③ 관계사의 쓰임
④ 관계사의 쓰임

모의! **70** One of the biggest challenges faced by organizations ① <u>is</u> how to transform raw data into information and eventually into knowledge, ② <u>which</u> if ③ <u>exploiting</u> correctly provides the capabilities ④ <u>to predict</u> customers' behaviour and business trends.

① 동사의 수 일치
② 관계사의 쓰임
③ 분사의 형태
④ to-v의 형용사적 용법

모의! **71** The location of senile mental deterioration ① <u>was</u> no longer the aging brain ② <u>but</u> a society that, through involuntary retirement, social isolation, and the loosening of traditional family ties, ③ <u>stripping</u> the elderly of the roles that ④ <u>had sustained</u> meaning in their lives.

*senile 노쇠한   deterioration 노화

① 동사의 수 일치
② 상관접속사의 쓰임
③ 동사의 파악
④ 동사의 시제

모의! **72** As ① <u>improbable</u> as this may seem, the bodily fluids of aquatic animals show a strong similarity to oceans, and indeed, most studies of ion balance in freshwater physiology ② <u>documents</u> the complex regulatory mechanisms ③ <u>by which</u> fish, amphibians and invertebrates attempt to maintain an inner ocean in spite of ④ <u>surrounding</u> fresh water.

*amphibian 양서류   invertebrate 무척추동물

① 보어의 형태
② 동사의 수 일치
③ 관계사의 쓰임
④ 명사를 수식하는 분사의 형태

---

68 complex 복잡한   sensory 감각의   analysis 분석   swallow 삼키다   reject 거부하다   **69** owe A to B A를 B에 빚지고 있다   namely 즉, 다시 말해서   package 꾸리다; 포장하다   **70** organization 조직   transform A into B A를 B로 바꾸다, 변형시키다   raw 날것의, 가공하지 않은   exploit 이용하다; 착취하다   capability 역량, 능력   behavio(u)r 행위   **71** location 위치, 장소   involuntary 본의 아닌   retirement 은퇴, 퇴직   isolation 고립   loosen 느슨하게 하다   strip A of B A에게서 B를 제거하다   sustain 유지하다   **72** improbable 있을 것 같지 않은   bodily fluid 체액   aquatic 수중의, 수생의   physiology 생리학   document (문서로) 뒷받침하다, 증명하다   regulatory 조절하는   mechanism (목적을 달성하기 위한) 방법, 메커니즘   surround 둘러싸다

Answer Key

각 Unit의 정답만 빠르게 확인해 보세요.

STAGE I 문장성분 중심의 구문

Chpater 01 주어의 파악

Unit 01 명사구 주어 pp.28~29

Ⓐ 03~05 해석 Rainbow Book p.6 확인

Ⓑ 06~09 해석 Rainbow Book p.7 확인

06 Considering issues in an appropriate context

07 passing large sums of wealth on to your children

08 Raising awareness of children about ~ act

09 To conquer oneself / to be vanquished ~ nature

Ⓒ 10 Investing   11 (A) makes (B) increases

12 is

Unit 02 명사절 주어 pp.30~31

Ⓐ 03~05 해석 Rainbow Book p.8 확인

Ⓑ 06~09 해석 Rainbow Book p.9 확인

06 Whoever acquires knowledge but does ~ it

07 What we ~ alone / what we have ~ the world

08 How the universe began

09 That witches ~ disasters and misfortunes

Ⓒ 10 is   11 we are   12 Whatever

Unit 03 가주어 it pp.32~33

Ⓐ 03~05 해석 Rainbow Book p.10 확인

Ⓑ 06~09 해석 Rainbow Book p.11 확인

06 to propose alternative ideas and then to ~ concepts

07 to leave the medicine where the children ~ it

08 that many people view any amount of visible fat ~ of

09 how much more ~ others say

Ⓒ 10 for   11 to create   12 whether

Unit 04 주어 + 형용사구 pp.34~35

Ⓐ 03~05 해석 Rainbow Book p.12 확인

Ⓑ 06~09 해석 Rainbow Book p.13 확인

06 in the evolution of modern man

07 to guard ~ ambitions

08 studying genes in yeast cells

09 introduced accidentally or intentionally ~ territories

Ⓒ 10 rely   11 is   12 is

Unit 05 주어 + 형용사절 1 pp.36~37

Ⓐ 03~05 해석 Rainbow Book p.14 확인

Ⓑ 06~09 해석 Rainbow Book p.15 확인

06 who have a high sense of self-efficacy

07 that freed men from most of their ancient fetters

08 where students feel involved and respected

09 that we behave in a given situation

Ⓒ 10 looks   11 influence   12 is

Unit 06 주어 + 형용사절 2 pp.38~39

Ⓐ 03~05 해석 Rainbow Book p.16 확인

Ⓑ 06~09 해석 Rainbow Book p.17 확인

06 that the first stages of human cloning ~ achieved

07 we now see

08 you speak to someone

09 we wish the world to be

Ⓒ 10 is   11 tells   12 is

Chapter 01 Review pp.40~41

A 01~04 해석 Rainbow Book p.18 확인

B 05 Learning   06 nourishes   07 become

C 08 Learning science through inquiry is a primary principle

09 difficult to see ourselves through the lenses of others

10 The belly fat disorder caused by lack of physical activity

D 11 ③   12 ②   13 ①

Chpater 02 동사 구문

Unit 07 전치사구와 짝을 이루는 동사 구문 pp.44~45

Ⓐ 03~05 해석 Rainbow Book p.22 확인

Ⓑ 06~09 해석 Rainbow Book p.23 확인

06 as the masters ~ fate, as threats, as challenges ~ opportunities

07 with the happy endings ~ our hearts

08 of your own strengths and successes

09 from the innocent, from the truthful

Ⓒ 10 from   11 to   12 with

Unit 08 조동사 구문
pp.46~47

Ⓐ [03~05 해석] Rainbow Book p.24 확인

Ⓑ [06~09 해석] Rainbow Book p.25 확인

06 might have been, might have been

07 can't have committed

08 might as well expect ~ as …

09 can hardly be valued too highly

Ⓒ 10 have originated   11 have taken   12 enter

Unit 09 수동태 구문
pp.48~49

Ⓐ [03~05 해석] Rainbow Book p.26 확인

Ⓑ [06~09 해석] Rainbow Book p.27 확인

06 is extracted or learned / is (then) transformed / is (eventually) used

07 can be stimulated, controlled, or suppressed

08 is (commonly) described

09 is estimated

Ⓒ 10 may not be taken   11 are still being written

12 are often referred to as

Chapter 02 Review
pp.50~51

A [01~04 해석] Rainbow Book p.28 확인

B 05 (A) with (B) of   06 should

07 must   08 (A) is designed (B) predetermined

C 09 was being updated

10 must have been invented

D 11 attributed changes in the climate to global warming

12 has often been compared to a super-computer

Chpater 03 목적어의 파악

Unit 10 명사구 목적어
pp.54~55

Ⓐ [03~05 해석] Rainbow Book p.32 확인

Ⓑ [06~09 해석] Rainbow Book p.33 확인

06 when to follow them and when to ignore them

07 stealing the car / driving it under the influence of alcohol

08 to turn off the oven / seeing the expression ~ to eat

09 checking for monsters under our bed

Ⓒ 10 to say   11 saying   12 to stand

Unit 11 명사절 목적어
pp.56~57

Ⓐ [03~05 해석] Rainbow Book p.34 확인

Ⓑ [06~09 해석] Rainbow Book p.35 확인

06 that we are still pioneers ~ behind us

07 whether they will ~ comedy, whether they will suffer ~ tears

08 no system of waste disposal can be ~ the future

09 whichever is more convenient for you

Ⓒ 10 that   11 whether   12 whatever

Unit 12 가목적어 it
pp.58~59

Ⓐ [03~05 해석] Rainbow Book p.36 확인

Ⓑ [06~09 해석] Rainbow Book p.37 확인

06 to avoid some form of publicity

07 not to clutter my mind ~ five minutes

08 to give them a dignified and hopeful future

09 that, no matter how violent, it is ~ shining

Ⓒ 10 easy   11 that   12 it

Unit 13 목적어 + 형용사구
pp.60~61

Ⓐ [03~05 해석] Rainbow Book p.38 확인

Ⓑ [06~09 해석] Rainbow Book p.39 확인

06 illustrative of the various temperaments of authors

07 to think with deep gratitude of those who ~ us

08 of blood flowing through your brain

09 released into the air and water

Ⓒ 10 to see   11 heading   12 applied

Unit 14 목적어 + 형용사절
pp.62~63

Ⓐ [03~05 해석] Rainbow Book p.40 확인

Ⓑ [06~09 해석] Rainbow Book p.41 확인

06 who has ~ 10,000 kicks once / who has ~ 10,000 times

07 which animals must have to survive

08 that are more expressive, like ~ 'wonderful'

09 at which conflict with the finite ~ inevitable

Ⓒ 10 ⓑ   11 ⓐ   12 ⓒ

Chapter 03 Review
pp.64~65

A [01~04 해석] Rainbow Book p.42 확인

B 05 working   06 to do   07 that   08 to happen

C 09 I had forgotten to lock the door

10 how the force of gravity affects all objects

11 think it necessary for people to realize

D 12 ⓑ   13 ⓐ   14 ⓒ

Chpater 04 보어의 파악

Unit 15 주격보어: 구   pp.68~69

Ⓐ [03~05 해석] Rainbow Book p.46 확인

Ⓑ [06~09 해석] Rainbow Book p.47 확인

06 unconvinced of the value and usefulness ~ bitcoin

07 to learn ~ experimentation

08 taking the first step

09 about waiting ~ to pass / about learning how to dance in the rain

Ⓒ 10 is to see it in use

11 is when to apply the knowledge

12 is having a good social network

Unit 16 주격보어: 절   pp.70~71

Ⓐ [03~05 해석] Rainbow Book p.48 확인

Ⓑ [06~09 해석] Rainbow Book p.49 확인

06 what we would expect to see ~ socially

07 how they win / how they handle defeat

08 what a Ferrari is to other cars

09 whatever the author intends ~ the poem

Ⓒ 10 is that we should try to see

11 is how well or poorly people express

12 what words are to the poet

Unit 17 목적격보어 1   pp.72~73

Ⓐ [03~05 해석] Rainbow Book p.50 확인

Ⓑ [06~09 해석] Rainbow Book p.51 확인

06 to go to the river / to drink from it

07 understand the details better

08 fill out an evaluation of every course they take

09 approach and stop outside

Ⓒ 10 to act   11 use   12 (A) merge (B) come

Unit 18 목적격보어 2   pp.74~75

Ⓐ [03~05 해석] Rainbow Book p.52 확인

Ⓑ [06~09 해석] Rainbow Book p.53 확인

06 beating / moving along our veins and arteries

07 barking fiercely

08 delivered fast / to arrive hot

09 spoken ill of by others

Ⓒ 10 (A) posted (B) published

11 (A) grazing (B) wandering

12 (A) feel (B) shaking

Unit 19 보어 + 형용사구   pp.76~77

Ⓐ [03~05 해석] Rainbow Book p.54 확인

Ⓑ [06~09 해석] Rainbow Book p.55 확인

06 (in the past responsible for ~ separated)

07 (to acquire guidance on how ~ their DNA)

08 (thought of as being closely ~ trade)

09 (without a single drop of honey left inside)

Ⓒ 10 making   11 used   12 to succeed

Unit 20 보어 + 형용사절   pp.78~79

Ⓐ [03~05 해석] Rainbow Book p.56 확인

Ⓑ [06~09 해석] Rainbow Book p.57 확인

06 (that deals with beauty, especially ~ arts)

07 (which I may not touch, but whose ~ the same)

08 (in which all kinds of composition ~ formed)

09 (we can be)

Ⓒ 10 ⓒ   11 ⓐ   12 ⓑ

Chapter 04 Review   pp.80~81

A [01~04 해석] Rainbow Book p.58 확인

B 05 splashing   06 delivered

07 jump

C 08 found car windows broken

09 allowed us to control some of the risks of life

10 is that it acts

D 11 ⓐ   12 ⓒ   13 ⓑ

STAGE Ⅲ 수식어 중심의 구문

Chpater 05 명사 수식어: 구

Unit 21 명사 + (형용사 +) 전치사구   pp.86~87

Ⓐ [03~05 해석] Rainbow Book p.64 확인

Ⓑ [06~09 해석] Rainbow Book p.65 확인

06 (on the front cover of each test)

07 (suitable for beginners and advanced users alike)

08 (in the sense ~ viewpoint) / (in the sense ~ the person)

09 (capable of transforming ~ a friend)

Ⓒ 10 depend   11 are   12 is

Unit 22 명사 + to-v[v-ing / v-ed]   pp.88~89

Ⓐ [03~05 해석] Rainbow Book p.66 확인

Ⓑ [06~09 해석] Rainbow Book p.67 확인

06 (judged to be functionally illiterate) / (required in everyday life)

07 (growing on a grape skin) / (originally processed ~ the fruit)

08 (written on the front page of your bill)

09 (to be crowned Best Picture at the Academy Awards)

C 10 to leave

11 (A) targeting (B) preparing

12 (A) handed (B) soaring

Chapter 05 *Review* pp.90~91

A 01~04 해석 Rainbow Book p.68 확인

B 05 (A) held (B) dedicated

06 to see

07 (A) processing (B) known

08 inhabiting

C 09 Changes to one part of our ecosystem

10 called ozone in the upper atmosphere protects

11 new policy restricting sales and content

Chpater 06 명사 수식어: 절

Unit 23 명사 + 관계대명사절 pp.94~95

A 03~05 해석 Rainbow Book p.72 확인

B 06~09 해석 Rainbow Book p.73 확인

06 (who wait) / (who fear) / (who grieve) / (who rejoice) / (who love)

07 (whose teeth are sound)

08 (which contains no medical ~ medication)

09 (that people now have with each other)

C 10 who **11** that **12** are

Unit 24 명사 + 전치사 + 관계대명사 pp.96~97

A 03~05 해석 Rainbow Book p.74 확인

B 06~09 해석 Rainbow Book p.75 확인

06 by which my feet are guided

07 with ~ concerned / by which ~ things

08 within which goods and services ~ consumed

09 with whom they could identify

C 10 ⓑ **11** ⓐ **12** ⓒ

Unit 25 명사 + 관계부사절 pp.98~99

A 03~05 해석 Rainbow Book p.76 확인

B 06~09 해석 Rainbow Book p.77 확인

06 (when the Power of Love ~ Power)

07 (where the monetary compensation ~ for)

08 (why we have "good days" ~ at work)

09 (that citizens can communicate ~ issues)

C 10 ⓒ **11** ⓑ **12** ⓐ

Unit 26 명사 + 관계사가 생략된 수식절 pp.100~101

A 03~05 해석 Rainbow Book p.78 확인

B 06~09 해석 Rainbow Book p.79 확인

06 people ✔ you trust and feel comfortable around

07 the faith ✔ people have in them / the expectations ✔ they have raised themselves

08 One reason ✔ most dogs are much happier than most people

09 the things ✔ he seeks to teach / all ✔ you ask of your students and more

C 10 ⓑ **11** ⓒ **12** ⓐ

Unit 27 명사와 관계사절의 분리 pp.102~103

A 03~05 해석 Rainbow Book p.80 확인

B 06~09 해석 Rainbow Book p.81 확인

06 (a part of a cell) that controls what it looks ~ develops

07 (patients) who are not expected to live ~ a year

08 (technology) that can allow devices and services ~ data

09 (the time) when people will see that my paintings ~ the paint

C 10 burn **11** which **12** create

Unit 28 명사, 관계사절 pp.104~105

A 03~05 해석 Rainbow Book p.82 확인

B 06~09 해석 Rainbow Book p.83 확인

06 which allows computers to ~ data

07 when he decided ~ writing / where he met many ~ the day

08 some of which you may not ~ for

09 which every normal child has

C 10 ⓑ **11** ⓒ **12** ⓐ

Chapter 06 *Review* pp.106~107

A 01~04 해석 Rainbow Book p.84 확인

B 05 whose **06** where

07 which **08** which

Answer Key **219**

C 09 through which we see the world

　10 when science and technology are developing with great rapidity

　11 all of which turned out to be false alarms

D 12 ⓒ　　13 ⓑ　　14 ⓐ

Chpater 07　부사적 수식어: 구

Unit 29　부사 역할을 하는 전치사구　pp.110~111

Ⓐ [03~05 해석] Rainbow Book p.88 확인

Ⓑ [06~09 해석] Rainbow Book p.89 확인

　06 from the planet as a result of human activity

　07 of my heart, to my heart, from my eyes

　08 Upon discovering his own ~ the architecture / for an architectural firm in Chicago

　09 Above all, with glittering eyes, in the most unlikely places

Ⓒ 10 ①　　11 ③　　12 ②

Unit 30　부사 역할을 하는 to-v의 의미　pp.112~113

Ⓐ [03~05 해석] Rainbow Book p.90 확인

Ⓑ [06~09 해석] Rainbow Book p.91 확인

　06 to avoid coming ~ about it

　07 to form a crystal structure

　08 to have you as a guest at the annual festival

　09 to have opportunity

Ⓒ 10 ⓒ　　11 ⓐ　　12 ⓑ

Unit 31　부사적 to-v의 관용 구문　pp.114~115

Ⓐ [03~05 해석] Rainbow Book p.92 확인

Ⓑ [06~09 해석] Rainbow Book p.93 확인

　06 versatile enough to adjust ~ medium / to vary ~ message

　07 too heavily, too quickly, to be ~ accounts

　08 are, willing to do yourself

　09 to make matters worse

Ⓒ 10 am realistic enough to know

　11 is just too exceptional to pass up

　12 not to mention the damage to the environment

Unit 32　부사 역할을 하는 분사구문의 의미　pp.116~117

Ⓐ [03~05 해석] Rainbow Book p.94 확인

Ⓑ [06~09 해석] Rainbow Book p.95 확인

　06 pretending to be ~ Josh's mom / happily forcing ~ thinks and feels

　07 seeing there are only four pieces of pie for five people

　08 Assumed to have a substantial amount of water

　09 speaking words of wisdom, "Let it be" / speaking words of wisdom, "Let it be"

Ⓒ 10 Fueled　　11 striking　　12 compared

Unit 33　분사구문의 다양한 형태 1　pp.118~119

Ⓐ [03~05 해석] Rainbow Book p.96 확인

Ⓑ [06~09 해석] Rainbow Book p.97 확인

　06 Turned down for countless jobs

　07 the two factors clearly being linked in harmony

　08 When faced with a bunch of watermelons / all promising delicious juiciness inside

　09 if applied to honest endeavor

Ⓒ 10 making　　11 being　　12 expelled

Unit 34　분사구문의 다양한 형태 2　pp.120~121

Ⓐ [03~05 해석] Rainbow Book p.98 확인

Ⓑ [06~09 해석] Rainbow Book p.99 확인

　06 With the industrial society ~ an information-based society

　07 Unable to write, or even to speak clearly

　08 each completely dependent on the other for survival

　09 Strictly speaking

Ⓒ 10 slipping　　11 Taking

　12 (A) collected (B) being

Chapter 07　Review　pp.122~123

A [01~04 해석] Rainbow Book p.100 확인

B 05 causing　　06 getting　　07 seen

C 08 in order to teach them effectively

　09 allowing you access to any information

　10 with my eyes closed

D 11 ⓒ　　12 ⓐ　　13 ⓑ

Chpater 08　부사적 수식어: 절

Unit 35　시간의 부사절　pp.126~127

Ⓐ [03~05 해석] Rainbow Book p.104 확인

Ⓑ [06~09 해석] Rainbow Book p.105 확인

　06 The moment you doubt whether you can fly

　07 Since the Industrial Revolution began ~ century

　08 once they are in hand

　09 By the time you get it built

Ⓒ 10 until　　11 when　　12 Whenever

Unit 36 이유의 부사절   pp.128~129

Ⓐ 03~05 해석 Rainbow Book p.106 확인

Ⓑ 06~09 해석 Rainbow Book p.107 확인

  06 because listeners or readers bring ~ encounter

  07 Just because you can hear ~ morning

  08 As the nature of sarcasm implies ~ message

  09 Now that genetically modified foods ~ shelves

Ⓒ 10 increase   11 fallible   12 important

Unit 37 조건의 부사절   pp.130~131

Ⓐ 03~05 해석 Rainbow Book p.108 확인

Ⓑ 06~09 해석 Rainbow Book p.109 확인

  06 If you wait for the mango fruits to fall

  07 unless you have information in your head to think about

  08 As far as we can discern

  09 in so far as it ~ negotiation / in so far as mediation ~ another

Ⓒ 10 ⓒ   11 ⓐ   12 ⓑ

Unit 38 목적 · 결과의 부사절   pp.132~133

Ⓐ 03~05 해석 Rainbow Book p.110 확인

Ⓑ 06~09 해석 Rainbow Book p.111 확인

  06 so that he could marry Mrs. Simpson ~ woman

  07 so that you can't take your eyes off her

  08 that we do not ~ us

  09 that the police ~ time

Ⓒ 10 ⓒ   11 ⓑ   12 ⓐ

Unit 39 반전 · 대조의 부사절   pp.134~135

Ⓐ 03~05 해석 Rainbow Book p.112 확인

Ⓑ 06~09 해석 Rainbow Book p.113 확인

  06 No matter what emotion you're feeling right now

  07 If we don't have the power to choose ~ from

  08 while in Einstein's theory ~ as a force

  09 whether it's sitting on a bench waving ~ shot

Ⓒ 10 Though   11 Whereas   12 Whatever

Unit 40 양태의 부사절   pp.136~137

Ⓐ 03~05 해석 Rainbow Book p.114 확인

Ⓑ 06~09 해석 Rainbow Book p.115 확인

  06 as they are / as we would like them to be

  07 Just as darkness ~ each day / Just as plants ~ life cycle

  08 as if what you do makes a difference

  09 as though there isn't a lot you can do ~ problems

Ⓒ 10 ⓑ   11 ⓒ   12 ⓐ

Chapter 08 Review   pp.138~139

A 01~04 해석 Rainbow Book p.116 확인

B 05 so   06 than   07 as though

C 08 Now that we are all part of the global village

  09 Much as I sympathize with your difficulties

  10 Leave things as they are

D 11 ⓐ   12 ⓒ   13 ⓑ

STAGE Ⅲ 주요 구문의 독파

Chpater 09 가정법 구문

Unit 41 If 가정법 과거 구문   pp.144~145

Ⓐ 03~05 해석 Rainbow Book p.122 확인

Ⓑ 06~09 해석 Rainbow Book p.123 확인

  06 understood, would be

  07 could survive, were

  08 were to rewind, were, would happen

  09 should find, can be obtained

Ⓒ 10 were   11 would   12 were to

Unit 42 If 가정법 과거완료 구문   pp.146~147

Ⓐ 03~05 해석 Rainbow Book p.124 확인

Ⓑ 06~09 해석 Rainbow Book p.125 확인

  06 Hadn't devoted, could have become

  07 had died, would have written

  08 would have been, had chosen

  09 had learned, would be using

Ⓒ 10 have been   11 have had   12 be

Unit 43 wish · as if 가정법 구문   pp.148~149

Ⓐ 03~05 해석 Rainbow Book p.126 확인

Ⓑ 06~09 해석 Rainbow Book p.127 확인

  06 could turn, give   07 had spent

08 were   09 had happened

C 10 could   11 had done   12 as if

Unit 44　**if가 없는 가정법 구문**　pp.150~151

A 03~05 해석 Rainbow Book p.128 확인

B 06~09 해석 Rainbow Book p.129 확인

06 but for Wells and Verne and the people ~ it

07 Without it

08 A hundred years ago

09 Born in better times

C 10 Otherwise   11 With   12 without

Chapter 09　**Review**　pp.152~153

A 01~04 해석 Rainbow Book p.130 확인

B 05 were   06 be

07 have called

C 08 wouldn't have run out of gas

09 I had known there was a sale

10 Had it not been for antibiotics

D 11 it were not for your donations / it not for your donations

12 you hadn't told me

13 I had not got caught in a traffic jam

Chpater 10　**비교 구문**

Unit 45　**원급 구문**　pp.156~157

A 03~05 해석 Rainbow Book p.134 확인

B 06~09 해석 Rainbow Book p.135 확인

06 as much about him or her as ~ behavior

07 not so much by great pieces ~ as by little advantages …

08 twice as much spending power as ~ 1950s

09 as simple and reassuring as ~ ended

C 10 as   11 dense   12 much

Unit 46　**비교급 구문 1**　pp.158~159

A 03~05 해석 Rainbow Book p.136 확인

B 06~09 해석 Rainbow Book p.137 확인

06 scarier, rather than ~ unharmed

07 more anxious ~ than ~ possess

08 much better than tedious disease

09 two to six times more grain, than ~ plants

C 10 more than one hundred times larger than the earth's

11 far more likely to come

12 less popular now than twenty years ago

Unit 47　**비교급 구문 2**　pp.160~161

A 03~05 해석 Rainbow Book p.138 확인

B 06~09 해석 Rainbow Book p.139 확인

06 the more / the harder

07 no lower than 28 degrees Celsius, no higher than 20

08 no more explain ~ than ~ the blind

09 no less plagued by pests than ~ farmers

C 10 the more frequently they are exposed

11 would be no better off than

12 not to be found in molecules any more than

Unit 48　**최상급 구문**　pp.162~163

A 03~05 해석 Rainbow Book p.140 확인

B 06~09 해석 Rainbow Book p.141 확인

06 Nobody is so miserable as

07 the hardest things in this world / nothing is more helpful ~ than

08 The most exciting phrase to hear in science

09 larger and more diverse than that of all the other river systems

C 10 the most   11 animal   12 than

Chapter 10　**Review**　pp.164~165

A 01~04 해석 Rainbow Book p.142 확인

B 05 (A) does (B) than

06 (A) effectively (B) secure

07 those   08 makes

C 09 twice as much energy as

10 the more job opportunities you'll find

11 No bread in the world is so sweet as

D 12 Nothing, as fear

13 than / any more than

14 as / so much as

Chpater 11　**특수 구문**

Unit 49　**도치 구문 1**　pp.168~169

A 03~05 해석 Rainbow Book p.146 확인

B 06~09 해석 Rainbow Book p.147 확인

---

06 must the solution be

07 will anyone's personal information ~ out

08 evolved the abstract algebra ~ structure

09 is a list of ~ words

C 10 has food   11 is   12 was

Unit 50 도치 구문 2 pp.170~171

A 03~05 해석 Rainbow Book p.148 확인

B 06~09 해석 Rainbow Book p.149 확인

06 is sniffing tied

07 does bathing

08 learning we cannot put

09 in terms of chemistry ~ as first love

C 10 quickly did he rush

11 have many plants taken the offensive

12 Sigmund Freud called the unconscious

Unit 51 강조 구문 pp.172~173

A 03~05 해석 Rainbow Book p.150 확인

B 06~09 해석 Rainbow Book p.151 확인

06 not work, but overwork / not hard work

07 the former

08 not until we're being massaged ~ our e-mail

09 only in the mysterious equation of love

C 10 It is the biography of Steve Jobs that[which] I have been looking for.

11 it is poetry and dreams that[which] have developed science

12 It is only in our darkest hours that we may discover the true strength of the brilliant light within ourselves.

Unit 52 동격 구문 pp.174~175

A 03~05 해석 Rainbow Book p.152 확인

B 06~09 해석 Rainbow Book p.153 확인

06 I-can-do-anything job applicant

07 listening to Mozart will make your child smarter

08 robot vehicles blindly programmed to preserve the selfish molecules known as genes

09 that it could be a threat to the traditional culture

C 10 the habit / taking an objective view of the past

11 analyze data and extract information ~ from them / learn

12 principle / concrete ~ ones, the shortest ~ the best

Unit 53 삽입 구문 pp.176~177

A 03~05 해석 Rainbow Book p.154 확인

B 06~09 해석 Rainbow Book p.155 확인

06 in my not so humble opinion

07 however little it might be

08 when they are fed patients' medical histories

09 we know

C 10 that   11 seems   12 who

Unit 54 생략·공통 구문 pp.178~179

A 03~05 해석 Rainbow Book p.156 확인

B 06~09 해석 Rainbow Book p.157 확인

06 if (it is) deprived

07 are not (supported by evidence), do not (get results)

08 whether (they are) happy or tragic

09 but (it takes) just as much (of bravery) ~ friends (as to stand up to our enemies)

C 10 only a tool of man   11 the reality

12 anything

Chapter 11 Review pp.180~181

A 01~04 해석 Rainbow Book p.158 확인

B 05 are   06 was   07 that

C 08 who they suspected had been

09 that makes life interesting

10 had we started out before

D 11 ⓒ   12 ⓐ   13 ⓑ

Chpater 12 기타 주요 구문

Unit 55 등위접속사 구문 pp.184~185

A 03~05 해석 Rainbow Book p.162 확인

B 06~09 해석 Rainbow Book p.163 확인

06 and   07 or   08 for, yet   09 for

C 10 do they   11 yet   12 Adopt

Unit 56 상관접속사 구문 pp.186~187

A 03~05 해석 Rainbow Book p.164 확인

B 06~09 해석 Rainbow Book p.165 확인

06 sunshine, cold nights and chilling showers / joy, trial and difficulty

07 serve us, cut us

08 in the result of their actions, in what ~ causes

09 the happy ending ~ love, the more ~ in "the real world"

C 10 nor 11 but 12 (A) but (B) Both

Unit 57 병렬 구문 pp.188~189

A 03~05 해석 Rainbow Book p.166 확인

B 06~09 해석 Rainbow Book p.167 확인

06 discordant sounds, false harmony, noisy ~ sounds

07 seat children all behind ~, dictate information ~, expect them to absorb ~ a sponge

08 in the length of days, in the use we make of them / long, very little

09 whether it exists, what the meaning of it is, whether ~ broken, what ~ party

C 10 concentrate 11 require 12 to induce

Unit 58 부정 구문 pp.190~191

A 03~05 해석 Rainbow Book p.168 확인

B 06~09 해석 Rainbow Book p.169 확인

06 All, not / Not all 07 not both

08 nothing but 09 scarcely, not

C 10 rarely succeed unless they have fun

11 Hardly any discovery is possible without

12 don't necessarily have a higher success rate

Unit 59 동명사 관용 구문 pp.192~193

A 03~05 해석 Rainbow Book p.170 확인

B 06~09 해석 Rainbow Book p.171 확인

06 is busy processing, forming

07 made a point of sending

08 It is no use saying

09 there's no knowing

C 10 enlightening your mind is worth reading

11 There is no telling

12 have a hard time letting go of their suffering

Unit 60 전치사 + 명사절 pp.194~195

A 03~05 해석 Rainbow Book p.172 확인

B 06~09 해석 Rainbow Book p.173 확인

06 up to whether both sides are ~ concessions

07 by what it eats and how it reproduces

08 with how the availability ~ organisms

09 in whatever I'm doing

C 10 ⓑ 11 ⓒ 12 ⓐ

Chapter 12 Review pp.196~197

A 01~04 해석 Rainbow Book p.174 확인

B 05 nor 06 seeing

07 expressing 08 helping

C 09 or by using the arrow keys

10 do not always tell you everything

11 nor can it be denied

D 12 ⓒ 13 ⓐ 14 ⓑ

어법 공략 십계명 pp.199~201

01 is, are, lies 02 occurs, donate, be donated 03 Establishing, has 04 reading, to change, come, running, using 05 being treated, compared, to have been 06 efficiency, making 07 that, whether, which, where, what, that 08 would accept, had been, practice, had done 09 clear, than 10 how a work is, did he know

Special Unit 01 pp.202~207

01 is 02 in which 03 (A) doing (B) that 04 be 05 considered 06 that 07 is 08 as 09 (A) have been (B) at which 10 using 11 (A) has been said (B) reveals 12 (A) breaking (B) left 13 what 14 (A) running (B) that 15 turning 16 had searched 17 (A) promote (B) depends 18 to be taken 19 is 20 helping 21 is interpreted 22 whose 23 (A) whispering (B) feel 24 which 25 leaving 26 are 27 lies 28 restricted 29 (A) producing (B) leaves 30 emerged 31 differ 32 (A) consuming (B) rely 33 come 34 (A) turn (B) proves 35 (A) which (B) generated 36 are

Special Unit 02 pp.208~214

37 ②	38 ③	39 ②	40 ④	41 ④	42 ④
43 ①	44 ③	45 ②	46 ②	47 ③	48 ①
49 ④	50 ④	51 ③	52 ②	53 ③	54 ③
55 ②	56 ④	57 ②	58 ③	59 ②	60 ①
61 ③	62 ③	63 ③	64 ③	65 ②	66 ④
67 ①	68 ②	69 ①	70 ③	71 ③	72 ②

224 Answer Key

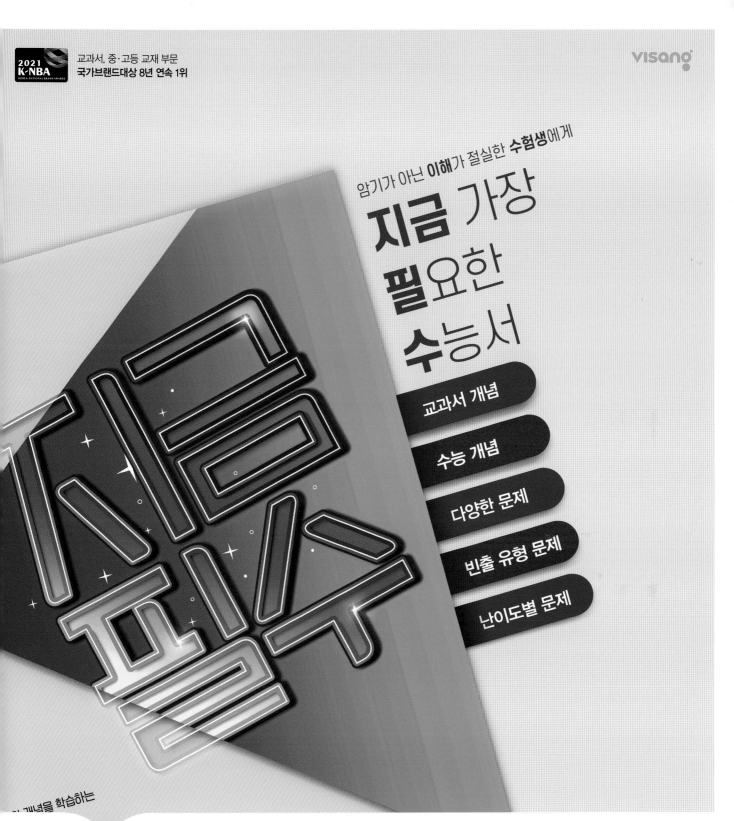

시리즈 소개

영어 문장 학습의 새로운 표준

마법같은 블록구문

기본편

1. 진짜 제대로 된
   영문법·구문 기초 확립
2. 단계적 학습으로
   좌절 없이 완주·성취
3. 최적 문장으로
   재미·감동·실력을 한꺼번에

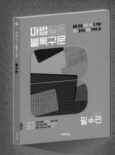

필수편

1. 영어 문장[구문]
   최적 기억 학습 프로그램
2. 최신·고전 명문장으로
   감동·교양·실력 다 잡기
3. 내신 실력 확립,
   1문장 1지문 수능 최강 적중

실전편

1. 정통적 & 효과적
   영어 구문 공략법
2. 수능 영어에 최적화된
   예문과 구문 적용 훈련
3. 구와 절 → 문장성분별
   구문독해 → 어법 문제 공략법

무료 부가서비스

 http://book.visang.com/

 m.book.visang.com

고등교재 〉 학습자료실 〉 학습자료 〉 영어에서
아래의 자료들을 내려받을 수 있습니다.

- **WORKBOOK(HWP):**
  Version 1. 영어문장을 한글로 해석하기
  Version 2. 우리말에 맞게 영어문장 배열하기
- **AUDIOBOOK(MP3):**
  Version 1. 영어문장 3회-한글해석 1회
  Version 2. 한글해석 1회-영어문장 3회

＊차별화된 음성자료로 책 없이도 언제 어디서든
  영어문장을 익힐 수 있어요!

마법같은 블록구문   컬러와 블록으로 완성하는 마법의 영어 문장

visang

비상교육
누리집에
방문해보세요

http://book.visang.com/

발간 이후에 발견되는 오류 비상교재 누리집 〉 학습자료실 〉 고등교재 〉 정오표
본 교재의 정답 비상교재 누리집 〉 학습자료실 〉 고등교재 〉 정답·해설

교재 설문에
참여해보세요

QR 코드
스캔하기

의견 남기기

선물 받기!

품질혁신코드 VS01QI21_4

마법같은 블록구문

컬러와 블록의 마법,
& 의미 기억의 힘

Rainbow Book

Marvel Book을 품고 있는 **자학자습용 해설서**
문장성분별 완전 컬러화

박세광

실전편

ABOVE IMAGINATION

우리는 남다른 상상과 혁신으로
교육 문화의 새로운 전형을 만들어
모든 이의 행복한 경험과 성장에 기여한다

마법같은 블록구문

Rainbow Book 실전편

STAGE I

문장성분 중심의 구문

Contents of Stage

Chapter **01** 주어의 파악	Unit 01	명사구 주어	
	Unit 02	명사절 주어	
	Unit 03	가주어 it	
	Unit 04	주어 + 형용사구	
	Unit 05	주어 + 형용사절 1	
	Unit 06	주어 + 형용사절 2	
Chapter **02** 동사 구문	Unit 07	전치사구와 짝을 이루는 동사 구문	
	Unit 08	조동사 구문	
	Unit 09	수동태 구문	
Chapter **03** 목적어의 파악	Unit 10	명사구 목적어	
	Unit 11	명사절 목적어	
	Unit 12	가목적어 it	
	Unit 13	목적어 + 형용사구	
	Unit 14	목적어 + 형용사절	
Chapter **04** 보어의 파악	Unit 15	주격보어: 구	
	Unit 16	주격보어: 절	
	Unit 17	목적격보어 1	
	Unit 18	목적격보어 2	
	Unit 19	보어 + 형용사구	
	Unit 20	보어 + 형용사절	

01

주어의 파악

• unit 01 명사구 주어
• unit 02 명사절 주어
• unit 03 가주어 it
• unit 04 주어+형용사구
• unit 05 주어+형용사절 1
• unit 06 주어+형용사절 2

■ 본격적인 구문 학습에 앞서, 각 유닛별 주요 단어를 확인하세요.

Unit 01

- ☐ performance 성과, 수행
- ☐ existence 존재
- ☐ vital 필수적인
- ☐ assess 판단하다

- ☐ latitude 자유
- ☐ flexibility 융통성
- ☐ context 맥락, 문맥
- ☐ pros and cons 찬반양론

- ☐ sum 액수, 금액
- ☐ potential ～이 될 수 있는
- ☐ noble 숭고한, 고귀한
- ☐ trivial 사소한

Unit 02

- ☐ density 밀도
- ☐ plough 갈다, 일구다
- ☐ sow 씨를 뿌리다
- ☐ immortal 영원한, 불멸의

- ☐ occupy (마음·주의를) 끌다
- ☐ prehistoric times 선사시대
- ☐ witch 마녀
- ☐ disaster 재난, 재해

- ☐ compose 구성하다
- ☐ organization 구성, 조직
- ☐ valued 소중한; 중요한
- ☐ confidence 자신감

Unit 03

- ☐ victim 희생양; 희생
- ☐ superstition 미신
- ☐ heed 주의하다
- ☐ matter 중요하다

- ☐ alternative 대신하는
- ☐ get rid of ～을 제거하다
- ☐ pause 잠시 멈추다
- ☐ latest 최신의

- ☐ prime minister 수상, 국무총리
- ☐ resignation 사직, 사임
- ☐ tactical 전술의, 전략적인
- ☐ move 조치; 이동

Unit 04

- ☐ candidate 지원자, 후보자
- ☐ qualification 자격 요건
- ☐ instantaneously 바로, 당장
- ☐ microwave 극초단파

- ☐ outstanding 두드러진
- ☐ simply (부정문) 도저히, 결코
- ☐ unsustainable 지속할 수 없는
- ☐ alien 외래의

- ☐ favorable 유리한
- ☐ speculation 고찰, 추측
- ☐ analogy 유사성
- ☐ give off ～을 배출하다

Unit 05

- ☐ cultivate 계발하다
- ☐ throughout ～ 동안, ～ 내내
- ☐ procurement 입수, 확보
- ☐ self-efficacy 자기 효능감

- ☐ pursue 추구하다
- ☐ fetter 족쇄
- ☐ realization 자각, 인식
- ☐ discipline 훈육; 징계

- ☐ ultimately 궁극적으로, 결국
- ☐ enhance 향상시키다
- ☐ contemporary 현대의; 동시대의
- ☐ near-sighted 근시안적인

Unit 06

- ☐ publication 출판물
- ☐ spectacular 장관을 이루는
- ☐ plural 복수형; 복수형의
- ☐ subsequent 뒤이어 일어나는

- ☐ perception 인식, 지각
- ☐ determine 밝히다, 알아내다
- ☐ announcement 발표, 공고
- ☐ complaint 불평, 불만

- ☐ erroneously 잘못되게, 틀리게
- ☐ static 고정된
- ☐ impractical 비현실적인
- ☐ scheme 체계

명사구 주어

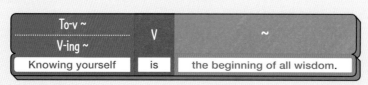

| To-v ~ / V-ing ~ | V | ~ |
| Knowing yourself | is | the beginning of all wisdom. |

네 자신을 아는 것은 / ~이다 / 모든 지혜의 시작

Standard Sentences

01 **Getting meaningful feedback on your performance** is a powerful strategy
의미 있는 피드백을 얻는 것은 / 당신의 성과에 대해 / 강력한 전략이다
for learning anything.
/ [어떤 것을 배우기 위한]

■ 주어로 동명사 Getting이 이끄는 명사구가 쓰였으며, 동명사 또는 to부정사가 이끄는 주어는 단수 취급한다.

performance 성과, 수행
strategy 전략

02 **To love and to be loved** is the greatest happiness of existence. *Sydney Smith*
사랑하고 사랑받는 것은 / 존재의 가장 큰 행복이다

■ 두 개의 to부정사가 주어로 쓰였다. and로 연결되는 주어는 복수로 취급하는 것이 원칙이지만, 합쳐서 하나의 의미를 나타낼 때는 단수 취급한다.
— 주어로 쓰이는 to부정사는 '가주어 – 진주어' 구문으로 바꿔 쓸 수 있다. / (= It is the greatest happiness of existence to love and to be loved.) ● Unit 03

existence 존재

A **03** **Knowing how climate has changed over millions of years** is vital to
아는 것은 / 기후가 수백만 년 동안 어떻게 변했는지를 / 필수적이다 /
properly assess current global warming trends.
제대로 현재의 지구 온난화 추세를 판단하기 위해

■ 주어로 쓰인 Knowing은 준동사이므로 뒤에 목적어가 올 수 있다. 명사절 how ~ years가 Knowing의 목적어이며, is가 문장의 동사이다.
— to-v의 부사적 용법으로 '목적(~하기 위해서)'의 의미로 쓰였다.

vital 필수적인; 생명의
assess 판단하다, 가늠하다
current 현재의; 흐름

수능! **04** **Giving people the latitude and flexibility to use their judgment and apply**
사람들에게 자유와 융통성을 주는 것은 / [그들의 판단력을 이용하고 / 그리고 그들의
their talents rapidly accelerates progress.
재능을 활용하는] / 빠르게 진전을 촉진시킨다

■ 주어로 쓰인 Giving은 간접목적어 people과 직접목적어 the latitude and flexibility ~ talents를 가진다.
— the latitude and flexibility는 to부정사구 to use ~ talents의 수식을 받는다.

latitude 자유; 위도
flexibility 융통성; 유연성
apply 활용하다; 지원하다
accelerate 촉진시키다

05 **To think that you know something without actually knowing it** is a serious
생각하는 것은 / 당신이 실제로 무언가를 알지 못하면서 그것을 안다고 / 심각한 실수이다
mistake.

■ 주어로 쓰인 To think가 목적어로 접속사 that이 이끄는 명사절을 취하고 있다.
— 전치사 without의 목적어로 동명사구 knowing it이 쓰였다.

serious 심각한, 위험한

B **06** Considering issues in an appropriate context will help you accurately
사안을 고려하는 것이 / 적합한 맥락 속에서 / 도울 것이다 / 당신이 정확하게
evaluate the pros and cons of a decision.
결정의 찬반양론을 평가하는 것을

appropriate 적합한
context 맥락, 문맥
pros and cons 찬반양론

- 주어로 쓰인 Considering은 전치사구 in ~ context의 수식을 받는다.
- help는 목적격보어로 to부정사 또는 동사원형을 가지며, 'O가 ~하는 것을 돕다'라고 해석한다.

07 Is passing large sums of wealth on to your children good for them or right
당신의 자녀들에게 많은 액수의 재산을 물려주는 것이 / 그들에게 좋거나 사회를 위해서
for society? *Bill Gates*
옳은가?

sum 액수, 금액; 합계
wealth 재산, 부

- 의문문의 어순 「Be동사[조동사] + 주어 ~?」에 따라 is가 주어 passing ~ children 앞에 쓰였다.
- 보어로 쓰인 good for them과 right for society가 등위접속사 or로 병렬 연결되어 있다.

> **Know More** 마이크로 소프트 윈도우의 창업주인 빌 게이츠(Bill Gates)는 자녀들에게 자신의 재산을 0.1 % 미만으로 물려주고, 99. 9%는 모두 기부할 것이라고 선언했다. 빌 게이츠 부부는 현재 세계 최대의 자선재단인 '빌 앤드 멜린다 게이츠 재단'을 설립해 저개발국을 주요 대상으로 교육, 보건, 개발 사업을 운영하는 데 힘쓰고 있다.

수능! **08** Raising awareness of children about the particular characteristics of SNS
아이들의 인식을 높이는 것은 / [SNS의 독특한 특성들에 관한
and the potential long-term impact of a seemingly trivial act is crucial.
/ 그리고 겉보기에 사소한 행위의 장기적으로 변할 수 있는 영향(에 관한)] / 매우 중요하다

awareness 인식
potential ~이 될 수 있는, 잠재적인
long-term 장기적인
trivial 사소한
crucial 매우 중요한

- 동명사 Raising이 이끄는 명사구가 주어이며, 동사는 is이다.
- about이 이끄는 전치사구 (about ~ act)는 awareness를 수식한다.

09 To conquer oneself is the best and noblest victory; to be vanquished by
스스로를 정복하는 것은 / 최고의 그리고 가장 숭고한 승리이다 / 자신의 본성에 의해 정복당하는 것은
one's own nature is the worst and most ignoble defeat. *Plato*
/ 최악의 그리고 가장 수치스러운 패배이다

conquer 정복하다
noblest 숭고한, 고귀한
vanquish 정복하다
ignoble (일이) 수치스러운, 명예롭지 못한; (사람의 행실, 성격이) 비열한

- 주어로 쓰인 To conquer는 목적어로 oneself를 가지고, to be vanquished는 to부정사의 수동태(to be v-ed)로 전치사구 by ~ nature의 수식을 받는다.

C **10** Investing regularly in learning opportunities is one of the greatest gifts you
정기적으로 투자하는 것은 / 학습 기회에 / 가장 큰 선물 중의 하나이다 / [당신이
can give yourself.
스스로에게 줄 수 있는]

invest 투자하다
regularly 정기적으로; 규칙적으로

- **풀이** 주어의 역할을 할 수 있는 명사구 또는 명사절이 되어야 하는데 부사(regularly)의 수식을 받고 있으므로, 준동사인 v-ing 형태가 적절하다.
- gifts 다음에는 목적격 관계대명사 that이 생략되었다. **⊙ Unit 26**

11 Having a large vocabulary makes reading more enjoyable and increases
많은 어휘를 아는 것은 / 독서를 더 즐겁게 만든다 / 그리고 자료의 영역을
the range of materials that you can explore.
증가시킨다 / [당신이 탐험할 수 있는]

range 영역, 범위

- **풀이** 동명사 주어는 단수 취급하며, and로 동사가 병렬 연결되므로 단수 동사 makes와 increases가 적절하다.

12 To say that AI will start doing what it wants for its own purposes is like
말하는 것은 / AI가 자기가 원하는 것을 하기 시작할 것이라고 / 자신의 목적을 위해서 / 말하는
saying a calculator will start making its own calculations. *Oren Etzioni*
것과 같다 / 계산기가 스스로 계산을 하기 시작할 것이라고

calculator 계산기
calculation 계산

- **풀이** to부정사가 이끄는 주어는 단수 취급하므로 단수 동사 is가 적절하다.
- 전치사구 like saying ~에서 saying 다음에 목적어절을 이끄는 접속사 that이 생략되어 있다.

unit 02
명사절 주어

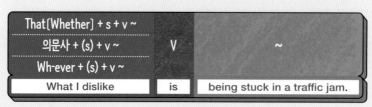

That[Whether] + s + v ~		
의문사 + (s) + v ~	V	~
Wh-ever + (s) + v ~		
What I dislike	is	being stuck in a traffic jam.

내가 싫어하는 것은 / ~이다 / 교통 혼잡에 꼼짝 못하게 되는 것

Standard Sentences

모의 01 **That some organisms must starve in nature is** deeply **regrettable and**
일부 유기체가 자연에서 굶주려야 한다는 것은 / 정말 유감스럽고 슬프다
sad.

■ That이 이끄는 명사절이 주어이다. that절이 주어인 경우에는 대개 '가주어–진주어' 구문으로 쓰인다. (= It is deeply regrettable and sad that some organisms must starve in nature.) **Unit 03**

starve 굶주리다
regrettable 유감스러운

모의 02 **What works for most job seekers is to look through their past experiences**
대부분의 구직자들에게 효과가 있는 것은 / 그들의 과거의 경험을 살펴보는 것이다
to help them build for the future.
/ 그들이 미래를 준비하는 것을 돕기 위해서

■ What이 이끄는 명사절이 주어이다. what은 '무엇' 또는 '~하는 것'으로 해석하는데, 여기서는 '~하는 것'으로 해석한다.

■ help는 목적격보어로 to부정사, 동사원형 둘 다 쓸 수 있으며 여기서는 동사원형인 build가 쓰였다.

job seeker 구직자

A 03 **Whether an object floats on water depends on the density of both the**
어떤 물체가 물에 뜨는지는 / 그 물체와 물의 밀도에 달려 있다
object and the water.

■ Whether가 이끄는 명사절이 주어로 쓰였다. whether가 명사절을 이끌 때는 '~인지 (아닌지)'의 뜻이고, 부사절을 이끌 때는 '~이든 (아니든)'의 뜻이다.

float 뜨다
density 밀도

04 **When Stonehenge was built is known, but why it was built remains a**
언제 스톤헨지가 건설되었는지는 알려져 있다 / 그러나 왜 그것이 건설되었는지는 미스터리로 남아있다
mystery.

■ 의문사 When과 why가 이끄는 간접의문문이 각각 문장에서 주어 역할을 하고 있다.

Know More 스톤헨지는 영국 런던의 남서쪽에 위치한 거대한 구조물 유적으로, 고대 앵글로 색슨 언어로 '매달려 있는 바윗돌'이라는 의미이다. 직경 98미터, 폭 6미터, 깊이 1.4미터의 도랑에 둘러싸인 원형 광장의 형태로, 어떻게 만들었는지는 밝혀지지 않았다. 스톤헨지가 세워진 곳 주변은 커다란 돌이나 산이 없고 들판만 있을 뿐이며, 스톤헨지에 쌓인 돌은 유적지에서 38km 떨어진 곳에서 가져온 것으로 확인되었다.

05 **Whatever is worth doing at all is worth doing well.** *Lord Chesterfield*
어쨌든 할 가치가 있는 것은 무엇이든 / 잘 할 가치가 있다

■ Whatever가 이끄는 절이 주어로 쓰였으며, 해석은 '~하는 것은 무엇이든'으로 한다.

be worth v-ing ~할 가치가 있다
at all (긍정문) 어쨌든

B **06** Whoever acquires knowledge but does not practice it is as one who

지식을 습득하지만 그것을 실천하지 않는 사람은 누구나 　　　　　　　　　　　 / 사람과 같다 　　 / [밭을

ploughs but does not sow. *Saadi*

갈지만 씨를 뿌리지 않는]

> ■ Whoever가 이끄는 절이 주어로 쓰였으며, 해석은 '~하는 사람은 누구나'로 한다.
> ━ as는 전치사로 '~처럼, ~와 같은'의 의미로 쓰였으며, who 이하는 one을 수식하는 형용사절이다.

plough(= plow) 갈다, 일구다
sow 씨를 뿌리다

07 What we have done for ourselves alone dies with us; what we have done

우리가 우리 자신만을 위해서 해온 것은 　　　　　　　　 / 우리와 함께 사라진다 / 우리가 다른 사람들과 세상을

for others and the world remains and is immortal.

위해서 해온 것은 　　　　　　　　 / 남아있다 그리고 영원하다

> ■ what은 '무엇' 또는 '~하는 것'으로 해석한다.

immortal 영원한, 불멸의

08 How the universe began is a fundamental question which has occupied the

우주가 어떻게 시작되었는가는 　　　　 / 근본적인 질문이다 　　　　　　 / [사람들의 마음을 끌어온

minds of men from prehistoric times.

　　　　　 / 선사시대부터]

> ■ 의문사 How가 이끄는 명사절이 주어로 쓰였다.
> ━ 관계대명사 which가 이끄는 형용사절이 보어인 a fundamental question을 수식한다.

fundamental 근본적인
occupy (마음·주의를) 끌다, 차
지하다
prehistoric times 선사시대

09 That witches caused disasters and misfortunes was widely believed among

마녀들이 재난과 불운을 초래했다는 것은 　　　　　　　　　 / 널리 믿어졌다 　　　　 / 초기

early American settlers.

미국 정착민들 사이에서

> ■ That이 이끄는 명사절이 주어 역할을 하고 있다. 명사절은 단수로 취급하므로 단수 동사 was로 받는다.

Know More 1692년 미국 매사추세츠주의 세일럼 빌리지에서 이루어진 마녀 재판에서 약 200명의 무고한 마을 사람들이
마녀로 고발되어 25명이 살해되었다. 이 사건은 인간의 집단적 광기, 종교 극단주의에 대한 경종을 울리며 정치적 수사학, 대중문
학, 심리학의 사례로 연구되고 있다.

witch 마녀
disaster 재난, 재해
misfortune 불운
settler 정착민, 이주민

C **10** What makes organisms different from the materials that compose them is

유기체들을 물질과 다르게 만드는 것은 　　　　　　　　　　　　 / [그것들을 구성하는] 　　 /

their level of organization.

그들의 구성의 수준이다

> **풀이** What이 이끄는 명사절이 주어로 쓰인 문장으로, 여기서 what은 'The thing which'를 의미하므로 단수 동사
> is가 적절하다.

compose 구성하다; 작곡하다
organization 구성, 조직

11 How successful we are at forming good relationships and how valued we

우리가 좋은 관계를 형성하는 데 얼마나 성공적인지 　　　　　　　 / 그리고 우리가 다른 사람들에 의해

feel by other people make a big difference in how good we feel about

얼마나 소중하다고 느끼는지는 　　 / 큰 차이를 만든다 　　　　　 / 우리가 스스로에 대해 얼마나 훌륭하다고

ourselves.

느끼는지에

> **풀이** 의문사 How가 이끄는 두 개의 명사절이 주어이다. 의문사가 이끄는 명사절은 간접의문문이며, 「의문사 + s + v」의
> 어순이어야 하므로 we are가 적절하다.

valued 소중한; 중요한

12 Whatever we expect with confidence becomes our own self-fulfilling

자신감을 가지고 우리가 기대하는 것은 무엇이든 　　　　　 / 우리 자신의 자기 충족 예언이 된다

prophecy.

> **풀이** 문장의 두 번째 동사 becomes가 있으므로 그 앞까지 주어 부분임을 알 수 있다. Whatever가 이끄는 명사절
> 은 주어 역할을 할 수 있지만, However가 이끄는 절은 부사절이며 주어 역할을 할 수 없다.

confidence 자신감
self-fulfilling prophecy 자
기 충족적 예언

unit 03
가주어 it

It	V	~	to-v[v-ing] ~
			that[whether / 의문사] + (s) + v ~
It	is	obvious	that the pollution is getting worse.

(…은) / ~이다 / 명백한 / 오염이 더 악화되고 있다는 것은

Standard Sentences

01 It is usual in this world for the weak to become the victim of the strong.
(…은) 이 세상에서 흔하다 / 약자가 강자의 희생양이 되는 것은

- 가주어 It은 명사구 진주어 to become 이하를 대신하며, to become 앞의 for the weak는 to부정사의 의미상 주어이다.
- 「the + 형용사」는 대개 '~한 사람들'의 뜻을 나타낸다. *ex.* the poor = poor people

victim 희생양; 희생

02 It is a common superstition that a black cat crossing your path is bad
(…은) 흔한 미신이다 / 검은 고양이가 / [당신의 길을 가로지르는] / 불운이라는
luck.
것은

- 가주어 It은 명사절 진주어 that ~ luck을 대신한다.
- a black cat은 형용사구 crossing your path의 수식을 받는다.

superstition 미신
path 길

A **03** It's fine to celebrate success but it is more important to heed the lessons
(…은) 좋다 / 성공을 축하하는 것은 / 그러나 (…은) 더 중요하다 / 실패의 교훈에 주의를 기울이는 것은
of failure. *Bill Gates*

- 첫 번째 가주어 It은 to celebrate success를 대신하며, 두 번째 가주어 it은 to heed ~ 이하를 대신한다.

heed ~에 주의를 기울이다

04 It's no use locking the stable door after the horse has bolted. *Irish Proverb*
(…은) 소용없다 / 마구간 문을 잠그는 것은 / 말이 달아난 후에

- 가주어 It은 locking ~ bolted를 대신한다. ➡ unit 59

stable 마구간, 외양간
bolt 달아나다, 도망치다

05 It matters not what someone is born, but what they grow to be.
(…이) 중요하다 / 누군가가 어떤 사람으로 태어나는지가 아니라 / 그들이 자라서 어떤 사람이 되는지가
the novel <Harry Potter and the Goblet of Fire>

- 가주어 It은 명사절 진주어 what~ born과 what ~ to be를 대신한다.
- not A but B: A가 아니라 B

matter 중요하다, 문제가 되다; 문제, 일

B **06** It is the essence of scientific thinking to propose alternative ideas and then to
(…은) 과학적 사고의 본질이다 / 대안을 제시하는 것 / 그리고 그것을

essence 본질, 정수
alternative 대신하는

test them against existing concepts.
실험하는 것은 / 기존의 개념과 비교하여

■ 가주어 It은 등위접속사 and로 연결된 to propose ~ 와 to test ~를 대신한다.

07 It was very careless of her to leave the medicine where the children could
(…은) 아주 조심성이 없었다 / 그녀가 그 약을 둔 것은 / 아이들이 그것을 집을 수 있는 곳에

careless 조심성이 없는

reach it.

■ It is[was] 다음에 사람의 성질이나 태도를 나타내는 형용사(good, kind, nice, clever, foolish, stupid, careful, careless, polite, rude 등)가 오면 to부정사의 의미상 주어를 「of + (대)명사」로 나타낸다.

모의 **08** With all the passion for being slim, it is no wonder that many people view
날씬해지고 싶은 모든 열정으로 / (…은) 놀랄 일이 아니다 / 많은 사람들이 자신의 몸에 있는 눈에

view A as B A를 B로 여기다
〔간주하다〕
get rid of ~을 제거하다

any amount of visible fat on the body as something to get rid of.
띄는 지방이 얼마만큼이든 여기는 것은 / 제거해야 할 무언가로

■ 가주어 It은 that 이하의 명사절을 대신한다.
— to get rid of는 something을 수식하는 형용사구이다.

모의 **09** It's amazing how much more you learn when you pause, quiet your mind,
(…은) 놀랍다 / 얼마나 더 많이 당신이 배우는가 / 당신이 잠시 멈춰서, 당신의 마음을 진정시키고,

pause 잠시 멈추다
quiet 진정시키다, 안심시키다

and listen to what others say.
다른 사람들이 말하는 것을 들을 때

■ 가주어 It은 명사절 진주어 how 이하를 대신한다.
— 진주어 안의 when절에는 동사 pause, quiet, listen to가 등위접속사 and로 병렬 연결되어 있다.

C **10** Grown-ups never understand anything by themselves, and it is tiresome for
어른들은 결코 스스로 아무것도 이해하지 못한다 / 그리고 (…은) 따분하다 /

tiresome 따분한

children to be always and forever explaining things to them. *the novel <The Little Prince>*
아이들이 늘 그리고 끊임없이 상황을 그들에게 설명하고 있는 것은

풀이 어른들에게 상황을 늘 설명해야 하는 행위가 따분하다는 것이며, 사람의 성질이나 태도를 나타내는 형용사가 온 것이 아니므로 「for + O」의 형태로 의미상의 주어를 나타내는 것이 적절하다.
— to be 뒤의 always and forever는 삽입된 부사구로 be explaining을 수식한다.

11 With today's latest virtual reality technologies, it is now possible for
오늘날의 최신 가상현실 기술로 / (…은) 이제 가능하다 /

latest 최신의
virtual reality 가상현실

designers to create real-world situations in a digital environment.
설계자들이 디지털 환경에서 실제 세계의 상황을 만들어내는 것은

풀이 가주어 it과 for designers라는 의미상의 주어가 쓰였으므로, 뒤에 진주어가 있음을 알 수 있다. 진주어 역할을 할 수 있는 것은 동사원형이 아닌 명사구, 명사절이므로 to create가 적절하다.

12 It's not yet clear whether the Prime Minister's resignation offer is a serious
(…은) 아직 분명하지 않다 / 그 수상의 사직 의사가 진지한 것인지

prime minister 수상, 국무총리
resignation 사직, 사임
offer 의사(표시), 제안
tactical 전술의, 전략적인
move 조치; 이동

one, or whether it's simply a tactical move.
/ 아니면 단순히 전술적인 조치인지는

풀이 가주어 it이 대신하는 진주어로 쓰일 명사절을 이끄는 접속사의 자리이며, that과 whether 둘 다 명사절을 이끌어 주어 역할을 할 수 있으므로 이어지는 문맥을 살펴보아야 한다. that 뒤에는 확실한 내용이 오고 whether 뒤에는 불확실한 내용이 오는데, 불확실한 추측의 내용이 이어지므로 whether가 적절하다.

unit 04
주어 + 형용사구

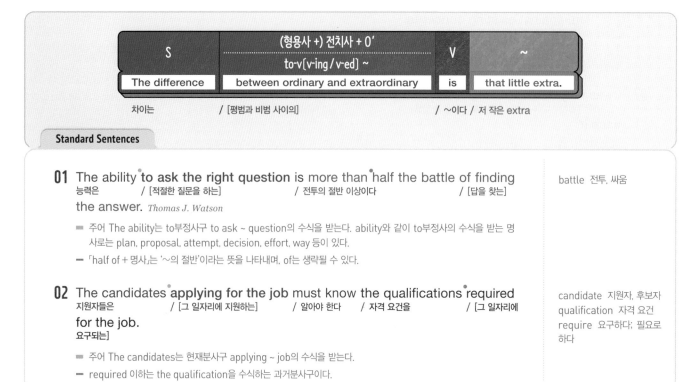

| S | (형용사 +) 전치사 + O'
to-v[v-ing / v-ed] ~ | V | ~ |
|---|---|---|---|
| The difference | between ordinary and extraordinary | is | that little extra. |
| 차이는 | / [평범과 비범 사이의] | / ~이다 / | 저 작은 extra |

Standard Sentences

01 The ability ˙to ask the right question is more than ˙half the battle of finding
능력은 / [적절한 질문을 하는] / 전투의 절반 이상이다 / [답을 찾는]
the answer. *Thomas J. Watson*

- 주어 The ability는 to부정사구 to ask ~ question의 수식을 받는다. ability와 같이 to부정사의 수식을 받는 명사로는 plan, proposal, attempt, decision, effort, way 등이 있다.
- 「half of + 명사」는 '~의 절반'이라는 뜻을 나타내며, of는 생략될 수 있다.

battle 전투, 싸움

02 The candidates ˙applying for the job must know the qualifications ˙required
지원자들은 / [그 일자리에 지원하는] / 알아야 한다 / 자격 요건을 / [그 일자리에
for the job.
요구되는]

- 주어 The candidates는 현재분사구 applying ~ job의 수식을 받는다.
- required 이하는 the qualification을 수식하는 과거분사구이다.

candidate 지원자, 후보자
qualification 자격 요건
require 요구하다; 필요로
하다

A 03 The simple act ˙of typing a few words into a search engine will virtually
[모에] 간단한 행위는 / [몇 개의 단어를 검색 엔진에 입력하는] / 거의 당장
instantaneously produce links ˙related to the topic at hand.
만들어낼 것이다 / 그 주제와 관련된 링크를 / 바로 쓸 수 있도록

- 주어 The simple act는 전치사구 of ~ engine의 수식을 받는다.
- 과거분사구 related ~ topic은 produce의 목적어인 links를 수식한다.

virtually 거의
instantaneously 바로, 당장
at hand 바로 쓸 수 있도록

04 The only way ˙to understand a word fully is ˙to see it in use in many contexts.
유일한 방법은 / [한 단어를 완전히 이해하는] / 그것이 많은 문맥 속에서 사용되는 것을 보는 것이다

- 주어 The only way는 to understand a word fully의 수식을 받는다.
- 보어 to see it에서 대명사 it은 a word를 가리킨다.

context 문맥, 맥락

05 The microwaves ˙emitted from mobile phones can interfere with sensitive
극초단파는 / [휴대폰에서 방출되는] / 지장을 줄 수 있다 / 민감한 전자
electronic equipment.
기기에

- 주어 The microwaves는 과거분사구 emitted ~ phones의 수식을 받는다.

microwave 극초단파
emit 방출하다
interfere with ~에 지장을
주다

B **06** An outstanding feature **in the evolution of modern man** is the growth of the
두드러진 특징은 / [현대 인류의 진화에서] / 뇌 크기의 증가이다
size of the brain.

outstanding 두드러진, 눈에
띄는
evolution 진화

➡ 주어 An outstanding feature는 전치사구 in ~ man의 수식을 받는다.

(수능!) **07** Many present efforts **to guard and maintain human progress, to meet**
현재의 많은 노력은 / [인류의 발전을 지키고 유지하려는 / 인간의 요구를
human needs, and to realize human ambitions are simply unsustainable
만족시키려는 / 그리고 인간의 야망을 실현하려는] / 도저히 지속할 수 없다
—in both rich and poor nations.
—부유한 국가와 가난한 국가 모두에서

simply (부정문) 도저히, 결코
unsustainable 지속할 수 없는

➡ 주어 Many present efforts는 등위접속사 and로 이어진 세 개의 to부정사구 to guard ~, to meet ~, and to
realize ~ ambitions의 수식을 받는다.

08 Scientists **studying genes in yeast cells** recently found a chemical **that**
과학자들은 / [효모 세포 속의 유전자를 연구하는] / 최근에 화학물질을 발견했다 /
seems to work with a longevity gene to increase the yeast cell's lifespan.
[장수 유전자와 함께 작동하는 것처럼 보이는 / 효모 세포의 수명을 늘리기 위해서]

yeast 효모
longevity 장수
lifespan 수명

➡ 주어 Scientists는 현재분사구 studying ~ cells의 수식을 받는다.
➖ that 이하는 a chemical을 수식하는 주격 관계대명사절이다.

09 Foreign, or alien, species **introduced accidentally or intentionally into new**
외부에서 온, 즉 외래종은 / [우연히 또는 의도적으로 새로운 영역에 유입된]
territories often do well in their new homes because conditions may be
/ 종종 그들의 새로운 서식지에서 잘 생육한다 / 여건이 아마 매우 유리하기
highly favorable to their growth and reproduction.
때문에 / 그들의 성장과 번식에

alien 외래의
introduced 도입하다; 소개하다
territory 영역, 지역
condition 여건; 환경
favorable 유리한; 호의적인

➡ 주어 Foreign, or alien, species는 과거분사구 introduced ~ territories의 수식을 받는다.

C **10** Speculations **about the meaning and purpose of prehistoric art** rely heavily
(수능!) 고찰은 / [선사시대 예술의 의미와 목적에 대한] / 굉장히 의존한다
on analogies **drawn with modern-day hunter-gatherer societies.**
/ 유사성에 / [현대의 수렵 채집 사회에서 끌어낸]

speculation 고찰, 추측
analogy 유사성; 비유
hunter-gatherer 수렵 채집

풀이 주어가 전치사구 about ~ art의 수식을 받는 Speculations이므로 복수 동사 rely가 적절하다.
➖ drawn 이하는 analogies를 수식하는 과거분사구이다.

11 The best way **to protect your computer from viruses and spyware** is to
최상의 방법은 / [당신의 컴퓨터를 바이러스와 스파이웨어로부터 보호하기 위한] /
install a recommended anti-virus program.
권장되는 안티바이러스 프로그램을 설치하는 것이다

spyware 스파이웨어(인터넷
사용자를 염탐하는 악성 소프트
웨어 프로그램)
install 설치하다

풀이 주어가 to부정사구 to protect ~ spyware의 수식을 받는 The best way이므로 단수 동사 is가 적절하다.

12 The carbon dioxide **given off when coal and oil are burned** is accumulating
이산화탄소는 / [배출되는 / 석탄과 석유가 연소될 때] / 대기 중에 축적되고 있다
in the atmosphere and causing temperatures to rise.
/ 그리고 기온이 상승하도록 초래하고 (있다)

give off ~을 배출하다, 발산
하다
accumulate 축적하다
atmosphere 대기; 분위기

풀이 주어가 과거분사구 given ~ burned의 수식을 받는 The carbon dioxide이므로 단수 동사 is가 적절하다.

unit 05
주어 + 형용사절 1

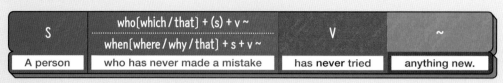

S	who[which / that] + (s) + v ~ when[where / why / that] + s + v ~	V	~
A person	who has never made a mistake	has never tried	anything new.

사람은 / [한 번도 실수를 한 적이 없는] / 결코 해본 적이 없는 것이다 / 새로운 어떤 것을

Standard Sentences

01 Species which have not been able to survive in changing living conditions
종들은 / [생존할 수 없었던 / 변화하는 생활 환경에서]
have become extinct.
/ 멸종되어왔다

■ 주어 Species는 관계대명사 which가 이끄는 절 which ~ conditions의 수식을 받는다.

species (단수·복수 동형) 종
survive 생존하다
extinct 멸종된

02 The reason why we have two ears and only one mouth is that we may
이유는 / [우리가 두 개의 귀와 오직 하나의 입을 가지고 있는] / ~이다 / 우리가 더 많이
listen more and talk less.
듣고 더 적게 말하려는 것

■ 주어 The reason은 관계부사 why가 이끄는 절 why ~ mouth의 수식을 받는다.
— that 이하는 보어 역할을 하는 명사절이다. **unit 16**

A 03 The creativity that children possess needs to be cultivated throughout their
수능 창의성은 / [아이들이 지닌] / 계발될 필요가 있다 / 그들의 성장 과정 동안
development.

■ 주어 The creativity는 관계대명사 that이 이끄는 절 that children possess의 수식을 받는다.
— 창의성은 계발되는 대상이므로 수동의 의미를 나타내기 위해 to부정사의 수동태 「to be v-ed」의 형태로 쓰였다.

possess 소유하다
cultivate 계발하다; 경작하다
throughout ~ 동안, ~ 내내

모의 04 A person who works on an assembly line is well aware of the efficiency
사람은 / [조립 라인에서 일하는] / 잘 알고 있다 / 효율성에 대해
that can be gained through repetition.
/ [반복을 통해 얻어질 수 있는]

■ 주어 A person은 관계대명사 who가 이끄는 절 who ~ line의 수식을 받는다.
— that 이하는 the efficiency를 수식하는 형용사절이다.

assembly line (공장의 대량 생산) 조립 라인; 일관된 작업 공정
be aware of ~을 알다

05 The one area where the Internet could be considered to be an aid to thinking
하나의 영역은 / [인터넷이 사고에 도움이 된다고 여겨질 수 있는]
is the rapid procurement of new information.
/ 새로운 정보의 신속한 입수이다

■ 주어 The one area는 관계부사 where가 이끄는 절 where ~ thinking의 수식을 받는다.
— aid 뒤의 to는 전치사이며, 목적어로 동명사 thinking이 쓰였다.

aid 도움; 돕다
procurement 입수, 확보

B 06 People **who have a high sense of self-efficacy** tend to pursue challenging
_{모의} 사람들은 / [높은 자기 효능감을 가진] / 도전적인 목표를 추구하는 경향이 있다
goals **that may be outside the reach of the average person.**
/ [아마 보통 사람의 도달 범위를 벗어나 있을]

self-efficacy 자기 효능감
pursue 추구하다

- 주어 People은 관계대명사 who가 이끄는 절 who ~ self-efficacy의 수식을 받는다.
- that 이하는 goals를 수식하는 형용사절이다.

07 The idealism **that freed men from most of their ancient fetters** awakened
이상주의는 / [남성들을 고대의 족쇄 대부분으로부터 자유롭게 만든] / 여성들을
women to a realization of their unequal position in society.
일깨웠다 / 사회에서 그들의 불평등한 위치를 자각하도록

idealism 이상주의
fetter 족쇄
awaken A to B A에게 B를 일깨우다[깨닫게 하다]
realization 자각, 인식; 실현

- 주어 The idealism은 관계대명사 that이 이끄는 절 that ~ fetters의 수식을 받는다.

Know More 18세기 계몽주의와 1789년 프랑스 혁명은 여성이 자신의 권리를 자각하게 된 계기가 되었다. 프랑스 혁명은 '모든 인간은 합리적 피조물로서 동일한 기본권을 가진다'고 공표하였고, 이에 등장한 자유주의와 여성주의로 여성은 정치에 참여할 권리 및 생존을 위한 경제적·사회적 권리를 주장하였다.

08 A classroom **where students feel involved and respected** will reduce
교실은 / [학생들이 참여하며 존중받는다고 느끼는] / 훈육의 문제를
discipline issues, increase student motivation, and ultimately enhance
감소시키고 / 학생의 동기 부여를 증가시키고 / 그리고 궁극적으로 학습을 향상시킬 것이다
learning.

involved 참여한; 관련된
discipline 훈육; 징계
ultimately 궁극적으로, 결국
enhance 향상시키다

- 주어 A classroom은 관계부사 where가 이끄는 절 where ~ respected의 수식을 받는다.
- 조동사 will과 이어지는 본동사 reduce, increase, enhance가 등위접속사 and로 병렬 연결되고 있다.

_{모의} 09 The way **that we behave in a given situation** is often influenced by how
방식은 / [우리가 주어진 상황 속에서 행동하는] / 종종 영향을 받는다 / 하나의 가치가
important one value is to us relative to others.
우리에게 얼마나 중요한가에 의해 / 다른 가치들에 비해서

relative to ~에 비하여; ~에 관하여

- 주어 The way는 that이 이끄는 관계부사절 that ~ situation의 수식을 받는다. 명사 way는 관계부사 how와 같이 쓸 수 없으며, 반드시 둘 중 하나를 생략하거나 how 대신 that 또는 in which로 써야 한다.
- 전치사 by의 목적어로 how가 이끄는 명사절이 쓰였으며, how 이하는 간접의문문의 어순 「how + 형용사/부사 + 주어 + 동사 ~」로 쓰였다.

C 10 Someone **who reads only newspapers and books by contemporary**
_{수능} 사람은 / [신문과 현대 작가가 쓴 책들만 읽는]
authors looks to me like a near-sighted person.
/ 나에게는 근시안적인 사람처럼 보인다

contemporary 현대의; 동시대의
near-sighted 근시안적인; 근시안의

- _{풀이} 주어가 관계대명사 who가 이끄는 절의 수식을 받는 Someone이며, 문장 전체의 동사가 필요하므로 단수 동사 looks가 적절하다.

11 The impressions **that a child receives from his environment during the first**
인상은 / [아이가 자신의 환경으로부터 받는] / 인생의 처음 몇 해 동안에]
years of life influence his intellectual development and character very basically.
/ 그의 지적 발달과 성격에 매우 근본적으로 영향을 끼친다

impression 인상

- _{풀이} 주어가 관계대명사 that이 이끄는 절의 수식을 받는 The impressions이므로 복수 동사 influence가 적절하다.

12 The period **when humans began growing crops, raising animals for food,**
기간은 / [인간이 농작물을 재배하고, 식량을 위해 동물을 사육하고, 석기 기술을 사용하기 시작한]
and using stone-tool technology is referred to as Neolithic period.
/ 신석기라고 일컬어진다

refer to A as B A를 B라고 부르다(수동태: A be referred to as B A는 B라고 불려지다)
Neolithic period 신석기

- _{풀이} 주어가 관계부사 when이 이끄는 절의 수식을 받는 The period이므로 단수 동사 is가 적절하다.

주어 + 형용사절 2

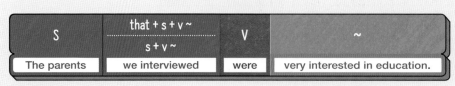

S	that + s + v ~ / s + v ~	V	~
The parents	we interviewed	were	very interested in education.

부모님들은 / [우리가 인터뷰한] / ~였다 / 교육에 아주 관심이 많은

Standard Sentences

01 The fact that a book or publication is popular does not necessarily make
사실이 / [= 어떤 책이나 출판물이 인기가 있다는] / 반드시 만드는 것은 아니다
it of value.
/ 그것을 가치 있게

■ 주어 The fact 다음에 동격의 that절 that ~ popular가 이어지고 있다. **Unit 52**

— not necessarily ~: 반드시 ~인 것은 아니다 (부분 부정) **Unit 58**

publication 출판물, 출판
of value 가치 있는, 귀중한

모의 02 The bodies of flowing ice we call glaciers are the most spectacular of natural
흐르는 얼음 덩어리는 / [우리가 빙하라고 부르는] / 가장 장관을 이루는 것이다 / [자연의 특징 중]
features.

■ 주어 The bodies of flowing ice는 관계사절 we call glaciers의 수식을 받으며, we 앞에는 목적격 관계대명사 which 또는 that이 생략되어 있다.

glacier 빙하
spectacular 장관을 이루는, 극적인
feature 특징

A 03 The rule that nouns form their plural by adding "s" does not apply to the
규칙은 / [= 명사들이 복수형을 만든다는 / 's'를 덧붙임으로써] / 'mouse'라는 단어에는 적용되지
word "mouse."
않는다

■ 주어 The rule 다음에 동격의 that절 that ~ adding 's'가 이어지고 있다.

Know More 캐나다의 인지과학자이자 언어학자인 스티븐 핑커(Steven Pinker)는 우리가 '불규칙' 복수라고 부르는 것들이 사실 '규칙' 복수형이었음을 밝혀냈다. 단어 mouse-mice, man-men과 같은 불규칙 복수형, 그리고 drink-drank와 seek-sought와 같은 불규칙 과거 시제형이라고 부르는 것들은 sink-sank, shrink-shrank / sing-sang, ring-rang / know-knew, grow-grew와 같이 규칙적으로 정리된다. 이렇게 규칙이 발견되는 이유는 현대 영어와 대부분 유럽어의 조상 언어인 원시 인도 유럽어에 하나의 모음을 다른 모음으로 대체해서 과거 시제를 만드는 규칙이 있었기 때문이다. 이 규칙이 적용된 단어들이 현대 영어에 남아 '불규칙'의 형태로 불리게 되었으며, 그 규칙 자체는 사라지게 되었다.

noun 명사
plural 복수형, 복수형의
mouse 쥐 (pl. mice)

모의 04 The first impressions we form about someone often affect our impression
첫 인상은 / [우리가 어떤 사람에 대해 만들어 내는] / 종종 우리의 인상에 영향을 미친다
of subsequent perceptions of that person.
/ [그 사람에 대해 뒤이어 일어나는 인식에 대한]

■ 주어 The first impressions는 관계사절 we ~ someone의 수식을 받으며, we 앞에는 목적격 관계대명사 which 또는 that이 생략되어 있다.

subsequent 뒤이어 일어나는, 다음의
perception 인식, 지각

05 One of the most important reasons we need to send humans to Mars is to
가장 중요한 이유 중의 하나는 / [우리가 화성에 인간을 보낼 필요가 있는] / 밝혀내는
determine whether there ever was or even still is life on Mars.
것이다 / 생명체가 있었는지 또는 아직도 있는지를 / 화성에

■ 주어 One of most important reasons는 관계부사절 we ~ Mars의 수식을 받으며, we 앞에는 관계부사 why가 생략되어 있다.

— whether절 안의 life는 was와 is의 공통 주어이다. **Unit 54**

determine 밝히다, 알아내다; 결정하다, 결심하다

B 06 The announcement ˚that the first stages of human cloning have been
발표는 / [= 인간 복제의 첫 단계가 달성되었다는]
achieved ˚leaves us wondering where it will all end.
/ 우리를 궁금하게 만든다 / 그것이 어디서 완전히 끝날지

> ▬ 주어 The announcement 다음에 동격의 that절 that ~ achieved가 이어지고 있다.
> ▬ leave + O + v-ing: O가 ~한 상태로 계속 있게 만든다[그대로 두다]

announcement 발표, 공고
clone 복제하다

07 The living organisms ˚we now see all have their structure ˚based upon the
살아 있는 유기체들은 / [우리가 지금 보는] / 모두 그들의 구조를 가지고 있다 / [탄소라는 원소에 기반한]
element carbon.

> ▬ 주어 The living organisms는 관계사절 we now see의 수식을 받으며, we 앞에는 목적격 관계대명사 which 또는 that이 생략되어 있다.
> ▬ based 이하는 their structure를 수식하는 과거분사구이다.

organism 유기체
element 원소; 요소
carbon 탄소

(모의) 08 The words ˚you speak to someone may have the potential to make or break
단어들은 / [당신이 누군가에게 말하는] / 그 사람을 만들거나 깨뜨리는 잠재력을 가지고 있을지도 모른다
that person, so ˚it is important ˚to choose words carefully.
/ 따라서 (…은) 중요하다 / 단어들을 신중히 선택하는 것은

> ▬ 주어 The words는 관계사절 you ~ someone의 수식을 받으며, you 앞에는 목적격 관계대명사 which 또는 that이 생략되어 있다.
> ▬ 등위접속사 so가 이끄는 절에서 가주어 it은 to choose 이하를 대신한다. **➔ Unit 03**

potential 잠재력; 잠재적인

(수능!) 09 The way ˚we wish the world to be is how, in the movies, it more often than
방식은 / [우리가 세상이 어떻게 되기를 소망하는] / 영화에서 그것(세상)이 대개 결국 존재하게 되는 방식이다
not winds up being.

> ▬ 주어 The way는 관계부사절 we ~ be의 수식을 받으며, we 앞에는 관계부사 how가 생략되어 있다.

more often than not 대개,
자주
wind up v-ing 결국 ~으로
되다, 끝나다[마무리되다]

C 10 The complaint **that immigrants take people's jobs** is, like similar complaints
(모의) 불평은 / [= 이민자들이 사람들의 일자리를 앗아간다는] / 기술에 관한 비슷한 불평처럼 근거하고 있다
about technology, based on an erroneously static view of the world.
/ 잘못 고정된 세계관에

> **풀이** 주어가 접속사 that이 이끄는 동격절 that ~ jobs의 수식을 받는 The complaint이므로 단수 동사 is가 적절하다.

complaint 불평, 불만
immigrant 이민자
erroneously 잘못되게, 틀리게
static 고정된, 고정적인

(수능!) 11 The seemingly impractical knowledge **we gain from space probes to other**
겉보기에 비현실적인 지식이 / [우리가 얻는 / 다른 세계로 간 우주 탐사기에서]
worlds tells us about our planet and our own role in the scheme of nature.
/ 우리에게 말해준다 / 우리의 행성과 우리의 역할에 대해서 / [자연의 체계 안에서의]

> **풀이** 주어가 목적격 관계대명사 which 또는 that이 생략된 관계사절 we ~ worlds의 수식을 받는 The seemingly impractical knowledge이므로 단수 동사 tells가 적절하다.

seemingly 겉보기에
impractical 비현실적인
space probe 우주 탐사기
scheme 체계; 계획

12 The reason **people give up so quickly** is ˚because they look at ˚how far they
이유는 / [사람들이 그렇게 빨리 포기하는] / 그들이 바라보기 때문이다 / 그들이 여전히 얼마나
still have to go, instead of ˚how far they have come.
멀리 가야 하는지를 / 얼마나 멀리 그들이 왔는지 대신에

> **풀이** 주어가 관계부사 why가 생략된 관계사절 people ~ quickly의 수식을 받는 The reason이므로 단수 동사 is가 적절하다.
> ▬ 여기서 because는 보어로 쓰이는 명사절을 이끌고 있다. 격식을 갖춘 문장에서는 that을 쓴다.
> ▬ how far they still have to go는 전치사 at의 목적어로 쓰인 명사절이고, how far they have come은 전치사 instead of의 목적어로 쓰인 명사절이다.

give up 포기하다

Chapter 01

A **01** *Whatever happens, happens for a reason.*
일어나는 것은 무엇이든지 / 일어난다 / 이유가 있기 때문에

■ Whatever가 이끄는 절이 주어로 쓰였으며, '~하는 것은 무엇이든지'의 의미로 해석한다.

02 *What people eat, when they eat, and how they eat are all patterned by*
사람들이 무엇을 먹는지, 그들이 언제 먹는지, 그리고 그들이 어떻게 먹는지는 / 모두 양식이 형성된다 /
culture.
문화에 의해서

■ 의문사 what, when, how가 이끄는 세 개의 명사절이 주어 역할을 하며, 등위접속사 and로 병렬 연결되어 있다.

pattern 양식[패턴]을 형성시키다

03 *Being able to predict how other people might feel, act, or react is a skill*
예측할 수 있는 것은 / 다른 사람들이 어떻게 느끼고, 행동하고, 반응할지를 / 기술이다
that helps us build better relationships.
/ [우리가 더 나은 관계를 형성하도록 돕는]

■ 동명사 Being이 이끄는 명사구 Being ~ react가 주어가 쓰였다.
― 의문사 how가 이끄는 명사절 how ~ react가 predict의 목적어로 쓰였다.

(모의) **04** *With a bit of unbiased examination of our motives, it is hard to deny that*
우리의 동기에 대해 좀 공정한 조사를 해 보면 / (…은) 어렵다 / 부인하는 것은
we have strong bias toward our individual interests.
/ 우리가 개인적인 이익을 향한 강한 성향을 가지고 있다는 것을

■ 가주어 it은 to deny 이하를 대신한다.
― deny는 that이 이끄는 명사절을 목적어로 가지고 있다.

unbiased 공정한, 편견이 없는
examination 조사; 시험
bias 성향; 편견

B **05** *Learning how to persuade people will earn you the support and respect of*
사람들을 설득하는 법을 배우는 것은 / 얻게 할 것이다 / 당신에게 / 지지와 존경을 [당신의 고객, 상사,
your customers, bosses, co-workers, colleagues and friends.
업무 협력자, 동료, 그리고 친구들의]

풀이 동사 will earn의 주어가 필요하므로 주어의 역할을 할 수 있는 동명사 Learning이 적절하다.

earn 얻게 하다, 가져오다
co-worker 업무 협력자
colleague (함께 일하는) 동료

06 *In nature, there is no such thing as waste. What dies or becomes useless*
자연에는 / 쓰레기와 같은 것은 없다 죽거나 쓸모없게 되는 것은
in one part of an ecosystem nourishes another part.
/ 생태계의 한 부분에서 / 다른 부분에 영양분을 공급한다

풀이 What이 이끄는 명사절 what ~ an ecosystem이 주어이며, 문장의 동사가 필요하므로 nourishes가 적절하다.

ecosystem 생태계
nourish 영양분을 공급하다

07 *Physical and physiological features or behaviors of an organism that once*
한 유기체의 물리적, 생리적 특징이나 행동은 / [예전에
may have contributed to its reproductive success but no longer do so
그 유기체의 번식 성공에 기여했을 수도 있는 / 그러나 더 이상은 그렇지 않은]
become susceptible to elimination by natural selection.
/ 자연 선택에 의해 제거되기 쉬워진다

풀이 주어가 that이 이끄는 형용사절 that ~ do so의 수식을 받는 Physical and physiological features or behaviors이므로 복수 동사 become이 적절하다.

physiological 생리적인
contribute 기여하다
reproductive 번식의
susceptible to ~되기 쉬운
elimination 제거
natural selection 자연 선택

C **08** Learning science through inquiry is a primary principle in education today.
탐구를 통해 과학을 배우는 것은 / 주된 원칙이다 / 오늘날 교육에서

inquiry 탐구; 조사
primary 주된, 주요한

> **풀이** '~하는 것'이라는 의미로 주어 역할을 하는 동명사구 Learning science 뒤에 이를 수식하는 전치사구 through inquiry가 오며, 이어 동사 is 다음에 보어 a primary principle이 오는 것이 자연스럽다.

09 It is difficult to see ourselves through the lenses of others.
(…은) 어렵다 / 다른 사람들의 눈으로 우리 자신을 보는 것은

> **풀이** 가주어 It이 쓰였으며 be동사 뒤에 보어 difficult가 오며, 이어 진주어 to see 이하를 쓴다. 진주어 to see 이하에서 전치사구 through ~ others는 see ourselves를 수식하는 부사이므로 문장의 끝에 오는 것이 적절하다.

(Up!) **10** The belly fat disorder caused by lack of physical activity leads to
복부 지방 질환은 / [신체 활동의 부족으로 인한] / 우리 신체의
a decreased rate of metabolism in our body.
신진대사율의 감소로 이어진다

belly fat 복부 지방
disorder (가벼운) 질환
metabolism 신진대사

> **풀이** '복부 지방 질환'에 해당하는 명사구 The belly fat disorder를 주어로 먼저 쓴다. '~으로 인한'이라는 의미는 caused by ~로 나타내며, by 뒤에는 원인인 lack of physical activity가 이어지는 것이 자연스럽다.

D **11** What traditional entertainment always promised was to transport us from
전통적인 오락이 항상 약속한 것은 / 우리를 이동시켜 주는 것이었다 /
our daily problems, to enable us to escape from the struggles of life.
우리의 일상적인 문제들로부터 / 즉 우리가 삶의 고투로부터 벗어날 수 있게 해주는 것

entertainment 오락, 연예
transport 이동시키다, 옮기다
struggle 투쟁, 분투

> ➡ What이 이끄는 명사절이 문장 전체의 주어로 쓰였다.
> ➡ 보어인 to transport ~ problems와 to enable ~ life는 콤마(,)로 연결된 동격 관계이다. **➡ Unit 52**

12 The discrepancy between the understanding of the writer and that of the
불일치는 / [작가의 이해와 독자의 이해 사이의]
audience is the single greatest impediment to accurate communication.
/ 정확한 의사소통에 대한 유일한 가장 큰 장애물이다

discrepancy 불일치, 차이
audience 독자; 청중
impediment 장애물
accurate 정확한

> ➡ 주어 The discrepancy는 전치사구 between ~ audience의 수식을 받는다.
> ➡ 지시대명사 that은 앞에 나온 the understanding을 가리킨다.

(모의) **13** Any scientist who announces a so-called discovery at a press conference
과학자는 누구든지 / [기자 회견에서 소위 발견을 발표하는
without first permitting expert reviewers to examine his or her claims is
/ 먼저 전문 검토자들이 그 사람의 주장을 검토하도록 허용하지 않고] /
automatically castigated as a publicity seeker.
자동적으로 혹평된다 / 명성을 쫓는 사람이라고

so-called 소위, 이른바
press conference 기자 회견
examine 검토하다, 조사하다
claim 주장; 요구
castigate 혹평하다; 징계하다
publicity 명성, 평판; 홍보
theoretical 이론적인

> ➡ 주어 Any scientist는 관계대명사 who가 이끄는 절의 수식을 받는다.

Chapter

02

동사 구문

- unit 07   전치사구와 짝을 이루는 동사 구문
- unit 08   조동사 구문
- unit 09   수동태 구문

■ 본격적인 구문 학습에 앞서, 각 유닛별 주요 단어를 확인하세요.

Unit 07

- ☐ ups and downs 기복, (길의) 오르내림
- ☐ generation 세대; 생성
- ☐ collect on 징수하다
- ☐ debt 빚
- ☐ competent 유능한
- ☐ caring 배려하는, 돌보는

- ☐ cherish (마음속에) 품다, 간직하다
- ☐ perceive 인지하다, 감지하다
- ☐ guilty 유죄인
- ☐ innocent 무죄인
- ☐ mental 정신적인
- ☐ attitude 태도
- ☐ extraordinary 비상한, 놀라운

- ☐ enhance 향상시키다
- ☐ associate 연상하다
- ☐ photographic (사진처럼) 선명한, 생생한
- ☐ self-worth 자아 존중감, 자부심
- ☐ tear apart 헐뜯다
- ☐ superior 우월한

Unit 08

- ☐ faulty 결함이 있는; 그릇된
- ☐ come through 전해지다, 통하다
- ☐ condemn 책망하다, 비난하다
- ☐ defeatist 패배주의적인
- ☐ harp on ~을 되뇌다
- ☐ resist 참다, 삼가다
- ☐ suspect 용의자

- ☐ commit a crime 범죄를 저지르다
- ☐ murder 살인
- ☐ backwards 거꾸로, 반대 방향으로
- ☐ content 만족시키다
- ☐ pen 가두다, 감금하다
- ☐ peak 최고점, 절정
- ☐ literature 문학

- ☐ value 평가하다
- ☐ compact 조밀한
- ☐ state 상태
- ☐ epidemic 전염병
- ☐ claim (목숨을) 앗아가다
- ☐ authority (pl.) 당국
- ☐ drift 떠돌다, 표류하다

Unit 09

- ☐ connect 연결하다
- ☐ neuron 뉴런, 신경세포
- ☐ solar 태양의
- ☐ alternative 대안
- ☐ rate 속도; 비율
- ☐ lumber 목재
- ☐ pasture land 목초지

- ☐ volcano 화산
- ☐ emit 내뿜다, 방출하다
- ☐ surface 표면
- ☐ extract 추출하다, 뽑다
- ☐ trigger 촉발하다
- ☐ sociability 사교성
- ☐ aggression 공격성

- ☐ stimulate 자극하다
- ☐ suppress 억압하다
- ☐ alter 변경하다, 바꾸다
- ☐ characterize 규정하다, 특징짓다
- ☐ judge 판단하다
- ☐ confirm 입증하다, 확인하다
- ☐ theory 이론

전치사구와 짝을 이루는 동사구문

S	V	O	전치사 + O'
We	regard	technology	as our extended body.

우리는 / 여긴다 / 기술을 / 우리의 확장된 신체로서

Standard Sentences

모예 01 Many experts in childhood development think of play **as the "work of**
많은 아동기 발달 전문가들은 / 놀이를 여긴다 / '아이들의 일로
children."

■ think of A as B: A를 B로 여기다

expert 전문가
development 발달, 발전

모예 02 Pride prevents individuals **from experiencing their true value or the true**
자만심은 개인들을 막는다 / 자신들의 참된 가치 또는 다른 사람들의 참된 가치를 경험하는 것으로부터
value of others.

■ prevent A from v-ing: A가 ~하는 것을 막다(하지 못하게 하다)

pride 자만심
individual 개인; 개인적인

A 03 We can compare life **to a roller coaster** because it has ups and downs, but
우리는 인생을 비유할 수 있다 / 롤러코스터에 / 왜냐하면 그것은 기복이 있기 때문에 / 그러나
it's your choice to scream or enjoy the ride.
(…은) 당신의 선택이다 / 소리를 지르거나 타는 것을 즐기는 것은

■ compare A to B: A를 B에 비유하다 / 수동태로 쓰일 때는 '비교하다'의 의미로도 쓰인다.
— 첫 번째 it은 life를 가리키는 대명사이고, 두 번째 it은 to scream 이하를 대신하는 가주어이다.

ups and downs 기복, (길의)
오르내림
scream 소리치다, 비명을 지르다

수능 04 Future generations may blame us **for our wasteful ways,** but they can never
미래 세대는 우리를 비난할지도 모른다 / 우리의 낭비하는 방식에 대해 / 그러나 그들은 결코 징수할
collect on our debt to them.
수 없다 / 그들에 대한 우리의 빚을

■ blame A for B: A를 B에 대해 비난하다

generation 세대; 생성
wasteful 낭비하는
collect on 징수하다; 모으다
debt 빚

05 Never deprive someone **of hope;** it might be all they have.
결코 어떤 사람에게서 희망을 빼앗지 마라 / 그것은 전부일지도 모른다 / [그들이 가진]

■ deprive A of B: A에게서 B를 빼앗다
— all 다음에 목적격 관계대명사 that이 생략되었다.

B 06 The competent, confident, and caring young adults **saw** themselves **as the**
[모의] 유능하고, 자신감 있고, 배려심이 있는 젊은이들은 자기 자신을 여겼다   / 자기
masters of their own fate and **viewed** negative events not **as threats** but
스스로의 운명의 주인으로   / 그리고 부정적인 사건들을 여겼다   / 위협이 아니라   / 도전과
as challenges and even opportunities.
심지어는 기회로

■ see[view] A as B: A를 B로 여기다

competent 유능한
caring 배려하는, 돌보는
fate 운명

---

07 Movies **provide** us **with the happy endings and the just solutions that we**
영화는 우리에게 제공한다   / 행복한 결말과 올바른 해결책을   / [우리가
cherish in our hearts.
우리의 마음속에 품고 있는]

■ provide A with B: A에게 B를 제공하다 (= provide B for[to] A)

cherish (마음속에) 품다, 간직
하다; 소중히 하다

---

08 If you feel threatened every time a perceived rival does well, **remind** yourself
만약 당신이 위협받는다고 느낀다면   / 인지된 경쟁 상대가 잘할 때마다   / 스스로에게 상기시켜라
of your own strengths and successes.
/ 당신 자신의 강점과 성공한 것들을

■ remind A of B: A에게 B를 상기시키다

threatened 위협받는
perceive 인지하다, 감지하다
strength 강점; 힘

---

09 Throughout history there have been efforts to **distinguish** the guilty from
역사를 통틀어   / 노력이 있어왔다   / [유죄인 사람들을 무죄인 사람들과 구별하는
the innocent and to **tell** the liars from **the truthful.**
/ 그리고 / 거짓말쟁이들을 진실된 사람들과 구별하는]

■ distinguish[tell] A from B: A를 B와 구별하다
― to distinguish ~ truthful은 efforts를 수식하는 형용사구이다.
― 「the + 형용사」는 '~한 사람들'을 의미한다. the guilty = guilty people, the truthful = truthful people

throughout ~동안 내내, ~을
통해서
guilty 유죄인 (↔ innocent
무죄인)

C 10 Nothing can **stop** the man with the right mental attitude **from achieving his**
어떤 것도 막을 수 없다   [올바른 정신적 태도를 가진 사람을]   / 그의 목표를 성취하는 것으로부터
goal; nothing on earth can help the man with the wrong mental attitude.
/ 지구상의 어떠한 것도 도울 수 없다   / 사람을   / [잘못된 정신적 태도를 가진]   *Thomas Jefferson*

풀이 stop A from v-ing: A가 ~하는 것을 막다(하지 못하게 하다)

mental 정신적인, 정신의
attitude 태도
achieve 성취하다

---

11 Most scientists **attribute** extraordinary memory performance **to an enhanced**
[모의] 대부분의 과학자들은 비상한 기억력을 덕분으로 여긴다   / 향상된 능력의
ability to associate or organize the information to be memorized, rather
/ [기억될 정보를 연상하거나 조직화하는]   / 사진처럼
than true photographic memory.
선명한 진정한 기억력이라기보다는

풀이 attribute A to B: A를 B의 덕분(탓)으로 여기다
- -
― to associate ~ memorized는 ability를 수식하는 형용사구이다.

extraordinary 비상한, 놀라운
enhance 향상시키다
associate 연상하다; 관련시키다
photographic (사진처럼) 선
명한, 생생한

---

12 When individuals have a true sense of self-worth, they do not need to
[모의] 개인들이 참된 의미의 자아 존중감을 가질 때   / 그들은 필요가 없다   / 스스로를
compare themselves **with others,** to tear others apart or feel superior.
타인들과 비교하거나   / 타인들을 헐뜯거나   / 우월하다고 느낄

풀이 compare A with B: A를 B와 비교하다

self-worth 자아 존중감, 자부심
tear apart 헐뜯다; 찢어놓다
superior 우월한

unit 08
조동사 구문

S	조동사 + ⓥ	~	
We	should have booked	our flight tickets	earlier.

우리는 / 예약했어야 했다 / 우리의 비행기 표를 / 더 일찍

Standard Sentences

01 You **shouldn't have driven** that car with the faulty brakes. You **might have**
당신은 그 차를 운전하지 말았어야 했다 / [브레이크에 결함이 있는] 당신은 심각한 사고를
had a serious accident.
당했을지도 모른다

■ should not have v-ed: ~하지 말았어야 했는데 (했다) / may[might] have v-ed: ~했을지도 모른다

faulty 결함이 있는; 그릇된
serious 심각한

02 I **would rather walk** with a friend in the dark, **than** alone in the light.
나는 차라리 걷겠다 / 어둠 속에서 친구와 함께 / 빛 속에서 혼자 걷느니

■ would rather A than B: B하느니 차라리 A하겠다(하고 싶다)
— than 다음에 동사 walk가 생략되었다.

🅐 03 I was **never** top of the class at school, but my classmates **must have seen**
나는 결코 학창 시절에 학급 수석이 아니었다 / 그러나 나의 급우들은 내게서 잠재력을 봤음에 틀림없다
potential in me, because my nickname was "Einstein." *Stephen Hawking*
/ 왜냐하면 나의 별명은 '아인슈타인'이었으니까

■ must have v-ed: ~했음에 틀림없다

potential 잠재력; 잠재적인

04 One's true feelings **cannot but come through** in **what** one says and does.
사람의 진정한 감정은 전해지지 않을 수 없다 / 사람이 말하고 행하는 것 속에

■ cannot but + ⓥ: ~하지 않을 수 없다 (= cannot help v-ing)
— what은 문맥에 따라 '무엇' 또는 '~하는 것'으로 해석한다.

come through 전해지다, 통하다

05 A man **may well be condemned,** not for doing something, but for doing
사람은 아마 책망 받을 것이다 / 어떤 일을 해서가 아니라 / 아무것도 하지 않기
nothing. *William Barclay*
때문에

■ may well + ⓥ: 아마 ~일 것이다, ~하는 것은 당연하다
— not A but B: A가 아니라 B / A와 B는 for가 이끄는 전치사구가 왔다.

condemn 책망하다, 비난하다

B **06** It's defeatist to harp on what **might have been, and yet,** it's hard to resist
(…은) 패배주의적이다 / 무슨 일이 있었을지도 모른다고 되뇌는 것은 / 그렇다 하더라도 (…은) 어렵다 / 무슨 일이
considering what **might have been.**
있었을지도 모른다고 생각하는 것을 참는 것은

defeatist 패배주의적인, 패배주의자의
harp on ~을 되뇌다
resist 참다, 삼가다

- may(might) have v-ed: ~했을지도 모른다
- It(it)은 가주어이고, to harp ~ have been, to resist ~ have been이 각각 진주어로 쓰였다.

07 The suspect **can't have committed** the crime as he was in another country
그 용의자가 그 범죄를 저질렀을 리가 없다 / 그가 다른 나라에 있었기 때문에
at the moment of the murder.
/ 살인의 순간에

suspect 용의자, 혐의자
commit a crime 범죄를 저지르다
murder 살인

- cannot have v-ed: ~했을 리가 없다

08 You **might as well expect rivers** to run backwards **as any man born free to**
당신은 강이 거꾸로 흐르는 것을 기대하는 것이 나을 것이다 / 자유롭게 태어난 어떤 사람이 가두어진
be contented penned up. *Chief Joseph*
채로 만족하는 것을 기대하느니

backwards 거꾸로, 반대 방향으로
content 만족시키다
pen 가두다, 감금하다

- may(might) as well A as B: B하느니 A하는 게 낫다
- as 다음의 「(expect) + O + to-v」 구문에서 expect가 생략되었으며, 목적어 any man은 뒤에 온 born free의 수식을 받는다.

09 *The Brothers Karamazov*, one of the peaks in the literature of the world, **can**
「카라마조프가의 형제들」은 / 세계 문학의 최고봉 중의 하나인 / 아무리
hardly be valued too highly. *Sigmund Freud*
높이 평가되어도 지나치지 않다

peak 최고점, 절정
literature 문학
value 평가하다

- cannot(can hardly) + ⓥ + too: 아무리 ~해도 지나치지 않다

C **10** The universe **must have originated from a more compact state** that we call
우주는 생겨났음에 틀림없다 / 더 조밀한 어떤 상태로부터 / [우리가 빅뱅이라고
the Big Bang.
부르는]

originate 생기다, 유래하다
compact 조밀한, 빽빽한
state 상태

- **풀이** '~했음에 틀림없다'라는 과거의 일에 대한 확실한 추측의 의미가 되도록 「must have v-ed」가 적절하다.
- that ~ Big Bang은 state를 수식하는 형용사절이다.

11 When the epidemic broke out, it claimed many lives. The authorities **ought**
그 전염병이 발생했을 때 / 그것은 많은 생명을 앗아갔다 당국이 예방조치를 취했어야 했다
to have taken precautions to prevent the epidemic.
/ 그 전염병을 예방하기 위해

epidemic 전염병
break out 발생하다
claim (목숨을) 앗아가다, 빼앗다
authority (pl.) 당국
precaution 예방조치

- **풀이** '~했어야 했는데 (하지 못했다)'라는 과거에 대한 후회의 뜻이 되도록 「ought to have v-ed」가 적절하다.

12 I **would rather** be a ghost, drifting by your side as a condemned soul, **than**
나는 차라리 유령이 되고 싶다 / 당신 곁을 떠돌면서 / 저주받은 영혼으로서 /
enter heaven without you. *the movie <Crouching Tiger, Hidden Dragon 와호장룡>*
당신이 없는 천국에 들어가느니

drift 떠돌다, 표류하다
condemned 저주받은; 비난받은

- **풀이** 'B하느니 차라리 A하고 싶다'를 뜻하는 「would rather A than B」에서 A와 B에는 둘 다 동사원형이 와야 하므로 enter가 적절하다.
- 현재분사 drifting이 이끄는 분사구문이 삽입되었으며, '~하면서'로 해석한다. **⊙ Unit 32**

수동태 구문

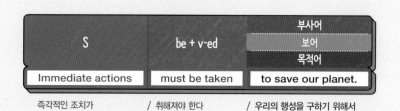

S	be + v-ed	부사어
		보어
		목적어
Immediate actions	must be taken	to save our planet.
즉각적인 조치가	/ 취해져야 한다	/ 우리의 행성을 구하기 위해서

Standard Sentences

01 We are all now connected by the Internet, like neurons in a giant brain.
우리는 모두 지금 연결되어 있다 / 인터넷에 의해 / 마치 거대한 뇌 속의 뉴런들처럼 *Stephen Hawking*

■ 수동태 문장은 「be동사 + v-ed」 형태로 쓰인다.

connect 연결하다
neuron 뉴런, 신경세포

02 Solar power and wind power are considered alternatives to fossil-
태양 에너지와 풍력은 / 대안으로 여겨진다 / [화석 연료
fuel-based energy generation.
기반의 에너지 생성에 대한]

■ 「동사 + 목적어 + 목적격보어(명사 / 형용사)」의 5형식 문장이 수동태로 바뀌면 「be동사 + v-ed + 명사(형용사)」의 2형식 문장이 되며, 과거분사 뒤의 명사나 형용사는 주어의 상태를 보충 설명해 주는 보어 역할을 한다.

solar 태양의
alternative 대안
fossil fuel 화석 연료
generation 생성, 발전

A 03 The best and most beautiful things in the world cannot be seen or even
세상에서 가장 좋고 가장 아름다운 것은 / 보이거나 심지어는 만져질 수도 없다
touched. They must be felt with the heart. *Helen Keller*
그것들은 마음으로 느껴져야 한다

■ 조동사가 쓰인 수동태는 「조동사 + be + v-ed」의 형태로 쓴다.

04 Unfortunately, the rain forests are being cut down at a shocking rate to
유감스럽게도 / 우림은 잘려져 나가고 있다 / 충격적인 속도로 / 인간
provide humans with lumber, pasture land, and farm land.
들에게 목재, 목초지, 그리고 농지를 제공하기 위해서

■ 현재진행형의 수동태는 「be동사 + being + v-ed」로 쓴다.
— to provide는 '목적'의 의미를 나타내는 부사적 용법으로 쓰여, '제공하기 위해서'로 해석한다.

rate 속도; 비율
provide A with B A에게 B를 제공하다
lumber 목재
pasture land 목초지

05 Geysers have often been compared to volcanoes because they both emit
간헐천은 종종 화산으로 비유되어 왔다 / 왜냐하면 그것들은 둘 다 뜨거운 액체를
hot liquids from below the Earth's surface.
분출하기 때문에 / 지구의 표면 아래로부터

■ 현재완료형의 수동태는 「have[has] been + v-ed」로 쓴다.

Know More 간헐천은 열수(熱水)가 수증기와 함께 일정한 시간 간격으로 공중에 분출하는 온천으로, 특히 화산 지대에서 볼 수 있는 지하의 깊은 곳에서 상승한 고온의 열수나 수증기가 비교적 얕은 곳에서 보통의 지하수와 혼합될 때 일어나는 현상이다.

geyser 간헐천
compare A to B A를 B에 비유하다
volcano 화산
emit 내뿜다, 방출하다
surface 표면

B 06 Information is extracted or learned from sources of data, and this captured
정보는 추출되거나 학습된다 　/ 자료의 원천으로부터 　/ 그리고 이 입수된 정보는
information is then transformed into knowledge that is eventually **used** to
곧이어 지식으로 바뀐다 　/ [마침내 행동 또는 결정을 촉발하기 위해
trigger actions or decisions.
사용되는]

- 접속사 and로 병렬 연결된 두 개의 절에 수동태가 쓰였으며, 앞 절의 is extracted or learned의 경우는 접속사 or로 두 개의 과거분사가 병렬 연결되어 is에 이어진다.
- that ~ decisions는 knowledge를 수식하는 형용사절로, that절 안에는 수동태가 쓰였다.

extract 추출하다, 뽑다
capture 획득하다; 붙잡다
transform 바꾸다, 변형시키다
trigger 촉발하다, 유발하다

모의 07 Genetic tendencies toward intelligence, sociability, and aggression **can be**
유전적 성향은 　/ [지능, 사교성, 그리고 공격성에 대한] 　/ 자극되거나
stimulated, controlled, or suppressed by parental response and other
통제되거나 또는 억압될 수 있다 　/ 부모의 반응이나 다른 환경적 영향에 의해서
environmental influences.

- 「조동사 + be + v-ed」의 조동사 수동태가 쓰인 문장으로, 과거분사 stimulated, controlled, suppressed가 콤마와 or로 can be에 이어진다.

genetic 유전의, 유전학적인
sociability 사교성
aggression 공격성
stimulate 자극하다
suppress 억압하다

08 Hacking is commonly described as the act of re-designing the configuration
해킹은 흔히 묘사된다 　/ 하드웨어 또는 소프트웨어 시스템의 환경 설정을 재설계하는 행위로서
of hardware or software systems to alter their intended function.
　/ 그것의 의도된 기능을 변경하기 위해

- 「be described as ~」는 '~로서 묘사되다'라는 의미로 쓰이는 수동태 표현이다.

configuration (시스템의) 환경 설정, 구성
alter 변경하다, 바꾸다

09 It is estimated that we have characterized only one percent of all bacterial
(…이) 추정된다 　/ 우리가 모든 박테리아 종들의 겨우 1%만을 규정해왔다는 것이
species that exist.
　/ [존재하는]

- 「It is estimated that ~」은 '~으로 추정되다'라는 의미로 쓰이는 수동태 표현이다.
- It은 가주어이고, that이 이끄는 절(that we have ~ that exist)이 진주어이다.

estimate 추정하다
characterize 규정하다, 특징짓다

C 10 Test papers **may not** be taken out of the examination room.
시험 문제지는 갖고 나가져서는 안 된다 　/ 시험장 밖으로

- **풀이** 조동사 may의 수동태는 「may be + v-ed」로 쓰며, 조동사가 쓰인 수동태에서 부정어 not의 위치는 조동사와 be동사 사이이다.

11 Don't judge people by their covers. Most of their books **are still being**
사람들을 판단하지 마라 　/ 그들의 겉모습으로 　그들의 책 대부분은 여전히 쓰이고 있는 중이다
written.

- **풀이** '~되고 있는 중이다'는 현재진행형 수동태인 「be동사 + being + v-ed」로 표현할 수 있다. 주어 Most of their books가 복수이므로, be동사는 are를 쓴다.

judge 판단하다

12 Confirmed scientific theories **are often referred to as** "laws of nature" or "laws
입증된 과학 이론들은 종종 일컬어진다 　/ '자연의 법칙' 또는 '물리학의 법칙'이라고
of physics."

- **풀이** 「refer to A as B」의 수동태: A be referred to as B(A는 B라고 일컬어지다[지칭되다]) / 주어 Confirmed scientific theories가 복수이므로, be동사는 are를 쓴다.

confirm 입증하다, 확인하다
theory 이론
refer to A as B A를 B라고 일컫다(-referred-referred)

Chapter 02

Review

A **01** Primitive societies tend to **view** man and beast, animal and plant, organic
원시 사회는 경향이 있다 / 사람과 짐승, 동물과 식물, 생물체와 무생물체의 영역을 여기는
and inorganic realms, **as participants in an integrated, animated totality.**
/ 통합된, 살아있는 총체 속의 참여자로

> ■ view A as B: A를 B로 여기다

tend to-v ∼하는 경향이 있다
primitive 원시의
realm 영역, 범위
integrate 통합하다
animate 생명을 주다

02 You can fail at what you don't want, so you might as well take a chance on
당신은 실패할 수 있다 / 당신이 원하지 않는 것에 / 따라서 당신은 운에 맡기고 해보는 편이 낫다 / 당신이
doing what you love. *Jim Carrey*
좋아하는 것을 하는 것을

> ■ may(might) as well + ⓥ: ∼하는 편이 낫다

take a chance on ∼을 운에
맡기고 해보다

03 I'd rather be hated for who I am, **than** loved for who I am not. *Kurt Cobain*
나는 차라리 미움을 받겠다 / 내 자신인 것으로 / 사랑받느니 / 내 자신이 아닌 것으로

> ■ would rather A than B: B하느니 차라리 A하겠다(하고 싶다) / 조동사 would는 주어 I와 결합하여 축약형으로 쓰였다.
> ■ loved 앞에 수동태를 나타내는 be가 생략된 것으로 볼 수 있다.

04 Quantum theory states that energy, such as light, **is given off and absorbed**
양자론은 명시한다 / 빛과 같은 에너지는 방출되고 흡수된다는 것을
in tiny definite units called quanta or photons.
/ 아주 작은 일정한 구성 단위 속에서 / [양자 또는 광자라고 일컬어지는]

> ■ 과거분사 given과 absorbed가 and로 병렬 연결되어 is에 이어지고 있다.
> ■ called ∼ photons는 units를 수식하는 형용사구로, 과거분사 called 앞에 which[that] are가 생략된 것으로 볼 수 있다.

quantum 양자(*pl.* quanta)
state 명시하다
give off 방출하다
definite 일정한; 명확한
photon 광자

B **05** A copyright **supplies** its holder **with a kind of monopoly over the created**
모의 저작권은 그것의 보유자에게 제공한다 / 일종의 독점을 / [창작된 저작물에 대한]
material, and it assures him or her of both control over its use and the
/ 그리고 그것은 그 사람에게 보증한다 / 그것의 이용에 대한 통제권과 그것에서 나오는 수익 둘 다를
benefits from it.

> 풀이 (A) supply A with B: A에게 B를 제공[공급]하다
> (B) assure A of B: A에게 B를 보증하다(확신시키다)

copyright 저작권
monopoly 독점
benefit 수익, 혜택

06 The show **is** all **booked up.** You **should have purchased** tickets earlier.
그 공연은 모두 예약이 매진되었습니다 당신은 더 일찍 표를 구매했어야 합니다
Would you like to be put on a waiting list?
당신은 대기자 명단에 오르기를 원하십니까?

> 풀이 「must have v-ed」는 '∼했음에 틀림없다'라는 과거에 대한 추측의 의미를 나타내고, 「should have v-ed」는 '∼했어야 했는데 (하지 않았다)'는 과거에 대한 후회의 의미를 나타낸다. 더 일찍 구매했어야 했는데 하지 않았다는 의미가 되어야 하므로 should가 알맞다.

be booked up 예약이 매진
되다
put ∼ on a waiting list ∼을
대기 명단에 올리다

07 Scientists assume that Earth **must have formed** from dry material and
과학자들은 추정한다 / 지구는 생겨났음에 틀림없다고 / 물기 없는 물질로부터 / 그리고
acquired its water through objects from more distant, icy reaches of the
물을 얻었음에 틀림없다고 / 물체들을 통해서 / [태양계의 더 먼, 얼음 구간대에서 온]
solar system crashing into Earth.
/ [지구로 충돌하는]

assume 추정하다, 가정하다

> **풀이** 과학자들이 과거에 지구가 어떻게 탄생했는지 배경을 추정하고 있는 내용이 와야 한다. '~했음에 틀림없다'라는
> 과거의 일에 대한 확실한 추측이 자연스러우므로 「must have v-ed」가 적절하다.
> ───
> — from ~ system과 crashing into Earth는 둘 다 objects를 수식하는 형용사구이다.

모의 08 The personal computer **is designed** for the general function of handling and
개인용 컴퓨터는 설계된다 / 정보를 다루고 처리하는 일반적인 용도를 위해서
processing information, but exactly how the PC is used **is not predetermined.**
/ 그러나 정확하게 PC가 어떻게 사용되는지는 미리 결정되지 않는다

predetermine 미리 결정하다

> **풀이** (A) 주어 The personal computer는 설계하는 것이 아니라 '설계되는' 것이므로 수동태가 적절하다.
> (B) 주어 the PC가 어떻게 사용되는지가 '미리 결정되지 않는' 것이므로 수동태가 적절하다.

C **09** I couldn't access the website because it **was being updated.**
나는 그 웹사이트에 접속할 수 없었다 / 그것이 업데이트 되고 있는 중이었기 때문에

access 접속하다

> **풀이** '~되고 있는 중이다'는 진행형의 수동태 「be being v-ed」로 쓸 수 있다. 과거의 일을 나타내므로 과거진행의
> 형태가 되어야 한다.

10 It **is** sometimes **alleged**, by linguists, that language **must have been**
(…이) 때때로 주장된다 / 언어학자들에 의해서 / 언어는 발명되었음에 틀림없다는 것이
invented at some recent point in the past.
/ 과거의 어떤 최근 시점에

allege 주장하다, 단언하다
linguist 언어학자

> **풀이** '~했음에 틀림없다'는 과거에 대한 확실한 추측을 나타내는 것으로 「must have v-ed」로 표현할 수 있는데, 언
> 어는 '발명되는' 대상이므로 수동태의 형태가 되어 must have been invented로 써야 한다.
> ───
> — It은 가주어이고, that ~ the past가 진주어이다.

D **11** The scientist **attributed** changes in the climate **to global warming and**
그 과학자는 기후 변화를 탓으로 돌렸다 / 지구 온난화와 대기 오염의
pollution of the atmosphere.

pollution 오염
atmosphere 대기; 분위기

> **풀이** attribute A to B: A를 B의 탓으로 돌리다

12 A spongy three-pound mass of fatty tissue, the brain **has** often **been**
해면 모양으로 생긴 3파운드의 지방 조직 덩어리인 뇌는 종종 비유되어왔다
compared to a super-computer.
/ 슈퍼컴퓨터에

spongy 해면 모양의; 스펀지 같은
mass 덩어리
fatty tissue 지방 조직

> **풀이** 「compare A to B」의 수동태는 「A be동사 compared to B」이며, 현재완료형 수동태는 「have[has] been
> v-ed」로 쓴다.
> ───
> — A spongy three-pound mass of fatty tissue는 the brain과 동격 관계이다.

03

목적어의 파악

- unit 10   명사구 목적어
- unit 11   명사절 목적어
- unit 12   가목적어 it
- unit 13   목적어 + 형용사구
- unit 14   목적어 + 형용사절

■ 본격적인 구문 학습에 앞서, 각 유닛별 주요 단어를 확인하세요.

Unit 10

- [ ] **abolish** (법률·제도를) 폐지하다
- [ ] **tariff wall** 관세 장벽
- [ ] **particularly** 특히
- [ ] **countryside** 시골 지역, 전원
- [ ] **mind** 싫어하다, 주의하다
- [ ] **preach at** ~에게 설교하다
- [ ] **storyline** (소설·연극 등의) 줄거리
- [ ] **instinct** 본능
- [ ] **ignore** 무시하다
- [ ] **admit** 시인하다, 인정하다
- [ ] **deny** 부인하다
- [ ] **consideration** 숙고, 고려
- [ ] **plenty of** 많은
- [ ] **mean** 비열한, 심술궂은
- [ ] **knock down** 쓰러뜨리다, 무너뜨리다

Unit 11

- [ ] **guilty** 유죄의
- [ ] **innocent** 무죄의
- [ ] **crime** 범행, 범죄
- [ ] **merely** 단지, 그저
- [ ] **astronomer** 천문학자
- [ ] **recede** 멀어지다
- [ ] **further** 여분의, 추가의
- [ ] **identification** 신분증명서
- [ ] **pioneer** 개척자
- [ ] **barely** 가까스로, 겨우
- [ ] **make merry** 즐겁게 놀다
- [ ] **shed tears** 눈물을 흘리다
- [ ] **disposal** 처리, 폐기
- [ ] **monetary** 통화의, 재정의
- [ ] **stability** 안정성

Unit 12

- [ ] **artificial intelligence** 인공지능
- [ ] **moral** 교훈적인; 도덕적인
- [ ] **consensus** (의견의) 일치
- [ ] **evident** 명백한, 분명한
- [ ] **engrave** 새기다, 명심하다
- [ ] **a deal of** 많은
- [ ] **pity** 동정
- [ ] **publicity** 광고, 홍보
- [ ] **clutter** 어지럽히다
- [ ] **dignified** 고귀한, 위엄 있는
- [ ] **bear ~ in mind** ~을 명심하다
- [ ] **violent** 맹렬한, 폭력적인
- [ ] **temporary** 일시적인
- [ ] **master** (감정을) 억누르다
- [ ] **magnify** 확장하다

Unit 13

- [ ] **carelessly** 부주의하게
- [ ] **foundation** 토대
- [ ] **a fair trial** 공정한 재판
- [ ] **a court of law** 법정
- [ ] **yield** (결과를) 낳다, 산출하다
- [ ] **illustrative** 분명히 보여주는
- [ ] **temperament** 기질
- [ ] **go out** (불·전깃불이) 꺼지다
- [ ] **rekindle** 다시 불붙이다
- [ ] **gratitude** 감사하는 마음
- [ ] **hazardous** 위험한
- [ ] **toxic** 유독한
- [ ] **uncanny** 뛰어난, 신비로운
- [ ] **asteroid** 소행성
- [ ] **manned** 유인의, 사람을 실은

Unit 14

- [ ] **approach** 다가가다
- [ ] **outperform** 능가하다
- [ ] **raw material** 원료, 원자재
- [ ] **underestimate** 과소평가하다
- [ ] **independently of** ~와 관계없이
- [ ] **fable** 우화
- [ ] **denote** 뜻하다
- [ ] **advance** 제시하다
- [ ] **expressive** 표현력이 있는
- [ ] **conflict** 갈등
- [ ] **finite** 한정된
- [ ] **inevitable** 불가피한
- [ ] **claim** 주장하다; 요구하다
- [ ] **proficient** 능숙한
- [ ] **disseminate** 퍼뜨리다

명사구 목적어

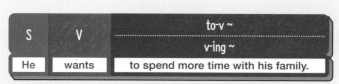

S	V	to-v ~ / v-ing ~
He	wants	to spend more time with his family.

그는 / 원한다 / 자신의 가족과 더 많은 시간을 보내기를

Standard Sentences

01 Both countries agreed **to abolish their tariff walls** within 5 years.
양국은 동의했다 / 그들의 관세 장벽을 철폐하는 것을 / 5년 내에

- agree는 to부정사를 목적어로 취하는 동사이다.

> **Know More** 관세 장벽이란 국내 산업 보호 및 국가의 재정수입을 도모할 목적으로 수입 상품에 높은 관세를 부과함으로써, 국내 수입품 가격을 높게 하여 수입을 억제하는 제도를 뜻한다.

abolish (법률·제도·관습을) 폐지하다
tariff wall 관세 장벽

02 I particularly enjoyed **driving through the countryside with you.**
나는 특히 즐겼다 / 당신과 함께 교외를 드라이브하는 것을

- enjoy는 동명사를 목적어로 취하는 동사이며. driving이 목적어로 쓰였다.

particularly 특히
countryside 시골 지역, 전원

A 03 I don't mind **listening to advice** that I've asked for, but I refuse **to be**
나는 조언을 경청하는 것을 싫어하지 않는다 / [내가 요청한] / 그러나 나는 훈계 듣는 것을
preached at.
거부한다

- mind는 동명사를 목적어로 취하는 동사이고, refuse는 to부정사를 목적어로 취하는 동사이다. to-v의 수동태는 'to be v-ed'로 쓴다.
- that ~ for는 advice를 수식하는 형용사절이다.

mind 싫어하다; 주의하다
preach at ~에게 훈계하다

04 I almost forgot the storyline of the Disney movie *Frozen*, but I **do remember**
나는 디즈니 영화 '겨울왕국'의 줄거리를 거의 잊었다 / 그러나 나는 줄을 서서 기다린
waiting in line to see the movie.
것을 정말 기억한다 / 그 영화를 보기 위해

- remember는 동명사와 to부정사 둘 다 목적어로 취할 수 있는 동사인데, 동명사가 목적어로 쓰이면 '(과거에) ~한 것을 기억하다'라는 의미이다.
- 동사 remember를 강조하기 위해 do가 쓰였다.

storyline (소설·연극·영화 등의) 줄거리

05 Politicians are the same all over. They promise **to build a bridge** even where
정치인들은 어디서나 똑같다 그들은 다리를 놓을 것을 약속한다 / 강이 없는 곳에도
there is no river. *Nikita Khrushchev*

- promise는 to부정사를 목적어로 취하는 동사이다.

politician 정치인

06 No one's instincts are always correct; so how do you know **when to follow**
어느 누구의 본능도 항상 올바르지는 않다 　　　　　/ 그렇다면 당신은 어떻게 아는가 　/ 언제 그것을 따라야 할지
them and when to ignore them?
　　/ 그리고 언제 그것을 무시해야 할지를?

instinct 본능
ignore 무시하다

■ when to follow와 when to ignore는 「의문사 + to-v」 형태의 명사구로서 '언제 ~해야 할지'로 해석하며, 이 문장에서는 동사 know의 목적어로 쓰였다.

---

07 The drunken man admitted **stealing the car**, but denied **driving it under the**
그 술 취한 남자는 그 차를 훔쳤음을 시인했다 　　　　　/ 하지만 그것을 운전한 것을 부인했다 / 술에 취한
influence of alcohol.
상태로

admit 시인하다, 인정하다
deny 부인하다
under the influence of
alcohol 술에 취한 상태로

■ admit과 deny는 동명사를 목적어로 취하는 동사이다.

---

08 Once I forgot **to turn off the oven** and I shall never forget **seeing the**
예전에 나는 잊었다 　/ 오븐을 끄는 것을 　　/ 그리고 나는 결코 잊지 못할 것이다 　/ 나머지 가족의
expression on the faces of the rest of the family when they realized they
얼굴 표정을 본 것을 　　　　　　　　　　　　　　　　/ 그들이 깨달았을 때 　　　　/ 자신들이
had nothing to eat.
먹을 것이 없다는 것을

turn off ~을 끄다
expression 표정; 표현
the rest 나머지

■ forget + to-v: (미래에) ~할 것을 잊다 / forget + v-ing: (과거에) ~한 것을 잊다
— realized 다음에 목적어 역할을 하는 명사절을 이끄는 접속사 that이 생략되어 있다.

---

09 We stopped **checking for monsters under our bed** when we realized they
우리는 괴물들을 살펴보는 것을 그만두었다 　　　　　　/ 우리의 침대 아래에서 / 우리가 깨달았을 때 　　/ 그것들이
were inside us. *the movie <The Dark Knight>*
우리 안에 있다는 것을

■ stop은 동명사를 목적어로 취하는 동사이며 '~하는 것을 그만두다'로 해석한다. / stop 다음에 to부정사가 올 경우에는 '~하기 위해서'의 목적의 의미를 나타낸다.

---

10 After careful consideration of your proposal, I regret **to say that we are**
당신의 제안에 대해서 심사숙고한 후에 　　　　　　　　　　　/ 나는 말하게 되어 유감이다 / 우리가 그것을
unable to accept it.
받아들일 수 없다고

consideration 숙고, 고려
proposal 제안

풀이 regret + to-v: ~하게 되어 유감이다 / regret + v-ing: ~한 것을 후회하다

---

11 I've never regretted **saying a kind word to someone**, but I have regretted
나는 결코 후회하지 않았다 　　　/ 누군가에게 다정한 말 한 마디를 한 것을 　　　　　/ 그러나 나는 후회해왔다
plenty of mean things I have said and done.
/ 많은 비열한 것들을 　　　　　/ [내가 말하고 행한]

plenty of 많은
mean 비열한, 심술궂은

풀이 regret + v-ing: ~한 것을 후회하다 / regret + to-v: ~하게 되어 유감이다

— things 다음에는 목적격 관계대명사 which 또는 that이 생략되어 있으며, I have ~ done은 things를 수식하는 형용사절이다.

---

12 Life will knock us down, but we can choose **whether or not to stand back**
인생은 우리를 쓰러뜨릴 것이다 　　　　　　/ 그러나 우리는 선택할 수 있다 　/ 우리가 다시 일어설지 말지를
up. *Jackie Chan*

knock down 쓰러뜨리다, 무너뜨리다

풀이 whether or not to stand는 「의문사 + to-v」 형태의 명사구로서 '~할지 말지'의 의미이다.

unit **11**

명사절 목적어

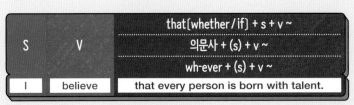

S	V	that[whether/if] + s + v ~
		의문사 + (s) + v ~
		wh-ever + (s) + v ~
I	believe	that every person is born with talent.

나는 / 믿는다 / 모든 사람은 재능을 갖고 태어난다는 것을

Standard Sentences

01 A judge must decide **whether a person is guilty or innocent of a crime.**
판사는 판결을 내려야 한다 / 어떤 사람이 유죄인지 무죄인지를 / 범행에 대해

■ 접속사 whether가 이끄는 명사절이 동사 decide의 목적어로 쓰였다.

guilty 유죄의
innocent 무죄의
crime 범행, 범죄

02 Your present circumstances don't determine **where you can go**; they
당신의 현재 상황이 결정하지 않는다 / 어디로 당신이 갈 수 있는지를 / 그것들은
merely determine **where you start.** *Nido Qubein*
단지 결정한다 / 어디서 당신이 시작하는지를

■ 의문사 where가 이끄는 명사절이 동사 determine의 목적어로 쓰였다.

determine 결정하다, 결심하다
circumstance 상황, 환경
merely 단지, 그저

A 03 The great astronomer Edwin Hubble discovered **that all distant galaxies**
위대한 천문학자 에드윈 허블은 발견했다 / 모든 먼 은하들이 멀어지고 있다는 것을
are receding from our Milky Way Galaxy.
/ 우리의 은하로부터

■ 접속사 that이 이끄는 명사절이 동사 discovered의 목적어로 쓰였다.

Know More '우리 은하(Milky Way Galaxy)'는 태양계가 속해 있는 은하로 우리가 속해 있는 곳이기 때문에 단순히 '은하' 또는 '은하계'라고도 불린다. 은하수는 지구에서 보이는 우리 은하의 부분으로, 천구를 가로지르는 밝은 띠로 보이며, 이 밝은 띠는 다수의 별들로 이루어져 있다.

astronomer 천문학자
galaxy 은하
recede 멀어지다; 후퇴하다

04 The woman who was on passport control asked me **if I had any further**
그 여자는 / [여권 심사대에 있던] / 내게 물었다 / 내가 또 다른 신분 증명 자료를
identification.
가졌는지를

■ '~인지 아닌지'를 뜻하는 접속사 if가 이끄는 명사절이 동사 asked의 목적어로 쓰였으며, 이때의 if는 whether로 바꿔 쓸 수 있다.
■ who ~ control은 The woman을 수식하는 형용사절이다.

passport control 여권 심사대
further 여분의, 추가의
identification 신분증명서

05 People who are satisfied appreciate **what they have in life** and don't worry
사람들은 / [만족하는] / 감사한다 / 그들이 인생에서 가진 것 / 그리고 걱정하지 않는다
about **how it compares to what others have.**
/ 그것이 어떻게 비교되는지에 대해서 / 다른 사람들이 가진 것과

■ what이 이끄는 명사절 what they have in life가 동사 appreciate의 목적어로 쓰였다.
■ 의문사 how가 이끄는 명사절이 전치사 about의 목적어로 쓰였고, what이 이끄는 명사절 what others have가 전치사 to의 목적어로 쓰였다.

appreciate 제대로 알다, 진가를 인식하다; 감사하다

B **06** Perhaps, we've just forgotten **that we are still pioneers,** **that we've barely**
아마도 / 우리는 그저 잊어버렸는지도 모른다 / 우리가 여전히 개척자들이라는 것을 / 우리가 가까스로 시작했다는
begun, and that our greatest accomplishments cannot be behind us.
것을 / 그리고 우리의 가장 위대한 성취는 우리의 뒤에 있을 수 없다[이미 일어난 것이 아니라]는 것을

the movie <Interstellar>

접속사 that이 이끄는 세 개의 명사절이 콤마와 and에 의해 병렬 연결되어 have forgotten의 목적어로 쓰였다.

pioneer 개척자
barely 가까스로, 겨우, 간신히;
거의 ~ 않는

07 Actors are so fortunate. They can choose **whether they will appear in**
배우들은 아주 운이 좋다 그들은 선택할 수 있다 / 자신들이 비극 또는 희극에 출연할 것인지를
tragedy or in comedy, whether they will suffer or make merry, laugh or
/ 그들이 고통을 겪을 것인지 또는 즐겁게 놀지 / 웃을지 아니면
shed tears. *Oscar Wilde*
눈물을 흘릴 것인지를

'~인지 아닌지'를 뜻하는 접속사 whether가 이끄는 명사절이 동사 choose의 목적어로 쓰였다.

make merry 즐겁게 놀다
shed tears 눈물을 흘리다

08 Environmentalists argue **no system of waste disposal can be absolutely**
환경 운동가들은 주장한다 / 어떠한 쓰레기 처리 시스템도 절대적으로 안전할 수는 없다고
safe, either now or in the future.
/ 지금이든 미래든

argue 다음에 목적어 역할을 하는 명사절(no system ~ the future)을 이끄는 접속사 that이 생략되어 있다.

disposal 처리, 폐기
absolutely 절대적으로

09 Either Saturday or Monday, choose **whichever is more convenient for you.**
토요일이나 월요일 중 / 선택해라 / 어느 것이든 네게 더 편한 쪽을

복합관계대명사 whichever가 이끄는 명사절이 동사 choose의 목적어로 쓰였다.

convenient 편리한

C **10** Indeed, a brief look at a dictionary will show you **that the majority of words**
[모의] 정말로 / 사전을 잠깐 살펴 보는 것은 당신에게 보여 줄 것이다 / 대다수의 단어가 사용된다는 것을
are used with more than one meaning.
/ 하나 이상의 의미로

풀이 동사 show의 직접목적어 역할을 하는 명사절을 이끄는 접속사 that이 빈칸에 알맞다.

indeed 정말로
brief look 잠깐 살펴 보는 것
majority 대다수

11 In times of social, cultural or religious sensitivity one might wonder **whether**
사회적, 문화적 또는 종교적 민감성의 시대에 / 사람들은 궁금해할 수도 있다 / (…이) 윤리적
it is ethical to avoid, or not to avoid, questions that might increase conflict.
인지 / 질문을 피하는 것 또는 피하지 않는 것이 / [갈등을 증가시킬 수도 있는]

풀이 동사 wonder의 목적어 역할을 하며 '~인지 아닌지'를 뜻하는 접속사 whether가 빈칸에 알맞다.

접속사 whether가 이끄는 명사절의 주어 자리에 쓰인 it은 가주어이고, to avoid ~ conflict가 진주어이며, that might increase conflict는 questions를 수식하는 형용사절이다.

religious 종교적인
sensitivity 민감성
ethical 윤리적인
conflict 갈등

12 The government will take **whatever action is necessary** to achieve monetary
정부는 취할 것이다 / 필요한 어떤 조치든지 / 통화와 금융의 안정성을
and financial stability.
확보하기 위해서

풀이 동사 take의 목적어 역할을 하는 명사절을 이끌면서 action을 수식할 수 있는 whatever가 빈칸에 알맞다. 여기서 whatever는 복합관계형용사로 쓰였다.

monetary 통화의, 재정의
stability 안정성

unit 12
가목적어 it

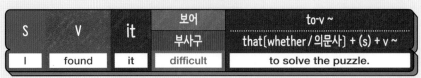

S	V	it	보어	to-v ~
			부사구	that[whether / 의문사] + (s) + v ~
I	found	it	difficult	to solve the puzzle.

나는 / 알았다　　　/ (…이) / 어렵다는 것을　/ 그 퍼즐을 푸는 것이

Standard Sentences

01 Artificial intelligence makes it possible for machines to learn from
인공지능은 만든다　　　　　/ (…을) 가능하게　/ 기계들이 경험으로부터 배우는 것을
experience and perform human tasks.
　　　/ 그리고 인간의 과제를 수행하는 것을

- 목적어 자리의 it은 가목적어이고, to부정사구 to learn ~ tasks가 진목적어이다. for machines는 to learn의 의미상 주어이다.

artificial intelligence
인공지능
perform 수행하다; 공연
하다
task 과제

02 We should not take it for granted that classic moral stories will
우리는 여겨서는 안 된다　　　/ (…을) 당연하게　/ 고전적인 교훈적 이야기들이 자동적으로 도덕적
automatically promote moral behaviors.
행동을 촉진할 것임을

- take it for granted that ~은 '~을 당연한 것으로 여기다'라는 의미로 가목적어 it이 쓰이는 관용표현이다. 이 문장의 진목적어는 접속사 that이 이끄는 명사절(that classic ~ behaviors)이다.

moral 교훈적인, 도덕적인
promote 촉진하다; 승진
시키다

A 03 The European Union has found it difficult to reach a consensus on
유럽연합은 알았다　　　　　　　　　/ (…이) 어렵다는 것을 / 의견 일치에 도달하는 것이　/ 경제
economic issues.
문제에 관해

- it이 가목적어이고, to reach ~ issues가 진목적어이다.

  Know More 유럽연합(EU)은 유럽의 정치·경제 통합을 실현하기 위해 1993년 11월에 발표된 마스트리히트 조약에 따라 유럽 12개국이 참가하여 출범한 연합 기구이다. 원래는 회원국 사이에 경제적 장벽이 없는 유럽 경제 공동체를 만들려는 것에서 출발하여 현재는 경제 정책뿐만 아니라 정치적·사회적으로도 하나의 정책을 추구해 가는 것으로 발전하여 27개국이 가입되어 있다.

consensus (의견의) 일치

04 Our research makes it evident that many imaginative children often invent
우리의 연구는 만든다　　　　/ (…을) 명백하게 / 상상력이 풍부한 많은 아이들이 종종 상상의 놀이 친구를 만들어 낸다는 것을
imaginary playmates.

- it이 가목적어이고, 접속사 that이 이끄는 명사절(that many ~ playmates)이 진목적어이다.

evident 명백한, 분명한
imaginative 상상력이 풍부
한, 창의적인
imaginary 상상의, 가상의

05 Engrave it on your heart that a little help is worth a deal of pity.
새겨라　　　/ (…을) 당신의 마음에　/ 작은 도움이 많은 동정의 가치가 있다는 것을

- it이 가목적어이고, 접속사 that이 이끄는 명사절(that ~ pity)이 진목적어이다.

engrave 새기다, 명심하다
a deal of 많은
pity 동정

B **06** Even if you don't read a newspaper or watch television, and walk around
비록 당신이 신문을 읽지 않거나 텔레비전을 시청하지 않는다고 하더라도 / 그리고 눈을 내리깐 채로
the streets with your eyes down, you'll find **it** impossible **to avoid some**
거리를 걸어 다닌다고 하더라도 / 당신은 알게 될 것이다 / (…이) 불가능하다는 것을 / 어떤 형태의
form of publicity.
광고를 피하는 것이

publicity 광고, 홍보

> 목적어 자리의 가목적어 it은 진목적어인 to avoid ~ publicity를 대신한다.

07 I make **it** a rule **not to clutter my mind with simple information that I can**
나는 삼는다 / (…을) 규칙으로 / 내 마음을 어지럽히지 않는 것을 / 간단한 정보로 / [내가 책에서
find in a book in five minutes. *Albert Einstein*
찾을 수 있는 / 5분 이내에]

clutter 어지럽히다

> make it a rule to-v는 '~을 규칙으로 하다'라는 의미로 가목적어 it이 쓰이는 관용표현이며, 이 문장에서 가목적어
> it은 진목적어인 not to clutter ~ five minutes를 대신한다.
> not to clutter처럼 to부정사는 to 앞에 not이나 never를 써서 부정을 나타낸다.

08 We owe **it** to our children **to give them a dignified and hopeful future.**
우리는 의무를 지고 있다 / (…을) 우리의 자녀들에게 / 그들에게 고귀하고 희망찬 미래를 제공할 것을 *Giorgio Napolitano*

owe A to B A를 B에게 빚지고 있다
dignified 고귀한, 위엄 있는

> 목적어 자리의 가목적어 it은 진목적어인 to give ~ future를 대신한다.

09 Bear **it** in mind when a life storm breaks **that, no matter how violent, it is**
품어라 / (…을) 마음 속에 / 인생의 폭풍이 일 때 / 아무리 맹렬하더라도 / 그것은
only temporary and that behind the clouds the sun is always shining.
단지 일시적이라는 것을 / 그리고 구름 뒤에는 태양이 항상 빛나고 있다는 것을

bear ~ in mind ~을 명심하다
no matter how 아무리 ~하더라도 (= however)
violent 맹렬한, 폭력적인
temporary 일시적인

> 목적어 자리의 가목적어 it은 진목적어인 두 개의 that이 이끄는 명사절(that ~ shining)을 대신한다.
> no matter how violent는 that절 속에 삽입된 것으로, how violent 다음에는 it may be가 생략되어 있다.
> 두 번째 it은 'a life storm'을 가리킨다.

C **10** The internet has made **it** easy **for us to hear whatever we like the most in**
인터넷은 만들어왔다 / (…을) 쉽게 / 우리가 듣는 것을 / 우리가 가장 좋아하는 무엇이든 /
mere seconds.
단 몇 초 내에

mere 단지, 겨우 ~의

> 풀이: 5형식 문장에서 가목적어 뒤에 목적격보어로 형용사가 와야 하므로 easy가 적절하다. / for us는 진목적어 to
> hear의 의미상 주어이다.
> whatever가 이끄는 명사절이 hear의 목적어로 쓰였다.

(모의) **11** At certain times in history, cultures have taken **it** for granted **that a person**
역사의 어떤 때에 / 문화는 여겨왔다 / (…을) 당연하게 / 사람이 충분하게
was not fully human unless he or she learned to master thoughts and
인간적이지 않았다는 것을 / 만약 그 사람이 배우지 않았다면 / 생각과 감정을 억누르는 것을
feelings.

master (감정을) 억누르다; 숙달하다

> 풀이: 3형식 문장에서 it이 가목적어이므로, 진목적어로 명사절을 이끄는 접속사 that이 적절하다. / 이어지는 절이 완
> 전하므로 which는 올 수 없다.

12 Every man who knows how to read has **it** in his power **to magnify himself,**
모든 사람은 / [글을 읽는 방법을 아는] / (…을) 그의 수중에 가진다 / 자신을 확장하는 것
to multiply the ways in which he exists, to make his life full, significant,
/ 방식을 다양화하는 것 / [자신이 존재하는] / 자신의 삶을 충만하고, 중대하고, 흥미롭게 만드는 것
and interesting. *Aldous Huxley*

magnify 확장하다, 확대하다
multiply 다양화하다, 증대시키다; 곱하다
significant 중대한; 의미심장한

> 풀이: 세 개의 to부정사인 to magnify, to multiply, to make가 이끄는 진목적어가 뒤에 왔으므로, 가목적어 it이
> 적절하다.

unit 13
목적어 + 형용사구

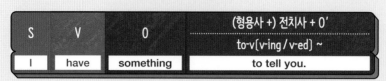

S	V	O	(형용사 +) 전치사 + O' to-v[v-ing / v-ed] ~
I	have	something	to tell you.
나는	가지고 있다	어떤 것을	[너에게 말할]

Standard Sentences

수능! 01 Our bodies have the natural ability **to fight off bacteria and diseases when**
우리의 신체는 타고난 능력을 가지고 있다 / [박테리아와 질병을 물리칠 / 그것들이
they enter our bodies.
우리의 몸에 들어올 때]

━ 목적어인 the natural ability를 to fight가 이끄는 형용사구가 수식하고 있다.

02 We often experience unexpected results **brought about by words carelessly**
우리는 종종 예상치 못한 결과를 경험한다 / [말에 의해서 초래되는 / [부주의하게
used.
사용된]]

━ 목적어인 unexpected results를 과거분사 brought가 이끄는 형용사구가 수식하고 있다.

bring about ~을 초래하다
carelessly 부주의하게

A 03 Healthy living in individuals lays the foundation **for healthy living throughout**
모의 개인들의 건강한 삶은 토대를 놓는다 / [사회와 세계의 모든 곳의 건강한 삶을 위한]
society and the world.

━ for 이하의 전치사구가 목적어인 the foundation을 수식한다.

individual 개인
foundation 토대

04 You have the right **to be given a fair trial by a court of law if you are**
당신은 권리를 가진다 / [공정한 재판을 받을 / 법정에 의해서] / 만약 당신이
accused of a crime.
범죄로 고발된다면

━ 목적어인 the right를 to be given이 이끄는 형용사구가 수식하고 있다.

Know More 공정한 재판을 위해 사법부를 분리하는 것뿐만 아니라 심급 제도(법원의 판결에 불복할 경우, 상급 법원에 다시 재판을 청구할 수 있는 제도)가 있으며, 공개 재판주의, 증거 재판주의를 원칙으로 하고 있다.

a fair trial 공정한 재판
a court of law 법정, 재판정
accuse A of B A를 B의 이유로 고발하다[기소하다]

05 I have received an email **offering me a job for an unknown company that I**
나는 이메일을 받았다 / [내게 무명의 회사의 일자리를 제안하는 / [내가
don't remember applying to.
지원한 기억이 나지 않는]]

━ 목적어인 an email을 현재분사 offering이 이끄는 형용사구가 수식하고 있다.
━ 목적격 관계대명사 that 이하는 an unknown company를 수식하는 형용사절이다.
━ remember v-ing: ~했던 것을 기억하다

apply 지원하다, 신청하다; 적용하다

B 06 The use of words itself yields, upon analysis, valuable results illustrative of
단어의 사용 그 자체는 낳는다 / 분석해보면 / 가치 있는 결과를 / [작가의 다양한
the various temperaments of authors.
기질을 분명히 보여 주는]

> 목적어인 valuable results를 형용사 illustrative가 이끄는 형용사구가 수식하고 있다.

yield 낳다, 산출하다; 굴복하다
illustrative 분명히 보여 주는, 설명적인
temperament 기질

07 At times our own light goes out and is rekindled by a spark from another
가끔 우리 자신의 빛이 꺼진다 / 그리고 재점화된다 / 다른 사람으로부터의 불꽃에 의해서
person. Each of us has cause to think with deep gratitude of those who
우리 각자는 이유를 가지고 있다 / [사람들에 대해 깊이 감사하는 마음으로 생각할 / [우리
have lighted the flame within us. *Albert Schweitzer*
안의 불꽃에 불을 붙여온]]

> 목적어인 cause를 to think가 이끄는 형용사구가 수식하고 있다.

at times 가끔
go out (불·전깃불이) 꺼지다
rekindle 다시 불붙이다
spark 불꽃
cause 이유, 원인
gratitude 감사하는 마음
flame 불꽃

08 Regular exercise increases the amount of blood flowing through your brain.
규칙적인 운동은 피의 양을 증가시킨다 / [당신의 뇌를 통하여 흐르는]

> 목적어인 the amount를 of blood가 수식하고, blood를 현재분사 flowing이 이끄는 형용사구가 수식하고 있다.

regular 규칙적인
amount 양; 금액

09 We should reduce hazardous and toxic chemicals released into the air and
우리는 위험하고 유독한 화학물질을 줄여야 한다 / [대기와 물속으로 방출되는]
water.

> 목적어인 hazardous and toxic chemicals를 과거분사 released가 이끄는 형용사구가 수식하고 있다.

hazardous 위험한
toxic 유독한
chemical 화학물질; 화학의
release 방출하다

C 10 Certainly, Leonardo da Vinci had an unusual mind and an uncanny ability to
[모의] 확실히 레오나르도 다빈치는 남다른 사고방식과 뛰어난 능력을 지녔다 / [다른
see what others didn't see.
사람들이 보지 못했던 것을 보는]

> 풀이 '보는'의 의미를 나타내고 목적어인 an unusual mind and an uncanny ability를 수식하는 형용사구로 to see가 적절하다.

> **Know More** 레오나르도 다빈치(1452~1519)는 르네상스 시대의 이탈리아를 대표하는 천재적 미술가·과학자·기술자·사상가로, 사람의 몸을 해부해 과학적으로 분석했고, 여기서 얻은 지식을 수많은 인체 소묘와 회화로 표현했으며, 음악, 화학, 천문학, 건축학 등 여러 방면에 걸쳐 다양한 연구를 하였다.

certainly 확실히
unusual 보통이 아닌, 특이한
uncanny 뛰어난; 신비로운

11 Scientists at NASA have spotted six asteroids heading in the direction of
NASA의 과학자들은 여섯 개의 소행성을 발견해왔다 / [지구 쪽으로 향하는]
Earth, with one of them having a size larger than the Empire State Building.
/ 그것들 중 하나는 엠파이어 스테이트 빌딩보다 더 큰 크기이다

> 풀이 '향하는'의 의미를 나타내고 목적어인 six asteroids를 수식하는 형용사구가 와야 하므로 현재분사 heading이 적절하다.
> ─ with one of them having은 '~한 채로'를 뜻하는 「with + O + v-ing / v-ed」 분사구문으로 쓰였다. 목적어가 분사의 의미상 주어이며, 목적어와 분사의 관계가 능동이면 v-ing, 수동이면 v-ed를 쓴다. **Unit 34**

spot 발견하다
asteroid 소행성
head 향하다

12 Google and other carmakers around the world are developing technologies
구글과 전 세계의 다른 자동차 제조사들은 기술을 개발하고 있다
applied to currently "manned" vehicles to permit drivers to take their
/ [현재 '유인' 차량에 적용되는] / 운전자들이 운전대로부터 손을 떼고 다른 업무에
hands off the wheel and focus on other tasks.
집중할 수 있도록

> 풀이 목적어인 technologies는 '적용되는' 대상이므로 수동의 의미를 나타내는 과거분사 applied가 적절하다.
> ─ to permit ~ other tasks는 to부정사의 부사적 용법으로 '목적'의 의미를 나타낸다.

currently 현재의
manned 유인의, 사람이 탑승한
vehicle 차량
permit 허용하다
wheel 자동차의 핸들; 바퀴

unit 14
목적어 + 형용사절

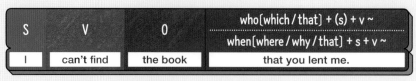

S	V	O	who[which / that] + (s) + v ~
			when[where / why / that] + s + v ~
I	can't find	the book	that you lent me.

나는 / 찾을 수 없다 / 그 책을 / [네가 내게 빌려준]

Standard Sentences

모의 01 We trust leaders who are real, who walk their talk, who act on their core
우리는 지도자들을 신뢰한다 [진실된 / 그들이 말한 것을 실행하는 / 그들의 핵심 가치대로 행동하는
values, and who tell us the truth.
/ 그리고 우리에게 진실을 말하는]

— 목적어 leaders를 콤마(,)와 and로 병렬 연결된 관계대명사 who가 이끄는 네 개의 형용사절이 수식하고 있다.

walk the talk 말한 것을 실행[실천]하다
core 핵심의, 중심적인

02 We are approaching the time when machines will be able to outperform
우리는 시대로 다가가고 있다 [기계가 인간을 능가할 수 있을
humans at almost any task.
/ 거의 모든 업무에서]

— 목적어 the time을 관계부사 when이 이끄는 형용사절이 수식하고 있다.

approach 다가가다, 접근하다
outperform 능가하다
task 업무, 과제

A 03 Basic scientific research provides the raw materials that technology and
수능 기초 과학 연구는 원료를 제공한다 / [기술과 공학이 활용하는
engineering use to solve problems.
/ 문제를 해결하기 위해서]

— 목적어인 the raw materials를 관계대명사 that이 이끄는 형용사절이 수식하고 있다.
— to solve problems는 목적을 나타내는 부사적 용법으로 쓰였다.

research 연구
raw material 원료, 원자재
engineering 공학

모의 04 Personality psychologists had underestimated the extent to which the
성격 심리학자들은 정도를 과소평가했다 / [사회적 상황이
social situation shapes people's behavior, independently of their personality.
사람들의 행동을 형성하는 / 그들의 성격과 관계없이]

— 목적어인 the extent를 「전치사 + 관계대명사」인 to which가 이끄는 형용사절이 수식하고 있다.
— 관계대명사가 전치사의 목적어로 쓰이는 경우, 전치사는 관계대명사 앞이나 관계사절의 끝에 올 수 있다.

psychologist 심리학자
underestimate 과소평가하다
extent 정도
independently of ~와 관계없이

05 The word "fable" frequently denotes a brief tale where animals or inanimate
'우화'라는 단어는 빈번하게 짧은 이야기를 뜻한다 / [동물 또는 무생물이 말을 하고 행동하는
objects speak and behave like humans, usually to advance a moral point.
/ 사람처럼 / 대개 어떤 교훈적인 의미를 제시하기 위해서]

— 목적어인 a brief tale을 관계부사 where가 이끄는 형용사절이 수식하고 있다.
— to advance는 to부정사의 부사적 용법 중에서 '~하기 위해서'라는 목적의 의미로 사용되었다.

fable 우화
denote 뜻하다, 나타내다
inanimate 무생물의
advance 제시하다; 나아가다

B **06** I fear not the man who has practiced 10,000 kicks once, but I fear the man
나는 사람을 두려워하지 않는다 / [한 번에 1만 번의 발차기를 연습한] / 그러나 나는 사람을 두려워한다
who has practiced one kick 10,000 times. *Bruce Lee*
/ [하나의 발차기를 1만 번 연습한]

■ 목적어인 the man을 관계대명사 who가 이끄는 형용사절이 각각 수식하고 있다.

07 Our atmosphere supplies most of the oxygen which animals must have to
우리의 대기는 대부분의 산소를 제공한다 / [동물들이 가져야 하는 / 생존
survive, as well as the carbon dioxide needed by plants.
하기 위해서] / 이산화탄소뿐만 아니라 / [식물이 필요로 하는]

■ 목적어인 most of oxygen을 관계대명사 which가 이끄는 형용사절이 수식하고 있다.
— the carbon dioxide를 과거분사 needed가 이끄는 형용사구가 수식하고 있다.

oxygen 산소
A as well as B B뿐만 아니라 A도
carbon dioxide 이산화탄소

(모의) **08** Choose words that are more expressive, like 'great' or 'terrific' or 'wonderful'
단어들을 선택하라 / [더욱 표현력이 있는 / 'great,' 'terrific,' 또는 'wonderful'처럼]
if you want to express pleasure.
/ 만약 당신이 즐거움을 표현하고 싶다면

■ 목적어인 words를 관계대명사 that이 이끄는 형용사절이 수식하고 있다.

expressive 표현력이 있는, 표현하는
terrific 굉장한; 무서운

(모의) **09** We will eventually reach a point at which conflict with the finite nature of
우리는 결국 지점에 이르게 될 것이다 / [자원의 한정성과의 갈등이 불가피한]
resources is inevitable.

■ 목적어인 a point를 「전치사 + 관계대명사」인 at which가 이끄는 형용사절이 수식하고 있다. at which는 관계부사 where로 바꿔 쓸 수 있다.

eventually 결국, 마침내
conflict 갈등
finite 한정된, 유한한
inevitable 불가피한

C **10** 'Jack-of-all-trades' means those who claim to be proficient at countless
'팔방미인'은 사람들을 의미한다 / [셀 수 없이 많은 일들에 능숙하다고 주장하는
tasks, but cannot perform a single one of them well.
/ 그러나 그것들 중 단 하나도 잘 해낼 수 없는]

■ 목적어 those를 수식하는 형용사절로 관계대명사 who가 이끄는 절이 온다.

jack-of-all-trades 팔방미인, 무엇이나 잘하는 사람
claim 주장하다; 요구하다
proficient 능숙한
countless 셀 수 없이 많은, 무수한

(모의) **11** We are thoroughly enjoying the immediate benefits of attractive consumer
우리는 매력적인 소비재의 목전의 혜택을 잘 누리고 있다
goods that we generate from producing and disseminating hazardous
/ [우리가 만들어 내는 / 위험한 화학물질을 생산하고 퍼뜨리는 것으로부터]
chemicals.

■ consumer goods를 관계대명사 that이 이끄는 형용사절이 수식한다.
— are enjoying의 목적어에 해당하는 the immediate benefits를 전치사 of가 이끄는 형용사구 of attractive consumer goods가 수식한다.

thoroughly 잘, 아주; 완전히
immediate 목전의, 즉각적인
consumer goods 소비재
disseminate 퍼뜨리다, 전파하다
hazardous 위험한

(모의) **12** School physical education programs should offer a balanced variety of
학교 체육 프로그램은 균형 잡힌 다양한 활동을 제공해야 한다
activities that allow young people to develop ability in lifetime activities
/ [젊은이들이 평생 활동 속에서 능력을 개발할 수 있게 하는
that are personally meaningful and enjoyable.
/ [개인적으로 의미 있고 즐거운]]

■ 목적어 a balanced variety of activities를 수식하는 형용사절로 관계대명사 that이 이끄는 절이 오고, that절의 lifetime activities를 또다른 관계대명사 that이 이끄는 절이 수식하고 있다.

physical education 체육
balanced 균형 잡힌

Chapter 03

Review

A **01** Remember **to look up at the stars and not down at your feet.** Try **to make**
기억해라   / 위로 별을 보고 아래로 네 발을 보지 말 것을   노력해라 / 네가 보는
sense of what you see and wonder about what makes the universe exist.
것을 이해하려고   / 그리고 생각해보라 / 무엇이 우주를 존재하게 만드는가에 대해서 *Stephen Hawking*

make sense of ~을 이해하다

■ remember + to-v: (미래에) ~할 것을 기억하다 / try + to-v: ~하려고 노력하다

수능! **02** Some people make **it difficult for others to tell them the truth** because they
어떤 사람들은 만든다   / (…을) 어렵게 / 다른 사람들이 그들에게 진실을 말하는 것을   / 왜냐하면 그들이
respond rudely or **emotionally to people who tell the truth.**
무례하게 또는 감정적으로 반응하기 때문이다   / 사람들에게 / [진실을 말하는]

respond 반응하다
rudely 무례하게
emotionally 감정적으로
tell the truth 진실을 말하다

■ it은 가목적어이고, to tell ~ the truth가 진목적어이다. for others는 to tell의 의미상 주어이다.
— 관계대명사 who가 이끄는 형용사절 who ~ truth가 people을 수식하고 있다.

03 Never tell people **how to do things.** Tell them **what to do** and they will
결코 사람들에게 일을 어떻게 해야 할지를 말하지 마라   그들에게 무엇을 해야 할지를 말해라 / 그러면 그들은 당신을
surprise you with their ingenuity. *George S. Patton*
놀라게 할 것이다 / 자신들의 창의력으로

ingenuity 창의력, 재간

■ how to-v: 어떻게 ~해야 할지 / what to-v: 무엇을 ~해야 할지

04 People will forget **what you said**, people will forget **what you did**, but people
사람들은 잊을 것이다   / 당신이 말한 것을   / 사람들은 잊을 것이다   / 당신이 행한 것을   / 그러나 사람들은
will **never forget how you made them feel.** *Maya Angelou*
절대 잊지 않을 것이다   / 당신이 그들이 어떻게 느끼게 했는지를

■ forget의 목적어로 각각 what과 how가 이끄는 명사절 what you said, what you did, how ~ feel이 쓰였다.

B **05** NASA said **the satellite stopped working within hours of its launch and**
NASA는 말했다 / 그 인공위성은 작동을 멈췄다고   / 그것을 발사한 지 몇 시간 내에   / 그리고
did not respond to attempts to communicate with it.
그것과 통신하려는 시도에 응답하지 않았다고

satellite 인공위성
launch 발사

풀이 stop은 동명사를 목적어로 취하는 동사로, '~하는 것을 그만두다'의 의미를 나타낸다. *cf.* stop to-v: ~하기 위해 멈추다

■ said 다음에 목적어절을 이끄는 접속사 that이 생략되어 있다.

06 Do regular maintenance **on your vehicles :** Do not skimp on or forget **to do**
당신의 차량에 정기적인 정비를 하라   지나치게 아끼지 마라   / 또는 잊지 마라 / 정기적인
regular oil changes.
오일 교체를 하는 것을

maintenance 정비, 보수
skimp 지나치게 아끼다, 인색
하게 굴다

풀이 forget은 to부정사와 동명사 둘 다 목적어로 취하지만 '~할 것을 잊다'는 의미로는 to부정사가 적절하다.

07 No one knows just **what impact the buildup of CO$_2$ will have,** but some
아무도 알지 못한다   / 정말 이산화탄소의 축적이 어떤 영향을 미칠지를   / 그러나 일부
scientists fear **that the globe will continue to warm up, bringing on**
과학자들은 염려한다   / 지구가 계속 온난해질 것을   / 기후 변화의 왜곡을
wrenching climatic changes.
야기하면서

buildup 축적; 증강
bring on ~을 야기하다
wrench 왜곡하다; 비틀다

풀이 동사 fear의 목적어로 접속사 that이 이끄는 명사절이 적절하다. / 이어지는 절이 완전하므로 what이 올 수 없다.
■ bringing ~ changes는 분사구문으로 앞의 사건과 동시에 발생하는 다른 사건을 서술한다. **Unit 32**

수능 **08** °Focusing on on-line interaction with people who are engaged in the same
사람들과 온라인상의 상호작용에 초점을 맞추는 것은 / [동일한 전문화된 분야에 종사하는]

specialized area can limit **potential sources of information and thus** make **it**
/ 정보의 잠재적 원천을 제한할 수 있다 / 그리고 따라서 만들 수 있다

less probable **for unexpected findings to happen.**
/ (…을) 가망이 더 적게 / 예상치 못한 발견이 일어나는 것을

> **풀이** make 다음의 it은 가목적어이므로, 진목적어 역할을 하는 to happen이 적절하다. / 'for ~ findings'는 to happen의 의미상 주어이다.
> ──
> ─ 문장의 주어로 Focusing이 이끄는 동명사구가 쓰였고, 관계대명사 who가 이끄는 절이 people을 수식하고 있다.

be engaged in ～에 종사하다
potential 잠재적인; 잠재력
probable 가망이 있는, 있음직한

C **09** I realized **I had forgotten to lock the door** before I'd only gone a few steps
나는 깨달았다 / 내가 문을 잠그는 것을 잊었다는 것을 / 내가 그 길로 단지 몇 걸음을 채 가기 전에

down the road.

> **풀이** realized 다음에 목적어 역할을 하는 명사절을 이끄는 접속사 that이 생략되어 있다. 문을 잠그는 것을 잊은 것이므로 had forgotten의 목적어로 to부정사를 쓴다.

10 The law of universal gravitation explains **how the force of gravity affects all**
만유인력의 법칙은 설명한다 / 어떻게 중력이 우주의 모든 물체에 영향을 미치는지를

objects in the universe.

> **풀이** explains의 목적어로 의문사 how가 이끄는 명사절이 이어져야 한다. 이때의 명사절은 간접의문문이므로 「의문사＋s＋v」의 어순으로 쓴다.

the law of universal gravitation 만유인력의 법칙
gravity 중력

11 I think **it** necessary **for people to realize what we are doing to the environment**
나는 생각한다 / (…이) 필요하다고 / 사람들이 깨닫는 것이 / 우리가 환경에 무엇을 하고 있는지를

each time we throw away plastic.
/ 우리가 플라스틱을 버릴 때마다

> **풀이** think의 목적어인 to부정사구가 길어 문장의 뒤로 보내진 것이므로 목적어 자리에 가목적어 it이 오고, 진목적어 to realize 뒤에 의문사 what이 이끄는 명사절이 이어지도록 한다. '깨닫는 것'의 주체는 사람들이므로 for people을 to부정사 앞에 쓴다.

each time ～할 때마다 (= every time, whenever)

D **12** Sometimes in the midst of life's chaos we forget °**to do the little things that**
때때로 인생의 혼돈의 한가운데에서 / 우리는 작은 것들을 해야 하는 것을 잊는다 / [우리에게

remind us °**we're part of something greater than ourselves.**
상기시켜 주는 / 우리는 우리 자신보다 더 큰 어떤 것의 일부라는 것을]

> ─ forget의 목적어로 to do the little things가 왔고, 관계대명사 that이 이끄는 절이 the little things를 수식한다.
> ─ 관계사절 내에서 us 다음에 직접목적어 역할을 하는 명사절을 이끄는 접속사 that이 생략되어 있다.

chaos 혼돈, 혼란
remind 상기시키다

모의 **13** Taking the time to truly understand another's point of view shows °**that you**
다른 사람의 관점을 진정으로 이해하기 위해서 시간을 들이는 것은 보여 준다 / 당신이 그가

value what he says and care about him as a person.
말하는 것을 소중하게 여긴다는 것을 / 그리고 그를 한 사람으로서 신경 쓴다는 것을

> ─ shows의 목적어로 접속사 that이 이끄는 명사절이 왔다.

point of view 관점
value 소중하게 여기다

모의 **14** Children °raised in households that foster communication find °it easier °to
가정에서 양육된 아이들은 / [소통을 장려하는] / 생각한다 / (…을) 더 쉽게 /

talk to others about their emotions later in life.
타인들과 얘기하는 것을 / 살면서 나중에 자신들의 감정에 대해서

> ─ it은 가목적어이고, to talk ~ in life가 진목적어이다.
> ─ 과거분사 raised가 이끄는 어구가 문장 전체의 주어인 Children을 수식하고 있다.

raise 양육하다, 기르다
foster 장려하다, 촉진하다

Chapter

04

보어의 파악

- unit 15   주격보어: 구
- unit 16   주격보어: 절
- unit 17   목적격보어 1
- unit 18   목적격보어 2
- unit 19   보어 + 형용사구
- unit 20   보어 + 형용사절

■ 본격적인 구문 학습에 앞서, 각 유닛별 주요 단어를 확인하세요.

Unit 15

- ☐ supreme 최고의, 최상의
- ☐ blur 흐릿하게 만들다
- ☐ account 계좌
- ☐ spread 유포하다, 퍼뜨리다

- ☐ closet 벽장
- ☐ primitive 원시의
- ☐ perspective 관점
- ☐ average 일반적인, 보통의

- ☐ observe 관찰하다
- ☐ context 문맥, 상황
- ☐ apply 적용하다
- ☐ factor 요소

Unit 16

- ☐ tragedy 비극
- ☐ challenge 도전
- ☐ overcome 극복하다
- ☐ design 설계하다, 계획하다

- ☐ acid test 진정한 척도, 시금석
- ☐ empathy 감정이입, 공감
- ☐ narcissism 자아도취
- ☐ measure 척도

- ☐ author 작가
- ☐ by means of ~에 의하여
- ☐ be stuck 꼼짝 못 하다
- ☐ competence 능력, 능숙함

Unit 17

- ☐ expand 확장하다
- ☐ power outage 정전
- ☐ brevity 덧없음, 짧음
- ☐ feed 먹이를 주다

- ☐ hatch 부화하다
- ☐ fill out ~을 작성하다
- ☐ punctually 정확하게
- ☐ parasite 기생충

- ☐ host 숙주
- ☐ ethnic group 인종 집단
- ☐ merge 어우러지다
- ☐ bond 유대; 접착

Unit 18

- ☐ beg 구걸하다
- ☐ debtor 채무자, 빚진 사람
- ☐ false teeth 틀니, 의치
- ☐ vein 정맥

- ☐ artery 동맥
- ☐ fiercely 사납게
- ☐ speak ill of ~을 욕하다
- ☐ post 게재하다, 게시하다

- ☐ graze 풀을 뜯다
- ☐ slope 비탈, 경사지
- ☐ meadow 목초지
- ☐ tense 긴장된

Unit 19

- ☐ rehearse 연습하다
- ☐ value (pl.) 가치관; 가치, 진가
- ☐ discard 버리다
- ☐ separate (따로) 떨어지다

- ☐ accumulate 축적하다
- ☐ ancestor 조상
- ☐ trade 무역, 거래
- ☐ pot 단지, 항아리

- ☐ device 기구, 장치
- ☐ term 용어
- ☐ treatment 치료제
- ☐ cure 치료하다

Unit 20

- ☐ vanquish 무찌르다
- ☐ ease 완화하다, 덜다
- ☐ friction 마찰
- ☐ bind 결속시키다, 묶다

- ☐ aesthetics 미학
- ☐ fragrance 향기
- ☐ composition 합성; 구성
- ☐ decomposition 분해; 부패

- ☐ immediate 당면한
- ☐ boundary 경계선
- ☐ a reference point 기준점
- ☐ collaboration 합작, 협력

unit 15
주격보어: 구

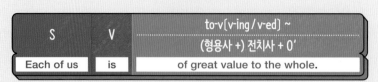

S	V	to-v(v-ing / v-ed) ~ (형용사 +) 전치사 + O'
Each of us	is	of great value to the whole.

우리들 각각은 / ~이다 / 전체에 대단히 중요한

Standard Sentences

01 The supreme accomplishment is to blur the line between work and play.
최고의 성취는 ~이다 / 경계를 흐릿하게 만드는 것 / [일과 놀이 사이의] *Arnold Toynbee*

■ to blur 이하는 주격보어로 쓰인 to부정사구이다.

supreme 최고의, 최상의
blur 흐릿하게 만들다
line 경계(선)

02 The most popular cyber crimes are hacking a person's personal account
가장 일반적인 사이버 범죄들은 ~이다 / 개인 계좌를 해킹하는 것
and spreading a computer virus.
/ 그리고 컴퓨터 바이러스를 유포하는 것

■ 동명사구 hacking ~ account와 spreading a computer virus가 and로 연결되어 주격보어로 쓰였다.

hack (컴퓨터를) 해킹하다
account 계좌
spread 유포하다, 퍼뜨리다

A 03 Knowledge of the world is only to be acquired in the world, and not in a
세상의 지식은 / 오로지 세상 속에서 획득될 수 있다 / 벽장 속에서가 아니라
closet. *Lord Chesterfield*

■ to be acquired 이하는 주격보어로 쓰인 to부정사구이다. 이처럼 be동사 바로 뒤에 이어져 형용사구로서 주어를 보충 설명하는 역할을 할 때, 이것을 「be + to-v 용법」이라고 한다.

acquire 획득하다, 얻다
closet 벽장

> **Grammar Plus** 「be + to-v 용법」의 의미
> ① 예정(~할 예정이다): The president **is to make** a speech next Monday.
> 　　　　　대통령은 다음 주 월요일에 연설할 예정이다.
> ② 가능(~할 수 있다): Not a sound **was to be heard** in that house.
> 　　　　　저 집에서는 아무 소리도 들을 수 없었다.
> ③ 의무(~해야 한다): You **are to take** this medicine regularly.
> 　　　　　당신은 이 약을 규칙적으로 복용해야 한다.
> ④ 의도 · 가정(~하려고 하다): If you **are to succeed**, you must be diligent.
> 　　　　　당신이 성공하려면, 당신은 부지런해야 한다.
> ⑤ 운명(~할 운명이다): All people **are to die** sometime.
> 　　　　　모든 사람들은 언젠가 죽을 운명이다.

04 From the perspective of the individual working person, the key to a great
근로자 개인의 관점에서 / 훌륭한 직장의 비결은 ~이다
workplace is feeling wanted and important.
/ 필요로 하고 중요하다고 느끼는 것

■ feeling 이하는 주격보어로 쓰인 동명사구이다.

perspective 관점
individual 개인

수능 05 Disease, action that might produce disease, and recovery from disease are
질병, 질병을 유발할 수도 있는 행동, 그리고 질병으로부터의 회복은 /
of vital concern to the whole primitive community.
중대한 관심사이다 / 원시 공동체 전체에게

■ of vital concern 이하는 주격보어로 쓰인 전치사구이다.
▬ 전치사 of 뒤에 추상명사가 오면 형용사구가 된다. *ex.* of importance = important, of value = valuable

recovery 회복
vital 중대한; 생명의
concern 관심사; 염려
primitive 원시의, 초기의

B 06 Average consumers all over the world **still remain** **unconvinced of the value**
전 세계의 일반 소비자들은 **여전히** 확신하지 못하는 상태이다   / 암호화폐의 가치와

and usefulness of cryptocurrencies such as bitcoin.
유용성을   / [비트코인과 같은]

■ 형용사 unconvinced가 이끄는 어구가 주격보어로 쓰였다.

Know More 암호화폐(cryptocurrency)는 '암호화'라는 뜻을 가진 crypto-와 '통화, 화폐'란 뜻을 가진 currency의 합성
어로, 컴퓨터 등에 정보 형태로 남아 실물 없이 사이버상으로만 거래되는 전자화폐의 일종으로, 초반에는 '디지털 화폐' 또는 '가상
화폐'로 불렸지만, 최근에는 암호화 기술을 사용하는 화폐라는 의미로 '암호화폐'라고 부르며 정부는 '가상통화'라는 용어를 사용하
고 있다.

average 일반적인, 보통의
unconvinced of ~을 확신하지 못하는, 납득하지 않은
crytocurrency 암호화폐
bitcoin 비트코인(디지털 화폐)

07 The goal of science is **to learn how nature works by observing the physical**
과학의 목적은   / 배우는 것이다 / 자연이 어떻게 작동하는지 / 물리적 세계를 관찰함으로써

world, and **to understand it through research and experimentation.**
                / 그리고 그것을 이해하는 것(이다) / 연구와 실험을 통해서

■ 두 개의 to부정사구 to learn ~ world, to understand ~ experimentation이 and로 연결되어 주격보어로 쓰였다.

observe 관찰하다

08 Faith is **taking the first step** even when you don't see the whole staircase.
신뢰는 첫발을 내딛는 것이다   / 당신이 전체의 계단을 보지 못하는 때조차도   *Martin Luther King Jr.*

■ taking the first step은 주격보어로 쓰인 동명사구이다.

staircase 계단

09 Life isn't **about waiting for the storm to pass.** It's **about learning** **how to**
삶은 기다리는 것에 관한 것이 아니다   / 폭풍이 지나가길   그것은 배우는 것에 관한 것이다 / 빗속에서

dance in the rain. *Vivian Greene*
어떻게 춤을 추어야 할지

■ 각 문장의 about 이하는 주격보어로 쓰인 전치사구이다.
— learning의 목적어로 '어떻게 ~해야 할지'를 뜻하는 「how + to-v」 구문이 쓰였다.

C 10 The only way to understand a word fully is **to see it in use in as many**
단어를 완전히 이해하는 유일한 방법은   / 사용되는 그것을 보는 것이다 / 가능한 한 많은

contexts as possible.
문맥 속에서

풀이 우리말 '사용되는 그것을 보는 것이다'의 의미에 해당하는 표현으로, 문장의 동사 is를 쓰고 주격보어로 to부정사
구 to see it in use를 써서 문장을 완성한다.

fully 완전히
context 문맥, 상황

11 **What the textbooks do not teach you is** **when to apply the knowledge.**
교과서가 당신에게 가르쳐 주지 못하는 것은   / 그 지식을 언제 적용하느냐이다

풀이 우리말 '그 지식을 언제 적용하느냐이다'에 해당하는 표현이므로, be동사 is를 문장의 동사로 쓰고 '언제 ~할지'
를 뜻하는 「when + to-v」를 주격보어로 쓴다.
— what이 이끄는 절 What ~ you가 문장의 주어로 쓰였다.

apply 적용하다

12 The most important factor in a happy life is **having a good social network**
행복한 삶의 가장 중요한 요소는   / 좋은 사회적 관계를 갖는 것이다

that you can depend on.
/ [당신이 의지할 수 있는]

풀이 우리말 '좋은 사회적 관계를 갖는 것이다'에 해당하는 표현으로, 문장의 동사 is를 쓰고 주격보어로 동명사
having이 이끄는 어구를 써서 문장을 완성한다.

factor 요소

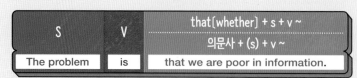

unit 16

주격보어: 절

S	V	that[whether] + s + v ~
		의문사 + (s) + v ~
The problem	is	that we are poor in information.

우리의 문제는 / ~이다 / 우리가 정보가 부족하다는 것

Standard Sentences

01 Life's tragedy is that we get old too soon and wise too late. *Benjamin Franklin*
인생의 비극은 ~이다 / 우리가 너무 빨리 늙고 너무 늦게 현명해진다는 것

— 접속사 that이 이끄는 절이 주격보어로 쓰였다.

tragedy 비극

02 Challenges are what make life interesting and overcoming them is what
도전은 ~이다 / 인생을 흥미롭게 만드는 것 / 그리고 도전을 극복하는 것은 ~이다 / 인생을
makes life meaningful. *Joshua J. Marine*
의미 있게 만드는 것

— 등위접속사 and로 연결된 두 개의 문장에서 what이 이끄는 두 개의 절 what ~ interesting, what ~ meaningful 이 각각의 주격보어로 쓰였다.

— 「what + (s) + v」는 '~하는 것'으로 해석한다.

challenge 도전
overcome 극복하다

(A) 03 If you don't design your own life plan, chances are you'll fall into someone
만약 당신이 자신의 인생 계획을 설계하지 않는다면 / 가능성은 ~이다 / 당신이 다른 사람의 계획에 빠지게 될
else's plan. *Jim Rohn*
것이라는 것

— you'll 이하가 주격보어로 쓰였으며, 그 앞에 보어절을 이끄는 접속사 that이 생략되었다.

design 설계하다, 계획하다
chance 가능성, 예상
fall into ~에 빠지다

04 Design is not just what it looks like and feels like. Design is how it works.
디자인은 ~아니다 / 단지 그것이 어떻게 보이고 느껴지느냐가 디자인은 ~이다 / 그것이 어떻게 작용하느냐
Steve Jobs

— 첫 번째 문장에서는 의문사 what이 이끄는 절이 주격보어로 쓰였고, 두 번째 문장에서는 의문사 how가 이끄는 절이 주격보어로 쓰였다.

Know More 애플의 전 최고 경영자인 스티브 잡스(1955-2011)는 스탠포드 대학의 졸업 축사에서 '점을 잇는 것(connecting dots)'에 관해 말했다. 그는 태어난 후 바로 입양되었으며, 입양 조건은 '대학 진학'이었다. 대학에 들어간 잡스는 6개월 뒤 중퇴했고, 캠퍼스를 돌아다니며 흥미를 느끼는 과목을 청강했다. 그 중 하나가 '서체학' 강의였고, 여러 서체와 글자 조합에 따른 자간 변화를 배웠다. 이것은 후에 서체가 가장 아름다운 최초의 PC '매킨토시'를 개발하는 일로 이어졌다. 그는 '결코 앞을 내다보면 점들을 이을 수 없고, 몰두하다가 뒤를 돌아보면 점들이 이어진 것을 볼 수 있다'고 하며 지금 열정을 가지고 하는 일들이 미래에 어떻게든 연결될 것이며, 그것을 믿고 실천하라는 명언을 남겼다.

work 작용하다

05 The acid test of a good driver is whether he or she remains calm in an
좋은 운전자를 보여주는 진정한 척도는 ~이다 / 그 사람이 침착함을 유지하는지 못하는지 / 비상시에
emergency.

— 접속사 whether가 이끄는 절이 주격보어로 쓰였다. whether가 명사절을 이끌 때는 '~인지 (아닌지)'로 해석한다.

acid test 진정한 척도, 시금석
calm 침착한
in an emergency 비상시에

B 06 A decline of empathy and a rise in narcissism are exactly **what we would**
모의 감정이입의 감소와 자아도취의 증가는 정확하게 ~이다 / 우리가 아이들에게서 볼
expect to see in children who have little opportunity to play socially.
것으로 예상하는 것 / [사회적으로 놀 기회가 거의 없는]

empathy 감정이입, 공감
narcissism 자아도취

- what이 이끄는 절이 주격보어로 쓰였다.
- 관계대명사 who가 이끄는 절이 선행사 children을 수식한다.

07 The measure of a true champion is **not how they win. It's how they handle**
진정한 챔피언의 척도는 ~아니다 / 그들이 어떻게 이기느냐가 그것은 ~이다 / 그들이 어떻게
defeat. *Garry Hall*
패배를 다루느냐

measure 척도; 재다
handle 다루다
defeat 패배

- 두 문장에서 의문사 how가 이끄는 절 how ~ win과 how ~ defeat이 각각 주격보어로 쓰였다.

08 The new processor is **to other processors what a Ferrari is to other cars:**
새로운 프로세서는 ~이다 / 다른 프로세서들에 대해서는 / 페라리가 다른 자동차들에 대한 것
i.e. faster.
/ 즉 더 빠르다

processor (컴퓨터의) 프로세서, 처리기
i.e. 즉

→ 새로운 프로세서와 다른 프로세서들의 관계는 페라리와 다른 자동차들의 관계와 같다. 즉 더 빠르다.

- A is to B what(as) C is to D: A와 B의 관계는 C와 D의 관계와 같다

09 The meaning of a poem is **whatever the author intends to communicate to**
시의 의미는 ~이다 / 작가가 독자에게 전달하려고 의도하는 무엇이나
the reader by means of the poem.
/ 시에 의하여

author 작가, 저자
by means of ~에 의하여, ~의 도움으로

- whatever가 이끄는 명사절이 주격보어로 쓰였다.
- whatever가 명사절을 이끌 때는 '~하는 무엇이나', 부사절을 이끌 때는 '무엇을 ~하더라도'로 해석한다.

C 10 An important lesson to remember is **that we should try to see the positives**
모의 기억해야 할 중요한 교훈은 ~이다 / 우리가 인생에서 긍정적인 것들을 보려고 노력해야 한다는 것
in life even while we are stuck in the middle of trouble.
/ 우리가 곤경의 한 가운데에 빠져 꼼짝 못 할 동안에도

positive 긍정적인; 긍정적인 것
be stuck 꼼짝 못 하다, 갇혀 있다

- 풀이 우리말 '우리가 노력해야 한다는 것이다'의 의미에 해당하는 표현이므로, 문장의 동사 is를 쓰고, 접속사 that이 이끄는 절이 주격보어가 되도록 「that + s + v」의 어순으로 단어를 배열한다.

수능 **11** One key social competence is **how well or poorly people express their**
하나의 중요한 사회적 능력은 ~이다 / 얼마나 잘 또는 형편없이 사람들이 자기 자신의 감정을 표현하느냐
own feelings.

competence 능력, 능숙함

- 풀이 우리말 '얼마나 잘 또는 형편없이 사람들이 표현하느냐이다'의 의미에 해당하는 표현으로, 문장의 동사 is를 쓰고, 의문사 how가 이끄는 절이 주격보어가 되도록 「의문사 + s + v」의 어순으로 단어를 배열한다. 의문사 how가 '어떻게'를 뜻하는 방법이 아닌 '얼마나'라는 정도를 나타낼 때는 「how + 형용사 / 부사」의 형태로 써야 한다.

12 Facts are **to the scientist what words are to the poet.**
사실들은 ~이다 / 과학자에 대해서는 / 단어들이 시인에 대한 것

→ 사실들과 과학자의 관계는 단어들과 시인과의 관계와 같다.

- 풀이 A is to B what(as) C is to D: A와 B의 관계는 C와 D의 관계와 같다

목적격보어 1

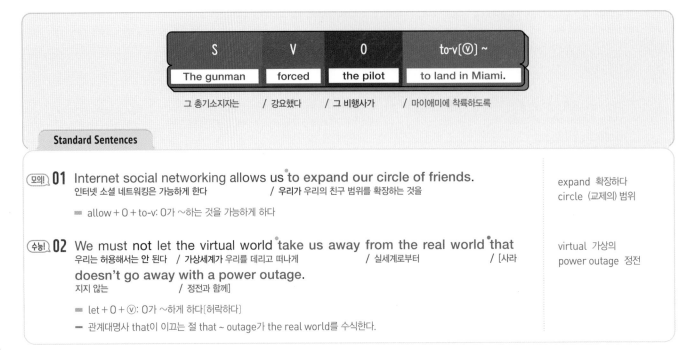

S	V	O	to-v(Ⓥ) ~
The gunman	forced	the pilot	to land in Miami.

그 총기소지자는 / 강요했다 / 그 비행사가 / 마이애미에 착륙하도록

Standard Sentences

모의 01 Internet social networking allows us to expand our circle of friends.
인터넷 소셜 네트워킹은 가능하게 한다 / 우리가 우리의 친구 범위를 확장하는 것을

■ allow + O + to-v: O가 ~하는 것을 가능하게 하다

expand 확장하다
circle (교제의) 범위

수능 02 We must not let the virtual world take us away from the real world that
우리는 허용해서는 안 된다 / 가상세계가 우리를 데리고 떠나게 / 실세계로부터 / [사라
doesn't go away with a power outage.
지지 않는 / 정전과 함께]

■ let + O + Ⓥ: O가 ~하게 하다[허락하다]
■ 관계대명사 that이 이끄는 절 that ~ outage가 the real world를 수식한다.

virtual 가상의
power outage 정전

A 03 If you used the same password on any other site, we encourage you to
모의 만약 당신이 어떤 다른 사이트에서 같은 비밀번호를 사용했다면 / 우리는 당신이 당신의 비밀번호를
change your password there as well.
바꾸기를 권장한다 / 거기서도 또한

■ encourage + O + to-v: O가 ~하기를 권장[장려]하다

encourage 격려하다

04 The realities of growing older and the sense of brevity of our own lives often
늙어간다는 현실 / 그리고 자신의 인생의 덧없음에 대한 의식은 / 종종
make us question the meaning of our existence.
시킨다 / 우리가 우리 존재의 의미를 묻게

■ make + O + Ⓥ: O가 ~하게 시키다

brevity 덧없음, 짧음; 간결함
existence 존재

모의 05 Day after day, I watched the parent birds feed their newly hatched chicks,
매일 / 나는 지켜봤다 / 어미 새들이 자신들의 갓 부화한 새끼들에게 먹이를 주는 것을
and I watched the chicks grow.
/ 그리고 나는 지켜봤다 / 그 새끼들이 자라는 것을

■ watch + O + Ⓥ: O가 ~하는 것을 지켜보다

feed 먹이를 주다
hatch 부화하다
chick 새끼 새; 병아리

B 06 You can force the horse to go to the river but you cannot force the horse to
당신은 강요할 수 있다 / 말이 강으로 가도록 / 그러나 당신은 강요할 수 없다 / 말이 그것에서
drink from it.
마시도록

➡ force + O + to-v: O가 ~하도록 강요하다

07 When you read, focusing on the main idea helps you understand the
당신이 글을 읽을 때 / 요지에 초점을 맞추는 것은 돕는다 / 당신이 세부사항들을 더 잘 이해하도록
details better.

➡ help + O + (to) ⓥ: O가 ~하는 것을 돕다 / help는 목적격보어로 to-v 또는 동사원형을 취한다.

main idea 요지
detail 세부사항

(모의) 08 Most universities have students fill out an evaluation of every course they
대부분의 대학들은 시킨다 / 학생들이 모든 강좌의 평가서를 작성하게 / [그들이
take.
수강하는]

➡ have + O + ⓥ: O가 ~하게 시키다
— course 다음에 목적격 관계대명사 which 또는 that이 생략되어 있다.

fill out ~을 작성하다[채우다]
evaluation 평가(서)

09 When the clock said ten minutes to five, punctually as always, she heard
시계가 5시 10분 전을 가리켰을 때 / 늘 그렇듯 정확하게 / 그녀는 들었다
the car approach and stop outside.
/ 그 자동차가 가까이 와서 밖에 멈추는 것을

➡ hear + O + ⓥ: O가 ~하는 것을 듣다 / 지각동사 hear는 목적어와 목적격보어의 관계가 능동일 때 목적격보어로 동사원형 또는 현재분사를 취한다.

punctually 정확하게, 시간을 엄수하여
as always 늘 그렇듯
approach 가까이 다가오다

C 10 To improve their own chances of survival, some parasites cause their hosts
(모의) 그들 자신의 생존 가능성을 높이기 위해서 / 어떤 기생충들은 시킨다 / 그들의 숙주들이
to act in ways that are very different from their normal behavior.
방식으로 행동하게 / [그들의 보통 행동과는 아주 다른]

풀이 cause + O + to-v: O가 ~하게 시키다
— 관계대명사 that이 이끄는 절이 ways를 수식한다.

survival 생존
parasite 기생충
host 숙주; 주인
normal 보통의, 정상의

11 Before you marry a person, you should first make them use a computer
당신이 어떤 사람과 결혼하기 전에 / 당신은 먼저 시켜야 한다 / 그들이 느린 인터넷 서비스로 컴퓨터를
with slow Internet service to see who they really are.
사용하게 / 그들이 정말 어떤 사람인지 보기 위해서

풀이 make + O + ⓥ: O가 ~하게 시키다
— to see 이하는 '~하기 위해서'를 뜻하는 목적을 나타내는 부사적 용법으로 쓰였다.

(수능) 12 I've seen couples from different ethnic groups merge into harmonious
나는 보아왔다 / 다른 인종 집단의 커플들이 조화로운 관계로 어우러지는 것을
relationships, and I've seen people from different religions come together
/ 그리고 나는 보아왔다 / 다른 종교의 사람들이 강하고 지속적인 유대를 위해 연합하는 것을
for a strong, lasting bond.

풀이 see + O + ⓥ: O가 ~하는 것을 보다

ethnic group 인종 집단
merge 어우러지다, 합병하다
lasting 지속적인, 영속적인
bond 유대; 접착

본책 74~75쪽을 함께 펴놓고 보세요!

unit 18

목적격보어 2

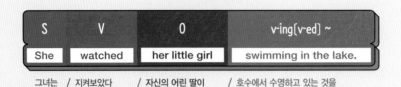

S	V	O	v-ing[v-ed] ~
She	watched	her little girl	swimming in the lake.

그녀는 / 지켜보았다 / 자신의 어린 딸이 / 호수에서 수영하고 있는 것을

Standard Sentences

예 01 In the downtown area I often see homeless people begging for money all
시내에서 / 나는 종종 본다 / 노숙자들이 돈을 구걸하고 있는 것을 /
around the stoplights.
모든 신호등 주변에서

━ see + O + v-ing: O가 ~하는 것을 보다 / O와 C의 관계가 능동·진행

beg 구걸하다; 간청하다
stoplight 신호등, 정지 신호

02 I saw a car pulled over on the side of the road while I was driving home.
나는 보았다 / 어떤 자동차가 길 한쪽에 세워진 것을 / 내가 집으로 운전하는 동안에

━ see + O + v-ed: O가 ~된 것을 보다 / O와 C의 관계가 수동

pull over (차를) 길가에 세
우다

Ⓐ 03 The front desk clerk was on the phone and kept us waiting to check in for
안내 데스크 직원은 통화중이었다 / 그리고 우리가 체크인하는 것을 계속 기다리게 했다 /
a long time.
오랫동안

━ keep + O + v-ing: O가 계속 ~하게 하다 / O와 C의 관계가 능동·진행

front desk 안내 데스크
clerk 직원
check in 체크인하다, 수속을
밟다

04 Many debtors of the bank now find themselves caught in a serious financial
많은 은행 채무자들은 지금 깨닫는다 / 자신들이 심각한 재정 상태에 빠져 있는 것을
position.

━ find + O + v-ed: O가 ~된 것을 깨닫다 / O와 C의 관계가 수동

debtor 채무자, 빚진 사람
financial 재정의, 재무의

05 Unless we take good care of our teeth we may have them all pulled out and
우리가 우리의 치아에 신경을 쓰지 않는다면 / 우리는 그것들이 모두 뽑히게 할지도 모른다 / 그리고
have a set of false teeth made to replace them.
틀니 세트를 맞춰지게 할지도 모른다 / 그것들을 대신하기 위해서

━ have + O + v-ed: O가 ~되게 하다 / O와 C의 관계가 수동

unless ~하지 않는다면(= if
~ not)
pull out ~을 뽑다
false teeth 틀니, 의치

> **Grammar Plus** have + O + v-ed의 의미
> ① 사역(~되게 하다): Where did you **have your hair cut**? 너는 어디에서 머리를 잘랐니?
> ② 수동(~당하다): I **had my watch stolen**. 나는 내 시계를 잃어버렸다.
> ③ 완료(~해버리다): I've **had my homework done**. 나는 숙제를 끝냈다.

B **06** The air we breathe in and out keeps our hearts beating and our blood
공기는 / [우리가 들이마시고 내뱉는] / 계속 우리의 심장이 뛰게 한다 / 그리고 우리의 피가
moving along our veins and arteries.
우리의 정맥과 동맥을 따라 움직이도록

- keep + O + v-ing: O가 계속 ~하게 하다 / O와 C의 관계가 능동·진행
- The air 다음에 목적격 관계대명사 which 또는 that이 생략되어 있다.

beat (심장이) 뛰다, 고동치다
vein 정맥
artery 동맥

07 I heard the dogs barking fiercely late at night, so I came outside to see what
나는 들었다 / 개들이 사납게 짖는 것을 / 늦은 밤에 / 그래서 나는 밖으로 나갔다 / 무슨 일이 일어나고
was going on.
있는지를 보기 위해서

- hear + O + v-ing: O가 ~하는 것을 듣다 / O와 C의 관계가 능동·진행
- what이 이끄는 절이 to see의 목적어로 쓰였다.

bark 짖다
fiercely 사납게, 격렬하게

(모의) **08** Customers want their food delivered fast, and they want it to arrive hot.
고객들은 원한다 / 그들의 음식이 빨리 배달되기를 / 그리고 그들은 원한다 / 그것이 따끈하게 도착하기를

- want + O + v-ed: O가 ~되기를 원하다 / O와 C의 관계가 수동
- want + O + to-v: O가 ~하기를 원하다 / O와 C의 관계가 능동 ⊙ (Unit 17)

09 Although I have known the judge for a long time, I never heard him spoken
비록 내가 그 재판관을 오랫동안 알아 왔지만 / 나는 전혀 듣지 못했다 / 그가 타인에
ill of by others.
의해서 나쁘게 말해지는 것을

- hear + O + v-ed: O가 ~된 것을 듣다 / O와 C의 관계가 수동

speak ill of ~을 욕하다, ~에 대해 나쁘게 말하다

C **10** Winners will have their essays posted on our website. Among the winners,
(모의) 입상자들은 할 것이다 / 그들의 에세이가 우리의 웹사이트에 게재되게 / 입상자들 중에서
only the first prize winner will have his or her essay published in our
/ 오직 1등 입상자만이 할 것이다 / 자신의 에세이가 우리의 잡지에 실리게
magazine.

풀이 목적어인 their essays와 his or her essay가 각각 웹사이트에 게재되고, 잡지에 실리는 대상이므로 수동의
관계를 나타내는 과거분사 posted와 published가 목적격보어로 알맞다.

post 게재하다, 게시하다
publish 싣다; 출판하다

(모의) **11** Up on the green, green shoulder of hill rising to the west I could see a small
언덕의 푸르고 푸른 등성이 위에 / [서쪽으로 솟은] / 나는 볼 수 있었다 / 작은 소
group of cattle grazing, and, below them on a gentler slope, several dozen
떼 무리가 풀을 뜯고 있는 것을 / 그리고 / 소 떼보다 아래쪽에 / 보다 완만한 비탈길에 / 수십 마리의 닭들이
chickens wandering down to the meadow.
/ 아래로 목초지까지 돌아다니고 있는 것을

풀이 see + O + v-ing: O가 ~하고 있는 것을 보다 / O와 C의 관계가 능동·진행

- and로 could see의 두 개의 목적어와 목적격보어가 병렬 연결되어 있다.

shoulder (산·언덕의) 등성이
cattle (집합적) 소
graze 풀을 뜯다, 방목하다
slope 비탈, 경사지
meadow 목초지, 초원

(모의) **12** Being in the spotlight made Tom feel tense. He tried to deliver his lines as
스포트라이트 속에 있는 것이 만들었다 / Tom이 긴장을 느끼게 그는 자신의 대사를 전달하려고 노력했다 /
best as he could, but he could feel his voice shaking.
그가 할 수 있는 한 가장 잘 / 그러나 그는 느낄 수 있었다 / 자신의 목소리가 떨리고 있는 것을

풀이 (A) make + O + ⓥ: O가 ~하게 만들다[하다]
(B) feel + O + v-ing: O가 ~하고 있는 것을 느끼다 / O와 C의 관계가 능동·진행

tense 긴장된

unit 19
보어 + 형용사구

S	V	C	(형용사 +) 전치사 + O' to-v(v-ing / v-ed) ~
The ugly frog	`turned out	to be a handsome prince	in disguise.
그 못생긴 개구리는 / 밝혀졌다		/ 잘생긴 왕자인 것으로	/ [위장한]

Standard Sentences

01 Painting is only a bridge `linking the painter's mind with `that of the viewer.
그림은 다리일 뿐이다 / [화가의 마음을 연결하는 / 보는 사람의 마음과]

Eugène Delacroix

- 현재분사구 linking ~ viewer가 보어 a bridge를 수식한다.
- that of the viewer의 that은 mind를 가리킨다.

Know More 외젠 들라크루아(Eugène Delacroix)는 19세기 낭만주의를 대표하는 프랑스 예술가로, 벽화 장식을 포함한 유화뿐만 아니라, 데생, 수채화, 파스텔, 판화 등 방대한 작품을 제작하였다. 그는 16세에 고전파 화가인 P. N.게랭에게 그림을 배웠고, 1816년 미술학교에 입학하여 루브르 박물관에 다니며 그림을 모사하기 시작했다. 들라크루아의 표현 방식은 인상주의자들의 작품에 영향을 끼쳤고, 1822년 최초의 낭만주의 회화인 〈단테의 작은 배〉를 발표하였다.

02 `Rehearsing what you want to say can help you find a better way `to say it.
연습하는 것은 / 당신이 말하고 싶은 것을 / 도울 수 있다 / 당신이 더 나은 방법을 찾는 것을 / [그것을 말하는]

rehearse 연습하다

- help의 목적격보어로 쓰인 find ~ way에서 a better way를 to say it이 수식하고 있다.
- 동명사 주어인 Rehearsing은 what이 이끄는 절 what ~ say를 목적어로 가진다.

Ⓐ 03 Knowledge workers are the ones `responsible for `keeping the high-tech
지식 근로자들은 사람들이다 / [첨단 기술 경제를 계속 돌아가게 하는 데 책임이 있는]
economy running.

responsible for ~에 책임이 있는; ~의 원인이 되는
high-tech 첨단 기술의

- responsible 이하의 형용사구가 보어 the ones를 수식한다.
- keep + O + v-ing: O가 계속 ~하게 하다

(모의) 04 In 1953, Jacqueline Cochran became `the first woman pilot `to break the
1953년에 / Jacqueline Cochran은 최초의 여성 조종사가 되었다 / [음속 장벽을 깬]
sound barrier. Additionally, she was `the first female `to pilot a jet across the
게다가 그녀는 최초의 여성이었다 / [대서양을 횡단하여 제트기를 조종한]
Atlantic.

pilot 조종사; 조종하다
sound barrier 음속 장벽(비행기의 속도가 음속에 가까워질 때 충격파가 발생하는 현상)
additionally 게다가

- 첫 번째 문장의 보어 the first woman pilot과 두 번째 문장의 보어 the first female을 각각 to break ~ barrier와 to pilot ~ Atlantic이 수식하고 있다.
- the first / last / only 등이 붙은 명사는 to부정사의 수식을 받으며 '~한(할) 최초의 / 마지막의 / 유일한 …'로 해석한다.

05 We should let our beliefs and values guide our decisions `about how to live
우리는 우리의 신념과 가치관이 우리의 결정을 이끌도록 허용해야 한다 / [우리의 삶을 어떻게 살아야
our life.
할지에 관한]

value (pl.) 가치관; 가치, 진가

- 동사 let의 목적격보어로 쓰인 guide our decisions에서 our decisions를 전치사구 about ~ life가 수식하고 있다.

B 06 Improved methods of transportation are forcing **man** to discard the concept
개선된 교통수단은 **사람들에게** 거리 개념을 버리도록 강요하고 있다

of distance **in the past responsible for keeping people separated.**
/ [과거에 사람들이 따로 떨어지게 한 원인인]

■ 목적격보어인 to discard the concept of distance에서 distance를 형용사구 in ~ separated가 수식하고 있다.

discard 버리다
separate (따로) 떨어지다, 분리시키다

07 Humans became the only species **to acquire guidance on how to live from**
인간은 유일한 종이 되었다 / [살아가는 방법에 관한 지침을 획득한 /

the accumulated knowledge of their ancestors, rather than just from their
그들의 조상들의 축적된 지식으로부터 / 단지 자신들의 DNA로부터라기보다는]

DNA.

■ 보어 the only species를 to acquire ~ DNA가 수식하고 있다.

guidance 지침, 안내
accumulated 축적하다
ancestor 조상

08 The global village is all the countries of the world **thought of as being**
지구촌은 세계의 모든 나라들이다 / [밀접하게 연결된 것으로 여겨지는

closely connected by modern communication and trade.
/ 현대의 통신과 무역으로]

■ 보어 all the countries of the world를 과거분사 thought가 이끄는 어구 thought ~ trade가 수식하고 있다.

think of A as B A를 B로 생각하다(여기다)
closely 밀접하게, 친밀히
trade 무역, 거래

09 A day without a friend is like a pot **without a single drop of honey left**
친구가 없는 하루는 단지와 같다 / [안에 남아 있는 꿀이 단 한 방울도 없는]

inside. *the short story collection <Winnie the Pooh>*

■ 보어 like a pot에서 a pot을 전치사구 without ~ inside가 수식하고 있다.
— left inside는 honey를 수식하고 있다.

pot 단지, 항아리

C 10 A mouse is a device **making it easier to select different options from**
마우스는 기구이다 / [(…을) 더 쉽게 만드는 / 컴퓨터 메뉴에서 여러 선택 사항들을 고르는 것을]

computer menus.

풀이 문장의 동사는 is이고, a device가 보어로 쓰인 문장으로 접속사 없이 동사 makes가 올 수는 없으므로, a device를 수식하는 형용사구가 되도록 현재분사 making이 적절하다.

device 기구, 장치
option 선택(할 수 있는 것), 선택권

Up! 11 Hindsight bias is a term **used in psychology to explain the tendency of**
사후인지 편향은 용어이다 / [심리학에서 사용되는 / 사람들의 경향을 설명하기 위해

people to overestimate their ability to have predicted an outcome that
/ [자신들의 능력을 과대평가하는 / [어떤 결과를 예측했던 /

could not possibly have been predicted.
[아마도 예측될 수 없었던]]]]

풀이 보어인 a term을 수식하는 분사구가 되어야 하는데, a term이 사용되는 대상이므로 과거분사 used가 알맞다.

hindsight bias 사후인지 편향
term 용어; 기간
overestimate 과대평가하다
outcome 결과

Know More 사후인지 편향(사후 과잉 확신 편향)은 '그럴 줄 알았어 효과(knew it all along effect)' 또는 '헤안 편파'로도 잘 알려져 있다. 이 현상은 어떤 사건의 결과를 알고 난 후 마치 처음부터 그 일의 결과가 그렇게 나타날 것이라는 걸 알고 있었던 것처럼 생각하는 경향을 말한다. 사후인지 편향이 발생하면 기억의 왜곡을 초래하여 내용의 회상과 재구성이 잘못된 결과로 이어지며, 심한 경우 정신질환으로 악화될 수도 있다.

12 Lots of countries wanted **their pharmaceutical companies** to be the first **to**
많은 나라들은 바랐다 / 자신의 제약회사들이 최초가 되길 / [코로나

succeed in developing vaccines and treatments for coronavirus.
바이러스에 대한 백신과 치료제 개발에 성공하는]

풀이 wanted의 목적격보어로 쓰인 to be the first에서 the first를 수식하는 어구로는 문맥상 미래 지향성을 함축하는 to-v 형태가 적합하며, 문장에 다른 접속사가 없으므로 동사인 succeed가 올 수 없다.

pharmaceutical company 제약회사
vaccine 백신
treatment 치료제

unit 20
보어 + 형용사절

S	V	O	C	who[which/that] + (s) + v ~ when[where/why/that] + s + v ~
He	asked	us	to help students	who can't read.

그는 / 요청했다 / 우리가 / 학생들을 도울 것을 / [읽지 못하는]

Standard Sentences

01 Education is the most powerful weapon **which you can use to change the**
교육은 가장 강력한 무기이다 / [당신이 세상을 바꾸기 위해서 사용할 수 있는]
world. *Nelson Mandela*

weapon 무기

- 보어인 the most powerful weapon이 관계대명사 which가 이끄는 절의 수식을 받는다.

수능! 02 Life is a game **where there are multiple winners.**
인생은 게임이다 / [다수의 승자가 존재하는]

multiple 다수의, 복수의

- 보어인 a game이 관계부사 where가 이끄는 절의 수식을 받는다.

Ⓐ 03 King Arthur was a legendary king **who brought peace to his kingdom by**
아서왕은 전설적인 왕이었다 / [자신의 왕국에 평화를 가져다준 /
vanquishing all forms of evil.
모든 형태의 악을 무찌름으로써]

legendary 전설의
vanquish 무찌르다, 패배시키다
evil 악

- 보어인 a legendary king이 관계대명사 who가 이끄는 절의 수식을 받는다.

Know More 아서왕은 중세 6세기경 영국의 전설적 인물이며, 켈트 민족에 속하는 영웅이다. 「아서왕 이야기」에는 아서왕의 출생부터 죽음뿐만 아니라, 당시 켈트족의 다양한 신화와 전설, 기독교 문화가 기록되어 있다. 그는 영국 브리튼 지방을 배경으로 한 중세 로맨스에서 원탁의 기사들을 다스리는 왕으로 나오며, 위풍당당하고 다른 사람을 배려하는 성격으로 부하들과 백성의 존경과 사랑을 받는 것으로 그려진다. 이 전설이 어떻게, 어디에서 유래했는지 그리고 그가 역사상의 실제 인물이었는지는 확실하지 않지만, 아서왕을 주제로 한 문학 작품은 르네상스기뿐만 아니라, 20세기 작가들에 의해서 계속 재생산되고 있다.

04 In family life, love is the oil **that eases friction,** the cement **that binds closer**
가정생활에서 / 사랑은 윤활유이다 [마찰을 완화시켜 주는] / 접합제(이다) / [더 가깝게 결속시키는]
together, and the music **that brings harmony.** *Eva Burrows*
/ 그리고 음악(이다) / [조화를 가져다주는]

ease 완화하다, 덜다
friction 마찰, 충돌, 불화
cement 접합(접착)제; 시멘트
bind 결속시키다, 묶다

- 콤마와 접속사 and로 병렬 연결된 보어 the oil, the cement, the music이 각각 관계대명사 that이 이끄는 절 that ~ friction, that ~ together, that ~ harmony의 수식을 받고 있다.

모의 05 Nutrition education in schools can **help** more students **eat balanced diets**
학교에서의 영양 교육은 도울 수 있다 / 더 많은 학생들이 균형식을 먹도록
that include more vegetables and have a healthy life.
/ [더 많은 채소를 포함하는] / 그리고 건강한 삶을 살도록

nutrition 영양
balanced diet 균형식(영양의 균형을 갖춘 식사)

- 동사 help의 목적격보어로 eat ~ vegetables와 have a healthy life가 쓰였으며, balanced diets를 관계대명사 that이 이끄는 절 that ~ vegetables가 수식하고 있다.
- help + O + (to) ⓥ: O가 ~하도록 돕다

B **06** According to one traditional definition, aesthetics is the branch of philosophy
[모의] 하나의 전통적인 정의에 따르면 / 미학은 철학의 한 부문이다
that deals with beauty, especially beauty in the arts.
/ [미(美)를, 특히 예술에서의 미를 다루는]

- 보어인 the branch of philosophy에서 명사 philosophy를 관계대명사 that이 이끄는 절이 수식하고 있다.

aesthetics 미학
branch 부문; 가지
philosophy 철학

07 Love is like a beautiful flower **which I may not touch, but whose fragrance**
사랑은 아름다운 꽃과 같다 / [내가 만질 수 없는 / 하지만 그 향기가 정원을 기쁨의
makes the garden a place of delight just the same. *Helen Keller*
장소로 만드는 / 마찬가지로]

- 보어인 like a beautiful flower에서 a beautiful flower를 관계대명사 which가 이끄는 절과 but으로 병렬 연결된 소유격 관계대명사 whose가 이끄는 절이 함께 수식하고 있다.

fragrance 향기
just the same 마찬가지로

08 I consider nature a vast chemical laboratory **in which all kinds of composition**
나는 자연을 광대한 화학 실험실로 여긴다 / [온갖 종류의 합성과 분해가 이뤄지는]
and decompositions are formed. *Antoine Lavoisier*

- 목적격보어인 a vast chemical laboratory를 in which 이하의 관계사절이 수식하고 있다.
- 「전치사 + 관계대명사」 형태인 in which는 장소를 나타내는 관계부사 where로 바꿔 쓸 수 있다.

vast 광대한
composition 합성; 구성
decomposition 분해; 부패

09 At the personal level, competition allows us to become the best individual
개인적 수준에서 / 경쟁은 우리가 최고의 개인이 되게 한다
we can be.
/ [우리가 될 수 있는]

- to become 이하가 목적격보어이며, 명사 individual을 관계사절 we can be가 수식하고 있다.
- individual 다음에 관계대명사 who 또는 that이 생략되었다.

C **10** In many situations the boundary between good and bad is a reference point
[수능] 많은 상황에서 / 선과 악 사이의 경계는 기준점이다
that changes over time and depends on the immediate circumstances.
/ [시간에 따라서 바뀌고 당면한 상황에 달려있는]

- 보어인 a reference point가 관계대명사 that이 이끄는 절의 수식을 받는다.

boundary 경계선
a reference point 기준점
immediate 당면한; 즉각적인

11 Better keep yourself clean and bright; you are the window **through which**
당신 자신을 깨끗하고 밝게 유지하는 것이 좋다 / 당신은 창문이다 / [당신이 세상을 봐야 하는]
you must see the world. *George Bernard Shaw*

- 보어인 the window를 through which 이하의 관계사절이 수식하고 있다. / 「전치사 + 관계대명사」에서 전치사는 관계사절의 끝에 위치할 수도 있다. (= ~ the window which you must see the world through.)
- 'Better + ⓥ'은 구어체 표현으로 'You had better + ⓥ'을 줄인 말로 '~하는 것이 좋다'라는 의미이다.

Know More 조지 버나드 쇼(George Bernard Shaw)는 아일랜드의 극작가로, 70에 가까운 긴 창작 기간 동안 진지하면서도 풍자의 묘미가 느껴지는 수준 높은 희곡들을 발표하여 영국 근대극을 확립하고 부흥시켰다는 평가를 받고 있으며, 1925년에 노벨 문학상을 수상하였다. 희곡 외에도 클래식과 미술, 문학 평론에 능했으며 당대의 사상가로 활약하였다.

12 Every novel is an equal collaboration **between the writer and the reader and**
모든 소설은 동등한 합작이다 / [작가와 독자 사이의] / 그리고
it is the only place in the world where two strangers can meet on terms of
그것은 세상에서 유일한 곳이다 / [두 명의 낯선 사람이 절대적인 친밀한 사이로 만날 수 있는]
absolute intimacy. *Paul Auster*

- and 다음의 절에서 보어인 the only place가 관계부사 where가 이끄는 절의 수식을 받는다.
- 첫 번째 절에서 보어인 collaboration이 전치사구 between ~ the reader의 수식을 받는다.

collaboration 합작, 협력
absolute 절대적인; 완벽한
on terms of intimacy 친한 사이로

Chapter 04

A **01** Words are to language what notes are to music.
단어는 ~이다 / 언어에 대해서는 / 음표가 음악에 대한 것

→ 단어와 언어의 관계는 음표와 음악의 관계와 같다.

■ A is to B what[as] C is to D: A와 B의 관계는 C와 D의 관계와 같다.

note 음표; 메모

02 Don't let what you can't do stop you from doing what you can do. *John Wooden*
내버려 두지 마라 / 당신이 할 수 없는 것이 / 당신이 할 수 있는 것을 하지 못하게 하도록

■ let + O + ⓥ: O가 ~하도록 내버려 두다[허락하다]
— stop + O + from + v-ing: O가 ~하지 못하게 하다
— 관계대명사 what이 이끄는 절 what you can't do는 let의 목적어이며, what you can do는 doing의 목적어이다.

03 A central lesson of science is that we must try to free our minds of dogma
과학의 가장 중요한 교훈은 ~이다 / 우리가 노력해야 한다는 것 / 우리의 정신을 독단으로부터 풀어주도록
and to guarantee the freedom to publish, to contradict, and to experiment.
/ 그리고 자유를 보장하도록 / [출판하고, 반박하고 그리고 실험하는]

■ 접속사 that이 이끄는 절이 보어로 쓰였다.
■ 콤마(,)와 and로 연결된 세 개의 to부정사 to publish, to contradict, to experiment가 the freedom을 수식한다.

dogma 독단, 신조
guarantee 보장하다
contradict 반박하다; 모순되다

04 Technological advances will allow high-performance athletes to move faster,
기술적 진보는 하게 할 것이다 / 높은 수준의 운동선수들이 더 빨리 움직이도록
jump higher, hit harder, and improve their consistency.
/ 더 높이 뛰도록 / 더 강하게 치도록 / 그리고 그들의 일관성을 향상하도록

■ allow + O + to-v: O가 ~할 수 있게 허락하다[가능하게 하다] / 네 개의 동사 move, jump, hit, improve가 콤마(,)와 and로 병렬 연결되어 to에 이어진다.

advance 진보, 전진
athlete 운동선수
consistency 일관성

B **05** Walking up the path and back to the car, they could still hear the fish
수능! 그 길을 걸어서 그 자동차로 다시 왔다 / (그때) 그들은 여전히 들을 수 있었다 / 물고기들이
splashing in the water.
물속에서 첨벙거리는 것을

풀이 지각동사 hear는 목적어와 목적격보어의 관계가 능동일 경우 목적격보어로 동사원형이나 현재분사를 쓴다.

splash (물속에서) 첨벙거리다;
첨벙 하는 소리

06 I didn't have time to shop at the market yesterday, so I phoned the store
나는 물건을 살 시간이 없었다 / 시장에서 / 어제 / 그래서 나는 가게에 전화했다
and had the groceries delivered.
/ 그리고 시켰다 / 식료품들이 배달되게

풀이 목적어인 식료품들은 배달되는 대상이므로 목적격보어로는 수동을 나타내는 과거분사 delivered가 알맞다.

grocery 식료품

모의! **07** The experience of eating a pile of unwanted cabbage until they feel sick is
원하지 않는 한 무더기의 양배추를 먹는 경험은 / 그들이 물릴 때까지 /
hardly going to make children jump for joy the next time it is served.
좀처럼 아이들이 기쁨으로 펄쩍 뛰게 만들지 않을 것이다 / 다음번에 그것이 제공될 때

풀이 사역동사 make는 목적격보어로 to부정사가 아닌 원형부정사를 취하므로 jump가 알맞다.

a pile of 한 무더기의
cabbage 양배추
hardly 좀처럼 ~ 않는

C

08 When the man returned to his car, he found car windows broken.
그 남자가 자신의 자동차로 돌아왔을 때 / 그는 알았다 / 차 유리창들이 깨진 것을

> **풀이** found의 목적어로 car windows가 오며, 차 유리창은 깨진 대상이므로 수동의 의미를 나타내도록 목적격보어로 break의 과거분사 broken이 오는 것이 자연스럽다.

09 The growth of scientific knowledge has allowed us to control some of the
과학 지식의 성장은 해 주었다 / 우리가 삶의 위험들의 일부를 통제하도록
risks of life.

> **풀이** allow + O + to-v: O가 ~하도록 허용하다[가능하게 하다]

10 One of the most fundamental characteristics of money is that it acts as an
돈의 가장 근본적인 특징 중 하나는 / 그것이 역할을 한다는 것이다 /
easily transportable store of value.
쉽게 운반 가능한 가치 저장소로서

fundamental 근본적인
store 저장소; 저장하다

> **풀이** 문장의 주어 One of ~ money는 단수로 취급하므로 be동사는 is를 쓰고, 보어로 접속사 that이 이끄는 명사절이 오도록 배열한다.

D

11 Yes and No are the two most important words that determine your destiny
'네'와 '아니오'는 두 개의 가장 중요한 단어들이다 / [인생에서 당신의 운명을 결정하는]
in life.

destiny 운명

> 보어인 the two most important words를 관계대명사 that이 이끄는 절이 수식하고 있다.

12 One of the principal aims of the sciences is to extend the range of our
과학의 주요한 목표 중 하나는 / 우리의 제한된 감각의 범위를 연장하는 것이다
limited senses by translating invisible and inaudible phenomena into
/ 보이지 않고 들리지 않는 현상을 사건으로 바꿈으로써
events that can be seen or heard.
/ [보이거나 들릴 수 있는]

principal 주요한
translate (다른 상태·성질로)
바꾸다, 변형하다
invisible 보이지 않는
inaudible 들리지 않는
phenomenon 현상
(pl. phenomena)

> to extend 이하는 보어로 쓰인 to부정사구이다.
> 주격 관계대명사 that이 이끄는 절이 events를 수식한다.

13 Nuclear weapons have turned war between superpowers into a mad act of
핵무기는 전쟁을 바꾸어왔다 / [초강대국 사이의] / 집단 자살이라는 광기 어린
collective suicide, and forced the most powerful nations on earth to find
행위로 / 그리고 강요해왔다 / 지구상의 가장 강력한 국가들이 평화로운 방법을 찾도록
peaceful ways to resolve conflicts.
/ [분쟁을 해결할]

nuclear weapon 핵무기
collective suicide 집단 자살
resolve 해결하다
conflict 갈등, 분쟁

> force + O + to-v: O가 ~하도록 강요하다
> to resolve conflicts는 peaceful ways를 수식한다.

STAGE II

수식어 중심의 구문

Contents of Stage

Chapter **05** 명사 수식어: 구	Unit 21	명사 + (형용사 +) 전치사구
	Unit 22	명사 + to-v[v-ing / v-ed]
Chapter **06** 명사 수식어: 절	Unit 23	명사 + 관계대명사절
	Unit 24	명사 + 전치사 + 관계대명사
	Unit 25	명사 + 관계부사절
	Unit 26	명사 + 관계사가 생략된 수식절
	Unit 27	명사와 관계사절의 분리
	Unit 28	명사, 관계사절
Chapter **07** 부사적 수식어: 구	Unit 29	부사 역할을 하는 전치사구
	Unit 30	부사 역할을 하는 to-v의 의미
	Unit 31	부사적 to-v의 관용 구문
	Unit 32	부사 역할을 하는 분사구문의 의미
	Unit 33	분사구문의 다양한 형태 1
	Unit 34	분사구문의 다양한 형태 2
Chapter **08** 부사적 수식어: 절	Unit 35	시간의 부사절
	Unit 36	이유의 부사절
	Unit 37	조건의 부사절
	Unit 38	목적 · 결과의 부사절
	Unit 39	반전 · 대조의 부사절
	Unit 40	양태의 부사절

05

명사 수식어: 구

- unit 21   명사 + (형용사 +) 전치사구
- unit 22   명사 + to-v[v-ing ~ / v-ed ~]

■ 본격적인 구문 학습에 앞서, 각 유닛별 주요 단어를 확인하세요.

Unit 21

- ☐ integrate 통합하다
- ☐ regardless of ~에 관계없이
- ☐ race 인종
- ☐ creed 신조, 신념
- ☐ affiliation 소속
- ☐ at the wheel (자동차의) 핸들을 잡고, 운전하여
- ☐ follow close behind 바짝 뒤따르다
- ☐ toxic 유독한
- ☐ flexible 마음대로 바꿀 수 있는
- ☐ user-friendly 사용하기 쉬운
- ☐ empathy 공감
- ☐ adopt 취하다, 채택하다
- ☐ compassion 동정심
- ☐ enemy 적; 장애물
- ☐ to a large extent 크게
- ☐ legitimate 타당한; 합법적인
- ☐ valid (근거가) 확실한
- ☐ fulfilled 성취감을 느끼는
- ☐ burn out 녹초가 되게 하다

Unit 22

- ☐ functionality 기능성
- ☐ sum 총합, 합계
- ☐ establish (기록·습관 등이) 자리를 잡다; 확립하다
- ☐ arise 발생하다, 생기다
- ☐ come up with 생각해내다
- ☐ in isolation 홀로, 고립되어
- ☐ case 사건, 사례
- ☐ illiterate 문맹의, 읽고 쓸 줄 모르는
- ☐ past-due 기일을 넘긴
- ☐ balance 잔금, 지불 잔액
- ☐ crown (영예를) 지니게 하다
- ☐ abandon 버리다
- ☐ assume (태도를) 취하다
- ☐ vessel 배, 선박
- ☐ launch 시작하다
- ☐ hand down 물려주다
- ☐ soar 날아오르다

unit 21
명사 + (형용사 +) 전치사구

~	명사	(형용사 +) 전치사 + O'
He has developed	software	useful to designers.
그는 / 개발해왔다	/ 소프트웨어를	/ [디자이너들에게 유용한]

Standard Sentences

01 Now the Internet has become a well-integrated technology **essential to**
현재 인터넷은 잘 통합된 기술이 되었다 / [전 세계적 사업과
global business and culture.
문화에 필수적인]

■ essential 이하의 형용사구가 a well integrated technology를 수식하고 있다.

integrate 통합하다

02 All people have the right **to medical care** **regardless of race, religion, creed**
모든 사람들은 권리를 가지고 있다 / [의료에 대한] / 인종, 종교, 신조 또는 정치적 소속에 관계없이
or political affiliation. *Doctors Without Borders*

■ 전치사구 to medical care가 the right를 수식하고 있다.
─ 전치사 regardless of의 목적어로 race, religion, creed, political affiliation이 or로 병렬 연결되어 있다.

medical care 의료
regardless of ~에 관계
없이
race 인종
creed 신조, 신념
affiliation 소속; 가입

A 03 A small blue car **with an unknown driver at the wheel** was following **close**
작은 파란색 자동차 한 대가 / [모르는 운전자가 핸들을 잡고 있는] / 내 차를 바짝 뒤따라오고 있었다
behind my car.

■ with가 이끄는 전치사구 with ~ the wheel이 A small blue car를 수식하고 있다.

at the wheel (자동차의) 핸들
을 잡고, 운전하여
follow close behind 바짝
뒤따르다

04 The greatest scientific discoveries are the product **of imagination, curiosity,**
가장 위대한 과학적 발견들은 산물이다 / [상상력, 호기심
and years of careful research.
/ 그리고 수년간의 세심한 연구의]

■ of 이하의 전치사구가 the product를 수식하고 있다.
─ of의 목적어인 imagination, curiosity, years of careful research가 and로 병렬 연결되어 있다.

curiosity 호기심

05 A global network **of non-government organizations** works **toward eliminating**
비정부기구들의 전 세계 네트워크는 일한다 / 생산과 사용을 없애기 위해서
the production and use of toxic chemicals harmful to human health and
/ [유독한 화학물질의 / [인간의 건강과 환경에 해로운]]
the environment.

■ 전치사구 of ~ organizations는 A global network를 수식한다.
■ 전치사구 of ~ the environment는 the production and use를 수식하고 있고, harmful 이하의 형용사구가 toxic chemicals를 수식하고 있다.
─ 전치사 toward의 목적어로 eliminating이 이끄는 동명사구가 쓰였다.

toxic 유독한
harmful 해로운

B **06** Read the instructions **on the front cover of each test** carefully.
지시 사항을 읽어라 　　　　/ [각 시험의 앞장에 있는] 　　　　　/ 주의 깊게

　■ 전치사구 on ~ test가 the instructions를 수식하고, of each test는 the front cover를 수식한다.

07 Microsoft Excel is a flexible and user-friendly software **suitable for beginners**
마이크로소프트의 엑셀은 마음대로 바꿀 수 있고 사용하기 쉬운 소프트웨어이다 　　　/ [초보자와 고급 사용자 모두에게
and advanced users alike.
적합한]

　■ suitable 이하의 형용사구가 a flexible and user-friendly software를 수식한다.

(모의) **08** Empathy **in the sense of adopting someone's viewpoint** is not the same as
다른 사람의 관점을 취한다는 의미에서 공감은 　　　　　　　　　　　　　/ 동일하지 않다 　　　/
empathy **in the sense of feeling compassion toward the person**, but the
그 사람에 대해 동정심을 느낀다는 의미에서의 공감과 　　　　　　　　　　　/ 그러나
first can lead to the second by a natural route.
전자는 후자로 향할 수 있다 　　　/ 자연스러운 방법으로

　■ 두 개의 전치사구 in ~ viewpoint와 in ~ the person이 각각 앞의 명사 empathy를 수식하고 있다.

09 Love is the only force **capable of transforming an enemy into a friend.**
사랑은 유일한 힘이다 　　　/ [적을 친구로 바꿔 놓을 수 있는] 　　　　　　　*Martin Luther King Jr.*

　■ capable 이하의 형용사구가 the only force를 수식한다.

　Know More 마틴 루터 킹(1929~1968)은 미국의 인권 운동가이자 목사로 1955년 보스턴 대학에서 신학 박사 학위, 하버드
대학에서 철학 박사 학위를 받고, 목사가 되었다. 1955년 '몽고메리 시에서 운행하는 버스에 흑인은 탈 수 없다'는 인종 차별적 규
칙에 반대하는 보이콧 운동을 시작으로, 전국의 흑인 인권 운동을 지도하다 몇 차례 투옥되기도 하였다. 흑인들의 정신적인 기둥으로
서 추앙받고 비폭력 운동의 지도자로서 1964년 노벨 평화상을 받았으나, 1968년 백인의 총에 맞아 37세의 나이로 숨을 거뒀다.
이후 미국에서는 1월의 세 번째 월요일을 공휴일로 정하여 그의 업적을 기리고 있다.

C **10** The particular strategies **appropriate to an organization** depend to a large
특정 전략들은 　　　　　/ [어떤 조직에 적합한] 　　　　　/ 크게 달려 있다
extent on the political and financial circumstances of the organization.
　　/ 그 조직의 정치적, 재정적인 상황에

　풀이 appropriate to an organization은 주어인 The particular strategies를 수식하는 형용사구이므로 복수
동사 depend가 적절하다.

(모의) **11** Challenges **to new ideas** are the legitimate business **of science** in building
도전은 　　/ [새로운 아이디어에 대한] / 과학의 타당한 일이다 　　　　　　/ 확실한 지식을
valid knowledge.
쌓는 데 있어서

　풀이 동사 바로 앞의 to new ideas는 주어인 Challenges를 수식하는 형용사구이고, 주어가 복수이므로 복수 동사
are가 적절하다.

(모의) **12** Often the difference **between feeling fulfilled at work and feeling empty,**
종종 차이는 　　　　　/ [일에서 성취감을 느끼는 것과 공허한 것, 어찌할 바를 모르는 것, 짜증이 나는 것, 그리고
lost, annoyed, and burned out is all about whether or not you're learning
녹초가 되었다고 느끼는 것 사이의] 　　　/ 모두 당신이 어떤 것을 배우고 있느냐 아니냐에 관한 것이다
anything.

　풀이 between ~ out은 주어인 the difference를 수식하는 형용사구이므로 단수 동사 is가 적절하다.

---

instruction (*pl.*) 지시 사항,
설명
front cover 앞장, 앞표지

flexible 마음대로 바꿀 수 있
는; 유연한
user-friendly 사용하기 쉬운
suitable 적합한
advanced 고급의
alike 양쪽 모두, 똑같이

empathy 공감, 감정이입
adopt 취하다, 채택하다
compassion 동정심, 연민
route 방법; 경로

capable of ~을 할 수 있는
transform A into B A를 B
로 바꾸다(변형시키다)
enemy 적; 장애물

depend on ~에 달려 있다
to a large extent 크게, 대
단히
circumstance 상황

legitimate 타당한; 합법적인
valid (근거가) 확실한, 타당한

fulfilled 성취감을 느끼는, 만
족하는
empty 공허한; 속이 빈
lost 어찌할 도리 없는, 난감한
burn out 녹초가 되게 하다,
에너지를 다 소진시키다

본책 88~89쪽을 함께 펴놓고 보세요!

unit 22

명사 + to-v[v-ing ~ / v-ed ~]

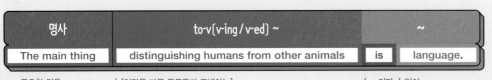

명사	to-v[v-ing / v-ed] ~		~
The main thing	distinguishing humans from other animals	is	language.

주요한 것은 / [인간을 다른 동물들과 구별하는] / ~이다 / 언어

Standard Sentences

수능 01 The human species is unique in its ability ˙to expand its functionality by
인간 종은 독특하다 / 그것의 능력에 있어서 / [그것의 기능성을 확대하는 /
inventing new cultural tools.
새로운 문화적 도구를 발명함으로써]

- to expand 이하가 its ability를 수식하고 있다.

functionality 기능성

02 Climate is the total sum of the weather ˙experienced over a long enough
기후는 날씨의 총합이다 / [충분히 오랜 기간 동안에 걸쳐 경험되는
time period ˙for the pattern to be established.
/ 경향이 자리잡을 정도로]

- 과거분사 experienced가 이끄는 어구가 the weather를 수식하고 있다.
- for the pattern은 to be established의 의미상 주어를 나타낸다.

sum 총합, 합계
establish (기록, 습관 등이) 자리를 잡다; 확립하다

ⓐ 03 Robots are not equipped with capabilities like humans ˙to solve problems
수능 로봇은 인간과 같은 능력을 갖추고 있지 않다 / [문제들을 해결할]
as they arise.
/ 그것들이 발생할 때

- to solve problems가 capabilities를 수식하고 있다.

be equipped with ~을 갖추고 있다
arise 발생하다, 생기다

모의 04 The common idea of a creative individual ˙coming up with great insights,
창의적인 개인이라는 통념은 / [대단한 통찰력, 발견, 작품 또는 발명을 생각해내는
discoveries, works, or inventions in isolation is wrong.
/ 홀로] / 잘못된 것이다

- 현재분사구 coming ~ isolation이 a creative individual을 수식하고 있다.

come up with ~을 생각해내다, 찾아내다
insight 통찰력
in isolation 홀로, 고립되어

05 The story ˙called *The Strange Case of Dr. Jekyll and Mr. Hyde* is the famous
이야기는 / [「지킬 박사와 하이드 씨의 이상한 사건」이라고 불리는 / 선량한 남성에 관한
story of a good man ˙sometimes turning into a horrible monster.
유명한 이야기이다 / [때때로 끔찍한 괴물로 변하는]

- 과거분사구 called ~ *Hyde*가 The story를 수식하고 있다.
- 현재분사구 sometimes ~ monster가 a good man을 수식하고 있다.

case 사건, 사례
horrible 끔찍한, 무서운

Know More 「지킬 박사와 하이드 씨의 이상한 사건」은 영국의 소설가이자 시인인 로버트 루이스 스티븐슨(Robert Louis Stevenson)이 1886년에 발표한 단편소설이다. 변호사인 찰스 어터슨이 그의 오랜 친구인 헨리 지킬 박사와 '저주받은 괴물'인 에드워드 하이드의 관계에 대해 의심을 품고 조사하는 과정을 담고 있으며, 선과 악의 첨예한 대립, 분열된 두 인물의 갈등을 그려 냄으로써 인간의 양면성을 다룬 걸작으로 꼽히고 있다.

B **06** People **judged to be functionally illiterate** lack the basic reading and
사람들은 / [기능적으로 문맹이라고 판단되는] / 기본적인 읽기와 쓰기 능력이 부족하다

writing skills **required in everyday life.**
/ [일상생활에서 요구되는]

- 과거분사구 judged ~ illiterate가 주어 People을 수식하고 있다.
- 과거분사 required 이하가 the basic reading and writing skills를 수식하고 있다.

functionally 기능적으로
illiterate 문맹의, 읽고 쓸 줄
모르는
lack 부족하다, ~이 없다

모의 **07** Yeast cells **growing on a grape skin** obtain energy from nutrient molecules
효모균 세포들은 / [포도 껍질에서 자라는] / 에너지를 얻는다 / 영양소 분자들로부터

originally processed within the grape leaves and stored within the fruit.
/ [원래 포도 나뭇잎 내부에서 가공되는 / 그리고 열매 안에 저장되는]

- 현재분사구 growing on a grape skin이 주어인 Yeast cells를 수식하고 있다.
- originally 이하의 과거분사구가 nutrient molecules를 수식하고 있다.

yeast 효모균
nutrient 영양소
molecule 분자

08 You must pay the past-due balance by the date **written on the front page**
당신은 기일을 넘긴 잔금을 지불해야 한다 / 날짜까지 / [당신의 청구서 앞면에 적혀 있는]

of your bill to avoid the late fee.
/ 연체료를 피하기 위해

- 과거분사구 written ~ bill이 the date를 수식하고 있다.

past-due 기일을 넘긴, 만기가
지난
balance 잔금, 지불 잔액; 균형
late fee 연체료

09 On February 9th, 2020, South Korean movie *Parasite* became the first
2020년 2월 9일에 / 남한의 영화 '기생충'은 / 최초의 외국어 영화가 되었다

foreign-language film **to be crowned Best Picture at the Academy Awards.**
/ [아카데미 시상식에서 최고 작품상의 영예를 받은] *the magazine <The Economist>*

- to be crowned 이하가 the first foreign-language film을 수식하고 있다.

crown (영예를) 지니게 하다,
~에게 왕관을 씌우다

C **10** The order **to abandon ship** automatically assumes two rules: women and
명령은 / [배를 버리라는] / 자동적으로 두 개의 규칙을 취한다 여성과 아이들이

children are first, **and** the captain is the last **to leave** or goes down with his
먼저이다 / 그리고 선장은 떠나는 최후의 사람이다 / 또는 자신의 배와 함께 침몰한다

vessel.

풀이 the last를 수식하는 형용사적 용법의 to부정사 to leave가 적절하다. 주어인 선장이 떠나는 주체이므로 수동
의 의미를 나타내는 과거분사 left는 적절하지 않다.

abandon 버리다
assume (태도를) 취하다
vessel 배, 선박

11 The company has decided to launch a new campaign **targeting inexperienced**
그 회사는 결정했다 / 새로운 캠페인을 시작하기로 / [경력이 없는 대학 졸업생을 겨냥하는

college graduates **preparing to enter the job market for the first time.**
/ [처음으로 취업 시장에 들어가려 준비하고 있는]]

풀이 (A) 새로운 캠페인이 겨냥하는 것이므로 능동의 의미를 나타내는 현재분사 targeting이 적절하다.
(B) 대학 졸업생들이 준비하는 주체이므로 능동의 의미를 나타내는 현재분사 preparing이 적절하다.

launch 시작하다, 착수하다
inexperienced 경력이 없는
graduate 졸업생

Up! **12** The desire **to fly** is an idea **handed down to us by our ancestors who**
날고자 하는 욕망은 생각이다 / [우리에게 전해진 / 우리 조상에 의해서 / [새들을

looked enviously on the birds soaring freely through space on the infinite
부러운 듯 바라보았던 / [자유롭게 공간을 날아오르는 / 하늘이라는 무한한

highway of the air. *Orville Wright*
고속도로 위에서]]]

풀이 (A) 생각은 전해져 내려오는 대상이므로 수동의 의미를 나타내는 과거분사 handed가 적절하다.
(B) 새들이 날아오르는 주체이므로 능동의 의미를 나타내는 현재분사 soaring이 적절하다.

- the infinite highway of the air는 동격의 of가 쓰여 '하늘이라는 무한한 고속도로'의 의미를 나타낸다. **Unit 52**

hand down 전하다, 물려주다
ancestor 조상
enviously 부러운 듯
soar 날아오르다
infinite 무한한

Chapter 05

A 01 We enclose here a copy of our illustrated catalogue ˙about the main items
저희가 여기에 삽화가 들어간 목록 한 부를 동봉합니다   / [주요 물품들에 관한

available at present.
/ 현재 구할 수 있는]

| enclose 동봉하다
| illustrate 삽화를 넣다
| catalogue 목록
| at present 현재

- 전치사구 about ~ present가 our illustrated catalogue를 수식한다.
- 형용사 available 이하가 the main items를 수식한다.

02 Two of the hardest tests ˙in life are the patience ˙to wait for the right moment
인생에서 가장 힘든 두 가지 시험은 ~이다   / 알맞은 순간을 기다리는 인내심

and the courage ˙to accept whatever you encounter.
/ 그리고 당신이 맞닥뜨리는 무엇이든 받아들이는 용기

| patience 인내심
| encounter 맞닥뜨리다

- 전치사구 in life가 Two of the hardest tests를 수식한다.
- to부정사구 to wait ~ moment가 the patience를, to accept ~ encounter가 the courage를 수식한다.

03 We listened to the sound ˙of the rain ˙beating down on the roof and thunder
우리는 소리를 들었다   / [지붕을 두드리는 비의   / 그리고 멀리서

rolling off in the distance.
우르릉대는 천둥의]

| beat 두드리다; (심장이) 뛰다
| thunder 천둥
| roll off (천둥이) 우르릉대다;
| 굴러떨어지다
| in the distance 멀리서

- 전치사 of가 이끄는 어구가 the sound를 수식한다.
- 현재분사구 beating ~ roof가 the rain을, rolling ~ distance가 thunder를 수식한다.

[모의] **04** Words acquire objective meanings because of the "pull" **exerted by social**
단어들은 객관적인 의미를 얻는다   / '영향력' 때문에   / [사회적 압력에 의해서 행사되는

pressures to conform to publicly approved usage.
/ [대중적으로 인정되는 용법에 순응하게 하는]]

| objective 객관적인
| pull 영향력
| exert (영향력을) 행사하다
| conform 순응하다
| approve 인정하다

- 과거분사 exerted가 이끄는 어구가 the "pull"을 수식한다.
- to conform 이하가 social pressures를 수식한다.

B 05 The Superhero Walkathon is an annual fundraising walking event **held to**
[모의] Superhero Walkathon은 해마다 열리는 기금 마련 걷기 행사이다   / [Active

support the Active Way, a charity **dedicated to granting the wishes of**
Way를 지원하고자 개최되는   / 소원을 들어주기 위한 자선단체인   /

terminally ill children.
[병이 중증인 어린이들의]

| fundraising 기금 마련, 모금
| dedicate 바치다, 헌신하다
| grant (소원, 간청을) 들어주다
| terminally ill (병이) 중증인,
| 말기의

> **풀이** (A) 걷기 행사는 개최되는 대상이므로 수동의 의미를 나타내는 과거분사 held가 적절하다.
> (B) 자선단체가 '~을 바치는' 것이 아니라 '~에 바쳐진, ~에 헌신된' 것이므로, 수동의 의미를 나타내는 과거분사
> dedicated가 알맞다.
> ----
> — the Active Way 다음에 콤마(,)에 의해 동격 어구인 a charity ~ children이 이어지고 있다. **● Unit 52**

06 Man's ability ˙to walk upright and use his hands, and his natural capacity ˙to
인간의 능력   / [직립 보행하며 손을 사용하는]   / 그리고 그 사람의 타고난 능력은 /

see into the distance instead of looking at the ground, became weapons
[먼 곳을 보는   / 땅을 보는 대신에]   / 생존의 무기가 되었다

of survival.

> **풀이** 문장의 동사는 became이며 동사 앞인 ground까지 주어가 되어야 하므로, his natural capacity를 수식하
> 는 to부정사의 형태인 to see가 적절하다.
> ----
> — to부정사구 to walk ~ hands가 Man's ability를, to see ~ ground가 his natural capacity를 수식하고 있다.

07 In the information age, reliance **on expert intuition** will gradually be replaced
정보화 시대에 / 전문가의 직관에 대한 의존은 점차 대체될 것이다
by computer programs **processing the relevant data using rules known as**
/ 컴퓨터 프로그램에 의해 / [관련된 자료를 처리하는 / 규칙들을 사용하여 / [알고리즘으로
algorithms.
알려진]]

> **풀이** (A) 컴퓨터 프로그램이 자료를 처리하는 주체이므로 능동의 의미를 나타내는 현재분사 processing이 알맞다.
> (B) 규칙들이 '알고 있는' 것이 아니라 알고리즘으로 '알려져 있는' 것이므로 수동의 의미를 나타내는 과거분사 known 이 알맞다.

reliance 의존
intuition 직관
relevant 관계가 있는
algorithm 알고리즘(문제 해결 절차 및 방법), 연산(법)

수능 **08** The visual preoccupation **of early humans** **with the nonhuman creatures**
초기 인류의 시각적 심취는 / [인간이 아닌 생물들에 대한
inhabiting their world becomes profoundly meaningful.
/ [그들의 세상에서 살고 있는]] / 상당히 중요해진다

> **풀이** 인간이 아닌 생물이 살고 있는 주체이므로 능동의 의미를 나타내는 현재분사 inhabiting이 적절하다.
> ━ 전치사구 of early humans와 with ~ world는 둘 다 주어인 The visual preoccupation을 수식하고 있다.

preoccupation 심취
inhabit 살다, 거주하다
profoundly 상당히, 완전히

C **09** Changes **to one part of our ecosystem,** even a small part, have consequences
우리 생태계의 한 부분에서의 변화는 / 심지어 작은 부분조차도 / 영향을 미친다
for everything else.
/ 다른 모든 것에

> **풀이** 주어인 Changes를 전치사 to가 이끄는 어구가 뒤에서 수식하도록 쓴다.
> ━ 주어와 동사 사이에 even a small part는 삽입된 어구이다.

have consequences for ~에 영향을 미치다

10 A layer of a gas **called ozone in the upper atmosphere** protects us from
가스층이 / [오존이라고 불리는] / [상층 대기에 있는] / 우리를 보호한다 / 태양의
harmful rays of the Sun.
해로운 광선으로부터

> **풀이** A layer of a gas가 불리는 대상이므로 수동의 의미를 나타내는 과거분사 called가 이끄는 어구가 뒤에서 수식하여 문장의 주어가 되도록 하고, 이어서 동사 protects를 쓴다.

layer 층
ray 광선, 빛살
atmosphere 대기

11 Facebook and Instagram announced new policy **restricting sales and**
페이스북과 인스타그램은 발표했다 / 새로운 정책을 / [담배와 주류 상품에 대한 판매와
content for tobacco and alcohol products.
정보를 제한하는]

> **풀이** 새로운 정책이 제한하는 주체이므로 능동의 의미를 나타내는 현재분사 restricting이 이끄는 어구가 new policy를 뒤에서 수식하도록 쓴다.

announce 발표하다, 알리다
restrict 제한하다
content (인터넷이나 컴퓨터 통신에서 제공되는) 정보, 내용물

Chapter

06

명사 수식어절

- Unit 23 명사 + 관계대명사절
- Unit 24 명사 + 전치사 + 관계대명사절
- Unit 25 명사 + 관계부사절
- Unit 26 명사 + 관계사가 생략된 수식절
- Unit 27 명사와 관계사절의 분리
- Unit 28 명사, 관계사절

■ 본격적인 구문 학습에 앞서, 각 유닛별 주요 단어를 확인하세요.

Unit 23

- ☐ social welfare 사회 복지
- ☐ offset 상쇄하다
- ☐ cognitive 인지의
- ☐ intrigue 호기심, 흥미
- ☐ intrinsically 본질적으로
- ☐ swift 빠른, 신속한
- ☐ grieve 슬퍼하다
- ☐ rejoice 기뻐하다
- ☐ eternity 영원
- ☐ sound 건강한, 이상 없는
- ☐ poverty-stricken 가난에 시달리는
- ☐ untapped 미개발의

Unit 24

- ☐ heroine 여주인공
- ☐ sincere 진정한, 진심의
- ☐ elicit 이끌어내다
- ☐ context 상황
- ☐ inherent 내재된, 내재하는
- ☐ but 오직, 단지
- ☐ deal with ~을 다루다
- ☐ consume 소비하다
- ☐ tremendous 엄청난
- ☐ identify with ~와 동일시하다
- ☐ clarity 명확성
- ☐ revise 바꾸다, 변경하다

Unit 25

- ☐ at the expense of ~의 희생으로
- ☐ embark ~에 들어서다, 착수하다
- ☐ fulfill 충족시키다
- ☐ look forward to ~을 기대하다
- ☐ replace 대체하다, 대신하다
- ☐ in general 일반적으로
- ☐ compensation 보수, 급여; 보상
- ☐ cycle 주기; 순환
- ☐ contain 담고 있다, 포함하다
- ☐ complement 보완하다
- ☐ make a fortune 거액을 벌다
- ☐ crave 간절히 원하다, 갈망하다

Unit 26

- ☐ fortune 행운의 여신; 행운
- ☐ frown 눈살을 찌푸리다
- ☐ calculate 추정하다; 계산하다
- ☐ regarding ~에 관하여
- ☐ discrepancy 차이; 불일치
- ☐ retail store 매장, 소매 상점
- ☐ raw material 원료, 원자재
- ☐ advent 출현
- ☐ intimate 친밀한
- ☐ external 외부의
- ☐ exemplify ~의 좋은 예가 되다
- ☐ distribute 배분하다

Unit 27

- ☐ at the moment 지금으로서는
- ☐ govern 통제하다; 통치하다
- ☐ discipline 규율하다; 훈련하다
- ☐ roar 포효하다, 으르렁거리다
- ☐ anticipate 예견하다, 예상하다
- ☐ care for ~을 돌보다
- ☐ suffer from ~으로 고통받다
- ☐ incurable 불치의
- ☐ ultimate 궁극적인
- ☐ authority 권위; 권한
- ☐ in terms of ~의 면에서
- ☐ rooted 자리잡은, 고착한

Unit 28

- ☐ urbanization 도시화
- ☐ surplus 잉여, 나머지
- ☐ division of labor 분업
- ☐ settlement 정착지; 해결
- ☐ autonomously 자체적으로
- ☐ symbolist 상징주의자
- ☐ permanent 영구적인
- ☐ tribal 부족의, 종족의
- ☐ assume 취하다
- ☐ remarkable 눈에 띄는
- ☐ aboriginal 원주민의
- ☐ misleading 오해의 소지가 있는

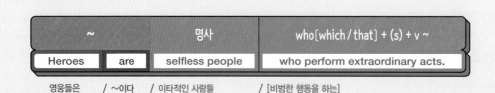

unit 23
명사 + 관계대명사절

~	명사	who[which / that] + (s) + v ~
Heroes are	selfless people	who perform extraordinary acts.
영웅들은 / ~이다	/ 이타적인 사람들	/ [비범한 행동을 하는]

Standard Sentences

01 Social welfare is a set of activities which have, in part, been directed to
사회 복지는 일련의 활동이다 / [부분적으로, 불공평한 분배의 상쇄를 지향해온]
offset unequal distribution.

■ which 이하는 선행사 a set of activities를 수식하는 주격 관계대명사절이다.

social welfare 사회 복지
offset 상쇄하다
distribution 분배

02 A Korean speaker uses different verb forms depending on his or her
한국어 사용자는 다른 동사의 형태를 사용한다 / 그 또는 그녀의 관계에 따라서
relationship to the person whom he or she is speaking to.
/ [그 사람에 대한 / [그 또는 그녀가 이야기하고 있는]]

■ 선행사 the person을 목적격 관계대명사 whom이 이끄는 절이 수식하고 있다. 관계대명사 whom은 who로 바
꿔 쓸 수 있으며, 관계대명사절의 뒤에 있는 전치사 to가 관계대명사 앞으로 이동하면 반드시 whom만 쓸 수 있
다. / (= the person to whom he or she is speaking)

verb 동사

A **03** Birds that in the breeding season fight one another to death over territory
[모의] 새들은 / [번식기에 영역을 두고 서로 죽을힘을 다해 싸우는]
may end up in the same flock during migration.
/ 결국 있게 될 것이다 / 동일한 무리 속에 / 이주기에는

■ 주격 관계대명사 that이 이끄는 형용사절 that ~ territory가 Birds를 수식하고 있다.

breeding season 번식기
territory 영역
end up 결국 (어떤 처지에) 처
하게 되다
flock 무리, 떼
migration 이주

04 Culture shock is the feeling of confusion felt by someone visiting a country
문화 충격은 혼란의 감정이다 / [어떤 사람이 느끼는 / [어떤 나라 또는 장소를
or place whose culture they do not know.
방문하는 / [그곳의 문화를 그들이 알지 못하는]]]

■ 소유격 관계대명사 whose가 이끄는 절 whose ~ know가 a country or place를 수식하고 있다.
– 과거분사구 felt by someone이 the feeling of confusion을 수식하고, 현재분사구 visiting a country or
place가 someone을 수식한다.

culture shock 문화 충격
confusion 혼란

수능! **05** We define cognitive intrigue as the wonder that stimulates and intrinsically
우리는 인지적 호기심을 경이로움으로 정의한다 [자극하고 / 본질적으로 동기를
motivates an individual to voluntarily engage in an activity.
부여하는 / 개인이 자발적으로 어떤 활동에 참여하도록]

■ 주격 관계대명사 that이 이끄는 형용사절이 선행사 the wonder를 수식하고 있다.
– 관계사절의 동사 stimulates와 motivates가 등위접속사 and로 병렬 연결되어 있다.

cognitive 인지의
intrigue 호기심. 흥미
intrinsically 본질적으로
voluntarily 자발적으로
engage in ~에 참여하다

B **06** Time is too slow for those ·who wait, too swift for those ·who fear, too long
시간은 너무 느리다 / 사람들에게는 [기다리는] / 너무 빠른 / 사람들에게는 [두려워하는] / 너무 긴

for those ·who grieve, too short for those ·who rejoice, but for those ·who
/ 사람들에게는 [슬퍼하는] / 너무 짧은 / 사람들에게는 [기뻐하는] / 그러나 사람들에게는 [사랑하는]

love, time is eternity. *Henry Van Dyke*
/ 시간은 영원이다

swift 빠른, 신속한
grieve 슬퍼하다
rejoice 기뻐하다
eternity 영원

> ▬ 주격 관계대명사 who가 이끄는 다섯 개의 절이 각각 앞의 선행사 those를 수식하고 있으며, those who는 '~하는 사람들'의 의미를 나타낸다.

07 The man with a toothache thinks that everyone ·whose teeth are sound is
치통이 있는 사람은 생각한다 / 모든 사람이 / [이가 건강한] /

happy. The poverty-stricken man makes the same mistake about the rich
행복할 거라고 가난에 시달리는 사람은 같은 실수를 한다 / 부자에 대해

man. *George Bernard Shaw*

sound 건강한, 이상 없는
poverty-stricken 가난에 시달리는

> ▬ 소유격 관계대명사 whose가 이끄는 절 whose teeth are sound가 선행사 everyone을 수식하고 있다.

08 The term "placebo" is used to describe a "pill" ·which contains no medical
'플라세보'라는 용어는 사용된다 / '알약'을 표현하기 위해 / [약 성분을 포함하지 않는

ingredients but ·which often produces the same effect as genuine medication.
/ 하지만 종종 진짜 약물과 같은 효과를 내는]

term 용어
placebo 가짜 약, 위약
genuine 진짜의

> ▬ 주격 관계대명사 which가 이끄는 두 개의 절 which ~ ingredients, which ~ medication이 등위접속사 but으로 연결되어 a "pill"을 수식하고 있다.

모의 **09** Flu and colds spread very quickly, especially with the large amount of
독감과 감기는 아주 빠르게 퍼진다 / 특히 많은 접촉으로 인해

contact ·that people now have with each other.
/ [사람들이 지금 서로 하는]

flu 독감
contact 접촉

> ▬ 목적격 관계대명사 that이 이끄는 절이 선행사 the large amount of contact를 수식하고 있다.

C **10** Andy Weir wrote *"The Martian"* for science fiction readers ·who want their
모의 앤디 위어는 「마션」을 썼다 / 공상 과학 소설 독자들을 위해 / [그들의 이야기가 확고히

stories ·firmly grounded in scientific fact.
근거하고 있기를 바라는 / 과학적 사실에]

firmly 확고하게
ground 근거를 두다; 땅

> **풀이** 선행사가 science fiction readers이고, 뒤에 주어가 빠진 절이 이어지므로 주격 관계대명사 who가 적절하다.
> ▬ 과거분사구 firmly grounded 이하는 want의 목적격보어에 해당한다.

> **Know More** 미국인 소설가 앤디 위어(Andy Weir)가 집필한 공상 과학 소설 「마션」은 2011년에 전자책으로 출판되었고, 2014년 종이책으로 나와 베스트셀러가 되었다. 화성을 탐사하러 왔다가 갑작스러운 모래 폭풍에 휘말려 동료들과 생이별을 한 우주인 마크 와트니의 생존기를 다루고 있으며, 이 책을 원작으로 한 동명의 영화가 2015년 개봉되었다.

11 A rain forest is a virtually untapped storehouse of evolutionary achievement
우림은 사실상 미개발의 저장소이다 / [진화적 업적의

that will prove increasingly valuable to mankind as it yields its secrets.
/ [점점 더 인류에게 소중한 것으로 판명될 / 그것이 자신의 비밀을 밝힘에 따라서]]

virtually 사실상, 거의
untapped 미개발의
storehouse 저장소
increasingly 점점 더
yield (비밀을) 밝히다; 낳다

> **풀이** 두 개의 절을 연결하는 접속사의 역할과 이어지는 절의 주어 역할을 동시에 할 수 있는 주격 관계대명사 that이 적절하다.

수능 **12** Those people, organizations, and countries that possess the highest-quality
그 사람들, 조직들, 그리고 국가들은 / [최고급의 정보를 소유하는]

information are likely to prosper economically, socially, and politically.
/ 경제적으로, 사회적으로, 정치적으로 번영할 것 같다

possess 소유하다
prosper 번영하다

> **풀이** 주격 관계대명사 that이 이끄는 절 that ~ information의 수식을 받는 주어 Those ~ countries가 복수이므로 복수 동사 are가 적절하다.

unit 24
명사 + 전치사 + 관계대명사절

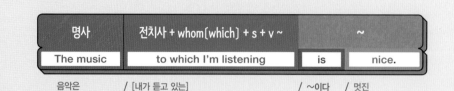

명사	전치사 + whom(which) + s + v ~	~	
The music	to which I'm listening	is	nice.

음악은 / [내가 듣고 있는] / ~이다 / 멋진

Standard Sentences

01 Many authors today are creating fairy stories in which the heroines are
많은 작가들이 오늘날 동화를 창작하고 있다 / [여주인공들이 보다 적극적인]
more active.

- 관계대명사 which가 이끄는 절이 전치사 in의 목적어로 쓰였으며, fairy stories를 수식한다.

author 작가, 저자
fairy story 동화
heroine 여주인공

02 It is often difficult to get books back from people to whom you have lent
(…은) 종종 어렵다 / 책들을 사람들에게서 돌려받는 것은 / [당신이 그것들을 빌려준]
them.

- 관계대명사 whom이 이끄는 절이 전치사 to의 목적어로 쓰였으며, people을 수식한다. / 전치사 to는 관계사절의 끝에 위치할 수도 있는데, 이때는 whom을 who로 바꿔 쓰거나 관계대명사를 생략할 수도 있다.
- It은 가주어이고 to get ~ them이 진주어이다.

Ⓐ 03 Sincere apologies are for those that make them, not for those to whom they
진정한 사과는 사람들을 위해서이다 / [그것을 하는] / 사람들을 위해서가 아니라 / [그것을 받는]
are made. *Greg LeMond*

- 관계대명사 whom이 이끄는 절이 전치사 to의 목적어로 쓰였으며, those를 수식한다.
- that make them은 those를 수식하는 주격 관계대명사절이다.

sincere 진정한, 진심의
apology 사과

04 Even the exact same question can elicit very different responses depending
완전히 똑같은 질문조차도 매우 다른 반응을 이끌어 낼 수 있다 / 상황에 따라서
on the context in which the question occurs.
/ [그 질문이 떠오르는]

- 관계대명사 which가 이끄는 절이 전치사 in의 목적어로 쓰였으며, the context를 수식한다. 이때 in which는 where로 바꿔 쓸 수 있다.

elicit 이끌어 내다
context 상황

모의 05 When a seed grows into a tree, it represents only a change in the degree
씨앗이 나무로 성장할 때 / 그것은 단지 변화를 나타낸다 / 정도에 있어서
to which its potential, always inherent in its original nature, is realized.
/ [그것의 잠재력이 / (늘 그것의 원래의 본성 속에 내재된) / 실현되는]

- 관계대명사 which가 이끄는 절이 전치사 to의 목적어로 쓰였으며, 선행사 the degree를 수식한다.
- which가 이끄는 관계사절 내에서 주어와 동사 사이에 always ~ nature가 삽입되어 있다. ⦿ Unit 53

potential 잠재력
inherent 내재된, 내재하는

B **06** I have but one lamp **by which my feet are guided,** and that is the lamp of
나는 오직 하나의 램프를 가지고 있다 / [그것으로 나의 발이 인도되는] / 그리고 그것은 경험의 램프이다

experience. *Patrick Henry*

but 오직, 단지
guide 인도하다, 안내하다

■ 관계대명사 which가 이끄는 절이 전치사 by의 목적어로 쓰였으며, 선행사 one lamp를 수식한다.

07 What makes a study scientific is **not** the nature of the things **with which it is**
어떤 연구를 과학적으로 만드는 것은 / 사물의 본성이 **아니다** / [그것이 관계된]

concerned, but the method **by which it deals with those things.**
/ 방식(이다) / [그것(연구)이 그러한 사물들을 다루는]

concern 관계하다; 걱정하다
deal with ~을 다루다

■ 전치사 with의 목적어로 쓰인 관계대명사절 which ~ concerned가 the things를 수식하며, 전치사 by의 목적어로
쓰인 관계대명사절 which ~ things가 the method를 수식하고 있다.
─ not A but B: A가 아니라 B / 주격보어인 the nature ~ concerned와 the method ~ things가 병렬 연결되어
있다.

모의 **08** All human societies have economic systems **within which goods and**
모든 인간 사회는 경제 체제를 가지고 있다 / [그 안에서 재화와 서비스가 만들어지고

services are produced, distributed, and consumed.
/ 분배되고 / 그리고 소비되는]

goods 재화, 상품
distribute 분배하다
consume 소비하다

■ 전치사 within의 목적어로 쓰인 관계대명사절 which ~ consumed가 economic systems를 수식한다.

09 *Spider-Man* was a tremendous hit with readers because it gave millions of
「스파이더맨」은 독자들에게 엄청난 히트였다 / 그것이 수백만의 십 대들에게 영웅을 선사했기

teenagers a hero **with whom they could identify.**
때문에 / [그들이 동일시할 수 있었던]

tremendous 엄청난
identify with ~와 동일시하다

■ 전치사 with의 목적어로 쓰인 관계대명사절 whom ~ identify가 a hero를 수식한다. / (= ~ a hero (whom) they
could identify with.)

C **10** The effectiveness of human society is largely dependent **upon the clarity,**
인간 사회의 유효성은 크게 의존한다 / 명확성,

accuracy, and efficiency with which language is used or understood.
정확성, 그리고 효율성에 / [언어가 사용되거나 이해되는]

be dependent upon ~에
의존하다(= depend on)
clarity 명확성
accuracy 정확성

■ 전치사 with의 목적어로 쓰인 관계대명사절 which ~ understood가 선행사 the clarity ~ efficiency를 수식한다.

모의 **11** Separation anxiety disorder is defined **as excessive worry and fear about**
분리 불안 장애는 정의된다 / 과도한 걱정과 두려움으로 / [사람들과

being apart from individuals to whom a child is most attached.
떨어져 있는 것에 대한 / [아이가 가장 애착을 가지고 있는]]

separation anxiety 분리 불안
disorder 장애, 질환
be apart from ~와[에서] 떨
어져 있다
be attached to ~에 애착을
가지다

■ 전치사 to의 목적어로 쓰인 관계대명사절 whom ~ attached가 선행사 individuals를 수식한다. / (= ~ individuals
(whom) a child is most attached to.)

Know More 분리 불안 장애란 집 또는 애착 대상과 분리되는 상황에서 불안의 정도가 일상생활을 위협할 정도로 심하고 지
속적인 경우를 의미한다. 지나치게 밀착된 가족, 부모의 과보호적 양육 태도, 아이의 의존적인 성향이 원인이 될 수 있다. 애착 대
상을 상실하거나 그들에게 해로운 일이 일어날 것에 대해 과도한 걱정을 하며, 분리되는 상황을 반복적인 악몽으로 꾸는 등 여러
증상으로 발견될 수 있다.

12 Social influence is the process **by which individuals adapt their opinion,**
사회적 영향은 과정이다 / [개인들이 그들의 의견을 조정하거나

revise their beliefs, or change their behavior as a result of social interactions
/ 그들의 신념을 바꾸거나 / 또는 그들의 행위를 변화시키는 / 다른 사람들과 맺는 사회적 상호작용의 결과로]

with other people.

adapt 조정하다
revise 바꾸다, 변경하다

■ 전치사 by의 목적어로 쓰인 관계대명사절 which ~ people이 선행사 the process를 수식한다.
─ or로 세 개의 동사 adapt, revise, change가 병렬 연결되어 있다.

unit 25
명사 + 관계부사절

명사	when[where / why / (how)] + s + v ~		~
The reason	why I'm calling	is	to make an appointment.
이유는	/ [내가 전화하고 있는]	/ ~이다	/ 약속을 정하는 것

Standard Sentences

01 We are living in the first century when the greatest skills will come from
우리는 첫 번째 세기에 살고 있다 　　　　　　／ [가장 위대한 기술들이 인간의 행동에서 생겨날
human actions rather than from nature.
　　　　　／ 자연으로부터라기보다는]

- 관계부사 when이 이끄는 절 when ~ nature가 선행사 the first century를 수식한다.
- A rather than B: B라기보다는 A / 동사 come에 from human actions와 from nature가 이어진다.

02 Competition becomes a zero sum game where one organization can only
경쟁은 제로섬 게임이 된다 　　　　　　　　／ [한 조직만 이길 수 있는
win at the expense of others.
　　　／ 다른 조직들의 희생으로]

- 관계부사 where가 이끄는 절 where ~ others가 선행사 a zero sum game을 수식한다. / 관계부사 where의 선행사로는 point(점), case(경우), circumstance(사정), situation(상황) 등의 추상적인 장소 개념도 쓰일 수 있다.

at the expense of ~의 희생으로

A 03 We are embarking on a time when each individual will have all their own
(모의) 우리는 시기에 들어서고 있다 　　　　／ [개인 각자가 가지게 될 　　　　／ 자기 자신의 모든
medical data and the computing power to process it in the context of
의료 정보와 　　　／ 그리고 그것을 처리하는 컴퓨터 사용 능력을 　　　／ 자기 자신의 세계라는 맥락
their own world.
속에서]

- 관계부사 when이 이끄는 절 when ~ world가 선행사 a time을 수식한다.
- to process는 the computing power를 수식하는 형용사적 용법의 to부정사로 쓰였다.

embark ~에 들어서다, 착수하다

04 The reason why worry kills more people than work is that more people
이유는 　　　／ [근심이 일보다 더 많은 사람을 죽이는] 　　　　　　／ 더 많은 사람이 일하기보다는
worry than work. *Robert Frost*
근심해서이다

- 관계부사 why가 이끄는 절 why ~ work가 선행사 The reason을 수식한다.
- 접속사 that이 이끄는 명사절 that ~ work가 문장의 보어 역할을 하고 있다.

05 The way people act is often influenced by experiences that they had in the
방식은 　　／ [사람들이 행동하는] 　종종 영향을 받는다 　／ 경험에 의해서 　／ [그들이 과거에 가진]
past and by the need to fulfill basic human needs.
／ 그리고 필요에 의해서 　／ [기본적인 인간의 욕구를 충족시킬]

- people act는 선행사 The way를 수식하는 관계부사절이며, people 앞에 관계부사 how가 생략되어 있다. 관계부사 how와 선행사 the way는 함께 쓸 수 없으며, 반드시 둘 중 하나를 생략해야 한다. *cf.* 선행사 the way가 있으면 how 대신에 that 또는 in which를 쓴다.
- 목적격 관계대명사절 that ~ past가 선행사 experiences를 수식하고 있다.

fulfill 충족시키다

B 06 We look forward to the time **when the Power of Love will replace the Love**
우리는 때를 기대한다 　　　　　　　　　/ [사랑의 힘이 힘에 대한 사랑을 대체할]
of Power. **Then will our world know the blessings of peace.**
　　　　　　그때는 우리 세계가 평화의 축복을 알게 될 것이다

look forward to ～을 기대
하다
replace 대체하다, 대신하다

- 관계부사 when이 이끄는 절 when ~ Power가 선행사 the time을 수식한다.
- 부사 Then이 문장 앞으로 나와 「조동사 + 주어 + 본동사」의 어순으로 도치되었다. ➔ **Unit 49**

(모의) 07 In general, people accept job offers **where the monetary compensation is**
일반적으로　　　　사람들은 일자리 제안을 받아들인다　　　　[금전적인 보수가 그 금액에 가까운
near the amount that they were hoping for.
　　　　　　　　　/ [그들이 바라고 있었던]]

in general 일반적으로
monetary 금전적인
compensation 보수, 급여;
보상
amount 금액; 양

- 관계부사 where가 이끄는 절 where ~ for가 선행사 job offers를 수식한다.
- 목적격 관계대명사절 that ~ for가 선행사 the amount를 수식한다.

08 Possibly, we all have high points and low points in our creative cycles. This
아마　　　　/ 우리 모두는 높은 지점과 낮은 지점을 지니고 있다　　　　/ 우리의 창의적인 주기에　　　　이것은
may be the reason why we have "good days" and "bad days" at work.
이유일 수도 있다　　　/ [우리가 근무 중에 '좋은 날'과 '나쁜 날'이 있는]

cycle 주기; 순환

- 관계부사 why가 이끄는 절 why ~ work가 선행사 the reason을 수식한다.

(모의) 09 In today's digital environment, appearing in the mainstream news is still an
오늘날의 디지털 환경에서　　　　　　/ 주류 뉴스에 출현하는 것은 여전히 중요한 방법이다
important way that citizens can communicate with a broader community
　　　　　　/ [시민들이 더 넓은 공동체와 소통할 수 있는
about events and issues.
/ 사건과 논쟁점에 대해]

mainstream 주류의

- 관계부사 that이 이끄는 절 that ~ issues가 선행사 an important way를 수식하며, 이때 관계부사 that은 선행사
the way와 함께 쓸 수 없는 관계부사 how를 대신하고 있다.

C 10 The best picture books contain words and pictures that complement each
(모의) 최고의 그림책은 단어와 그림을 담고 있다　　　　　　　/ [서로를 보완하는]
other and are dependent upon each other to the point that one would be
/ 그리고 서로에 의존적이다　　　　　/ 정도로　　　/ [하나가 다른 하나 없이는
ineffective without the other.
효과가 없게 되는]

contain 담고 있다, 포함하다
complement 보완하다

- 관계부사 that이 이끄는 절이 선행사 the point를 수식하고 있다. 이때 that은 관계부사 where 대신 쓰였다.
- 관계대명사 that이 이끄는 절 that ~ other가 선행사 words and pictures를 수식한다.

11 The food industry has made a fortune because we retain Stone Age bodies that
식품 산업은 거액을 벌어왔다　　　　　　　/ 우리가 석기 시대의 신체를 유지하고 있기 때문에　　　/
crave sugar but live in a Space Age world where sugar is cheap and plentiful.
[설탕을 간절히 원하는] / 하지만 우주 시대 세계에 살고 있기 때문에 / [설탕이 저렴하고 풍부한]

make a fortune 거액을 벌다,
재산을 모으다
crave 간절히 원하다, 갈망하다
plentiful 풍부한

- 관계부사 where가 이끄는 절 where ~ plentiful이 선행사 a Space Age world를 수식한다.
- Stone Age bodies는 관계대명사 that이 이끄는 형용사절 that crave sugar의 수식을 받고 있다.

12 Friendship is born at that moment **when one says to another, "What! You**
우정은 그 순간에 생겨난다　　　　　　/ [한 사람이 다른 사람에게 말하는　　　/ "뭐라고! 너도야?
too? I thought I was the only one." *C. S. Lewis*
　　　나는 생각했어　/ 내가 유일한 사람이라고"]

- 관계부사 when이 이끄는 절 when ~ one이 선행사 that moment를 수식한다.
- 동사 thought 다음에 명사절을 이끄는 접속사 that이 생략되어 있다.

unit 26
명사 + 관계사가 생략된 수식절

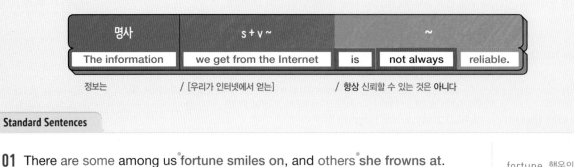

명사	s + v ~	~		
The information	we get from the Internet	is	not always	reliable.

정보는 / [우리가 인터넷에서 얻는] / 항상 신뢰할 수 있는 것은 아니다

Standard Sentences

01 There are some among us fortune smiles on, and others she frowns at.
우리 중에 몇몇이 있다 / [행운의 여신이 미소 짓는] / 그리고 다른 사람들이 (있다) / [그녀가 눈살을 찌푸리는]

■ 각각의 선행사 some과 others 다음에 목적격 관계대명사 whom 또는 that이 생략되었다.

fortune 행운의 여신; 행운; 재산
frown 눈살을 찌푸리다

02 Scientists can answer when and how the universe began, but cannot
과학자들은 답할 수 있다 / 언제 그리고 어떻게 우주가 시작되었는지 / 그러나 이유를
calculate the reason it began.
추정할 수는 없다 / [그것이 시작된]

■ 선행사 the reason 다음에 관계부사 why가 생략되었다.
■ answer의 목적어로 「의문사 + s + v」 어순의 간접의문문이 쓰였다.

calculate 추정하다; 계산하다

A 03 I am writing to you regarding a price discrepancy I encountered between
나는 당신에게 편지를 쓰고 있다 / 가격 차이에 관하여 / [내가 맞닥뜨린] / 당신의
an item offered in your retail store and the same item offered on your
매장에서 제공되는 물품과 / 당신의 웹사이트에서 제공되는 동일한 물품 간의]
website.

■ 선행사 a price discrepancy 다음에 목적격 관계대명사 which 또는 that이 생략되었다.
■ an item과 the same item은 각각 과거분사 offered가 이끄는 어구 offered ~ store와 offered ~ website의 수식을 받고 있다.

regarding ~에 관하여
discrepancy 차이; 불일치
retail store 매장, 소매 상점

04 This country imports about two-thirds of the raw materials it needs and
이 나라는 수입한다 / 원료의 약 2/3를 / [그 나라가 필요로 하는]
exports approximately three-fifths of the machinery it produces.
/ 그리고 수출한다 / 기계류의 약 3/5을 / [그 나라가 생산하는]

■ 선행사 the raw materials와 the machinery 다음에 각각 목적격 관계대명사 which 또는 that이 생략되었다.

raw material 원료, 원자재
approximately 대략
machinery 기계류

05 The advent of driverless cars and other vehicles promises to revolutionize
운전자 없는 자동차와 다른 차량의 출현은 가망이 있다 / 방식을 변화시킬
the way the world transports itself goods every day.
/ [세계가 직접 매일 상품을 운송하는]

■ 선행사 the way 다음에 관계부사 how가 생략되어 있으며, 이 둘은 함께 쓰일 수 없다.

advent 출현, 도래
promise ~할 가망이 있다
revolutionize 혁명을 일으키다

B **06** One of the most effective ways to calm down from stress is intimate contact
스트레스로부터 진정하는 가장 효과적인 방법 중 하나는 / 사람들과의 친밀한 접촉이다

with people you trust and feel comfortable around.
/ [주변에 당신이 신뢰하고 그리고 편안하게 느끼는]

intimate 친밀한

- 선행사 people 다음에 목적격 관계대명사 who(m) 또는 that이 생략되었다.
- 「one of + the + 최상급 + 복수 명사」는 '가장 ~한 … 중 하나'의 의미이며, 주어로 쓰일 때 단수 취급한다.

07 Leaders need to safeguard the faith people have in them by acting in
지도자들은 신념을 보호할 필요가 있다 / [사람들이 지도자들에게서 갖고 있는] / 행동함으로써 /

accordance with the expectations they have raised themselves.
기대에 따라 / [그들이 스스로 고양시킨]

safeguard 보호하다, 지키다
in accordance with ~에 따라, ~와 일치하여
raise 고양시키다; 일으키다

- 선행사 the faith와 the expectations 다음에 각각 목적격 관계대명사 which 또는 that이 생략되었다.

수능 **08** One reason most dogs are much happier than most people is that dogs
하나의 이유는 / [대부분의 개들이 대부분의 사람들보다 훨씬 더 행복한] / 개들은 영향을

aren't affected by external circumstances the way we are.
받지 않기 때문이다 / 외부의 환경에 의해서 / 우리가 영향을 받는 것처럼

external 외부의
circumstance 환경, 상황

- 선행사 One reason 다음에 관계부사 why가 생략되었다.
- 보어 역할을 하는 that절에서 the way는 접속사로 쓰여 '~처럼(= as)'의 의미를 나타낸다.

09 An instructor should exemplify the things he seeks to teach. It will be of
강사는 일들에 본보기가 되어야 한다 / [그가 가르치려고 하는] / (…은) 대단한

great advantage if you yourself can do all you ask of your students and
이점이 될 것이다 / 만약 당신 스스로 모든 것을 할 수 있다면 / [당신이 당신의 학생들 그리고 그 이상의 사람들에게

more. *Bruce Lee*
요구하는]

instructor 강사, 교사
exemplify ~의 좋은 예가 되다

- 첫 문장에서 선행사 the things 다음에 목적격 관계대명사 which 또는 that이 생략되었다.
- 두 번째 문장에서는 It은 가주어이고, if절이 진주어에 해당한다.

C **10** Before a job interview, it is a good idea to find out some background
구직 면접 전에 / (…은) 좋은 생각이다 / 그 회사에 관한 약간의 배경 정보를 알아 보는 것은

information about the company you would be working for.
/ [당신이 일하고자 하는]

- 선행사 the company 다음에 목적격 관계대명사 which 또는 that이 생략되었다.
- it은 가주어이고 to find 이하가 진주어이다.

11 Because of the huge volume of clouds it generates, the Amazon River
막대한 구름의 양 때문에 / [그것이 생성하는] / 아마존 수계는 중대한

system plays a major role in the way the sun's heat is distributed around
역할을 한다 / 방식에 있어서 / [태양열이 전 지구에 배분되는]

the globe.

huge 거대한
volume 분량
generate 발생시키다
river system 수계(한 지역을 흐르는 지표면의 하천이나 고여 있는 표층수 및 지류)
distribute 배분하다

- 선행사 the huge volume of clouds 다음에 목적격 관계대명사 which 또는 that이 생략되었다.
- 선행사 the way 다음에 관계부사 how가 생략되었다.

모의 **12** Do you think that being able to list all the reasons you love a person
당신은 생각하는가 / 모든 이유를 열거할 수 있다는 것이 / [당신이 어떤 사람을 사랑하는]

enables you to love that person more or differently?
/ 당신이 그 사람을 더 많이 또는 다르게 사랑할 수 있게 해 준다고?

list 열거하다

- 선행사 all the reasons 다음에 관계부사 why가 생략되었다.
- 동명사구 being ~ a person이 that절의 주어로 쓰였다.

본책 102~103쪽을 함께 펴놓고 보세요!

unit 27
명사와 관계사절의 분리

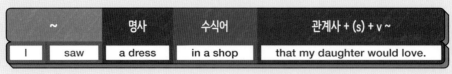

~	명사	수식어	관계사 + (s) + v ~
I	saw	a dress	in a shop	that my daughter would love.

나는 / 보았다 / 드레스를 / 가게에서 / [내 딸이 아주 좋아할]

Standard Sentences

01 I can't think of any good film at the moment that I'd like to see.
나는 어떤 좋은 영화가 생각나지 않는다 / 지금으로서는 / [내가 보고 싶은]

■ 선행사 any good film을 수식하는 목적격 관계대명사 that이 이끄는 절 that ~ see가 수식어구 at the moment로 인해 떨어져 있는 구조이다.

> at the moment 지금으로서는, 바로 지금

02 That government is best which governs least, because its people discipline
그러한 정부가 제일이다 / [가장 적게 통제하는] / 왜냐하면 그 국민이 스스로를 규율하기 때문에
themselves. *Thomas Jefferson*

■ 선행사 That government를 수식하는 관계대명사 which가 이끄는 절 which ~ least가 문장의 서술어 is best 뒤로 보내진 구조이다.

> govern 통제하다; 통치하다
> least 가장 적게; 최소로
> discipline 규율하다; 훈련하다

A **03** Some people recognize humans as the only one among the living organisms
[모의] 어떤 사람들은 인간을 인지한다 / 유일한 것으로 / 살아 있는 유기체 중에서
that can change its behavior to preserve other species.
/ [다른 종을 보존하기 위해 자신의 행동을 바꿀 수 있는]

■ 선행사 the only one을 수식하는 주격 관계대명사 that이 이끄는 절 that ~ species가 전치사구 among the living organisms로 인해 떨어져 있는 구조이다.

> recognize A as B A를 B로 인지하다

04 Courage doesn't always roar. Sometimes courage is the little voice at the
용기가 항상 포효하지는 않는다 때때로 용기는 작은 목소리이다 / 하루의
end of the day that says "I'll try again tomorrow." *Mary Anne Radmacher*
끝에 / ['나는 내일 다시 시도해 볼 거야'라고 말하는]

■ 선행사 the little voice를 수식하는 주격 관계대명사 that이 이끄는 절 that ~ tomorrow가 수식어구 at the end of the day로 인해 떨어져 있는 구조이다.

> roar 포효하다, 으르렁거리다

05 Creative solutions are required which not only answer yesterday's questions
창의적인 해결책이 요구된다 / [어제의 질문에 답할 뿐만 아니라
but also anticipate tomorrow's needs.
/ 내일의 필요를 예견하기도 하는]

■ 선행사 Creative solutions를 수식하는 주격 관계대명사 which가 이끄는 절 which ~ needs가 서술어 are required 뒤로 보내진 구조이다.
— not only A but (also) B: A뿐만 아니라 B도 / 두 개의 동사구 answer ~ questions와 anticipate ~ needs가 but으로 연결되어 있다.

> anticipate 예견하다, 예상하다

B **06** A gene is a part of a cell in a living thing that controls what it looks like,
유전자는 세포의 일부이다 / [생명체 안에 있는] / [통제하는 / 그것이 어떻게 생겼는지
how it grows, and how it develops.
/ 그것이 어떻게 자라는지 / 그리고 그것이 어떻게 발달하는지]

- 선행사 a part of a cell을 수식하는 주격 관계대명사 that이 이끄는 절 that ~ develops가 수식어구 in a living thing 뒤로 보내진 구조이다.
- 세 개의 간접의문문(what it looks like, how it grows, how it develops)이 등위접속사 and로 병렬 연결되어 있다.

07 Hospices care for patients suffering from incurable diseases who are not
호스피스는 환자들을 돌본다 / [불치병으로 고통받고 있는] / [1년 넘게 살 것으로
expected to live for more than a year.
예상되지 않는]

- 선행사 patients를 수식하는 주격 관계대명사 who가 이끄는 절이 수식어구로 쓰인 현재분사구 suffering from incurable diseases 뒤로 보내진 구조이다.
- 현재분사구 suffering ~ diseases는 patients를 수식한다.

hospice 호스피스(말기 환자들을 전문으로 돌보는 특수 병원)
care for ~을 돌보다
suffer from ~으로 고통받다
incurable 불치의

08 From smart cities to self-driving cars, technology is needed that can allow
스마트 도시부터 자율 주행 자동차까지 / 기술이 요구된다 / [장치와 서비스가 대량의
devices and services to access great volumes of data.
데이터에 접근할 수 있게 해 주는]

- 주어인 technology를 수식하는 주격 관계대명사 that이 이끄는 절 that ~ data가 서술어 is needed 뒤로 보내진 구조이다.

09 The time will come when people will see that my paintings are worth more
때가 올 것이다 / [사람들이 알게 될 / 나의 그림들이 가치가 있다는 것을 / 물감
than the price of the paint. *Vincent van Gogh*
가격 이상의]

- 주어인 The time을 수식하는 관계부사 when이 이끄는 절 when ~ the paint는 주어가 너무 길어져 서술어 will come 뒤로 보내진 구조이다.

C **10** The ultimate life force lies in tiny cellular factories of energy, called
(수능!) 궁극적인 생명력은 아주 작은 에너지 세포 공장에 있다 / 미토콘드리아
mitochondria, that burn nearly all the oxygen we breathe in.
라고 불리는 / [거의 모든 산소를 연소시키는 / [우리가 들이마시는]]

(풀이) 과거분사구인 called mitochondria는 삽입어구이며, 주격 관계대명사 that이 이끄는 절이 선행사 tiny cellular factories (of energy)를 수식하는 구조이므로, 관계사절의 동사는 복수 동사 burn이 적절하다.

ultimate 궁극적인
tiny 아주 작은

11 Most professors see themselves in a position of professional authority over
대부분의 교수들은 스스로를 인지한다 / 자신들의 학생들을 넘어서는 전문적인 권위의 입장에서
their students which they earned by many years of study.
/ [그들이 오랜 세월의 연구로 얻은]

(풀이) 그들이 오랜 세월의 연구로 얻은 것은 professional authority이므로 목적격 관계대명사로는 사물을 나타내는 which가 적절하다. over their students는 professional authority를 꾸며 주는 수식어구이다.

authority 권위; 권한

(모의) **12** Art has mostly been considered in terms of seeking beauty, but there are other
예술은 주로 고려되어 왔다 / 아름다움을 추구하는 것의 측면에서 / 그러나 다른 이유가 있다
reasons deeply rooted in the human experience that create needs for art.
/ [인간의 경험 속에 깊이 자리잡은] / [예술에 대한 필요성을 창조하는]

(풀이) 예술에 대한 필요성을 창조하는 것이 reasons이므로, 주격 관계대명사 that이 이끄는 절이 other reasons를 수식하도록 복수 동사 create가 와야 한다. 과거분사구 deeply ~ experience는 reasons를 꾸며 주는 수식어구이다.

in terms of ~의 면에서, ~의 관점에서
rooted 자리잡은, 고착한

unit 28
명사, 관계사절

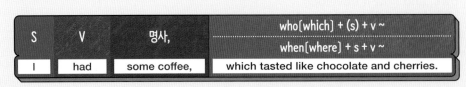

S	V	명사,	who[which] + (s) + v ~ when[where] + s + v ~
I	had	some coffee,	which tasted like chocolate and cherries.

나는 / 마셨다 / 약간의 커피를 / 그리고 그것은 초콜릿과 체리 같은 맛이 났다

Standard Sentences

모의 01 Costa Rica was discovered and named by Christopher Columbus, who
코스타리카는 발견되었다 그리고 명명되었다 / 크리스토퍼 콜럼버스에 의해 / 그리고
thought it might be a land rich with gold.
그는 생각했다 / 그것이 금이 풍부한 땅일 것이라고

- 주격 관계대명사 who가 이끄는 절이 Christopher Columbus를 보충 설명한다.
- 관계사절 내의 동사 thought 다음에 명사절을 이끄는 접속사 that이 생략되어 있다.

name 명명하다, ~에 이름을 붙이다

모의 02 Change, which is an essential part of our life, can have both positive and
변화는 / 그것은 우리 삶의 필수적인 부분인데 / 긍정적인 영향과 부정적인 영향을 둘 다
negative effects.
미칠 수 있다

- 관계대명사 which가 이끄는 절 which ~ life는 삽입절로, 주어인 Change를 보충 설명한다.

A 03 Yesterday is history, tomorrow is a mystery, today is a gift of God, which is
어제는 역사이다 / 내일은 미스터리이다 / 오늘은 신의 선물이다 / 그리고 그것이
why we call it the present. *Bill Keane*
우리가 오늘을 present(선물)라고 부르는 이유이다

- 콤마 뒤의 관계대명사 which는 앞의 절 today is a gift of God를 대신하며, which가 이끄는 절이 이에 대한 보충 설명을 하고 있다.

present 선물; 현재; 주다

모의 04 Urbanization has been taking place since the Neolithic Revolution, when
도시화는 일어나고 있는 중이다 / 신석기 혁명 이래로 / 그리고
agriculture enabled food surpluses to create a division of labor in
그때 농업이 잉여 식량으로 정착지에서 분업이 생겨날 수 있게 했다
settlements.

- 콤마 뒤의 관계부사 when이 이끄는 절이 the Neolithic Revolution에 대한 보충 설명을 하고 있으며, 이때 when은 and then의 의미이다.

urbanization 도시화
surplus 잉여, 나머지
division of labor 분업
settlement 정착지; 해결

05 Homer's *Iliad*, which contained descriptions of actual places, was the basis
Homer의 「일리아드」는 / 그것은 실제 장소에 대한 서술을 포함했는데 / 많은 초기 지도에 대한
for many early maps.
기반이었다

- 관계대명사 which가 이끄는 절 which ~ places는 삽입절로서 Homer's *Iliad*를 보충 설명한다.

Know More 「일리아드(Iliad)」는 고대 그리스 시인 Homer가 BC 900년경에 집필한 작품으로 그리스 최대의 민족 대서사시이다. 트로이의 도시를 정복하러 온 그리스 군대와 그 영웅들의 활약상을 주로 다루며, 신이 아닌 인간의 눈으로 세상을 바라보기 시작한 '인간주의적' 접근을 시도한 최초의 작품으로 꼽힌다. 총 1만 5,693행으로 24권에 달하는 이 작품은 유럽 서사시의 모범이 되어 유럽 문학에 큰 영향을 끼쳤다.

B 06 Cognitive computing is supported by machine learning and deep learning
인지 컴퓨팅은 뒷받침된다 / 기계 학습과 딥 러닝 기술에 의해
technology, **which allows computers to autonomously learn from data.**
그리고 그것은 컴퓨터가 자체적으로 데이터로부터 학습할 수 있게 해 준다

- 콤마 뒤의 주격 관계대명사 which가 이끄는 절은 앞 문장 전체 Cognitive ~ technology를 보충 설명한다.
- 관계사절 내에 to autonomously learn은 분리부정사로 to부정사에서 to와 동사 사이에 부사가 들어간 것이다. 부사의 의미를 강조하기 위해 구어체에서 주로 쓰인다.

cognitive 인지의
machine learning 기계 학습(자신의 동작을 스스로 개선할 수 있는 슈퍼컴퓨터의 능력)
autonomously 자체적으로

모의 07 Maurice Maeterlinck studied law and worked as a lawyer until 1889, **when**
Maurice Maeterlinck는 법학을 공부했다 / 그리고 변호사로 일했다 / 1889년까지 / 그리고
he decided to devote himself to writing. In 1897, he went to Paris, **where**
그때 그는 결심했다 / 글쓰기에 전념하기로 1897년에 그는 파리로 갔다 / 그리고
he met many of the leading symbolist writers of the day.
거기서 그는 만났다 / 그 당시의 여러 주요한 상징주의 작가들을

- 첫 번째 문장에서 관계부사 when이 이끄는 절은 1889년에 대한 보충 설명이며, 두 번째 문장에서 관계부사 where가 이끄는 절은 Paris에 대한 보충 설명이다.

devote oneself to ~에 전념하다
leading 주요한, 이끄는
symbolist 상징주의자

수능 08 Jobs may not be permanent, and you may lose your job for countless
일자리는 영구적이지 않을 수도 있다 / 그리고 당신은 당신의 일자리를 잃을 수도 있다 / 수많은 이유로
reasons, **some of which you may not even be responsible for.**
/ 그리고 그것들 중의 일부에 대해 당신은 심지어 책임이 없을 수도 있다

- some of which는 '~ 중 일부'로 해석하며, and some of countless reasons로 바꿔 쓸 수 있다. / 관계대명사 앞에 부정대명사가 올 때는 「부정대명사 + of + 관계대명사」의 어순으로 쓴다.

permanent 영구적인
countless 수많은, 무수한

09 The spontaneous wish to learn, **which every normal child has,** as shown in
배우고 싶다는 자연스러운 소망은 / 그것은 평범한 아이들 모두가 갖고 있는데 / 아이들의 걷고 말하는
their efforts to walk and talk, should be the driving force in education.
노력에서 보이는 것처럼 / 교육에 있어서 추진력이 되어야 한다

- 콤마로 삽입된 관계대명사 which가 이끄는 절 which ~ has가 주어 The spontaneous ~ learn을 보충 설명한다.
- 접속사 as 다음에 'it is'가 생략된 것으로 볼 수 있다. ○ Unit 53

spontaneous 자연스러운; 자발적인
driving force 추진력

C 10 The bodies of all living creatures are organized into many different systems,
모든 살아 있는 생물의 몸은 조직되어 있다 / 여러 가지 다른 체계로
each of which has a certain function.
/ 그리고 각각의 체계는 특정 기능을 가진다

- each of which는 '각각의 ~'로 해석하며, and each of many different systems로 바꿔 쓸 수 있다.

모의 11 One remarkable aspect of aboriginal culture is the concept of "totemism,"
원주민 문화의 한 가지 눈에 띄는 면은 / '토테미즘'이라는 개념이다
where the tribal member at birth assumes the soul and identity of a part
/ 그리고 거기(토테미즘)에서 부족 구성원은 출생 시에 자연의 일부의 영혼과 정체성을 취한다
of nature.

- 관계부사 where가 이끄는 절이 totemism을 보충 설명한다.

remarkable 눈에 띄는
aboriginal 원주민의
totemism 토테미즘(유럽 사회에서 동식물이나 자연을 신성시함으로써 형성되는 종교 및 사회 체제)
tribal 부족의, 종족의
assume 취하다

모의 12 The television crime drama isn't such a hit with police officers, **who have**
텔레비전 범죄 드라마는 경찰관들에게는 대단한 히트작이 아니다 / 그리고 그들은 그
criticized the series for presenting a highly misleading image of how
시리즈를 비판해왔다 / 대단히 오해의 소지가 있는 모습을 보여 준다는 이유로 / 범죄가
crimes are solved.
어떻게 해결되는지에 대한

- 주격 관계대명사 who가 이끄는 절이 콤마 앞의 명사 police officers를 보충 설명한다.
- 의문사 how가 이끄는 명사절 how ~ solved가 전치사 of의 목적어로 쓰였다.

criticize 비판하다
misleading 오해의 소지가 있는; 현혹시키는

Chapter 06

A **01** There is only one thing **that makes a dream impossible to achieve**: the fear
오직 한 가지가 있다 / [꿈을 이루는 것을 불가능하게 하는] / 실패에 대한
of failure. *the novel <The Alchemist>*
두려움

> ■ 관계대명사 that이 이끄는 절 that ~ achieve가 주어 only one thing을 수식한다.
> ■ only one thing과 the fear of failure는 콜론(:)으로 이어진 동격 관계이다. **○ Unit 52**

02 Radioactive waste disposal has become one of the key environmental
방사성 폐기물 처리는 주요한 환경 문제의 전쟁터 중 하나가 되어왔다
battlegrounds **over which the future of nuclear power has been fought.**
/ [원자력의 미래에 맞서 싸워 온]

> ■ 전치사 over의 목적어로 관계대명사 which가 이끄는 절이 쓰여 선행사 the key environmental battlegrounds 를 수식한다.

radioactive 방사성의, 방사능이 있는
disposal 처리, 처분
battleground 전쟁터
nuclear power 원자력

03 Fate is like a strange, unpopular restaurant filled with odd little waiters **who**
운명은 이상하고 인기가 없는 식당과 같다 / [이상한 작은 종업원들로 가득찬 /
bring you things you never asked for and don't always like. *Lemony Snicket*
[당신에게 어떤 것들을 갖다주는 / [당신이 결코 요청하지 않은 / 그리고 항상 좋아하는 것은 아닌]]]

> ■ 관계대명사 who가 이끄는 절이 선행사 odd little waiters를 수식한다.
> ■ things 다음에 목적격 관계대명사 which 또는 that이 생략되어 있다.

fate 운명
filled with ~으로 가득 찬
odd 이상한

(모의) 04 Multitasking is another way of saying you are going to complete several
멀티태스킹은 말하는 또 다른 방법이다 / 당신이 몇 가지 일을 마무리하려고 하는데
tasks, **none of which are going to be very good.**
/ 그러나 그것들 중 어떤 것도 그다지 훌륭하진 않을 것이라고

> ■ none of which는 '~ 중 아무것도 … 않은'으로 해석하며, and none of several tasks로 바꿔 쓸 수 있다.
> ■ saying 다음에 명사절을 이끄는 접속사 that이 생략되어 있다.

multitasking 멀티태스킹, 다중 작업
complete 완료하다

B **05** Man is the only animal **whose desires increase as they are fed**; the only
인간은 유일한 동물이다 / [욕망이 증가하는 / 욕망이 충족되었을 때] 즉 유일한 동물
animal **that is never satisfied.** *Henry George*
/ [결코 만족하지 않는]

> **풀이** 이어지는 절에 주어나 목적어가 빠져 있지 않기 때문에 주격 또는 목적격 관계대명사가 올 자리는 아니다. 선행사인 the only animal과 이어지는 명사 desires 사이에 소유의 의미 관계(동물의 욕망)가 성립하므로 소유격 관계대명사 whose가 적절하다.

feed 충족시키다, 만족시키다

(모의) 06 We're heading toward a world **where an extensive trail of information**
우리는 세상을 향해 나아가고 있다 / [우리에 관한 정보 조각들의 광범위한 자국이
fragments about us will be forever preserved on the Internet, displayed
/ 인터넷상에 영원히 보존될 / 검색 결과로
instantly in a search result.
즉각 보이는]

> **풀이** 선행사가 a world이고, 뒤에 완전한 절이 이어지므로 관계부사 where가 적절하다.

extensive 광범위한
trail 자국
fragment 조각, 파편
instantly 즉각

(모의) 07 Angela mentioned that for a long time she had wanted to get back into
Angela는 언급했다 / 오랫동안 자신은 연극으로 돌아가고 싶어 했다고
acting, **which she used to do in college.**
/ 그것을 그녀는 대학 시절에 했었다

mention 언급하다
used to 과거 한때[예전에] ~했었다, ~하곤 했다

> 풀이: 콤마 앞의 선행사 acting에 대한 보충 설명이 이어지므로 관계대명사로 which가 적절하다. that은 콤마 뒤에서 선행사에 대한 부가 정보를 주는 관계대명사로 쓸 수 없다.
>
> ─ 동사 mentioned의 목적어로 접속사 that이 이끄는 명사절이 쓰였다.

08 Penicillin, the first antibiotic to be discovered, kills a broad spectrum of
페니실린은 / 발견된 최초의 항생제인 / 광범위의 박테리아를 죽인다
bacteria, many of which cause disease in humans.
/ 그리고 그것들 중 다수는 인간에게 질병을 유발한다

antibiotic 항생제
spectrum 범위

> 풀이: 이어지는 절이 주어가 없는 불완전한 절이므로, 주어 역할을 하면서 동시에 두 절을 연결하는 접속사 역할을 하는 관계대명사 which가 적절하다.
>
> ─ Penicillin과 the first ~ discovered는 동격 관계이다.

C 09 Values and their supporting beliefs are lenses **through which we see the world.**
가치관과 그것들을 뒷받침하는 신념은 렌즈다 / [우리가 세상을 보는]

> 풀이: 선행사 lenses를 전치사 through의 목적어로 관계대명사 which가 이끄는 절이 뒤에서 수식하도록 배열한다.

10 In this information age **when science and technology are developing with**
이 정보 시대에 / [과학과 기술이 엄청난 속도로 발전하고 있는]
great rapidity, network has become an important symbol of modern life.
/ 네트워크는 현대의 삶에서 중요한 상징이 되어왔다

with great rapidity 엄청난 속도로

> 풀이: 관계부사 when이 이끄는 절이 this information age를 수식하도록 배열한다.

11 The police received a number of bomb warnings, **all of which turned out to**
경찰은 다수의 폭발물 예고를 받았다 / 그런데 그것들 모두 허위 신고로 밝혀졌다
be false alarms.

a number of 다수의, 많은
warning 예고, 경고
turn out ~으로 밝혀지다

> 풀이: '~ 모두[전부]'의 의미를 나타내는 all of which를 써서 warnings를 보충 설명하도록 쓴다.

D 12 Science operates within the context of the culture **it exists in;** it does not
과학은 작동한다 / 문화의 상황 내에서 / [그것이 존재하는] 그것은 진공에서
exist in a vacuum **where pure absolute objectivity prevails.**
존재하지 않는다 / [완전한 절대적 객관성이 지배적인]

vacuum 진공
pure 완전한; 순수한
absolute 절대적인
prevail 지배적이다, 만연하다

> ─ 선행사 culture 다음에 목적격 관계대명사 which 또는 that이 생략되었다.
> ─ 관계부사 where가 이끄는 절 where ~ prevails가 선행사 a vacuum을 수식한다.

[모의] 13 For every one thing **we think we have done on our own,** there are a dozen
모든 것에 있어서 / [(우리가 생각하기에) 우리가 스스로 해온] / 수십 개의 일이 있다
things **that had to be provided for us by others.**
/ [타인들에 의해 우리에게 제공되었어야 하는]

> ─ 선행사 every one thing 다음에 목적격 관계대명사 which 또는 that이 생략되었으며, we think는 관계사가 이끄는 절에 삽입된 절이다.
> ─ 주격 관계대명사 that이 이끄는 절 that ~ others가 선행사 a dozen things를 수식한다.

14 The brain modifies its structure in response to the different tasks **it is**
뇌는 자신의 구조를 수정한다 / 서로 다른 임무에 응하여 / [뇌가
required to do.
수행하도록 요구되는]

modify 수정하다
in response to ~에 응하여, ~에 대한 응답으로

> ─ 선행사 the different tasks 다음에 목적격 관계대명사 which 또는 that이 생략되었다.

부사적 수식어: 구

- Unit 29   부사 역할을 하는 전치사구
- Unit 30   부사 역할을 하는 to-v의 의미
- Unit 31   부사적 to-v의 관용 구문
- Unit 32   부사 역할을 하는 분사구문의 의미
- Unit 33   분사구문의 다양한 형태 1
- Unit 34   분사구문의 다양한 형태 2

■ 본격적인 구문 학습에 앞서, 각 유닛별 주요 단어를 확인하세요.

Unit 29

- [ ] photosynthesis 광합성
- [ ] convert 전환하다
- [ ] make sense of ~을 이해하다
- [ ] prospect 가망, 가능성

- [ ] repay 빚을 갚다
- [ ] planet 세상; 행성
- [ ] glitter 반짝이다
- [ ] unlikely 있을 법하지 않은

- [ ] rigorously 엄격히
- [ ] hold onto ~을 계속 유지하다
- [ ] impulse 충동
- [ ] impatient 초조하게 기다리는

Unit 30

- [ ] desperate 절망적인
- [ ] stimulus 자극 (pl. stimuli)
- [ ] bits and pieces 이런저런 것들
- [ ] at length 마침내; 상세히
- [ ] settle 합의를 보다

- [ ] carving 조각품
- [ ] stick with ~을 계속하다
- [ ] hasty 성급한
- [ ] come to a conclusion 결론에 도달하다

- [ ] near 가까워지다
- [ ] crystal 결정, 결정체
- [ ] further 더 심한
- [ ] criticize 지적하다
- [ ] dodge 피하다, 기피하다

Unit 31

- [ ] span of life 수명
- [ ] versatile 다재다능한
- [ ] medium 매체
- [ ] tone 어조

- [ ] draw on ~을 이용하다
- [ ] overdrawn 초과 인출된
- [ ] bankrupt 파산시키다
- [ ] optimistic 낙관적인

- [ ] stand out 눈에 띄다, 두드러지다
- [ ] deal 거래
- [ ] exceptional 파격적인, 예외적인
- [ ] mention 언급하다

Unit 32

- [ ] tap 톡톡 두드리다
- [ ] impatience 성급함
- [ ] dissatisfaction 불만
- [ ] be pressed for time 시간에 쫓기다

- [ ] deadlock 교착 상태
- [ ] hybrid 혼합의
- [ ] narrative 서사의
- [ ] asthma 천식

- [ ] promptly 바로
- [ ] substantial 상당한
- [ ] spectacular 극적인
- [ ] come apart 부서지다

Unit 33

- [ ] sustain 유지하다
- [ ] ecological 생태적인
- [ ] consume 소비하다
- [ ] wad ~을 뭉치다

- [ ] crawl 기어가다
- [ ] bunch 무더기, 다발
- [ ] lament 한탄하다
- [ ] lot 운명, 운

- [ ] yield (결과를) 낳다
- [ ] splendid 정말 멋진
- [ ] mutual 상호의
- [ ] dispute 논쟁

Unit 34

- [ ] adolescent 청소년
- [ ] immerse oneself in ~에 몰두하다, 열중하다
- [ ] fairly 꽤
- [ ] promising 유망한

- [ ] vulnerable 공격받기 쉬운
- [ ] desperate 필사적인
- [ ] conceited 자만하는
- [ ] relativity 상대성 이론; 상대성
- [ ] geometry 기하학

- [ ] ultimate 궁극적인
- [ ] symbiotic 공생의
- [ ] overstate 과장하다
- [ ] under threat 위협받고 있는
- [ ] disseminate 유포하다

unit 29
부사 역할을 하는 전치사구

전치사 + O' ~	S	V	전치사 + O' ~
After an hour	I	arrived	at the airport.
한 시간 후에	/ 나는	/ 도착했다	/ 공항에

Standard Sentences

01 By means of photosynthesis, plants convert the radiant energy of the sun
광합성에 의해　　　　　　　　　　/ 식물은 태양의 복사 에너지를 전환한다
into chemical energy.
/ 화학 에너지로

■ 두 개의 전치사구 By ~ photosynthesis와 into ~ energy가 동사 convert를 수식한다.

> by means of ~에 의해서
> photosynthesis 광합성
> convert 전환하다, 바꾸다
> radiant energy 복사 에너지

02 From the moment that we are born, we begin to make sense of the world
그 순간부터　　　　　　　/ [우리가 태어나는]　/ 우리는 우리 주변의 세상을 이해하기 시작한다
around us by associating the unknown with the known.
　　　　　　/ 알려지지 않은 것을 알려진 것과 연관시킴으로써

■ 전치사구 From ~ born은 문장 전체를 수식하고, by ~ known은 to make sense를 수식한다.
— the moment 다음의 that은 관계부사로 선행사 the moment를 수식하는 형용사절을 이끌고 있다.

> make sense of ~을 이해하다
> associate A with B A를 B와 연관시키다

A **03** Fossil fuels form beneath the ground from dead plants and animals that
화석 연료들은 형성된다　/ 땅 밑에서　　/ 죽은 식물과 동물로부터　　　　　　　/
do not break down completely.
[완전히 분해되지 않은]

■ 두 개의 전치사구 beneath the ground와 from ~ completely가 동사 form을 수식한다.
— dead plants and animals를 관계대명사 that이 이끄는 절이 수식한다.

> fossil fuel 화석 연료
> break down 분해되다; 고장나다

04 Despite its high price, this new cell phone sells like hot cakes because of
높은 가격에도 불구하고　　/ 이 신형 휴대폰은 팔린다　/ 핫케이크처럼　/ 그것의 고품질 때문에
its high quality.

■ despite는 '~에도 불구하고'라는 의미의 전치사이며, Despite ~ price가 문장 전체를 수식한다.
■ like hot cakes와 전치사 because of가 이끄는 어구는 둘 다 동사 sells를 수식한다. / because of는 뒤에 목적어로 명사를 취하지만, 접속사 because는 뒤에 「s + v」가 온다.

> sell like hot cakes 날개 돋친 듯이 팔리다(방금 구워져 따뜻한 팬케이크가 빠르게 팔리는 현상에서 유래한 표현)

수능! **05** We borrow environmental capital from future generations with no intention
우리는 환경 자본을 빌린다　　　　　　/ 미래 세대에게서　　　/ 빚을 갚으려는 의도나
or prospect of repaying.
가망도 없이

■ 두 개의 전치사구 from future generations, with ~ repaying이 동사 borrow를 수식한다.

> capital 자본; 수도
> prospect 가망, 가능성
> repay 빚을 갚다, 돌려주다

B **06** Each year about 50,000 species of plants and animals disappear from the
매년 / 약 5만 종의 식물과 동물들이 사라진다 / 세상으로부터

planet as a result of human activity.
/ 인간 활동의 결과로

▬ from the planet과 '~의 결과로'를 뜻하는 as a result of가 이끄는 전치사구가 동사 disappear를 수식한다.

planet 세상; 행성

07 Sometimes my eyes get jealous of my heart because you always remain
때때로 / 나의 눈은 내 심장을 질투하게 된다 / 왜냐하면 당신은 항상 나의 심장과 가까이 있고

close to my heart and far from my eyes.
나의 눈에서는 멀리 있기 때문이다

▬ 세 개의 전치사구 of my heart, to my heart, from my eyes는 각각 형용사 jealous, close, far를 수식한다.

모예 **08** Upon discovering his own passion and talent for architecture, Frank Lloyd
자기 자신의 열정과 재능을 발견하자마자 / [건축을 향한] / Frank Lloyd

Wright dropped out of school and went to work for an architectural firm in
Wright는 학교를 그만두었다 / 그리고 시카고에 있는 건축 회사로 근무하러 갔다

Chicago.

▬ 「upon+v-ing」는 '~하자마자'를 뜻하는 전치사구로 Upon ~ architecture가 문장 전체를 수식하며, 전치사구 for ~ Chicago는 동사 to work를 수식한다.

architecture 건축
drop out of school 학교를
그만두다, 중퇴하다
firm 회사; 확고한

09 Above all, watch with glittering eyes the whole world around you because
무엇보다도 / 반짝이는 눈으로 당신 주변의 온 세상을 주시하라 / 왜냐하면

the greatest secrets are always hidden in the most unlikely places. *Roald Dahl*
가장 큰 비밀들은 항상 감춰져 있기 때문이다 / 가장 있을 법하지 않은 곳에

▬ 전치사구 Above all은 문장 전체를 수식한다.
▬ 두 개의 전치사구 with glittering eyes와 in ~ places는 각각 동사 watch와 are hidden을 수식한다.

glitter 반짝이다
unlikely 있을 법하지 않은; 가
망이 없는

C **10** In a democratic environment, old ideas can be challenged and rigorously
민주적인 환경에서 / 오래된 개념은 도전을 받을 수 있다 / 그리고 엄격히 비판받을

criticized, though there are some difficulty due to the human desire to hold
(수 있다) / 비록 약간의 어려움이 있더라도 / 인간의 욕구 때문에 / [오래된

onto old ideas, especially by the original proposers.
개념을 유지하려는 / 특히 최초 제안자에 의해]

▬ 전치사구 In ~ environment는 문장 전체를 수식하고, due to(~ 때문에)가 이끄는 전치사구가 문장 끝에 쓰였다.

democratic 민주적인
rigorously 엄격히
hold onto ~을 계속 유지하다

모예 **11** In spite of the rare case of receiving rewarding email, we cannot resist the
가치 있는 이메일을 받을 경우가 드물더라도 / 우리는 이메일을 확인하려는

impulse to check email because our behaviors are maintained with the
충동을 참지 못한다 / 왜냐하면 우리의 행동이 유지되기 때문이다 / 보상으로

reward presented in an unpredictable way.
/ [예측할 수 없는 방식으로 제공되는]

▬ 전치사구 In spite of ~ email이 문장 전체를 수식하며, with ~ way는 동사 are maintained를 수식한다.
▬ with가 이끄는 전치사구 내에서 in an unpredictable way는 과거분사 presented를 수식한다.

rewarding 가치가 있는, 보람
이 있는 (cf. reward 보상)
resist 참다, 견디다
impulse 충동, 자극

모예 **12** With the advent of social media, our children become impatient for an
소셜 미디어의 출현으로 / 우리 아이들은 초조하게 기다리게 되었다 / 즉각적인

immediate answer or "Like" within minutes of sending an urgent piece of
응답 또는 '좋아요'를 / 다급한 정보를 발송하고 수 분 이내에

information out.

▬ With ~ social media는 문장 전체를 수식한다.
▬ for an ~ "Like"는 형용사 impatient를 수식하며, within이 이끄는 전치사구는 동사를 수식한다.

advent 출현, 도래
impatient 초조하게 기다리는
immediate 즉각적인
urgent 다급한, 긴급한

unit 30
부사 역할을 하는 to-v의 의미

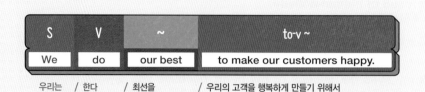

S	V	~	to-v ~
We	do	our best	to make our customers happy.

우리는 / 한다 / 최선을 / 우리의 고객을 행복하게 만들기 위해서

Standard Sentences

수능! 01 Charles Dickens used his desperate experience as a child laborer in
찰스 디킨스는 자신의 절망적인 경험을 활용했다 / [빅토리아 시대의 영국에서 아동
Victorian England **to write** *David Copperfield*.
노동자로서의] / 『데이비드 코퍼필드』를 쓰기 위해서

■ to write 이하는 '~하기 위해'라는 목적을 나타낸다.

> **Know More** 「데이비드 코퍼필드」는 영국 작가 찰스 디킨스(1812-1870)의 자전적 장편소설로, 19세기 영국 중산층 사람들의 애환이 잘 담겨 있는 풍속 소설이기도 하다. 이 작품의 주인공을 통해 작가는 어린 시절에 겪은 가난과 시련, 성장 과정을 고스란히 녹여 보여주며, 이 작품을 '가장 마음 속 깊이 사랑하는 자식'이라고 언급하기도 하였다. 찰스 디킨스는 주인공 데이비드 뿐만 아니라 고생을 이겨내고 중산계층에 합류하는 미코버, 충실한 가정부 페고티, 가련한 소녀 에밀리 등 개성 있는 인물들을 생생하게 묘사하였다.

desperate 절망적인
laborer 노동자

02 That Friday morning, I awoke **to find** myself caught in the middle of a
그 금요일 아침에 / 나는 깨어나서 내가 처해 있다는 것을 알게 되었다 / 소셜 미디어 폭풍의 한가운데에
social media storm.

■ awake 뒤에 나오는 to find 이하는 '~해서 …하다'라는 결과를 나타낸다.

awake (잠에서) 깨다

A 03 Our brain organizes the available sensory information and environmental
우리의 뇌는 이용 가능한 감각 정보와 환경 자극을 체계화한다
stimuli **so as to make sense out of** millions of bits and pieces of data.
/ 수백만 개의 이런저런 자료들을 이해하기 위해서

■ to make 이하는 '~하기 위해'라는 목적을 나타내는데, 목적의 의미를 명확히 하고자 so as가 to-v 앞에 쓰였다.

stimulus 자극 (*pl.* stimuli)
make sense (out) of ~을 이해하다
bits and pieces 이런저런 것들, 일부분

수능! 04 When at length the deal was settled, Dr. Paul was delighted **to purchase**
마침내 그 거래가 합의에 이르렀을 때 / Paul 박사는 기뻤다 / 그 조각품을 적절한
the carving at a reasonable price.
가격에 구입하게 되어

■ 형용사 delighted 뒤에 온 to purchase 이하는 '~하게 되어'라는 감정의 원인을 나타낸다.

at length 마침내; 상세히
settle 합의를 보다
carving 조각품, 조각
reasonable (가격이) 적절한; 합리적인

05 If an activity is easy **to perform**, easy **to fit** into your schedule, and easy **to**
만약 어떤 활동이 하기 쉽고 / 당신의 일정에 맞추기 쉬우며 / 그리고 좋아하기
love, you're more likely to stick with it.
쉽다면 / 당신은 그것을 더욱 계속할 것이다

■ 세 개의 to부정사구 to perform, to fit ~, to love는 '~하기에'라는 의미로 각각 바로 앞의 형용사 easy를 수식한다.

fit into ~에 맞추다
stick with ~을 계속하다

B 06 We should carefully think about the reason for someone's behavior **to avoid**
우리는 조심스럽게 생각해야 한다 / 어떤 사람의 행동의 이유에 대해 / 성급한 결론에
coming to a hasty conclusion about it.
도달하는 것을 피하기 위해서 / [그것에 대한]

■ to avoid 이하는 '~하기 위해'라는 목적을 나타낸다.

hasty 성급한
come to a conclusion 결론
에 도달하다(이르다)

07 When temperatures near 0℃, water molecules start bonding with one
온도가 섭씨 0도에 가까워질 때 / 물 분자는 서로 결합되기 시작한다
another to form a crystal structure.
/ 그래서 결정 구조를 형성한다

■ to form 이하는 '~해서 …하다'라는 결과를 나타낸다.

near 가까워지다
molecule 분자
bond 결합되다, 이어지다
crystal 결정, 결정체; 수정

08 We would be honored **to have you as a guest at the annual festival.**
저희는 영광일 것입니다 / 당신을 손님으로 모신다면 / 해마다 열리는 축제에

■ to have 이하는 '~한다면'이라는 '가정'의 의미를 나타내는데, 문장의 동사에 쓰인 would가 그 단서이다. / (= We would be honored if we had you ~.)

honor 영광을 주다; 존경하다

09 If you are fortunate **to have opportunity,** it is your duty to make sure other
만약 당신이 운이 좋다면 / 기회를 가지는 데 / (…은) 당신의 의무이다 / 반드시 하는 것은 / 다른
people have those opportunities as well. *Kamala Harris*
사람들도 또한 그러한 기회를 갖도록

■ to have opportunity는 '~하는 데'라는 의미로 형용사 fortunate를 수식한다.
■ it은 가주어이고, to make sure 이하가 진주어이다.
■ make sure 다음에는 접속사 that이 생략되어 있다.

make sure 반드시 ~하도록
하다, ~을 확실히 하다
as well 또한, 마찬가지로

C 10 We can't help but think **James must have his head in the clouds to talk like**
우리는 생각하지 않을 수 없다 / James가 틀림없이 공상에 잠긴 것이라고 / 그렇게 말하다니
that.

■ to talk 이하는 '~하다니'라는 판단의 근거를 나타낸다.
■ think 다음에 목적어 역할을 하는 명사절을 이끄는 접속사 that이 생략되었다.

cannot (help) but ⓥ ~하지
않을 수 없다
have one's head in the clouds
공상에 잠기다

모의 11 Have you ever found yourself speaking to someone at length **only to realize**
당신은 발견한 적이 있는가 / 자신이 어떤 사람에게 상세히 말하고 있는 것을 / (그러나) 결국 깨닫게 된
they haven't heard a single thing you've said?
/ 그들이 하나도 듣지 않았다는 것을 / [당신이 말한]?

■ only to realize 이하는 '(…했으나) 결국 ~하게 되다'라는 결과를 나타낸다.
■ realize 다음에 명사절을 이끄는 접속사 that이 생략되었고, a single thing 다음에 목적격 관계대명사 which 또는 that이 생략되었다.

수능 12 A child **who has been repeatedly criticized for poor performance on math**
아이는 [수학에서의 부진한 (학업) 성취로 인해 반복해서 야단을 맞아온]
may learn to dodge difficult math problems in order to avoid further
/ 배울지도 모른다 / 어려운 수학 문제들을 피하는 것을 / 더 심한 처벌을 면하기 위해
punishment.

■ to avoid 이하는 '~하기 위해'라는 목적을 나타내며, 목적의 의미를 명확히 하고자 in order가 to-v 앞에 쓰였다.
■ A child를 관계대명사 who가 이끄는 절 who ~ math가 수식하고 있다.

criticize 지적하다, 비난하다
dodge 피하다, 기피하다
further 더 심한; 추가의
punishment 처벌

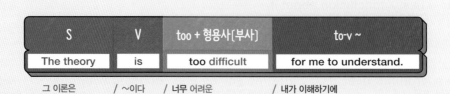

unit 31
부사적 to-v의 관용 구문

S	V	too + 형용사[부사]	to-v ~
The theory	is	too difficult	for me to understand.
그 이론은	/ ~이다	/ 너무 어려운	/ 내가 이해하기에

Standard Sentences

01 Our span of life is brief, but is long **enough for us to live well and**
우리의 수명은 짧다 / 그러나 길다 / 우리가 멋지게 그리고 정직하게 살기에는 충분히
honestly. *Cicero*

- 형용사 + enough to-v: ~할 정도로[하기에] 충분히 …한[하게] / enough 다음의 for us는 to live의 의미상 주어이다.

span of life 수명
honestly 정직하게

02 Some kinds of viruses are **too small to be seen by the naked eye.**
어떤 종류의 바이러스는 / 너무 작다 / 보이기에는 / 맨눈으로

- too + 형용사 + to-v: 너무 ~해서 …할 수 없는 / (= Some kinds of viruses are so small that they can't be seen by ~.)

Know More 바이러스는 동물, 식물, 세균 등 살아 있는 세포에 기생하고, 세포 안에서만 증식이 가능한 미생물로, 일반 광학현미경으로는 볼 수 없다. 그것은 그 크기가 세균의 100분의 1에서 1,000분의 1 정도로 아주 작기 때문에 바이러스의 크기는 나노미터(nm)로 표시한다. 1nm는 1mm의 100만분의 1의 크기이며, 독감 바이러스의 크기는 약 100nm로 알려져 있다.

naked eye 맨눈

A 03 You are **never too old to set another goal or to dream a new dream.**
당신은 결코 너무 나이가 많지 않다 / 다른 목표를 정하거나 새로운 꿈을 꾸기에

- never + too + 형용사[부사] + to-v: 너무 ~해서 …할 수 없는 것은 아닌

set (목표 등을) 정하다, 설정하다

04 Change is the law of life. And those who look only to the past or present **are**
변화는 삶의 법칙이다 그리고 사람은 / [과거 또는 현재만을 바라보는] /
certain to miss the future. *John F. Kennedy*
반드시 미래를 놓치게 된다

- be certain to-v: 반드시 ~하다 (= be sure to-v)

05 **To make a long story short,** Beauty fell in love with the Beast, **who turned**
간단히 말해서 / 미녀는 야수와 사랑에 빠졌다 / 그리고 그는 잘생긴
out to be a handsome prince.
왕자인 것으로 밝혀졌다

- to make a long story short: 간단히 말해서 (= to be brief, to put it simply)
- 관계대명사 who가 이끄는 절이 the Beast를 보충 설명한다.

turn out ~으로 밝혀지다[드러나다]

B 06 Copywriters must be **versatile** enough to adjust to each new product and
카피라이터는 다재다능해야 한다 / 각각의 새로운 상품과 매체에 적응할 정도로 충분히
모의
medium and to vary the language and tone of each message.
/ 그리고 각 메시지의 용어와 어조를 바꿀 정도로

- 형용사 + enough to-v: ~할 정도로[하기에] 충분히 …한[하게]
- to adjust와 to vary가 이끄는 어구가 and로 enough에 병렬 연결되어 있다.

copywriter 카피라이터, 광고의 글귀를 만드는 사람
versatile 다재다능한
medium 매체; 중간
vary 바꾸다
tone 어조

수능! 07 People draw **too heavily, too quickly**, on already overdrawn environmental
사람들이 너무 많이, 너무 빠르게 이용한다 / 이미 초과 인출된 환경의 자원 계좌들을
resource accounts to be affordable far into the future without bankrupting
/ 먼 미래에 감당하기에는 / 그러한 계좌들을 파산시키지 않고서
those accounts.

- too + 부사 + to-v: 너무 ~해서 …할 수 없는
- without + v-ing: ~하지 않고서

draw on ~을 이용하다
overdrawn 초과 인출된
account 계좌
affordable 감당할 수 있는
bankrupt 파산시키다

08 It is not fair to ask of others what you are not willing to do yourself.
(…은) 공정하지 않다 / 타인들에게 요구하는 것은 / 당신이 직접 기꺼이 하려고 하지 않는 것을

- be willing to-v: 기꺼이 ~하다 (↔ be unwilling[reluctant] to-v: ~하기를 꺼리다)
- It은 가주어이고, to ask 이하가 진주어이다. what이 이끄는 명사절은 to ask의 목적어이다.

09 The team has lost the last two games and, **to make matters worse**, two of
그 팀은 마지막 두 경기를 졌다 / 그리고 설상가상으로 / 최고
its best players are injured.
선수들 중 두 명이 부상 중이다

- to make matters worse: 설상가상으로

injure 부상을 입히다

C 10 I always like to look on the optimistic side of life, but I am **realistic** enough
나는 항상 좋아한다 / 인생의 낙관적인 면을 보는 것을 / 그러나 나는 현실적이다 / 알 정도로
to know that life is a complex matter. *Walt Disney*
충분히 / 인생은 복잡한 문제라는 것을

- 형용사 + enough to-v: ~할 정도로[하기에] 충분히 …한[하게]
- 접속사 that이 이끄는 절 that ~ matter가 동사 to know의 목적어로 쓰였다.

optimistic 낙관적인
complex 복잡한

Know More 월트 디즈니(1901-1966)는 애니메이션과 관련 업계를 주도하는 회사인 월트 디즈니를 만든 전설의 경영자이자 애니메이션 연출가, 제작자, 애니메이션의 스토리와 캐릭터를 구상한 창업주이다. 세계적으로 가장 널리 알려진 캐릭터 미키 마우스를 탄생시킨 장본인이며, 애니메이션이라는 새로운 문화 장르를 개척했고, 꿈을 현실로 이루어낸 디즈니랜드를 건설하였다.

모의 11 The bargain must truly stand out in the consumer's mind as a good deal
염가판매는 정말로 눈에 띄어야 한다 / 소비자의 마음속에 / 좋은 거래로서
that is just too exceptional to pass up.
/ [정말 너무나 파격적이어서 놓칠 수 없는]

- too + 형용사 + to-v: 너무 …해서 ~할 수 없는

stand out 눈에 띄다, 두드러지다
deal 거래
exceptional 파격적인; 예외적인
pass up (기회를) 놓치다; 거절하다

12 Pollution has a negative effect on the health of everyone living in the city,
오염은 부정적인 영향을 미친다 / 모든 사람의 건강에 / [도시에 살고 있는]
not to mention the damage to the environment.
/ 환경에 대한 손상은 말할 것도 없이

- not to mention: ~은 말할 것도 없이 (= to say nothing of, not to speak of)
- 현재분사구 living in the city가 everyone을 수식한다.

pollution 오염
have an effect on ~에 영향을 미치다
damage 손상
mention 언급하다

unit 32
부사 역할을 하는 분사구문의 의미

V-ing(V-ed) ~,	S	V	~
Walking on the street	I	met	a friend of mine.

길을 걸었다 / (그때) 나는 / 만났다 / 내 친구 한 명을

Standard Sentences

01 **Tapping his fingers loudly on the desk top**, he made his impatience and
자신의 손가락으로 시끄럽게 톡톡 두드렸다 / 책상 위를 / (그러면서) 그는 자신의 성급함과 불만이 알려지게
dissatisfaction known.
했다

- 주어 he가 두드리는 것이므로 현재분사 Tapping이 쓰여 '~하면서'의 의미를 나타낸다.
- 목적어인 his impatience and dissatisfaction이 알려지는 대상이므로 목적격보어로 과거분사 known이 쓰였다.

tap 톡톡 두드리다; 박자를 맞추다
impatience 성급함, 조바심
dissatisfaction 불만, 불평

[모의] 02 **Pressed for time and stuck in a deadlock**, she had no idea how to finish
시간에 쫓기고 교착 상태에 갇혔다 / (그래서) 그녀는 알지 못했다 / 그 논문을 어떻게
the paper.
끝내야 할지

- 주어 she가 시간의 압박을 받고 교착 상태에 갇힌 대상이므로 과거분사 Pressed와 stuck이 쓰여 '~하게 되어'의 의미를 나타낸다. / (= Because she was pressed for time and stuck in a deadlock, she ~.)

be pressed for time 시간에 쫓기다
deadlock 교착 상태

Ⓐ 03 **Being a hybrid art as well as a late one**, film has always been in a dialogue
[수능] 혼합 예술이다 / 후발 예술일 뿐만 아니라 / (그래서) 영화는 항상 대화를 해왔다
with other narrative genres.
/ 다른 서사 장르와

- 현재분사 Being이 이끄는 어구는 이어지는 내용에 대한 이유·원인을 나타내므로, '~하여, ~하므로'라고 해석한다.

hybrid 혼합의
A as well as B B뿐만 아니라 A도
narrative 서사의, 이야기체의

04 **Taken daily**, according to a new study, vitamin D can help treat severe
매일 섭취된다 / 새로운 연구에 따르면 / (그러면) 비타민 D는 심한 천식을 치료하는 것을 도울
asthma.
수 있다

- 주어 vitamin D가 섭취되는 대상이므로 과거분사 Taken이 쓰였으며, '~된다면'으로 해석한다.
- help의 목적어로 동사가 올 때 to부정사나 to가 생략된 원형부정사의 형태로 쓸 수 있다. / (= If vitamin D is taken daily, according to a new study, it can ~.)

severe 심각한
asthma 천식

05 **Originally raised mainly for their meat**, sheep and goats became valuable
원래 주로 고기를 위해 사육되었다 / (그러나) 양과 염소는 귀중하게 되었다
also for their milk and wool.
/ 그것들의 우유와 털 때문에도

- 주어 sheep and goats가 사육되는 대상이므로 과거분사 raised가 쓰였으며, 이어지는 문장과 상반되는 내용이므로 '~일지라도'라고 해석한다. / (= Though sheep and goats were originally raised mainly for their meat, they became ~.)

originally 원래
raise (가축을) 사육하다

B **06** Children at play often take on other roles, **pretending to be Principal Walsh**
놀이 중인 아이들은 종종 다른 역할을 맡는다 　　　　/ Walsh 교장 선생님이나 Josh의 엄마인
[모의]

or Josh's mom, happily forcing themselves to imagine how someone else
체하면서 　　　/ (그러면서) 행복하게 스스로가 상상하도록 한다 　　/ 다른 사람이 어떻게 생각하고

thinks and feels.
느끼는지

■ 주어 Children이 다른 사람인 체하고 스스로가 상상하게 하는 것이므로 현재분사 pretending과 forcing이 쓰여
'~하면서'의 의미를 나타낸다.

take on ~을 맡다
pretend ~인 체하다

07 A mother is a person who **seeing** there are only four pieces of pie for five
어머니는 사람이다 　　　　　/ [다섯 명이 있는데 파이가 네 조각만 있는 것을 본다

people, promptly announces she never did care for pie.
　　　/ (그때) 바로 알리는 　　　/ 자신은 한 번도 파이를 좋아한 적이 없었다고]

■ 주어 A mother가 네 조각의 파이를 본 것이므로 현재분사 seeing이 쓰여 '~할 때'라는 의미를 나타낸다.
― seeing과 announces 다음에 각각 목적어 역할을 하는 명사절을 이끄는 접속사 that이 생략되었다.

promptly 바로, 즉시
announce 알리다, 발표하다
care for ~을 좋아하다; ~을
돌보다

08 **Assumed to have a substantial amount of water, Mars is probably most**
상당한 양의 물을 가진 것으로 추정된다 　　　　　　　/ (그래서) 화성은 아마도 가장 살기에

habitable out of all the planets in our solar system.
적합할 것이다 　/ 우리 태양계의 모든 행성들 중에서

■ 주어인 Mars가 추정되는 대상이므로 과거분사 assumed가 쓰였으며, '~ 때문에'의 의미를 나타낸다.

assume 추정하다, 가정하다
substantial 상당한
habitable 살기에 적합한

09 When I find myself in times of trouble, mother Mary comes to me, **speaking**
내 자신이 곤경에 처한 것을 알게 될 때 　　　　/ 어머니 Mary가 내게 오신다 　　/ (그리고 나서)

words of wisdom, "Let it be." And in my hour of darkness she is standing
지혜의 말씀을 주신다 　/ "내버려 두라" 　　그리고 내가 어둠의 시간에 있을 때 　　/ 그녀는 내 바로 앞에

right in front of me, speaking words of wisdom, "Let it be." *the song <Let It Be>*
서 계신다 　　/ (그리고 나서) 지혜의 말씀을 주신다 　/ "내버려 두라"

■ 주어 mother Mary와 she가 말하는 것이므로 각각 현재분사 speaking이 쓰여, '~하면서'의 의미를 나타낸다.

wisdom 지혜

Know More 〈렛 잇 비(Let it be)〉는 1960년 영국의 리버풀에서 결성된 록 밴드 비틀즈(The Beatles)가 1970년에 발표한
동명 앨범에 수록된 타이틀곡이다. 비틀즈의 멤버인 폴 매카트니(Paul McCartney)가 작사, 작곡하였는데, 팀 내 불화로 어려운
시기를 보내고 있던 와중에 돌아가신 어머니 매리 매카트니(Mary McCartney)가 꿈에 나와 "Let it be"라고 말하며 안심시켜
주었던 것을 바탕으로 쓰인 것이다.

C **10** **Fueled by drought and development, wildfires in the West are getting bigger**
가뭄과 개발로 부채질된다 　　　　　/ (그래서) (미국) 서부의 들불은 점점 더 커지고 더 강력해지고 있다

and more aggressive.

풀이 분사구문의 의미상 주어가 문장의 주어와 같은 wildfires이고, 그 들불이 부채질되는 대상이므로 과거분사
Fueled가 적절하다.

fuel 부채질하다, 연료를 공급
하다
drought 가뭄
aggressive 강력한, 공격적인

11 Seconds after its spectacular launch, the spacecraft with seven astronauts
극적인 발사 수초 후에 　　　　　/ 일곱 명의 우주비행사들이 탑승한 그 우주선은 폭발하였다

on board blew up and came apart, striking the viewers dumb with shock.
/ 그리고 부서졌다 　　/ (그래서) 시청자들이 갑자기 충격으로 말문이 막히게 했다

풀이 두 문장을 연결해 주는 접속사가 없으므로 준동사가 와야 하는 자리이며, 주어인 the spacecraft가 시청자들의
말문을 막히게 한 것이므로 현재분사 striking이 적절하다.

spectacular 극적인; 장관인
launch 발사
come apart 부서지다, 흩어지다
strike 갑자기 ~가 되게 하다
dumb 말문이 막힌; 말을 못하는

12 The very real genetic differences between races or genders are insignificant
매우 실질적인 유전적 차이들은 　　　　/ [인종 또는 성별 사이의] 　　　　/ 사소하다

compared with the similarities in our minds.
/ 우리의 정신적 유사성과 비교될 때

풀이 주어 The very real genetic differences가 비교되는 대상이므로 과거분사 compared가 적절하다.

gender 성별, 성(性)
insignificant 사소한, 중요하
지 않은
compare 비교하다
similarity 유사성

unit 33
분사구문의 다양한 형태 1

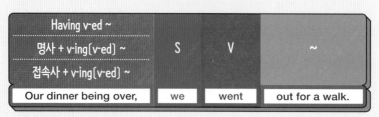

Having v-ed ~			
명사 + v-ing[v-ed] ~	S	V	~
접속사 + v-ing[v-ed] ~			
Our dinner being over,	we	went	out for a walk.

우리의 저녁 식사가 끝났다 / (그러고 나서) 우리는 / 나갔다 / 밖으로 산책을 하러

Standard Sentences

01 **Not having been to the city before**, I needed some tourist pamphlets.
전에 그 도시에 가본 적이 없었다 / (그래서) 나는 몇 개의 여행자용 팸플릿이 필요했다

■ 주어 I가 그 도시에 가본 적이 없다는 것이 팸플릿이 필요한 과거 시제보다 이전의 일이므로, 완료분사구문 having been이 쓰였다. / (= Because I hadn't been to the city before, I needed ~.)
■ 분사구문의 부정은 not이나 never를 분사 앞에 써서 나타낸다.

pamphlet 팸플릿, 소책자

(모의) 02 Can we sustain our standard of living in the same ecological space **while**
우리는 우리의 생활 수준을 유지할 수 있을까 / 동일한 생태적 공간에서 / 그 공간의
consuming the resources of that space?
자원을 소비하면서?

■ 분사구문의 의미를 분명히 하기 위해 consuming 앞에 접속사 while이 쓰였다. / (= ~, while we are consuming the resources of that space?)

sustain 유지하다, 지속하다
standard 수준, 표준
ecological 생태적인
consume 소비하다

A 03 The fundamental problem most patients face is an inability to love themselves,
근본적인 문제는 / [대부분의 환자들이 직면하는] / 자신을 사랑하지 못하는 것이다
having been unloved by others during some crucial part of their lives.
/ (왜냐하면) 사랑받지 못했다 / 다른 사람들에 의해서 / 그들의 삶의 어떤 결정적인 기간 동안에

■ 문장의 동사는 is로 현재를 나타내는데, 대부분의 환자들이 사랑을 받지 못한 것은 그 이전의 일이며 수동의 관계이므로 완료 수동 분사구문 having been unloved가 쓰였다.
문장의 주어인 'The fundamental problem'이 분사구문의 주어는 아니지만, 이 문장처럼 분사구문의 주어가 문장 전체의 주어와 다른 경우에도 글의 흐름이 자연스러우면 별도의 주어를 쓰지 않으며, 이런 문장을 '현수분사구문'이라고 한다.
■ The fundamental problem 다음에 목적격 관계대명사 which 또는 that이 생략되었다.

fundamental 근본적인
crucial 결정적인, 중대한

(모의) 04 I sat quietly in a chair, **my only actions consisting of taking notes and**
나는 의자에 조용히 앉아 있었다 / (그러면서) 나의 유일한 행동은 필기를 하는 것이었고 / 그리고
stuffing my ears with wadded toilet paper.
내 귀를 똘똘 뭉친 화장지로 채우는 것이었다

■ 문장의 주어 I와 분사구문의 주어 my only actions가 서로 다르므로 현재분사 consisting 앞에 분사구문의 의미상 주어를 쓴 구조이다.
■ 전치사 of의 목적어로 두 개의 동명사구 taking notes와 stuffing ~ paper가 and로 병렬 연결되어 있다.

consist of ~으로 구성되다
stuff A with B A를 B로 채우다
wad ~을 뭉치다, 뭉치로 만들다

05 **Though seriously injured**, the pilot crawled out of the wreckage and was
비록 심하게 다쳤지만 / 그 조종사는 잔해에서 기어나왔다 / 그리고
flown by helicopter to a nearby medical center.
헬리콥터에 태워져 이송되었다 / 근처의 의료 센터로

■ 분사구문이 '비록 ~이긴 하지만, 비록 ~일지라도'라는 양보의 의미를 나타내고 있음을 명확히 하기 위해 접속사 Though가 과거분사 injured 앞에 쓰였다. 주어 the pilot이 다친 대상이므로 수동의 의미를 나타내는 injured가 쓰였으며, 앞에 현재분사 being이 생략된 것으로 볼 수 있다. (= Though he was seriously injured, ~.)

crawl 기어가다, 기다
wreckage (사고 자동차·비행기 등의) 잔해

B 06 **Turned down for countless jobs,** Jenny didn't give up hope and is now a
무수한 일자리를 거절당했다 / (그러나) Jenny는 희망을 포기하지 않았다 / 그리고 지금은
successful architect.
성공한 건축가이다

turn down 거절하다
countless 무수한, 셀 수 없는
architect 건축가

> ■ 일자리를 거절당한 것이 희망을 포기하지 않은 것보다 이전의 일이고 주어 Jenny와 수동의 관계이므로, 완료 수동 분사구문인 Having been turned down ~으로 쓰며, 과거분사 앞의 Having been이 생략된 형태로 볼 수 있다. (= Though Jenny had been turned down ~.)

(모의) 07 **In recent history, countries with the highest net inward migration have also**
최근의 역사에서 / 순유입이 가장 높았던 나라들이 / 또한 가장 높은
had the highest growth rates, the two factors clearly being linked in
성장률을 보였다 / (그래서) 그 두 요소는 분명 조화롭게 연결되어 있다
harmony.

net inward migration 순유
입(純流入)
growth rate 성장률
in harmony 조화롭게, 조화를
이루어

> ■ 문장의 주어 countries와 분사구문의 주어 the two factors가 서로 다르므로 분사 being linked 앞에 분사구문의
> 의미상 주어를 쓴 구조이다.

(모의) 08 **When faced with a bunch of watermelons, all promising delicious**
한 무더기의 수박을 마주 대하게 될 때 / 모두 속에 맛있는 과즙이 있을 것 같은데
juiciness inside, how do you know which one to pick?
/ 당신은 어떻게 아는가 / 어느 것을 골라야 할지?

bunch 무더기, 다발
promise ~일 것 같다, ~의
가망성이 있다

> ■ faced가 이끄는 분사구문의 의미를 분명히 하기 위해서 '~할 때'를 뜻하는 접속사 when이 분사 앞에 쓰였다.
> ■ all promising ~ inside는 삽입어구로 쓰인 분사구문으로 all을 의미상의 주어로 하고 있다.

09 **The time spent in lamenting their lot, if applied to honest endeavor,** would
시간은 / [자신의 운명을 한탄하면서 보낸] / 만약 정직한 노력에 쓰인다면 / 정말
yield splendid results and give them **proper places in the world.**
멋진 결과를 낳을 텐데 / 그리고 그들에게 세상에서 적절한 자리를 줄 텐데

lament 한탄하다, 슬퍼하다
lot 운명, 운
yield (결과를) 낳다; 양보하다
splendid 정말 멋진, 화려한

> ■ 분사구문의 의미를 분명히 하기 위해 '~한다면'을 뜻하는 접속사 if가 쓰인 분사구문이 주어와 동사 사이에 삽입되었다.
> ─ 주어 The time을 과거분사 spent가 이끄는 어구가 수식하고 있다.
> ─ 가정법 과거의 문장의 주절의 동사 형태이다. (➔ Unit 41)

C 10 **The making of a contract requires the mutual agreement of two or more**
계약을 하는 것은 필요로 한다 / 둘 이상의 사람이나 단체의 상호 합의를
(수능!)
persons or parties, one of them ordinarily making an offer and another accepting.
/ 그들 중 한쪽이 보통 제안을 한다 / 그리고 다른 한쪽은 받아들인다

contract 계약
mutual 상호의, 서로의
agreement 합의, 동의
party 단체, 일행; 당사자

> **풀이** 두 문장을 연결해 주는 접속사가 없으므로 준동사가 와야 하는 자리이며, one of them을 주어로 하는 분사구문
> 이 되려면 현재분사 making이 적절하다.

11 **There being a dispute over a topic of environment,** the country **is to make**
환경이라는 주제에 대해서 논쟁이 있다 / (그래서) 그 나라는 효과적인 법률을
an effective law for its sustainable development.
만들 예정이다 / 지속 가능한 개발을 위해서

dispute 논쟁
sustainable 지속 가능한, 지
탱할 수 있는

> **풀이** 두 문장을 연결해 주는 접속사가 없으므로 준동사가 와야 하는 자리이다. 문장의 주어 the country와 주어가 일
> 치하지 않는 분사구문임을 표시하기 위해 현재분사 being 앞에 There가 그대로 쓰인 것이다.
> ─ is to make ~는 「be to-v 용법」으로 '예정'의 의미를 나타낸다. (➔ Unit 15)

12 **When expelled from the nucleus of an atom,** a neutron is unstable and
원자핵에서 방출되었을 때 / 중성자는 불안정하다 / 그리고
decayed to form a proton and an electron.
자연 붕괴된다 / 그 결과 양성자와 전자를 형성한다

nucleus 핵
neutron 중성자
unstable 불안정한
decay (방사능 물질이) 자연 붕
괴하다
proton 양성자

> **풀이** 주어인 a neutron이 방출되는 대상이므로 과거분사 expelled가 와야 한다. 분사구문의 의미를 분명히 하기
> 위해 과거분사 앞에 접속사 When이 쓰인 것이다.

unit 34
분사구문의 다양한 형태 2

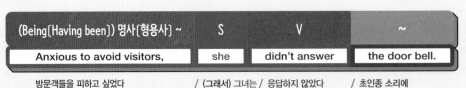

(Being(Having been)) 명사[형용사] ~	S	V	~
Anxious to avoid visitors,	she	didn't answer	the door bell.
방문객들을 피하고 싶었다	/ (그래서) 그녀는	/ 응답하지 않았다	/ 초인종 소리에

Standard Sentences

〔모의〕 01 Adolescents have been quick to immerse themselves in technology with
청소년들은 재빨랐다 　　　　　　　 / 기술에 몰두하는 것에 　　　　　　 / 대부분
most using the Internet to communicate.
인터넷을 사용하면서 　　　 / 소통하기 위해서

- with + 명사 + v-ing: ~가 …하면서[한 채로], ~가 …하여
- most는 most of adolescents를 가리키고, to communicate는 목적을 나타내는 부사적 용법의 to부정사 이다.

adolescent 청소년
immerse oneself in ~에 몰두하다, 열중하다

02 Judging from his latest novel that I have read, he seems to be a fairly
그의 최신 소설로 판단하건대 　　　　 / [내가 읽은] 　　　 / 그는 꽤 유망한 작가인 것 같다
promising writer.

- judging from: ~으로 판단하건대

fairly 꽤
promising 유망한

Ⓐ 03 〔수능!〕 While afloat, the reindeer is uniquely vulnerable, moving slowly with its
물에 떠 있는 동안 　 / 순록은 특히 공격받기 쉽다 　　　　　　 / (왜냐하면) 천천히 움직인다 / 뿔을 높이
antlers held high as it struggles to keep its nose above water.
받쳐 든 채로 　　　　　 / 순록이 코를 유지하려고 애쓰면서 　　　 / 물 위로

- with + 명사 + v-ed: ~가 …된 채로[하면서] / its antler가 hold high의 대상이므로 과거분사인 held가 왔다.
- While 다음에 it is가 생략되었다. 한편 afloat 앞에 being이 생략된 분사구문으로 볼 수 있다.
- 주어인 the reindeer가 움직이는 주체이므로 현재분사 moving이 쓰여 '~ 때문에'의 의미를 나타낸다.

afloat (물에) 뜬
reindeer 순록
vulnerable 공격받기 쉬운, 취약한
antler (가지진) 뿔

〔모의〕 04 Desperate to keep himself and his family from starving, Erich took any
필사적이었다 　 / 자기 자신과 가족이 굶주리지 않게 하려고 　　　　　　 / (그래서) Erich는 구할
available job.
수 있는 어떠한 일자리라도 취했다

- 형용사 Desperate 앞에 분사구문을 이끄는 Being이 생략되었다. / (= Since he was desperate to keep ~.)

desperate 필사적인; 절망적인
keep ~ from v-ing ~가 …하지 못하게 하다
starve 굶주리다

05 Granted that you've made some progress, you should not be conceited.
네가 어느 정도 진전을 이루었다는 것이 인정된다 　　　　　 / (그러나) 너는 자만해서는 안 된다

- granting (that): ~을 인정한다고 하더라도

progress 진전, 발전
conceited 자만하는

B 06 **수능!** **With the industrial society evolving into an information-based society**, the
산업 사회가 진화하면서 / 정보 기반 사회로 /

concept of information as a product, a commodity with its own value, has emerged.
정보의 개념이 / [생산물로서 / 즉 그 자체의 가치를 가진 상품(으로서)] / 나타났다

■ with + 명사(구) + v-ing: ∼가 …하면서[한 채로]

commodity 상품
emerge 나타나다; 떠오르다

07 **Unable to write, or even to speak clearly**, Stephen Hawking was leaping
쓸 수도 혹은 명확하게 말을 수도 없었다 / (그러나) 스티븐 호킹은 도약하고 있었다

beyond relativity, beyond quantum mechanics, beyond the Big Bang, to the
/ 상대성 이론을 넘어 / 양자 역학을 넘어 / 빅뱅을 넘어 / '기하학의

'dance of geometry' that created the universe.
춤'으로 / [우주를 창조한]

■ 형용사 Unable 앞에 분사구문을 이끄는 Being이 생략되었으며, '비록 ∼이지만'의 의미를 나타낸다. / (= Although
he was unable to write, ~.)

leap (어떤 점, 상태로) 도약하다; 도달하다
relativity 상대성 이론; 상대성
quantum mechanics 양자 역학
geometry 기하학

Up! **08** Some pioneers in computer usage see the ultimate relation between man
일부 개척자들은 / 컴퓨터 사용에 있어서 / 인간과 컴퓨터 사이의 궁극적인 관계를 여긴다

and computer as a symbiotic union of two living species, **each completely**
/ 두 개의 살아 있는 종의 공생 결합으로 / (왜냐하면) 각각은 완전히

dependent on the other for survival.
상대방에 의존하고 있다 / 생존을 위해

■ 문장의 주어는 Some pioneers이고, 분사구문의 의미상 주어는 each로 서로 다르므로 being이 생략된 분사구문
completely dependent ~ 앞에 의미상 주어인 each가 쓰였다.

see A as B A를 B로 여기다
ultimate 궁극적인, 최후의
symbiotic 공생의
union 결합; 조합

09 **Strictly speaking**, Great Britain consists of Scotland, Wales and England,
엄격히 말하자면 / Great Britain은 스코틀랜드, 웨일스, 그리고 잉글랜드로 구성된다

and the United Kingdom consists of Great Britain and Northern Ireland.
/ 그리고 the United Kingdom은 Great Britain과 북아일랜드로 구성된다

■ strictly speaking: 엄격히 말하자면

consist of ∼으로 구성되다

C 10 **수능!** The role of science can **sometimes** be overstated, **with its advocates slipping**
과학의 역할은 때때로 과장될 수 있다 / 그 지지자들이 과학(만능)주의에 빠져들면서

into scientism.

풀이 「with + 명사 + v-ing」 구문으로, advocates가 과학만능주의에 빠져드는 주체이므로 현재분사 slipping이 알
맞다.

overstate 과장하다
advocate 지지자, 옹호자
slip into ∼에 빠지다
scientism 과학(만능)주의

11 **Taking into account growing population numbers, climate change and**
늘어나는 인구의 수, 기후 변화, 자연재해를 고려할 때

natural disasters, global food security is under threat.
/ 전 세계의 식량 안보가 위협받고 있다

풀이 taking ~ into account: ∼을 고려하면(= considering) / Taking의 목적어 growing ~ disasters가 길어
서 into account 뒤로 이동한 형태이다.

natural disaster 자연 재해
food security 식량 안보(국가
가 필요로 하는 식량을 항상 확
보하여 유지하는 것)
under threat 위협받고 있는

12 **With so much data collected about us and with anybody being able to**
우리에 관해 너무나 많은 자료가 수집된 상태에서 / 그리고 누구라도 그것을 유포할 수 있는 상태에서

disseminate it around the globe, is there anything we really can do to
/ 전 세계에 / 어떤 것이 있는가 / [우리가 정말로 할 수 있는] /

protect privacy?
사생활을 보호하기 위해서?

풀이 (A) 「with + 명사(구) + v-ing[v-ed]」 구문이 and로 병렬 연결된 문장이다. so much data는 수집되는 대상
이므로 과거분사인 collected가 와야 한다.
(B) anybody는 유포할 수 있는 주체이므로 현재분사인 being이 와야 한다.

collect 수집하다, 모으다
disseminate 유포하다, 퍼뜨
리다
privacy 사생활

Chapter 07

Review

A **01** Holding on to anger is like grasping a hot coal **with the intent of throwing it**
분노를 계속 유지하는 것은 뜨거운 석탄을 쥐고 있는 것과 같다   / 그것을 누군가에게 던지려는 의도로
at someone else; you are the one who gets burned. *Buddha*
당신이 사람이다   / [화상을 입게 되는]

   ■ 전치사구 with ~ else가 동명사 grasping을 수식한다.

hold on to ~을 유지하다
grasp 꽉 쥐다
coal 석탄
intent 의도

02 I can't change the direction of the wind, but I can adjust my sails **to always**
나는 바람의 방향을 바꿀 수 없다   / 그러나 나는 돛을 조정할 수 있다   / 항상 나의
reach my destination. *Jimmy Dean*
목적지에 도착하기 위해

   ■ to always reach 이하는 '~하기 위해'라는 의미의 목적을 나타낸다.

adjust 조정하다
sail 돛; 항해(하다)

03 The virus is **too small to carry all the molecular machinery required to**
바이러스는 너무 작다   / 모든 분자적 조직을 갖기에는   / [스스로를 복제하는
replicate itself, which is why it needs a host cell **to multiply.**
데 필요한]   / 그리고 그것이 바이러스가 숙주 세포를 필요로 하는 이유이다 / 증식하기 위해서

   ■ too + 형용사 + to-v: 너무 ~해서 …할 수 없는 / (= The virus is so small that it can't carry ~.)
   ■ to multiply는 '~하기 위해'라는 의미의 목적을 나타낸다.

molecular 분자의
machinery 조직; 기계
replicate 복제하다
host 숙주; 주인
multiply 증식(번식)하다

04 Plants communicate, **signaling to remote organs within an individual,**
식물들은 소통한다   / 개체 내에서 멀리 떨어진 기관에 신호를 보내면서
eavesdropping on neighboring individuals, and exchanging information
/ 이웃하는 개체의 이야기를 엿들으면서   / 그리고 다른 유기체와 정보를 교환하면서
with other organisms.

   ■ 주어 Plants가 신호를 보내고, 이야기를 엿듣고, 정보를 교환하는 주체이므로, 현재분사 signaling,
   eavesdropping, exchanging이 쓰여 '~하면서'의 의미를 나타낸다.

signal 신호를 보내다; 신호
remote 멀리 떨어진, 먼
organ 기관
eavesdrop 이야기를 엿듣다

B **05** A foreign exchange market gets influenced **by a real world event, and has**
외환 시장은 영향을 받는다   / 실제 세상의 사건에   / 그리고
an impact on the economy of a nation, **causing the value of its money to**
영향을 끼친다   / 한 나라의 경제에   / 그 나라의 화폐 가치가 오르내리게 하면서
rise and fall.

   풀이 앞에 접속사가 없으므로 동사는 올 수 없고 준동사가 와야 하는 자리이며, 주어인 A foreign exchange
   market이 화폐의 가치를 오르내리게 하는 주체이므로 현재분사인 causing이 적절하다.

foreign exchange market
외환 시장

06 With so many people getting their information online, there may not be a
너무나 많은 사람들이 온라인에서 정보를 얻고 있어서   / 수요가 없을지도 모른다
need for traditional newspapers.
    / [전통적인 신문에 대한]

   풀이 「with + 명사 + v-ing」 구문으로 many people이 온라인에서 정보를 얻는 주체이므로 현재분사 getting이 와
   야 한다.

07 When seen near the horizon, the moon appears strikingly larger than **when**
지평선 근처에서 보일 때   / 달은 현저하게 더 커 보인다   / 머리 위로 보일
viewed overhead.
때보다

   풀이 접속사 When이 의미를 명확히 하기 위해 생략되지 않고 분사 앞에 쓰였으며, 주어인 the moon이 수평선 근
   처에서 보이는 대상이므로 과거분사 seen이 와야 한다.

horizon 지평선, 수평선
strikingly 현저하게, 두드러지게

C **08** Teachers need to know their students well **in order to teach them effectively**.
교사들은 자신의 학생들을 잘 알 필요가 있다 / 학생들을 효과적으로 가르치기 위해서

> 풀이 to부정사는 '~하기 위해'라는 목적을 나타내며, 목적의 의미를 더 분명히 할 때 to 앞에 in order를 쓴다.

09 The Internet is a modern luxury abounding with information, **allowing you**
인터넷은 현대의 사치품이다 / [정보가 풍부한] / (그래서) 여러분이 모든
access to any information, all with the ease of a simple finger click.
정보에 접근할 수 있게 해준다 / 단지 간단한 손가락 클릭만으로 쉽게

luxury 사치품
abound with ~이 풍부하다
access 접근

> 풀이 두 문장을 연결해 주는 접속사가 없으므로 준동사인 분사구문의 형태가 되어야 하는데, 주어인 The Internet이
> 정보에 접근할 수 있게 해 주는 주체이므로 현재분사 allowing이 이끄는 어구로 쓴다.
> ─ 현재분사구 abounding with information이 a modern luxury를 수식한다.

10 It took me **a little while** to get used to this job, **but now I could do it with my**
(…은) 내게 잠깐의 시간이 걸렸다 / 이 일에 익숙해지는 것은 / 하지만 이제 나는 그 일을 할 수 있다 / 눈을
eyes closed.
감은 채로

get used to ~에 익숙해지다

> 풀이 with + 명사 + v-ed: ~가 …된 채로

D **11** All species are seen as having rights as people do, **environmental welfare**
모든 종은 여겨진다 / 권리를 가진 것으로 / 사람들처럼 / (따라서) 환경적 복지는 인간의 복지에
thus coming before human welfare.
우선한다

welfare 복지
thus 따라서

> 문장의 주어는 All species이고, coming이 이끄는 분사구문의 의미상 주어는 environmental welfare이다.
> environmental welfare가 인간의 복지에 우선하는 주체이므로 현재분사 coming이 쓰인 것이다.
> ─ people do는 people have rights의 의미이다.

12 Have you ever experienced the frustration of offering to help someone only
너는 좌절을 경험해 본 적이 있니 / [누군가를 도와주겠다고 제안하였는데] / 그러나
to be told to mind your own business?
결국 네 자신의 일에나 신경 쓰라는 말을 듣게 된]?

frustration 좌절
mind 신경 쓰다

> only to be 이하는 '(…했으나) 결국 ~하게 되다'라는 결과를 나타낸다.
> ─ 전치사 of의 목적어로 동명사구 offering to ~ business가 쓰였다.

모의 **13** **Faced with information that relates to what the old already know**, their brains
정보에 직면한다 / [노인들이 이미 알고 있는 것과 관계가 있는] / (그때) 그들의 뇌는
tend to work quicker and smarter, **discerning patterns and jumping to the**
더 빠르고 더 현명하게 작동하는 경향이 있다 / 양상을 구분하고 논리적인 결론 부분으로 도약하면서
logical end point.

be faced with ~에 직면하다
relate to ~와 관계가 있다
discern 구분하다, 식별하다
logical 논리적인

> 주어 their brains가 정보에 직면하는 대상이므로 과거분사 Faced가 쓰였으며, '~할 때'의 의미를 나타낸다.
> 주어 their brains가 양상을 구분하고 결론 부분으로 도약하는 주체이므로 현재분사 discerning과 jumping이 쓰였으며, '~하면서'의 의미를 나타낸다.
> ─ what이 이끄는 명사절 what ~ know가 전치사 to의 목적어로 쓰였다.

Chapter

08

부사적 수식어: 절

- unit 35   시간의 부사절
- unit 36   이유의 부사절
- unit 37   조건의 부사절
- unit 38   목적·결과의 부사절
- unit 39   반전·대조의 부사절
- unit 40   양태의 부사절

■ 본격적인 구문 학습에 앞서, 각 유닛별 주요 단어를 확인하세요.

Unit 35

- ☐ abandon 폐기하다
- ☐ hypothesis 가설
- ☐ phase 단계, 국면
- ☐ chill 냉기, 서늘함
- ☐ creep 서서히 다가오다
- ☐ proportion 비율
- ☐ carbon 탄소
- ☐ spectator 관객
- ☐ lecture 강의
- ☐ unlock (비밀 등을) 밝히다
- ☐ molecule 분자
- ☐ better 개선하다

Unit 36

- ☐ argument 논쟁; 주장
- ☐ opponent 상대, 적수
- ☐ geological 지질학의
- ☐ interactive 쌍방향의, 대화형의
- ☐ consciously 의식적으로
- ☐ chirp (새가) 지저귀다
- ☐ sarcasm 빈정거림, 비꼼
- ☐ contradiction 모순
- ☐ nonverbal 비언어적인
- ☐ equilibrium 균형
- ☐ fallible 틀릴 수 있는
- ☐ equation 방정식

Unit 37

- ☐ interest rate 이자율
- ☐ contribute 기여하다
- ☐ motion 발의, 제안; 움직임
- ☐ withdraw 철회하다
- ☐ commence 시작되다
- ☐ amend 수정하다
- ☐ parallel ~와 유사하다
- ☐ advocacy 옹호
- ☐ take up (입장을) 취하다
- ☐ settle 결제하다
- ☐ constant 일정한
- ☐ charge 청구하다

Unit 38

- ☐ fulfilling 성취감을 주는
- ☐ portable 휴대용의
- ☐ thorough 철저한
- ☐ monarch 군주
- ☐ throne 왕위
- ☐ abdicate (왕위·권리를) 포기하다
- ☐ divorce 이혼하다
- ☐ nothing but 바로 ~인
- ☐ in no time 즉시, 당장
- ☐ integrate 통합하다
- ☐ obligation 의무
- ☐ inseparable 분리할 수 없는

Unit 39

- ☐ measure up to ~에 필적하다
- ☐ pass down 전하다
- ☐ score 악보
- ☐ transparent 투명한
- ☐ be composed of ~으로 구성되다
- ☐ namely 즉
- ☐ count on ~을 믿다
- ☐ mass 질량
- ☐ exert (힘 따위를) 쓰다
- ☐ considerable 상당한
- ☐ state 진술하다
- ☐ poetry (집합적) 시

Unit 40

- ☐ sword 칼
- ☐ edge (칼의) 날; 예리함
- ☐ mutually 상호간에, 서로
- ☐ intend ~하려고 하다, 의도하다
- ☐ dawn 새벽
- ☐ seed 씨
- ☐ emerge 나타나다
- ☐ at a time 한 번에
- ☐ preference 선호
- ☐ be aware of ~을 알다
- ☐ particularly 특히
- ☐ gossip 소문, 험담

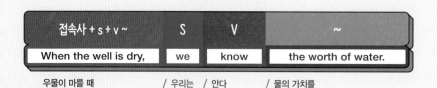

unit 35
시간의 부사절

접속사 + s + v ~	S	V	~
When the well is dry,	we	know	the worth of water.
우물이 마를 때	/ 우리는	/ 안다	/ 물의 가치를

Standard Sentences

01 Once you replace negative thoughts with positive ones, you'll start having
일단 당신이 부정적인 생각을 긍정적인 생각으로 대체하면   / 당신은 긍정적인 결과를
positive results. *Willie Nelson*
가지기 시작할 것이다

■ once + s + v ~: 일단 ~하면, ~하자마자

> replace A with B A를 B 로 대체하다
> negative 부정적인; 소극적인
> positive 긍정적인; 적극적인

02 You never really understand a person until you consider things from his
당신은 결코 정말로 어떤 사람을 이해하지 못한다   / 당신이 그의 관점으로 상황을 고려할 때까지
point of view. *the novel <To Kill a Mockingbird>*

■ until + s + v ~: ~할 때까지

> consider 고려하다
> point of view 관점

> **Know More** 「앵무새 죽이기(To kill a mockingbird)」는 미국 작가 하퍼 리(Harper Lee)의 소설로, 1960년에 출판되어 풀리처상을 수상했다. 대공황 직후 미국의 작은 도시를 배경으로 백인 변호사가 백인 여성을 성폭행한 혐의를 받는 흑인 남성을 변호하면서 일어나는 일을 어린 소녀의 시선으로 쓴 일종의 성장소설이며, 인종 차별과 흑백 갈등을 그리고 있다.

A **03** We must be ready to abandon or modify our hypothesis as soon as it is
[모의!] 우리는 준비가 되어 있어야 한다 / 우리의 가설을 폐기하거나 수정할   / 가설이 사실과 일치하지
shown to be inconsistent with the facts.
않는다는 것으로 증명되자마자

■ as soon as + s + v ~: ~하자마자

> abandon 폐기하다, 버리다
> modify 수정하다
> hypothesis 가설
> inconsistent 일치하지 않는

04 Lunar eclipses occur each time the Earth blocks the sun's light from the
월식은 일어난다   / 지구가 태양의 빛을 막을 때마다   / 달로부터
moon during the moon's full phase.
/ 달의 만월 단계 동안에

■ each time + s + v ~: ~할 때마다 / each time은 whenever와 같은 의미의 접속사로 시간의 부사절을 이끈다.
─ during은 '~ 동안에, ~ 중에'를 뜻하는 전치사로 뒤에 명사가 온다.

> lunar eclipse 월식
> block 막다
> phase 단계, 국면

05 No sooner had I spoken the words than I felt an icy chill creep to my heart.
내가 그 말을 내뱉자마자   / 나는 얼음 같은 냉기가 서서히 다가오는 것을 느꼈다 / 나의 심장으로
the short story <The IMP of the Perverse>

■ no sooner ~ than ...: ~하자마자 ...하다 / 부정어인 no sooner가 문장 앞으로 나오면서 「조동사 + 주어 + 본동사」의 어순으로 도치되었다.
─ 지각동사 felt의 목적어로 an icy chill, 목적격보어로 동사원형인 creep이 왔다.

> chill 냉기, 서늘함
> creep 서서히 다가오다

B **06** **The moment you doubt whether you can fly,** you cease forever to be able
당신이 의심하자마자　　　　／ 당신이 날 수 있는지를　　　／ 당신은 영원히 멈춘다　　／ 그것을 할 수

to do it. *the novel <Peter Pan>*
있는 것을

■ the moment + s + v ~: ～하자마자 / the moment는 as soon as와 같은 의미의 접속사로 시간의 부사절을 이끈다.

cease 멈추다, 중단하다
forever 영원히, 영구히

모의 **07** **Since the Industrial Revolution began in the eighteenth century, CO₂**
산업 혁명이 18세기에 시작된 이래로　　　　　　　　　　　　　　　／ 산업

released during industrial processes has greatly increased the proportion of
공정 중에 배출된 이산화탄소는 크게 증가시켰다　　　　　　　　／ 대기 중의 탄소의 비율을

carbon in the atmosphere.

■ since + s + v ~: ～ 이래로
━ 주어인 CO₂는 과거분사구 released ~ processes의 수식을 받는다.

Industrial Revolution 산업
혁명
release 배출하다
proportion 비율
carbon 탄소

08 Each player must accept the cards life deals him or her; but once they are
각각의 경기자는 카드들을 받아들여야 한다　　／ [인생이 그 사람에게 나눠주는]　／ 그러나 일단 그것들이 수중에

in hand, he or she alone must decide how to play the cards in order to win
있으면　　　／ 그 사람은 홀로 결정해야 한다　　　／ 그 카드들을 어떻게 사용할 것인지 / 그 게임을 이기기 위해서

the game. *Voltaire*

■ once + s + v ~: 일단 ～하면
━ the cards 다음에는 목적격 관계대명사 which 또는 that이 생략되었다.
━ 「in order to-v」는 '～하기 위해서'라는 목적을 나타내는 부사적 용법이다.

deal (카드를) 나눠주다, 돌리다

09 You can't just ask customers what they want and then try to give that to
당신은 단지 고객에게 물어볼 수 없다　　　／ 그들이 원하는 것을　　／ 그리고 나서 그들에게 그것을 주려고 시도할 (수는

them. By the time you get it built, they'll want something new. *Steve Jobs*
없다)　　당신이 그것이 만들어지게 할 무렵에는　／ 그들은 새로운 어떤 것을 원할 것이다

■ by the time + s + v ~: ～할 무렵에는
━ get의 목적어인 it(고객이 원하는 것)이 만들어지는 대상이므로 목적격보어로 과거분사 built가 쓰였다.

C **10** Art does not come to life until a spectator, a listener, or an audience breathes
예술은 살아 움직이지 않는다　　　／ 관객, 청취자, 혹은 청중이 그것에 생명을 불어넣을 때까지

life into it by experiencing it.
　　　　／ 그것을 경험함으로써

→ 예술은 관객, 청취자, 혹은 청중이 그것을 경험함으로써 그것에 생명을 불어넣고 나서야 비로소 살아 움직인다.

풀이 until + s + v ~: ～할 때까지 / not A until B: B할 때까지 A하지 않다, B하고 나서야 비로소 A하다

come to life 살아 움직이다,
활기를 띠다
spectator 관객, 구경꾼
breathe (생명 따위를) 불어넣다;
호흡하다

11 **Hardly** had everybody taken their seats when the professor began his
모든 사람이 자기 자리에 앉자마자　　　　　　　／ 그 교수는 자신의 강의를 시작했다

lecture.

풀이 hardly ~ when ...: ～하자마자 …하다 / 부정어인 hardly가 문두에 나오면서 「Hardly + 조동사 + 주어 + 본
동사」의 어순으로 도치되었다.

take a seat 자리에 앉다
lecture 강의

수능 **12** **Whenever a geneticist unlocks new secrets of the DNA molecule,** it adds
유전학자가 DNA 분자의 새로운 비밀들을 밝힐 때마다　　　　　　　　　　　／ 그것은

to our knowledge base and enables us to better the human condition.
우리의 지식 기반에 더해진다　　　　　／ 그리고 우리가 인간의 여건을 개선하는 것을 가능하게 한다

풀이 whenever + s + v ~: ～할 때마다

geneticist 유전학자
unlock (비밀 등을) 밝히다
molecule 분자
better 개선하다

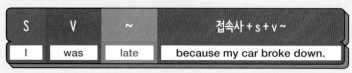

unit 36
이유의 부사절

S	V	~	접속사 + s + v ~
I	was	late	because my car broke down.

나는 / ~였다 / 늦은 / 왜냐하면 내 차가 고장 났기 때문에

Standard Sentences

01 As people are walking all the time, in the same spot, a path appears.
사람들이 늘 걷고 있기 때문에 / 같은 장소에서 / 길이 생긴다 *John Locke*

　■ as + s + v ~: ~이기 때문에 / as는 이유의 의미뿐만 아니라, 시간, 비교, 반전, 양태 등 다양한 의미를 나타낸다.

all the time 늘, 항상
spot 장소
path 길

02 Don't take the wrong side of an argument just because your opponent
논쟁의 잘못된 면을 선택하지 마라 / 단지 당신의 상대방이 올바른 면을 취했다고 해서
has taken the right side. *Baltasar Gracian*

　■ not A because B: B라고 해서 A는 아니다 / because 앞에는 just, only, merely 등의 부사가 더해질 수 있다.

argument 논쟁; 주장
opponent 상대, 적수

Ⓐ **03** Knowing another language is a window into another culture, since how a
다른 언어를 아는 것은 다른 문화를 보는 창문이다 / 한 사회가 세상을
society thinks and views the world is expressed through its language.
어떻게 생각하고 바라보는지가 표현되기 때문에 / 그것의 언어를 통해서

　■ since + s + v ~: ~이기 때문에 / 접속사 since는 '~ 이래로'라는 의미로 시간의 부사절을 이끌기도 한다.
　─ 의문사 how가 이끄는 명사절 how ~ world가 이유를 나타내는 부사절의 주어이고, is expressed가 동사이다.

모의 **04** The time scales of geological activity are important for environmental
지질학적 활동의 시간 척도들은 중요하다 / 환경 지질학자들에게
geologists because they provide a way to measure human impacts on the
　　　　　/ 그것들이 방법을 제공하기 때문에 / [인간의 영향을 측정하는 / [자연계에
natural world.
미친]]

　■ because + s + v ~: ~이기 때문에
　─ they는 The time scales를 가리킨다.

scale 척도; 규모
geological 지질학의
geologist 지질학자

05 Now that tablet PCs, 3D VR glasses, and interactive whiteboards are so
태블릿 PC, 3차원 가상현실 안경, 그리고 쌍방향의 화이트보드는 현대 교실에서 너무나도 많은 부분이기 때문에
much a part of the modern classroom, many people fear reading books
　　　　　　　　　　　　　　　　/ 많은 사람들은 염려한다 / 책을 읽는 것이 더 이상
will no longer be as important.
중요하지 않을까 봐

　■ now that + s + v ~: ~이기 때문에, ~이므로
　─ fear 다음에 명사절을 이끄는 접속사 that이 생략되었으며, as important 다음에 as now가 생략되었다.

interactive 쌍방향의, 대화형의
fear 염려하다
no longer 더 이상 ~ 않는

B **06** Words can carry meanings beyond those consciously intended by speakers
단어들은 의미를 전달할 수 있다 / 의식적으로 의도된 의미를 넘어서 / 화자 또는 필자에

or writers because listeners or readers bring their own perspectives to the
의해 / 청자 또는 독자가 그들 자신의 시각을 언어에 가져오기 때문에

language they encounter.
/ [그들이 맞닥뜨리는]

- because + s + v ~: ~이기 때문에
- 과거분사구 consciously intended ~ writers가 those를 수식한다.

consciously 의식적으로
perspective 시각, 관점
encounter 맞닥뜨리다, 마주치다

07 Just because you can hear your robins, goldfinches, and sparrows chirping
단지 당신이 울새, 오색방울새, 그리고 참새가 행복하게 지저귀는 것을 들을 수 있다는 이유로

away happily in the garden every morning, don't be fooled into thinking
/ 매일 아침 정원에서 / 생각하도록 속아 넘어가지 마라

that all is well in 'birdworld.'
/ '조류 세상'에서는 모든 것이 다 괜찮다고

- just because + s + v: 단지 ~라는 이유로, 오로지 ~이므로
- 지각동사 hear의 목적격보어로 현재분사가 쓰였다.

robin 울새
goldfinch 오색방울새
sparrow 참새
chirp (새가) 지저귀다
fool ~ into 속여서 ~하게 하다

08 As the nature of sarcasm implies a contradiction between intent and
빈정거림의 본질은 모순을 암시하기 때문에 / [의도와 메시지 사이의]

message, nonverbal cues may "leak" and reveal the speaker's true mood.
/ 비언어적 신호는 '새어나가게' 그리고 드러나게 할지도 모른다 / 화자의 진정한 기분을

- as + s + v ~: ~이기 때문에

sarcasm 빈정거림, 비꼼
contradiction 모순
nonverbal 비언어적인, 말을 쓰지 않는
cue 신호
reveal 드러내다

09 Now that genetically modified foods are on our supermarket shelves, the
유전자 조작 식품이 우리의 슈퍼마켓 선반에 있기 때문에 /

genie is out of the bottle and cannot be put back in.
genie는 병 밖으로 나와 있다 / 그리고 안으로 다시 넣어질 수 없다

→ 이미 유전자 조작 식품이 슈퍼마켓에서 팔리고 있기 때문에, 돌이키기 어려운 상황이다.

- now that + s + v ~: ~이기 때문에, ~이므로

genetically modified food
유전자 조작 식품
the genie is out of the bottle
돌이킬 수 없는 문제가 발생하다

C **10** As price is decided by bringing demand and supply into equilibrium, an
가격은 결정되기 때문에 / 수요와 공급을 균형에 맞춰놓음으로써 /

increase in supply leads to a fall in price and increase in equilibrium quantity.
공급의 증가는 이어진다 / 가격의 하락과 균형 생산량의 증가로

풀이 가격이 수요와 공급의 균형에 의해 결정된다고 하였으므로, 가격의 하락과 균형 생산량의 증가는 공급의 증가에
의한 것임을 알 수 있다. 따라서 '증가'를 뜻하는 increase가 알맞다. decrease는 '감소, 하락'을 뜻한다.

demand and supply 수요와 공급
equilibrium 균형, 평형
lead to ~으로 이어지다
quantity 양, 수량

11 If we are not to become 'slaves to the machine', we should keep in mind
만약 우리가 '기계의 노예'가 되지 않으려면 / 우리는 명심해야 한다

that since computer programs are designed by people, they, too, are fallible.
/ 컴퓨터 프로그램은 사람에 의해서 설계되므로 / 그것들도 또한 틀릴 수 있다는 것을

풀이 컴퓨터 프로그램이 사람에 의해 설계되는 것이므로 그것은 완벽할 수 없고, 틀릴 수 있다는 것을 명심해야 한다는
내용이 자연스러우므로 '틀릴 수 있는'을 뜻하는 fallible이 알맞다.

- if절의 are (not) to become은 '~하려고 하다'의 의도를 나타내는 be to-v 용법으로 쓰였다.

keep ~ in mind ~을 명심하다
fallible 틀릴 수 있는

12 Now that labor's clout has significantly diminished, knowledge workers
노동의 영향력이 상당히 줄어들었기 때문에 / 지식 근로자들이 더 중요한

have become the more important group in the economic equation.
집단이 되었다 / 경제 방정식에서

풀이 노동의 영향력이 줄면서 상대적으로 지식 근로자들이 더 중요한 집단이 되었다고 하는 것이 자연스러우므로 '중
요한'을 뜻하는 important가 알맞다. trivial은 '사소한, 하찮은'을 뜻한다.

clout 영향력
diminish 줄어들다, 약해지다
equation 방정식; (고려해야 할 요소가 많은) 상황

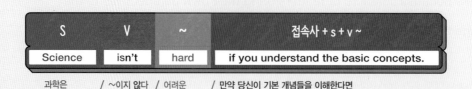

unit 37
조건의 부사절

S	V	~	접속사 + s + v ~
Science	isn't	hard	if you understand the basic concepts.
과학은	/ ~이지 않다	/ 어려운	/ 만약 당신이 기본 개념들을 이해한다면

Standard Sentences

01 Differences of habit and language are nothing at all **if our aims are**
습관과 언어의 차이는 전혀 아무것도 아니다   / 만약 우리의 목표가 같다면
identical and our hearts are open. *the novel <Harry Potter and the Goblet of Fire>*
/ 그리고 우리의 마음이 열려 있다면

- if + s + v ~: 만약 ~라면

at all (부정문) 전혀
identical 같은, 동일한

02 A life devoted to the acquisition of wealth is useless, **unless we know how**
부의 획득에 바쳐진 인생은 쓸모없다   / 만약 우리가 알지 못한다면 / 어떻게
to turn it into joy.
그것을 즐거움으로 바꾸는지

- unless + s + v ~: 만약 ~가 아니라면, 만약 ~하지 않으면 / unless는 if ... not으로 바꿔 쓸 수 있다. / (= if we don't know ~)
- 과거분사구 devoted ~ wealth가 주어 A life를 수식한다.

devote 바치다
acquisition 획득
turn A into B A를 B로
바꾸다

A **03** In so far as changes in interest rates affect expectations, lower interest
이자율의 변화가 기대에 영향을 미치는 한에서   / 더 낮은 이자율은
rates may still contribute to higher investment.
여전히 기여할 것이다   / 더 높은 투자에

- in so far as + s + v ~: ~하는 한에 있어서, ~한다는 점에서

interest rate 이자율
contribute 기여하다
investment 투자

04 I don't care who you are, where you're from or what you did **as long as you**
나는 상관없다   / 당신이 누구인지   / 당신이 어디 출신인지   / 또는 당신이 무엇을 했는지 / 당신이 나를 사랑하는 한
love me. *the song <As Long As You Love Me>*

- as(so) long as + s + v ~: ~하는 한, ~하기만 하면 / (= if only you love me)
- 의문사 who, where, what이 이끄는 세 개의 절이 or로 병렬 연결되어 동사 care의 목적어 역할을 하고 있다.

care 상관하다, 관심을 가지다

05 A motion may be withdrawn by its proposer at any time before voting on it
발의는 철회될 수도 있다   / 그 제안자에 의해서 / 언제라도   / 그것에 대한 투표가 시작되기
has commenced, **provided that the motion has not been amended.**
전에   / 만약 그 발의가 수정되지 않았다면

- provided(providing) that + s + v ~: 만약 ~라면 / (= if the motion has not been amended)
- 접속사 before가 이끄는 절의 주어로 동명사구 voting on it이 쓰였다.

motion 발의, 제안; 움직임
withdraw 철회하다, 취소하다
commence 시작되다
amend 수정하다

06 **If you wait for the mango fruits to fall,** you'd be wasting your time **while**
당신이 망고 열매가 떨어지기를 기다린다면 / 당신은 당신의 시간을 낭비하고 있는 것이다 / 다른

others are learning how to climb the tree. *Michael Bassey Johnson*
사람들이 배우고 있는 동안에 / 어떻게 그 나무에 올라갈지를

- if + s + v ~: 만약 ~라면
- while은 '~하는 동안에'의 의미로 시간의 부사절을 이끄는 접속사이다. ➔ **Unit 35**

07 You can't think creatively about information **unless you have information in**
당신은 정보에 대해서 창의적으로 생각할 수 없다 / 만약 당신이 머릿속에 생각할 정보가 없다면

your head to think about.

- unless + s + v ~: 만약 ~가 아니라면, 만약 ~하지 않으면 / (= if you don't have information ~)

08 **As far as we can discern,** the sole purpose of human existence is **to kindle**
우리가 식별할 수 있는 한 / 인간 존재의 유일한 목적은 빛을 밝게 하는 것이다

a light in the darkness of mere being. *Carl Jung*
/ 단순한 존재의 어둠 속에서

- as(so) far as + s + v ~: ~하는 한

discern 식별하다, 분간하다
sole 유일한
existence 존재
kindle 밝게 하다; (불을) 붙이다
mere 단순한

09 Mediation parallels advocacy **in so far as it tends to involve a process of**
중재는 옹호와 유사하다 / 그것이 협상의 과정을 수반하는 경향이 있다는 점에서

negotiation, but differs **in so far as mediation involves adopting a neutral**
/ 그러나 다르다 / 중재가 중립적인 역할을 취하는 것을 수반한다는 점에서

role between two opposing parties rather than **taking up the case of one**
/ 대립하는 두 당사자들 사이에서 / 한쪽 편의 입장을 취하기보다는

party against another.
/ 다른 편에 반대하여

- in so far as + s + v ~: ~하는 한에 있어서, ~한다는 점에서
- 동명사구 adopting ~ parties와 taking ~ another이 rather than(~라기 보다는)으로 병렬 연결되었다.

mediation 중재
parallel ~와 유사하다; ~에 평행하다
advocacy 옹호
involve 수반하다
adopt 채택하다
neutral 중립적인
take up (입장을) 취하다

10 An object that is moving at constant speed will **eventually** slow down and come
물체는 / [일정한 속도로 움직이고 있는] / 마침내 느려지고 멈추게 될 것이다

to a stop **unless there is something to keep it moving at constant speed.**
/ 만약 어떤 것이 없다면 / [그것을 일정한 속도로 계속 움직이게 하는]

- unless + s + v ~: 만약 ~가 아니라면, 만약 ~하지 않으면 (= if ... not)

constant 일정한
eventually 마침내
come to a stop 멈추다, 정지하다

11 Change may hurt us a little **when** it occurs, but **if we accept it as a growth**
변화는 우리를 약간 아프게 할 수도 있다 / 그것이 일어날 때 / 그러나 만약 우리가 그것을 성장 과정으로

process, it will bring benefits in the long run.
받아들인다면 / 그것은 결국에는 이익을 가져다줄 것이다

- if + s + v ~: 만약 ~라면
- when it occurs는 '~할 때'를 뜻하는 접속사 when이 이끄는 시간의 부사절이다. ➔ **Unit 35**

in the long run 결국에는

12 There is no fee for the card and no interest is charged **provided that the**
카드에 대한 수수료가 없다 / 그리고 이자가 청구되지 않는다 / 만약 그 계좌가 결제된다면

account is settled in full every month.
/ 매월 전액

- provided(providing) that + s + v ~: 만약 ~라면 (= if)

charge 청구하다
account 계좌
settle 결제하다; 해결하다

unit 38
목적·결과의 부사절

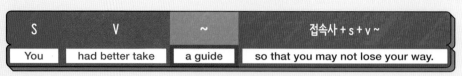

S	V	~	접속사 + s + v ~
You	had better take	a guide	so that you may not lose your way.

너는 / 가져가는 게 나을 것이다 / 여행 안내서를 / 네가 길을 잃지 않기 위해서

Standard Sentences

01 We do what we have to do **so that we can do** what we want to do.
우리는 한다 / 우리가 해야 하는 것을 / 우리가 할 수 있도록 / 우리가 하고 싶은 것을

- so that + s + can + ⓥ ~: ~하도록, ~하기 위해서 / (= in order that we can do ~)
- what이 이끄는 두 개의 명사절 what we have to do, what we want to do는 각각 do의 목적어로 쓰였다.

02 It was **so** quiet in the room **that I could** hear the leaves being blown off
방안이 아주 조용했다 / 그래서 나는 들을 수 있었다 / 바깥에서 나뭇잎이 나무들로부터 날리고
the trees outside.
있는 것을

- so + 형용사 + that + s + v ~: 아주 …해서 ~하다
- 지각동사 hear가 「hear + O + v-ing」 구문으로 쓰였으며, 목적어인 leaves가 날리는 대상이고, 날리는 상황이 진행 중인 것이므로 현재분사의 수동태 being blown이 쓰였다.

blow off (바람에) 날려 보내다, 날리다

Ⓐ 03 [모의] A scientific understanding of emotional intelligence may allow us to train
정서 지능의 과학적 이해는 우리가 우리의 감성적 기술들을 훈련하게 할 수도 있을 것이다
our emotional skills **so that we can live** more fulfilling and productive lives.
/ 우리가 살아갈 수 있도록 / 더 성취감을 주고 더 생산적인 삶을

- so that + s + can + ⓥ ~: ~하도록, ~하기 위해서 / (= in order that we can live ~)
- allow + O + to-v: O가 ~하는 것을 허용하다

emotional intelligence 정서 지능
fulfilling 성취감을 주는
productive 생산적인

04 The personal computer becomes far smaller and much more portable, **so**
개인용 컴퓨터는 훨씬 더 작고 훨씬 더 휴대하기 쉽게 된다 /
that some people such as writers or stock dealers are able to work
그래서 일부 사람들은 / [작가 또는 증권 중개인과 같은] / 일할 수 있다
wherever they are.
/ 그들이 있는 어디서나

- ~, so that + s + v …: ~해서 …하다 / 접속사 so that이 결과를 나타낼 때는 대개 그 앞에 콤마(,)를 둔다.
- 비교급 smaller, more portable 앞에 각각 비교급 강조 부사 far와 much를 써서 '훨씬 더 ~한'의 의미로 강조하였다.

portable 휴대용의
stock dealer 증권 중개인

05 Some people are making **such** thorough preparation for rainy days **that they**
어떤 사람들은 하고 있다 / 아주 철저한 준비를 / [비 오는 날을 대비하는] / 그래서
aren't enjoying today's sunshine. *William Feather*
그들은 오늘의 햇빛을 즐기지 못하고 있다

- such + (a) + 형용사 + 명사 + that + s + v ~: 아주 …해서 ~하다

thorough 철저한

06 In 1936, King Edward VIII became the very first British monarch to
1936년에　　　/ 국왕 에드워드 8세는 바로 최초의 영국 군주가 되었다　　　/
voluntarily give up his throne when he abdicated **so that he could marry**
[자발적으로 자신의 왕위를 포기한]　　/ 그가 퇴위했을 때　　/ 그가 이혼한 미국인 여성, Simpson
Mrs. Simpson, a divorced American woman.
부인과 결혼하기 위해서

■ so that + s + can + ⓥ ~: ~하도록, ~하기 위해서 / (= in order that he could marry ~)

monarch 군주
voluntarily 자발적으로
throne 왕위
abdicate (왕위·권리를) 포기
하다, 버리다
divorce 이혼하다

07 Her eyes are nothing but a pure emerald shining in the rays of the sun and
그녀의 눈은 바로 순수한 에메랄드이다　　/ [햇살과 달빛 속에서 빛나는]
the moon **so that you can't take your eyes off her.**
　　/ 그래서 당신은 그녀에게서 눈을 뗄 수 없다

■ ~(,) so that + s + v ...: ~해서 …하다
─ 현재분사 shining ~ the moon이 a pure emerald를 수식한다.

nothing but 바로 ~인, 그저
[단지] ~일 뿐인
take one's eyes off ~에서
눈을 떼다

08 When one door of happiness closes, another opens; but often we look **so**
행복의 한쪽 문이 닫히면　　/ 또 다른 문이 열린다　　/ 그러나 종종 우리는 아주 오래 닫힌
long at the closed door that we do not see the one which has been opened
문을 바라본다　　/ 그래서 우리는 그것(문)을 보지 못한다　　/ [우리를 위해 열린]
for us. *Helen Keller*

■ so + 부사 + that + s + v ~: 아주 …해서 ~하다
─ 관계대명사 which가 이끄는 절이 the one을 수식한다.

09 The witness described the suspect in **such detail that the police were able**
목격자는 용의자를 묘사했다　　/ 아주 상세하게　　/ 그래서 경찰은 그의 위치를 알아낼 수 있었다
to locate him in no time.
　　/ 즉시

■ such + (a) + (형용사) + 명사 + that + s + v ~: 아주 …해서 ~하다

witness 목격자
suspect 용의자
in detail 상세하게
locate ~의 위치를 알아내다
in no time 즉시, 당장

10 Rights and obligations should be **so inseparable that a demand for one is**
권리와 의무는 아주 불가분적이어야 한다　　/ 그래서 하나에 대한 요구는 항상 수반되게
always accompanied by a statement of the other.
　　/ 다른 하나의 표명에 의해

■ so + 형용사 + that + s + v ~: 아주 …해서 ~하다

right 권리
obligation 의무, 책임
inseparable 분리할 수 없는
accompany 수반하다, 동반
하다
statement 표명; 진술

11 If you live to be a hundred, I want to live to be a hundred minus one day **so**
만약 당신이 100세까지 산다면　　/ 나는 100세에서 하루를 뺀 날까지 살고 싶다　　/
I never have to live without you. *the short story <Winnie the Pooh>*
내가 결코 살아야 하지 않도록　　/ 당신 없이

■ so (that) + s + have to + ⓥ ~: ~해야 하도록 / 목적을 나타내는 접속사 so that에서 that이 생략된 형태이다.

12 When you are reading for study purposes, it is critical to read systematically,
당신이 학습 목적으로 글을 읽고 있을 때　　/ (…은) 중요하다　　/ 체계적으로 읽는 것은
so you are able to integrate the new knowledge you acquire with what
/ 당신이 새로운 지식을 통합할 수 있도록　　/ [당신이 획득하는]　　/ 당신이 이미
you already know.
알고 있는 것과

■ so (that) + s + be able to + ⓥ ~: ~하도록, ~하기 위해서 / '~할 수 있다'는 의미의 조동사 can 대신에 be able to가 쓰였다.
─ knowledge 다음에 목적격 관계대명사 which 또는 that이 생략되었다.

critical 중요한; 비판적인
integrate 통합하다
acquire 얻다, 획득하다

unit 39
반전·대조의 부사절

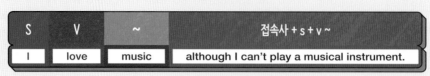

S	V	~	접속사 + s + v ~
I	love	music	although I can't play a musical instrument.

나는 / 사랑한다 / 음악을 / 비록 내가 악기를 연주할 수 없을지라도

Standard Sentences

수능! 01 **Even though a speech can be effective,** all the words in the world cannot
비록 연설이 효과적일 수 있을지라도 / 세상의 모든 말은 필적할 수 없다
measure up to the example of a leader.
/ 지도자의 본보기에

■ even though + s + v ~: 비록 ~일지라도

measure up to ~에 필적하다, ~에 달하다

02 **However hard you shop for an item,** after you've bought it, it will be on
아무리 열심히 당신이 어떤 물품을 사러 가더라도 / 당신이 그것을 사고 난 후에 / 그것은 할인 중일
sale somewhere cheaper.
것이다 / 어딘가에서 더 싸게

■ however + 부사 + s + v ~: 아무리 ~하더라도

on sale 할인 중인; 판매 중인

A 03 **Even if it turns out that time travel is impossible,** it is important that we
비록 (…이) 판명될지라도 / 시간 여행이 불가능하다는 것이 / (…은) 중요하다 / 우리가
understand why it is impossible. *Stephen Hawking*
이해하는 것은 / 왜 그것이 불가능한가를

■ even if + s + v ~(가정의 내용): 비록 ~일지라도
─ 두 개의 it은 가주어이고, 각각 뒤에 나오는 that절이 진주어이다.
─ 의문사 why가 이끄는 절이 동사 understand의 목적어로 쓰였다.

turn out 판명되다

수능! 04 **Before sound recording, classical music was passed down through written**
음원 녹음 이전에 / 고전 음악은 전해졌다 / 기록된 악보를 통해서
scores, **whereas early jazz mainly relied on live performance.**
/ 반면에 초기의 재즈는 주로 라이브 공연에 의존했다

■ whereas[while] + s + v ~: ~인 반면에

pass down 전하다, 전해 주다
score 악보
rely on ~에 의존하다

05 **Strange as it may sound,** the diamond, so clear and transparent, is
비록 이상하게 들릴 수도 있지만 / 다이아몬드는 / 아주 깨끗하고 투명한데 /
composed of the same material as coal and soot, namely carbon.
동일한 물질로 구성되어 있다 / 석탄과 검댕과 / 즉 탄소로

■ 형용사 + as + s + v ~: 비록 ~이지만 / (= Though it may sound strange ~)

transparent 투명한
be composed of ~으로 구성되다
soot 검댕, 매연
namely 즉

06 **No matter what emotion you're feeling right now,** you can count on one
당신이 어떤 감정을 느끼고 있다 하더라도 　　　　　　　　　　　　　／ 바로 지금 　　　／ 당신은 한 가지를 믿을 수 있다
thing—it will change.
／ 즉, 그것은 바뀔 것이다

　■ no matter what + 명사 + s + v ~: 무슨 …을 ~하더라도 / (= Whatever emotion you're feeling ~)
　— one thing 다음에 오는 대시(—)는 동격을 나타낸다. ◑ Unit 52

07 **If we don't have the power to choose where we come from,** we can still
비록 우리가 선택할 힘은 없을지라도 　　　　　　　　　　　／ 우리가 어디서 오는지를 　　　／ 우리는 여전히
choose where we go from there.
선택할 수 있다 ／ 우리가 거기에서 어디로 갈지

　■ (even) if + s + v ~(가정의 내용): 비록 ~일지라도
　— 두 개의 명사절 where we come from과 where we go from there가 각각 동사 choose의 목적어로 쓰였다.

08 **Newton imagined that masses affect each other by exerting a force, while**
뉴턴은 상상했다 　　　　／ 질량은 서로 영향을 미친다고 　　　　／ 힘을 씀으로써 　　　　／ 반면에
in Einstein's theory the effects occur through a bending of space and
아인슈타인의 이론에서는 　　　／ 그 영향이 일어난다 　　　　／ 공간과 시간의 휘어짐을 통해
time and there is no concept of gravity as a force.
／ 그리고 중력의 개념은 없다 　　　　　　／ 힘으로서

　■ while[whereas] + s + v ~: ~인 반면에
　— 명사절 that ~ a force가 동사 imagined의 목적어로 쓰였다.

09 **I'll do whatever it takes to win games, whether it's sitting on a bench waving a**
나는 할 것이다 ／ 게임을 이기는 데 필요로 하는 것은 무엇이든 ／ 그것이 벤치에 앉아 있는 것이든 　　　／ 수건을 흔들면서
towel, handing a cup of water to a teammate, or hitting the game-winning
／ 팀 동료에게 물 한 잔을 건네는 것이든 　　　　　　／ 결승 슛을 하는 것이든
shot. *Kobe Bryant*

　■ whether it is A, B, or C: 그것이 A이든 B이든 C이든
　— whatever it takes ~는 명사절로서 동사 do의 목적어로 쓰였다. 이때 whatever는 '~하는 것은 무엇이든'을 뜻한다.

10 **Though most people agree that clothes do not make the person,** they spend
비록 대부분의 사람들이 동의할지라도 　　　／ 옷이 사람을 만들지 않는다는 것에 　　　　／ 그들은 상당한
considerable time and money dressing themselves in the newest fashion.
시간과 돈을 쓴다 　　　／ 스스로 옷을 차려 입는 데 　　／ 최신 패션으로

　풀이 '비록 ~일지라도'의 의미로 반전의 부사절을 이끄는 접속사 Though가 적절하다.
　— spend + O + v-ing: O를 ~하는 데 쓰다

11 **Whereas science is concerned with finding and stating the facts,** poetry's
과학은 관련이 있는 반면에 　　　　　　　／ 사실들을 찾고 진술하는 것과 　　　　／ 시의 과제는
task is to give you the look, the smell, the taste, and the "feel" of those facts.
당신에게 주는 것이다 　／ 모양, 냄새, 맛, 그리고 '느낌'을 　　　　／ [그러한 사실들의]

　풀이 빈칸이 속한 문장과 뒤의 문장이 서로 대조를 이루므로 '~인 반면에'의 의미로 대조의 부사절을 이끄는 접속사
　whereas가 적절하다.

12 **Whatever you want to do,** if you want to be great at it, you have to love it
당신이 무엇을 하고 싶은지 간에 　　　／ 만약 당신이 그것에 뛰어나길 원한다면 　　　／ 당신은 그것을 사랑해야 한다
and be able to make sacrifices for it. *Maya Angelou*
／ 그리고 희생할 수 있(어야 한다) 　　　／ 그것을 위해서

　풀이 do의 목적어가 없는 불완전한 문장이 빈칸 다음에 이어지므로, 빈칸에는 Whatever가 적절하다. whatever는
　'무엇을 ~하더라도'의 의미로 반전의 부사절을 이끈다. / (= No matter what you want ~)

count on ~을 믿다

mass 질량; 다수
exert (힘 따위를) 쓰다, 발휘하다
theory 이론
bending 구부림, 굽힘

hand 건네다
game-winning 경기를 승리
로 이끈, 결정적인

considerable 상당한; 고려할
만한

be concerned with ~와 관
련되다
state 진술하다
poetry (집합적) 시 cf. poem
(한 편의) 시

make sacrifices 희생하다

unit 40
양태의 부사절

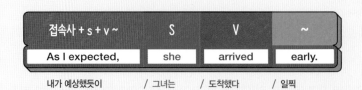

접속사 + s + v ~	S	V	~
As I expected,	she	arrived	early.

내가 예상했듯이 / 그녀는 / 도착했다 / 일찍

Standard Sentences

01 A mind needs books **as a sword needs a whetstone**, if it is to keep its
정신은 책을 필요로 한다 / 칼이 숫돌을 필요로 하는 것처럼 / 그것이 날을 유지하려고 한다면
edge. *the novel <A Game of Thrones>*

sword 칼
whetstone 숫돌
edge (칼의) 날; 예리함

- as + s + v ~: ~처럼, ~이듯이, ~ 대로
- is to keep은 be to-v 용법으로 '~하려고 하다'를 뜻하는 의도의 의미를 나타낸다.

> **Know More** 「왕좌의 게임(A Game of Thrones)」은 미국의 소설가 조지 R. R. 마틴(George R. R. Martin)의 판타지 소설 시리즈인 <얼음과 불의 노래>의 1부로, 1996년 8월 1일에 처음 출판되었다. 방대한 세계관과 판타지의 공식을 깨부수는 전개로 작가에게 '금세기 최고의 걸작'이라는 극찬을 안겨 준 이 책은 미국 HBO 채널에서 <왕좌의 게임> 시리즈로 드라마화되면서 전 세계적인 인기를 얻게 되었다.

02 Most textbooks are written **as if science is a set of truths** to be memorized.
대부분의 교과서는 쓰여 있다 / 마치 과학이 일련의 사실들인 것처럼 / [암기되어야 할]

- as if + s + v ~: 마치 ~인 것처럼 (= as though + s + v ~)
- a set of truths는 암기되는 대상이므로 to-v의 수동태인 to be memorized가 a set of truths를 수식한다.

A **03** The horse-drawn carriage was itself a technological innovation, **as were the**
말이 끄는 마차는 그 자체로 기술적 혁신이었다 / 말이 없는 차와
(모의)
horseless carriage and later automobiles.
나중의 자동차가 그랬듯이

carriage 마차, 차
innovation 혁신

- as + s + v ~: ~이듯이, ~처럼, ~ 대로 / 양태의 접속사 as 다음에 오는 주어가 길면 종종 주어와 동사가 도치된다.

(모의) **04** Just as a flesh-and-blood beast influences and is influenced by its
꼭 현재 살아 있는 짐승이 영향을 주고 받는 것처럼 / 환경과
environment, so too do science and society mutually influence one another.
/ 과학과 사회도 또한 / 상호간에 서로 영향을 미친다

flesh-and-blood 현재 살아 있는
mutually 상호간에, 서로

- just as + s + v ~, so + V + S ...: 꼭 ~인 것처럼 ...하다
- its environment는 influence와 is influenced by의 공통 목적어이다.
- do는 주어 science and society와 동사 influence가 도치되면서 쓰인 조동사이다.

05 Live **as though you intend to live forever**, and work **as though your strength**
살아라 / 마치 당신이 영원히 살고자 하는 것처럼 / 그리고 일하라 / 마치 당신의 힘이 무한한 것처럼
were limitless.

intend ~하려고 하다, 의도하다

- as though + s + v ~: 마치 ~인 것처럼 (= as if)

B **06** We need to see people **as they are**, not **as we would like them to be.**
우리는 사람들을 볼 필요가 있다 / 있는 그대로 / 우리가 그들이 어떠하길 바라는 대로가 아니라

⚡ as + s + v ~: ~ 대로, ~처럼, ~이듯이

(모의) **07** **Just as darkness comes at the end of each day, so** also comes the dawn
꼭 어둠이 오듯이 / 하루의 끝에 / 또한 새벽이 온다
to spread light across the land. **Just as plants must die at the end of their**
/ 온 땅에 빛을 퍼뜨리기 위해 / 꼭 식물들이 틀림없이 죽는 것처럼 / 생명 주기의 끝에
life cycle, the seeds they have produced will emerge as new plants in the
/ 씨들이 / [그들이 만들어 낸] / 나타날 것이다 / 봄에 새로운 식물들로
spring.

dawn 새벽
spread 퍼뜨리다
seed 씨
emerge 나타나다

⚡ just as + s + v ~, so + V + S ...: 꼭[반드시] ~인 것처럼 …하다
━ the seeds 다음에 목적격 관계대명사 which 또는 that이 생략되었다.

08 Act **as if what you do makes a difference.** It **does.** *William James*
행동하라 / 마치 당신이 하는 것이 변화를 가져오는 것처럼 / 그것은 그러하다(변화를 가져온다)

make a difference 변화를 가져오다

⚡ as if + s + v ~: 마치 ~인 것처럼
━ as if가 이끄는 양태의 부사절 내에서 what이 이끄는 명사절 what you do가 주어이다.
━ It은 what you do를 가리키고, does는 makes a difference를 대신하는 대동사이다.

09 Even when you feel **as though there isn't a lot you can do to change unhappiness**
당신이 느낄 때조차도 / 마치 많은 것이 있지 않은 것처럼 / [당신이 할 수 있는 / 불행 또는 문제를 바꾸기 위해서]
or problems, you can always do a little—and a little at a time eventually
/ 당신은 항상 작은 것을 할 수 있다 / 그리고 한 번에 조금씩은 / 결국 큰 변화를
makes a big difference.
만들어 낸다

at a time 한 번에
eventually 결국, 마침내

⚡ as though + s + v ~: 마치 ~인 것처럼
━ a lot 다음에 목적격 관계대명사 which 또는 that이 생략되었다.

C **10** **As there are differing tastes and preferences among different peoples**
다른 취향과 선호가 있는 것처럼 / 세상의 여러 민족과 지역 사이에
and regions of the world, so do tastes and preferences evolve over the
/ 취향과 선호는 진화한다 / 수 세기에 걸쳐서
course of centuries.

preference 선호
evolve 진화하다, 발전하다

⚡ (just) as + s + v ~, so + V + S ...: (꼭) ~인 것처럼 …하다

11 We usually take for granted our ability to produce and understand speech,
우리는 대개 우리의 능력을 당연한 것으로 여긴다 / [말을 만들어 내고 이해하는]
just as we are not particularly aware of the action of our hearts, brains, or
/ 마치 우리가 작동을 특히 알아차리지 못하는 것처럼 / [우리의 심장, 뇌, 또는 다른 필수적인
other essential organs.
기관들의]

take ~ for granted ~을 당연한 것으로 여기다
be aware of ~을 알다
particularly 특히, 특별히
organ 기관

⚡ as + s + v ~: ~처럼, ~이듯이, ~ 대로

12 Once you have listened to the gossip for some time, you will soon feel **as if**
일단 당신이 소문에 귀를 기울여왔다면 / 얼마간 / 당신은 곧 느낄 것이다 / 마치
you know everyone, even if you have never met them.
당신이 모두를 아는 것처럼 / 비록 당신은 결코 그들을 만난 적이 없을지라도

gossip 소문, 험담

⚡ as if[as though] + s + v ~: 마치 ~인 것처럼
━ once는 '일단 ~하면, ~하자마자'의 뜻으로 시간의 부사절을 이끄는 접속사이다.
━ even if는 '비록 ~일지라도'의 의미로 가상의 일, 즉 가정해서 말할 때 쓰이는 접속사로 반전의 부사절을 이끈다.

Chapter 08

Review

A **01** Celebrate what you've accomplished, but raise the bar a little higher each
축하하라   / 당신이 성취한 것을   / 하지만 장애물을 약간 더 높여라   / 당신이

time you succeed.
성공할 때마다

- each time + s + v: ~할 때마다
- what이 이끄는 명사절 what you've accomplished가 Celebrate의 목적어로 쓰였다.

celebrate 축하하다
bar 장애물; 막대기

02 A broken heart is just the growing pains necessary so that you can love
상심은 단지 필요한 성장통이다   / 당신이 더 완전하게 사랑할 수 있기

more completely when the real thing comes along. *J. S. B. Morse*
위해서   / 진정한 것이 다가올 때

- so that + s + can[will / may] + ⓥ ~: ~하기 위해서, ~하도록 / (= in order that you can love ~)
- when + s + v ~: ~할 때
- 형용사 necessary가 the growing pains를 뒤에서 수식한다.

broken heart 상심, 실연
growing pains 성장통

03 The rights guaranteed in the Bill of Rights—freedom of speech, assembly,
권리장전에 보장된 권리들은   / —언론, 집회, 종교, 기타 등등의 자유—

religion, and so on—fall within negative rights, as do the rights to freedom
/ 소극적인 권리에 해당한다   / 상해로부터의 그리고 사생활의 자유에 대한

from injury and to privacy.
권리들이 그런 것처럼

- as + s + v ~: ~처럼, ~이듯이, ~ 대로 / 양태의 접속사 as 다음에 오는 주어가 길면 종종 주어와 동사가 도치된다.
- 과거분사구 guaranteed ~ Rights가 주어 The rights를 수식한다.

guarantee 보장하다
the Bill of Rights (영국) 권리장전
assembly 집회; 의회
and so on 기타 등등
negative rights 소극적 권리
(자유를 침해받지 않을 권리; 표현의 자유, 종교의 자유, 재산권 등)

[모의] **04** Food unites as well as distinguishes eaters because what and how one
음식은 먹는 사람들을 구별지을 뿐만 아니라 결속시킨다   / 왜냐하면 사람이 무엇을 어떻게 먹느냐가 형성하기

eats forms much of one's emotional tie to a group identity, be it a nation
때문이다   / 그 사람의 감정적 유대의 많은 것을   / [집단 정체성에 대한]   / 그것이 국가이든 민족

or an ethnicity.
집단이든

- because + s + v ~: ~이기 때문에
- be it A or B: A이든 B이든 (= whether it be[is] A or B) / (= whether it be[is] a nation or an ethnicity)

unite 결속시키다
tie 유대
identity 정체성
ethnicity 민족 집단; 민족성

B **05** The noise of barking and yelling from the park at night is **so** loud and
[수능] 밤중에 공원에서 개가 짖어대는 소리와 (사람들이) 소리치는 소음이   / 너무 시끄럽고 불편하게

disturbing **that I cannot relax in my apartment.**
한다   / 그래서 나는 나의 아파트에서 쉴 수 없다

- 풀이 '너무 ~해서 …하다'라는 결과의 의미를 나타내도록 so ~ that을 써서 「so + 형용사[부사] + that + s + v ….」으로 표현한다.

bark 개가 짖다; 짖는 소리
yell 소리 지르다
disturb 불편하게 하다; 방해하다

06 The teacher had **no sooner** gone out of the classroom **than all of the**
그 선생님이 교실 밖으로 나가자마자   / 모든 학생들이 갑자기

students burst out laughing.
웃기 시작했다

- 풀이 '~하자마자 …하다'라는 의미로 시간을 나타내는 표현은 「no sooner ~ than ….」을 쓴다.

burst out v-ing 갑자기 ~하기 시작하다

07 **If you are stuck in a pattern of doing the same things every day and you**
만약 당신이 패턴 속에 갇혀 있다면 / [매일 똑같은 것들을 하는] / 그리고 당신이
feel as though you are becoming dull, perhaps it is time to stop and
느낀다면 / 마치 당신이 무뎌지고 있는 것처럼 / 아마도 시간일 것이다 / [멈춰서 당신의
sharpen your axe.
도끼를 갈아야 할]

> **풀이** '마치 ~인 것처럼'의 의미가 되도록 양태를 나타내는 접속사 as though가 알맞다. even though는 반전의 접속사로 '비록 ~일지라도'를 뜻한다.

be stuck in ~에 갇혀 있다
dull 무딘
ax(e) 도끼

C **08** **Now that we are all part of the global village,** everyone becomes a neighbor.
우리는 모두 지구촌의 일원이기 때문에 / 모든 사람이 이웃이 된다

> **풀이** now that + s + v ~: ~이기 때문에, ~이므로

09 **Much as I sympathize with your difficulties,** there is little I can do to help
나는 너의 어려움에 매우 공감하지만 / 내가 너를 돕기 위해 할 수 있는 것이 거의 없다
you.

> **풀이** 부사 + as + s + v ~: 비록 ~이지만 / (= Though I sympathize with your difficulties much, ~)
> — little은 명사로 쓰였으며, 그 뒤에 목적격 관계대명사 which 또는 that이 생략되었다.

sympathize 공감하다

10 Leave things **as they are until the police arrive.**
물건들을 둬라 / 있는 그대로 / 경찰이 도착할 때까지

> **풀이** as + s + v ~: ~ 대로, ~처럼, ~이듯이 / until + s + v ~: ~할 때까지

D **11** Adolescents are **so primed to learn that they are also extremely vulnerable**
청소년들은 배울 준비가 아주 잘 되어 있다 / 그래서 그들은 또한 극히 취약하다
to learning the wrong things.
/ 잘못된 것들을 배우는 것에도

> so + 형용사[부사] + that + s + v ~: 아주 …해서 ~하다

primed 준비가 되어 있는, ~할
의향이 있는
extremely 극히, 극도로
vulnerable 취약한

12 **Unless an actor speaks and moves in the manner in which the imaginary**
만약 배우가 말하고 움직이지 않는다면 / 방식으로 / [가상의 등장인물이
character whose part he is playing would do, the story will not be clearly
/ [그 역할을 그가 연기하고 있는] / 할 것 같은] / 그 이야기는 분명하게 전달되지 않을 것이다
communicated to the audience.
/ 관객에게

> unless + s + v ~: 만약 ~가 아니라면, 만약 ~하지 않으면 / unless는 if ... not으로 바꿔 쓸 수 있다. (= If an actor doesn't speak and move ~)
> — the manner를 in which가 이끄는 관계사절 in which ~ would do가 수식하고 있다.
> — 소유격 관계대명사 whose가 이끄는 절 whose ~ playing이 the imaginary character를 수식하고 있다.

imaginary 가상의, 상상의
audience 관객, 청중

13 **While physics and mathematics may tell us how the universe began,** they
물리학과 수학이 우리에게 말해 줄 수도 있는 반면에 / 우주가 어떻게 시작되었는지 / 그것들은
are not much use in predicting human behavior **because there are far too**
그다지 소용이 없다 / 인간의 행동을 예측함에 있어서는 / 풀어야 할 너무나 많은 방정식이
many equations to solve. *Stephen Hawking*
있기 때문에

> while[whereas] + s + v ~: ~인 반면에
> because + s + v ~: ~이기 때문에

use 유용함, 효용

STAGE III

주요 구문의 독파

Contents of Stage

Chapter 09 가정법 구문	Unit 41	if 가정법 과거 구문
	Unit 42	if 가정법 과거완료 구문
	Unit 43	wish · as if 가정법 구문
	Unit 44	if가 없는 가정법 구문
Chapter 10 비교 구문	Unit 45	원급 구문
	Unit 46	비교급 구문 1
	Unit 47	비교급 구문 2
	Unit 48	최상급 구문
Chapter 11 특수 구문	Unit 49	도치 구문 1
	Unit 50	도치 구문 2
	Unit 51	강조 구문
	Unit 52	동격 구문
	Unit 53	삽입 구문
	Unit 54	생략 · 공통 구문
Chapter 12 기타 주요 구문	Unit 55	등위접속사 구문
	Unit 56	상관접속사 구문
	Unit 57	병렬 구문
	Unit 58	부정 구문
	Unit 59	동명사 관용 구문
	Unit 60	전치사 + 명사절

Chapter

09

가정법 구문

- Unit 41   if 가정법 과거 구문
- Unit 42   if 가정법 과거완료 구문
- Unit 43   wish·as if 가정법 구문
- Unit 44   if가 없는 가정법 구문

■ 본격적인 구문 학습에 앞서, 각 유닛별 주요 단어를 확인하세요.

Unit 41

- [ ] asteroid 소행성
- [ ] diameter 직경
- [ ] collide 충돌하다
- [ ] maternal instinct 모성 본능
- [ ] rewind 되돌리다, 되감다
- [ ] laws of nature 자연의 법칙
- [ ] opponent 경쟁자, 상대
- [ ] two-faced 위선적인, 두 얼굴을 가진
- [ ] self-deprecatingly 자조적으로
- [ ] wed 결혼하다, 혼인하다
- [ ] successive 이어지는
- [ ] note 주목하다
- [ ] any number of 꽤 많은
- [ ] intoxicate 열광하게 하다
- [ ] delight 환희, 기쁨

Unit 42

- [ ] lung 폐
- [ ] eye-opening 놀랄 만한
- [ ] nail 못; 손톱
- [ ] remove 제거하다
- [ ] save 구하다; 절약하다
- [ ] devote oneself to ~에 헌신하다
- [ ] assume 생각하다, 가정하다
- [ ] better off 더 나은
- [ ] workout 운동
- [ ] sign up for ~을 신청하다
- [ ] agonize 고심하다
- [ ] take chance 위험을 무릅쓰다
- [ ] go after ~을 추구하다
- [ ] gravity 중력
- [ ] ignorant 무지한

Unit 43

- [ ] masterpiece 걸작
- [ ] light 밝게 하다
- [ ] burst into 갑자기 ~을 터뜨리다
- [ ] high-pitched (음이) 아주 높은
- [ ] fraction 일부, 작은 부분
- [ ] on one's deathbed ~의 임종에
- [ ] stumble 발이 걸리다
- [ ] pick oneself up 일어서다
- [ ] hurry off 서둘러 떠나다
- [ ] take risk 위험을 감수하다
- [ ] administration (미국) 집권 정부
- [ ] all told 모두 통틀어
- [ ] fiber-optic cable 광섬유 케이블
- [ ] plug ~와 연결하다; 플러그를 꽂다
- [ ] fire 쏘다, 발사하다

Unit 44

- [ ] come true 실현되다
- [ ] incite 자극하다
- [ ] sore 아픈
- [ ] confront 직면하다
- [ ] own 가지다, 소유하다
- [ ] multi-million 수백만의
- [ ] voyage 항해
- [ ] immortal 영원히 기억되는
- [ ] assure 장담하다
- [ ] operation 수술
- [ ] snatch 잡아채다
- [ ] creep 기어가다
- [ ] concrete 구체적인
- [ ] disease-ridden 질병이 들끓는
- [ ] pollination 수분

unit 41
if 가정법 과거 구문

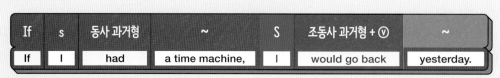

If	s	동사 과거형	~	S	조동사 과거형 + ⓥ	~
If	I	had	a time machine,	I	would go back	yesterday.
만약 ~라면	내가	가지고 있다	타임머신을	나는	돌아갈 텐데	어제로

Standard Sentences

01 If people knew how hard I had to work to gain my mastery, it would not
만약 사람들이 안다면 / 내가 얼마나 열심히 일해야 했는지 / 나의 숙련된 솜씨를 얻기 위해 / 그것은 전혀 매우
seem so wonderful at all. *Michelangelo*
놀랍게 보이지 않을 텐데

- If + s + 동사 과거형 ~, S + 조동사 과거형 + ⓥ ...: 만약 ~라면, ...할 텐데
- 의문사 how가 이끄는 명사절 how ~ mastery가 동사 knew의 목적어이다.

> mastery 숙련, 숙달; 전문적 지식

02 If thunder should occur, it would be better to find a shelter as soon as
혹시라도 천둥이 친다면 / (···이) 더 나을 것이다 / 대피소를 찾는 것이 / 가능한 한 빨리
possible and avoid dangerous places.
/ 그리고 위험한 장소를 피하는 것이

- If + s + should + ⓥ ~, S + 조동사 과거형 + ⓥ ...: (혹시라도) 만약 ~라면, ...할 텐데 / if절에 쓰인 should는 happen to의 의미이며, should 가정법 구문에서는 주절에 명령문 또는 직설법이 올 수 있다.
- 가주어 it이 진주어인 to find ~ places를 대신한다.

> shelter 대피소; 거처

Ⓐ 03 I heard a young boy on television say, "If I were President, I'd give
나는 텔레비전에서 어린 남자아이가 말하는 것을 들었다 / 제가 만약 대통령이라면 / 저는 모든
everybody enough money to buy whatever they want."
사람에게 줄 거예요 / 사기에 충분한 돈을 / 그들이 원하는 무엇이든

- If + s + 동사 과거형 ~, S + 조동사 과거형 + ⓥ ...: 만약 ~라면, ...할 텐데 / 현재의 사실이나 상황과 반대되는 가정이나 상상을 나타내는 가정법 과거 구문이 쓰였다. 가정법 과거 구문에서 if절의 be동사는 주어의 인칭이나 수와 관계없이 were를 쓰는 것이 원칙이다. (단, 구어체에서는 was를 쓰기도 한다.)

04 If an asteroid with a diameter of 30 km were to collide with the Earth, it
만약 직경 30km의 소행성이 지구와 충돌한다면 /
would probably bring an end to human civilization.
그것은 아마 종말을 초래할 텐데 / 인간 문명에

- If + s + were to + ⓥ ~, S + 조동사 과거형 + ⓥ ...: (불가능한 일이지만) 만약 ~라면, ...할 텐데 / if절에 「were to + ⓥ」가 오는 가정법은 있을 법하지 않은 가상의 미래 상황을 가정한다.

> asteroid 소행성
> diameter 직경, 지름
> collide 충돌하다

05 Should you meet a jaguar in the jungle, just turn slowly, walk away, and
만약 당신이 정글에서 재규어를 만난다면 / 그저 천천히 돌아서 / 걸어가고 / 그리고
never look back.
결코 뒤돌아보지 마라

- Should + s + ⓥ ~, 명령문: (혹시라도) 만약 ~라면, ...해라 / if절의 동사가 should일 때 접속사 if를 생략할 수 있는데, if가 생략되면 주어와 동사가 도치된다. (= If you should meet a jaguar ~.)

> jaguar 재규어, 아메리카표범

B **06** **If young people understood how doing well in school makes the rest of**
만약 젊은이들이 이해한다면 / 어떻게 학교에서 잘하는 것이 / 그들의 여생을 정말 흥미롭게

their life so much interesting, they would be more motivated. *Bill Gates*
만드는지를 / 그들은 더욱 동기부여가 될 텐데

the rest of one's life ~의 여생

> If + s + 동사 과거형 ~, S + 조동사 과거형 + ⓥ …: 만약 ~라면, …할 텐데

07 Many species of animals **could not survive were it not for the strong maternal**
많은 종의 동물들은 생존할 수 없을 것이다 / 강한 모성 본능이 없다면

instinct to protect the young.
/ [새끼를 보호하려는]

maternal instinct 모성 본능

> Were it not for ~, S + 조동사 과거형 + ⓥ …: ~이 없다면(아니라면), …할 텐데 / if it were not for ~에서 if가 생략되면서 주어와 동사가 도치된 것으로, without이나 but for와 바꾸어 쓸 수 있다. (= if it were not for the strong maternal instinct ~)

08 **If the universe were to rewind back to the beginning and the laws of nature**
만약 우주가 처음으로 되돌아간다면 / 그리고 자연의 법칙이 동일하다면

were the same, would everything happen in the exact same way?
/ 모든 것이 일어날까 / 정확히 같은 방식으로?

rewind 되돌리다, 되감다
laws of nature 자연의 법칙

> If + s + were to + ⓥ ~, S + 조동사 과거형 + ⓥ …: (불가능한 일이지만) 만약 ~라면, …할 텐데

09 **Should you find our service useful, further information can be obtained by**
만약 당신이 저희의 서비스가 유용하다고 생각하시면 / 추가 정보가 얻어질 수 있습니다 /

contacting our office.
저희 사무실에 연락함으로써

further 추가의, 그 이상의; 더 먼
obtain 얻다, 획득하다

> Should + s + ⓥ ~, S + 조동사 과거형 + ⓥ …: (혹시라도) 만약 ~라면, …할 텐데 / 접속사 if가 생략되고 조동사 should가 주어 앞으로 도치된 문장이다. 조건절에 should가 쓰였을 때 주절에는 can be obtained와 같은 직설법 현재 시제가 올 수 있다.

C **10** When Stephen Douglas, Abraham Lincoln's opponent in the presidential
에이브러햄 링컨의 경쟁자였던 스티븐 더글러스가 / 대통령 선거에서

election, accused Lincoln of being two-faced during a debate, Lincoln
/ 링컨을 위선적이라고 비난했을 때 / 토론 중에 / 링컨은

self-deprecatingly responded like this. "Honestly, **if I were two-faced, would I**
자조적으로 이렇게 응답했다 / 솔직히 말해서 / 만약 내가 얼굴이 두 개라면 / 내가

be wearing this one?"
이 얼굴을 하고 있겠는가?

opponent 경쟁자, 상대
accuse A of B A를 B라는 이유로 비난하다
two-faced 위선적인, 두 얼굴을 가진
self-deprecatingly 자조적으로, 자신을 비하하여

> 풀이 주절의 동사에 「조동사 과거형 + ⓥ」인 would be가 쓰였고, 현재 사실과 반대되는 상황을 가정하고 있으므로 if가 이끄는 조건절에는 가정법 과거를 나타내는 be동사의 과거형 were가 적절하다.

11 Delicious autumn! My very soul is wedded to it, and **if I were a bird I would**
달콤한 가을! 나의 영혼은 가을과 결혼했다 / 그리고 만약 내가 새라면 / 나는 지구

fly about the earth seeking the successive autumns. *George Eliot*
여기저기를 날아다닐 텐데 / 이어지는 가을을 찾아서

wed 결혼하다, 혼인하다
successive 이어지는, 연속하는

> 풀이 if가 이끄는 조건절에 동사 과거형 were가 쓰였으므로, 주절에는 「조동사 과거형 + ⓥ」인 would fly가 오는 것이 적절하다.

12 **If a man were to come back from the past and watch the modern world,**
만약 어떤 남자가 과거로부터 돌아와서 현대 세계를 지켜본다면

he would note any number of things that would intoxicate him with wonder
/ 그는 주목하게 될 것이다 / 꽤 많은 것들을 / [그를 경이로움과 환희로 열광하게 할]

and delight.

note 주목하다
any number of 꽤 많은
intoxicate 열광하게 하다; 취하게 하다
delight 환희, 기쁨

> 풀이 주절의 동사가 「조동사 과거형 + ⓥ」인 would note이고, 있을 법하지 않은 가상의 미래 상황은 조건절에 「were to + ⓥ」를 쓴다.

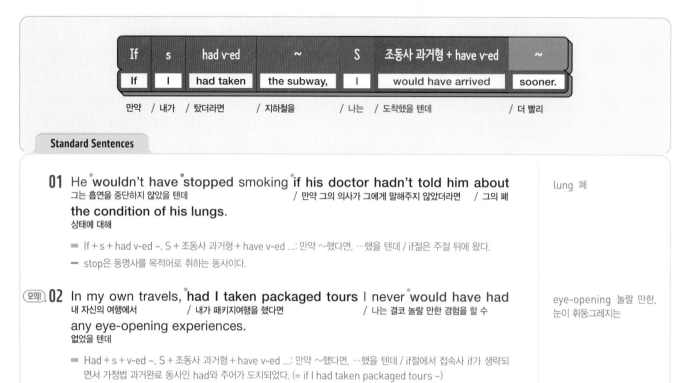

본책 146~147쪽을 함께 펴놓고 보세요!

unit 42
if 가정법 과거완료 구문

If	s	had v-ed	~	S	조동사 과거형 + have v-ed	~
If	I	had taken	the subway,	I	would have arrived	sooner.
만약 / 내가 / 탔더라면			/ 지하철을	/ 나는	/ 도착했을 텐데	/ 더 빨리

Standard Sentences

01 He wouldn't have stopped smoking if his doctor hadn't told him about
그는 흡연을 중단하지 않았을 텐데 / 만약 그의 의사가 그에게 말해주지 않았더라면 / 그의 폐
the condition of his lungs.
상태에 대해

lung 폐

- If + s + had v-ed ~, S + 조동사 과거형 + have v-ed ...: 만약 ~했다면, ...했을 텐데 / if절은 주절 뒤에 왔다.
- stop은 동명사를 목적어로 취하는 동사이다.

(모의) **02** In my own travels, had I taken packaged tours I never would have had
내 자신의 여행에서 / 내가 패키지여행을 했다면 / 나는 결코 놀랄 만한 경험을 할 수
any eye-opening experiences.
없었을 텐데

eye-opening 놀랄 만한, 눈이 휘둥그레지는

- Had + s + v-ed ~, S + 조동사 과거형 + have v-ed ...: 만약 ~했다면, ...했을 텐데 / if절에서 접속사 if가 생략되면서 가정법 과거완료 동사인 had와 주어가 도치되었다. (= if I had taken packaged tours ~)

A 03 If the truck driver had only taken a few minutes to get the nail removed,
만약 그 트럭 운전사가 단 몇 분을 들였더라면 / 그 못을 제거하기 위해서
he most likely would not have had a flat tire yesterday.
/ 그는 아마도 어제 타이어 펑크를 겪지 않았을 텐데

nail 못; 손톱
remove 제거하다
flat tire 펑크난 타이어

- If + s + had v-ed ~, S + 조동사 과거형 + have v-ed ...: 만약 ~했다면, ...했을 텐데
- to get의 목적어인 the nail이 제거되는 대상이므로 과거분사 removed가 목적격보어로 쓰였다.

04 As a firefighter, I have seen many people die in fires. Most could have saved
소방관으로서 / 나는 많은 사람들이 화재 속에서 죽는 것을 봐왔다 대부분은 자신을 구할 수 있었을 텐데
themselves had they been prepared.
/ 그들이 준비되어 있었더라면

firefighter 소방관
save 구하다; 절약하다

- Had + s + v-ed ~, S + 조동사 과거형 + have v-ed ...: 만약 ~했다면, ...했을 텐데 / (= ~ if they had been prepared.)
- 지각동사 have seen의 목적어인 many people이 죽는 것이므로, 목적격보어로 동사원형 die가 쓰였다.

(모의) **05** Can you imagine what the world today would be like if Leonardo da Vinci
너는 상상할 수 있니 / 오늘날 세상이 어떠할까를 / 만약 레오나르도 다빈치가 농부가
had become a farmer or Wolfgang Amadeus Mozart a banker?
되었다면 / 또는 볼프강 아마데우스 모차르트가 은행원이 되었다면?

- If + s + had v-ed ~, S + 조동사 과거형 + ⓥ ...: 만약 (과거에) ~했다면, (지금) ...할 텐데 (혼합 가정법) / 과거의 사실이나 행동의 결과가 현재에 영향을 미치는 것을 상상하여 가정할 때 쓴다.
- Wolfgang Amadeus Mozart와 a banker 사이에 had become이 생략되어 있다.

B **06** **If I am a great man,** it is all thanks to my mother. **Hadn't she devoted**
만약 내가 위대한 인물이라면 / 그것은 모두 나의 어머니 덕분이다 그녀가 나를 부양하는 데 헌신하지
herself to supporting me, I could never have become what I am.
않았더라면 / 나는 **결코** 현재의 내가 될 수 없었을 것이다

thanks to ~ 덕분에(= due to)
devote oneself to ~에 헌신하다

> ■ Had + s + v-ed ~, S + 조동사 과거형 + have v-ed ...: 만약 ~했다면, ...했을 텐데 /(= If she hadn't devoted herself to supporting me, ~.)
> ■ 첫 번째 문장은 조건절의 내용이 현실적인 단순 조건문이다.

(모의) **07** We must assume that we had one chance each for *The Divine Comedy* and
우리는 생각해야 한다 / 우리가 「신곡」과 「리어 왕」에 대해 각각 한 번의 기회가 있었다고
King Lear. **If Dante and Shakespeare had died before they wrote those**
만약 단테와 셰익스피어가 사망했다면 / 그들이 그 작품들을 쓰기 전에
works, nobody ever would have written them.
/ 아무도 지금까지 그것들을 쓰지 않았을 것이다

assume 생각하다, 가정하다
divine 신의, 신성한

> ■ If + s + had v-ed ~, S + 조동사 과거형 + have v-ed ...: 만약 ~했다면, ...했을 텐데

08 Some economists discovered that gym goers **would have been** better off,
어떤 경제학자들은 발견했다 / 헬스클럽에 가는 사람들은 더 나았을 것이라는 것을
financially, **had they chosen to pay per workout rather than signing up for**
/ 금전적으로 / 만약 그들이 운동할 때마다 지불하는 것을 선택했더라면 / 월 또는 연 단위의 회원권을 신청하는 대신에
monthly or annual memberships.

better off 더 나은
workout 운동
sing up for ~을 신청하다

> ■ S + 조동사 과거형 + have v-ed ...., had + s + v-ed ~ : ...했을 텐데, 만약 ~했다면 / (= if they had chosen to pay ~.)

(모의) **09** **If Louise had not learned the effective parenting skills taught in the**
만약 Louise가 효과적인 양육 기술을 배우지 않았더라면 / [세미나에서 교수 받은]
seminars, she would probably be using similarly ineffective threatening
/ 그녀는 아마도 비슷하게 비효율적인 위협하는 기술을 사용하고 있을 것이다
techniques with her own children today.
/ 오늘날 자신의 자녀들에게

similarly 비슷하게

> ■ If + s + had v-ed ~, S + 조동사 과거형 + ⓥ ...: 만약 (과거에) ~했다면, (지금) ...할 텐데 (혼합 가정법)

C **10** **If our ancestors hadn't agonized over losses and instead had taken too**
만약 우리의 조상들이 손실에 대해 고심하지 않았다면 / 그리고 대신에 너무나 많은 위험을 무릅썼다면
many chances in going after the big gains, they'd have been more likely to
/ 큰 이익을 추구하면서 / 그들은 실패하여 결코 어떤 사람의 조상이 되지
lose out and never become anyone's ancestor.
못했을 가능성이 더욱 컸을 것이다

agonize 고심하다, 고뇌하다
take chance 위험을 무릅쓰다
go after ~을 추구하다
lose out 실패하다

> 풀이 If + s + had v-ed ~, S + 조동사 과거형 + have v-ed ...: 만약 ~했다면, ...했을 텐데

11 **Had it not been for Newton,** Einstein **might never have had** his own miracle
만약 뉴턴이 없었더라면 / 아인슈타인은 결코 자신의 기적의 해를 갖지 못했을 것이다
year that completely revolutionized our view of gravity, space, matter, and time.
/ [완전히 근본적으로 바꾼 / 중력, 공간, 물질 그리고 시간에 대한 우리의 시각을]

revolutionize 근본적으로 바꾸다, 대변혁을 일으키다
gravity 중력
matter 물질

> 풀이 Had it not been for ~, S + 조동사 과거형 + have v-ed ...: 만약 ~이 없었다면(아니었다면), ...했을 텐데 / If it had not been for ~에서 if가 생략되고 주어와 동사가 도치되었다. (= If it had not been for Newton, ~.)

12 Copernicus doubted that the earth was the center of the universe. **If it had**
코페르니쿠스는 의심했다 / 지구가 우주의 중심이라는 것을 만약 의심이
not been for doubt, we should be now even more ignorant than we really are.
없었더라면 / 우리는 지금 훨씬 더 무지할 것이다 / 실제의 우리보다

ignorant 무지한

> 풀이 If it had not been for ~, S + 조동사 과거형 + ⓥ ...: 만약 (과거에) ~이 없었다면, (지금) ...할 텐데 (혼합 가정법) / 조건절은 과거에 대한 가정이므로 과거완료 시제가 왔으나, 주절에는 현재를 나타내는 now가 있으므로 가정법 과거의 동사 형태인 should be가 적절하다.

unit 43
wish · as if 가정법 과거 구문

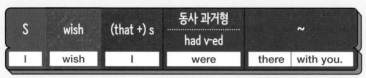

S	wish	(that +) s	동사 과거형 had v-ed	~
I	wish	I	were	there | with you.

나는 / 좋을 텐데 / 내가 / 있다면 / 거기에 너와 함께

Standard Sentences

01 I wish I **were endowed** with an artistic talent for painting masterpieces like
나는 좋을 텐데 / 내가 예술적 재능을 타고났다면 / [걸작을 그리기 위한 /
Pablo Picasso's.
[파블로 피카소의 것과 같은]]

- S + wish (that) + s + 동사 과거형 ~: ~라면 좋을 텐데 (주절과 같은 시점)

endow A with B A에게 B(재능, 자질, 권리 등)를 주다(부여하다)
masterpiece 걸작

모의 02 The woman smiled and he felt **as if she lit up the world around her.**
그 여자는 미소를 지었다 / 그러자 그는 느꼈다 / 마치 그녀가 밝히는 것처럼 / 그녀 주변의 세상을

- as if + s + 동사 과거형 ~: 마치 ~인(하는) 것처럼 (주절과 같은 시점)

light 밝게 하다

A 03 I wish I **had accepted** your invitation, rather than running away with my tail
나는 좋을 텐데 / 내가 너의 초대를 받아들였다면 / 도망치는 것 대신에 / 겁을 먹고
between my legs.

- S + wish + s + had v-ed ~: ~했다면 좋았을 텐데 (주절보다 앞선 시점)

run away 도망치다, 달아나다
with one's tail between one's legs 겁을 먹고, 기가 죽어서

04 Even though I don't personally believe in the Lord, I try to behave **as though**
비록 내가 개인적으로 하느님을 믿지 않을지라도 / 나는 행동하려고 노력한다 / 마치 그가
He was watching. *Christopher Reeve*
지켜보고 있는 것처럼

- as though + s + 동사 과거형 ~: 마치 ~인(하는) 것처럼 (주절과 같은 시점) / 가정법 과거 문장에서 if절의 be동사는 were를 쓰는 것이 원칙이지만, 구어체에서는 주어가 1인칭, 3인칭 단수일 때 was를 쓰기도 한다.
- as though가 이끄는 절의 주어 He는 앞에 나온 Lord를 가리키며, 신을 의미할 때 대문자로 쓴다.

05 He burst into a high-pitched laugh, **as though he'd said something funny.**
그는 갑자기 고음의 웃음을 터뜨렸다 / 마치 자신이 웃긴 어떤 것을 말했던 것처럼

- as though + s + had v-ed ~: 마치 ~였던(했던) 것처럼 (주절보다 앞선 시점)

burst into 갑자기 ~을 터뜨리다(내뿜다)
high-pitched (음이) 아주 높은; (감정이) 격렬한, 강렬한

06 I wish I could turn the clock back and give Mom a fraction of what she
나는 좋을 텐데 / 내가 예전으로 돌아갈 수 있다면   / 그래서 엄마에게 일부라도 드릴 수 있다면 / [그녀가 내게 준 것의]
gave to me.

■ S + wish + s + 조동사 과거형 + ⓥ ~: ~라면 좋을 텐데 (주절과 같은 시점) / 종속절의 동사로 「조동사 과거형+ ⓥ」
인 could turn과 (could) give가 and로 연결되어 있다.

turn the clock back 예전
[과거]으로 돌아가다; 시곗바늘
을 되돌리다
fraction 일부, 작은 부분; 아주
조금

07 No one on his deathbed ever said, "I wish I had spent more time on my
임종에 어느 누구도 지금껏 말한 적이 없었다   / 나는 좋을 텐데 / 내가 나의 사업에 더 많은 시간을 썼다면
business."

■ S + wish + s + had v-ed ~: ~했다면 좋을 텐데 (주절보다 앞선 시점)

on one's deathbed ~의 임
종에, ~의 죽음에 임하여

08 To achieve great things we must live as though we were never going to die.
위대한 것들을 성취하기 위해서 / 우리는 살아야 한다 / 마치 우리가 절대 죽지 않을 것처럼

Marquis de Vauvenargues

■ as though + s + 동사 과거형 ~: 마치 ~인[하는] 것처럼 (주절과 같은 시점)

09 Men occasionally stumble over the truth, but most of them pick themselves
사람들은 가끔 진실에 발이 걸린다   / 그러나 그들 대부분은 스스로 일어선다
up and hurry off as if nothing had happened. *Winston Churchill*
/ 그리고 서둘러 떠난다 / 마치 아무 일도 일어나지 않았던 것처럼

■ as if + s + had v-ed ~: 마치 ~였던(했던) 것처럼 (주절보다 앞선 시점)

stumble 발이 걸리다, 발을 헛
디디다
pick oneself up 일어서다
hurry off 서둘러 떠나다

ⓒ 10 I've lived my life taking risks and I wish I could tell you they were all
[모의] 나는 내 인생을 위험을 감수하며 살아왔다   / 그리고 나는 좋을 텐데 / 내가 당신에게 말할 수 있다면 / 그것들은 모두
successful, but they weren't.
성공적이었다고   / 그러나 그것들은 그렇지 않았다

풀이 I wish 다음에 가정법 과거나 과거완료 형태의 동사가 와야 하므로, 조동사 과거형인 could가 적절하다.
— you 다음에는 목적어절을 이끄는 접속사 that이 생략되었다.
— weren't 다음에는 successful이 생략되었다.

take risk 위험을 감수하다

11 Toward the end of their administrations, every president I think I've ever
집권 정부가 끝날 무렵에   / 모든 대통령은   / [내가 생각하기에 / 내가
known was disappointed and wished they had done some things differently.
알아온] / 실망했다   / 그리고 바랐다 / 그들이 어떤 것들을 달리했었기를

Billy Graham

풀이 소망의 시점(wished)보다 they ~ differently의 내용이 더 이전의 일이므로 과거완료인 had done이 적절하다.
— 주어인 every president 다음에 관계대명사 that이 생략되었으며, 그 뒤의 I think는 삽입절이다.

administration (미국) 집권
정부; 관리

[모의] 12 All told, every second, our senses transmit an estimated 11 million bits of
모두 통틀어 / 매 초   / 우리의 감각은 어림잡아 천백만 비트의 정보를 전송한다
information to our poor brains, as if a giant fiber-optic cable were plugged
/ 우리의 불쌍한 뇌에   / 마치 거대한 광섬유 케이블이 뇌에 직접 연결된 것처럼
directly into them, firing information at full speed.
/ 정보를 전속력으로 쏘면서

풀이 단수 주어 a giant fiber-optic cable 뒤에 복수 동사 were가 쓰였으므로 '마치 ~인 것처럼'의 의미로 가정법
을 나타내는 as if가 적절하다. even if는 '~에도 불구하고, 비록 ~이지만'의 뜻으로 반전의 부사절을 이끈다.
— 주어 a giant fiber-optic cable이 정보를 쏘는 것이므로 현재분사 firing이 쓰여 '~하면서'의 의미를 나타낸다.

transmit 전송하다
all told 모두 통틀어
fiber-optic cable 광섬유 케
이블
plug ~와 연결하다; 플러그를
꽂다
fire 쏘다, 발사하다

unit 44

if가 없는 가정법 구문

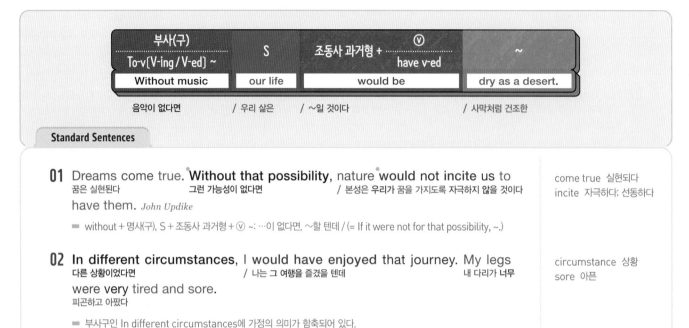

부사(구) To-v[V-ing / V-ed] ~	S	조동사 과거형 + have v-ed (v)	~
Without music	our life	would be	dry as a desert.
음악이 없다면	/ 우리 삶은	/ ~일 것이다	/ 사막처럼 건조한

Standard Sentences

01 Dreams come true. **Without that possibility,** nature would not incite us to
꿈은 실현된다 　　　　그런 가능성이 없다면 　　　　/ 본성은 우리가 꿈을 가지도록 자극하지 않을 것이다
have them. *John Updike*

━ without + 명사(구), S + 조동사 과거형 + ⓥ ~: …이 없다면, ~할 텐데 / (= If it were not for that possibility, ~.)

come true 실현되다
incite 자극하다; 선동하다

02 In different circumstances, I would have enjoyed that journey. My legs
다른 상황이었다면 　　　　　　/ 나는 그 여행을 즐겼을 텐데 　　　　내 다리가 너무
were very tired and sore.
피곤하고 아팠다

━ 부사구인 In different circumstances에 가정의 의미가 함축되어 있다.

circumstance 상황
sore 아픈

Ⓐ **03** Coronavirus is a completely different type of virus. **Otherwise** it would be
코로나는 완전히 다른 형태의 바이러스이다 　　　　　　　　　그렇지 않다면 　　/ 그것은 독감이라고
called flu.
불릴 것이다

━ Otherwise + S + 조동사 과거형 + ⓥ ~: 그렇지 않다면 ~할 텐데 / (= If coronavirus were not a completely
different type of virus, ~.)

04 Only a fool would ignore his past experience when confronted with a new
오직 바보만이 자신의 과거 경험을 무시할 것이다 　　　　　　　　/ 새로운 상황에 직면했을 때
situation.

━ 주어 Only a fool에 가정의 의미가 함축되어 있다. / (= If he were only a fool, he would ignore ~.)
━ when confronted ~는 접속사 when이 그 의미를 명확히 하기 위해 남아있는 분사구문이다.

confront 직면하다

05 To see her walking around in her old clothes, you'd never guess she owned a
그녀가 자신의 낡은 옷을 입고 걸어 다니는 것을 본다면 　　　　/ 당신은 결코 추측하지 못할 것이다 / 그녀가 수백만
multi-million dollar business.
달러의 사업체를 가지고 있다는 것을

━ to-v ~, S + 조동사 과거형 + ⓥ …: ~한다면, …할 텐데 / To see 이하의 부정사구에 가정의 의미가 함축되어 있다.
(= If you saw her walking ~.)
━ guess 다음에는 명사절을 이끄는 접속사 that이 생략되었다.

own 가지다, 소유하다; 자신의
multi-million 수백만의

B 06 We would not have had men on the Moon but for Wells and Verne and the
우리는 인간을 달에 있게 할 수 없었을 것이다 　　　　/ 만약 웰스와 베른 그리고 사람들이 없었다면
people who write about this and made people think about it. *Arthur C. Clarke*
　　/ [이것에 대해서 쓰고 　　　　　/ 그리고 사람들이 그것에 대해서 생각하게 만든]

> 가정법 과거완료 + but for + 명사(구): 만약 ～이 없었다면, …했을 텐데 / (= if it had not been for Wells and Verne ~)

Know More 허버트 조지 웰스(Herbert George Wells)는 영국의 소설가이자 비평가로, 「타임머신」, 「우주 전쟁」 등을 통해 과학 소설의 독자적인 영역을 개척하고 제1차 세계대전 후에는 「세계사 대계」, 「생명의 과학」 등의 계몽적인 작품을 저술하였다.

07 All great achievers in past ages possessed singleness of purpose without
위대한 성취자들은 　　　　/ [옛날의] 　　/ 단 하나의 목적을 갖고 있었다 　　　/ 예외 없이
exception. Without it, Columbus wouldn't have started upon the voyage
　　　　그것이 없었다면 　/ 콜럼버스는 항해를 출발하지 않았을 것이다
that made his name immortal.
/ [그의 이름을 영원히 기억되게 한]

> without + 명사(구), + 가정법 과거완료: 만약 ～이 없었다면, …했을 텐데 / (= If it had not been for it ~)

exception 예외
voyage 항해
immortal 영원히 기억되는, 불후의; 불멸의

08 A hundred years ago not a doctor in the world could have assured a
백 년 전이라면 　　　　/ 세상의 어떤 의사도 환자에게 장담할 수 없었을 것이다
patient that an operation would be painless.
　　　　/ 어떤 수술이 고통스럽지 않을 거라고

> 부사구인 A hundred years ago에 가정의 의미가 함축되어 있다.

assure 장담하다, 보장하다
operation 수술

09 Born in better times, he would have done credit to society.
더 좋은 시대에 태어났더라면 　　/ 그는 사회에 명예로운 인물이 되었을 텐데

> v-ed ~, S + 조동사 과거형 + have v-ed …: ～했다면, …했을 텐데 / 과거분사 Born이 이끄는 분사구문 앞에 Having been이 생략되어 있다. (= If he had been born in better times, ~.)

do credit to ～에 명예로운 인물이 되다

C 10 In the past it never occurred to me that every casual remark of mine would
과거에 　　/ (…이) 내게 결코 떠오르지 않았다 　/ 나의 모든 무심코 한 말이 　　　　/ 잡아채여지고
be snatched up and recorded. Otherwise I would have crept further into
　　　/ 그리고 기록될 것이 　그렇지 않았다면 　/ 나는 기어갔을 텐데 　　/ 더 한층 나의
my shell. *Albert Einstein*
껍질 속으로

> 풀이 앞에 나온 내용에 대한 반대를 가정하는 흐름이 되어야 하므로 '그렇지 않았다면'을 뜻하는 otherwise가 적절하다. / (= If it had occurred to me that ~.)

occur (생각이) 떠오르다; 발생하다
casual remark 무심코 한 말
snatch 잡아채다
creep 기어가다 (-crept-crept)

11 With the right software, I could help students form a concrete idea of
알맞은 소프트웨어가 있다면 　　　/ 나는 도울 수 있을 텐데 / 학생들이 사회에 대한 구체적인 인상을 형성하도록
society by displaying on-screen a version of the city in which they live.
　　/ 화면으로 도시의 형태를 보여 줌으로써 　　　　/ [그들이 살고 있는]

> 풀이 with + 명사(구), + 가정법 과거: ～이 있다면, …할 텐데 / (= If I had the right software, ~.)

concrete 구체적인
display 보여 주다

모의 12 Ironically, while many of us perceive insects as harmful pests—dangerous,
역설적이게도 　/ 우리 중 많은 사람들이 곤충을 해충으로 인지하는 반면에 　　　　　/ ㅡ위험한, 흉한,
ugly, and disease-ridden—in reality, without the service of pollination
그리고 질병이 들끓는 　　　/ ㅡ실제로는 　　/ 수분의 공로가 없다면
which they provide, humankind might cease to exist.
/ [그들이 제공하는] 　　　/ 인류는 존재하기를 멈출지도 모른다

> 풀이 without + 명사(구) ~, + 가정법 과거: ～이 없다면, …할 텐데

ironically 역설적이게도
pest 해충
disease-ridden 질병이 들끓는
pollination 수분
cease 멈추다, 중지하다

A **01** **If everything** **given to us by research were to be taken away**, civilization
만약 연구에 의해서 우리에게 주어진 모든 것이 빼앗긴다면 　　　　　　　　　　／ 문명은 무너질

would collapse and we **would stand** naked, searching for caves again.
것이다 　　　　　／ 그리고 우리는 벌거벗은 상태가 될 것이다 　／ 다시 동굴을 찾으면서

■ If + s + were to + ⓥ ~, S + 조동사 과거형 + ⓥ ...: (불가능한 일이지만) 만약 ~라면, ...할 텐데
— everything은 과거분사구 given ~ research의 수식을 받는다.

take away ~을 빼앗다
collapse 무너지다
naked 발가벗은

02 **It** was wonderful to find America, but **it** **would have been** more wonderful **to**
(...은) 멋졌다 　　　　　／ 아메리카를 발견한 것은 ／ 그러나 (...은) 더 멋졌을 텐데 　　　　　／

miss it. *Mark Twain*
그것을 지나쳤다면

■ to miss it이 가정의 의미를 함축하고 있다. (= if people had missed it)
— 등위접속사 but으로 연결된 두 등위절의 맨 앞에 있는 It[it]은 가주어이고, to부정사인 to find America와 to miss it이 각각 진주어이다.

03 He drowsed off, but then woke up abruptly, **as though someone had called**
그는 졸았다 　　　／ 그러나 그때 갑자기 깨어났다 　　／ 마치 누군가가 그의 이름을 불렀던 것처럼

his name.

■ as though + s + had v-ed ~: 마치 ~했던 것처럼 (주절보다 앞선 시점)

drowse 졸다
abruptly 갑자기

04 The sun, the moon and the stars **would have disappeared** long ago, **had**
태양, 달, 그리고 별들은 사라졌을 것이다 　　　　　　　　　　／ 오래전에 ／ 만약

they happened to be within reach of predatory human hands. *Havelock Ellis*
그것들이 마침 있었다면 　　　／ 인간의 약탈하는 손이 미치는 범위 내에

■ S + 조동사 과거형 + have v-ed ...., had + s + v-ed ~: 만약 ~했다면, ...을 텐데 / 가정법 과거완료의 조건절에서 if가 생략되면서 had와 주어가 도치되었다. (= if they had happened to be ~)

reach (팔이) 미치는 범위[거리]
predatory 약탈하는; 포식성의

B **05** When two cultures come into contact, they do not exchange every cultural
수능! 두 문화가 접촉할 때 　　　　　　　　／ 그것들이 모든 문화적 항목을 교환하지는 않는다

item. **If that were the case, there would be** no cultural differences in the
만약 그것이 사실이라면 　　　／ 어떠한 문화적 차이도 없을 것이다 　　　　　／ 오늘날

world today.
세계에는

풀이 If + s + 동사 과거형 ~, S + 조동사 과거형 + ⓥ ...: 만약 ~라면 ...할 텐데 / 주절의 동사가 가정법 과거를 나타내는 「조동사 과거형 + ⓥ」인 would be이므로, if가 이끄는 조건절의 동사로는 과거형인 were가 적절하다.

come into contact 접촉하다, 만나다
the case 사실, 실정

모의 **06** Indeed, **if our early African ancestors hadn't been good at fixing all their**
정말로 　　／ 만약 우리의 초기 아프리카의 조상들이 능숙하지 않았다면 　　　／ 그들의 모든 주의를 고정

attention on the just-ripened fruit or the approaching predators, we
하는 것에 　　　／ 막 익은 열매 또는 다가오는 포식자들에게 　　　　　　　　／

wouldn't be here.
우리는 여기에 없을 것이다

풀이 If + s + had v-ed ~, S + 조동사 과거형 + ⓥ ...: 만약 (과거에) ~했다면, (지금) ...할 텐데 (혼합 가정법) / if가 이끄는 조건절은 과거의 일을 가정하는 과거완료(hadn't been)이지만, 주절은 우리가 여기 없을 것이라는 현재에 대한 가정이므로 「조동사 과거형 + ⓥ」 형태의 wouldn't be가 되어야 한다.

indeed 정말로
ancestor 조상
ripen 익다
predator 포식자

07 I wish I **could have called** my family more often while I was away from
나는 좋을 텐데 / 내가 나의 가족들에게 더 자주 전화했다면 / 내가 집에서 떠나 있던 동안에
home.

> **풀이** S + wish + s + 조동사 과거형 + have v-ed ~: ~했다면 좋을 텐데 (주절보다 앞선 시점) / wish 이후의 내용이 소망하는 시점인 현재보다 더 이전의 일이므로 가정법 과거완료가 되도록 「조동사 과거형 + have v-ed」 형태가 되어야 한다.

C

08 If we had stopped at the service station, we wouldn't have run out of gas.
만약 우리가 주유소에 들렀다면 / 우리는 가솔린이 바닥나지 않았을 텐데

> If + s + had v-ed ~, S + 조동사 과거형 + have v-ed ...: 만약 ~했다면, ...했을 텐데

service station 주유소
run out of ~을 바닥내다, ~을 다 써 버리다

09 I wish I **had known** there was a sale. I **would have gone** with you.
나는 좋을 텐데 / 내가 할인 판매가 있다는 것을 알았다면 / 나는 너와 함께 갔을 텐데

> S + wish + s + had v-ed ~: ~했다면 좋을 텐데 (주절보다 앞선 시점)

10 Had it not been for antibiotics, medicine would not have made such
만약 항생제가 없었다면 / 의학은 이루지 못했을 것이다 / 그런
remarkable progress.
놀라운 발전을

> Had + s + v-ed ~, S + 조동사 과거형 + have v-ed ...: 만약 ~했다면, ...했을 텐데 /(= If it had not been for antibiotics, ~)

antibiotic 항생제
remarkable 놀라운, 주목할 만한

D **11** Without your donations, many more children would go hungry.
만약 너의 기부가 없다면 / 더욱 많은 아이들이 굶주리게 될 것이다
= If it were not for your donations, many more children would go hungry.
= Were it not for your donations, many more children would go hungry.

> Without + 명사(구), + 가정법 과거: 만약 ~이 없다면, ...할 텐데 /(= If it were not for ~, Were it not for ~)

donation 기부

12 You told me how the film ends; it would have been better if you had not
당신은 내게 그 영화가 어떻게 끝나는지 말했다 / (...이) 더 나았을 텐데 / 만약 당신이 내게 얘기
told me.
하지 않았다면
= I wish you hadn't told me how the film ends.
나는 좋을 텐데 / 당신이 내게 얘기하지 않았다면 / 그 영화가 어떻게 끝나는지

> If + s + had v-ed ~, S + 조동사 과거형 + have v-ed ...: 만약 ~했다면, ...했을 텐데
> S + wish + s + had v-ed ~: ~했다면 좋을 텐데 (주절보다 앞선 시점)
> — 이 문장에서 it은 if절을 가리킨다. if절은 보통 부사절로 가정의 의미를 나타내지만, 구어체에서 진주어로 사용될 수 있다.

13 I got caught in a traffic jam; **otherwise** I **would have been** here sooner.
나는 교통 체증에 걸렸다 / 그렇지 않았다면 / 나는 도착했을 텐데 / 여기에 더 일찍
= I got caught in a traffic jam; **if I had not got caught in a traffic jam**, I
나는 교통 체증에 걸렸다 / 내가 교통 체증에 걸리지 않았다면 /
would have been here sooner.
나는 도착했을 텐데 / 여기에 더 일찍

traffic jam 교통 체증

> Otherwise + S + 조동사 과거형 + have v-ed ~: 그렇지 않았다면 ~했을 텐데
> If + s + had + not + v-ed ~, S + 조동사 과거형 + have v-ed ...: 만약 ~하지 않았다면, ...했을 텐데

10

비교 구문

• Unit 45 원급 구문
• Unit 46 비교급 구문 1
• Unit 47 비교급 구문 2
• Unit 48 최상급 구문

■ 본격적인 구문 학습에 앞서, 각 유닛별 주요 단어를 확인하세요.

Unit 45

- ☐ poetry (집합적) 시
- ☐ absurd 어리석은; 불합리한
- ☐ manners 예의
- ☐ fortune 행운; 재산
- ☐ advantage 좋은 점, 이점

- ☐ depressed 우울한
- ☐ reassuring 안심시키는
- ☐ consequence 결과, 결론
- ☐ interaction 상호작용
- ☐ foresee 예측하다, 예견하다

- ☐ nearly 거의
- ☐ dense 밀집한, 고밀도의
- ☐ insomnia 불면증
- ☐ symptom 증상; 징후
- ☐ medication 약물; 투약

Unit 46

- ☐ infancy (발달의) 초기; 유아기
- ☐ humanity 인류; 인간성
- ☐ honorable 명예로운
- ☐ trustworthy 신뢰할 수 있는
- ☐ relentlessly 가차없이

- ☐ in terms of ~의 관점에서
- ☐ distinguished 유명한, 성공한
- ☐ purchase 얻다; 구입하다
- ☐ perpetual 끊임없는
- ☐ tedious 시시한, 따분한

- ☐ grain 곡물; 낟알
- ☐ equivalent 동등한, 상응하는
- ☐ observe (소견을) 말하다, 진술하다
- ☐ diameter 직경
- ☐ mind-wandering 멍한, 딴 생각하는

Unit 47

- ☐ tick (시계가 째깍째깍) 움직이다
- ☐ reed 갈대
- ☐ jigsaw puzzle 조각 그림 퍼즐
- ☐ struggle 안달복달하다
- ☐ call upon 요청하다

- ☐ blind 눈이 먼, 맹인의
- ☐ organic 유기 농법의
- ☐ plague 괴롭히다
- ☐ pest 해충
- ☐ conventional 재래 농법의

- ☐ discriminate 구별하다; 차별하다
- ☐ expose 노출시키다
- ☐ be better off 더 낫다
- ☐ subhuman 유인의, 사람에 가까운
- ☐ molecule 분자

Unit 48

- ☐ sincere 진실한, 진정한
- ☐ ignorance 무지
- ☐ conscientious 양심적인; 진지한
- ☐ stupidity 어리석음
- ☐ empower 힘을 더해 주다

- ☐ religion 종교
- ☐ institution 제도, 관습; 기관
- ☐ miserable 비참한, 불쌍한
- ☐ long 바라다, 갈망하다
- ☐ other than ~이 아닌

- ☐ resolve 해결하다
- ☐ phrase 말; 어구
- ☐ herald 알리다
- ☐ funny 신기한, 이상한
- ☐ timely 시기적절한, 때맞춘

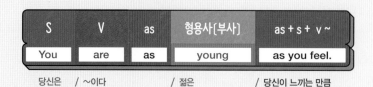

unit 45
원급 구문

S	V	as	형용사[부사]	as + s + v ~
You	are	as	young	as you feel.

당신은 / ~이다 / 젊은 / 당신이 느끼는 만큼

Standard Sentences

01 What you get by achieving your goals is **not as** important **as** what you
당신이 얻는 것은 / 당신의 목표를 성취함으로써 / 중요하지 않다 / 당신이 되는 것만큼
become by achieving your goals. *Zig Zigler*
/ 당신의 목표를 성취함으로써

■ not + as[so] + 형용사[부사] + as ~: ~만큼 …하지 않은[않게] / 주어로 쓰인 명사절 What ~ goals와 두 번째
as 뒤의 what ~ goals가 비교되고 있다.

02 The human brain cell can hold **five times as** much information **as** the
인간의 뇌세포는 보유할 수 있다 / 5배 많은 정보를 / 브리태니커
Encyclopaedia Britannica.
백과사전보다

■ 배수사 + as + 형용사 + as ~: ~보다 몇 배 더 …한

A **03** To ask what is the use of poetry should be **as** absurd **as** asking what is the
묻는 것은 / 시의 효용이 무엇인지를 / 아마 어리석을 것이다 / 묻는 것만큼 / 무지개나 바다
use of a rainbow, or the sea, or a nice dress. *Cecil Day-Lewis*
또는 근사한 옷의 효용이 무엇인지를

■ as + 형용사 + as ~: ~만큼 …한 / 주어로 쓰인 to부정사구 To ask ~ poetry와 동명사구 asking ~ dress가 비교
되고 있다.

poetry (집합적) 시 *cf.* poem
(한 편의) 시
absurd 어리석은; 불합리한

04 The International Space Station is **almost four times as** large **as** the Russian
국제 우주 정거장은 거의 네 배만큼 크다 / 러시아의 우주 정거장
space station Mir and **about five times as** large **as** the U.S. Skylab.
Mir보다 / 그리고 약 5배만큼 크다 / 미국의 스카이랩보다

■ 배수사 + as + 형용사 + as ~: ~보다 몇 배 더 …한

space station 우주 정거장

05 It is important **not so much** to give a man bread, **as** to put him in the way of
(…은) 중요하다 / 어떤 사람에게 빵을 주는 것보다는 / 오히려 그 사람이 스스로 그 빵을 얻을 수
earning it for himself.
있도록 해주는 것이

■ not so much A as B: A라기보다는 오히려 B / 진주어로 쓰인 to give a man bread와 as 뒤의 to put ~
himself가 비교되고 있다.

put A in the way of A가
~할 수 있도록 해주다
earn 얻다

B 06 A person's choice and use of words tells **as** much about him or her **as do**
어떤 사람의 단어 선택과 사용은 말한다 / 그 사람에 대해 많이 / 예의,

manners, dress, and general behavior.
복장, 그리고 일반적인 행동이 말하는 만큼

> as + 부사 + as + v + s: ~만큼 …하게 / 두 번째 as 뒤에 주어와 동사가 도치되었으며, do는 tell을 대신한다.

manners 예의, 예절
general 일반적인

07 Happiness is produced **not so much** by great pieces of good fortune **that**
행복은 만들어진다 / 행운이라는 큰 조각들에 의해서가 아니라 / [드물

seldom happen, **as** by little advantages that occur every day. *Benjamin Franklin*
게 생기는] / 작은 좋은 점들에 의해서 / [매일 일어나는]

> not so much A as B: A라기보다 오히려 B
> great ~ fortune과 little advantages가 각각 주격 관계대명사 that이 이끄는 형용사절의 수식을 받는다.

fortune 행운; 재산
seldom 드물게, 좀처럼 ~ 않는
happen 생기다, 발생하다
(= occur)
advantage 좋은 점, 이점

08 While people today have **twice as** much spending power **as** they did in the
오늘날 사람들이 두 배 더 많은 구매력을 가지고 있는 반면에 / 그들이 1950년대에 그랬던

1950s, they are ten times more likely to be depressed.
것보다 / 그들은 10배 더 우울한 것 같다

> 배수사 + as + 형용사 + as ~: ~보다 몇 배 더 …한 / 두 번째 as 뒤에 did는 대동사로 had를 대신한다.

depressed 우울한, 의기소침한

09 A hero can be anyone, even a man doing something **as** simple and reassuring
영웅은 누구든지 될 수 있다 / 심지어 어떤 사람도 / [간단하고 안심시켜주는 무언가를 하는

as putting a coat on a young boy's shoulders to let him know that the world
/ 어린 소년의 어깨에 외투를 걸쳐주는 것만큼 / 그에게 알려주기 위해서 / 세상이 끝나지 않았다는

hadn't ended. *the movie <The Dark Knight Rises>*
것을]

> as + 형용사 + as ~: ~만큼 …한 / a man을 수식하는 doing something과 putting 이하가 비교되고 있다.
> anyone 뒤의 even a man 이하의 어구는 콤마로 anyone과 동격의 관계를 나타낸다. **Unit 52**

reassuring 안심시키는, 불안
감을 없애 주는

C 10 The consequences of interaction can be difficult to foresee because they
[모의] 상호작용의 결과는 예측하기 어려울 수 있다 / 왜냐하면 그것들은

depend **as** much on the behavior of others **as** on oneself.
타인의 행동에 많이 달려 있기 때문이다 / 자기 자신에 만큼

> [풀이] as + 부사 + as ~: ~만큼 …하게
> 전치사구 on the behavior of others와 on oneself가 비교되고 있다.

consequence 결과, 결론
interaction 상호작용
foresee 예측하다, 예견하다

11 Singapore has nearly 8,000 people per km^2, and is **more than 200 times as**
싱가포르는 평방킬로미터 당 거의 8,000명을 보유하고 있다 / 그리고 200배 이상 밀집되어 있다

dense **as** the U.S.
/ 미국보다

> [풀이] 배수사와 함께 쓰인 원급 구문에서 is의 보어가 들어갈 자리이므로 형용사 dense가 적절하다.
> more than은 '~ 이상의'라는 뜻으로 배수사를 꾸며주고 있다.

nearly 거의
dense 밀집한, 고밀도의

12 Most insomnia is **not** an illness or a physical condition **so much as** a
대부분 불면증은 질환이나 건강 문제가 아니다 / 오히려 다른 문제에

symptom of another problem that may simply be a reaction to certain
대한 증상(이다) / [단순히 특정한 약물에 대한 반응

medications, anxiety about travel, or stress before a job interview.
/ 여행에 대한 불안 / 또는 취업 면접 전의 스트레스일 수 있는]

> [풀이] not A so much as B: A라기보다는 오히려 B

insomnia 불면증
condition (몸의) 문제, 질병
symptom 증상; 징후
anxiety 불안; 갈망

unit 46
비교급 구문 1

S	V	비교급	than ~
Prevention	is	better	than cure.
예방은	/ ~이다	/ 더 나은	/ 치료보다

Standard Sentences

01 According to recent research, the universe is expanding **faster** today **than**
최근의 연구에 의하면 / 우주는 오늘날 더 빠르게 팽창하고 있다 / 우주가
it did in its infancy.
초기에 그랬던 것보다

■ 비교급 + than ~: ~보다 더 …한[하게]

infancy (발달의) 초기; 유아기

02 The energy in sunlight arriving on earth contains **about twelve thousand**
햇빛 속의 에너지는 / [지구에 도달하는] / 약 12,000배 더 많은 에너지를 포함하고 있다
times more energy **than** humanity uses in a year.
/ 인류가 1년에 사용하는 에너지보다

■ 배수사 + 비교급 + than ~: ~보다 몇 배 더 …한[하게]

humanity 인류; 인간성

A 03 It is **more important** to be honorable and trustworthy **than** to look important
(…은) 더 중요하다 / 명예롭고 신뢰할 수 있는 것은 / 대단해 보이는 것보다
for one small minute.
/ 짧은 순간 동안에

■ 비교급 + than ~: ~보다 더 …한[하게]
— It은 가주어이고 to be honorable and trustworthy가 진주어이다.

honorable 명예로운
trustworthy 신뢰할 수 있는

04 Learning to study effectively is **even more important than** merely acquiring
효과적으로 공부하는 것을 배우는 것이 / 훨씬 더 중요하다 / 단지 특정한 양의 정보를 습득하는
a particular body of information.
것보다

■ 비교급 강조 부사(even) + 비교급 + than ~: ~보다 훨씬 더 …한[하게] / 비교급 앞에 even, far, much, still, a lot을 써서 '훨씬 더 ~한'의 의미로 강조할 수 있다.

merely 단지
body of ~의 (많은) 양, 모음

모의 05 Champion golfers are **much less likely than** average golfers to blame their
챔피언 골프 선수들은 일반 골프 선수들보다 자신들의 문제들을 훨씬 덜 탓할 것 같다
problems on the weather, the course, or chance factors. Instead they focus
/ 날씨, 코스, 또는 뜻밖의 요소에 대해 / 대신에 그들은 가차없이 초점을
relentlessly on their own performance.
맞춘다 / 자신들의 실력에

■ 비교급 강조 부사(much) + less + 원급 + than ~: ~보다 덜 …한[하게]

average 일반의, 보통의
blame A on B A를 B의 탓으로 돌리다
chance 뜻밖의, 우연한
factor 요소
relentlessly 가차없이, 냉정하게

B **06** Medical procedures may sound `scarier` when `presented in terms of the risk
의료 시술은 더 무섭게 들릴 수도 있다 / 제시될 때 / 사망 위험의 관점에서
of dying, rather **than** the likelihood of coming through unharmed.
/ 무사히 성공할 가능성보다

> ▪ 비교급 + than ~: ~보다 더 …한[하게]
> ▪ 접속사 when과 presented 사이에 they are가 생략되어 있으며, they는 Medical procedures를 가리킨다.

procedure (의학) 시술, 수술
in terms of ~의 관점에서
likelihood 가능성
come through 성공하다, 극복하다
unharmed 무사한

07 We are always `more anxious to be distinguished for a talent which we do not
우리는 늘 유명해지기를 더욱 열망한다 / 한 가지 재능으로 / [우리가 갖고 있지 않은]
possess, **than** to be praised for the fifteen which we `do possess. *Mark Twain*
/ 15개의 재능으로 칭찬받기보다는 / [우리가 정말 가지고 있는]

> ▪ 비교급 + than ~: ~보다 더 …한[하게] / 보어로 쓰인 to be distinguished와 to be praised가 비교되고 있다.
> ▪ which we do possess의 do는 강조의 의미를 더하는 조동사로 쓰였다.

anxious 열망하는; 불안해하는
distinguished 유명한, 성공한

08 What some call health, `if purchased by perpetual anxiety about diet, isn't
일부가 건강이라고 부르는 것이 / 만약 식단에 대한 끊임없는 불안으로 얻어지는 것이라면 / 훨씬
`much better than tedious disease. *George Prentice*
더 좋지는 않다 / 시시한 병보다

> ▪ 비교급 강조 부사(much) + 비교급 + than ~: ~보다 훨씬 더 …한[하게] / 비교급 표현 앞에 not이 있어서 '훨씬 더 좋지는 않다'는 부정의 의미를 나타낸다.
> ▪ if ~ diet는 삽입어구인데, 접속사 if가 부가된 분사구문 또는 if 다음에 'it is'가 생략된 부사절로 볼 수 있다. **○ Unit 53, 54**

purchase 얻다; 구입하다
perpetual 끊임없는; 영원한
tedious 시시한, 따분한

모의 **09** It takes `two to six times more grain to produce food value through animals
(…은) 두 배에서 여섯 배 더 많은 곡물을 필요로 한다 / 영양가를 만들어 내는 것은 / 동물을 통해서
than to get the equivalent value directly from plants.
/ 직접 동등한 영양가를 얻는 것보다 / 식물에서

> ▪ 배수사 + 비교급 + than ~: ~보다 몇 배 더 …한[하게] / 진주어로 쓰인 to produce ~ animals와 than 뒤의 to get ~ plants가 비교되고 있다.

grain 곡물; 낟알
food value (식품의) 영양가
equivalent 동등한, 상응하는

> **Know More** 미국 농무부는 소고기 1kg을 생산하는 데 곡물 10~12kg과 10만 ℓ의 물이 필요하며, 닭고기 1kg을 생산하는 데는 곡물 2~3kg과 3500 ℓ의 물이 필요하다고 밝혔다. 또한 전 세계에서 수확되는 곡물의 3분의 1이 가축을 위한 사료로 쓰인다는 통계도 있다. 브라질 아마존 강 유역은 매년 목초지로 개발되고 있으며, 여기서 생산되는 곡물들은 유럽과 일본으로 수출되어 가축의 사료로 쓰인다. 여러 환경운동가들은 물 부족과 무분별한 산림 개발로 인해 생태계가 파괴될 것이라고 경고하고 있다.

C **10** Astronomers observe that the sun's diameter is **more than one hundred**
천문학자들은 말한다 / 태양의 직경은 100배 이상 더 크다고
times larger than the earth's.
/ 지구의 직경보다

> ▪ 배수사 + 비교급 + than ~: ~보다 몇 배 더 …한 / the earth's 뒤에 diameter가 생략되었다.

observe (소견을) 말하다, 진술하다; 관찰하다
diameter 직경

11 Insights are **far more likely** to come when you are in the mind-wandering
통찰력은 생길 가능성이 훨씬 더 높다 / 당신이 멍한 상태일 때
mode **than** in the task-focused mode.
/ 과제에 집중하는 상태일 때보다

> ▪ 비교급 강조 부사(far) + 비교급 + than ~: ~보다 훨씬 더 …한

insight 통찰력, 직관
mind-wandering 멍한, 딴 생각하는

12 Big cars that use a lot of petrol are **less popular** now **than** twenty years ago.
대형차들은 / [많은 휘발유를 사용하는] / 현재 덜 인기가 있다 / 20년 전보다

> ▪ less + 원급 + than ~: ~보다 덜 …한

petrol 휘발유, 가솔린

unit 47
비교급 구문 2

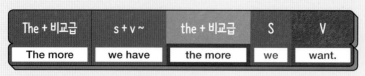

The + 비교급	s + v ~	the + 비교급	S	V
The more	we have	the more	we	want.

더 많은 것을 / 우리가 가질수록 / 더 많은 것을 / 우리는 / 원한다

Standard Sentences

01 *The more we use certain parts of our brain, *the more developed and
더 많이 / 우리가 뇌의 특정 부분들을 사용할수록 / 더욱더 발달하고 더 효율적으로
efficient those parts of the brain become.
/ 뇌의 그 부분들이 된다

- the + 비교급 ~, the + 비교급 ...: ~하면 할수록, 더욱더 …하다 / (= As we use certain parts of our brain more, those parts of the brain become more developed and efficient.)

02 A collection of facts is *no more science **than** a dictionary is poetry.
사실들의 모음은 과학이 아니다 / 사전이 시가 아닌 것만큼

collection 모음, 수집

- A no more ~ than B ...: A가 ~이 아닌 것은 B가 …이 아닌 것과 같다 / (= A collection of facts is not science any more than a dictionary is poetry. = Just as a dictionary is not poetry, a collection of facts is not science.)

A **03** According to Einstein's Special Theory of Relativity, *the faster a spaceship
아인슈타인의 특수 상대성 이론에 따르면 / 우주선이 더 빠르게 갈수록
goes, *the slower its clock ticks and the shorter its length in the direction of
/ 그것의 시계는 더 느리게 움직인다 / 그리고 그것의 이동 방향의 길이가 더 짧아진다
travel gets.

tick (시계가 째깍째깍) 움직이다
length 길이
travel 이동; 여행

- the + 비교급 ~, the + 비교급 ...: ~하면 할수록, 더욱더 …하다

04 Man is *no more than a reed, the weakest in nature, **but** he is a thinking
인간은 갈대에 불과하다 / 자연에서 가장 연약한 존재 / 그러나 그는 생각하는 갈대이다
reed. *Blaise Pascal*

reed 갈대

- no more than: ~일 뿐(= only)
- a reed 뒤의 명사구 the weakest in nature는 콤마로 연결되어 a reed와 동격을 이루고 있다.

05 Air pollution does *no less harm to birds and animals **than** it does to human
대기 오염은 조류와 동물에게 마찬가지로 해를 끼친다 / 그것이 인간에게 해를 끼치는 것과
beings.

harm 해, 손상

- A no less ~ than B ...: A가 ~인 것은 B가 …인 것과 같다, A는 B와 마찬가지로 ~이다

B **06** Anyone who has tried to complete a jigsaw puzzle as the clock ticked on
누구든 / [조각 그림 퍼즐을 완성하려고 애썼던] / 시계가 마감 시간을 향해 째깍째깍
toward a deadline knows that **the more** they struggle to find the missing
움직일 때] / 안다 / 그들이 더욱더 안달복달할수록 / 빠진 조각들을 찾느라
pieces, **the harder** it is to find them.
/ 더욱더 힘들다는 것을 / 그것들을 찾는 것이

- the + 비교급 ~, the + 비교급 ...: ~하면 할수록, 더욱더 …하다
- the harder가 이끄는 절에서 it은 가주어이며, to find them이 진주어이다.

complete 완성하다
jigsaw puzzle 조각 그림 퍼즐
struggle 안달복달하다, 몸부림치다

07 We have called upon the people to set their air conditioners at **no lower**
우리는 사람들에게 그들의 에어컨을 설정하도록 요청해왔다 / 여름에는 섭씨
than 28 degrees Celsius in the summer and **no higher than** 20 in the winter.
28도보다 조금도 낮지 않게 / 그리고 겨울에는 20도보다 조금도 높지 않게

- no + 비교급 + than ~: ~보다 조금도 …하지 않은(않게)

call upon 요청하다
degree (온도의) 도; 정도
Celsius 섭씨

08 We can **no more** explain a passion to a person who has never experienced
우리는 어떤 이에게 열정을 설명할 수 없다 / [그것을 한 번도 경험하지 않은]
it **than** we can explain light to the blind. *T. S. Eliot*
/ 마치 우리가 눈이 먼 사람에게 빛을 설명할 수 없는 것만큼

- A no more ~ than B ...: A가 ~이 아닌 것은 B가 …이 아닌 것과 같다

passion 열정
blind 눈이 먼, 맹인의

> **Know More** 미국계 영국인인 T. S. 엘리엇은 20세기 모더니즘에 지대한 영향을 끼친 시인·극작가·문학평론가로 시어·문체·운율 등을 실험하여 영국 시에 활력을 불어넣었고 '4개의 4중주(Four Quartets)'로 1948년에 메리트 훈장과 노벨 문학상'을 받았다.

모에 **09** Organic farmers grow crops that are **no less plagued** by pests **than** those
유기 농법을 사용하는 농부들은 작물을 재배한다 / [마찬가지로 해충에 시달리는 / 재래 농법을
of conventional farmers; insects generally do not discriminate between
사용하는 농부들의 작물과] / 곤충들은 대개 구별하지 않는다 / 유기 농법인지
organic and conventional as well as we do.
재래 농법인지를 / 우리가 그런 것만큼 잘

- A no less ~ than B ...: A가 ~인 것은 B가 …인 것과 같다, A는 B와 마찬가지로 ~이다
- as well as 이하는 원급 구문이며, do는 discriminate를 대신한 대동사로 쓰였다.

organic 유기 농법의
plague 괴롭히다; 전염병
pest 해충
conventional 재래 농법의; 전통적인
discriminate 구별하다; 차별하다

C **10** **The closer** the people in the world become, **the more frequently** they are
세상 사람들이 더 가까워질수록 / 그들은 더욱더 자주 노출된다
exposed to people from other cultures.
/ 다른 문화권의 사람들에게

- 풀이 the + 비교급 ~, the + 비교급 ...: ~하면 할수록, 더욱더 …하다

expose 노출시키다

11 If all our knowledge stopped at the level of the senses, we would be **no**
만약 우리의 모든 지식이 멈춘다면 / 감각의 수준에서 / 우리는 조금도 더 낫지
better off than the subhuman members of the animal kingdom.
않을 것이다 / 동물 세계의 유인원보다

- 풀이 no + 비교급 + than ~: ~보다 조금도 …하지 않은(않게)
- 현재 사실과 반대로 가정하는 가정법 과거의 문장이다.

be better off 더 낫다, 더 좋은 상태이다
subhuman 유인의, 사람에 가까운

Up! **12** Mind is **not** to be found in molecules **any more than** the works of Shakespeare
정신은 분자 속에서 발견될 수 없다 / 셰익스피어의 작품들이 그의 유전자 속에서 발견될
were to be found in his genes.
수 없었던 것만큼

- 풀이 A not ~ any more than B ...: A가 ~이 아닌 것은 B가 …이 아닌 것과 같다 (= A no more ~ than B ...)

molecule 분자
work (집합적) 작품

unit 48
최상급 구문

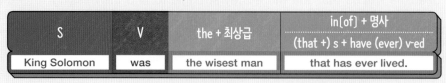

S	V	the + 최상급	in[of] + 명사 (that +) s + have (ever) v-ed
King Solomon	was	the wisest man	that has ever lived.

솔로몬 왕은 / ~이었다 / 가장 현명한 사람 / [여태껏 살았던 사람들 중]

Standard Sentences

01 Global warming is considered to be the most serious threat facing humanity
지구온난화는 여겨진다 / 가장 심각한 위협으로 / [인류를 향한]
by many environmentalists.
/ 많은 환경 운동가들에 의해

■ the + 최상급 + 명사: 가장 ~한 …

humanity 인류; 인간성
environmentalist 환경
운동가, 환경 보호가

02 Nothing in all the world is more dangerous than sincere ignorance and
세상의 어떤 것도 더 위험하지는 않다 / 성실하면서 무지한 것과
conscientious stupidity. *Martin Luther King Jr.*
양심적이면서 어리석은 것보다

■ 부정 주어 + ~ 비교급 + than …: 어떤 것도 …보다 더 ~하지 않은

sincere 진실한, 진정한
ignorance 무지
conscientious 양심적인;
진지한
stupidity 어리석음

Ⓐ 03 Personal computers have become the most empowering tool we've ever
개인용 컴퓨터는 되었다 / 가장 힘을 더해 주는 도구가 / [우리가 지금껏
created. *Bill Gates*
만들어 낸 것 중]

■ the + 최상급 + (that +) s + have (ever) v-ed: (지금껏) ~해 본 중에서 가장 …한 / 「the + 최상급」 뒤의 that은 목
적격 관계대명사로 종종 생략된다.

empower 힘을 더해 주다; 권
한을 주다

04 Next to religion, baseball has had a greater impact on our American way of
종교 다음으로 / 야구는 우리 미국인의 생활 방식에 더 큰 영향을 미쳐왔다
life than any other American institution. *Herbert Hoover*
/ 다른 어떤 미국의 제도보다

■ 비교급 + than + any other + 단수 명사: 다른 어떤 ~보다 더 …한

religion 종교
institution 제도, 관습; 기관

05 No other writer's plays have been produced so many times or read so
다른 어떤 작가의 희곡도 여러 번 상연되거나 널리 읽히지 않았다
widely in so many countries as Shakespeare's.
/ 아주 많은 국가에서 / 셰익스피어의 희곡만큼

■ 부정 주어 + ~ so + 원급 + as …: 어떤 것도 …만큼 ~하지 않은 / (= Shakespeare's plays have been
produced the most times and read the most widely in so many countries.)

produce 상연하다

06 Nobody is **so** miserable **as** he who longs to be somebody and something
어느 누구도 비참하지는 않다 / 사람만큼 / [누군가 그리고 무언가가 되기를 바라는
other than the person he is in body and mind. *Angelo Patri*
/ 자기 자신이 아닌 / 몸과 마음에서]

■ 부정 주어 + ~ so + 원급 + as ...: 어떤 것도 …만큼 ~하지 않은
─ the person 다음에는 관계대명사 who 또는 that이 생략되었다.

miserable 비참한, 불쌍한
long 바라다, 갈망하다
other than ~이 아닌, ~ 이
외의

07 One of **the hardest** things in this world is to admit you are wrong. And
이 세상에서 가장 어려운 것들 중의 하나는 / 받아들이는 것이다 / 당신이 틀렸다는 것을 그리고
nothing is more helpful in resolving a situation **than** its frank admission.
어떤 것도 더 도움이 되지는 않는다 / 어떤 상황을 해결하는 데 / 그것의 솔직한 인정보다 *Benjamin Disraeli*

■ the + 최상급 + 명사 + in + 명사: ~에서 가장 …한
■ 부정 주어 + ~ 비교급 + than ...: 어떤 것도 …보다 더 ~하지 않은

admit 인정하다 *cf.* admission
인정
resolve 해결하다; 결심하다
frank 솔직한

08 **The most exciting** phrase to hear in science, the one that heralds new
가장 흥미진진한 말은 / [과학에서 듣는] / 즉 새로운 발견을 알리는 말은
discoveries, is not "Eureka!"(I found it!) but "That's funny." *Isaac Asimov*
/ '유레카!'(내가 그걸 찾았어!)가 아니라 '그거 신기하네'이다

■ the + 최상급 + 명사 + 범위: ~ 중에서 가장 …한
─ the one ~ discoveries는 앞의 어구와 콤마로 연결된 동격 어구이다.

phrase 말; 어구
herald 알리다; 예고하다
not A but B A가 아니라 B
funny 신기한, 이상한; 재미있는

09 The Amazon's aquatic life, such as freshwater dolphins, 400-pound catfish,
아마존의 수생 생물은 / 민물 돌고래, 400 파운드의 메기, 거대한 뱀장어와 같은
giant eels, is **larger and more diverse than** that of **all the other** river
/ 더 크고 더 다양하다 / 세계의 다른 모든 하천 수생 생물보다
systems in the world.

■ 비교급 + than + all the other + 복수 명사: 다른 모든 ~보다 더 …한
─ that은 aquatic life를 대신하는 지시대명사로 쓰였다.

aquatic 수생의, 물의
freshwater 민물에 사는; 민
물의
catfish 메기
eel 뱀장어
diverse 다양한

10 Of all the wonderful and unique characteristics of man, his ability to communicate
인간의 모든 놀랍고 독특한 특성들 중에서 / 인간의 의사소통 능력은
through the use of language is perhaps **the most important**.
/ [언어의 사용을 통한] / 아마 가장 중요할 것이다

풀이 the + 최상급 + of + 명사: ~ 중에서 가장 …한
■ 최상급의 범위를 나타내는 of 이하의 전치사구가 강조를 위해 문장의 맨 앞에 쓰였다.

characteristic 특성; 특징적인

11 Although humans are not the only animals who use tools, our species has
비록 인간이 유일한 동물은 아닐지라도 / [도구를 사용하는] / 인류는 이 기술을 발전시
developed this skill to a **far greater** extent **than any other** animal.
켜왔다 / 훨씬 더 훌륭한 정도로 / 다른 어떤 동물보다

풀이 비교급 강조부사(far) + 비교급 + than + any other + 단수 명사: 다른 어떤 ~보다 훨씬 더 …한

species (the ~, our ~) 인류;
(분류상의) 종
to ~ extent ~한 정도로

12 In today's industry, where technology and speed of information are critical
오늘날의 산업에서 / 거기서는 기술과 정보의 속도가 중대한 요소인데
factors, **nothing** is **more valuable** to our clients **than** providing timely and
/ 어떤 것도 우리의 고객에게 더 유용하지는 않다 / 시기적절하고 정확한 정보를 제공하는 것보다
accurate information.

풀이 부정 주어 + ~ 비교급 + than ...: 어떤 것도 …보다 더 ~하지 않은

critical 중대한; 비판적인
valuable 유용한; 가치 있는
client 고객
timely 시기적절한, 때맞춘
accurate 정확한

Chapter 10

Review

A

01 An individual neuron sending a signal in the brain uses **as** much energy **as** a
개별적인 뉴런은 / [뇌에서 신호를 보내는] / 많은 에너지를 사용한다 / 다리

leg muscle cell running a marathon.
근육 세포만큼 / [마라톤을 뛰는]

> ▪ as + 형용사 + as ~: ~만큼 …한
> ▪ An individual neuron과 a leg muscle cell은 각각 sending과 running이 이끄는 형용사구의 수식을 받는다.

individual 개별적인; 개인의
signal 신호

02 Knowledge can **no more** be planted in the human mind without labor **than** a
지식은 심겨질 수 없다 / 인간의 정신 속에 / 노력 없이 / 밀밭이

field of wheat can be produced without the previous use of the plow.
만들어질 수 없는 것만큼 / 쟁기를 먼저 쓰지 않고서

> ▪ A no more ~ than B …: A가 ~이 아닌 것은 B가 …이 아닌 것과 같다

plant 심다
wheat 밀
previous 먼저의, 이전의
plow 쟁기; (밭을) 갈다

(수능!) 03 126 different studies of more than 36,000 people found that **the more prone**
36,000명 이상의 사람들에 대한 126개의 여러 연구들이 밝혀냈다 / 어떤 사람이 불안해하는

to anxieties a person is, **the poorer** his or her academic performance is.
성향일수록 / 그 사람의 학업 성취는 더 떨어진다는 것을

> ▪ the + 비교급 ~, the + 비교급 …: ~하면 할수록, 더욱더 …하다

prone to ~하는 경향이 있는,
~하기 쉬운
academic performance 학
업 성취

04 There is **no other** quality **so** essential to success of any kind **as** the quality of
다른 어떤 자질은 없다 / [어떤 종류의 성공에 필수적인] / 끈기라는 자질만큼

perseverance. It overcomes almost everything, even nature. *John D. Rockefeller*
그것은 거의 모든 것을 극복한다 / 심지어 본성조차도

> ▪ 부정 주어 + ~ as[so] + 원급 + as …: 어떤 것도 …만큼 ~하지 않은
> ▪ almost는 부사이지만 한정적으로 쓰여 뒤에 온 everything을 수식해 준다.

quality 자질; 특성
perseverance 끈기, 인내

B

05 Solids, like wood for example, transfer sound waves **much better than** air
고체는 / 예를 들어 목재와 같은 / 음파를 훨씬 더 잘 전달한다 / 공기가

typically does because the molecules in a solid substance are **much closer**
일반적으로 하는 것보다 / 왜냐하면 고체 물질 속 분자들은 훨씬 더 가깝기 때문이다

and **more tightly** packed together **than** they are in air.
/ 그리고 더욱 밀집되게 채워져 있기 (때문이다) / 그것들이 공기 속에서 그런 것보다

> **풀이** (A) 주절의 동사가 일반동사인 transfer이므로 than 뒤의 대동사로 does가 적절하다.
> (B) 앞에 비교급인 closer와 more tightly가 쓰였으므로, 이와 짝을 이루는 than이 적절하다.

solid 고체
transfer 전달하다
typically 일반적으로, 보통은
molecule 분자
substance 물질

(수능!) 06 **The more effectively** parents communicate their loving authority, **the more**
더 효과적으로 / 부모들이 자신의 애정 어린 권위를 전할수록 / 더 안전하게

secure the child feels.
/ 그 자녀는 느낀다

> **풀이** (A) 「the + 비교급 ~, the + 비교급 …」 구문으로, 동사 communicate를 수식하는 부사 effectively가 적절하다.
> (B) 동사 feels의 보어에 해당하므로 형용사 secure가 적절하다.

authority 권위, 권한
secure 안전한, 확실한

모의 07 The brain's running costs are **about eight to ten times as** high, per unit
뇌의 유지 비용은 약 8~10배 높다 / 단위 질량당
mass, **as** those of the body's muscles.
/ 신체 근육의 유지 비용보다

running cost 유지비
per ~당, ~마다
unit 단위
mass 질량; 다수

> **풀이** 「배수사 + as + 형용사[부사] + as ~」의 원급 구문이 쓰여 뇌와 신체 근육의 유지 비용을 비교하고 있으므로,
> 앞에 나온 명사 running costs를 대신하는 지시대명사로 복수형인 those가 적절하다.

08 Having children makes you **no more** a parent **than** having a piano makes
자녀가 있는 것은 당신을 부모로 만들지 않는다 / 피아노가 있는 것이 당신을 피아니스트로
you a pianist.
만들지 않는 것만큼

> **풀이** 「A no more ~ than B ... (A가 ~이 아닌 것은 B가 …이 아닌 것과 같다)」 구문이 쓰였으며, 그 자체로 주절과
> than이 이끄는 절 둘 다를 부정하므로 than 다음에 부정어를 중복하여 쓰지 않는다.

C 09 Recycling plastic saves **twice as** much energy **as** it takes to burn it.
플라스틱을 재활용하는 것은 절약시켜 준다 / 두 배 많은 에너지를 / 그것을 소각하는 데 필요로 하는 것보다

> **풀이** 배수사 + as + 형용사[부사] + as ~ : ~보다 몇 배 더 …한[하게]

10 **The more** experience you have, **the more** job opportunities you'll find.
더 많은 경험을 / 네가 가질수록 / 더 많은 일자리 기회를 / 너는 찾을 것이다

> **풀이** the + 비교급, the + 비교급 ...: ~하면 할수록, 더욱더 …하다

11 No bread in the world is **so** sweet **as** that earned by his own labor.
세상의 어떤 빵도 달콤하지 않다 / 자신의 노동으로 얻은 빵만큼

labor 노동, 수고, 노력

> **풀이** 부정 주어 ~ + so + 원급 + as ...: 어떤 것도 …만큼 ~하지 않은
> --
> → that은 bread를 대신하는 지시대명사이며, 뒤에 온 과거분사구의 수식을 받는다.

D 12 Fear defeats **more** people **than any other** one thing in the world.
두려움은 패배시킨다 / 더 많은 사람들을 / 세상에서 다른 어떤 것보다
= **Nothing** in the world defeats **so many** people **as** fear.
세상의 어떤 것도 패배시키지 않는다 / 많은 사람들을 / 두려움만큼

defeat 패배시키다

> **풀이** 최상급의 의미를 나타내는 「비교급 + than + any other + 단수 명사」는 「부정 주어 + ~ so + 원급 + as ...」로
> 쓸 수 있다.

13 Just as a horse is not a fish, a whale is not a fish either.
말이 물고기가 아닌 것처럼 / 고래도 또한 물고기가 아니다
= A whale is **no more** a fish **than** a horse is.
고래가 물고기가 아닌 것은 말이 물고기가 아닌 것과 같다
= A whale is **not** a fish **any more than** a horse is.
고래가 물고기가 아닌 것은 말이 물고기가 아닌 것과 같다

> **풀이** 양쪽의 부정을 나타내는 표현은 「A no more ~ than B ...」나 「A not ~ any more than B ...」로 쓸 수 있다.

14 She is a realist **rather than** a pessimist.
그녀는 오히려 현실주의자이다 / 비관론자라기보다는
= She is **not so much** a pessimist **as** a realist.
그녀는 비관론자라기보다는 / 현실주의자이다
= She is **not** a pessimist **so much as** a realist.
그녀는 비관론자라기보다는 / 현실주의자이다

realist 현실주의자
pessimist 비관주의자

> **풀이** 「B rather than A」 구문은 「not so much A as B」나 「not A so much as B」로 쓸 수 있다.

Chapter 11

특수 구문

- Unit 49 도치 구문 1
- Unit 50 도치 구문 2
- Unit 51 강조 구문
- Unit 52 동격 구문
- Unit 53 삽입 구문
- Unit 54 생략·공통 구문

■ 본격적인 구문 학습에 앞서, 각 유닛별 주요 단어를 확인하세요.

Unit 49

- ☐ trustworthy 신뢰할 수 있는
- ☐ ecology 생태학
- ☐ triumph 업적
- ☐ third party 제3자
- ☐ express 명시된
- ☐ fundamental 원리; 근본적인
- ☐ abstract 추상적인
- ☐ misspell 철자를 틀리다
- ☐ at the expense of ~을 희생하여
- ☐ meadow 목초지
- ☐ dotted 점점이 있는
- ☐ contented 만족한

Unit 50

- ☐ equation 방정식, 등식
- ☐ gaze 응시하다
- ☐ in awe 경탄하며
- ☐ atomic 원자의
- ☐ existing 기존의
- ☐ sniff 코를 킁킁거리다
- ☐ odor 냄새
- ☐ vessel 용기, 그릇
- ☐ on earth 도대체
- ☐ in terms of ~의 관점에서
- ☐ offensive 공격 태세; 공격적인
- ☐ unconscious 무의식

Unit 51

- ☐ fatal 결정적인
- ☐ count 중요하다
- ☐ untiring 지칠 줄 모르는
- ☐ unwilling 마음이 내키지 않는
- ☐ heritage 유산
- ☐ artefact 인공물
- ☐ the former 전자
- ☐ the latter 후자
- ☐ infinity 무한
- ☐ biography 전기
- ☐ deprive A of B A에게서 B를 빼앗다
- ☐ brilliant 눈부신, 반짝반짝 빛나는

Unit 52

- ☐ brain wave 뇌파
- ☐ frequency 진동수
- ☐ moderate 적당한
- ☐ voltage 전압
- ☐ reciprocally 서로
- ☐ devise 고안하다
- ☐ observe 관찰하다
- ☐ jack-of-all-trades 만물박사
- ☐ distort 왜곡하다
- ☐ hype 과장 광고, 과대 선전
- ☐ warrant 보장하다
- ☐ ground 이유; 땅

Unit 53

- ☐ fallacy 오류
- ☐ aura 기운, 분위기
- ☐ undeserved 자격이 없는
- ☐ idealist 이상주의자, 공상가
- ☐ humble 겸손한; 보잘 것 없는
- ☐ inexhaustible 무궁무진한
- ☐ remedy 치료하다
- ☐ reliably 확실하게, 믿을 수 있게
- ☐ resemble 닮다
- ☐ liable ~하기 쉬운
- ☐ acquire (몸에) 익히다, 지니게 되다
- ☐ acquaintance 지인, 아는 사람

Unit 54

- ☐ object 목적, 목표
- ☐ extend 연장하다
- ☐ appealing 매력적인
- ☐ adequate 적절한, 충분한
- ☐ myth 신화; 통념
- ☐ faith 신앙, 신념
- ☐ realm 영역
- ☐ tragic 매우 슬픈, 비극적인
- ☐ stand up to ~에게 맞서다
- ☐ immediate 즉각적인
- ☐ concern 관심사
- ☐ be convinced of ~을 확신하다

unit 49
도치 구문 1

부정의 어구	be동사	S	~
	조동사	S	본동사	
Never	will	I	forget	your kindness.

결코 ~ 않는 / ~할 것이다 / 나는 / 잊지 / 너의 친절을

Standard Sentences

01 **On no account** must you give your banking details to anyone over the
결코 당신은 당신의 은행 정보를 줘서는 안 된다   / 누군가에게   / 전화로 또는
phone or by email.
이메일로

  ■ 부정의 어구 (On no account) + 조동사 + S + 본동사

on no account 결코[무
슨 일이 있어도] ~ 않는

02 **Trustworthy** are those who give not only compliments but also bitter
신뢰할 수 있는 것은 사람들이다   / [칭찬뿐만 아니라 쓴 조언도 주는]
advice.

  ■ 보어 (Trustworthy) + be동사 + S

trustworthy 신뢰할 수
있는
compliment 칭찬, 찬사
bitter 쓴

A 03 **Not until the rise of ecology at the beginning of the twentieth century** did
생태학이 등장하고 나서야 비로소   / 20세기 초에   /
people begin to think seriously of land as a natural system with interconnecting
사람들은 땅을 진지하게 여기기 시작했다   / 서로 연결된 부분들을 가진 자연계로서
parts.

  ■ 부정의 어구 (Not until ~) + 조동사 + S + 본동사 / not A until B에서 부정어 not과 함께 until B 부분이 문장 앞으로
   나가 도치된 문장이다. (= People did not begin to think seriously of land as a natural system with
   interconnecting parts until the rise of ecology ~.)

ecology 생태학
think of A as B A를 B로 여
기다
interconnect 서로 연결하다

04 Every cell is a triumph of natural selection, and we're made of trillions of cells.
모든 세포는 자연 선택의 업적이다   / 그리고 우리는 수조 개의 세포로 이뤄져 있다
Within us, is a little universe. *Carl Sagan*
우리 안에   / 작은 우주가 있다

  ■ 장소의 부사 (Within us) + be동사 + S

   Know More 자연 선택(natural selection)이란 다윈(Charles Darwin)의 진화론 중 하나의 갈래로, 자연이 한 개체의 변
   이와 성장을 '선택'했다는 의미이다. 어떤 종 안에서 일어나는 생존 경쟁에서 환경에 적응한 것이 생존하여 자손을 남기게 되고,
   그렇지 못한 것은 사라지게 되는 현상을 가리킨다.

triumph 업적, 승리
natural selection 자연 선택
trillion 조(兆)

05 Natural ability is necessary to become an expert in anything, but **no less**
타고난 재능은 필수적이다   / 어떤 것에서 전문가가 되기 위해   / 그러나 기꺼이
important is the willingness to study.
연구하려는 의사가 마찬가지로 중요하다

  ■ 보어 (no less important) + be동사 + S

expert 전문가
willingness 기꺼이 하기[하
는 마음 상태]

ⓑ 06 For a computer to solve a problem, **not only** must the solution be very
컴퓨터가 어떤 문제를 해결하기 위해서 / 해결 방법이 아주 자세해야 할 뿐만 아니라
detailed, but it must also be written in a form the computer can understand.
/ 그것은 또한 쓰여야 한다 / 형태로 / [그 컴퓨터가 이해할 수 있는]

■ 부정의 어구 (not only) + 조동사 + S + 본동사

07 **Under no circumstances** will anyone's personal information be given out to
어떤 상황에서도 누군가의 개인 정보는 배포되지 않을 것이다 /
any third party without the express permission of the person concerned.
제3자에게 / 명시적 허락 없이는 / [관계자의]

■ 부정의 어구 (Under no circumstances) + 조동사 + S + 본동사

under no circumstances
어떠한 상황에서도 ~ 않는
third party 제3자
express 명시된, 명확한
the person concerned 관
계자

08 **Out of the fundamentals of elementary algebra** evolved the abstract algebra
기초 대수학의 원리로부터 / 오늘날 사용되는 추상 대수학과 대수 구조의
used today and the concept of an algebraic structure.
개념이 발전했다

■ 장소의 부사 (Out of the fundamentals of elementary algebra) + V + S / '기초 대수학의 원리'가 추상적 장소
로 개념화되었다.

fundamental 원리; 근본적인
elementary 기초의, 초급의
abstract 추상적인
algebra 대수학

09 **Included in this chapter** is a list of frequently misspelled words, which you
이 장(章)에 포함되어 있다 / 자주 철자를 틀리는 단어들의 목록이 / 그리고 당신은
may find it helpful to memorize.
그것을 암기하는 것이 유용하리라는 것을 알게 될 것이다

■ 분사 (Included in this chapter) + be동사 + S / (= A list of frequently misspelled words is included in
this chapter, which ~.)
― it은 가목적어이고 to memorize가 진목적어로 쓰였다.

misspell 철자를 틀리다, 철자를
잘못 쓰다

ⓒ 10 **Only in the last few decades**, in the primarily industrially developed economies,
[모의] 겨우 지난 몇 십 년 동안에서야 / 주로 산업적으로 발전된 국가에서
has food become so plentiful and easy to obtain as to cause fat-related
/ 음식은 아주 풍부하고 얻기 용이하게 되었다 / 지방과 관련된 건강 문제를 일으킬 만큼
health problems.

풀이 Only를 포함하는 부사구가 문장 앞으로 나온 것으로, 주어와 동사는 「조동사 + S + 본동사」의 어순으로 도치되
어야 하므로 has food become이 적절하다.

decade 10년
economy (경제 주체로서의)
국가; 경제
primarily 주로
plentiful 풍부한

[모의] 11 **Fundamental to most moral approaches** is the idea that human life has a
대부분의 도덕적 접근의 근간이 되는 것은 / 생각이다 / [= 인간의 삶은 특별한 존엄성과
special dignity and value that is worth preserving even at the expense of
가치를 가진다는 / [보존할 가치가 있는] / 심지어 자기 이익을 희생하고서라도]]
self-interest.

풀이 보어인 Fundamental ~ approaches가 문장 앞으로 나와 「be동사 + S」의 어순으로 주어와 동사가 도치된
것으로, 문장의 주어는 the idea이므로 단수 동사인 is가 적절하다.
― the idea 다음에 동격의 that절이 이어지고 있다. ➔ Unit 52

dignity 존엄성
at the expense of ~을 희생
하여, ~을 대가로
self-interest 자기 이익, 사리
사욕

[모의] 12 **Laid before me** was(, I realized,) a scene of almost classical rural beauty―
내 앞에 놓여졌다 / 나는 깨달았다 / 거의 전형적인 시골의 아름다운 장면이―
the meadows dotted with contented animals, the woods in the background,
/ (배불러) 만족한 동물들이 점점이 있는 목초지 / 그 뒤편의 숲
a twisting stream threading through it all.
/ 그 모두의 사이를 구불구불 흘러 지나가는 시냇물

풀이 과거분사 Laid가 이끄는 어구가 문장 앞으로 나와 「be동사 + S」의 어순으로 도치된 문장으로, 삽입어구인 I
realized를 괄호로 묶으면 문장의 주어는 전치사구 of 이하의 수식을 받는 a scene이므로 단수 동사 was가 적절하다.

rural 시골의
meadow 목초지
dotted 점점이 있는; 점을 찍은
contented 만족한
twisting 구불구불한
thread 뚫고 지나가다; 실

본책 169 ∽ Unit 49 **147**

unit 50
도치 구문 2

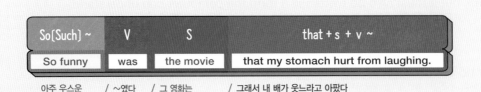

So[Such] ~	V	S	that + s + v ~
So funny	was	the movie	that my stomach hurt from laughing.
아주 우스운	~였다	그 영화는	그래서 내 배가 웃느라고 아팠다

Standard Sentences

모의 01 The present moment does not exist in the equations of physics, and
현재의 순간은 존재하지 않는다 / 물리학 방정식에 / 따라서
therefore **neither** does the flow of time.
시간의 흐름도 그렇지 않다

■ Neither + 조동사 + S: ~도 역시 그렇지 않다 / (= ~ therefore the flow of time doesn't exist in the equations of physics either.)

equation 방정식, 등식

02 What the caterpillar calls the end of the world the world calls a butterfly.
애벌레가 세상의 종말이라고 부르는 것을 / 세상은 나비라고 부른다   *Richard Bach*

■ 목적어 (What the caterpillar calls the end of the world) + S + V / 목적어가 강조를 위해 문장의 앞으로 나온 구조로, 목적어가 부정어를 동반하지 않는 한, 주어와 동사는 도치되지 않는다.

caterpillar 애벌레

A 03 Such was the power of his voice that even those at the back of the room
그의 목소리의 힘은 대단했다 / 그래서 그 방의 뒤쪽에 있는 사람들조차도 그 연사를 경탄하며 응시했다
gazed at the speaker in awe.
그의 목소리의 힘은 대단했다

■ Such + be동사 + S + that + s + v ~ / (= The power of his voice was such that ~.)

such (that과 함께 쓰여) 대단한, 굉장한
gaze 응시하다
in awe 경탄하며, 경외하며

04 Philosophy, which is understood to be the desire to acquire wisdom, is a
철학은 / 그것은 욕망으로 이해되는데 / [지혜를 얻으려는] / 인간의
fundamental part of the human being, and **so** is science.
근원적인 부분이다 / 그리고 과학도 역시 그러하다

■ So + be동사 + S: ~도 역시 그렇다 / (= ~ science is a fundamental part of the human being too.)
━ which가 이끄는 절 which ~ wisdom이 주어 Philosophy를 부연 설명하고 있다.

fundamental 근원적인

05 The release of atomic energy has **not** created a new problem. It has **merely**
원자 에너지의 방출이 새로운 문제를 만들어 내지 않았다 / 그것은 단지 더 긴급하게
made more urgent the necessity of solving an existing one.
만들었을 뿐이다 / 기존의 문제를 해결해야 하는 필요성을

■ S + V + 목적격보어 + 목적어 / 목적어가 길어져서 목적격보어와 위치가 바뀐 구조이다.

release 방출
atomic 원자의
merely 단지
urgent 긴급한
existing 기존의, 현존하는

B **06** **So closely** is sniffing tied to odor perception that people routinely sniff
[모의] 매우 밀접하게 / 코를 킁킁거리는 것은 냄새 지각과 연관되어 있다 / 그래서 사람들은 일상적으로 코를 킁킁거린다

when they are asked to imagine a smell.
/ 그들이 어떤 냄새를 상상해 보라는 요청을 받을 때

■ So + 부사 + be동사 + S ~ + that + s + v ... / (= Sniffing is so closely tied ~.)

sniff 코를 킁킁거리다; 냄새를 맡다
odor 냄새
perception 지각, 인식
routinely 일상적으로

07 People often say that motivation doesn't last. Well, **neither** does bathing—
사람들은 종종 말한다 / 동기 부여는 오래가지 않는다고 음, 목욕하는 것도 역시 그렇지 않다—

that's why we recommend it daily. *Zig Ziglar*
/ 그것이 우리가 그것을 매일 권장하는 이유이다

■ Neither + 조동사 + S: ~도 역시 그렇지 않다 / (= ~ bathing doesn't last either.)
— it은 bathing을 가리키는 대명사이다.

last 오래가다, 지속되다

08 We carry home what we have bought in some vessel, but **learning** we
우리는 집으로 가져간다 / 우리가 구매한 것을 / 용기에 담아서 / 그러나 배운 것을 우리는

cannot put in any other vessel but our minds.
둘 수 없다 / 다른 어떤 용기 속에 [우리의 정신 이외의]

■ 목적어 (learning) + S + V

vessel 용기, 그릇; 배
but ~ 이외에, ~을 제외하고

09 How on earth are you ever going to explain in terms of chemistry and
도대체 당신은 어떻게 설명할 것인가 / 화학과 물리학의 관점에서

physics so important a biological phenomenon as first love? *Albert Einstein*
/ 첫사랑과 같은 중요한 생물학적인 현상을?

■ explain의 목적어 so ~ love가 길어서 부사구 뒤로 보내진 구조이다.
— so + 형용사 + a(n) + 명사 = such + a(n) + 형용사 + 명사 / (= such an important biological phenomenon)

on earth 도대체
in terms of ~의 관점에서

C **10** **So quickly** did he rush out of the office that he forgot to lock up and set the
아주 서둘러서 / 그는 사무실에서 나왔다 / 그래서 그는 잊어버렸다 / 문을 잠그고 경보 장치를 설정하는

alarm.
것을

[풀이] So가 문장의 앞에 쓰였으므로 뒤에 so의 수식을 받는 부사를 쓰고, 주어와 동사는 「조동사 + S + 본동사」의 어순으로 도치되어야 한다.

11 Unlike animals, plants cannot pick up their roots and race for safety. **Nor**
[모의] 동물과 달리 / 식물은 자신의 뿌리를 집어 들 수 없다 / 그리고 안전을 위해서 질주할 (수 없다) 많은

have many plants taken the offensive and become predators.
식물은 공격 태세를 취한 적이 없다 / 그리고 포식자가 된 (적도 없다)

[풀이] 부정어 Nor가 앞에 있으므로 「조동사 + S + 본동사」의 어순으로 도치되어야 한다.

offensive 공격 태세; 공격적인
predator 포식자; 약탈자

12 The large part of our thoughts and feelings that we do not know and cannot
우리의 생각과 감정의 커다란 부분을 / [우리가 알지 못하고 통제할 수 없는]

control Sigmund Freud called the unconscious.
/ 지그문트 프로이트는 무의식이라고 불렀다

[풀이] 문장의 목적어 The large ~ control이 강조되어 문장의 앞으로 나왔으며, 목적어가 이동될 경우 주어와 동사의 도치는 일어나지 않으므로 주어와 동사를 먼저 쓰고, 이어 목적격보어를 쓰는 것이 적절하다.

unconscious 무의식

강조 구문

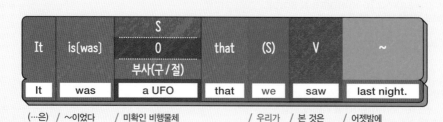

It	is[was]	**S** **O** **부사(구/절)**	that	(S)	V	~
It	was	a UFO	that	we	saw	last night.

(…은) / ~이었다 / 미확인 비행물체 / 우리가 / 본 것은 / 어젯밤에

Standard Sentences

01 **It is** the interaction between our genes and the environment **that**
(…은) 바로 상호작용이다 / [우리의 유전자와 환경 사이의] / 결정

determines whether we develop an illness.
하는 것은 / 우리가 병이 생길지 어떨지

■ 「It is ~ that …」 강조 구문이 쓰였으며, 주어 the interaction ~ the environment를 강조하고 있다.

> develop an illness 병이
> 생기다, 발병하다

02 **It was** not until the twelfth century **that** the magnetic compass was used
(…은) 바로 12세기가 될 때까지는 아니었다 / 자기 나침반이 사용된 것은

for navigation.
/ 항해를 위해

→ 12세기가 되어야 비로소 자기 나침반이 항해를 위해 사용되었다.

■ 「It is ~ that …」 강조 구문이 쓰였으며, 부사구 not until the twelfth century를 강조하고 있다. / (= The magnetic compass wasn't used for navigation until the twelfth century.)

> magnetic compass 자기
> 나침반

A **03** Success is not final, failure is not fatal: **it is** the courage to continue **that**
성공은 최종적이지 않다 / 실패는 결정적이지 않다 / (…은) 바로 계속하려는 용기이다 / 중요한

counts. *Winston Churchill*
것은

■ 「It is ~ that …」 강조 구문이 쓰였으며, 주어 the courage to continue를 강조하고 있다.

> fatal 결정적인; 치명적인
> count 중요하다; 세다

04 **It is** not the number of books which a young man reads **that** makes him
(…은) 바로 책의 권수가 아니다 / [젊은이가 읽는] / 그를 지적이고 박식하게

intelligent and well-informed, but the number of well-chosen ones that he
만드는 것은 / 정선된 책의 권수(이다) / [그가

has mastered.
완전히 익힌]

→ 젊은이를 지적이고 박식하게 만드는 것은 그가 읽는 책의 권수가 아니라, 그가 완전히 익힌 정선된 책의 권수이다.

■ 「It is ~ that …」 강조 구문이 쓰였으며, not A but B의 not A에 해당하는 부분인 not the number of books which a young man reads를 강조하고 있다.

> well-informed 박식한
> well-chosen 정선된, 잘 골
> 라낸
> master 완전히 익히다, 통달
> 하다

05 **It is** through his untiring effort **that** the singer has succeeded in becoming
(…은) 바로 그의 지칠 줄 모르는 노력을 통해서이다 / 그 가수가 성공한 것은 / 현재의 그가 되는 것에

what he is now, getting out of what he was.
/ 예전의 자신의 상태에서 벗어나

■ 「It is ~ that …」 강조 구문이 쓰였으며, 부사구 through his untiring effort를 강조하고 있다.

> untiring 지칠 줄 모르는, 지치
> 지 않는

B 06 It is not work, but overwork, **that** is hurtful; and it is not hard work **that** is
(…은) 바로 일이 아니라 과로이다 / 상하게 하는 것은 / 그리고 (…은) 바로 힘든 일이 아니다 / 해롭게 하는

injurious so much as unwilling work.
것은 / 오히려 마음이 내키지 않는 일(이다)

- 「It is ~ that ...」 강조 구문이 쓰였으며, not A but B로 연결된 주어 not work, but overwork를 강조하고 있다.
- 「It is ~ that ...」 강조 구문이 쓰였으며, not A so much as B에서 not A에 해당하는 부분인 not hard work를 강조하고 있다. **Unit 45**

not A so much as B A라기보다는 오히려 B
unwilling 마음이 내키지 않는, 마지못해 하는

07 Heritage is more concerned with meanings than material artefacts. **It is** the
유산은 의미와 더욱 관련이 있다 / 물질적인 인공물보다는 (…은) 바로

former **that** give value, either cultural or financial, to the latter and explain
전자이다 / 가치를 주는 것은 / 문화적이든 금전적이든 / 후자에게 / 그리고 설명하는 (것은)

why they have been selected from the near infinity of the past.
/ 왜 그것들이 선택되었는지를 / 거의 무한에 가까운 과거의 산물에서

- 「It is ~ that ...」 강조 구문이 쓰였으며, 주어 the former를 강조하고 있다.
- the former는 meanings를 가리키고, the latter는 material artefacts를 가리킨다.

heritage 유산; 전통
artefact 인공물, 가공품
the former 전자; 앞선
the latter 후자; 후반의
infinity 무한

08 **It's** not until we're being massaged by warm water, unable to check our
(…은) 바로 우리가 따뜻한 물로 마사지를 받고 있을 때까지는 아니다 / 우리의 이메일을 확인할 수 없는

e-mail, **that** we're finally able to hear the quiet voices in the backs of our
상황에서 / 우리가 마침내 조용한 목소리를 들을 수 있는 것은 / 우리의 머리 뒤편에서의

heads telling us about the insight.
/ [통찰에 대해 우리에게 말을 건네는]

→ 우리가 따뜻한 물로 마사지를 받고 있느라 우리의 이메일을 확인할 수 없는 때가 되어서야, 우리는 마침내 통찰에 대해 우리에게 말을 건네는 우리의 머리 뒤편에서의 조용한 목소리를 들을 수 있게 된다.

- 「It is ~ that ...」 강조 구문이 쓰였으며, 부사구 not until we're being massaged by warm water, unable to check our e-mail을 강조하고 있다. / (= We're not finally ~ until we're being massaged by ....)

insight 통찰(력)

09 I've made the most important discovery of my life. **It's** only in the mysterious
나는 내 인생의 가장 중요한 발견을 해냈다 (…은) 바로 사랑이라는 신비한 방정식

equation of love **that** any logical reasons can be found. *John Nash*
속에서뿐이다 / 어떤 논리적 이유도 발견될 수 있는 것은

- 「It is ~ that ...」 강조 구문이 쓰였으며, 부사구 only in the mysterious equation of love를 강조하고 있다.

equation 방정식
logical 논리적인

C 10 It is the biography of Steve Jobs **that**[**which**] I have been looking for.
(…은) 바로 스티브 잡스의 전기이다 / 내가 찾고 있었던 것은

풀이 전치사 for의 목적어를 is와 that 사이에 써서 「It is ~ that ...」 강조 구문으로 만든다. 강조되는 것이 사물이면 that 대신에 which를 쓸 수 있다.

biography 전기

11 Some people say science deprives man of his dreams and of his poetry, but
어떤 사람들은 말한다 / 과학이 인간에게서 꿈과 시를 빼앗는다고 / 그러나

we can also say **it is** poetry and dreams **that**[**which**] have developed
우리는 또한 말할 수 있다 / (…은) 바로 시와 꿈이라고 / 과학을 발전시켜 온 것은

science.

풀이 강조하고자 하는 주어를 is와 that 사이에 써서 「It is ~ that ...」 강조 구문으로 만든다.
- 접속사 but으로 연결된 두 절의 동사 say 다음에 각각 목적어절을 이끄는 접속사 that이 생략되었다.

deprive A of B A에게서 B를 빼앗다

12 It is only in our darkest hours **that** we may discover the true strength of the
(…은) 바로 오로지 우리의 가장 어두운 시간들 속에서이다 / 우리가 눈부신 빛의 진정한 힘을 발견할 수 있는 것은

brilliant light within ourselves.
/ 우리 자신의 내부에서

풀이 강조하고자 하는 부사구를 is와 that 사이에 써서 「It is ~ that ...」 강조 구문으로 만든다.

brilliant 눈부신, 반짝반짝 빛나는

unit 52
동격 구문

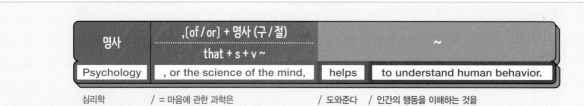

명사	,(of / or) + 명사 (구 / 절) that + s + v ~		~
Psychology	, or the science of the mind,	helps	to understand human behavior.
심리학	/ = 마음에 관한 과학은	/ 도와준다	/ 인간의 행동을 이해하는 것을

Standard Sentences

01 Alpha rhythm, a brain wave frequency of moderate voltage, is characteristic
알파 리듬은 / = 적당한 전압의 뇌파 진동수인 / 사람의 특징이다
of a person who is awake but relaxed.
/ [깨어 있지만 안정된]

- Alpha rhythm 다음에 콤마(,)에 의해 동격 어구가 이어지고 있다.

brain wave 뇌파
frequency 진동수; 빈도
moderate 적당한, 온건한
voltage 전압

모의 02 Coevolution is the concept that two or more species of organisms can
공진화는 개념이다 / [= 둘 이상의 유기체 종들이 서로 상대방의 진화 방향에 영향을 줄 수 있다고
reciprocally influence the evolutionary direction of the other.
하는]

- the concept 다음에 동격의 that절이 이어지고 있다.
- 동격의 that절을 이끄는 명사로는 사고나 생각 등을 나타내는 추상명사인 fact, news, idea, belief, thought, theory, proposal, suggestion, opinion, doubt 등이 주로 쓰인다.

coevolution 공진화(서로 밀접한 관계를 갖는 둘 이상의 종이 상대 종의 진화에 영향을 주며 진화하는 것)
reciprocally 서로

A 03 Throughout history, people have been intrigued by the question of whether
역사를 통틀어 / 사람들은 질문에 강한 흥미를 느껴왔다 / [= 지적생명체가
there is intelligent life elsewhere in the universe.
있는지의 / 우주 어딘가 다른 곳에]

- the question 다음에 전치사 of에 의해 whether가 이끄는 동격절이 이어지고 있다.

intrigue 강한 흥미를 불러일으키다
elsewhere (어딘가) 다른 곳에

모의 04 Scientists tried to extract knowledge by devising theories, that is, building
과학자들은 지식을 끌어내려고 노력했다 / 이론을 고안해 냄으로써 / = 즉, 자료를 설명하는
models to explain the data they observed.
모델을 만듦으로써 / [그들이 관찰한]

- devising theories 다음에 동격의 관용표현 that is(즉, 다시 말해서)에 의해 동격 어구가 이어지고 있다.

extract 끌어내다; 추출하다
devise 고안하다
observe 관찰하다; 준수하다

05 As humans, we respond to everything in our environment in one of two
인간으로서 / 우리는 모든 것에 반응한다 / 환경 속에서 / 두 가지 기본 방식 중의
basic ways: we either approach stimuli or we avoid stimuli.
하나로 / = 우리는 자극에 다가간다 / 또는 우리는 자극을 피한다

- one of two basic ways 다음에 동격의 구두점 콜론(:)에 의해 동격절이 이어지고 있다.

stimulus 자극 (*pl.* stimuli)

B **06** Don't try to be a jack-of-all-trades, I-can-do-anything job applicant, also
만물박사가 되려고 하지 마라 / = 나는 무엇이든 할 수 있다는 구직자 / [또한
known as a "slash" person.
'여기 저기 발을 걸친' 사람으로 알려진]

jack-of-all-trades 만물박사
applicant 지원자
slash 사선(/)

■ a jack-of-all-trades 다음에 콤마(,)에 의해 동격 어구 I-can-do-anything job applicant가 이어지고 있다.

Know More slash person이란 하나의 직업만을 가진 것이 아니라, 여러 분야의 경험이 있어 /(슬래시)로 경력을 나열할 수 있는 사람을 가리킨다.

모의 **07** The so-called Mozart effect—listening to Mozart will make your child
이른바 모차르트 효과는 / —모차르트 음악을 듣는 것이 당신의 자녀를 더 영리하게 만들 것이라는
smarter—is a good example of a scientific finding being distorted by the
/ —과학적 결과물의 좋은 예이다 / [대중매체에 의해서 왜곡되고 있는
media through hype not warranted by the research.
/ 과장 광고를 통해서 / [연구 조사에 의해 보장되지 않은]]

so-called 이른바, 소위
distort 왜곡하다
hype 과장 광고, 과대 선전
warrant 보장하다

■ The so-called Mozart effect 다음에 대시(—)에 의해 동격절이 이어지고 있다.

08 We are survival machines, robot vehicles blindly programmed to preserve
우리는 생존 기계들이다 / = 로봇 매개체들 / [맹목적으로 프로그램된 / 이기적 분자들을
the selfish molecules known as genes. *Richard Dawkins*
보존하기 위해서 / [유전자로 알려진]]

vehicle 매개체, 수단; 탈 것
blindly 맹목적으로, 무분별하게

■ survival machines 다음에 콤마(,)에 의해 동격 어구가 이어지고 있다.

09 The first time rock 'n' roll came into being, it received much criticism on the
로큰롤이 처음 출현했을 때 / 그것은 많은 비판을 받았다 / 이유로
grounds that it could be a threat to the traditional culture, just as jazz did
/ [= 그것이 전통적인 문화에 위협이 될 수 있다는] / 35년 전에 재즈가 그랬듯이
thirty-five years ago.

come into being 출현하다, 생기다
criticism 비판
ground 이유; 땅

■ the grounds 다음에 동격의 that절이 이어지고 있다.
— just as가 이끄는 절의 did는 대동사로 received much criticism을 대신한다.

C **10** Only the smallest fraction of the human race has ever acquired the habit of
인류의 오직 가장 적은 일부만이 획득한 적이 있었다 / 과거에 대해서
taking an objective view of the past.
객관적인 견해를 취하는 습관을

fraction 일부, 부분
objective 객관적인; 목표

풀이 the habit과 taking ~ the past가 전치사 of에 의해 동격으로 연결되어 있다.

모의 **11** There is a growing interest in computer programs that can analyze data and
늘어나는 관심이 있다 / 컴퓨터 프로그램에 / [자료를 분석하고 그것들부터 자동적으로
extract information automatically from them—in other words, learn.
정보를 뽑아낼 수 있는 / 다시 말해서 / = 배울 수 있는]

extract 뽑아내다; 추출

풀이 analyze ~ them과 동격을 이루는 learn이 대시(—)로 연결되어 있으며, in other words는 삽입어구이다.

12 In writing or speaking English, there is only the general principle that
영어를 쓰거나 말하는 데 있어 / 일반적인 원칙이 있을 뿐이다 /
concrete words are better than abstract ones, and that the shortest way
[= 구체적인 단어들이 추상적인 단어들보다 더 낫다는 / 그리고 어떤 것을 말하는 가장 짧은 방식이
of saying anything is always the best.
항상 최선이라는]

concrete 구체적인
abstract 추상적인

풀이 the general principle과 and로 연결된 두 개의 that절이 동격으로 연결되어 있다.

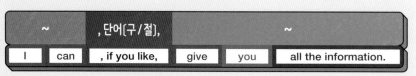

unit 53
삽입 구문

| ~ | , 단어[구/절], | ~ |

| I | can | , if you like, | give | you | all the information. |

나는 / ~할 수 있다 / (당신이 원한다면) / 주다 / 당신에게 / 모든 정보를

Standard Sentences

01 The little reed(, **bending to the force of the wind,**) soon stood upright again
작은 갈대는 / (바람의 힘에 구부러지는) / 곧 다시 똑바로 섰다

when the storm had passed over. *Aesop*
/ 폭풍이 지나갔을 때

■ 주어와 동사 사이에 현재분사구 bending ~ the wind가 삽입되어 있다.

reed 갈대
upright 똑바로

02 A fallacy is an idea that (**a lot of people think**) is true but which is false.
오류는 생각이다 / [(많은 사람들이 생각하기에) / 진실인 / 그러나 잘못된]

■ 관계대명사 that 다음에 a lot of people think가 삽입되어 있다.

fallacy 오류

A **03** What's dangerous about the Internet is(, **because it has the aura of**
수능! 인터넷에 대해 위험한 것은 ~이다 / (그것이 기술이라는 기운을 두르고 있기 때문에)

technology around it,) it has a totally undeserved instant credibility.
/ 그것이 전혀 자격이 없는, 즉각적인 신뢰성을 지닌다는 것

■ 동사 is와 보어 역할을 하는 명사절(it ~ credibility) 사이에 접속사 because가 이끄는 부사절이 삽입되어 있다.
▬ it has 앞에 보어절을 이끄는 접속사 that이 생략되어 있다.

aura 기운, 분위기
undeserved 자격이 없는
instant 즉각적인
credibility 신뢰성

04 An idealist is one who(, **on noticing that a rose smells better than a**
이상주의자는 사람이다 / [(알아차리자마자 / 장미가 양배추보다 더 좋은 냄새가 난다는 것을)

cabbage,) concludes that it will also make better soup. *Henry L. Mencken*
/ 결론을 내리는 / 그것(장미)이 또한 더 좋은 수프가 될 것이라고]

■ 관계대명사 who 다음에 부사구 on ~ a cabbage가 삽입되어 있다.

idealist 이상주의자, 공상가
cabbage 양배추
conclude 결론짓다

05 Your work is going to fill a large part of your life, and the only way to be truly
당신의 일은 당신의 인생의 큰 부분을 채울 것이다 / 그리고 진정으로 만족하는 유일한 방법은 하는

satisfied is to do what (**you believe**) is great work. *Steve Jobs*
것이다 / (당신이 믿기에) 멋진 일인 것을

■ what과 is 사이에 you believe가 삽입되어 있다.

B **06** Words are(, **in my not so humble opinion,**) our most inexhaustible source of

말은 ~이다 / (나의 주제넘은 의견으로는) / 우리의 가장 무궁무진한 마법의 원천

magic, capable of both influencing injury, and remedying it.

/ [마음의 상처에 영향을 줄 수도 있고, 그것을 치료할 수도 있는]

the novel <Harry Potter and the Deathly Hallows>

humble 겸손한; 보잘 것 없는
inexhaustible 무궁무진한, 다 쓸 수 없는
remedy 치료하다

■ 동사와 보어 사이에 관용표현 in my not so humble opinion이 삽입되어 있다.

Grammar Plus 삽입되는 관용표현: in my opinion 내 생각에는, so to speak 말하자면 (= as it were), after all 결국, if any 만약 있다면, if ever 설령 ~하는 일이 있더라도, as far as I know 내가 아는 한

07 We can share what we know(, **however little it might be,**) with someone who

우리는 공유할 수 있다 / 우리가 알고 있는 것을 / (그것이 아무리 작을지라도) / 사람과 /

has need of that knowledge.

[그 지식을 필요로 하는]

■ what이 이끄는 명사절 안에 however가 이끄는 양보의 부사절이 삽입되어 있다.

08 There are computer programs which(, **when they are fed patients' medical**

컴퓨터 프로그램들이 있다 / [(그 컴퓨터들이 환자의 병력을 제공받았을 때)

histories,) can predict health issues such as heart attacks more reliably than

/ 심장 마비와 같은 건강 문제들을 예측할 수 있는 / 의사들보다 더 확실하게]

doctors.

feed (정보를) 제공하다
medical history 병력
heart attack 심장 마비
reliably 확실하게, 믿을 수 있게

■ 관계대명사 which 다음에 when이 이끄는 시간의 부사절이 삽입되어 있다.

09 It looks like water was on Mars, because the surface features resemble

(…이) 보인다 / 물이 화성에 있었던 것처럼 / 왜냐하면 표면 지형들이 지구상의 지형들과 닮았기 때문에

those on Earth that (**we know**) are made by water.

/ [(우리가 알기로는) / 물에 의해서 만들어진]

feature 지형; 특징
resemble 닮다

■ 관계대명사 that 다음에 we know가 삽입되어 있다.

C **10** Our judgments are so liable to be influenced by many considerations

Up! 우리의 판단들은 많은 고려 사항들에 의해서 영향을 받기 무척 쉽다

(, **which almost**(, **without our knowing it,**) **are unfair,**) that it is necessary to

/ (그것들은 거의 / (우리가 그것을 알지 못한 채로) / 불공정하다) / 그래서 (…이) 필요하다 /

keep a guard upon them.

그것들에 대해 경계하는 것이

judgment 판단
liable ~하기 쉬운
consideration 고려 사항

풀이 which ~ unfair는 삽입절이며, 절 내에 without ~ it이 삽입되어 있다. 이어지는 절에 빠진 문장 성분이 없으므로, 접속사 that이 들어가 「so + 형용사[부사] + that + s + v ~」 구조를 이루는 것이 적절하다.

모의 **11** People may change the kinds of games they are playing, but an interest in

사람들은 게임의 종류를 바꿀지도 모른다 / [그들이 하고 있는] / 그러나 쌍방향의 오락 매체에

interactive entertainment media(, **once acquired,**) seems never to fade.

대한 흥미는 / (일단 습득되면) / 결코 사라지지 않는 것 같다

acquire (몸에) 익히다, 지니게 되다; 얻다
fade 사라지다, 약해지다

풀이 once acquired는 삽입 어구이며, 문장의 주어가 an interest ~ media이므로 단수 동사 seems가 적절하다.

— once는 '일단 ~하면'을 뜻하는 접속사이고, 그 뒤에 it is가 생략되어 있다.

모의 **12** I recently saw a news interview with an acquaintance who (**I was certain**)

나는 최근에 지인과의 뉴스 인터뷰를 보았다 / [(내가 확신하기로는)

was going to lie about a few particularly sensitive issues, and lie she did.

/ 몇 가지 특히 민감한 문제들에 대해서는 거짓말을 할] / 그리고 그녀는 정말 거짓말을 했다

acquaintance 지인, 아는 사람
particularly 특히

풀이 I was certain은 삽입절이며, 이어지는 절에서 주어가 빠져 있으므로 주격 관계대명사 who가 적절하다.

— 동사 앞에 do동사를 써서 강조한 she did lie에서 lie를 더욱 강조하기 위해 lie를 주어 앞으로 보낸 형태이다.

unit 54
생략·공통 구문

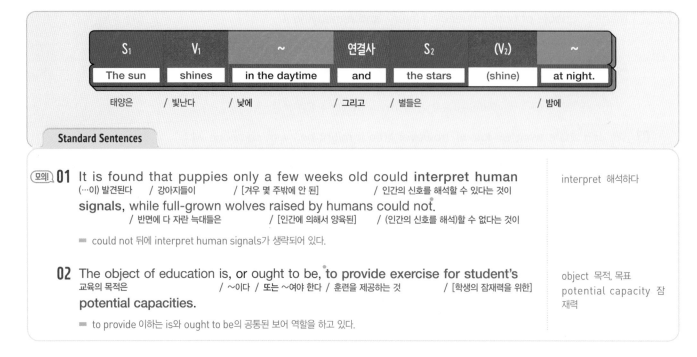

S₁	V₁	~	연결사	S₂	(V₂)	~
The sun	shines	in the daytime	and	the stars	(shine)	at night.
태양은	/ 빛난다	/ 낮에	/ 그리고	/ 별들은		/ 밤에

Standard Sentences

모의 01 It is found that puppies only a few weeks old could **interpret human**
(…이) 발견된다 / 강아지들이 / [겨우 몇 주밖에 안 된] / 인간의 신호를 해석할 수 있다는 것이
signals, while full-grown wolves raised by humans could not.
/ 반면에 다 자란 늑대들은 / [인간에 의해서 양육된] / (인간의 신호를 해석)할 수 없다는 것이

　■ could not 뒤에 interpret human signals가 생략되어 있다.

interpret 해석하다

02 The object of education is, or ought to be, to provide exercise for student's
교육의 목적은 / ~이다 / 또는 ~여야 한다 / 훈련을 제공하는 것 / [학생의 잠재력을 위한]
potential capacities.

　■ to provide 이하는 is와 ought to be의 공통된 보어 역할을 하고 있다.

object 목적, 목표
potential capacity 잠재력

A 03 Marshall McLuhan noted that clothes **are people's** extended skin, wheels
모의 마셜 매클루언은 언급했다 / 옷은 사람들의 연장된 피부이고 / 바퀴는
extended feet, camera and telescopes extended eyes.
연장된 발(이며) / 카메라와 망원경은 연장된 눈(이라고)

　■ wheels와 telescopes 뒤에 각각 are their가 생략되어 있다.

extend 연장하다
telescope 망원경

> **Know More** 마셜 매클루언(1911~1980)은 캐나다의 미디어 이론가로, 커뮤니케이션 연구, 문화 연구 등을 통해 미디어가 우리 인간과 사회에 어떤 영향을 미치는지를 관찰하였다. 그는 인류가 무비판적으로 미디어를 수용할 경우, 이는 사회적 해악이 될 것이므로 전 인류가 미디어를 비판적으로 사고할 자질을 갖추어야 한다고 주장하였다. 현재 사후 30여년이 지난 오늘날에도 가장 영향력 있는 미디어 이론가로 여겨지고 있다.

모의 04 A snack with the label "99% natural" **seems** more appealing than it would if
'99% 천연인'이라는 라벨이 붙은 과자는 더욱 매력적으로 보인다 / 그것이 그럴 것보다
labeled "1% unnatural."
만약 '1% 천연이 아닌'이라고 라벨이 붙여진다면

　■ would 뒤에 seem appealing이 생략되어 있다.
　— 가정법 과거의 의미를 나타내는 if 뒤에는 주어와 be동사 it were가 생략되어 있다.

snack 과자, 간식
appealing 매력적인

05 Mathematics is **an area of study** that I'm attracted to, interested in, and
수학은 학문의 한 분야이다 / [내가 끌리는, 관심이 있는, 그리고 잘하는]
good at, though I have not explored it in depth.
/ 비록 내가 그것을 탐구하지 않았지만 / 깊게

　■ an area of study는 전치사 to, in, at의 공통된 목적어 역할을 하고 있다.

attract 끌다; 매혹하다

B **06** Sleep is to the brain what food is to the body. That is to say, if deprived of
수면은 ~이다 / 뇌에 대해　　/ 음식과 신체의 관계　　　　다시 말해서　　　/ 만약 (뇌가) 적절한
adequate sleep, the brain cannot function properly.
수면을 빼앗긴다면　　/ 뇌는 제대로 기능할 수 없다

- if 뒤에 it is가 생략되어 있다.
- A is to B what C is to D: A의 B에 대한 관계는 C의 D에 대한 관계와 같다

deprive 빼앗다, 박탈하다
adequate 적절한, 충분한

07 Scientific beliefs are **supported by evidence**, and they **get results**. Myths
과학적 신념은 증거에 의해 뒷받침된다　　　　　　　/ 그리고 그것들은 결과를 얻는다　　신화와
and faiths are not and do not. *Richard Dawkins*
신앙은 (증거에 의해서 뒷받침되지) 않으며, (결과를 얻지) 못한다

- are not 뒤에 supported by evidence가 생략되어 있으며, do not 뒤에 get results가 생략되어 있다.

myth 신화; 통념
faith 신앙, 신념

모의 08 In the realm of human psychology, research has long noted the essential
인간 심리학의 영역에서　　　　　　　　　　/ 연구는 오랫동안 주목해왔다　　　/ 본질적인 특성을
trait of adapting to life's events, whether happy or tragic.
　　/ [인생의 사건들에 적응하는]　　/ (그 사건들이) 행복한 것이든 매우 슬픈 것이든

- whether 뒤에 they are가 생략되어 있다.

realm 영역
psychology 심리학
trait 특성, 특징
adapt to ~에 적응하다
tragic 매우 슬픈, 비극적인

Up! 09 It takes a great deal of **bravery** to stand up to our enemies, but just as
(…은) 많은 용기를 필요로 한다　　　/ 우리의 적에게 맞서는 것은　　　/ 그러나 꼭 같은
much to stand up to our friends. *the novel <Harry Potter and the Sorcerer's Stone>*
양의 (용기를 필요로 한다) / 우리의 친구에게 맞서는 것은

- but 뒤에 it takes가 생략되어 있으며, much 뒤에는 bravery가 생략되어 있다.
- friends 뒤에는 as to stand up to our enemies가 생략되어 있다.

a great(good) deal of (양이) 많은
stand up to ~에게 맞서다(저항하다)

C **10** The computer is only a fast idiot; it has no imagination; it cannot originate
컴퓨터는 단지 빠른 멍청이일 뿐이다　　　　　/ 그것은 상상력이 없다　　　/ 그것은 행동을 일으킬 수 없다
action. It is, and will remain, **only a tool of man.**
　　　그것은 ~이다 / 그리고 남아 있을 것이다 / 단지 인간의 도구로

- only a tool of man은 is와 will remain의 공통된 보어 역할을 하고 있다.

idiot 멍청이, 바보
originate 일으키다; 유래하다

모의 11 Pride causes individuals to be out of touch with the reality of who they truly
자만심은 개인들이 현실성과 접촉하지 못하게 만든다　　　　　　　　　　/ [= 자신들이 진정으로
are and of what really brings happiness.
누구인지의 / 그리고 무엇이 정말로 행복을 가져다주는지의]

- the reality는 동격의 of에 의해 두 개의 동격절 who ~ are와 what ~ happiness에 공통으로 연결되어 있다.

모의 12 Only after the immediate concerns of the unconscious have been satisfied
무의식의 즉각적인 관심사들이 충족된 후에서야
can the conscious mind begin to be convinced of, or interested in, **anything.**
/ 의식적인 마음은 어떤 것이든 확신하거나 흥미를 갖기 시작할 수 있다

- anything은 전치사 of와 in의 공통된 목적어 역할을 하고 있다.
- only를 포함한 부사절(Only ~ satisfied)이 문두에 와서 주절은 「조동사 + S + 본동사」의 어순으로 도치되었다.

immediate 즉각적인, 당면한
concern 관심사; 염려
unconscious 무의식
conscious 의식적인
be convinced of ~을 확신하다

A **01** `At the heart of individualism` lies the belief `that each individual person`
모의 개인주의의 핵심에 / 신념이 놓여 있다 / [= 각 개인은 자신의 우주의 중심을 구성한다는]
constitutes the center of one's universe.

> 장소의 부사 (At the heart of individualism) + V + S / the belief 다음에 동격의 that절이 이어지고 있다.

02 `It is` not what he has, `nor` even what he does, **which** directly expresses the
(…은) 바로 그가 가진 것이 아니다 / 심지어는 그가 하는 것도 아니다 / 어떤 사람의 가치를 직접 나타내는 것은
worth of a man, but what he is. *Henri-Frédéric Amiel*
/ 그가 어떤 사람인지이다

→ 어떤 사람의 가치를 직접 나타내는 것은 그의 재산이 아니고, 심지어는 그의 행위도 아니고, 그의 사람됨이다.

> 「It is ~ that ....」 강조 구문이 쓰였으며, 강조되는 어구가 사물 또는 상황인 경우 that 대신 which를 쓸 수 있다.
> — not A, nor B, but C: A도 아니고, B도 아니고 C

03 `It's a common misconception that money is` **every entrepreneur's metric for**
(…은) 흔한 오해이다 / 돈이 성공에 대한 모든 기업인의 측정 기준이라는 것은
success. `It's not,` and **nor** should `it be.`
그것은 아니다 / 그리고 그것이 그래서도 안 된다

> not과 be 뒤에는 every entrepreneur's metric for success가 생략되어 있다.
> 부정의 어구 (nor) + 조동사 + S + 본동사
> — 첫 문장에서 It은 가주어이며, 두 번째 문장에서 It[it]은 money를 가리키는 대명사이다.

04 Don't get caught up in thinking that any success you experience as a student
생각하는 것에 말려들지 마라 / 어떠한 성공이 / [당신이 학생으로서 경험하는]
has no bearing on, or relationship to, **future success in the "real" world.**
/ 관련이나 관계가 없다고 / '현실' 세계에서 미래의 성공과

> future success in the "real" world는 전치사 on과 to의 공통된 목적어 역할을 하고 있다.

B **05** Break the 'big, fat, terrible book' down into sections that (**you feel**) are more
'크고, 두툼하고, 지겨운 책'을 부분들로 쪼개라 / [(당신이 느끼기에) / 보다 감당할
manageable and read through them one at a time.
수 있는] / 그리고 하나씩 그것들을 통독하라

> 풀이 you feel은 삽입절이며, sections를 수식하는 관계대명사 that절의 동사로 복수 동사 are가 적절하다.

06 Even more significant **than the ability to communicate knowledge by**
훨씬 더 중요한 것은 / 지식을 전달하는 능력보다 /
means of signs and sounds was the development of a means of preserving
기호와 음성으로 / 수단의 발전이었다 / [문서 기록을 통해
the knowledge through written records.
지식을 보존하는]

> 풀이 「보어 + be동사 + S」의 어순으로 도치되었으며, 문장의 주어가 the development이므로 단수 동사 was가 알맞다.

Up! 07 **It is** in our ancient myths **that** many writers find the core of the human
(…은) 바로 우리 고대의 신화 속이다 / 많은 작가들이 인간의 분투의 핵심을 발견하는 것은
struggle to make sense of the world and to find one's role—(**in short,**) a road
/ [세상을 이해하고 자신의 역할을 찾으려는] / —(간단히 말해) / 인간
map to the human psyche.
정신세계로 가는 도로 지도를

---

constitute 구성하다

misconception 오해, 오인
entrepreneur 기업인
metric 측정 기준

get caught up in ~에 말려들다; ~에 열중하다
bearing 관련, 영향; 태도

section 부분, 구획
manageable 감당할 수 있는, 처리하기 쉬운
one at a time 하나씩, 차례로

significant 중요한, 의미심장한
by means of ~으로, ~을 수단으로 하여

ancient 고대의, 옛날의
core 핵심
in short 간단히 말해
psyche 정신(세계)

풀이 「It is ~ that ....」 강조 구문이 쓰였으며 부사구 in our ancient myths를 강조하고 있다. 부사구를 강조할 경우 that을 쓰며, that 대신에 which를 쓸 수 없다.

—— in short는 삽입된 관용표현이며, the core ~ one's role 다음에 대시(—)로 동격 어구와 연결되어 있다.

C 08
The police arrested a man who (**they suspected**) had been at the crime
경찰은 한 남자를 체포했다 / [(그들이 의심했던) / 범행 현장에 있었던 것으로]
scene.

풀이 a man을 수식하는 형용사절을 이끄는 관계대명사 who 다음에 they suspected를 삽입하고, 이어서 동사 had been이 오는 것이 자연스럽다.

arrest 체포하다
suspect 의심하다, 혐의를 두다;
용의자
crime scene 범행 현장

09
It's the possibility of having a dream come true **that** makes life interesting.
(…은) 바로 꿈을 실현하도록 하는 가능성이다 / 인생을 흥미롭게 만드는 것은

풀이 「It is ~ that ....」 강조 구문이 주어 the possibility ~ true를 강조하고 있으므로, that 이하에 서술부에 해당하는 「V+O+C」를 써서 완성한다.

10
Scarcely had we started out before the sky became overcast and **down**
우리가 출발하자마자 / 하늘이 흐려졌다 / 그리고 비가 다시
came the rain again.
내렸다

풀이 부정의 어구 (Scarcely)+조동사+S+본동사 ~+before[when] ...: ~하자마자 …하다 / 부정어인 scarcely가 문장의 앞으로 나와 있으므로, 주어와 조동사를 도치해서 쓴다.

—— 장소의 부사 (down)+장소·이동의 V (came)+S

overcast 흐린, 구름으로 뒤덮인

D 11
모의 Any discussion of coevolution quickly runs into what philosophers call a
공진화에 대한 어떠한 토론도 곧 충돌한다 / 철학자들이 '인과 관계 딜레마'라고 부르는
"causality dilemma," a problem we recognize from the question, "Which
것과 / = 문제인 / [우리가 질문에서 인식하는 / = 어떤
came first, the chicken or the egg?"
것이 먼저냐 / 닭이냐 달걀이냐?]

—— a causality dilemma 다음에 콤마(,)에 의해 동격 어구가 이어지고 있고, the question 다음에 콤마(,)에 의해 동격 어구가 이어지고 있다.

coevolution 공진화
run into ~와 충돌하다; 우연히
만나다
causality 인과 관계
dilemma 딜레마, 진퇴양난

12
The wise **are instructed** by reason; ordinary minds, by experience; the stupid,
현명한 사람들은 이성에 의해 교육된다 / 평범한 사람들은 경험에 의해서 (교육된다) / 어리석은 사람들은
by necessity; and brutes, by instinct.
필요에 의해서 (교육된다) / 그리고 짐승 같은 사람들은 본능에 의해서 (교육된다)

—— ordinary minds, the stupid, brutes 뒤의 콤마는 각각 are instructed가 생략되어 있음을 나타낸다.

instruct 교육하다, 가르치다
ordinary 평범한, 보통의
mind 사람; 마음
brute 짐승 같은 사람; 짐승
instinct 본능

13
In my experience, **it's** not what happens to you in life, **but** how you deal with
나의 경험으로는 / (…은) 바로 인생 동안 당신에게 일어나는 것이 아니라 / 당신이 그것을 어떻게 처리하느냐
it, **that** makes you a survivor and a winner.
이다 / 당신을 생존자이자 승자로 만드는 것은

—— 「It is ~ that ....」 강조 구문이 쓰였으며, 주어로 쓰인 not A but B 구문(not what happens to you in life, but how you deal with it)을 강조하고 있다.

12

기타 주요 구문

- unit 55 등위접속사 구문
- unit 56 상관접속사 구문
- unit 57 병렬 구문
- unit 58 부정 구문
- unit 59 동명사 관용 구문
- unit 60 전치사 + 명사절

■ 본격적인 구문 학습에 앞서, 각 유닛별 주요 단어를 확인하세요.

Unit 55

- [ ] **repent** 후회하다
- [ ] **criminalize** 범죄로 간주하다
- [ ] **immoral** 비도덕적인
- [ ] **heavenly** 하늘의
- [ ] **endure** 견디다, 참다
- [ ] **appreciation** 감사; 감상
- [ ] **acknowledge** 인정하다
- [ ] **rough** 힘든, 고된
- [ ] **constant** 계속되는; 일정한
- [ ] **physiological** 생리학의
- [ ] **maxim** 격언, 금언
- [ ] **adopt** (자세·입장을) 취하다

Unit 56

- [ ] **naive** 순진한
- [ ] **ambiguous** 애매한
- [ ] **tell** (정확히) 알다
- [ ] **wretched** 비참한, 끔찍한
- [ ] **starve to death** 굶어 죽다
- [ ] **chilling** 서늘한, 냉랭한
- [ ] **trial** 시련
- [ ] **mishap** 불행, 재난
- [ ] **grasp** 붙잡다
- [ ] **conservative** 보수적인
- [ ] **dominant** 주류의
- [ ] **inheritance** 유전; 상속

Unit 57

- [ ] **false** 허위의, 틀린
- [ ] **claim** 주장
- [ ] **cover up** ~을 은폐하다[감추다]
- [ ] **discordant** 조화되지 않는
- [ ] **dictate** 받아쓰게 하다
- [ ] **contract** 계약
- [ ] **compensation** 보상
- [ ] **due** 지불되어야 할
- [ ] **thermostat** 자동 온도 조절기
- [ ] **recharging** 재충전
- [ ] **suggest** 시사하다; 제안하다
- [ ] **induce** 유도하다; 유발하다

Unit 58

- [ ] **official** 관리자
- [ ] **fairy-tale** 동화
- [ ] **code of ethics** 윤리 규범
- [ ] **distinction** 구별
- [ ] **sensible** 합리적인
- [ ] **take ~ into account** ~을 고려하다
- [ ] **glitter** 반짝이다
- [ ] **wander** 방황하다
- [ ] **monetary** 통화[화폐]의
- [ ] **stabilize** 안정시키다
- [ ] **intuitive** 직관적인
- [ ] **outcome** 결과, 성과

Unit 59

- [ ] **leak** 새다
- [ ] **figure out** 알아내다, 이해하다
- [ ] **mean** 의도하다; 의미하다
- [ ] **state** 명시하다, 말하다
- [ ] **in practice** 실제로
- [ ] **attend** 참석하다
- [ ] **succeed in** ~에 성공하다
- [ ] **keep one's feet** 똑바로 서 있다
- [ ] **sweep** 휩쓸어 가다; 쓸다
- [ ] **enlighten** 깨우치게 하다
- [ ] **let go of** ~을 놓아주다
- [ ] **familiar** 익숙한

Unit 60

- [ ] **classify** 분류하다
- [ ] **commodity** 상품, 산물
- [ ] **security** 유가증권; 안전
- [ ] **publicly** 공개적으로
- [ ] **at once** 바로, 즉시
- [ ] **metaphor** 은유
- [ ] **converse** 반대의; 대화하다
- [ ] **concession** 양보
- [ ] **niche** 적합한 환경, 적소
- [ ] **be engaged in** ~에 몰입하다
- [ ] **construct** 구성하다
- [ ] **ethics** 윤리, 도덕

unit 55
등위접속사 구문

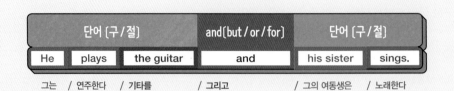

단어 [구 / 절]			and(but / or / for)	단어 [구 / 절]	
He	plays	the guitar	and	his sister	sings.
그는	/ 연주한다	/ 기타를	/ 그리고	/ 그의 여동생은	/ 노래한다

Standard Sentences

01 Be thankful for what you have **and** you'll end up having more. *Oprah Winfrey*
감사하라 / 당신이 가진 것에 대해서 / 그러면 당신은 결국 더 많이 갖게 될 것이다

- 명령문, and + S + V ~: …해라, 그러면 ~할 것이다
- what you have는 전치사 for의 목적어이다.

end up 결국 ~하게 되다

02 I am the wisest man alive, **for** I know one thing, **and** that is that I know
나는 현존하는 가장 현명한 사람이다 / 왜냐하면 나는 한 가지를 알기 때문이다 / 그리고 그것은 ~이다 / 내가 아무
nothing. *Socrates*
것도 모른다는 것

- S + V ~, for + S + V …: ~, 왜냐하면 …이기 때문에 / 접속사 for가 이끄는 절은 앞에 오는 절의 이유·근거를 나타
내며, 그 절의 앞에 쓰지 않는다. *cf.* 접속사 because가 이끄는 절은 주절의 앞 또는 뒤에 올 수 있다.

(A) 03 Cut your coat according to your cloth, **or** you'll repent some day. *Proverb*
네 코트를 잘라라 / 네 옷감에 맞춰서 / 그렇지 않으면 너는 언젠가 후회할 것이다
→ 분수에 맞게 살아라!

- 명령문, or + S + V ~: …해라, 그렇지 않으면 ~할 것이다 / or는 '또는'이라는 뜻 외에 '즉', '그렇지 않으면'의 뜻으로
도 쓰인다.

according to ~에 맞춰서, ~에
따라; ~에 의하면
repent 후회하다, 뉘우치다

04 Everyone admits that love is wonderful and necessary, **yet** no one agrees
모두가 인정한다 / 사랑은 아름답고 필연적인 것임을 / 하지만 아무도 의견이 일치하지 않는다
on just what it is. *Diane Ackerman*
/ 정확하게 그것이 무엇인지에 대해

- S + V ~, yet + S + V …: ~, 하지만 …

05 Criminalizing a behavior does **not** make it immoral, **nor** is all immoral
어떤 행동을 범죄로 간주하는 것이 만들지 않는다 / 그 행동을 비도덕적으로 / 그리고 모든 비도덕적
behavior **necessarily** criminalized.
행동이 반드시 범죄로 간주되지도 않는다

- not(never) ~, nor + V + S: …도 또한 아니다 /(= ~, and all immoral behavior is not necessarily criminalized
either.)

criminalize 범죄로 간주하다;
유죄로 하다
immoral 비도덕적인
necessarily 반드시

B **06** Change the way you look at things **and** the things you look at change. *Wayne Dyer*
방식을 바꿔라 / [당신이 상황을 바라보는] / 그러면 상황은 / [당신이 바라보는] / 바뀐다

- 명령문, and + S + V ~: …해라, 그러면 ~할 것이다
- the way와 관계부사 how는 함께 쓰일 수 없으며, 선행사가 the way일 때 관계부사 how는 생략하거나 that 또는 in which로 바꿔 쓸 수 있다. ➜ Unit 25

07 When a finger is pointing a way to the moon, don't concentrate on the
손가락이 달 쪽을 향해 가리키고 있을 때 / 그 손가락에 집중하지 마라
finger **or** you will miss all that heavenly glory!
/ 그렇지 않으면 당신은 저 모든 하늘의 장관을 놓치게 될 것이다!

heavenly 하늘의, 천국의
glory 장관; 영광

- 명령문, or + S + V ~: …해라, 그렇지 않으면 ~할 것이다

08 I will love the light **for** it shows me the way, **yet** I will endure the darkness
나는 빛을 사랑할 것이다 / 왜냐하면 그것은 내게 길을 보여주기 때문에 / 하지만 나는 어둠을 견딜 것이다
for it shows me the stars. *Og Mandino*
/ 왜냐하면 그것은 내게 별들을 보여주기 때문에

endure 견디다, 참다

- S + V ~, for + S + V …: ~, 왜냐하면 …이기 때문에
- S + V ~, yet + S + V …: ~, 하지만 …

09 Appreciation is the highest form of prayer, **for** it acknowledges the presence
감사는 가장 고귀한 형식의 기도이다 / 왜냐하면 그것은 선의 존재를 인정하기 때문에
of good wherever you shine the light of your thankful thoughts. *Alan Cohen*
/ 당신이 감사하는 마음의 빛을 비추는 어디서나

appreciation 감사; 감상; 식별
acknowledge 인정하다
presence 존재; 참석

- S + V ~, for + S + V …: ~, 왜냐하면 … 이기 때문에
- it은 앞에 나온 appreciation을 가리킨다.

C **10** The rough times must be endured and taken **as** they come, but they are **not**
[모의] 힘든 시간들은 견뎌져야 하고 감수되어야 한다 / 그것들이 올 때 / 그러나 그것들이 계속되지는
constant, **nor** do they last forever.
않는다 / 그리고 그것들은 영원히 지속되지도 않는다

rough 힘든, 고된, 괴로운; 거친
constant 계속되는; 일정한

- **풀이** not(never) ~, nor + V + S: …도 또한 아니다 / (= ~, and they don't last forever either.)

11 We sometimes think of aging as a process applying uniformly to the whole
우리는 때때로 노화를 여긴다 / 과정으로 / [유기체 전체에 균일하게 적용되는]
organism, **yet** physiological studies show that different parts of the body
/ 하지만 생리학 연구들은 보여준다 / 신체의 여러 부분들이 노화한다는 것을
age at different rates.
/ 별개의 속도로

aging 노화 *cf.* age 노화하다
uniformly 균일하게, 한결같이
physiological 생리학의

- **풀이** S + V ~, yet + S + V …: ~, 하지만 …

[모의] **12** The old maxim "I'll sleep when I'm dead" is unfortunate. Adopt this mindset,
'나는 죽을 때 잠에 들 것이다'라는 옛 격언은 유감스럽다 / 이러한 마음가짐을 취해 보라
and you will be dead **sooner and** the quality of that life will be worse.
/ 그러면 당신은 더욱 빨리 죽게 될 것이다 / 그리고 그 삶의 질은 더욱 나빠질 것이다

maxim 격언, 금언
unfortunate 유감스러운; 불행한
adopt (자세·입장을) 취하다; 입양하다

- **풀이** 명령문, and + S + V ~: …해라, 그러면 ~할 것이다

unit 56
상관접속사 구문

S	V	both / either / neither ...	단어 (구 / 절)	and / or / nor ...	단어 (구 / 절)
You	can take	either	soup	or	salad.
당신은	/ 가져갈 수 있다		/ 수프를	/ 또는	/ 샐러드를

Standard Sentences

01 The athletes competed to gain honor **both** for themselves **and** for their
그 운동선수들은 경쟁했다 / 명예를 얻기 위해서 / 자기 자신들을 위해서도 / 그리고 자신들의 나라를
countries rather than achieve great wealth.
위해서도 / 큰 부를 성취하기 위해서라기보다는

- both A and B: A와 B 둘 다
- A rather than B: B라기보다는 오히려 A / A가 to부정사일 때 B에는 to부정사 또는 동사원형이 올 수 있다.

수능 02 The Internet is the greatest tool we have **not only** for making people
인터넷은 가장 위대한 도구이다 / [우리가 가진 / 사람들을 더 빨리 더 똑똑하게 만들기 위해서일
smarter quicker, **but also** for making people dumber faster.
뿐만 아니라 / 사람들을 더 빨리 더 멍청하게 만들기 위해서도]

- not only A but also B: A뿐만 아니라 B도
- tool 다음에 목적격 관계대명사 that이 생략되어 있다.

A 03 The stupid **neither** forgive **nor** forget; the naive forgive and forget; the wise
어리석은 자는 용서하지도 잊지도 않는다 / 순진한 자는 용서하고 잊어버린다 / 현명한 자는
forgive but do not forget. *Thomas Szasz*
용서하지만 잊지 않는다

naive 순진한

- neither A nor B: A도 B도 아닌

모의 04 A word isn't ambiguous by itself **but** is used ambiguously: it is ambiguous
어떤 단어는 그 자체로 애매한 것이 아니라 / 애매하게 사용되는 것이다 / 그 단어는 애매하다
when one cannot tell from the context what sense is being used.
/ 사람이 문맥에서 알 수 없을 때 / 어떤 의미가 쓰이고 있는지를

ambiguous 애매한, 모호한
by itself 그 자체로, 저절로
tell (정확히) 알다, 판단하다

- not A but B: A가 아니라 B
- what sense is being used는 tell의 목적어로 쓰인 명사절로, 목적어가 길어 부사구 뒤로 보내진 형태이다.

05 Life on a desert island is wretched. You **either** starve to death **or** live like
무인도에서의 삶은 비참하다 당신은 굶주려서 죽게 되거나 또는 로빈슨 크루소처럼 산다
Robinson Crusoe, waiting for a boat which never comes.
/ 보트를 기다리면서 / [결코 오지 않는]

desert island 무인도
wretched 비참한, 끔찍한
starve to death 굶어 죽다

- either A or B: A이거나 B

> **Know More** ◄ 로빈슨 크루소는 18세기 영국 작가 다니엘 디포의 소설 「요크의 선원 로빈슨 크루소의 생애와 이상하고 놀라운 모험(The Life and Strange Surprising Adventures of Robinson Crusoe of York)」의 주인공이다. 그는 중산층의 보장된 생활을 택하지 않고 선원이 되기를 자처하여 해외로 가던 와중에 무인도에 갇히게 된다. 이 소설은 28년간의 무인도 생활을 사실적으로 묘사했을 뿐만 아니라, 당시 영국의 해상 교역 활동과 유럽의 식민지 개척 경쟁 등 시대상이 담겨 있어 영국 근대 소설의 대표작으로 인정받고 있다.

06 As fruit needs **not only** sunshine **but** cold nights and chilling showers to
열매가 햇살뿐만 아니라 서늘한 밤과 차가운 소나기도 필요로 하듯이 /
ripen it, so character needs **not only** joy **but** trial and difficulty to mellow it.
그것을 익히기 위해서 / 인격은 기쁨뿐만 아니라 시련과 곤경도 필요하다 / 그것을 원숙하게 하기 위해서

- not only A but (also) B: A뿐만 아니라 B도
- (just) as ~, so ...: (꼭) ~인 것처럼 …하다 **Unit 40**

chilling 서늘한, 냉랭한
ripen 익히다, 숙성시키다
trial 시련; 재판
mellow 원숙하게 하다; 원만한

07 Mishaps are like knives that **either** serve us **or** cut us as we grasp them by
불행은 칼과 같다 / [우리에게 쓸모가 있거나 또는 우리를 베는 / 우리가 그것을 붙잡을 때 /
the handle or blade.
손잡이 또는 날로]

- either A or B: A이거나 B

mishap 불행, 재난
grasp 붙잡다; 이해하다
blade (칼 등의) 날

08 The true mark of heroes lies **not** necessarily in the result of their actions, **but**
영웅들의 진정한 특징은 있다 / 반드시 그들의 행동의 결과가 아니라 /
in what they are willing to do for others and for their chosen causes.
그들이 기꺼이 하고자 하는 것에 / 남을 위해서 그리고 자신들이 선택한 대의를 위해서

- not A but B: A가 아니라 B
- 전치사 in의 목적어로 what이 이끄는 명사절 what ~ causes가 쓰였다. **Unit 60**

cause 대의, 목적; 원인

09 Movies offer **both** the happy ending that we love **and** the more conservative
영화는 제공한다 / 행복한 결말과 / [우리가 사랑하는] / 그리고 주류 문화에 대한 더욱 보수적인
support of the dominant culture that guides behavior in "the real world."
지지를 / ['현실 세계'에서의 행동을 좌우하는]

- both A and B: A와 B 둘 다

conservative 보수적인
dominant 주류의, 우세한
guide (사상·감정을) 좌우하다;
안내하다

10 **Neither** a wise man **nor** a brave man lies down on the tracks of history to
현명한 사람도 용감한 사람도 누워 있지 않는다 / 역사라는 철로 위에 /
wait for the train of the future to run over him. *Dwight D. Eisenhower*
미래라는 기차가 자신을 치고 가기를 기다리기 위해

- 풀이 neither A nor B: A도 B도 아닌 / neither A nor B가 주어일 때 동사는 B의 수에 일치시킨다.
- the tracks of history와 the train of the future는 동격의 of가 쓰인 표현이다. **Unit 52**

track 선로; 자국
run over (차 등이) ~을 치다

11 The whole aim of good teaching is to turn the young learner into an
훌륭한 교육의 완전한 목표는 젊은 학습자를 독립적인 사람으로 바꾸는 것이다
independent man, who doesn't **merely** learn **but** works by himself.
/ 그리고 그 사람은 배울 뿐만 아니라 스스로 공부한다

- 풀이 not merely A but (also) B: A뿐만 아니라 B도
- 관계대명사 who 이하는 an independent man에 대한 부가 설명이다. **Unit 28**

aim 목표, 목적
by oneself 스스로, 홀로

12 The language which every human being speaks is **not** an individual inheritance,
언어는 / [모든 인간이 말하는] / 개인적 유산이 아니라
but a social acquisition from the group in which he grows up. **Both** language
/ 집단으로부터 사회적으로 습득된 것이다 / [인간이 성장한] 언어와 환경 둘 다 도움을
and environment help to determine the character of his thought.
준다 / 인간의 사고의 성격을 결정짓는 데

- 풀이 (A) not A but B: A가 아니라 B (B) both A and B: A와 B 둘 다

inheritance 유전; 상속
acquisition 습득, 획득

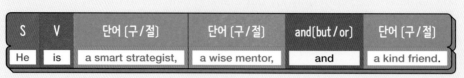

unit 57
병렬 구문

S	V	단어 [구 / 절]	단어 [구 / 절]	and[but / or]	단어 [구 / 절]
He	is	a smart strategist,	a wise mentor,	and	a kind friend.

그는 / ~이다 / 영리한 전략가 / 현명한 멘토 / 그리고 / 좋은 친구

Standard Sentences

01 Creative solutions come from **viewing something differently and discovering**
창의적인 해결책은 나온다 / 어떤 것을 다르게 보는 것으로부터 / 그리고 발견하는 것으로부터
what others have missed.
/ 다른 사람들이 놓친 것을

■ and로 동명사구 viewing ~ differently와 discovering 이하가 병렬 연결되어 있다.

[수능!] 02 Testing allows us **not merely** to confirm our theories **but to weed out** those
실험은 우리가 우리의 이론을 입증하도록 해 줄 뿐만 아니라 / 이론들을 제거하게도 해 준다
that do not fit the evidence.
/ [그 증거에 부합하지 않는]

■ not merely A but (also) B: A뿐만 아니라 B도 / to부정사구 to confirm ~ theories와 to weed out ~ evidence 가 병렬 연결되어 있다.
— those는 our theories를 가리킨다.

confirm 입증하다, 확인하다
weed out ~을 제거하다
fit 부합하다; 꼭 맞다; 적합한

[A] 03 Some drug companies have **frequently** been caught **making false claims**
[모의] 몇몇 제약 회사들은 자주 목격되어왔다 / 자신들의 제품에 대한 허위 주장을
about their products or hiding information to cover up their dangers.
하는 것이 / 또는 그것들의 위험을 감추기 위해서 정보를 은폐하는 것이

■ or로 분사구 making ~ products와 hiding 이하가 병렬 연결되어 있다.
— be caught + v-ing: ~하는 것이 목격되다

false 허위의, 틀린
claim 주장; 요구
cover up ~을 은폐하다[감추다]

04 Many people who have type II diabetes are advised to control their blood
많은 사람들은 / [제2형 당뇨병을 가진] / 그들의 혈당 수준을 통제하라고 조언을 받는다
sugar levels by following a healthy diet, taking exercise and losing weight.
/ 건강한 식단을 실천함으로써, 운동을 함으로써, 그리고 살을 뺌으로써

■ and로 세 개의 동명사구 following ~, taking ~, losing ~이 병렬 연결되어 있다.

blood sugar 혈당
diabetes 당뇨병

05 The world is a dangerous place to live; **not because of the people who are**
세상은 살기에 위험한 곳이다 / 사람들 때문이 아니라 / [악한]
evil, but because of the people who don't do anything about it. *Albert Einstein*
/ 사람들 때문에 / [악에 대해서 아무것도 하지 않는]

■ not A but B: A가 아니라 B / 전치사구 because of ~ evil과 because of ~ it이 병렬 연결되어 있다.

evil 악한; 악

ⓑ 06 In music, cacophony is **discordant sounds,** **false harmony,** **or noisy and**
음악에서 / 불협화음은 ~이다 / 조화되지 않는 소리 / 잘못된 화음 / 또는 시끄럽고 가락이
inharmonious combinations of sounds.
맞지 않는 음들의 조합

■ or로 세 개의 명사구 discordant sounds, false harmony, noisy ~ sounds가 병렬 연결되어 있다.

cacophony 불협화음
discordant 조화되지 않는; 일
치하지 않는
harmony 화음; 조화
inharmonious 가락이 맞지
않는

07 Teachers cannot **seat children all behind desks in a classroom,** **dictate**
교사들은 ~할 수 없다 / 아이들 모두를 앉게 하고 / 교실에서 책상 뒤에 / 그들에게
information to them and expect them to absorb all of it like a sponge.
지식을 받아쓰게 하고 / 그리고 그들이 스펀지처럼 그것 모두를 흡수하기를 기대할

■ and로 세 개의 동사구 seat ~ classroom, dictate ~ them, expect ~ sponge가 병렬 연결되어 있다.

dictate 받아쓰게 하다; 지시
하다

08 The value of life is **not in the length of days,** **but in the use we make of them;**
인생의 가치는 날들의 길이에 있는 것이 아니라 / 우리가 그 날을 사용하는 데 (있다)
a man may live **long yet very little.** *Michel de Montaigne*
사람은 오래 살 수도 있지만 아주 적게 살 수도 있다

■ not A but B: A가 아니라 B / 전치사구 in ~ days와 in ~ them이 병렬 연결되어 있다.
■ yet으로 동사 may live를 꾸며주는 부사 long과 very little이 병렬 연결되어 있다.

length 길이
make use of ~을 이용하다

수능 09 The law about a contract considers such questions as **whether it exists,**
계약에 관한 법은 문제들을 고려한다 / [계약이 존재하는지
what the meaning of it is, whether it has been broken, and what compensation
/ 그것의 의미가 무엇인지 / 그것이 깨졌는지 / 그리고 어떤 보상이 피해를 입은
is due to the injured party.
당사자에게 지불되어야 하는지와 같은]

■ and로 네 개의 명사절 whether ~ exists, what ~ is, whether ~ broken, what ~ party가 병렬 연결되어 있다.

contract 계약
compensation 보상
due 지불되어야 할; ~할 예정인
party 당사자, 상대방; 정당; 파티

ⓒ 10 By sensing **whether people are in the house or which rooms they are in,** a
감지함으로써 / 사람들이 집에 있는지 / 또는 그들이 어떤 방에 있는지를 /
smart thermostat can **either switch off heating or cooling completely or**
똑똑한 자동 온도 조절기는 난방 또는 냉방장치를 완전히 끌 수 있거나 / 또는
concentrate on the rooms where the people are.
방에 집중할 (수 있다) / [그 사람들이 있는]

풀이 「either A or B」 구조가 쓰였으며, 동사원형 switch와 병렬 연결되도록 동사원형 concentrate가 적절하다.

sense 감지하다; 감각
thermostat 자동 온도 조절기

모의 11 Electric cars have **several limitations that reduce their popularity. Some of**
전기차는 몇 가지 한계를 지니고 있다 / [그들의 인기를 떨어뜨리는] 이러한 불리한
these disadvantages are that the autos are expensive, are relatively slow,
점들의 일부는 ~이다 / 그 자동차들이 비싸고 / 상대적으로 느리고
and require constant recharging.
/ 그리고 끊임없는 재충전이 필요하다는 것

풀이 and로 두 개의 are와 병렬 구조를 이뤄야 하므로 주어 the autos와 이어지는 동사 require가 적절하다.

popularity 인기
disadvantages 불리, 불편
relatively 상대적으로
constant 끊임없는
recharging 재충전

모의 12 Recently, researchers have suggested that the purpose of laughter is **not**
최근에 / 연구자들은 시사했다 / 웃음의 목적은 전달하는 것일 뿐만 아니라
just to communicate that one is in a playful state, but to induce this state
/ 어떤 이가 쾌활한 상태에 있다는 것을 / 이 상태를 남들에게서 또한 유도해 내려는
in others as well.
것이기도 하다는 것을

풀이 「not just A but (also) B」 구조가 쓰였으며, but으로 to communicate와 병렬 연결되어야 하므로 to부정사
형태인 to induce가 적절하다.

suggest 시사하다; 제안하다
induce 유도하다; 유발하다

unit 58
부정 구문

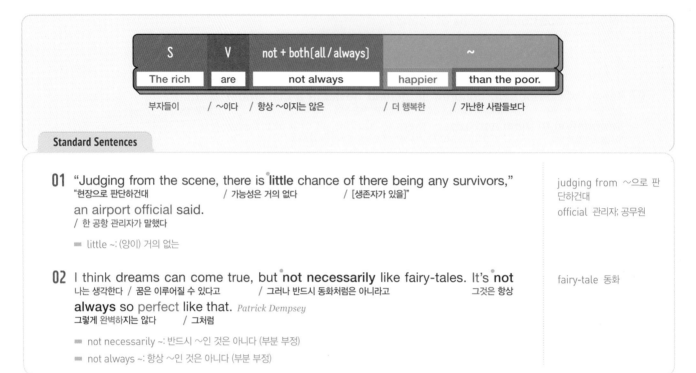

S	V	not + both[all / always]		~
The rich	are	not always	happier	than the poor.
부자들이	/ ~이다	/ 항상 ~이지는 않은	/ 더 행복한	/ 가난한 사람들보다

Standard Sentences

01 "Judging from the scene, there is **little** chance of there being any survivors,"
"현장으로 판단하건대 / 가능성은 거의 없다 / [생존자가 있을]"
an airport official said.
/ 한 공항 관리자가 말했다

- little ~: (양이) 거의 없는

judging from ~으로 판단하건대
official 관리자; 공무원

02 I think dreams can come true, but **not necessarily** like fairy-tales. It's **not**
나는 생각한다 / 꿈은 이루어질 수 있다고 / 그러나 반드시 동화처럼은 아니라고 그것은 항상
always so perfect like that. *Patrick Dempsey*
그렇게 완벽하지는 않다 / 그처럼

- not necessarily ~: 반드시 ~인 것은 아니다 (부분 부정)
- not always ~: 항상 ~인 것은 아니다 (부분 부정)

fairy-tale 동화

Ⓐ 03 There have been **few**, **if any**, human societies that have not had their own
거의 없었다 / 있다 하더라도 / 인간 사회는 / [그들 자신의 윤리 규범이 없는]
codes of ethics. There are **few**, **if any**, human beings not interested in
거의 없다 / 있다 하더라도 / 인간은 / [옳은 것과 그른 것 사이의
distinctions between right and wrong.
구별에 관심이 없다]

- few ~: (수가) 거의 없는
- few와 human societies 그리고 human beings 사이에 관용표현 if any가 삽입되어 있다.

if any 있다 하더라도
code of ethics 윤리 규범
distinction 구별

04 When the ancestors of the cheetah first began pursuing the ancestors of the
치타의 조상이 처음 가젤의 조상을 뒤쫓기 시작했을 때
gazelle, **neither** of them could run as fast as they can today. *Richard Dawkins*
/ 그들 중 어느 쪽도 달릴 수 없었다 / 그들이 오늘날 할 수 있는 만큼 빠르게

- neither ~: 어느 쪽도 ~ 아닌 (양자 부정)

ancestor 조상
pursue 뒤쫓다; 추구하다
gazelle 가젤, 영양

05 **No** sensible decision can be made any longer **without** taking into account
합리적인 결정은 더 이상 내려질 수 없다 / 고려하지 않고서는
not only the world as it is, but the world as it will be. *Isaac Asimov*
/ 세상을 현재 그대로 뿐만 아니라 / 세상이 앞으로 어떻게 될 것인지도

- no ~ without ...: ...하지 않고는 ~하지 않다 (이중 부정) / take의 목적어인 not only ~ will be가 길어져 account 뒤에 왔다.

sensible 합리적인, 분별 있는
take ~ into account ~을 고려하다

B 06 All that is gold does **not** glitter. **Not all** those who wander are lost.
금으로 된 모든 것이 반짝이는 것은 아니다   방황하는 사람들 모두가 길을 잃은 것은 아니다
the movie <The Lord of the Rings: The Fellowship of the Ring>

glitter 반짝이다
wander 방황하다, 헤매다

- not all: 모두 ~인 것은 아니다 (부분 부정)
- 첫 번째 문장에서 관계대명사 that이 이끄는 절 that is gold가 All을 수식하고, 두 번째 문장에서 관계대명사 who 가 이끄는 절 who wander가 all those를 수식한다.

07 With free capital flows, monetary policy could be directed **either** at stabilizing
자유로운 자본 흐름으로   / 통화 정책은 방향짓게 될 수 있다   / 환율을 안정화하는 것으로
an exchange rate **or** controlling inflation, but **not both**.
              / 또는 인플레이션을 통제하는 것으로 / 그러나 둘 다는 아니다

capital 자본
flow 흐름
monetary 통화[화폐]의
stabilize 안정시키다
exchange rate 환율

- not both: 둘 다 ~은 아니다
- 「either A or B」 구조가 쓰였으며, 전치사구 at stabilizing과 or로 연결되는 controlling inflation에서 at이 생략 되어 있다.

08 A new idea comes suddenly and in a rather intuitive way. But intuition is
새로운 아이디어는 찾아온다   / 갑자기 그리고 다소 직관적인 방식으로   그러나 직관은 결과일
nothing but the outcome of earlier intellectual experience. *Albert Einstein*
뿐이다   / [이전의 지적 경험의]

intuitive 직관적인 *cf.* intuition
직관
outcome 결과, 성과

- nothing but: ~일 뿐 (= only)

Up! 09 No one has given so much care to the study of composition as I. There is
어느 누구도 많은 관심을 주지는 않았다   / 작곡 연구에   / 나만큼 음악계에서
scarcely a famous master in music whose works I have **not** frequently and
유명한 거장은 거의 없다   / [그들의 작품을 내가 자주 그리고 부지런하게 연구하지 않은]
diligently studied. *Wolfgang Amadeus Mozart*

composition 작곡, 작문; 구성
frequently 자주
diligently 부지런하게

- scarcely ~ not ...: …하지 않은 것은 거의 ~ 않다 (이중 부정)
- 부정 주어 ~ + as[so] + 원급 + as ...: 어떤 것도 …만큼 ~하지 않은

C 10 People **rarely** succeed **unless** they have fun in what they are doing.
사람들은 좀처럼 성공하지 못한다   / 그들이 즐거움을 느끼지 않으면 / 자신이 하고 있는 것에

unless ~하지 않는다면

- rarely ~ unless ...: …하지 않는다면 좀처럼 ~하지 않다
- 전치사 in의 목적어로 what이 이끄는 명사절이 왔다.

Up! 11 **Hardly** any discovery is possible **without** making use of knowledge gained
거의 어떠한 발견도 가능하지 않다   / 지식을 활용하지 않고서   / [다른
by others.
사람들에 의해 얻어진]

make use of ~을 활용하다

- hardly ~ without ...: …하지 않고는 거의 ~ 않다 / hardly가 문장 앞에 있더라도, 문장 전체가 아니라 주어만 부정 할 경우 주어와 동사는 도치되지 않는다.

모의 12 Geniuses don't **necessarily** have a higher success rate than other creators;
천재들이 반드시 더 높은 성공률을 가진 것은 아니다   / 다른 창작자들보다
they simply do more—and they do a range of different things.
그들은 단지 더 많은 것을 한다   / —그리고 그들은 여러 다양한 것들을 한다

- not necessarily: 반드시 ~인 것은 아니다

unit 59
동명사 관용 구문

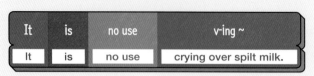

It	is	no use	v-ing ~
It	is	no use	crying over spilt milk.

(…은) / ~이다 / 소용없는 / 엎질러진 우유를 두고 우는 것은

Standard Sentences

모의 01 We are used to thinking of light as always going in straight lines. But it
우리는 빛을 생각하는 것에 익숙하다 / 항상 직선으로 가는 것이라고 그러나 그것은
doesn't.
그렇지 않다

- be used to + v-ing: ~하는 데 익숙하다 / cf. be used to-v: ~하기 위해 사용되다
- 두 번째 문장에서 doesn't 다음에 go in straight lines가 생략되어 있다.

02 It's no use carrying an umbrella if your shoes are leaking. *Irish Proverb*
(…은) 소용없다 / 우산을 갖고 다니는 것은 / 만약 당신의 신발이 새고 있다면

- It is no use v-ing: ~해도 소용없다 / (it은 가주어, v-ing 이하가 진주어이다.)

leak 새다

A 03 Those who don't set goals, will have a difficult time figuring out how to
목표를 설정하지 않는 사람들은 어려움을 겪을 것이다 / 그것에 어떻게 도달할지 알아내는 데
reach them. *JJ Goldwag*

- have a difficult time + v-ing: ~하는 데 어려움을 겪다

figure out 알아내다. 이해하다

04 Don't waste your time looking back at what you lost. Move on. Life is not
당신의 시간을 낭비하지 마라 / 되돌아보는 데 / 당신이 잃은 것을 나아가라 인생은 뒤로
meant to be traveled backwards.
돌아가도록 되어 있지 않다

- waste + 시간 + v-ing: ~하는 데 …을 낭비하다[쓰다]

mean ~을 의도하다; 의미하다

05 It goes without saying that stating a problem is not the same thing as
(…은) 말할 것도 없다 / 어떤 문제를 명시하는 것이 같은 것이 아니라는 것은 /
solving it in practice.
그것을 실제로 해결하는 것과

- It goes without saying that ~: ~은 말할 것도 없다 / It은 가주어, that절이 진주어이다.
- A not the same ~ as B: A는 B와 같지 않은 ~

state 명시하다, 말하다; 상태
in practice 실제로

ⓑ 06 During sleep, while the body rests, the brain is busy processing information
자는 동안 　 / 몸은 쉬고 있는 반면에 　 / 뇌는 바쁘다 　 / 낮에 만들어진 정보를 처리하느라
from the day and forming memories.
　 / 그리고 기억을 구성하느라

process 처리하다; 과정

> ■ be busy v-ing: ~하느라 바쁘다
> ― and로 processing ~ day와 forming memories가 병렬 연결되어 있다.

07 She made a point of sending thank-you notes to everyone who attended
그녀는 감사 편지 보내는 일을 반드시 했다 　 / 모두에게 　 / [자신의 파티에 참석한]
her party.

attend 참석하다; 주의하다

> ■ make a point of v-ing: 반드시[으레] ~하다, ~을 규칙적으로 하다 (= make it a rule to-v)

08 It is no use saying, "We are doing our best." You have got to succeed in
(…은) 소용없다 　 / 말하는 것은 　 / "우리는 최선을 다하고 있다"고 　 당신은 성공해야 한다 　 /
doing what is necessary. *Winston Churchill*
필요한 일을 하는 것에

succeed in ~에 성공하다

> ■ It is no use v-ing: ~해도 소용없다
> ― have got to는 의무를 나타내는 표현인 have to를 조금 더 강조해서 쓰는 구어체 표현이며, have to와 달리 현재 시
> 제의 긍정문에만 쓸 수 있다.

09 It's a dangerous business, Frodo, going out your door. You step onto the
(…은) 위험한 일이야 　 / 프로도 　 / 문 밖으로 나가는 것은 　 네가 길을 나서면
road, and if you don't keep your feet, there's no knowing where you might
　 / 그리고 만약 네가 똑바로 서 있지 않으면 　 / 아는 것은 불가능해 　 / 네가 어디로 휩쓸려 가게 될지
be swept off to. *the movie <The Lord of the Rings: The Fellowship of the Ring>*

keep one's feet 똑바로 서
있다[걷다], 넘어지지 않다
sweep 휩쓸어 가다; 쓸다
(swept-swept)

> ■ There is no v-ing: ~하는 것은 불가능하다, ~할 수 없다
> ― 첫 번째 문장에서 It은 가주어이고, going out your door가 진주어이다.

ⓒ 10 A good book enlightening your mind is worth reading over again and again.
좋은 책은 　 / [당신의 정신을 깨우치게 하는] 　 / 반복해서 읽을 가치가 있다

enlighten 깨우치게 하다, 계
몽하다

> ■ be worth v-ing: ~할 가치가 있다

11 There is no telling how far science and technology will have progressed by
말하는 것은 불가능하다 　 / 과학과 기술이 어디까지 진보했을지 　 /
the end of this century.
금세기 말에

progress 진보하다

> ■ There is no v-ing: ~하는 것은 불가능하다, ~할 수 없다
> ― how far 이하는 명사절로서 동명사 telling의 목적어이다.

12 People have a hard time letting go of their suffering. Out of a fear of the
사람들은 어려움을 겪는다 　 / 자신들의 고통을 놓아주는 데 　 미지에 대한 두려움으로
unknown, they prefer suffering that is familiar. *Thich Nhat Hanh*
　 / 그들은 고통을 더 좋아한다 　 / [익숙한]

let go of ~을 놓아주다
familiar 익숙한

> ■ have a hard time + v-ing: ~하는 데 어려움을 겪다

unit 60
전치사 + 명사절

S	V	전치사 + that[whether / 의문사 등] + (s) + v ~
You	may dance	with whomever you like.
너는	/ 춤춰도 된다	/ 네가 좋아하는 누구나와

Standard Sentences

01 There have been many debates °as to whether cryptocurrency should be
많은 토론이 있어왔다   / [암호화폐가 분류되어야 하는지에 관한
classified as property, commodity, money, or security.
   / 자산, 상품, 돈, 또는 유가증권으로서]

  ■ as to + whether + s + v ~: ~인지에 관한 / many debates를 수식하는 형용사 역할을 하고 있다.

cryptocurrency 암호화폐
classify 분류하다
commodity 상품, 산물
security 유가증권; 안전

02 Ecosystems are dynamic °in that their various parts are always changing.
생태계는 역동적이다   / 그것의 다양한 부분들이 항상 변하고 있다는 점에서

  ■ in + that + s + v ~: ~라는 점에서 / 이유·근거를 나타내는 부사절이다.

dynamic 역동적인

Ⓐ 03 One day President Roosevelt told me that he was asking publicly for
어느 날 루즈벨트 대통령이 내게 말했다   / 자신이 공개적으로 의견을 구하고 있다고
suggestions °about what the war should be called. I said at once "The
    / [그 전쟁이 무엇으로 불려야 하는지에 대한]   나는 바로 '불필요한 전쟁'이라고
Unnecessary War." *Winston Churchill*
말했다

  ■ 전치사 about의 목적어로 what이 이끄는 명사절이 왔다.

publicly 공개적으로; 공적으로
at once 바로, 즉시

모예 04 Technology is the basis of many of our metaphors and is important °in terms
기술은 우리의 은유 대부분의 토대이다   / 그리고 중요하다   / 어떻게 우리가
of how we think and how our ideas progress.
생각하는가 그리고 어떻게 우리의 생각이 나아가는가의 관점에서

  ■ in terms of의 목적어로 how가 이끄는 두 개의 명사절이 왔다.

metaphor 은유
in terms of ~의 관점에서

05 What you do for a living is critical °to where you settle and how you live—
생계를 위해 당신이 하는 것은 대단히 중요하다   / 당신이 어디에 정착하는지와 어떻게 사는지에—
and the converse is also true.
/ 그리고 그 반대 또한 진실이다

  ■ 전치사 to의 목적어로 의문사 where와 how가 이끄는 두 개의 명사절이 왔다.

critical 대단히 중요한, 중대한
settle 정착하다
converse 반대의; 대화하다

ⓑ 06 The success of the talks is up to whether both sides are willing to make
대화의 성공은 　　　　　　 / 양측이 기꺼이 약간의 양보를 하려고 하는지에 달려 있다
some concessions.

be up to ~에 달려 있다
concession 양보

- 전치사 up to의 목적어로 whehter가 이끄는 명사절이 왔다.
- whether는 명사절을 이끌며 '~인지 아닌지'를 뜻하고, 부사절을 이끌 경우에는 '~이든 아니든'의 뜻으로 쓰인다.

07 In biology, the "niche" of a species is broadly defined by what it eats and
생물학에서 　　 / 어떤 종의 '적합한 환경'은 폭넓게 정의된다 　　　　　 / 그것이 무엇을 먹는지와 그것이
how it reproduces.
번식하는 방식에 의해

niche 적합한 환경, 적소
reproduce 번식하다; 복제하다

- 전치사 by의 목적어로 의문사 what과 how가 이끄는 두 개의 명사절이 왔다.

모의 08 Competition is basically concerned with how the availability of resources,
경쟁은 기본적으로 관련된다 　　　　　　 / 어떻게 자원의 입수 가능성이
such as food and space, is reduced by other organisms.
/ [먹이와 공간 같은] 　　　　　 / 다른 생물체로 인해 줄어드는지와

be concerned with ~와 관련되다
availability 입수 가능성, 유용성

- 전치사 with의 목적어로 의문사 how가 이끄는 명사절이 왔다.
- how가 이끄는 명사절 내에서 such as ~ space는 삽입 어구이다.

09 Winning is important to me, but what brings me real joy is the experience of
승리하는 것은 내게 중요하다 　　　 / 그러나 내게 진정한 기쁨을 주는 것은 완전히 몰입하고 있는 경험이다
being fully engaged in whatever I'm doing. _Phil Jackson_
/ 무엇이든지 내가 하고 있는 것에

be engaged in ~에 몰입하다, ~에 종사하다

- 전치사 in의 목적어로 whatever가 이끄는 명사절이 왔다.

ⓒ 10 In choosing which path to take with some of life's decisions, ethics are
선택할 때 　　 / 어느 길을 취할 것인가 　　 / 인생의 몇몇 결정들에 　　　　　　 윤리가 종종 중심에
often at the center; heavily influencing our choices between what is right
있다 　　　　　　 / 우리의 선택에 크게 영향을 미치면서 　　　　　 / [옳은 것과 그릇 것 사이의]
and what is wrong.

path 길, 경로
ethics (보통 복수 취급) 윤리, 도덕; (단수 취급) 윤리학

- 「between A and B」 구문에서 전치사의 목적어로 what이 이끄는 명사절이 왔다. / our choices를 수식하는 형용사 역할을 하고 있다.

11 We hunger to understand, so we invent myths about how we imagine the
우리는 이해하는 데 굶주려 있다 　　　 / 그래서 우리는 신화들을 지어낸다 / [우리가 상상하기에 세상이 어떻게
world is constructed. _Carl Sagan_
구성되었는지에 관한]

myth 신화; 통념
construct 구성하다

- 전치사 about의 목적어로 의문사 how가 이끄는 명사절이 왔다.
- how 다음에 we imagine이 삽입되어 있다.

12 The knowledge you have acquired will enable you to be successful in whatever
지식은 　　　　 / [당신이 습득한] 　　　 / 당신이 성공할 수 있게 해 줄 것이다 　　　 / 당신이 진입하게
field you may enter.
될 어떠한 분야에서든지

field 분야; 들판

- 전치사 in의 목적어로 whatever가 이끄는 명사절이 왔다.
- The knowledge 다음에 목적격 관계대명사 which 또는 that이 생략되어 있다.

Chapter 12

Review

A **01** People are often blinded by love, **making** bad judgments and wrong
사람들은 종종 사랑에 눈이 먼다 / 부적절한 판단과 잘못된 선택을 하면서
choices, **or doing** stupid and foolish things, under the influence of love.
/ 또는 어리석고 바보 같은 일을 하면서 / 사랑의 영향으로

■ or로 현재분사구 making ~ choices와 doing 이하가 병렬 연결되어 있다.

02 Blockchain technology is **not** a company, **nor** is it an app, **but rather** an
블록체인 기술은 회사가 아니다 / 그것은 응용 프로그램도 아니다 / 오히려 인터넷상에서
entirely new way of documenting data on the Internet.
자료를 기록하는 완전히 새로운 방식(이다)

■ not A, nor B, but C: A도 아니고, B도 아니고, C이다
■ not(never) ~, nor + V + S: …도 또한 아니다

> app 응용 프로그램
> (= application)
> entirely 완전히, 전적으로
> document 기록하다; 서류, 문서

[수능!] **03** Material wealth in and of itself does **not necessarily** generate meaning **or**
물질적인 부유함은 그 자체로 그리고 저절로 / 반드시 의미를 만들어 내거나 감정적인 부유함으로 이끌지는 않는다
lead to emotional wealth.

■ not necessarily ~: 반드시 ~인 것은 아니다 (부분 부정)
■ or로 동사 generate와 lead가 병렬 연결되어 있다.

> in itself 그 자체로; 본래
> of itself 저절로

04 You probably wouldn't worry **about what people think of you** if you could
당신은 아마 걱정하지 않을 텐데 / 사람들이 당신을 어떻게 생각하는지에 대해 / 만약 당신이 알 수
know how seldom they do.
있다면 / 그들이 얼마나 드물게 그렇게 하는지

■ 전치사 about의 목적어로 what이 이끄는 명사절이 왔다.
■ do는 think of you를 대신하는 대동사로 쓰였다.

B **05** Energy can **neither** be created **nor** destroyed, **but** can merely be transformed
[모의] 에너지는 창조될 수도 파괴될 수도 없다 / 단지 변형될 수 있을 뿐이다
from one state to another.
/ 하나의 상태에서 다른 상태로

■ **풀이** neither A nor B: A도 B도 아닌

> transform 변형시키다

[수능!] **06** Just **walking** through a garden **or**, for that matter, **seeing** one out your
단지 정원을 걷는 것 / 또는 실제로 / 창밖으로 정원을 보는 것은
window, can **lower** blood pressure, **reduce** stress, **and ease** pain.
/ 혈압을 낮출 수 있다 / 스트레스를 줄인다 / 그리고 고통을 완화시킨다

■ **풀이** or로 동명사 walking과 병렬 연결되어 있으므로 동명사 seeing이 적절하다.

> for that matter 실제로; 그것
> 에 관해서는
> blood pressure 혈압
> ease 완화하다, 덜해지다; 쉬움

07 **Having grown** up in a culture that appreciates modesty and reserve, he was
문화에서 성장했기 때문에 / [겸손함과 신중함을 높이 평가하는] / 그는
not **accustomed to expressing** emotions in public.
익숙하지 않았다 / 공개적으로 감정을 표현하는 것에

■ **풀이** be accustomed to + v-ing: ~하는 데 익숙하다(= be used to + v-ing)
■ 주절의 동사보다 먼저 발생한 일을 나타내는 완료 분사구문이다.

> appreciate 높이 평가하다; 감
> 사하다
> modesty 겸손함; 소박함
> reserve 신중함, 자제; 남겨두
> 다, 보류하다

08 Introducing drones to our emergency services could save lives by **transporting**
드론을 우리의 긴급 구조대에 도입하는 것은 생명을 구할 수 있다 / 혈액과 AED와 같은

materials like blood and AEDs more quickly, **locating** people inside burning
물자를 더 빨리 운송함으로써 / 화재가 난 건물 안에 있는 사람들의 위치를

buildings, **and helping** the police track suspects.
알아냄으로써 / 그리고 경찰이 용의자를 추적하는 것을 도움으로써

> 풀이 and로 앞의 두 개의 동명사 transporting, locating과 병렬 연결되어 있으므로 동명사 helping이 적절하다.

emergency services 긴급 구조대
AED(Automated External Defibrillator) 심장 충격기
locate 위치를 알아내다
track 추적하다
suspect 용의자

C **09** You can move the cursor **either** by using the mouse **or** by using the arrow
당신은 커서를 움직일 수 있다 / 마우스를 사용함으로써 / 또는 키보드 위의 화살표 키를 사용

keys on the keyboard.
함으로써

> 풀이 「either A or B」 구조가 쓰였으며, by using the mouse와 병렬 연결되어 있으므로 by 뒤에 동명사구 using 이하가 오는 것이 자연스럽다.

cursor (컴퓨터 화면의) 커서

10 Advertisements do **not always** tell you everything you need to know in order
광고가 항상 당신에게 말해 주지는 않는다 / 모든 것을 [당신이 알 필요가 있는] / 당신이

to make a wise choice.
현명한 선택을 하기 위해서]

> 풀이 not always는 '항상 ~인 것은 아니다'의 의미로 부분 부정을 나타내며, 빈도부사 always는 조동사 뒤, 일반동사 앞에 위치하므로 do not always tell로 쓴다.
> — everything 다음에 목적격 관계대명사 that이 생략되어 있다.

in order to ~하기 위해서

11 True love cannot be found where it does not exist, **nor** can it be denied
진정한 사랑은 발견될 수 없다 / 그것이 존재하지 않는 곳에서 / 그리고 그것은 부인될 수도 없다

where it does. *Torquato Tasso*
/ 그것이 존재하는 곳에서

> 풀이 (not[never] ~) nor + V + S: …도 또한 아니다 / 조동사가 쓰였을 경우에는 「조동사 + S + 본동사」 순으로 도치된다.
> — where it does에서 does는 exists를 대신하는 대동사로 쓰였다.

deny 부인하다

D **12** A hypothesis **not only** should fit the facts which brought about its creation
가설은 사실에 들어맞아야 할 뿐만 아니라 / [그 가설을 생겨나게 한]

but should **also** be compatible with the rest of the body of science.
/ 또한 양립할 수 있어야 한다 / 과학의 대다수의 나머지 것들과

> not only A but also B: A뿐만 아니라 B도

fit 들어맞다, 적합하다
hypothesis 가설
compatible 양립할 수 있는, 호환될 수 있는
body 대다수, 대부분; 총체

모의 **13** When people are overwhelmed with the volume of information confronting
사람들이 압도당할 때 / 그들과 마주하고 있는 정보의 양에

them, they have **difficulty knowing** what to focus on.
/ 그들은 어려움을 겪는다 / 무엇에 집중해야 할지 판단하는 데

> have difficulty v-ing: ~하는 데 어려움을 겪다

overwhelm 압도하다
volume 양; 부피; 음량
confront 직면하다

14 Where the degree of competition is particularly intense, a zero-sum game
경쟁의 정도가 특히 치열한 곳에서 / 제로섬 게임은

can quickly become a negative sum game, **in that everyone in the market**
곧 네거티브섬 게임이 될 수 있다 / 시장에 있는 모든 이가 추가 비용에 직면한다는 점에서

is faced with additional costs.

> in + that + s + v ~: ~라는 점에서

degree 정도
intense 치열한
negative sum game 참여한 모든 사람이 손해를 보는 게임

Special
Stage

- 어법 공략 십계명
- Special Unit 01 ········· 01 - 36제
- Special Unit 02 ········· 37 - 72제

Special Stage

01 is, are, lies   **02** occurs, donate, be donated   **03** Establishing, has   **04** reading, to change, come, running, using   **05** being treated, compared, to have been   **06** efficiency, making   **07** that, whether, which, where, what, that   **08** would accept, had been, practice, had done   **09** clear, than   **10** how a work is, did he know

---

01-1 **Reading** books aloud to children **is** a powerful source for vocabulary
아이들에게 소리내어 책을 읽어주는 것은 / 강력한 원천이다 / [어휘 발달을 위한]
development.
풀이 동명사 Reading이 주어를 이끌고 있으며, 동명사구는 단수로 취급한다.

01-2 **Clues** to past environmental change **are** well preserved in many different
과거의 환경 변화에 대한 단서들은 잘 보존되어 있다 / 많은 다양한 종류의 암석 속에
kinds of rocks.
풀이 문장의 주어는 복수 명사인 Clues이므로 복수 동사가 와야 한다.

clue 단서
preserve 보존하다, 보호하다

01-3 In the middle of every difficulty **lies** opportunity.
모든 어려움의 한 가운데에 / 기회가 놓여 있다
풀이 장소의 부사구가 맨 앞으로 나와서 '동사 + 주어'로 도치된 문장이다.

02-1 A lunar eclipse **occurs** when the earth passes between the sun and the
월식은 일어난다 / 지구가 지날 때 / 태양과 달 사이를
moon.
풀이 occur는 자동사이므로 수동태로 쓸 수 없다.

lunar eclipse 월식
cf. solar eclipse 일식

02-2 • We **will donate** all profits to charity.
우리는 모든 수익을 기부할 것이다 / 자선단체에
풀이 주어 We가 '기부하는' 주체이고 뒤에 목적어 all profits가 있으므로 능동태 동사가 적절하다.
• All profits **will be donated** to charity.
모든 수익은 기부될 것이다 / 자선단체에
풀이 주어 All profits가 '기부되는' 대상이며 뒤에 목적어가 없으므로 수동태 동사가 적절하다.

donate 기부하다
profit 수익, 이득
charity 자선(단체)

03-1 **Establishing** protected areas with intact ecosystems **is** essential for
온전한 생태계를 가진 보호구역을 확립하는 것은 / 종 보존에 필수적이다
species conservation.
풀이 뒤에 동사 is가 있으므로 주어 역할을 하는 동명사가 적절하다.

establish 확립하다, 설립하다
intact 온전한, 손상되지 않은
ecosystem 생태계
conservation 보호, 보존

03-2 **Having** a fine library **does** not prove **that its legal owner has** a mind
좋은 도서관을 소유하고 있다는 것이 입증하지 않는다 / 그것의 법적 소유자가 정신을 소유하고 있다는 것을
enriched by books.
/ [책으로 인해 풍부해진]
풀이 접속사(that)가 한 개 있으므로 prove 외에 또 다른 동사가 필요하다. has는 목적어 역할을 하는 that절의 동사이다. / 동사의 개수 = 접속사의 개수 + 1

legal 법률의, 합법적인

04-1 I vaguely remember **reading** something about it in the paper.
나는 어렴풋이 기억한다 / 신문에서 그것에 관한 뭔가를 읽었던 것을
풀이 remember는 과거의 내용(~했던 것)이 오면 목적어로 동명사를 취한다.

vaguely 어렴풋이

04-2 • What **caused you to change** your mind?
무엇이 당신이 마음을 바꾸도록 만들었는가?
풀이 5형식 문장에서 cause는 목적격보어로 to-v를 취한다.

• A positive attitude can **really make dreams come** true.
긍정적인 태도는 정말로 꿈이 실현되게 만들 수 있다
풀이 사역동사 make의 목적어와 목적격보어가 능동의 관계일 경우, 목적격보어로 동사원형을 취한다.

positive 긍정적인
attitude 태도

• He **felt the cold sweat running** down his back.
그는 식은땀이 자신의 등 아래로 흐르는 것을 느꼈다
풀이 지각동사 feel의 목적어와 목적격보어가 능동의 관계일 경우, 목적격보어로 동사원형 또는 현재분사를 취한다.

sweat 땀

04-3 We are used **to using** audio to present examples of language in use.
우리는 오디오를 사용하는 것에 익숙하다 / 사용되는 언어의 실례를 제시하기 위해서
풀이 be used to + v-ing: ~하는 것에 익숙하다 *cf.* be used to-v: ~하기 위해 사용되다

present 제시하다; 주다

05-1 • My son dislikes **being treated** like a son.
나의 아들은 싫어한다 / 아이처럼 취급받는 것을
풀이 주어 My son이 누구를 아이처럼 취급하는 것이 아니라 아이처럼 '취급받는' 것을 싫어한다는 의미이므로, dislikes의 목적어로 동명사의 수동형 being treated가 오는 것이 적절하다.

• The earth is only a baby **compared with many other stars.**
지구는 아기에 불과하다 / 많은 다른 별들과 비교될 때
풀이 분사구문의 의미상 주어 The earth는 '비교되는' 대상이므로 수동의 의미를 나타내는 과거분사가 적절하다.

• Judging from his appearance, he **seems to have been** ill for quite a long time.
겉모습으로 판단하건대 / 그는 아팠던 것 같다 / 꽤 오랫동안
풀이 문장의 동사 seems보다 먼저 일어난 일은 완료부정사(to have v-ed)로 나타낸다.

judging from ~으로 판단하건대
appearance 외모

06-1 Computer buyers expect **versatility, simplicity, and energy efficiency** as
컴퓨터 구매자들은 다용도성, 단순성, 그리고 에너지 효율성을 기대한다 / 새로운
essential components of new equipment.
장비의 필수적인 구성 요소로서
풀이 and에 의해 expect의 목적어 역할을 하는 명사(구)가 병렬적으로 연결되어야 하므로 efficiency가 적절하다.

versatility 다용도성
simplicity 단순성
efficiency 효율성
component 구성 요소

06-2 Recycling is much more energy efficient than **making** from raw
재활용은 훨씬 더 에너지 효율적이다 / 원료로 만드는 것보다
materials.
풀이 than 뒤에는 주어 Recycling과 비교되는 대상이 오므로 같은 문법적 형태인 making이 적절하다.

raw material 원료

07-1 • We think **that the company has a bright future.**
우리는 생각한다 / 그 회사는 밝은 전망을 갖고 있다고
풀이 이어지는 내용이 확실한 내용이므로 접속사 that이 와야 한다.

• Please decide **whether the following statements are true or false.**
결정하시오 / 다음의 진술들이 참인지 거짓인지를
풀이 이어지는 내용이 의문시되는 것이므로 접속사 whether가 와야 한다.

statement 진술; 성명(서)

07-2 • We'll go to a restaurant **which has a children's menu.**
우리는 식당에 갈 것이다 / [어린이용 메뉴가 있는]
풀이 이어지는 절에 주어가 빠져 있으므로 주격 관계대명사 역할을 하는 which가 적절하다.

• I'd like to go to a restaurant **where I will be offered great services.**
나는 가고 싶다 / 식당에 / [내가 훌륭한 서비스를 받을]
풀이 이어지는 절이 완전하므로 장소(a restaurant)를 선행사로 하는 관계부사 where가 적절하다.

07-3 • Don't discount **what you might consider "small" successes.**
경시하지 마라 / 당신이 '작은' 성공들로 여길 수도 있는 것을
풀이 앞에 선행사가 없고, 이어지는 절에 consider의 목적어가 없으므로 what이 적절하다.

cf. Toys are cultural objects **that children learn to play with.**
장난감은 문화적인 사물이다 / [아이들이 갖고 노는 것을 배우는]
풀이 앞에 선행사 objects가 있고, 이어지는 절에서 전치사 with의 목적어가 없어서 불완전하므로 관계대명사 that
이 적절하다.

discount 무시하다, 경시하다

object 사물, 물건

08-1 • **If I were** in your shoes, I **would accept** the invitation.
만약 내가 네 입장이라면 / 나는 그 초청을 수락할 텐데
풀이 If절에 가정법 과거형 be동사인 were가 왔으므로, 주절에는 would accept가 적절하다.

• Emma **would have gotten** the job **if she had been** better prepared.
Emma는 그 일자리를 얻었을 텐데 / 만약 그녀가 더 잘 준비되어 있었더라면
풀이 주절에 '조동사 과거형 + have v-ed'가 왔으므로, 가정법 과거완료 시제 had been이 적절하다.

08-2 • The piano teacher **required that** her student **practice** every day.
그 피아노 교사는 요구했다 / 자신의 학생이 날마다 연습하도록
풀이 주절에 '요구'의 동사(required)가 왔고, that절이 '소망'의 내용을 나타내므로 '(should) + ⓥ'가 와야 한다.

cf. Sam **insisted that** he **had done** nothing wrong.
Sam은 주장했다 / 자신이 그릇된 어떤 것도 하지 않았다고
풀이 주절에 insisted가 왔지만, that절의 내용이 '의향·소망'이 아니라 '사실'에 해당하므로 시제 일치에 맞춰 과
거완료 동사가 와야 한다.

09-1 Deleting unnecessary words will make **your writing** more **clear.**
불필요한 단어들을 삭제하는 것이 / 당신의 글을 더 명확하게 만들 것이다
풀이 목적어 your writing을 보충 설명하는 목적격보어가 와야 할 자리이므로 형용사가 적절하다.

delete 삭제하다, 지우다

09-2 The modern adult owes **more** to the experience of his culture **than** does
현대의 성인은 더 많은 것을 자신의 문화의 경험에 신세를 지고 있다 / 원시인이 그런
primitive man.
것보다
풀이 앞에 more가 왔으므로 비교급과 짝을 이루는 than이 적절하다.

owe A to B A를 B에게 빚지
다, A는 B의 덕분이다

10-1 Computer technology can improve **how a work is** performed, broadcast,
컴퓨터 기술은 개선할 수 있다 / 작품이 공연되고, 방송되고, 경험되는 방식을
and experienced.
풀이 how 이하는 목적어로 쓰인 명사절로서 간접의문문이므로 '의문사 + s + v'의 어순이 되어야 한다.

broadcast 방송하다

10-2 **Little** did he know that he was giving his son unseen stress.
전혀 그는 알지 못했다 / 자신이 아들에게 보이지 않는 스트레스를 주고 있다는 것을
풀이 부정의 부사 Little이 문장의 맨 앞에 나왔으므로 '조동사 + 주어 + 본동사'의 어순으로 도치되어야 한다.

01 is　　02 in which　　03 (A) doing (B) that　　04 be　　05 considered　　06 that　　07 is　　08 as
09 (A) have been (B) at which　　10 using　　11 (A) has been said (B) reveals　　12 (A) breaking (B) left　　13 what
14 (A) running (B) that　　15 turning　　16 had searched　　17 (A) promote (B) depends　　18 to be taken　　19 is
20 helping　　21 is interpreted　　22 whose　　23 (A) whispering (B) feel　　24 which　　25 leaving
26 are　　27 lies　　28 restricted　　29 (A) producing (B) leaves　　30 emerged　　31 differ　　32 (A) consuming
(B) rely　　33 come　　34 (A) turn (B) proves　　35 (A) which (B) generated　　36 are

---

[모의] **01** According to Pierre Pica, **understanding** quantities approximately in terms
Pierre Pica에 따르면　　/ 수량을 대략 이해하는 것은　　/ 비율을
of estimating ratios **is** a universal human intuition.
가능하는 면에서　　/ 보편적인 인간의 직관이다

[풀이] 주어가 동명사구(understanding ~ ratios)이므로 단수 동사 is가 적절하다.

quantity 수량, 양
in terms of ~의 관점에서
estimate 어림잡다, 가능하다
ratio 비율
intuition 직관

02 The truth is not simply what you think it is; it is also the circumstances in
진리는 단지 ~은 아니다　　/ 당신이 생각하기에 그것이 어떠한 것　　/ 그것은 또한 상황이다　　/
which it is said, and to whom, why and how it is said. *Vaclav Havel*
[그것이 이야기되는　　/ 그리고 누구에게, 왜, 그리고 어떻게 그것이 이야기되는지]

[풀이] 앞에 선행사 the circumstances가 있고, 이어지는 절이 완전하므로 in which가 적절하다. in which는 관계부사 where로 바꿔 쓸 수 있다.

circumstance 상황

03 Sometimes we are **so** used **to doing** the things that we think we should do,
때때로 우리는 일들을 하는 것에 아주 익숙하다　　/ [우리가 생각하기에 / 우리가 해야 하는]
that we can forget about the things that we really want to do.
/ 그래서 우리는 일들에 대해서 망각할 수 있다　　/ [우리가 정말로 하고 싶은]

[풀이] (A) be used to + v-ing: ~하는 것에 익숙하다
(B) 앞에 나온 so와 연결되어 '결과'를 나타내는 접속사 that이 적절하다.

04 The airline **requests** that all baggage **be kept** in the overhead compartments.
그 항공사는 요청한다　　/ 모든 수하물을 보관되도록　　/ 짐칸에

[풀이] 주절에 requests가 왔고 that절이 '소망'을 담고 있으므로, that절의 동사는 '(should) + ⓥ'가 되어야 한다.

airline 항공사
baggage 수하물
compartment (보관용) 칸

05 Most of the animal-training practices **considered** good and normal in our
대부분의 동물 훈련 관행은　　/ [우리의 세상에서 적절하고 정상적으로 여겨지는]
world do not take the animals' viewpoint into account.
/ 동물들의 관점을 고려하지 않는다

[풀이] 뒤에 동사 do not take가 있으므로 주어를 수식하는 준동사가 와야 한다. practices는 '여겨지는' 대상이므로 과거분사가 적절하다.

viewpoint 관점
take ~ into account ~을 고려하다

06 It is a paradoxical but profoundly true and important principle of life **that**
(…은) 역설적이지만 매우 참되며 중요한 삶의 원리이다 / 목표에
the most likely way to reach a goal is to be aiming not at that goal itself but
도달하는 가장 유망한 방법은 ~이다 / 겨누는 것 / 그 목표 그 자체가 아니라 / 그
at some more ambitious goal beyond it. *Arnold Toynbee*
너머의 좀 더 야심찬 목표를

풀이 맨 앞의 It은 가주어이므로 진주어를 이끄는 접속사 that이 적절하다.

paradoxical 역설적인
profoundly 깊게
aim at ~을 겨누다
ambitious 야심적인

(모의) **07** **The tendency** to give more attention and weight to data that support our
자료에 더 많은 관심과 중요성을 부여하는 경향은 / [우리의 믿음을 뒷받침하는]
beliefs than we do to contrary data **is** especially dangerous **when our**
/ 우리가 반대의 자료에 대해서 하는 것보다 / 특히 위험하다 / 우리의 믿음이
beliefs are little more than prejudices.
편견에 불과할 때

풀이 주어부가 The tendency ~ data로 길지만 The tendency가 핵심 주어이므로 단수 동사 is가 적절하다.

weight 중요성
contrary 반대의
little more than ~에 지나
지 않는(= only)
prejudice 편견

(모의) **08** If one looks at the Oxford definition, one gets the sense that post-truth is
옥스퍼드 사전의 정의를 본다면 / 누구나 느낌을 받는다 / [= 탈진실이란 주장이라기
not so much a claim that truth does not exist **as** that facts are subordinate
보다는 / [= 진실이 존재하지 않는다는] / [= 사실이 우리의 정치적 관점에 종속적이라는
to our political point of view.
(주장이라는)]

풀이 not so much A as B: A라기보다는 오히려 B / A는 a claim that truth does not exist, B는 (a claim)
that facts are subordinate ~로 that은 동격의 명사절을 이끄는 접속사로 쓰였다.

post-truth 탈진실(왜곡된 정
보, 개념, 인식 등)
claim 주장; 요구
subordinate 하위의, 종속적인

09 People, Homo sapiens and our past ancestors and relatives, **must always**
사람들은, 즉 호모 사피엔스이며 우리의 과거의 조상들 및 친척들은 / 항상 물을 관리해
have been managing water in some manner as far back as six million years,
왔음에 틀림없다 / 어떤 방식으로 / 6백만 년을 거슬러 올라가서
the date **at which we shared a common ancestor with the chimpanzee.**
/ 시기인 / [우리가 침팬지와 공동의 조상을 가졌던]

풀이 (A) 과거에 대한 추측은 '조동사 + have v-ed'로 쓰는데, 과거로부터 현재까지 쭉 진행되고 있는 일이므로 '조
동사 + have been v-ing' 형태가 왔다.
(B) 선행사(the date)가 있고, 이어지는 절이 완전하므로 관계부사 when 또는 '전치사 + 관계대명사'가 적절하다.

ancestor 조상
relative 친척

(모의) **10** Children learn the meanings of words by trial and error, **by hypothesizing** a
아이들은 단어의 의미를 배운다 / 시행착오에 의해서 / 즉 단어와 대상 사이의 적합성에
fit between word and object **and using** the feedback they get from others
가설을 세움으로써 / 그리고 피드백을 활용함으로써 / [그들이 타인들로부터 얻는
to refine the abstract category for which the word stands.
/ 추상적인 범주를 가다듬기 위해서 / [그 단어가 의미하는]]

풀이 by의 목적어 역할을 하는 hypothesizing과 and에 의해 병렬로 연결되어야 하므로 using이 적절하다.

trial and error 시행착오
hypothesize 가설을 세우다
fit 적합(성)
refine ~를 가다듬다, 세련되
게 하다; 정제하다
abstract 추상적인
stand for ~을 나타내다

(모의) **11** **It has been said** that eye movements are windows into the mind, because
(…이) 말해져 왔다 / 눈의 움직임은 마음의 창이라는 것이 / 왜냐하면
where people look reveals what environmental information they are
사람들이 어디를 바라보느냐가 드러내기 때문이다 / 어떤 환경적 정보에 그들이 주의를 기울이는지
attending to.

풀이 (A) It은 가주어이고 that 이하가 진주어인 문장으로, that절은 '말해져 온' 내용이므로 수동태가 적절하다.
(B) because가 이끄는 절에서 주어가 명사절(where people look)이므로 단수 동사 reveals가 적절하다.

reveal 드러내다
attend to ~에 주의를 기울
이다

12 Supplies of salts that plants use to build up their substance can **only** be
소금의 공급은 / [식물들이 그들의 물질을 증식하기 위해서 사용하는] / 유지될 수 있을 **뿐이다**
maintained through the activities of bacteria **breaking down the organic**
/ 박테리아의 활동을 통해서 / [유기 물질을 분해하는
matter left in the soil by other living things.
/ [다른 생물들에 의해 토양에 남겨진]]

> **풀이** (A) bacteria가 '분해하는' 주체이므로 능동의 의미를 나타내는 현재분사 breaking이 적절하다.
> (B) the organic matter가 다른 생물들에 의해 '남겨진' 대상이므로 수동의 의미를 나타내는 과거분사 left가 적절하다.

substance 물질
maintain 유지하다
break down 분해하다; 고장
나다

(수능!) **13** If you are known as someone who is easily offended, you will **never** know
만약 당신이 사람으로서 알려져 있다면 / [쉽사리 기분이 상하는] / 당신은 **결코** 알지 못할 것이다
what others are really thinking or feeling because they will distort the truth
/ 다른 사람들이 정말로 생각하거나 느끼고 있는 것을 / 왜냐하면 그들은 진실을 왜곡할 것이기 때문에
to escape from your negative reaction.
/ 당신의 부정적인 반응으로부터 피하기 위해

> **풀이** 앞에 선행사가 없고, 이어지는 절이 목적어가 빠져 불완전하므로 what이 적절하다.

offend 기분을 상하게 하다
distort 왜곡하다

---

14 Many people, in their rise to success, **are so busy running** to the top,
많은 사람들은 / 성공으로 나아가면서 / 너무 분주하다 / 정상으로 달음질하고
stepping on their competitors, stepping on their enemies, and saddest of
경쟁자들을 밟고 / 적들을 밟고 / 그리고 가장 슬프게도
all, stepping on their friends and loved ones, **that** when they get to the top,
친구들과 사랑하는 사람들을 밟느라 / 그들이 정상에 이르렀을 때
they look around and discover that they are extremely lonely and unhappy.
/ 그들은 주위를 둘러보고 발견한다 / 자신들이 대단히 외롭고 불행하다는 것을   *Berry Gordy*

> **풀이** (A) be busy v-ing: ~하느라고 바쁘다
> (B) 앞의 so와 연결되어 '너무 ~해서 …하다'의 결과를 나타내는 접속사 that이 적절하다. 이어지는 절이 완전하므로 what은 올 수 없다.

step on ~을 밟다
competitor 경쟁자
extremely 극도로

(모의) **15** It is **not at all** rare for investigators to adhere to their broken hypotheses,
(…은) 전혀 드물지 않다 / 조사원들이 / 자신들의 어그러진 가설을 고수하는 것은
turning a blind eye to contrary evidence, and not altogether unknown for
/ 반대의 증거를 못 본 체하면서 / 그리고 전적으로 알려져 있지 않은 것은 아니다 / 그들이
them to deliberately suppress contrary results.
고의로 반대의 결과들을 은폐한다는 것은

> **풀이** 앞에 접속사가 없으므로 또 다른 동사는 올 수 없고, investigators를 의미상 주어로 하는 분사구문이 이어지는 것이 적절하다.

investigator 조사원, 수사관
adhere to ~을 고수하다
hypothesis 가설
(*pl.* hypotheses)
turn a blind eye to ~을 못
본 체하다
altogether 완전히, 전적으로
deliberately 고의로
suppress (정보 등을) 은폐하다

---

16 Whoever it was who searched the heavens with a telescope and found no
누구든지 / [하늘을 망원경으로 탐색하고 신을 발견하지 못한]
God **would not have found** the human mind if he **had searched** the brain
/ 인간의 마음을 찾지 못했을 것이다 / 만약 그가 현미경으로 뇌를 탐색했다면
with a microscope. *George Santayana*

> **풀이** 앞에 가정법 과거완료의 주절의 동사 형태인 'would not have found'가 왔으므로 if가 이끄는 절의 동사로는 'had v-ed' 형태가 적절하다.

telescope 망원경
microscope 현미경

(모의) **17** **Whether** we develop **effective communication skills** that **promote** healthy
우리가 효과적인 의사소통 기술을 개발시킬지는 / [건강한 상호작용을 증진시키는]
interactions **depends** largely on how we learn to communicate.
/ 주로 ~에 달려 있다 / 우리가 어떻게 의사소통하는 법을 배우는지

> **풀이** (A) 주격 관계대명사 다음에 오는 동사는 선행사(effective communication skills)에 그 수를 일치시키므로 복수 동사가 와야 한다.
> (B) 주어가 Whether가 이끄는 명사절이므로 단수 동사가 와야 한다.

promote 증진시키다
interaction 상호작용

18 The use of artificial intelligence technology makes **it** possible **for repetitive**
인공지능 기술의 사용은 / (…을) 가능하게 한다 / 반복적이지만 위험한
but hazardous activities to be taken over by computers or robots.
활동들이 / 컴퓨터 또는 로봇에게 인계되도록 하는 것을

> **풀이** it이 가목적어이고 to-v가 진목적어, 'for ~ activities'가 to-v의 의미상 주어인 문장에서, activities는 '인계되는' 대상이므로 수동의 의미를 나타내는 'to be v-ed' 형태가 적절하다.

artificial intelligence 인공지능
repetitive 반복적인
hazardous 위험한
take over ~을 인계받다

19 One of the greatest discoveries a man makes, one of his great surprises, **is**
가장 위대한 발견들 중의 하나는 / [사람이 행하는] / 즉 그의 대단히 놀랄만한 일 중의 하나는 ~이다
to find he can do what he was afraid he couldn't do. *Henry Ford*
/ 그가 할 수 있음을 깨닫는 것 / 그가 두려워 한 것을 / 자신이 할 수 없다고

> **풀이** 주어는 맨 앞에 있는 단수 명사 One이므로 단수 동사가 와야 한다. a man 앞에는 목적격 관계대명사 that이, to find와 afraid 뒤에는 접속사 that이 각각 생략되어 있다.

20 Concerning charity, it means **not only providing** immediate assistance to
자선에 관하여 / 그것은 의미한다 / 빈곤한 사람들에게 즉각적인 도움을 제공하는 것뿐만 아니라
the impoverished, **but also helping** the poor in ways that will enable them
/ 가난한 사람들을 돕는 것도 / 방법으로 / [그들이 스스로를 부양하고 더 이상
to support themselves and no longer need help.
도움을 필요로 하지 않게 할 수 있을]

> **풀이** means의 목적어가 상관접속사 'not only A but also B'로 연결되었고, A에 동명사구(providing ~ impoverished)가 왔으므로 B에도 동명사구가 오는 것이 적절하다.

concerning ~에 관한
charity 자선 (단체)
assistance 도움, 원조
impoverished 빈곤한
enable ~할 수 있게 하다
no longer 더 이상 ~ 않는
(= not ~ any longer)

(모의) **21** The brain wants rewards **and anything** that is learned, good or bad, that
뇌는 보상을 원한다 / 그리고 어떠한 것이든 / [좋든 나쁘든 학습되는 / 즉
stimulates the production of dopamine **is interpreted** by the brain as a
도파민의 생성을 자극하는] / 뇌에 의해서 해석된다 / 보상으로
reward.

> **풀이** anything을 주어로 하는 동사가 와야 하는데, anything은 '해석되는' 대상이므로 수동태 동사가 적절하다.

reward 보상
stimulate 자극하다
dopamine 도파민(신경 전달 기능을 하는 체내 유기 화합물)
interpret 해석하다

(모의) **22** A sovereign state is usually defined as **one whose citizens** are free to
주권국가는 대개 정의된다 / 국가로 / [그곳의 시민들이 자신들의 일을 마음대로 결정
determine their own affairs without interference from any agency beyond
할 수 있는 / 어떤 기관으로부터도 간섭받지 않고 / [그곳의 국경
its territorial borders.
너머에 있는]

> **풀이** 앞의 선행사(one)와 뒤의 명사 사이에 소유의 관계(one's citizens)가 성립하므로, 소유격 관계대명사가 적절하다.

sovereign state 주권국, 독립국
affair 일, 문제
interference 방해, 간섭
agency 정부 기관; 대행사
territorial 영토의

23 Students **often perceive a textbook as a huge, insurmountable obstacle**
학생들은 종종 교과서를 인식한다 / 거대한, 넘을 수 없는 장애물로서
that sits on their desk softly **whispering** their name just to **make** them **feel**
/ [그들의 책상 위에 앉아 있는 / 나지막하게 그들의 이름을 속삭이면서 / 단지 그들이 가책을 느끼도록 하기 위해서
guilty every time they walk past it.
/ 그들이 그것을 지나칠 때마다]

> **풀이** (A) '앉아서 ~하면서'의 동시 상황을 나타내는 분사구문이 오는 것이 적절하다. 앞에 접속사가 없으므로 또 다른 동사는 올 수 없다.
> (B) 사역동사 make의 목적격보어 자리이므로 동사원형이 적절하다.

perceive A as B A를 B로 인식하다
insurmountable 넘을 수 없는, 극복할 수 없는
obstacle 장애물
whisper 속삭이다
guilty 가책을 느끼는; 유죄의

24 Although commonsense knowledge may have merit, it also has drawbacks,
비록 상식적 지식이 장점을 가지고 있을지라도 / 그것은 또한 결점들도 가지고 있다
not **the least of which** is that it often contradicts itself.
/ 그리고 그것들 중 작지 않은 것은 ~이다 / 상식이 종종 그 자체로 모순된다는 것

> **풀이** drawbacks를 대신하는 대명사 역할을 하는 동시에 앞의 절과 이어지는 절을 연결하는 접속사 역할을 할 수 있는 관계대명사가 적절하다.

commonsense 상식적인
merit 장점
drawback 결점
contradict 모순되다; 반박하다

25 In childhood, a considerable number of languages may be learned one
어린 시절에는 　/ 상당한 수의 언어들이 차례로 학습될 수도 있다
after another, **without** the preceding language **leaving** any trace of its
　　　　　/ 선행하는 언어가 남기지 않고서　　　　　　　　　/ 그것의 문법 또는 소리
grammar or sound system on the one that succeeds.
체계의 어떤 자취도　　　　　　　/ 뒤에 오는 언어에

풀이 전치사 without의 목적어 역할을 하는 것이므로 동명사가 적절하다. the preceding language는 동명사의
의미상 주어이다.

considerable 상당한
one after another 차례로
precede 선행하다. 앞서다
trace 자취, 흔적
succeed 이어지다, 뒤에 오다;
성공하다

모의 26 Individuals who believe they control their own destinies and generally
개인들은　　　　/ [믿는　　　　　/ 자신들이 스스로의 운명을 통제하고 일반적으로 삶에서 최상의 것을 기대하는]
expect the best from life **are**, in fact, more likely to gain control of their
　　　　　　　　　　　　/ 사실상 자신들의 스트레스 요인들을 통제할 가능성이 더 높다
stressors and experience positive stress rather than distress.
　　　/ 그리고 고통보다는 긍정적인 스트레스를 경험할 (가능성이 더 높다)

풀이 주어는 관계사절의 수식을 받고 있는 복수 명사 Individuals이므로 복수 동사가 적절하다.

destiny 운명
gain control of ~을 통제하다
stressor 스트레스 요인
distress 고통, 골칫거리

27 **Hidden** within every astronomical investigation, sometimes so deeply
모든 천문학 연구 안에 감춰진 채로　　　　　　　　　/ 때때로 너무 깊이 파묻혀 있어서
buried that the researcher himself is unaware of its presence, lies a kernel
　/ 연구자 자신도 그것의 존재를 알지 못한다　　　　　　　　　　　/ 경외감의 핵심이 있다
of awe. *Carl Sagan*

풀이 원래의 문장은 'A kernel of awe lies hidden within ~'인데, 보어로 쓰인 hidden 이하가 문장의 맨 앞으로
와서 도치가 된 것이므로 동사 lies가 와야 한다.

astronomical 천문학의
investigation 연구, 조사
be unaware of ~을 알지 못
하다
presence 존재; 출석
kernel 핵심, 알맹이
awe 경외감, 두려움

모의 28 Creativity is strange in that it finds its way in any kind of situation, **no**
독창성은 이상하다　　　　/ 그것이 어떠한 상황에서든 자신의 길을 찾는다는 점에서　　　/ 아무리
matter how restricted, just as the same amount of water flows faster and
(그 상황이) 제한되어 있을지라도　　/ 마치 동일한 양의 물이 더 빠르고 더 강하게 흐르는 것처럼
stronger through a narrow strait than across the open sea.
　　　　　/ 좁은 해협을 통해서　　　　　/ 망망대해를 가로지르는 것보다

풀이 '~일지라도'의 의미를 나타내는 no matter how 뒤에 주어와 동사인 'it is'가 생략되어 있는데, 주어
it(situation)은 문맥상 '제한되는' 대상이므로 수동의 의미를 갖는 과거분사 restricted가 적절하다.

creativity 독창성, 창의력
in that ~라는 점에서
restrict 제한하다
strait 해협

29 Making new paper from recycled materials **uses** less energy than **producing**
재활용된 재료로 새 종이를 만드는 것은 더 적은 에너지를 사용한다　　　　　/ 사용된 적 없는 목제품으로
paper from virgin tree products and **leaves** more trees to absorb excess
종이를 생산하는 것보다　　　　　　　/ 그리고 더 많은 나무들이 초과한 이산화탄소를 흡수하도록 둔다
carbon dioxide.

풀이 (A) 비교되는 대상인 Making과 병렬적으로 연결되도록 than 뒤에 동명사가 와야 한다.
(B) 동사 uses와 and로 병렬적으로 연결되어야 하므로 leaves가 적절하다.

material 물질, 재료
virgin 쓰인 적이 없는; 처녀의
absorb 흡수하다
excess 초과한
carbon dioxide 이산화탄소

모의 30 With the evolution of more settled rural societies based on agriculture,
보다 안정된 시골 사회의 발전과 더불어　　　　　　　　　　　　/ [농업에 기반을 둔]
other characteristics, other traditions of form appropriate to the new
　/ 다른 특징들이　　　　/ 즉 새로운 삶의 방식에 적합한 형태의 다른 전통들이
patterns of life, rapidly **emerged**.
　　　　　　/ 신속하게 나타났다

풀이 other characteristics를 주어로 하는 동사가 와야 하므로 emerged가 적절하다.

evolution 발전, 진전
settled 안정된, 자리를 잡은
agriculture 농업
characteristic 특징
appropriate 적합한
emerge 나타나다

모의 31 Lie detector tests base judgments of honesty on **blood pressure, pulse,**
거짓말 탐지기 테스트는 정직성 판단의 기초를 혈압, 맥박, 호흡, 그리고 목소리의 높이에 둔다
respiration, and vocal pitch, which the test assumes **differ** when people lie
/ 그리고 그 테스트는 그것들이 다르다고 추정한다 / 사람들이 거짓말할 때와
and when they tell the truth.
그들이 진실을 말할 때

> **풀이** 관계대명사 which 다음에 삽입된 the test assumes을 괄호로 묶어보면, 선행사(blood pressure ~ vocal pitch)가 복수이기 때문에 복수 동사가 와야 함을 알 수 있다.

lie detector 거짓말 탐지기
base A on B A의 기초를 B에
두다
pulse 맥박
respiration 호흡
vocal pitch 목소리의 높이
assume 추정하다

모의 32 **With pests** often **consuming** up to 40 percent of the crops grown in the
해충이 종종 농작물의 40퍼센트까지 먹어치우고 있어서 / [미국에서 재배되는]
United States most organic farmers **cannot but rely on** chemicals as
/ 대부분의 유기농 농작물을 재배하는 농부들은 화학물질에 의존하지 않을 수 없다 / 그들의
necessary supplements to their operations.
조업에 필요한 보충물로서

> **풀이** (A) 'with + O' + 분사'에서 pests가 '먹어치우는' 주체이므로 능동의 의미를 나타내는 현재분사가 적절하다.
> (B) cannot but + ⓥ: ~하지 않을 수 없다(= cannot help v-ing)

pest 해충
consume 먹어버리다; 소비하다
crop 농작물
organic 유기농의
chemical 화학물질
supplement 보충물, 보충제
operation 조업, 운용, 경영

33 Only a man who knows what it is like to be defeated **can reach** down to
오직 사람만이 / [아는 / 패배를 당한다는 것이 어떤가를] / 자신의 영혼의 밑바닥까지 아래로
the bottom of his soul and **come up with** the extra ounce of power it takes
닿을 수 있다 / 그리고 젖 먹던 힘을 만들어낼 수 있다 / [이기는 데
to win when the match is even. *Muhammad Ali*
필요한 / 그 시합이 대등할 때]

> **풀이** (can) reach와 and로 병렬로 연결되므로 come이 적절하다.

defeat 패배시키다
come up with ~을 만들어
내다
ounce 아주 적은 양; (무게의
단위) 온스

34 Our expectations are **often** deceived. **Things** which **we feared** might do us
우리의 기대는 종종 기만당한다 일들이 / [우리에게 손해를 입힐까봐 우리가 두려워했던]
hurt **turn out** to be our advantage, and **what we thought** would save us
우리의 이득으로 드러난다 / 그리고 우리를 구해줄 것으로 우리가 생각한 것이 우리의 파멸의
proves our ruin.
원인으로 판명된다

> **풀이** (A) Things를 주어로 하는 동사가 와야 하므로 turn이 적절하다. 'which ~ hurt'는 Things를 수식하는 형용
> 사절이며, 그 안에 'we feared'는 삽입절이다.
> (B) what이 이끄는 명사절을 주어로 하는 동사가 와야 하므로 proves가 적절하다. what 다음의 'we thought'
> 도 삽입절이다.

deceive 기만하다, 속이다
hurt 손해, 피해
advantage 이득, 이익
ruin 파멸(의 원인)

모의 35 Modern psychological theory states that the process of understanding is a
현대의 심리학 이론은 분명히 말한다 / 이해의 과정은 구성의 문제이지
matter of construction, not reproduction, **which** means that the process of
/ 재생의 문제가 아니라고 / 그리고 그것은 의미한다 / 이해의 과정은
understanding takes the form of the interpretation of **data coming** from the
/ 자료를 해석하는 형태를 취함을 / [외부에서 들어오며 우리의
outside **and generated** by our mind.
정신에 의해서 생성되는]

> **풀이** (A) 앞의 절을 대신하고, 앞의 절과 이어지는 절을 연결하는 접속사 역할을 할 수 있는 관계대명사가 와야 한다.
> (B) and에 의해서 coming과 병렬로 연결되어 data를 수식하는 분사구인데, data는 '생성되는' 대상이므로
> 수동의 의미를 나타내는 과거분사가 적절하다.

psychological 심리학의
state 분명히 말하다
construction 구성; 건설
reproduction 재생; 번식
interpretation 해석
generate 발생시키다, 일으키다

수능 36 At the root of many of our blind spots **are a number of emotions or**
우리들의 많은 맹점들의 뿌리에는 / 수많은 감정들 또는 태도들이 있다
attitudes—fear being the most obvious, but also pride, self-satisfaction,
두려움이 가장 명백한 것이지만, 또한 자부심, 자기만족, 그리고 불안(도 있다)
and anxiety.

> **풀이** 장소의 부사구 At the root of ~ spots가 문장의 맨 앞으로 와서 주어와 동사가 도치되었으므로, 복수 주어
> a number of emotions or attitudes의 수에 맞게 복수 동사가 와야 한다.

blind spot 맹점
obvious 명백한
anxiety 불안; 갈망

37 ②	38 ③	39 ②	40 ④	41 ④	42 ④	43 ①	44 ③	45 ②	46 ②	47 ③	48 ①
49 ④	50 ④	51 ③	52 ②	53 ③	54 ③	55 ②	56 ④	57 ②	58 ③	59 ②	60 ①
61 ③	62 ③	63 ③	64 ③	65 ②	66 ④	67 ①	68 ②	69 ①	70 ③	71 ③	72 ②

수능! 37 When we learn to say no to ① what we don't feel like ② to do(→ doing) in
우리가 '아니오'라고 말하는 것을 배울 때 / 우리가 하고 싶지 않은 것에
order to say yes to our true self, we feel ③ empowered, and our
참된 자아에게 '예'라고 말하기 위해서 / 우리는 권한이 부여된 것으로 느낀다 / 그리고 우리의
relationships with others ④ improve.
타인들과의 관계가 개선된다

> **풀이** ② feel like + v-ing: ~하고 싶다

> **오답노트** 앞에 선행사가 없고 이어지는 절에서 feel like doing의 목적어가 없으므로, what(~하는 것)이 적절하다.
③ 수동의 의미를 나타내는 과거분사가 보어로 쓰였다. ④ our relationships를 주어로 하는 동사이다.

empowered 권한이 주어진
improve 개선하다; 나아지다

모의! 38 Every parent ① knows that lying to their kids about everything from the
모든 부모는 알고 있다 / 그들의 자녀들에게 모든 것에 대해서 거짓말을 하는 것은 / 산타클로스의
arrival of Santa Claus to the horrible things that will happen ② if they don't
도착에서부터 / 끔찍한 일들까지 / [일어나게 될 / [만약 그들이 완두콩을
eat their peas ③ are(→ is) a key component of ④ raising a child.
먹지 않는다면] / 자녀를 양육하는 것의 주된 구성 요소라는 것을

> **풀이** ③ 주어가 lying이므로 단수 동사가 와야 한다. 'to their kids ~ peas'가 lying을 수식한다.

> **오답노트** ① every가 붙은 명사는 단수로 취급한다. ② 조건절을 이끄는 접속사이다. ④ 전치사 of의 목적어 역할을 하는 동명사이다.

horrible 끔찍한
pea 완두콩
component 구성요소

모의! 39 ① Making a choice that is 1 percent better or 1 percent worse seems
선택을 하는 것은 / [1퍼센트 더 나은 또는 1퍼센트 더 나쁜] / 그 순간에는
② insignificantly(→ insignificant) in the moment, but over the span of moments
중요하지 않은 것 같다 / 그러나 순간들의 기간에 걸쳐서
that ③ make up a lifetime these choices ④ determine the difference between
/ [일생을 구성하는] / 이러한 선택들은 차이를 결정한다 / [당신이 어떤
who you are and who you could be.
사람인지와 당신이 어떤 사람이 될 수 있는지 사이의]

> **풀이** ② 주격보어 자리이므로 부사가 아닌 형용사가 와야 한다.

> **오답노트** ① 주어로 쓰인 동명사이다. ③ 주격 관계대명사절에 쓰인 동사이므로 복수 선행사(moments)에 맞춰 복수 동사가 왔다. ④ 복수형 명사(these choices)를 주어로 하는 동사이다.

insignificant 중요하지 않은
span (어떤 일이 지속되는) 기간
make up ~을 구성하다

40 Understanding the trait of human nature ① is essential to ② realizing why
인간 본성의 특징을 이해하는 것은 필수적이다 / 깨닫는 데 / 왜
people click on a link, hit the "like" button, share a post, or ③ comment on
사람들이 링크에 클릭을 하거나, '좋아요' 버튼을 누르거나, 게시물을 공유하거나, 또는 원가에 댓글을 다는지를
something someone else ④ has been said(→ has said) on social media.
/ [다른 누군가가 소셜 미디어에 말한]

> **풀이** ④ 주어 someone else가 '말한' 주체이므로 동사는 능동태가 되어야 한다.

> **오답노트** ① 동명사(Understanding)가 이끄는 주어는 단수로 취급한다. ② 전치사 to의 목적어 역할을 하는 동명사이다. ③ 동사 click, hit, share와 or에 의해 병렬로 연결되어 있다.

trait 특징
comment on ~에 의견을 달다

모의 41 When ① delighted by the way one's beautiful idea ② offers promise of
방식으로 매우 즐거워 할 때 / [어떤 이의 멋진 아이디어가 더 나아간 진전의 전망을 제공하는]
further advances, it is tempting to overlook an observation ③ that does not
/ (…은) 솔깃하다 / 어떤 관찰을 간과하는 것은 / [짜여진 패턴에 부합
fit into the pattern woven, or ④ trying(→ to try) to explain it away.
하지 않는] / 또는 그것을 둘러대려고 애쓰는 것은

풀이 ④ 진주어에 해당하는 부분으로 앞의 to overlook과 or로 병렬로 연결되어야 하므로 (to) try가 되어야 한다.

오답노트 ① by 이하에 의해서 즐거운 감정을 느끼게 된 것이므로 과거분사가 적절하다. When 뒤에 'we are'가 생략된 것으로 볼 수 있다. ② one's beautiful idea를 주어로 하는 동사이다. one' beautiful idea ~ advances는 the way를 수식한다. ③ an observation을 선행사로 하는 주격 관계대명사이다.

advance 진전, 발전
tempting 솔깃한, 유혹하는
overlook 간과하다
observation 관찰
fit into ~에 부합하다
weave 짜다, 엮다
(-wove-woven)
explain away ~을 둘러대다, 해명하다

---

42 ① What astounds and dismays us is ② that, knowing so well that war is
우리를 경악하고 당황하게 하는 것은 ~이다 / 너무나 잘 알고 있으면서 / 전쟁이 나쁘다는
wrong, and fearing and ③ hating it more than anything else, we seem
것을 / 그리고 그것을 다른 어떤 것보다 더 두려워하고 싫어하면서 / 우리는, 우리
④ compelling(→ compelled), in spite of ourselves, to go on waging it.
자신도 모르게, 계속해서 전쟁을 벌이도록 강요받는 것 같다는 것

풀이 ④ 주어인 we는 강요하는 주체가 아니라 '강요받는' 대상이므로 수동의 의미를 갖는 과거분사가 와야 한다.

오답노트 ① '~하는 것'이라는 의미의 What이 명사절을 이끌어 주어 역할을 하고 있다. ② 보어 역할을 하는 명사절을 이끄는 접속사로 쓰였다. ③ fearing과 and로 병렬로 연결된 분사이다.

astound 경악하다, 크게 놀라게 하다
dismay 당황하게 하다
compel 강요하다, 억지로 시키다
in spite of oneself 자기도 모르게
wage (전쟁 등을) 벌이다

---

43 An interesting aspect of human psychology is ① what(→ that) we tend to
인간 심리의 흥미로운 측면은 ~이다 / 우리가 어떤 것들을 더 좋아하고
like things more and find them more ② appealing if everything about those
그것들이 더 매력적임을 깨닫는 경향이 있다는 것 / 만약 그런 것들에 관한 모든 것이 명백하지
things ③ is not obvious the first time we experience ④ them.
않으면 / 처음으로 우리가 그것들을 경험할 때

풀이 ① 이어지는 절이 완전하므로 접속사 that이 와서 보어절을 이끌어야 한다.

오답노트 ② 목적격보어로 쓰인 현재분사형 형용사이다. ③ everything을 주어로 하는 동사로, every가 붙은 명사는 단수로 취급한다. ④ 복수인 those things를 받는 대명사이다.

aspect 측면
psychology 심리
tend to-v ~하는 경향이 있다
appealing 매력적인
obvious 명백한

모의 44 ① Deciding ② whether to spend Saturday afternoon relaxing with your
정하는 것은 / 토요일 오후를 당신의 가족과 편히 쉬면서 보낼지
family or ③ to exercise(→ exercising) will be determined by the relative
/ 또는 운동을 하면서 보낼지를 / 결정될 것이다 / 상대적 중요성에 의해서
importance ④ that you place on family versus health.
/ [당신이 가족 대 건강에 부여하는]

풀이 ③ relaxing과 or로 병렬로 연결되도록 exercising이 되어야 한다. / spend + O + v-ing: ~하는 데 O를 쓰다

오답노트 ① 주어로 쓰인 동명사이다. ② 「whether + to-v」는 명사구이며 '~할지'로 해석한다. ④ 목적격 관계대명사이다.

relative 상대적인
versus ~ 대(對), ~에 대한
place (중요성·가치 등을) 두다

모의 45 ① It is no coincidence that countries ② which(→ where[in which]) sleep time has
(…은) 우연의 일치가 아니다 / 나라들은 / [수면 시간이 가장 극적으로 감소한
declined most dramatically over the past century ③ are also those ④ suffering
/ 지난 세기에 걸쳐] / 또한 나라들이다 / [가장 큰 증가로
the greatest increase in rates of physical diseases and mental disorders.
고통 받고 있는 / 신체적 질병과 정신적 질환의 비율 면에서]

풀이 ② 이어지는 절이 완전하므로, countries를 선행사로 하는 관계부사나 '전치사 + 관계대명사'가 적절하다.

오답노트 ① It은 가주어이며, that절이 진주어이다. ③ countries가 주어이므로 복수 동사가 적절하다. ④ those를 수식하는 현재분사이다.

coincidence 우연의 일치
dramatically 극적으로
suffer 고통 받다, 겪다
rate 비율; 속도
disorder 질환; 무질서

---

46 The fact ① that life evolved out of nearly nothing, some 10 billion years after
사실은 / [= 생명이 거의 무로부터 진화했다는 / 우주가 문자 그대로 무로부터 전개된
the universe evolved out of literally nothing, ② are(→ is) a fact so staggering
100억여 년 후] / 사실이다 / [너무나 충격적인
③ that I ④ would be mad to attempt words to do it justice. *Richard Dawkins*
/ 그래서 나는 미치게 될 / 만약 그것을 정당하게 대하기 위해서 표현을 시도한다면]

풀이 ② 주어가 The fact이므로 단수 동사 is가 되어야 한다.

오답노트 ① 동격절을 이끄는 접속사이다. ③ 앞의 so와 연결되어 '너무 ~해서 …하다'의 결과를 나타낸다. ④ 가정법 과거의 주절의 동사이다. to attempt 이하에 '가정'의 의미가 함축되어 있다. (= if I attempted words ~)

evolve 진화하다, 발달하다
nearly 거의
literally 문자 그대로
staggering 충격적인, 믿기 어려운
do ~ justice ~을 정당하게 대하다

수능! 47 The Chinese saw the world as ① consisting of continuously ② interacting
중국인들은 세상을 보았다 / 계속해서 상호작용하는 물질로 구성되어 있는 것으로
substances, so their attempts to understand it ③ causing(→ caused) them
/ 그래서 그것을 이해하려는 그들의 시도는 그들로 하여금 전체의 '계(界)'의 복잡성을 지향하게 야기했다
④ to be oriented toward the complexities of the entire "field," that is, the
/ 다시 말해서,
context or environment as a whole.
전체로서의 맥락 또는 환경인

풀이 ③ their attempts를 주어로 하는 동사가 와야 한다.

오답노트 ① 전치사 as의 목적어로 동명사가 왔다. ② 뒤에 나온 명사(substances)를 수식하는 현재분사이다. ④ caused의 목적격보어로 to-v가 왔으며, orient는 '~을 향해 있다'의 의미일 때는 수동태로 쓰인다.

continuously 계속해서, 끊임없이
interact 상호작용하다
substance 물질
orient (수동태로) ~을 지향하게 하다, ~을 향해 있다
complexity 복잡성
that is 다시 말해서
context 문맥, 맥락

---

48 Only through accurately understanding our feelings ① we can learn(→ can
오직 우리의 감정을 정확하게 이해하는 것을 통해서만 / 우리는 우리 자신을 부정적인
we learn) to free ② ourselves from negative emotions, ③ which provides
감정으로부터 자유롭게 하는 것을 배울 수 있다 / 그리고 그것은 더 많은
more creative energy, as well as the opportunity for limitless personal
창의적인 에너지를 제공한다 / 무한한 개인적 성장을 위한 기회뿐만 아니라
growth, and, ultimately, ④ connects us to our higher selves.
/ 그리고 궁극적으로 우리를 우리의 더 높은 자아와 연결시켜 준다

풀이 ① Only가 이끄는 부사구가 문장의 맨 앞에 있으므로 '조동사 + 주어 + 본동사'의 어순으로 도치되어야 한다.

오답노트 ② to free의 목적어가 그 의미상 주어(we)와 같아 재귀대명사가 쓰였다. ③ 앞의 절 전체를 선행사로 하는 주격 관계대명사이다. ④ 관계대명사절 내의 앞에 있는 동사 provides와 and로 병렬로 연결되는 동사이다.

accurately 정확하게
free ~에서 자유롭게 하다, 제거하다
limitless 무한한
ultimately 궁극적으로
self 자기, 자아 *pl.* selves

49 ① Knowing that the depth of our thought ② is tied directly to the intensity
알고 있기 때문에 / 우리의 사고의 깊이는 우리의 주의력의 강도와 직접적으로 결부되어 있다는 것을
of our attentiveness, it's hard not ③ to conclude that as we adapt to the
/ (…은) 어렵다 / 결론을 내리지 않는 것은 / 우리가 인터넷의 지능적 환경에
intellectual environment of the Net our thinking ④ becoming(→ becomes)
적응함에 따라서 / 우리의 사고는 점점 더 피상적으로 된다고
shallower.

intensity 강도, 세기
attentiveness 주의력, 조심성
adapt to ~에 적응하다
intellectual 지능의, 지적인
the Net 인터넷
shallow 피상적인, 얕은

> **풀이** ④ conclude의 목적어 역할을 하는 that절에서 our thinking을 주어로 하는 동사가 와야 할 자리이다.
> **오답노트** ① '이유'의 분사구문을 이끄는 현재분사이다. ② the depth of our thought는 '결부되는' 대상이므로 수동태가 적절하다. ③ 앞에 있는 it이 가주어이고, not to conclude 이하가 진주어이다.

(모의) 50 As with a crossword, so with the physical universe, we find that the
십자낱말풀이에서처럼 / 물질적 우주에서도 / 우리는 발견한다 / 독립
solutions to independent clues ① link together in a consistent and
적인 단서들에 대한 해법들이 함께 연결되어 있음을 / 일관되고 지지하는 방식으로
supportive way ② to form a coherent unity, ③ so that the more clues we solve,
/ 그래서 결국 일관성 있는 통일성을 이루는 / 따라서 더 많은 단서들을 우리가 해결할수록
④ the more easily(→ the easier) we find it to fill in the missing features.
/ 빠진 모양들을 채우는 것이 더 쉽다는 것을 우리는 알게 된다

consistent 한결같은, 일관된
supportive 지지하는, 힘을 주는
coherent 일관성 있는, 논리
정연한
unity 통일(성)
feature 생김새; 특징

> **풀이** ④ 이어지는 절에서 가목적어(it)와 진목적어(to fill ~ features) 사이에 목적격보어가 빠져 있으므로, 목적격보어로 형용사의 비교급이 와야 한다.
> **오답노트** ① 복수 명사인 the solutions를 주어로 하는 동사이다. ② '결과'를 나타내는 to-v의 부사적 용법이다. ③ '따라서'라는 의미의 결과를 나타내는 접속사이다.

51 Helping a child ① to acknowledge what they can change, and ② explore
아이를 돕는 것은 / 그들이 바꿀 수 있는 것을 인정하도록 / 그리고 방식을 바꾸는
how to change the way ③ how(→ (that[in which])) they respond to
법을 탐구하도록 / [그들이 영속적인 상황에 대응하는]
permanent situations, ④ will create a shift in outlook and life experience.
/ 변화를 만들어 낼 것이다 / [관점과 인생 경험에서의]

acknowledge 인정하다
explore 탐험하다, 조사하다
permanent 영구적인, 불변의
shift 변화, 전환
outlook 관점, 견해; 전망

> **풀이** ③ 선행사가 the way일 때 관계부사 how는 같이 쓸 수 없으므로, that 또는 in which로 쓰거나 생략한다.
> **오답노트** ① Helping의 목적격보어로 to-v가 왔다. ② to acknowledge와 or에 의해 병렬로 연결되므로 (to) explore의 형태를 취해야 한다. ④ Helping a child ~ permanent solutions를 주어로 하는 문장 전체의 동사이다.

52 How the universe as we know it now ① evolved ② being(→ is) a complex
어떻게 우주가 / 우리가 현재 아는 바의 / 전개되었느냐는 / 복잡한 문제이다
question ③ involving study by vastly different branches of physics ④ including
/ [물리학의 매우 다양한 부문들의 연구를 관련시키는 / 입자물리학,
particle physics, nuclear physics and cosmology.
핵물리학 그리고 우주론을 포함하여]

involve 포함하다; 관련시키다
vastly 대단히, 엄청나게
branch 부문; 가지
including ~을 포함하여
particle physics 입자물리학
cosmology 우주론

> **풀이** ② 의문사 How가 이끄는 명사절을 주어로 하는 동사가 와야 할 자리이다. / as ~ now는 앞의 명사(the universe)를 한정하는 절이다.
> **오답노트** ① How가 이끄는 명사절에서 the universe를 주어로 하는 동사이다. ③ question을 수식하는 현재분사이다. ④ 현재분사 형태의 전치사이다.

53 It is common knowledge ① that walnuts, also ② called "super food" and
(…은) 상식이다 / 호두가 / 또한 '슈퍼 푸드' 그리고 '신들을 위한 음식'으로 일컬어
"food for the gods," ③ contains(→ contain) more antioxidants of higher
지는 / 더 높은 질의 항산화제를 더 많이 포함하고 있다는 것은
quality than ④ any other nut.
/ 다른 어떤 견과류보다

풀이 ③ that절에서 walnuts가 주어이므로 복수 동사가 와야 한다. 콤마로 연결된 삽입어구(also ~ gods)를 괄호로 묶으면 '주어-동사'의 연결이 잘 드러난다.

오답노트 ① 진주어를 이끄는 접속사이다. ② walnuts를 수식하는 형용사구를 이끄는 분사로, 호두는 '일컬어지는' 대상이므로 과거분사가 쓰였다. ④ 비교급 + than + any other + 단수명사

common 흔한
antioxidant 항산화제
quality 질

모의 **54** Evolution is largely the result of natural selection that ① takes place
진화는 주로 자연 선택의 결과이다 / [발생하는]
because humans, during their history of development as a species, ② have
/ 인간들이 / 한 종으로서 발전의 역사를 거치는 동안에 / 생물
been part of biotic communities ③ which(→ in which[where]) their interactions
군집의 일부였기 때문에 / [그들의 다른 동식물 종들과 상호작용이 결정해온
with other species of animals and plants have decided ④ whether or not
/ 그들이 생존하고 번식할지
they survived and reproduced.
여부를]

풀이 ③ 앞에 선행사(biotic communities)가 있고, 이어지는 절이 완전하기 때문에 관계부사 또는 '전치사 + 관계대명사'가 와야 할 자리이다.

오답노트 ① 주격 관계대명사에 이어지는 동사로서, 선행사 natural selection에 수를 일치시켜 단수 동사가 왔다. ② humans를 주어로 하는 동사이다. ④ have decided의 목적어절을 이끄는 접속사이다.

evolution 진화
natural selection 자연 선택
take place 일어나다, 발생하다
biotic community 생물 군집
interaction 상호작용
survive 생존하다
reproduce 번식하다

---

55 Patents for novel ideas, processes and methodologies ① are simply the
참신한 아이디어, 과정, 그리고 방법론에 대한 특허권은 그야말로 실재하는 결과물이다
tangible results of someone ② seen(→ seeing) something differently ③ than
/ [어떤 사람이 뭔가를 다르게 본 것의 / 세상이
the world had ever seen ④ it before.
전에 그것을 보아온 것과는]

풀이 ② 전치사 of의 목적어로 동명사가 와야 한다. someone은 동명사의 의미상 주어이다.

오답노트 ① Patents를 주어로 하는 동사이므로 복수 동사가 왔다. ③ differently의 뒤에 와서 '~와는 다른, ~이외의'의 의미를 나타내는 접속사로 쓰였다. ④ 앞에 나온 something을 가리키는 대명사이다.

patent 특허(권)
novel 참신한, 새로운
methodology 방법론, 절차
tangible 실재하는, 분명히 보이는

---

56 An instrument is efficient to the extent ① to which the using of it ② enables
기구는 효율적이다 / 정도로 / [그것을 사용하는 것이 목적을 가능하게 하는
the purpose, ③ for which the instrument was designed, ④ to achieve(→ to
/ 그 기구가 설계된 / 성취되도록]
be achieved).

풀이 ④ enables의 목적격보어로 to-v가 적절한데, 목적어 the purpose가 '성취되는' 대상이므로 수동의 의미를 나타내도록 to-v의 수동태가 와야 한다.

오답노트 ① 관계대명사에 이어지는 절이 선행사인 the extent와 전치사 to와 함께 연결되기 때문에 '전치사 + 관계대명사'가 되었다. ② 'the using of it'을 주어로 하는 동사이다. ③ 'for which ~ designed'는 삽입절로, 관계대명사에 이어지는 절이 선행사인 the purpose와 전치사 for와 함께 연결되어 '전치사 + 관계대명사'가 되었다.

instrument 기구, 도구
efficient 효율적인
extent 정도
achieve 성취하다

모의 57 When she reached her car, it occurred to her that she ① might have
그녀가 자신의 자동차에 이르렀을 때 / (…이) 그녀에게 생각났다 / 자신이 가스레인지 끄는 것을 잊었을지도
forgotten ② turning(→ to turn) off the gas range. With a sigh, she climbed
모른다는 것을 / 한숨을 내쉬며 / 그녀는 숨을 헐떡이며
breathlessly up the stairs, only ③ to find that the range ④ had been turned off.
계단 위로 올라갔다 / 결국 알게 되었다 / 가스레인지가 꺼져 있었음을

풀이 ② '~해야 할 것을 잊다'의 문맥이 되어야 하므로, 목적어로 to-v가 와야 한다. *cf.* forget + v-ing: ~했던 것을 잊다

오답노트 ① 과거의 일에 대한 약한 추측은 'may[might] have v-ed'로 쓴다. ③ '결과'를 나타내는 to-v의 부사적 용법이다. ④ 가스레인지가 '꺼진' 대상이고, 주절의 동사보다 먼저 일어난 일이므로 과거완료 수동태가 쓰였다.

occur (생각이) 떠오르다
turn off ~을 끄다(↔ turn on ~을 켜다)
sigh 한숨
breathlessly 숨을 헐떡이며

모의 58 The reason ① that we keep making the same error repeatedly ② is that
이유는 / [우리가 되풀이하여 동일한 실수를 계속 저지르는] / ~이다 /
associations form between the ideas in the chain of thoughts and become
사고의 사슬 속에서 생각들 간에 연계가 형성되는 것 / 그리고 더 견고해지는 것
③ more firmly(→ firmer) each time they are used, until finally the connections
/ 그것이 사용될 때마다 / 마침내 그 연계는 너무나 잘 확립되어
are so well established ④ that the chain is very difficult to break.
/ 그 사슬은 깨기가 아주 어려워질 때까지

풀이 ③ 주격보어 자리이므로 부사가 아닌 형용사의 비교급이 와야 한다.

오답노트 ① 관계부사 why를 대신해서 쓰인 관계부사이다. ② The reason을 주어로 하는 동사이다. ④ 앞에 있는 so와 연결되어 '결과'의 의미를 나타내는 접속사이다.

association 연계, 연관
firm 굳은, 견고한
connection 연결
establish 확립하다

모의 59 Psychological studies indicate ① that it is knowledge possessed by the
심리적 연구는 나타낸다 / (…은) 바로 개인이 소유한 지식이다
individual ② what(→ that) determines which stimuli become the focus of
/ 결정하는 것은 / 어떤 자극들이 개인의 관심의 초점이 되는지를
that individual's attention, ③ what significance he or she assigns to these
/ 어떤 중요성을 그 사람이 이러한 자극들에 부여하는지를
stimuli, and ④ how they are combined into a larger whole.
/ 그리고 어떻게 그것들이 더 큰 전체로 결합되는지를

풀이 ② 'it is ~ that' 강조 구문의 that이 와야 할 자리이다.

오답노트 ① 명사절을 이끄는 접속사이다. ③ significance를 수식하는 의문형용사로 쓰였다. ④ 명사절을 이끄는 의문사이다.

psychological 심리적인
indicate 나타내다
possess 소유하다
stimulus 자극 *pl.* stimuli
significance 중요성
assign 부여하다
combine 결합하다

모의 60 In response to variations in chemical composition, temperature and most
화학적 구성, 온도, 그리고 무엇보다도 압력의 변화에 반응하여
of all pressure, volatile substances ① containing(→ contained) in the magma
/ 휘발성 물질들은 / [물 또는 이산화탄소처럼 마그마 안에 포함되어 있는]
like water or carbon dioxide ② can be released to form gas bubbles, ③ producing
/ 방출되어 기포를 형성할 수 있다 / 마그마의
great changes in the properties of the magma and in many cases ④ leading
속성에 큰 변화를 일으키며 / 그리고 많은 경우에 분출을 초래하면서
to an eruption.

풀이 ① volatile substances가 마그마 안에 '포함되어 있는' 대상이므로 수동의 의미를 나타내는 과거분사가 와야 한다.

오답노트 ② volatile substances를 주어로 하는 동사로, '방출될 수 있다'의 의미가 되어야 하므로 수동태가 적절하다. ③ '~하며'의 의미의 분사구문을 이끄는 현재분사이다. ④ producing과 and에 의해 병렬로 연결되어 있다.

variation 변화
composition 구성
volatile 휘발성의
substance 물질
release 방출하다
property 속성, 특성
eruption 분출

61 The ability to see the situation as the other side sees ① it, as ② difficult as
상황을 보는 능력은 / 상대편이 그것을 보는 것처럼 / 비록 그것은 어렵겠지만
it may be, ③ being(→ is) one of the most important ④ skills a negotiator has
/ 가장 중요한 기술 중의 하나이다 / [교섭자가 보유해야 하는]
to possess.

> **풀이** ③ 양보의 부사절이 삽입된 문장에서, 주어 The ability와 연결되는 동사가 와야 한다.

> **오답노트** ① the situation을 가리키는 대명사이다. ② 보어로 쓰인 형용사이다. difficult 다음의 as는 '양보'의 접속사
이다. ((as) difficult as it may be = though it may be difficult) ④ one of + 형용사의 최상급 + 복수 명사

negotiator 교섭자, 협상가

수능! **62** In addition to ① protecting the rights of authors ② so as to encourage the
저자의 권리를 보호하는 것뿐만 아니라 / 새로운 창작품의 출판을 장려하기 위해
publication of new creative works, copyright ③ also supposes(→ is also
/ 저작권은 또한 합리적인 시간제한을 두기로 되어 있다
supposed) to place reasonable time limits on those rights so that outdated
/ 그러한 권리에 / 기한이 지난 작품들이 새로운
works ④ may be incorporated into new creative efforts.
창의적 노력 안으로 통합될 수 있도록 하기 위해서

> **풀이** ③ 주어인 copyright가 시간 제한을 두는 것으로 '전제되는' 대상이므로 수동태가 되어야 한다.

> **오답노트** ① 앞의 to가 전치사이기 때문에 목적어로 동명사가 적절하다. ② so as to-v: ~하기 위해서(= in order
to-v) ④ 주어인 outdated works가 '통합되는' 대상이므로 수동태가 적절하다.

in addition to ~에 더하여, ~뿐만 아니라
publication 출판
copyright 저작권
outdated 기한이 지난; 구식의
incorporate 통합하다

63 It is not men's faults ① that ruin them so much ② as the manner ③ which(→ (that
(…은) 바로 사람들의 잘못이 아니다 / 그들을 그렇게 많이 망가뜨리는 것은 / 오히려 방식이다 / [그들이 직접 행하는
[in which])) they conduct themselves after the faults ④ have been
/ 그 잘못이 저질러진 후에]
committed.

> **풀이** ③ 앞에 선행사(the manner)가 있고, 이어지는 절이 완전하므로 관계부사 that 또는 in which가 오거나 생
략할 수 있다. the manner[way]와 how는 함께 쓸 수 없다.

> **오답노트** ① 'it is ~ that' 강조 구문의 that이다. ② not A so much as B: A라기보다는 오히려 B (= not so much
A as B) ④ the faults가 '저질러지는' 대상이므로 수동태가 적절하다.

fault 잘못, 책임
ruin 망가뜨리다
conduct 행동하다, 처신하다
commit (잘못·범죄를) 저지르다

64 There is no good reason why we should fear the future, but there is every
합당한 이유가 없다 / [우리가 미래를 두려워해야 할] / 그러나 온갖 이유가 있다
reason why we should face ① it seriously, neither ② hiding from ourselves
/ [우리가 그것에 진지하게 직면해야 할] / 문제들의 중대성을 스스로에게 감추지 않고
the gravity of the problems before us ③ or (→ nor) fearing to approach these
/ [우리 앞에 있는] / 이러한 문제에 다가서는 것을 두려워하지도 않고
problems with the unbending, unflinching purpose to solve ④ them aright.
/ 불굴의, 움츠러들지 않는 의지력을 가지고 / [그것들을 올바르게 해결하려는]

Theodore Roosevelt

> **풀이** ③ 앞에 있는 neither와 짝을 이루는 상관접속사는 nor가 되어야 한다.

> **오답노트** ① the future를 가리키는 대명사이다. ② 분사구문을 이끄는 현재분사이다. ④ problems를 가리키는 대명
사이다.

gravity 중대함, 심각성; 중력
approach 접근하다, 다가서다
unbending 굽히지 않는, 불굴의
unflinching (위험한 상황에도) 움츠리지 않는
purpose 의지력, 결단력; 목적
aright 올바르게, 틀림없이

모의 65 There is a widely ① accepted theory in social psychology known as the
사회 심리학에서 광범위하게 수용되는 이론이 있다 / [엉덩방아 찧기 효과
pratfall effect, ② that(→ which) actually states that making certain kinds of
라고 알려진] / 그리고 그것은 실제로 분명히 말한다 / 특정한 종류의 실수를 하는 것은 당신을 더욱
mistakes ③ makes you more ④ likable because you are relatable in your
호감이 가게 만든다고 / 왜냐하면 당신은 당신의 취약함으로 공감대를 형성하기
vulnerability.
때문에

풀이 ② that은 콤마 다음에 선행사를 보충 설명하는 관계사절을 이끌 수 없다.

오답노트 ① theory가 '받아들여지는' 대상이므로, 과거분사형 형용사가 적절하다. ③ making이 이끄는 동명사구가 주어이므로 단수 동사가 왔다. ④ makes의 목적격보어로 형용사가 왔다.

pratfall 엉덩방아 찧기
relatable 공감대를 형성하는
vulnerability 취약함

---

66 ① Despite our precision mathematics and experiments, new surprises in
우리의 정밀 계산과 실험에도 불구하고 / 현대 물리학과 우주론에서
modern physics and cosmology ② have emerged that ③ compel some of
새로운 놀라운 일들이 일어났다 / [가장 유능한 물리학자들의 일부로
the most able physicists ④ resort(→ to resort) to myth making to try and
하여금 헛된 신화 만들기에 의지하도록 부추기는] / 혼란스럽게 하는
explain the mind-bending information they have uncovered about the
정보를 애써 설명하기 위해서 / [그들이 우주의 속성에 대해 밝혀낸]
nature of the universe.

풀이 ④ compel의 목적격보어 자리이므로 to-v가 되어야 한다.

오답노트 ① '~에도 불구하고'의 의미의 전치사구로 뒤에 명사구가 온다. ② new surprises를 주어로 하는 동사이다. ③ 주격 관계대명사 that에 이어지는 동사로서 선행사인 new surprises가 복수이므로 복수 동사가 쓰였다. 긴 주어를 회피하기 위해서 관계사절이 분리되어 짧은 서술어(have emerged) 뒤에 온 문장 구조이다.

despite ~에도 불구하고(= in spite of)
precision 정확, 정밀
mathematics 계산; 수학
cosmology 우주론
emerge 나타나다
compel 강요하다
resort to ~에 의지하다
myth 근거 없는 믿음, 통념; 신화
mind-bending (마음·상황을) 혼란스럽게 하는, 환각성의
uncover (비밀 등을) 알아내다, 밝혀내다

모의 67 The objection to ① include(→ to including) ethics among the sciences ② is
윤리학을 과학에 포함하는 것에 대한 반대는 ~이다
that, ③ whereas science deals with what is, ethics, it is said, ④ is concerned
/ 과학은 현실을 다루는 것에 반하여 / 윤리학은 / 그것이 이야기되기에 / 당위와 관련된다는 것
with what ought to be.

풀이 ① 앞에 있는 to가 전치사이기 때문에 목적어로 동명사가 와야 한다.

오답노트 ② The objection이 주어이므로 단수 동사가 왔다. ③ 대조의 접속사이다. ④ ethics를 주어로 하는 동사이며, 'be concerned with ~'는 '~와 관련되다'는 의미이다.

objection 반대
ethics 윤리(학)
whereas ~임에 반하여
deal with ~을 다루다

수능 68 ① Based on a complex sensory analysis that is not only restricted to the
복잡한 감각 분석에 근거하여 / [미각에 국한되는 것뿐만 아니라
sense of taste but also ② included(→ includes) smell, touch, and hearing,
/ 후각, 촉각, 그리고 청각도 포함하는]
the final decision ③ whether to swallow or reject food ④ is made.
/ 음식을 삼킬 것인가 거부할 것인가의 최종 결정이 내려진다

풀이 ② 상관접속사 'not only A but also B'로 연결된 문장에서, A는 동사 is restricted이므로, B도 동사가 와야 한다. A를 과거분사 restricted로 보고 B에도 과거분사 included를 쓰면, 이어지는 목적어(smell, touch, and hearing)와 연결되지 않는다.

오답노트 ① 분사구문을 이끄는 과거분사이다. ③ 의문사 whether가 이끄는 명사구(whether ~ food)는 the final decision과 동격 어구로 쓰였다. ④ 주어인 the final decision이 '내려지는' 대상이므로 수동태가 적절하다.

complex 복잡한
sensory 감각의
analysis 분석
swallow 삼키다
reject 거부하다, 거절하다

69 Blockchain owes its name to ① how does it work(→ how it works) and the
블록체인은 그것의 이름을 신세지고 있다 / 그것이 어떻게 작동하는지에 / 그리고 방식에
manner ② in which it stores data, namely ③ that the information is
/ [그것이 데이터를 저장하는 / 즉, 정보가 블록들 안으로 꾸려지는]
packaged into blocks, ④ which link to form a chain with other blocks of
/ 그리고 그것들은 유사한 정보의 다른 블록과 연결되어 사슬을 형성한다
similar information.

풀이 ① 간접의문문이므로 「의문사＋s＋v」의 어순이 되어야 한다.

오답노트 ② 선행사가 the manner인 경우, 관계부사 that이나 in which를 쓰거나 이를 생략할 수도 있다. ③ the manner를 선행사로 하는 관계부사이다. ④ 선행사 blocks를 보충 설명하는 절을 이끄는 관계대명사이다.

owe A to B A를 B에 빚지고 있다
namely 즉, 다시 말해서
package 꾸리다; 포장하다

모의 70 One of the biggest challenges faced by organizations ① is how to transform
조직이 당면한 가장 큰 도전들 중의 하나는 ~이다 / 어떻게 미가공 데이터를
raw data into information and eventually into knowledge, ② which if ③ exploiting
정보로 그리고 마침내는 지식으로 바꿀 것인가 / 그리고 그것은 / 만약 올바르게
(→ exploited) correctly provides the capabilities ④ to predict customers' behaviour
이용된다면 / 역량을 제공한다 / [고객의 행동과 사업의 경향을 예측하는]
and business trends.

풀이 ③ if 다음에 'it is'가 생략되었는데, 여기서 it은 knowledge를 가리킨다. knowledge는 '이용되는' 대상이므로 과거분사가 적절하다.

오답노트 ① One이 주어이므로 단수 동사가 적절하다. ② 선행사 knowledge에 대해 보충 설명하는 절을 이끄는 관계대명사이다. ④ capabilities를 수식하는 형용사적 용법으로 쓰였다.

organization 조직
transform A into B A를 B로 바꾸다, 변형시키다
raw 날것의, 가공하지 않은
exploit 이용하다; 착취하다
capability 역량, 능력
behavio(u)r 행위

모의 71 The location of senile mental deterioration ① was no longer the aging brain
노년기의 정신적인 노화가 일어나는 곳은 더 이상 노화하고 있는 뇌가 아니라 사회였다
② but a society that, through involuntary retirement, social isolation, and
/ [비자발적 퇴직, 사회적, 고립, 그리고 전통적인 가족 유대의 약화를 통해서
the loosening of traditional family ties, ③ stripping(→ stripped) the elderly of
/ 노인들에게서 역할들을 제거한
the roles that ④ had sustained meaning in their lives.
/ [그들의 삶에서 의미를 유지해왔던]]

풀이 ③ 삽입어구인 'through ~ ties'를 괄호로 묶어보면, 주격 관계대명사 that 다음에 동사가 와야 함을 알 수 있다.

오답노트 ① 주어가 The location이므로 단수 동사가 적절하다. ② 앞의 no longer과 짝을 이루어 '더 이상 ~이 아니라 …'의 의미를 나타낸다. ④ 관계사절의 동사 stripped 보다 먼저 일어난 일이므로 과거완료 시제가 쓰였다.

location 위치, 장소
senile 노년기의
deterioration 노화
involuntary 본의 아닌
retirement 은퇴, 퇴직
isolation 고립
loosen 느슨하게 하다
strip A of B A에게서 B를 제거하다
sustain 유지하다

모의 72 As ① improbable as this may seem, the bodily fluids of aquatic animals
비록 이것은 있을 법 하지 않지만 / 수생 동물의 체액은 바다와 강한 유사성을 보여준다
show a strong similarity to oceans, and indeed, most studies of ion balance
/ 그리고 정말로 담수 생리학에서 이온 균형에 대한 대부분의 연구들은
in freshwater physiology ② documents(→ document) the complex regulatory
복잡한 조절 메커니즘을 뒷받침한다
mechanisms ③ by which fish, amphibians and invertebrates attempt to
/ [어류, 양서류 그리고 무척추동물이 내부의 바다를 유지하려고 시도하는
maintain an inner ocean in spite of ④ surrounding fresh water.
/ 둘러싸고 있는 담수에도 불구하고]

풀이 ② document는 동사로 쓰였는데, 주어가 복수(most studies)이므로 복수 동사로 써야 한다.

오답노트 ① 주격보어로 쓰인 형용사이다. (= Though this may seem improbable ~) ③ 선행사인 'the complex regulatory mechanisms'와 이어지는 절이 전치사 by로 연결되기 때문에 '전치사＋관계대명사'가 쓰였다. ④ fresh water가 '둘러싸는' 주체이므로 능동의 의미를 나타내는 현재분사가 쓰였다.

improbable 있을 것 같지 않은
bodily fluid 체액
aquatic 수중의, 수생의
physiology 생리학
document (문서로) 뒷받침하다, 증명하다
regulatory 조절하는
mechanism (목적을 달성하기 위한) 방법, 메커니즘
amphibian 양서류
invertebrate 무척추동물
surround 둘러싸다

Memo